ACRONYMS AND ABBREVIATIONS

ABS	NYSE's Automated Bond Syste
ACAT	NSCC's Automated Customer /
ADR	American depository receipt
Amex	American Stock Exchange
AON Order	"All or none" order
Arb	Arbitrageur or arbitrage
ARIEL	A London-based computerized block-trading system
AutEx	An electronic system that enables block traders to seek trading interest
AUTOPER	American Stock Exchange's automated small order handling system
Beacon	Boston Stock Exchange's automated execution system
CAES	NASD's computer-assisted execution system for NASDAQ/NMS and exchange listed securities.
CAP Order	Convert and parity order
CAPM	Capital Asset Pricing Model
CATS	Toronto Stock Exchange's Computer Assisted Trading System
Cats	Salomon Brothers' Certificates of Accrual on Treasury Securities
CBOE	Chicago Board Options Exchange
CBOT	Chicago Board of Trade
CFTC	Commodity Futures Trading Commission
CLOB	Consolidated limit order book
CMA	Merrill Lynch's Cash Management Account
CME	Chicago Mercantile Exchange
CNS	Continuous net settlement
COLT	Herzog, Heine, & Geduld's order execution system
COMEX	Pacific Stock Exchange's order-routing system
CQS	Consolidated Quotations System
CRT	Cathode ray tube
CTS	Consolidated Transactions System
DBCCs	NASD's District Business Conduct Committees
DNR	Do not reduce
DOT	NYSE's automated small order handling system
ECU	European currency unit
EDGAR	SEC's Electronic Data Gathering, Analysis, and Retrieval System
EF	Efficient frontier
EMH	Efficient market hypothesis
FDIC	Federal Deposit Insurance Corporation
FOK Order	Fill or kill order
GNMA	Government National Mortgage Association
GTC	Good til cancelled
Instinet	An electronic system that provides order routing and a fourth market trading facility

(continued in back)

D1457323

EQUITY MARKETS

EQUITY MARKETS
Structure, Trading, and Performance

Robert A. Schwartz
Graduate School of Business Administration
New York University

HARPER & ROW, PUBLISHERS, New York
Cambridge, Philadelphia, San Francisco, Washington,
London, Mexico City, São Paulo, Singapore, Sydney

1817

Sponsoring Editor: *John Greenman*
Project Editor: *Donna DeBenedictis/Ellen MacElree*
Cover Design: *Lucy Krikorian*
Text Art: *Fine Line Illustrations, Inc.*
Production Manager: *Jeanie Berke*
Production Assistant: *Paula Roppolo*
Compositor: *Waldman Graphics, Inc.*
Printer and Binder: *R. R. Donnelley & Sons Company*

Equity Markets: Structure, Trading, and Performance

Library of Congress Cataloging in Publication Data

Schwartz, Robert A. (Robert Alan), 1937–
  Equity markets: structure, trading, and performance / Robert A.
Schwartz.
      p.   cm.
  Includes index.
  ISBN 0-06-041322-0
  1. Securities—United States.   2. Stock-exchange—United States.
I. Title.
HG4963.S38   1988
332.64'0973—dc19   87-23173
                                                    CIP

88 89 90 91 9 8 7 6 5 4 3 2 1

*To my wife, Christine,
and my daughter, Emily Liane*

About the Author

Robert A. Schwartz is Professor of Economics and Finance at the Graduate School of Business Administration of New York University. He has been a member of the NYU faculty since 1965. He is co-author of *The Microstructure of Securities Markets,* Prentice-Hall (1986) and is co-editor of *Impending Changes for Securities Markets: What Role for the Exchanges?* JAI Press (1979), and *Market Making and the Changing Structure of the Securities Industry,* Lexington Books (1985). He has over 40 publications, including articles in such journals as the *Journal of Finance, Journal of Financial Economics, Journal of Financial and Quantitative Analysis, Journal of Political Economy,* and *Journal of Portfolio Management.* For the past five years, he has been an associate editor of the *Journal of Finance.*

Contents

9. Information and Prices   270

10. Prices and Returns   307

11. Liquidity, Execution Costs, and the Volatility of Security Prices   355

PART THREE   MARKET STRUCTURE   385

12. The Economics of Market Making   387

13. Market Architecture   425

14. Regulation   478

15. Price Discovery   514

Preface

Starting in the mid-1970s, competitive, technological, and regulatory change have transformed the U.S. equity markets. Today, trading has attained central importance in the leading securities firms. Similar developments are now occurring rapidly in a number of international financial centers. This book describes and analyzes the equity markets. Its objective is to develop a framework for understanding trading and price determination in an environment where day-to-day operations are affected by the impediments of an imperfect world—commissions, taxes, and other transaction costs; regulatory blockages and other restrictions; and uncertainty about order execution and transaction prices.

The first five chapters of *Equity Markets* present institutional description. The following six chapters analyze individual trading decisions, the determination of market prices, and market performance. The last four chapters focus on issues concerning market design and regulation.

Chapter 1 sets forth the importance of the equity markets to individual firms, shareowners, and the aggregate economy, and reviews the increased importance of trading in recent years. Chapter 2 describes the basic design features of a securities trading system, and Chapter 3 gives further detail on the functions of a trading system and on the operations of the U.S. stock exchange and over-the-counter markets.

Chapter 4 surveys the operations of the firms that comprise the securities industry, identifies the securities that are traded, discusses trading activities, and describes post-trade clearance and settlement operations.

Chapter 5 presents the historical context. The discussion begins with the industry's early development in the United States and extends through the current era of change that started in the 1970s.

Chapters 6 and 7 provide foundation material. Chapter 6 establishes the conceptual framework and reviews the specific tools of microeconomic theory that are utilized. Chapter 7 considers the pricing of risky assets; in the process, it reviews relevant aspects of portfolio and capital asset pricing theory and paves the way for an analysis of an investor's trading decision.

The trading decision itself is analyzed in Chapter 8. Trading in a frictionless market is first examined, and then the impact of trading costs is assessed. This chapter establishes that order placement in a nonfrictionless environment requires that strategic decisions be made, and that the strategies used by traders depend on the institutional design of the market— that is, on how orders are handled and translated into trades.

Chapter 9 deals with the relationship between information and security prices. The discussion further links the investment and trading decisions of individuals to prices that are established in the market.

The analysis then turns to the behavior of market prices. Chapter 10 shows specifically how returns (price changes) are defined and measured, analyzes the factors that cause prices to change, and considers how returns are affected by the workings of the market. Chapter 10 also pays particular attention to the volatility of share prices, to the determinants of bid-ask spreads, and to the correlation over time of security returns. This discussion completes the theoretical demonstration that price behavior in actual markets differs from what one would expect in a frictionless environment.

Chapter 11 presents an empirical analysis of price behavior in three market centers: the New York Stock Exchange, the American Stock Exchange, and the National Association of Securities Dealer's NASDAQ National Market System, the most prestigious segment of the over-the-counter market. This chapter also discusses the concept of ''liquidity'' and presents evidence on the size of execution costs. Chapter 11 establishes empirically that price behavior in actual markets differs from what one would expect in a frictionless environment.

The problems involved in trading having been established, we then analyze the effect of market design and regulation on the operational efficiency of a trading system. Chapter 12 is devoted exclusively to one design feature of particular importance: the role of dealers and specialists as market makers. Chapter 13 then considers additional features of a market's architecture: the geographic consolidation of orders, the time batching of orders, the technology used to display orders and to execute trades, and the stabilization of prices. Chapter 14 next turns to the regulation of the securities markets; various causes of market and of government failure are analyzed, and four recent regulatory issues of particular importance are discussed—elimination of fixed commissions, off-board trading, shelf registration, and insider trading.

Chapter 15 reviews the previous analysis in relation to one special function of the markets—discovery of the prices at which trades are made. After considering why the importance of price discovery has not been widely recognized, we conclude by highlighting some of the major issues concerning price discovery and the market's microstructure for which answers do not currently exist.

ACKNOWLEDGMENTS

My first debt of gratitude is to my coauthors of many years: Edward I. Altman, Yakov Amihud, Ernest Bloch, Kalman J. Cohen, William K. H. Fung, Joel Hasbrouck, Gabriel A. Hawawini, Thomas S. Y. Ho, Steven F. Maier, Walter L. Ness, Jr., Hitoshi Okuda, Paul S. Schreiber, and David K. Whitcomb. I also thank the students who have struggled with me through the development of much of the subject matter. I am grateful to Ingo Walter and Marti Subrahmanyam who, as successive chairmen of the Finance Department, at NYU's Graduate School of Business, have provided an environment where experimentation is possible, and who have encouraged me to develop the course on the microstructure of securities markets from which this book has evolved.

Much of the conceptual framework for the book was worked out in discussion with Thomas S. Y. Ho and Kalman J. Cohen, my close friends and coauthors. Their support of this project is deeply appreciated. Stephen L. Williams, of Bridge Data, also made extensive and detailed comments for which I am most grateful. Finally, on various occasions, I have learned much from having jointly taught the course with Thomas S. Y. Ho and Stephen L. Williams.

Parts of the research reported in the book were funded by grants from the American Stock Exchange, Instinet, the New York Stock Exchange, and the Nomura Research Institute. Arnold Sametz and the Salomon Brothers Center for the Study of Financial Institutions at New York University have also provided support that aided the development of this book. Richard Torrenzano of the New York Stock Exchange gave much appreciated assistance. Frederick Eickelberg of the New York Institute of Finance provided helpful source material. I have had the privilege to learn from two leading market makers: Donald Stone of the New York Stock Exchange and Alan Streusand of the American Stock Exchange. Kalman J. Cohen, Robert Jarrow, Seymour Smidt, and Mustafa Gultekin had the graciousness and the courage to use earlier drafts of the manuscript in their classes at

Duke University (Cohen), Cornell University (Jarrow and Smidt), and the University of North Carolina (Gultekin).

Every page of this book reflects the advice, changes, and suggestions of one of our doctoral students at the Graduate Business School, Corinne Bronfman; without her help as my research assistant for over two years, this project would have been completed with appreciably less success and considerably more difficulty. Many others have commented on previous drafts. In particular, I thank Yakov Amihud (New York University and Tel Aviv University), Ernest Bloch (New York University), G. Geoffrey Booth (Syracuse University), Joel Hasbrouck (New York University), Marcia Kramer (The American Stock Exchange), Mario Lavallée (École des Hautes Études Commerciales, Montréal), Kelly Price (Wayne State University), Seymour Smidt (Cornell University), Stephen Smith (The University of Texas at Austin), Hans Stoll (Vanderbilt University), Donald Stone (The New York Stock Exchange), and Gautam Vora (Pennsylvania State University). I also thank John Greenman, my editor at Harper & Row, and Ellen MacElree, my project editor, for their patience and understanding. Most of all, I thank my wife, Christine, who has edited each draft of this manuscript. Without her encouragement and support, this project may never have been undertaken and might not have been completed.

Robert A. Schwartz

one

INSTITUTIONAL CONTEXT

chapter *1*

Secondary Markets

New shares of a financial asset are issued in the primary market; existing shares are traded in a secondary market. The securities exchanges and the over-the-counter market comprise the secondary markets in the United States. The efficiency of the secondary markets is essential to firms that raise funds in the primary market, and to individuals who invest their savings in marketable financial assets. This book is about trading in the secondary markets for equity shares.

This chapter establishes the importance of secondary markets to individual firms and the aggregate economy, and considers the importance of secondary markets to the share owner population. Market structure and performance are also discussed, as is the increased importance of trading in recent years.

THE IMPORTANCE OF SECONDARY MARKETS TO CORPORATIONS AND THE ECONOMY

The efficient allocation of plant, equipment, and working capital across firms in the economy depends on the efficiency with which financial capital is distributed across firms. The amount of funds a firm seeks to raise by the sale of a security depends on the profitability with which the funds can be used, and on the firm's cost of financial capital. If the level of financial capital costs is too high, aggregate investment will be insufficient, and the real economic growth of the country will be jeopardized. If the relative

3

capital costs of individual firms are inaccurately assessed, the distribution of funds and of real investment across firms will be distorted.

The cost of capital for a corporation depends on the price it receives for its newly issued shares. Therefore, for individual firms and for the economy in aggregate, real investment in plant, equipment, and working capital will be optimal only if the primary market for financial capital operates efficiently.

The primary market, in turn, requires an efficient secondary market. There are two reasons for this; the first involves the marketability of shares, and the second involves the accuracy of share valuation. Accurate share valuation is also important to corporations as a measure of managerial performance. We consider the marketability of shares first.

Marketability

The public in aggregate can liquidate its investment in a firm only if the firm repurchases its equity shares and/or retires its shares of a callable issue. Firms typically make major alterations in plant and equipment only infrequently and buy back their securities only upon occasion.[1] In the meantime, the total number of shares that have been issued by a corporation must be held by the public. From the aggregate public point of view, the total financial investment in a firm is as illiquid as the firm's assets themselves.

Any individual investor, however, wants to be able to alter his or her own portfolio holdings as changing liquidity needs and assessments of corporate prospects suggest. Must an individual investor be locked into a financial investment to the same extent that an individual firm is locked into its physical investment in plant and equipment? No; a secondary market for financial assets provides individual investors with the desired flexibility. With a secondary market, any investor who buys shares when they are issued is free to sell those shares any time the market is open, at the market determined price. And any investor who did not purchase shares when they were issued is free to buy them, at the market determined price.

The marketability of shares is of tremendous value to investors, who consequently pay higher prices for shares that are marketable. Therefore, marketability—*which is provided by a secondary market*—increases share prices in the primary market and reduces the cost of financial capital for firms. For this reason, corporations individually, and the economy in aggregate, have a major stake in the viability of the secondary markets. Without efficient secondary markets, the economic growth of the country could be seriously impaired.

---

[1]Shares can also be repurchased with internally generated funds (earnings and depreciation).

Share Valuation

For firms in specific and for the economy in aggregate, trading in a secondary market fulfills another important function: it is the process by which shares are valued.

Shares of a security could be evaluated by an appraiser. Such a valuation would, of course, reflect that individual's particular judgment. Or several independent appraisers might be used. This would not necessarily solve the judgment problem, however, and it would raise a second difficulty: if the various appraisers do not agree, how might differences in their opinions be resolved?

The difficulty of evaluating shares according to an appraiser's opinion is illustrated by one situation where no alternative exists—when a company first goes public with an *initial public offering* (IPO). An IPO involves the issuance of shares in the primary market with the aid of an investment banking firm. The investment banking firm organizes and handles the marketing of the shares, stabilizes share price during the offering period, and assumes the risk of the issue's not being fully purchased by the public. The investment banking firm also prices the shares. The pricing decision is based on an analysis of the firm's financial, operational, and managerial capabilities; on an assessment of the firm's market and industry; and on an evaluation of aggregate economic conditions. Ultimately, the pricing decision depends on the investment banker's judgment of the public's willingness to hold the company's shares.

After an IPO is complete, the accuracy of the appraiser's evaluation can be assessed in relation to the price established in the secondary market. Not infrequently, surprises are experienced. For instance, Morgan Stanley went public on March 21, 1986, with an IPO of 4,500,000 shares priced at $56½ a share. On its first day of trading, Morgan Stanley common closed on the New York Stock Exchange at $71¼ a share. Using the closing price, the appraiser had underassessed the stock relative to the market's valuation by more than 20 percent.[2]

In addition to mistakes, appraisals are costly. It would be inconceivable to value shares by such a process with any frequency (on a daily basis, for instance). Fortunately, a far better alternative exists: shares are valued by the prices established by traders in the secondary markets.

Trading and price determination are concomitant processes in the equity markets. The buying pressure exerted by investors who believe a corporation's shares are underpriced causes share prices to rise; the selling

[2]On March 21, Morgan Stanley traded at a high of 74¼. The valuation mistake resulted in a sizable profit for investors who bought at the offering price, and in a loss for Morgan Stanley; the company received less than it might have from its IPO, and thus its cost of capital was unnecessarily high.

pressure exerted by investors who believe a corporation's shares are over-priced causes share prices to fall. As traders meet and exchange shares according to their individual desires to buy and to sell at market prices, two things happen simultaneously: (1) individual share holdings are adjusted, and (2) share prices attain market clearing values.

In a market environment, each investor, rather than only a few professional appraisers, forms his or her own opinion of a company's prospects and expresses that opinion by the trades he or she seeks to make. The market process in turn establishes a *consensus opinion* across all investors; the consensus opinion is the market determined price. With a well-functioning market, it is not necessary to rely on ad hoc procedures to resolve the different judgments of professional appraisers.

The market determined price is *informationally efficient* if it fully reflects existing information. When prices are informationally efficient, no investor can consistently realize above normal returns by trading on the basis of existing information.

Informationally efficient prices are important to issuing firms for assessing the cost of capital generated either internally or by the issuance of new shares. Accurate share valuation is also important to investors for reassessing their portfolio holdings. Market prices are used as well to valuate estate held shares and mutual fund shares (for redemption) and to serve various other legal purposes.

In addition, informationally efficient prices reflect the market's assessment of managerial performance. The broadest measure of a firm's achievements over a period of time is the extent to which the firm has developed its earnings potential for the future while controlling its risk. Investors evaluate equity shares in relation to the expected level, and uncertainty, of future earnings. Consequently, change in share value over a period of time is in certain respects a more comprehensive and forward-looking measure of profits than the earnings figure reported on a firm's income statement for the period. This is a major reason why firms closely track the price of their equity shares in the secondary market. The association between stock price changes and corporate success also leads firms to compensate top executives and other key personnel with corporate stock and stock options.

THE IMPORTANCE OF SECONDARY MARKETS
TO THE SHARE OWNER POPULATION

Individuals, as share owners, are affected by the efficiency of the secondary markets for reasons relating to (1) the informational accuracy of share valuation, (2) the stability of the market, and (3) the cost of trading.

Informational Efficiency

The previous section defined *informationally efficient security prices:* prices that fully reflect existing information, such that above normal returns cannot be consistently realized by trading on the basis of existing information. In the dynamic context of the market, prices are continuously perturbed by the arrival of news, and informational efficiency is regained as prices adjust to news. During the adjustment process, profits are realized by investors who have an advantageous position vis-à-vis the information flow. These profits are the reward for information gathering activities and are the incentive that keeps share prices in line with the fundamental determinants of share value.

The dynamic adjustment of prices to new information, however, enables some investors to profit at the expense of others. If informational imbalances endure too long, and if they consistently favor some investors over others, those who are at an informational disadvantage may be driven from the market. This would decrease the aggregate demand to hold shares and lower share prices for all.

Pricing Stability

The stability of a market depends in part on its operational efficiency. Prices are generally more volatile in markets where the quality of price determination is poor, where buyers and sellers locate each other only with difficulty, and where information on recent trades and current price quotations is not widely disseminated. The price volatility attributable to operational inefficiency has an effect similar to the disorderly pricing attributable to informational inefficiency: the aggregate demand to hold shares is reduced, and share prices are lowered for all.

Trading Costs

Trading costs are classified either as *explicit transaction costs* or as *implicit execution costs*. Explicit transaction costs are visible and easily measured; they include, for example, commissions and taxes. Implicit execution costs are not easily measured; they exist because orders may, as a result of their size and/or the sparsity of counterpart orders on the market, execute at relatively high prices (if they are buy orders) or at relatively low prices (if they are sell orders).

Trading costs reduce returns to all investors. Furthermore, these costs lead investors to adjust their portfolios less frequently and, accordingly, to hold portfolios that would not be optimal in a frictionless environment.

Share Owner Profile

The informational and operational efficiency of the secondary markets affects the welfare of share owners, as discussed previously. This is true whether a share owner is a large or a small investor, whether he or she directly owns shares in public corporations, or indirectly owns shares through a mutual fund. Individuals are also affected by the performance of the secondary markets because of savings they have accumulated in pension funds, individual retirement accounts (IRAs), and Keogh plans. In recent years, the market has been dominated by large institutional investors; however, such investors, for the most part, represent a large number of small individuals. In total, the financial fortunes of a very substantial proportion of the population are affected by the performance of the secondary securities market.

Information on the share owner population is given in Table 1.1.[3] The data describe the *numbers* of share owners in each category, not the distribution of shares or of portfolio wealth. The information is of interest because it shows that participation in the secondary financial markets is indeed broad based in the United States.

In 1985, more than 47 million individuals in the United States owned shares of stock traded in the U.S. secondary markets. This total accounted for over 20 percent of the U.S. population of 233 million. As seen in Table 1.1, the shareholder population spans a wide range of age, education, income, occupational, and geographic classifications. Shareholders are evenly divided between male and female; large numbers have portfolios worth less than $5000; relatively few have portfolios worth $50,000 and over. More than two-thirds of all investors own shares of New York Stock Exchange listed securities; almost one-third own mutual fund shares; and almost one-quarter own shares traded in the over-the-counter market. All in all, the efficient operation of the secondary markets is a matter of importance to a sizable proportion of the United States population.

MARKET STRUCTURE AND PERFORMANCE

A Nonfrictionless Market

Because of the importance of the secondary markets to the economy, we next consider the efficiency of market operations.

Standard microeconomic decision models and market equilibrium models consider the value of a resource to consumers, the cost to firms of producing the resource, and the determination of the resource's market clearing price

---

[3]The information in Table 1.1 was assembled by the New York Stock Exchange for mid-1985; see *Shareownership 1985*, New York Stock Exchange, 1986.

Table 1.1   SHARE OWNER STATISTICS (1985)

	Individual share owners	
	Number (000)	Percentage of total
Type of security		
New York Stock Exchange listed	25,263	52.8
Other stock exchange listed	3,224	6.7
Over-the-counter	8,344	17.5
Stock mutual funds	10,994	23.0
Total[a]	47,825	100.0
Age of shareholders		
Under 21 years	2,260	4.8
21–44 years	22,075	46.9
45–64 years	16,116	34.3
65 years and older	6,589	14.0
Total	47,040	100.0
By sex		
Adult males	22,484	47.8
Adult females	22,509	47.8
Minor males	1,215	2.6
Minor females	832	1.8
Total	47,040	100.0
Schooling completed		
3 years high school or less	2,513	5.7
4 years high school	7,869	17.8
1–3 years college	13,937	31.6
4 years college or more	19,854	44.9
Total[b]	44,173	100.0
Household income		
Under $10,000	2,151	5.0
$10,000–$14,999	1,193	2.8
$15,000–$24,999	7,116	16.5
$25,000–$49,999	21,369	49.5
$50,000 and over	11,321	26.2
Total[b]	43,150	100.0
Occupation		
Professional and technical	9,725	22.5
Managers, officials, and proprietors	8,399	19.4
Clerical and sales	6,288	14.6
Craftsworkers and supervisors	2,821	6.5
Operatives and laborers	2,346	5.4
Service workers	1,372	3.2
Farmers and farm laborers	382	0.9
Homemakers, retired workers, and nonemployed adults	11,819	27.5
Total[b]	43,152	100.0

[a]Total exceeds 47,040,000 because some share owners fit into more than one category.
[b]Total does not include minors and portfolios not classified by enumerated categories.

Table 1.1 (Continued)

	Individual share owners	
	Number (000)	**Percentage of total**
Portfolio size		
Under $5,000	17,173	45.0
$5,000–$9,999	7,119	18.6
$10,000–$24,999	5,888	15.4
$25,000–$49,999	3,450	9.0
$50,000 and over	4,569	12.0
Total[b]	38,199	100.0
By region		
New England	3,112	6.6
Middle Atlantic	8,998	19.1
South Atlantic	7,462	15.9
East North Central	7,997	17.0
West North Central	3,081	6.5
East South Central	1,861	4.0
West South Central	4,520	9.6
Mountain	2,299	4.9
Pacific	7,710	16.4
Total	47,040	100.0

[a]Total exceeds 47,040,000 because some share owners fit into more than one category.
[b]Total does not include minors and portfolios not classified by enumerated categories.
Source: Shareownership 1985, New York Stock Exchange, 1986.

and output by market forces. *Market forces* is an abstract concept that means that if demand exceeds supply, competition between buyers will cause prices to rise and, if supply exceeds demand, competition between sellers will cause prices to fall.

Little formal analysis of the specific ways in which the orders of buyers and sellers are actually submitted to the market and translated into trades exists in traditional economic theory. The reason is that, for the most part, a market process has implicitly been assumed to be frictionless. This is true whether the resource is a good such as oranges, a service such as haircuts, a factor of production such as chemical engineers, a physical asset such as cars, or a financial asset such as shares of a corporation's common stock.

Much microeconomic analysis is based on the perfect competition paradigm: for a homogeneous resource (such as wheat), the number of buyers and sellers is taken to be large enough that no individual buyer or seller is significant in relation to the market. Being insignificant, no individual buyer or seller can have any observable impact on the market determined price. Thus, in a perfectly competitive environment, all buyers and sellers are price takers. *Price takers* in the perfectly competitive model make only one decision with respect to the market: the quantity of the resource to buy (demand) or to sell (supply) at the market clearing price.

The *market clearing price* is itself determined by the intersection of the market's demand and supply curves for the resource.

A market center such as the New York Stock Exchange (NYSE) is commonly cited as an example of a perfectly competitive environment. At first throught, the NYSE would certainly seem to fit the description: standardized resources are traded on the Big Board (any share of IBM common is like any other share of IBM common), and a very large number of investors own and trade shares of IBM common (as of March 9, 1987, over 605 million shares of IBM common were outstanding, and these shares were owned by over 787,000 shareholders). Therefore, one might expect that the price of IBM shares would be determined by the intersection of investors' demand and supply curves for the stock.

To an extent share prices are determined by demand and supply. To an appreciable degree, however, standard demand-supply analysis oversimplifies the way in which the NYSE market operates. The reason is that the NYSE, like all financial markets, is not a frictionless environment.

For all securities markets, friction exists in the form of taxes and commissions, order handling and clearance costs, trading halts and other blockages, trading restrictions, and the adverse price impact a trader's order might have in a relatively thin market. The trading costs are a wedge between prices paid by buyers and prices received by sellers.

But the impact of friction is greater. Unlike the theoretical decision maker of traditional microeconomic theory, traders do not submit complete buy and sell order curves to the market. Rather, investors write *point orders* (typically one quantity, at a single price). Furthermore, when writing their point orders, traders are uncertain as to (1) the price at which their orders might execute at any moment in time or (2) the price at which their orders might have executed if they had been priced, sized, timed, or in other respects qualified differently. Consequently, as is not the case in the standard competitive paradigm, investors use trading strategies when they approach the market. Understanding the existence, nature, and impact of the strategic trading decisions sheds much light on the behavior of the secondary markets and on the operations of its participants.

The perfectly competitive model does describe broad, underlying forces that govern price determination in the equity markets. Standard demand-supply analysis might provide a good explanation of why, for instance, a stock's price has moved from $25¼ to $68½ over the course of a year. Within this broader context, however, moment-to-moment and even day-to-day price determination is largely explained by the strategic decisions of traders reacting to the realities of a nonfrictionless environment.[4]

---

[4]The specific path from $25¼ to $68½ depends on the particular sequence of trades that were made. And the returns realized by those who participated in the trades depend, not only on longer run price movements, but also on the success of each participant's trading strategy relative to that of others.

The Effect of Market Design

The strategic trading decisions made by market participants in a nonfrictionless environment depend both on the prices that are expected to prevail in the market and on the particular way in which orders are handled and translated into trades. Consequently, market performance depends on market design.

Few markets are as elaborately structured and monitored as the secondary financial markets in the United States. Nowhere is online electronic surveillance of trading so extensive, or is the reporting of events so nearly simultaneous with their occurrence. Nowhere do market events occur with such rapidity. On the trading desks, decisions involving millions of dollars are made in a moment. Orders are transmitted to a market center with electronic speed. On an exchange's trading floor, trades are made with hand signals, a few words, or the nod of a head, and, almost instantaneously, new transaction prices, volume, and current market quotations are disseminated electronically throughout the country and the world.

The complexities of trading in such an environment call for an elaborate set of institutional arrangements. And a wide spectrum of alternative trading arrangements are used in the U.S. and international markets. Some markets are based on auction principles; others are dealer systems. Some markets allow for continuous trading during the trading day; others batch orders for simultaneous execution at periodic market calls. Many markets allow for direct trader-to-trader interaction; others are telephone markets; and some are computerized markets. In some systems, the order flow for a company's stock is consolidated in one market center; in other systems, the order flow is dispersed across competing dealers and/or exchanges. Some systems disseminate a great deal of current trading information; others disseminate very little. Some markets have elaborate rules for order handling and trade execution; others do not. Some markets are closely regulated; others are not. Some markets are large and resilient; others are small and thin.

None of these attributes would matter if trading were a costless activity. But in the nonfrictionless, dynamic environment of securities trading, each affects costs and market performance.

THE IMPORTANCE OF TRADING

Because the equity markets operate imperfectly, trading is a complex activity, and separable from investing. Investment decisions involve stock selection and portfolio formation with respect to longer term risk and return relationships. Trading involves the implementation of investment decisions, and buying and selling to exploit short run price swings and arbitrage possibilities. The long run for an investment manager may be the better part of a year or more. The long run for a trader, as of 9:30 A.M., may be early afternoon.

Some excellent investment managers would make very poor traders. Some excellent traders would be failures as investment managers. Successful trading requires special skills and attitudes. Good traders can sense a market, spot pricing discrepancies, and make lightning fast decisions. Good traders (like good investment managers) know when to cut their losses and get out of a bad situation. Those who survive the daily pressures of trading do not look over their shoulders and agonize over their mistakes. Traders are generally young, highly energetic, and physically strong. For many, a powerful voice is a definite asset; for some, size also has economic value.

Until recent years, far more attention has been given in both the securities industry and academia to investing rather than to trading or to the daily operations of financial markets. Currently, however, trading is one of the most important and profitable activities of the largest securities firms. This development may be seen most simply in the increased flow of orders to the market.

March 16, 1830, will be remembered as the dullest day in New York Stock Exchange history: 31 shares traded (5 shares of Morris Canal and Banking Co. and 26 shares of United States Bank). December 15, 1886, was the first million plus share day (1.2 million shares traded). August 18, 1982, was the first 100 million plus share day (132.7 million shares traded). On September 19, 1986, over 85 million shares traded during the last minute of trading in the session. January 23, 1987, was the first 300 million plus share day (302.4 million shares traded). On October 19 and 20, 1987, 604.3 and 608.1 million shares traded, respectively.

Table 1.2 presents data for 1975 through 1986 for New York Stock Exchange average daily volume, average number of trades per day, average size of trades, and highest daily volume for the year. Over this period, average daily volume increased from 18.6 million shares to 141.0 million shares. In part, this increase is accounted for by an increase in the average number of trades per day (from 37,474 trades to 74,988 trades). More striking, however, is the increase in the average size of trades (from 495 shares per trade to 1,881 shares per trade).[5] Also striking is the increase in peak daily volume—from 35.2 million shares in 1975 to 244.3 million shares in 1986. Tremendous demands are now being made on the markets.

In the early 1970s, securities firms were primarily involved in providing traditional agency services, in conducting stock research, in advising customers about investment opportunities, and in managing customer accounts and their own portfolios. Only within the last decade has trading

---

[5]This increase reflects the growing importance of institutional trading in the market.

Table 1.2   ORDER FLOW TO THE NEW YORK STOCK EXCHANGE

Year	Average daily volume (000)	Average number of trades per day	Average size of trades	Highest daily volume (000)
1975	18,551	37,474	495	35,158
1976	21,186	37,892	559	44,513
1977	20,928	32,626	641	35,261
1978	28,591	39,879	717	66,370
1979	32,237	40,986	787	81,619
1980	44,871	51,443	872	84,297
1981	46,853	46,230	1,013	92,881
1982	65,052	49,838	1,305	149,385
1983	85,334	59,489	1,434	129,411
1984	91,190	51,201	1,781	236,565
1985	109,169	58,130	1,878	181,027
1986	141,028	74,988	1,881	244,293

Sources: NYSE *Fact Book,* 1983 and 1987.

grown at an astonishing rate and have the standard investment operations of securities firms lost relative position. Several factors account for this development.

Fixed commissions were precluded with the passage by Congress of the Securities Acts Amendments of 1975. This regulatory change reduced the explicit costs of trading and spurred an increased flow of orders to the market. At the same time, the deregulation has reduced the commission income received by brokerage houses for handling the large orders of institutional investors. As a consequence, the brokerage houses have turned to trading for their own accounts as an alternative source of income.

During the past decade, the industry has been transformed by the introduction of new financial instruments such as futures and options. These instruments have greatly expanded the range of trading decisions that can be made and, in so doing, have increased the importance of the trading desk. The new instruments have also created complex arbitrage opportunities that are exploited by traders, not investment managers. Futures and options are short term instruments; if they are used, they are traded with some frequency.

The large scale institution of computer technology has integrated markets, accelerated the dissemination and analysis of information, expanded the range of trading decisions investors can make, and enabled the market centers to handle the explosive growth of the order flow. The increased importance of trading could not have occurred without modern computer technology, and, with this technology, trading will remain one of the most important operations of securities firms.

The current era of deregulation and the advent of computer technology, in combination, have resulted in the globalization of trading. Market centers around the world are being linked electronically, and trading is becoming a 24 hour affair. Complex, multicurrency financing plans are now routinely arranged for multinational corporations by multinational commercial and investment banks. International trading and arbitrage with multicurrency settlements are natural adjuncts to the operation.

The introduction of new and sophisticated financial instruments, the advent of computer technology, and the globalization of the markets have opened an exciting new era for the financial markets. These trends are continuing with no end in sight. The challenges and opportunities involved have attracted a special group of people to the industry. This, in and of itself, will continue to enhance the importance of trading.

CONCLUSION

The secondary markets are vital to the economy: (1) They provide the marketability of shares. (2) Share valuations established in the secondary markets are important pricing guides for the issuance of new shares and for the portfolio decisions of investors; they are also used for various legal purposes (for instance, the valuation of estate held shares and the redemption of mutual fund shares). (3) Share valuations reflect the market's assessment of managerial performance. (4) The shareholder population is large—over one person in five in the United States owns shares that are traded in the secondary markets.

The secondary markets for financial assets do not behave like the perfectly competitive markets of frictionless economics. Despite the power of modern technology, various trading costs impede the behavior of market participants and necessitate their making strategic decisions when they approach the market to trade. These decisions depend upon the market's architecture—the rules that determine how orders are handled and translated into trades. As is not the case in a frictionless environment, the institutional design of a market matters—it affects the market's operational efficiency.

Market architecture differs widely among the various market centers throughout the world, and a wide range of alternatives is available to those involved with market design. There has been considerable change, innovation, and experimentation with market design in recent years, and clear advances have been made. Nevertheless, much still remains to be learned about how a securities market operates, and certain basic issues have yet to be resolved.

The scope and importance of trading have increased dramatically in recent years. The profession offers tremendous challenge and reward. It is hoped that this book will yield some insight into what is involved.

chapter 2

Trading Systems

This chapter presents an overview of the design features of a trading system. Further institutional detail is given in Chapter 3 ("The U.S. Stock Exchange and Over-the-Counter Markets"), and analyses of the comparative advantages of alternative systems are presented in Chapter 12 ("The Economics of Market Making"), Chapter 13 ("Market Architecture"), and Chapter 14 ("Regulation").

In this chapter basic terms concerning prices, orders, and trading priority rules are identified. Dealer markets are differentiated from agency markets; then call markets are differentiated from continuous markets. Issues involving the consolidation/fragmentation of orders in the market are considered. Alternative procedures used for order display and trade execution are described, and finally the alternative procedures used for price stabilization are identified.

PRICES, ORDERS, AND TRADING PRIORITY RULES

Prices

The prices at which traders state they would be willing to transact are *quotation prices*:

- An *ask quotation* is an offer to sell at a specific price, the *ask price*.
- A *bid quotation* is an offer to buy at a specific price, the *bid price*.

The prices at which transactions are made are *transaction prices*. Usually, but not always, transactions are made at previously announced bid or ask quotations.

Orders

A public trader gives an order to a broker who, as the trader's agent, directs the order to a market center where a trade may be arranged. A trader must, of course, specify the exact number of shares to be bought or sold. In addition, the public trader must tell the broker how the order is to be handled in the market. Instructions may be very specific (for example, buy 300 shares at the market opening only, and only if the price is 49⅞ or lower). Alternatively, the order may give the trader's agent the freedom to use his or her own judgment and may be worked as a discretionary order by a professional on the trading floor.

Most orders are written either as limit orders or as market orders. Limit orders set a limit on the price at which they can be executed. A limit buy order sets the *maximum* price at which the trader will buy; a limit sell order sets the *minimum* price at which the trader will sell. Price limits for buy orders are usually set below the current price at which shares can be bought; price limits for sell orders are usually set above the current price at which shares can be sold. A price limit may also be placed on a large order to avoid the risk of the order's causing a large price change if it were to execute immediately. Limit orders that do not execute upon arrival are held on the market by being entered in a *limit order book,* a file of orders sequenced by price and time of arrival. Limit orders remain active on the book until they execute, are withdrawn, or expire. *Day orders* are automatically cancelled at the end of the day in which they are submitted; *good till cancelled* (GTC) orders remain on the book until cancelled.

A market order to buy or to sell is to be executed *at market,* namely, at the best price established on the market. For a market order seller, the best price is the highest bid posted by a buyer; for a market order buyer, the best price is the lowest ask posted by a seller. Market order traders usually face some uncertainty concerning the exact price at which they will transact, but, unlike limit order traders, they are assured of transacting.

Trading Priority Rules

The Price Priority Rule   With *price priority,* buyers posting higher bids have priority over buyers posting lower bids, and sellers posting lower asks have priority over sellers posting higher asks. This assures that traders who are willing to pay the highest prices will be the first to receive shares, that sellers willing to accept the lowest prices will be the first to sell shares, and that market order traders will buy at the lowest currently available prices and sell at the highest currently available prices.

Secondary Trading Priority Rules   A *secondary trading priority rule* specifies the sequence to be followed for orders that have been submitted at the same price. The secondary priority rule most commonly used is *time priority:* the first order placed is the first to execute. An alternative rule that is sometimes used is *size priority:* the largest order is the first to execute. A third alternative is *pro rata* execution of all orders tied at a price. In addition, certain classes of traders (for example, public traders) may be given priority over other classes of traders (such as market professionals on a trading floor).

DEALER MARKETS VERSUS AGENCY MARKETS

Dealers and Brokers

A *broker* is a trader's agent. In an *agency market,* public orders go to a broker's broker, who matches them with other public orders. Market professionals do not participate in trading in an agency market.

A *dealer,* unlike a broker, participates in trades as a principal, not as an agent. As a principal, a dealer satisfies a public order by buying for his or her own inventory, or by selling from his or her own inventory. In a *dealer market,* public traders do not trade directly with each other, but rather trade with a dealer who serves as intermediary.

Dealer Markets

The United States *over-the-counter* (OTC) market is a dealer market. When the public (through a broker) buys or sells shares in the OTC, they buy from a dealer or sell to a dealer. OTC dealers are allowed to handle public limit orders, but they do not do so in the normal course of business.

An Agency Market

The Tokyo Stock Exchange (TSE) is a pure agency market. The market on the TSE is established by the limit order book. The floor officials who oversee the books on the TSE (called *Saitori*) are not allowed to participate in trades for stocks assigned to them. Rather, they only maintain the limit order books and monitor trading.

Exchange Markets

Most securities exchanges are essentially agency/auction markets. This is because the flow of public orders is typically consolidated on an exchange's trading floor so as to allow the direct interaction of public buy and sell orders in an auction environment. The unfilled limit orders of some public traders establish the prices at which other public traders can transact by market orders. In addition, orders held by floor traders can be matched in an auction process.

The United States exchanges are also dealer markets. In a system that is unique to the U.S. exchanges, trading is structured around the *stock exchange specialist,* a market professional who functions as both a dealer and a broker's broker. As dealer, a specialist posts quotes on the market and buys for and sells from inventory. As a broker's broker, a specialist also handles limit orders for the stocks assigned to his or her trading post. Accordingly, the specialist maintains the limit order book (as do the *Saitori* on the Tokyo Stock Exchange). Unlike those of the *Saitori,* however, the posted quotes may be the specialist's own quotes. In addition, the U.S. specialist has the affirmative obligation to intervene in trading to make a fair and orderly market.

The New York Stock Exchange (NYSE) and the American Stock Exchange (Amex), as agency/auction markets, also allow for the direct interaction of traders on the trading floor. The professional floor traders may trade from their own accounts or may handle orders for other floor traders.[1] In addition, some floor traders are agents for member firms (brokerage houses such as Merrill Lynch or Morgan Stanley). When trading in an issue is active, the floor traders form a "crowd" that competes with the specialist and the limit order book in the purchase and sale of shares.

CONTINUOUS MARKETS VERSUS CALL MARKETS

One of the most basic design features of a trading system is whether it is structured as a call or as a continuous market. A *continuous market* allows trades to be made at any time during a trading day that counterpart orders cross in price. In a *call market,* orders are batched for simultaneous execution at the points in time when the market is "called." Call markets typically have one or two calls for a stock in a trading day.

The U.S. financial markets (both the securities exchanges and the OTC markets) are continuous trading systems. Major call markets include the stock exchanges in Austria, Belgium, France, Germany, and Israel.

---

[1]To avoid conflicts of interest, the floor professionals are prohibited from acting as both principal and agent in the same stock on the same day.

Continuous Markets

Both dealer and auction markets can be *continuous*. In a dealer market, each dealer making a market in a stock has an obligation to maintain a continuous, two-sided market for the stock. This necessitates that the dealer continuously maintain both a bid quotation (at which the public can sell shares) and an ask quotation (at which the public can buy shares). Continuous, two-sided markets are maintained in an agency market by the public limit orders that have been entered on the limit order books, and/or by floor traders in the crowd.

With a continuous market, traders can observe the behavior of bid and ask quotations, transaction prices, and trading volume over the course of the trading day. This information on current market conditions—called *floor information*—is valuable to traders in writing their orders.

Furthermore, the posting of quotes in a continuous market gives traders the option of placing market orders and thereby of being certain of achieving a transaction. In an orderly market, market order traders also have a good indication of the prices at which their orders will execute. Market order traders do not have complete certainty, however, because the availability of information is limited, the dissemination of floor information is not instantaneous, and order transmission is not immediate.

Call Markets

Call markets are primarily agency, not dealer, markets. The essence of a call is that orders that have accumulated over a period of time are batched for simultaneous execution, and all crossing orders are executed at the same price. Because public orders interact directly with other public orders in the batching process, a dealer need not participate in trading as an intermediary.

Trading in a call market can be either by written auction or by verbal auction. On the Paris Bourse, for instance, a verbal auction is used for actively traded issues, and a written auction is used for the smaller issues. The verbal auction is more expensive to operate, but also more desirable for floor traders, who are able to adjust their orders as the call searches for a clearing price. Traders in the written auction must, in ignorance of current market conditions, specify the price and size of their orders before trading begins (as must traders who are not present on the floor in the verbal auction).

Both limit and market orders can be submitted to a call. As with continuous trading, the *limit orders* specify a maximum price for buy orders, and a minimum price for sell orders. *Market orders* also have the same meaning: they are to transact at whatever price is established at the call. Compared with continuous trading, however, market order traders are far less certain about the prices at which their orders will transact: advance indications are generally not posted in currently existing call markets, and bid-ask quotations are not revealed until the market is called. In fact, market order traders may not even be assured of a transaction: call markets generally have a provision that no trading will be allowed at a given call if the price established at that call differs by more than a maximum allowable amount from the price established at the previous call. Consequently, a market order submitted to a call market does not resemble a market order submitted to a continuous market; rather, it is equivalent to a limit order written at the highest allowable call price (for a buy order) or at the lowest allowable call price (for a sell order).

Whether written or verbal, the orders for an issue are revealed to an auctioneer (an exchange official) when the market is called. Much as in the process depicted in standard microeconomics, buy and sell orders are matched so that a price that most closely equates the aggregate number of shares offered for sale (at that price and below) with the aggregate number of shares sought for purchase (at that price and above) may be found. Then, all market orders to buy and all buy limit orders at the clearing price or higher are executed, as are all market orders to sell and all sell limit orders at the clearing price or lower. In a call market, buyers and sellers all trade at the same clearing price.

Therefore, the price priority rule is strictly adhered to in call market trading. A secondary priority rule is also required for call market trading because with discrete order size and minimum allowable price changes,[2] no price at which the total number of buy orders precisely equals the total number of sell orders may exist. Therefore, orders on the "heavy" side of the market must be either rationed or absorbed. The excess of buys over sells (or of sells over buys) is typically rationed by random selection, or pro rata execution,[3] or else is absorbed by professional traders acting in a dealer capacity.[4]

Mixed Systems

Some exchange systems are mixtures of continuous and batched trading. Call markets such as the German and Austrian exchanges allow for continuous trading (referred to as a *call back period*) after the call market trading has been completed for certain larger issues. On the Geneva Stock Ex-

---

[2]The minimum allowable price change is one-eighth of a point for most issues traded in most U.S. equity markets.

[3]Some call markets assure that an execution will be realized by all market order traders and limit order traders with prices better than the clearing price and therefore ration only those limit orders with prices equal to the clearing price.

[4]A time priority rule is not possible because orders are not posted in the market until the market is called.

change, traders standing around an oval counter announce their buy and sell orders as an exchange official sequentially calls the market for listed securities; any trader can, however, interrupt the list whenever desired and reactivate trading in any issue for which the market has already been called.

Some continuous exchange markets operate as a call at one particularly critical moment during the trading day—at the market opening. The opening bell rings at 9:30 A.M. on the NYSE and Amex, but the market for individual stocks does not open until the specialist has found an opening price. In the opening procedure, orders that have been placed before the start of the trading session are batched together, tentative price indications may be given out to the "crowd" of brokers and floor traders, and the buy/sell desires of floor traders are assessed. Much like the call market auctioneer in a batched trading regime, the specialist starts trading at a price that best balances the buy and sell desires expressed at the time when the market opens.

The Tokyo Stock Exchange is a continuous trading system. However, for the six most heavily traded securities on the TSE, both a morning and an afternoon session are opened and closed with a formal market call.

CONSOLIDATION/FRAGMENTATION OF ORDERS

Orders are *consolidated* in a trading system if they are brought together for execution in one market. There are two dimensions to consolidation: time (temporal) and space (spatial). We considered temporal consolidation in the previous section, which deals with the distinction between continuous markets and call markets. Here we consider the spatial consolidation/fragmentation of orders.

A trading system is *spatially fragmented* if orders can be routed to different markets. For instance, the OTC competitive market maker system in the United States is a spatially fragmented market. The flow of orders to a securities exchange is consolidated at a single trading post;[5] nevertheless, the order flow may be fragmented for exchange listed issues: issues may be *cross-listed* (listed on more than one exchange); brokerage firms that are not exchange members may make off-board markets for listed securities (they are allowed to in the United States); and member firms may make in-house markets for listed securities (they are allowed to for some issues in the United States).

A trading system is also fragmented if some orders are handled differently than other orders. For instance, in the United States markets, small orders are typically routed to a specialist's post for immediate execution as a market order or are placed on the specialist's limit order book; medium

---

[5]The U.S. exchanges have experimented, but never successfully, with a system of competing specialists for a single issue.

size orders may be worked in the crowd by a floor trader; and large block trades are commonly negotiated off-board in the upstairs market and then brought to an exchange for execution as *put throughs*.[6]

Fragmented markets may be (and typically are) interlinked, both by telephone communication and by computer. The *National Association of Securities Dealers' Automated Quotations System* (NASDAQ) enables dealers and traders in the OTC market to see prices being set by other dealers. For exchange listed securities, the *Intermarket Trading System* (ITS) displays quotes posted in different markets to market makers on the national exchanges, the regional exchanges, and the OTC markets. ITS also provides an electronic linkage for intermarket executions. The *Consolidated Quotations System* (CQS) gives public traders floor information for exchange listed issues that are traded in different markets.

These electronic linkages enable prices set in one market center to be in tune with prices being set in other market centers. The linkages also make it feasible for arbitrageurs to keep prices in different market centers in close alignment. Accordingly, price setting may be efficient in a fragmented system, and, if orders are adequately exposed to the market in a fragmented system, price priorities may be preserved.

Electronic linkages, however, do not transform a fragmented market into a consolidated market. The actual consolidation of orders in one market allows the use of order handling and price determination procedures that are not possible in a fragmented system. For one thing, secondary priority rules such as the time priority rule can be instituted in a consolidated system, but not in a fragmented system. Furthermore, price movements may be stabilized in consolidated systems in ways that are not feasible in a fragmented system (for example, by the intervention of a designated market maker). The consolidation of trading in one market arena also facilitates the surveillance and monitoring of a market from a regulatory point of view. On the other hand, interdealer competition is stronger in a fragmented system, and a fragmented market may offer traders more flexibility for order handling than is possible in a consolidated system.

Achieving an optimal balance between fragmentation and consolidation is a difficult structural matter. The issue is dealt with further in Chapter 13 ("Market Architecture") and in Chapter 14 ("Regulation").

ORDER DISPLAY AND TRADE EXECUTION

This section focuses on the way in which orders are revealed to traders within a trading system. The methods used for order display vary widely among the equity markets.

---

[6]Block trades are all trades of 10,000 shares or more.

Dealer Markets

Orders displayed in the U.S. OTC market are the dealers' own bid and ask quotations. Quotes for NASDAQ issues are shown on NASDAQ.

Until October 1986, on the London Stock Exchange (a dealer market), jobbers (the dealers) displayed only the average of the bid and ask quotes (called the *midspread price*) on a chalkboard by their trading posts. Floor traders with customer orders could ask for the quotes and receive oral quotations before making a trade.[7] The holding back of floor information in the British system was undesirable from the viewpoint of traders, and deeper problems with the system led to the changes that were instituted in 1986.[8]

Exchange Markets

Call Market Systems   Orders are not displayed in batched trading until the market is called. At the market call, professionals on the trading floor reveal their orders at each price until the market clearing price is determined.

Order Book   In continuous markets such as the NYSE, Amex, and the TSE, public limit orders are stored in an order book. The book is open to floor traders on the TSE, but the NYSE and Amex books are closed, and only the price and size of the best quotes are revealed. On the U.S. exchanges, the displayed quotes may not be from the order book: they may alternatively be the specialist's own quotes or the quotes of floor traders, if these are better than the best quotes on the book.

The order book is a bilateral matching process that results in specific buyers' trading with specific sellers. Typically, two parties are involved in a trade, although a large buy (sell) order may be matched with two or more sell (buy) orders.

Board Display   Some continuous markets such as the Toronto, Hong Kong, Sydney, and Singapore exchanges use board trading systems.[9] With *board trading* (which is also a bilateral matching process), orders are posted so that they can be seen by all traders on the exchange floor. Usually orders

---

[7]Jobbers generally did not reveal the number of shares they were willing to buy or to sell at the quotes, but as a rule serviced an order in its entirety if it was not a large block.

[8]On October 27, 1986, the jobbers were required to disclose actual bids and offers in active securities (midspread prices continue to be shown for other securities); market professionals were for the first time given the freedom to operate in the dual capacity of both dealer and broker; and the era of fixed commissions ended.

[9]The Montreal Exchange, which also used a board trading system, changed to a specialist-type system in 1983.

are displayed at the best and second best bid quotations, and at the best and second best ask quotations. Multiple orders at a quote are usually written in time sequence, and the time priority rule usually determines the sequence in which they execute.

Quotations are displayed electronically in some board systems (for example, the Canadian exchanges) and by the physical writing of orders in other systems (such as the Hong Kong Exchange). On the Hong Kong Exchange, members have seats arranged in front of a chalkboard that spans the long front wall of the trading hall. There is a telephone for communicating with the member firm's home office at each member's seat, and a television monitor that enables distant sections of the board to be seen. Brokers themselves write orders on the board, putting their firm's initials by an order.

Only the two best bids and asks are displayed on the Hong Kong Exchange. If the arrival of a new order establishes a bid that is higher than the existing bid, the orders at what would be the third highest bid are erased (as are the orders at what would be the third lowest ask if a new and lower asking price were to be established). Trades are made when an exchange member accepts a quote written on the board; the price and quantity of the transaction are recorded on a "transactions" section on the bottom of the chalk board, forms are filled out, and the exchange is notified. The exchange personnel, however, are involved in neither the order entry process, the price setting procedures, nor the dissemination of floor information.

Crowd Trading   The Zurich Stock Exchange provides a good example of a bilateral matching system that uses crowd rather than board trading. Each security traded on the Zurich exchange is assigned to one of three trading rings. An official clerk opens trading in a security by calling the issue's name. However, unlike call market trading, the traders themselves announce their bid and ask quotations and seek counterparties to a trade. Because it is a matching system, each trade is bilateral, although a large buyer (seller) may deal with two or more sellers (buyers) simultaneously. There is no attempt to find a common price at which trades are made, and the deals struck for an issue may be made at different prices.

Issues on the Zurich exchange are divided into groups. The official clerk sequentially calls the market for each stock in a trading group. After trading has been completed for an issue, the exchange official calls out the next issue on the list. However, any trader may call back the market for any issue in a trading group, after that issue has already been called, until the trading session for the group has been completed.

The crowd system retains some of the advantages of the temporal order batching that characterizes a call market system, and it is a desirable arrangement for markets where there are not a large number of actively traded issues. By itself, crowd trading is not a practical method for the larger securities exchanges. Crowd trading is used, however, on the U.S. exchanges, along with the specialist/dealer system and the limit order book: floor traders gather by a specialist's post to participate in the auction process; they are free to agree on bilateral trades that bypass both the specialist and the book (so long as price priorities are maintained, and certain precedence requirements are met).

Pit Trading   In the United States, pit trading is used by commodities exchanges such as the Chicago Mercantile Exchange and the Chicago Board of Trade; in options exchanges, such as the Chicago Board Options Exchange; and in futures exchanges, such as the NYSE's New York Futures Exchange. *Pit trading* is a form of crowd trading: traders standing in a tiered, semicircular structure cry out buy/sell orders to each other and make bilateral trades.

Exchange members in the pit can trade from their own accounts or can handle customer orders as brokers. Because the market is continuous, trading continues throughout the session as new orders are brought into the crowd and as market professionals rebalance their inventories and react to new information and changing expectations.

The large number of traders typically gathered in a pit gives depth to the market, and neither a limit order book nor the services of a dealer/specialist are needed or used. Because it has both the depth of call market trading and the accessibility and informational advantages of continuous trading, pit trading has some very desirable characteristics. A particularly large flow of orders is required, however, to sustain the number of traders needed to make a pit work. For this reason, pit trading is used primarily for issues that have a large following in the market, and for which investor expectations change frequently. In the United States, for example, pit trading is used for futures contracts on market indexes for which there is a great deal of trading interest. Unfortunately there is not sufficient volume to sustain pit trading for even the most actively traded stocks such as IBM.

Negotiated Trades

Block orders are commonly negotiated away from the primary market centers because bringing them directly to the market would, because of their size, result in unacceptably large adverse price effects. In the United States, block trades are typically negotiated in the *upstairs market,* the network of trading desks that can communicate with each other and with institutional investors by means of electronic display systems and the telephone. In their bilateral negotiations, the upstairs traders use floor information, whatever other knowledge they can gather of market conditions, their detailed knowledge of their institutional clients' holdings and likely trading interests, and a good deal of strategy as they play the negotiation game.

Electronic Trading

Much electronic equipment has been introduced in recent years for order handling, information display, market surveillance, post trade clearance and, increasingly, for order matching and trading. Advances in computer technology and the sheer growth of trading over the past decade account for this development.

On the New York Stock Exchange, for instance, an *Opening Automated Report Service* (OARS) and *Designated Order Turnaround System* (DOT) electronically route orders to specialist posts for display and execution. With the launching of SuperDot 250 in November 1984, the NYSE obtained the capacity to handle daily trading volume of more than 250 million shares. Touch screen technology now exists at specialist posts on the NYSE, Amex, and other exchanges, and the era of fully automated workstations is approaching. State-of-the-art technology will include electronic display booths and electronic communication between member firms and specialist posts.

The computerized routing and display of orders are different, however, from computerized trading per se. In *computerized trading,* orders electronically entered in the system are executed, not by a market maker or by the traders themselves, but by the computer. The computer in this capacity has been referred to as a *black box,* and traders have been fearful of it: allowing the machine to handle trade execution restricts the exercise of human judgment at the most critical moment in the market process.

One of the first totally electronic trading systems, the *Computer Assisted Trading System* (CATS), was instituted in 1977 by the Toronto Stock Exchange. CATS is a continuous market system that stores orders on an electronic book, displays the orders to public traders via cathode-ray tube (CRT) devices, and enables public traders to cross orders on the book and thereby to achieve executions without the interference of exchange personnel.

CATS was developed by the Toronto Exchange for one simple reason: the exchange was running out of room on its trading floor. The system met with much opposition from floor traders, however, and has been used only for issues with the smallest average trading volume. But CATS has survived, and a modified version of it was in fact adopted by the Tokyo Stock Exchange in 1982. The Tokyo CATS has also been used for smaller issues, although the TSE extended the system in 1985 to all but 250 of its most heavily traded issues.

There are other electronic trading systems. In 1978 the Cincinnati

Stock Exchange started experimentation with its fully automated system, the *National Securities Trading System* (NSTS). The National Association of Securities Dealers (NASD) instituted its *Computer Assisted Execution System* (CAES) in 1983, and its *Small Order Execution System* (SOES) in late 1984. Currently, one of the fastest growing electronic intermarket linkage and trade execution systems is *Instinet,* a private firm that primarily provides an electronic block-trading facility for institutional investors and dealers. ARIEL, a London-based computerized block-trading system, was started in 1974. INTEX, the world's first fully automated futures exchange, started its Bermuda-based operations in October 1984.

With all these developments, however, computerized trading still faces problems. Traders in the equity markets do not submit orders with the same ease with which travelers, for instance, make airline reservations. Flight information has long since been computerized, and reservations can be made electronically for flights from virtually anywhere, to almost anywhere, from most places around the world. However, there is a major difference between the market for airline seats and the equity markets: the price of a plane ticket is predetermined (all the traveler need do is to book a seat); the price of asset shares, on the other hand, is determined while trading takes place.

Because the trading of shares and determining of price are concomitant processes, major traders in the equity markets are reluctant to enter orders in a black box system. Consequently, the computerized markets have had difficulty attracting the order flow needed to make markets. This has been particularly true for the larger issues, for which orders are commonly worked on the trading floor or are negotiated in the upstairs market.

PRICE STABILIZATION

Most securities exchanges have design features, including certain trading rules, that are intended to reduce the short term fluctuation of security prices. Although the rationale for these design features is often expressed in terms of the need to make an orderly market rather than in terms of price stabilization per se, the intent is the same: to prevent short run aberrations in the order flow from generating price changes that do not reflect broader market realities.

Maximum Price Change Limits

We have already noted one way in which prices are stabilized in call market trading: price change limits that prevent trading if the current price would differ from a previous price by an unacceptably large amount are imposed. Such limits are common in call market trading. A good example of their use occurred on the two trading days following the May 10, 1981, presidential election in France of the Socialist François Mitterand. Virtually no shares were traded May 11 on the Paris Bourse (a call market), as prices were marked down 10 percent (the maximum allowable price change) from their previous levels. The marked-down prices became the base prices for the trading session on May 12, at which point most shares were marked down an additional 10 to 20 percent.[10] Clearing prices were finally found for most issues on May 13, and trading was resumed for virtually all issues.

The imposition of maximum price change limits gives some protection to market order traders. Disallowing trades and announcing "buyers only" (when an upper limit has been hit) or "sellers only" (when a lower limit has been hit) also give the public a chance to learn of and to react to order imbalance. The additional orders that are then entered often serve to stabilize the market.

The Batching of Orders

The batching of the order flow itself helps to stabilize a market. As we have noted, orders can be batched *spatially* (by being consolidated in one market center) or *temporally* (by being consolidated over time in call market–type trading). Spatial order batching stabilizes price movements when it is associated with superior information flows and more orderly market conditions. Temporal order batching also mitigates instability caused by the sparsity of the order flow over short intervals of time.

Special Market Opening Procedures

Special opening procedures used by continuous market systems such as the NYSE facilitate price determination when trading resumes after the overnight period. Because prices that deviate from equilibrium values are generally more volatile, setting prices that best reflect broad demand/supply conditions is consistent with price stabilization.

The special opening procedure of the NYSE resembles call market–type trading, as noted. At the opening, orders that have accumulated while the exchange has been closed are brought together at one moment in time, and a price that best balances the accumulated buy and sell pressures is found.

---

[10]The maximum price change on any given day is greater if trading on the previous day has been disallowed.

Trading Halts

A *trading halt* in a continuous market environment is similar to the trading blockage that occurs in call market trading when a price limit has been hit. In the presence of major informational change the market cannot efficiently find new prices and handle trades at the same time. Furthermore, traders themselves may need time to assess a changing situation and to write their orders properly in relation to new market conditions.

The procedure for reopening the market at the end of a trading halt is the same as that used to open the market after the overnight period. During trading halts on the NYSE, the specialist assesses market conditions and tests the water by sending out price indications. When a reasonable price level is found, trading is resumed.

The Affirmative Obligation of Stock Exchange Specialists

Perhaps the most explicit stabilization procedure is the intervention of stock exchange specialists on the U.S. exchanges. Specialists have the affirmative obligation to make fair and orderly markets for the stocks assigned to them. "Fair and orderly" is viewed, not as price stabilization per se, but rather as the absence of excessively large and erratic price changes over a small number of shares traded. It is clear that, in providing a fair and orderly market, a specialist does dampen the short run volatility of prices.

Specialists do not, however, *peg* prices. That is, if the underlying market pressure for a price to change to a new level is present, the price indeed changes to the new level. What the specialist does is to make the transition to the new level more orderly. By the same token, the specialist keeps prices from fluctuating unduly if the equilibrium price for a stock has not in fact changed. This stabilization is of value to market order traders because it gives them greater assurance that prices will not behave erratically while their orders are in the process of being transmitted to the specialist posts. The stabilization is beneficial to all market participants because "noisy" prices transmit confusing signals of current market conditions.

Refusal to Allow Destabilizing Orders

Exchange rules exist to prevent the placing of orders that could have a destabilizing effect on price. In the U.S. and Canadian exchanges, for instance, market makers are strongly discouraged from reinforcing price trends by buying at a higher price after a price increase or by selling at a lower price after a price decrease. On the Tel Aviv Exchange, traders are not allowed to increase the size of their buy orders when the auctioneer calls out higher prices or to increase the size of their sell orders when the auctioneer calls out lower prices.

Stabilizing Speculation and the Participation of Other Large Traders

A larger order flow to a market results in greater market depth and therefore helps to stabilize prices. Accordingly, most market systems allow *speculating traders* to operate on the exchange floor. These traders are typically given advantages in the form of lower trading costs and preferred access to some market information.

Other market participants also buy and sell shares for the explicit purpose of stabilizing the market. OTC dealers to some extent freely do so in the U.S. markets. Making a better market increases their order flow and enhances relationships for dealers who are also investment bankers for particular firms.

Major securities firms in Japan and major banks in Israel also participate in trading to stabilize price fluctuations. Corporations, although they may wish to, are not allowed to stabilize the price of their own stock because of the possibilities for price manipulation that would be presented. In general, there is a fine line between price stabilization, price pegging, and price manipulation. Some students of the market are nervous when a well capitalized institution enters the scene.

CONCLUSION

Markets throughout the world use very different trading systems. The systems represent a wide array of viable alternatives, and opportunities (primarily with regard to electronic trading) that have not as yet been fully exploited exist. No one system is clearly superior, however, and the systems that have been used internationally depend, to a large extent, on circumstances that are unique to the various countries.

One principle is universal, however: in all markets, the orders that are submitted to a system, the prices that are established by a system, and the trades that are made depend upon the trading arrangements. This would not be the case if trading were a costless process; in a frictionless environment, the institutional design of a market should not matter.

SUGGESTED READING

D. Ayling, *The Internationalization of Stockmarkets: The Trend Towards Greater Foreign Borrowing and Investment*, Cambridge, England: Gower Publishing Company Limited, 1986.

K. Cohen, S. Maier, R. Schwartz, and D. Whitcomb, *The Microstructure of Securities Markets,* Englewood Cliffs, N.J.: Prentice-Hall, 1986.

K. Garbade, *Securities Markets,* New York: McGraw-Hill, 1982.

S. Smidt, ''Trading Floor Practices on Futures and Securities Exchanges: Economics, Regulation and Policy Issues,'' in A. Peck, Ed., *Futures Markets: Regulatory Issues,* Washington, D.C.: American Enterprise Institute, 1985.

chapter 3

The U.S. Stock Exchange and Over-the-Counter Markets

The U.S. secondary markets are classified as follows:

First market: refers to trades for exchange listed issues that are made on the floor of an exchange.

Second market: refers to OTC trades for OTC issues.

Third market: refers to trades in exchange listed issues that take place off the exchange floor (OTC) with the aid of brokers.

Fourth market: refers to trades in exchange listed issues that are arranged by buyers and sellers, off the exchange floor, without the aid of brokers.[1]

[1]None of these refers to the *upstairs market,* the network of trading desks that negotiate the block transactions. Trades negotiated in the upstairs market are generally taken to a market center to be executed.

There are two national stock exchanges:

> New York Stock Exchange (NYSE)
>
> American Stock Exchange (Amex)

and five regional exchanges:

> Boston Stock Exchange (B)
>
> Cincinnati Stock Exchange (C)
>
> Midwest Stock Exchange (M) (headquartered in Chicago)
>
> Pacific Stock Exchange (P) (headquartered in San Francisco with trading floors in San Francisco and Los Angeles)
>
> Philadelphia Stock Exchange (X)

The over-the-counter (OTC) market comprises:

1. Inactive issues that are usually traded in regional brokerage offices.
2. Thinner issues that command some national trading interest: bid and ask quotations are reported daily in "pink sheets" mailed nationally to brokers by the National Quotation Bureau.
3. Actively traded issues that are listed on the National Association of Securities Dealers' (NASD) Automated Quotation System (NASDAQ).
4. The most actively traded issues that are listed on the NASDAQ National Market System (NMS).

This chapter focuses on the operations of the U.S. stock exchange and over-the-counter markets. Their objectives are the same, but the exchange and OTC markets follow very different approaches to market making. We establish the objectives and compare the systems.

The chapter considers the functions of the trading systems and outlines the organizational structure of the market centers. The order handling procedures that are used are explained, as is the dissemination of information. The chapter identifies the revenues and costs associated with market making and contrasts the exchange and OTC systems.

WHAT A MARKET CENTER DOES

Order Handling and Trade Execution

Three steps comprise the transaction process: (1) receipt of customer orders by brokerage houses and transmission of the orders to a market center, (2) order handling and trade execution within a market center, and (3) post-trade clearance and settlement. Only the second step is handled by the market centers themselves.

Order handling and trade execution are the most visible and obvious functions of the trading systems. Related activities include the dissemination of floor information and dealer/specialist intervention in the transaction process. Floor information enables public traders to write their orders in light of current market conditions. Dealer/specialist intervention makes it easier for public orders to transact quickly and at reasonable prices during the trading day.

Monitoring the Integrity of Member Firms, Listed Firms, and Traders

The U.S. market centers are *self-regulatory organizations* (SROs). The stock exchanges are SROs for the exchange markets. The SRO for the OTC market is the National Association of Securities Dealers (NASD).

In their SRO capacity, the exchanges and the NASD impose, monitor, and enforce a variety of requirements with which the broker/dealer firms and listed companies must comply:

- Broker/dealer firms must meet minimum capital requirements, satisfy certain standards and licensing requirements, and follow various training and disciplinary procedures.
- The listed companies must satisfy various listing and disclosure requirements.

The SROs also monitor trading to guard against unfair trading practices:

- Price manipulation
- Inflation of trading volume to create the impression of interest (''painting the tape'')
- Unfair exploitation of information that has not been made public

The stock exchanges monitor specialists to ensure adequate compliance with their affirmative obligation to make a fair and orderly market. The exchanges demand an explanation from a specialist whenever a price change does not appear reasonable, rate the specialists, and give preference to better specialist units in their stock allocation procedures. When poor performance necessitates it, an exchange can take a stock away from the specialist firm to which it has been assigned.

The NASD conducts field examinations of its member firms at least once a year. Infractions are brought to the *District Business Conduct Committees* (DBCCs), of which there are 14 district offices. The DBCCs can censure, fine, suspend, or even expel a broker/dealer firm from the NASD. In 1985, the NASD introduced its *Equity Audit Trail,* an automated, online system that monitors trading activity in the NASDAQ market. This surveillance facility provides an integrated data base of second-by-second trade data (quotes and transactions) for all NASDAQ securities.

Substantial resources are required for the oversight of member firms, for the surveillance of the market makers, and for the stock watch over public traders. These operations of the SROs are also reinforced by oversight systems of the Securities and Exchange Commission (SEC), the federal regulatory agency in Washington, D.C.

Price Discovery

Price discovery—the determination of the prices at which trades are made—is one of the most important but least understood functions of the market centers. For two reasons price determination in the equity markets is more complex than in many competitive markets: (1) prices are established while trading takes place, and (2) the desire of traders to buy and to sell shares is continually in flux.

As discussed in Chapter 1, price determination in a securities market depends on the design of the marketplace—in particular, on the extent to which orders are consolidated in the market, on the market information that is disseminated, on dealer/specialist participation in trading, and on market protocols that govern the way in which orders are permitted to interact. These and related design features are critical: buy/sell propensities change rapidly in the markets, and equilibrium prices, if not found quickly, may not be found at all because the target is perpetually moving.

Liquidity

Broadly defined, the *liquidity* of a market is the ease with which shares can be traded at prices that are reasonable in relation to underlying demand conditions. Liquid markets are characterized by depth, breadth, and resiliency:

> *Depth:* A market has depth if a sufficient number of orders exists at prices above and below the price at which shares are currently trading.
>
> *Breadth:* A market has breadth if these orders exist in substantial volume (that is, if the orders are sufficiently large).
>
> *Resiliency:* A market has resiliency if temporary price changes due to temporary order imbalances quickly attract new orders to the market.

In illiquid markets, traders incur transaction costs above explicit costs such as commission fees. The hidden costs of trading, called *execution costs,* are incurred by buyers who pay higher prices for the shares they receive and by sellers who receive lower prices for the shares they deliver. Execution costs are attributable to three factors:

1. *The bid-ask spread:* With a spread, market order traders buy at higher prices ("at the ask") and sell at lower prices ("at the bid"). The market spread for an issue is wide when the market lacks sufficient depth.

2. *Market impact effects:* Market impact means that an order, because of its size, executes at an inferior price (large buyers pay a price premium, and large sellers accept a price reduction to attract a counterparty to the trade). Similarly, the chance arrival of a sequence of buy orders moves price up, and the chance arrival of a sequence of sell orders moves price down. Market impact effects are substantial when the market lacks sufficient breadth.

3. *Inaccurate price discovery:* Inaccurate prices can prevail if a market, lacking sufficient resiliency, does not quickly receive additional stabilizing orders when trades are made at disequilibrium prices.

The liquidity of a marketplace is enhanced by the willingness of dealers and specialists to supply capital to market making, by the integration of submarkets, and by information systems that allow traders to stay in tune with current market conditions.

Technological Development and Implementation

The market centers have devoted major resources to improving their trading systems. The NASD's introduction of NASDAQ in 1971 has had a tremendous impact on the efficiency of the OTC markets. NASDAQ has integrated the dealer markets and has enabled the largest OTC broker/dealer firms to gain national recognition. With NASDAQ, spreads have tightened, the quality of executions realized by public traders has improved, and the OTC has become competitive with the exchanges as a market center.[2]

The NASD has recently made further improvements in the efficiency of NASDAQ. It has also developed *CAES,* its *Computer Assisted Execution System* for NASDAQ/NMS and exchange listed issues, and *SOES,* its *Small Order Execution System.* In 1985, SOES was expanded to include all NASDAQ issues. SOES trades are "locked in" (that is, they do not require subsequent confirmation by both sides, as do oral trades), reported to NASDAQ, and transmitted to a clearing corporation. The NASD has now developed the computer capability to support a 200 million share day for its NASDAQ market.

---

[2]Competition between the market centers primarily involves the listings of the firms whose shares are traded.

The exchange markets were interlinked in the late 1970s with the institution of the *Intermarket Trading System* (ITS) and the *Consolidated Quotations System* (CQS). In addition, the exchanges have transformed their trading floors with the introduction of electronic equipment for order routing, information display, and small order execution. Technological change in the exchange markets has not been confined to the trading systems, however. In recent years, new financial instruments referred to as *derivative products*—options, futures on stock market indexes and subindexes, and options on futures—have been introduced.

The era of change in the securities markets is far from over. Pressures for change have come, and will continue to come, from five sources:

1. *Government:* In the early 1970s, the industry was prodded by the federal government (Congress and the SEC) to reduce barriers to competition, to integrate the markets, to display quotes widely, and generally to improve the efficiency of operations. Government pressure, though somewhat abated, has continued. In part this is the result of the SEC's continuing participation in monitoring the markets to guard against fraud, manipulation, and the abuse of position.
2. *Order flow:* Growth of the order flow (which in part is the result of technological and regulatory change that has reduced the cost of trading) has put continuing pressure on the trading systems.
3. *Intermarket competition:* Intermarket competition has intensified, primarily between the two major alternative systems, the exchange markets and the NASD.
4. *Advent of new systems:* The emergence of independent firms (such as Instinet) that provide electronic order routing and trade execution services has put new competitive pressures on the exchanges and the NASD.
5. *Globalization of trading:* The interlinking of international markets and the attending growth of international trading have created new opportunities and new competitive pressures for the domestic market centers.

The incentive for technological change is now endogenous to the industry. Fostering the development of new financial instruments and of superior trading systems has become a major function of the market centers.

ORGANIZATIONAL STRUCTURE

The Stock Exchanges

The structures of the various U.S. stock exchanges are similar (although differences do exist). Thus, for simplicity, we make reference only to the New York Stock Exchange for the remainder of this chapter.

Exchange Members   The NYSE is a corporation governed by a board of directors that sets policy and supervises operations. Members of the Exchange are individuals. A member may own a membership sometimes called a *seat,* or be a nominee of a firm that owns the seat. A securities firm is called a *member firm* and can do business on the trading floor, if either a partner or an officer of the firm is a member.

Some member firms, primarily those that operate retail networks, are referred to as *wire houses,* a term that developed in the days when a special hard wire connection (teletype) was used to transmit orders from the various offices of the brokerage houses to the Exchange. The major wire houses and other NYSE member firms are also members of the NASD. Thus many broker/dealer firms are simultaneously members of the Exchange, customers of the Exchange, and competitors of the Exchange.

The number of seats on the NYSE is fixed at 1366. Seats can be bought, sold, or leased, and their price, as set by buyers and sellers, reflects the demand to own a seat. In addition to the regular Exchange members, 96 individuals, by paying an annual fee, have obtained either physical or electronic access to the Exchange's trading floor.

Trading Systems   The NYSE comprises three major trading systems:

1. *Main trading floor:* The largest trading arena on the Exchange is the main trading floor, where stocks, warrants, and American Depository Receipts (ADRs) are traded.[3] Trading on the floor is handled at the specialist posts.
2. *Automated Bond System (ABS):* ABS is a computerized system that provides current quotations and trade information and gives electronic executions for listed bonds. ABS is used primarily for smaller orders that can be handled electronically (the major bond market is OTC).[4]
3. *New York Futures Exchange (NYFE):* NYFE (pronounced "knife") is the market where futures contracts for the NYSE composite index, other stock market indexes, and a commodity price index are exchanged in pit trading. NYFE, the most recent of the Exchange's operations, opened on August 7, 1980. On January 28, 1983, NYFE also started trading options on the NYSE composite index futures contract. The NYSE also trades options on the NYSE composite index, on the NYSE High Beta Index, and on several stocks.

---

[3]An ADR is a certificate, issued by a U.S. bank that represents ownership of a foreign security in the bank's possession. ADRs facilitate trading in foreign stocks; they are registered in the name of the individual owner, pay dividends declared on the underlying stock, but do not convey voting rights to the individual owner.

[4]In addition to ABS, the NYSE also has *cabinet trading* for infrequently traded bonds (the system derives its name from the fact that orders to buy and to sell are physically entered on paper forms that are filed in cabinets) and *crowd trading* for a few actively traded issues.

The Floor Traders   Exchange members who operate on the trading floor include the following:

1. *Specialists:* The specialists function as both brokers and dealers; they have the affirmative obligation to make a fair and orderly market for stocks assigned to them.
2. *Commission brokers:* These brokers, employed by the brokerage houses, are the link between the brokerage houses and the specialist posts. The commission brokers operate from booths along the outside walls of the trading floor, where they receive orders from their firms' clients.
3. *Two-dollar brokers:* The two-dollar brokers perform the same functions as the commission brokers but are not employed by a brokerage house. Rather, for a commission (which used to be two dollars an order), they execute orders for commission brokers who are not able to handle all of the orders that have been transmitted to their firms.
4. *Registered traders:* These traders deal for their own account and may also be two-dollar brokers or even specialists. They may not act as both agent and principal on the same stock on the same day.
5. *Registered Competitive Market Makers (RCMMs):* There are currently 22 RCMMs who, as nonspecialist floor members, can be called upon to aid the specialist firms by adding liquidity to the market at times of particular stress.

The Listed Companies   A company can have shares traded on the NYSE only if it is listed with the Exchange. To be listed, a company must satisfy minimum standards of quality and size, must be willing to release adequate information about its operations, and must attract sufficient public interest. The following minimum requirements are imposed by the Exchange:

1. Market value of publicly held shares: $18 million
2. Net tangible assets: $16 million
3. Number of shares publicly held: 1.1 million
4. Earnings before federal income tax for latest fiscal year: $2.5 million
5. Earnings before federal income tax for each of the two preceding years: $2 million
6. Number of stockholders who hold 100 shares or more: 2000

The stock of a newly listed company is allocated by the Exchange's stock allocation committee to a specialist unit that is then responsible for making the market in the stock. Interested specialist firms apply for the allocation of newly listed securities. The committee's allocation procedure takes into account the specialist firm's prior performance record and characteristics (such as industry identification) of the issues currently assigned to the specialist firm.

Delisting is also possible, but it occurs infrequently and only with difficulty if a stock continues to satisfy the listing criteria.[5] The NYSE does, however, grant a delisting request if the following conditions are met:

1. At least two-thirds of the holders of outstanding shares vote in favor of delisting.
2. No more than 10 percent of the holders of outstanding shares object to delisting.
3. Delisting is approved by a majority of the company's board of directors.

The Over-the-Counter Market

The OTC market comprises thousands of geographically dispersed securities firms that are linked primarily by telephone. The term *over-the-counter* originated in an earlier era when stocks and bonds were commonly bought and sold in banks, and the certificates were passed "over the counter." The term does not apply in today's sophisticated markets, but has remained to describe all secondary market trading other than that which takes place on the organized exchanges.

The Issues Traded Corporate common stock, warrants, preferred stock, ADRs, and some bonds are traded in both the exchange and the OTC markets. Options and futures are traded in exchange markets. Most corporate bonds, municipal bonds, and government securities are traded OTC, as are mutual funds, virtually all bank stocks (except for the large money center banks), and insurance company stocks. Real Estate Investment Trusts (REITs) also trade mostly over-the-counter.

OTC dealers operate both in the primary market (where new shares are issued) and in the secondary market (where shares that have already been issued are traded). In contrast, the stock exchange specialists are allowed to operate only in the secondary market.

The OTC is the major market for stocks with regional but not national appeal, and for the stocks of newer firms that do not meet the listing requirements of the exchanges. The OTC market, however, also includes several hundred major companies that qualify for exchange listing, but that have elected to remain on the OTC.

[5]Delisting is not impeded on the Amex.

The premier market in the OTC is the NASDAQ/NMS list. Issues on this list, which are the most actively traded of the OTC stocks, must meet criteria set by the SEC.[6] Unlike other OTC issues, stocks traded in the NASDAQ/NMS are subject to last-sale price and volume reporting, in addition to bid and ask quotations. The number of issues in the NASDAQ and NASDAQ/NMS markets has grown rapidly in recent years. Currently, these markets comprise the second largest stock market in the United States: their share volume is exceeded only by that of the NYSE and is considerably greater than that of the Amex.

The NASD   The 1938 Maloney Act Amendments to the Securities and Exchange Act of 1934 allowed for self-regulation in the securities industry, under the supervision of the SEC. The NASD, which is headquartered in Washington, D.C., was established under the authority granted by this act. As the SRO for the OTC markets, the NASD has provided an organizational structure for its member firms, has imposed a uniform set of rules, and has developed information, order routing, and execution systems.

The NASD does not have a statutory monopoly on self-regulation— multiple SROs would be allowed under the authority granted by the 1938 Maloney Act. However, NASD rules that restrict or prohibit dealings between members and nonmembers have put nonmembers at a substantial disadvantage in obtaining the order flow necessary to create a liquid market. Therefore, for all intents and purposes, the NASD is the sole SRO for the OTC market.

As an SRO, the NASD has established the *Rules of Fair Practice* for its members. The rules apply to the financial integrity of member firms, to sales practices and customer services (including the suitability of recommendations and execution of orders), and to market making and underwriting activities.

Unlike the exchange specialists, OTC dealers do not have an affirmative obligation to make a fair and orderly market. OTC market makers in a stock must, however, maintain quotes during the trading day. The NASD's *Rules of Fair Practice* also include the 5 percent *markup policy,* which prevents NASD members from profiting unreasonably at the expense of their customers.[7] Another NASD rule is that a firm cannot act as both a

---

[6]See Table 3.1 for the listing requirements.

[7]A *markup* is the percentage difference between a market maker's purchase price of shares and the (higher) price at which the shares are subsequently sold; a *markdown* is the percentage difference between the price at which a market maker sells short and the (lower) price at which the shares are subsequently bought. The *5 percent markup policy* is a guideline used to determine whether or not a dealer's markup or markdown is reasonable. Other factors considered relate to the risk of the issue, the liquidity of the market, and the cost of processing an order.

broker and a dealer in the same transaction. Therefore, if a firm sells stock from its own inventory, it is not allowed to receive a brokerage commission on the same transaction.

The NASD, like the exchanges, maintains surveillance of the markets. Prices and volume are monitored; a surveillance staff is alerted by an automated system to any unusual trading activity; and quotes can be halted while the NASD seeks an explanation.

The OTC Dealers   As of 1986, over 6600 broker/dealer firms were members of the NASD, and over 404,000 people were registered with the NASD as registered representatives (sales personnel). Public traders buy or sell shares in the OTC by trading with the broker/dealer firms. Public traders generally do not have direct access to these firms, however—a public order must be entered by a broker who is known by the dealer house.

OTC dealers specialize in the stocks they handle; a dealer that specializes in an issue is known as a *market maker* for that issue. Unlike the exchange system, issues are not assigned to the dealer firms, but rather are selected by the firms. When a dealer firm is established as a market maker for an issue, it must make a continuous two-sided market (it must continuously post both bid and ask quotations) for the issue.

Typically, between 2 and 20 dealers make a market in an OTC stock, with more actively traded stocks attracting a larger number of dealers. With over 6600 firms in the industry, and given the ease with which any particular firm can start making a market for any given issue, the dealer market is, indeed, competitive—both actual competition and the threat of potential competition limit the returns dealers can expect to realize from making markets for individual stocks.

NASDAQ   *NASDAQ,* the NASD's Automated Quotation System, is a nationwide electronic system that displays dealer quotes on terminals in brokerage offices across the country. For an issue to be included in the NASDAQ system, the issuing company must satisfy certain minimum listing requirements:

1. Number of publicly held shares: 100,000
2. Total assets: $2 million
3. Capital and retained earnings: $1 million
4. Number of market makers for its shares: 2
5. Shareholders of record: 300

To join the NASDAQ system, OTC market makers must satisfy the following requirements:

1. Maintain a minimum net capital of $2500 for each security in which they make a market or $100,000, whichever is less.
2. Continuously maintain both bid and ask quotations during the trading day.
3. Submit stabilizing quotes when the market is temporarily affected by a buy/sell order imbalance.
4. Report daily and monthly trading volume.

Currently, there are 500 market makers in NASDAQ issues; most of them are located in New York City.

NASDAQ/NMS   The largest, most actively traded OTC stocks are on the NASDAQ *National Market System* (NMS) list. The NASDAQ/NMS market differs from other OTC markets in reporting procedures and listing requirements. In addition to the information required for all NASDAQ issues, NASDAQ/NMS market makers must report transaction prices and size within 90 seconds of the transaction's occurrence. NASDAQ terminals also provide high, low, last-sale, and cumulative volume figures (as well as bid/ask quotations) for the NASDAQ/NMS stocks. In addition, trade data for these issues are now reported on a daily basis in many newspapers across the country. The listing requirements for the NASDAQ/NMS stocks are shown in Table 3.1.

ORDERS AND ORDER HANDLING

The exchanges, as agency/auction markets, handle limit orders, consolidate the order flow, and allow orders to be worked in the crowd on the trading floor. Consequently, a more varied set of orders can be written, and the

Table 3.1   QUALIFICATION STANDARDS FOR NATIONAL MARKET SYSTEM ISSUES

Standard	Alternative 1	Alternative 2
Publicly held shares	350,000	800,000
Market value of publicly held shares	$2 million	$8 million
Minimum bid	$3	—
Total assets	$2 million	$8 million
Capital and surplus	$1 million	$8 million
Net income	$300,000 in latest or 2 of 3 last fiscal years	—
Market makers	2	2
Shareholders of record	300	300
Operating history	—	4 years

Source: National Association of Securities Dealers, Inc., *1987 Fact Book.*

rules of order execution are more complex for the exchanges than for the OTC. For the most part, therefore, the discussion in this section applies to the stock exchanges. We continue to describe the NYSE's procedures in particular.

Order Types

There are three categories of orders in addition to the limit and market orders that are described in Chapter 2: not held orders, percentage orders, and stop orders.

Not Held Orders *Not held orders* (which are marked *NH*) indicate that the broker is not held responsible if the order is not executed while the broker attempts to obtain a better price. A not held limit order and not held market order give the commission broker the freedom to work the order on the floor; a not held limit order also instructs the broker not to go beyond the limit price. Orders may not be given to the specialist on a not held basis; a broker holding an NH order may, on his or her own judgment, give all or part of it to the specialist, but only on a "held" basis.

Percentage Orders A *percentage order* must be *elected* (turned into a limit order) before it can be executed. It is elected by another transaction for the same issue being made on the same exchange to which the order has been submitted. As its name implies, a percentage order is elected in parts. "The percentage" establishes the amount of the order that is elected in relation to trading volume on the exchange for the issue.

For example, if a 50 percent order for 8000 shares is specified, 100 shares of the order become a limit order with each 100 shares that transact on the exchange. This guarantees that the trader who placed the percentage order will participate in no more than 50 percent of the trades in the stock. If the ask quotation on the market decreases below the limit price of a buy percentage order, or if the bid quotation rises above the limit price of a sell percentage order, the elected portion of the percentage order is in effect a market order and executes immediately to the extent possible.

A percentage order may, if a public trader so instructs, be converted into a limit order without an electing trade. For example, an investor may submit the percentage order to buy 8000 shares of an issue at $40, with instructions that the order be converted, in whole or in part, into a limit order at that price if any order to sell 10,000 or more shares comes on the market. This conversion arrangement allows the trader who submits the percentage order to participate in a block transaction. A percentage order may also give the specialist permission to be *on parity* with the order (that is, to buy or to sell stock along with the converted portion of the percentage order). In this case the percentage order is known as a *convert and parity (CAP)* order.

A percentage order allows the public trader to have an order "worked" in the market without requiring that a floor trader stand continuously by the specialist's post. In essence, it enables a specialist to fulfill the role of a floor trader without using his or her own discretion. The reason for the elaborate order specification is that specialists are not allowed to handle customer orders on a not held basis.

Percentage orders enable investors to participate in the market without initiating trades at new price levels. These orders are commonly used by institutional traders to minimize price impact and to ensure that the average prices of their executions are in reasonable conformity with the average prices of all trades for an issue for a trading session.

Stop Orders *Stop orders* to buy at market are written at prices above the current quotes, and stop orders to sell at market are written at prices below the current quotes. The prices at which the orders are written are *stop prices*. Stop orders are usually transmitted to the specialist and entered on the limit order book.

A stop order is activated when the price on the market reaches the stop price. This can be illustrated in the case of a buy stop order. For instance, assume that the market ask quotation for XYZ stock is 50, and that a stop order to buy 100 shares has been entered at 55 (the order would be written "Buy 100 XYZ stop 55"). If the market price rises to 55, the stop order is activated by being converted into a market order and then executed against the best available ask on the market.

Stop orders can also be written as stop limit orders. When a stop limit order is activated, it is converted into a limit rather than a market order. A stop limit order to buy 100 shares of XYZ stock might read "Buy 100 XYZ at 55 stop, limit 55." Assume XYZ is currently trading at 50. The order would be activated if the price of XYZ were to rise to 55; it would then become an order to buy 100 shares at a maximum (limit) price of 55. Setting a limit price on the stop order puts a maximum on the price the buyer will pay if the order is activated.

The term *stop order* reflects the defensive use to which these orders are commonly put: to stop the loss that can occur in the advent of an adverse price movement. For instance, assume an investor has sold a stock short. If the price of the stock were to go down, the investor would buy it back cheaply, repay his or her debt, and enjoy a profit. The risk the investor runs is that the stock may go up in price. The investor can obtain some protection against this risk by placing a stop order to buy at a higher price. Then, if the price of the stock starts to rise, the order is automatically activated and the investor's loss is limited.

The stop order can also be used to protect a gain. Assume an investor has already made paper profits on a short position and, for some reason, expects the price of a stock to go down in the short run and then later to rise. Thus, while the investor is holding out for a better price, the gains from the short sale can be protected by placing a stop order to buy. Similarly, an investor who has made paper profits on a long position can achieve some protection against an unexpected downturn by placing a stop order to sell at a stop price below the current market price.

Order Qualifications and Instructions

The following qualifications and instructions are used for orders submitted to the exchanges:[8]

Day Orders   Limit orders are accepted by market makers as either day orders or good-til-cancelled orders. *Day orders,* if unexecuted, expire at the end of the day they have been received on the market. Unless otherwise marked, an order is presumed to be a day order.

Good-Til-Cancelled Orders (GTC)   GTC orders remain in force until cancelled. Regardless of when they were placed, however, GTC orders on the specialists' books are automatically cancelled (unless renewed by the brokerage firm that placed the order) on the last business day of April and of October so that old orders that have been forgotten will be eliminated from the books.

Fill or Kill (FOK)   *FOK* orders to buy (sell) at a particular price must either be entirely filled immediately or entirely cancelled.

Immediate or Cancel (IOC)   *IOC* orders are similar to FOK orders, except that partial execution is acceptable, and only the unexecuted portion of the order is to be cancelled.

All or None (AON)   *AON* orders are similar to FOK orders in that they do not allow for partial execution; however, they are not to be cancelled if they do not execute immediately.[9]

At the Opening   The *at the opening* instruction, which applies to both market and limit orders, directs the order to be executed only at the opening; any unfilled portion of the order that remains after the opening is to be cancelled.

---

[8]Other qualifications regarding the terms of settlement may also be specified.
[9]All or none orders are not reflected in market quotations.

Market-on-Close The order is to be executed as close to the market closing as possible.

Limit or Market-on-Close The *limit or market-on-close* order is placed as a limit order, but if it does not execute during the trading day, it is to be executed as a market order as near to the close as possible.

Limit or Better Assume the market bid for a stock is 50. A *limit or better order* to sell might be written at 49 OB. The customer expects to sell at 50 but is protected by the limit of 49; the "or better" identification is added so that the floor broker will not think the price is a mistake.

Do Not Reduce (DNR) Ordinarily, the prices of limit buy orders and of stop orders to sell are automatically reduced for dividends on the ex-dividend date; the *DNR* instruction tells the specialist not to do this. The instruction applies only to the dividend adjustment, however; the price of the order is still reduced for other distributions (stock dividends or rights).

Rules of Order Execution

For limit orders, the primary trading priority rule is that best priced offers execute first; thus a market order to sell executes against the highest bid, and a market order to buy executes against the lowest ask.

The secondary priority rules used by the NYSE to determine the sequence in which orders written at the same price will execute are the rules of priority, parity, and precedence.[10] To see how these rules work, assume that five limit buy orders for XYZ stock have been placed at 42 and that they have entered the book in the following sequence:

Time	Buy order	Size of buy order
11:05	A	100 shares
11:30	B	100 shares
11:32	C	300 shares
12:00	D	300 shares
12:15	E	500 shares

Assume a trade at 12:20 eliminates a limit buy order at $42\frac{1}{8}$ and that the market bid becomes 42. Now let a market order to sell 400 shares arrive at 12:30.

---

[10]The Amex uses a strict time priority rule only for orders tied at a price. The NYSE uses the term *priority* in a specific way that should not be confused with the more general use we make of the term in this and other chapters of the book.

Priority   *Priority* is given to the first limit order placed at a price. The first counterpart order that triggers a trade at the price must execute against the limit order that has priority. In the preceding example, order A has priority, and 100 shares of the 400 share market sell order execute against order A.

Parity   The rule of *parity* applies to all orders, at a price, that are large enough to satisfy the remaining part of a market order. In the preceding example, orders C, D, and E have parity. The orders that have parity are executed according to the time sequence in which they are placed; therefore, order C (which was placed before orders D and E) executes against the remaining 300 shares of the market sell order.

Precedence   If the market order to sell had been for 700 shares, order A would still have priority and so would execute first. But no other order would be large enough to satisfy the remainder, and consequently none would have parity. In this case the rule of precedence would apply. By the *rule of precedence,* the sequence is determined by order size. In the preceding example, order E (for 500 shares) is the largest, and it executes after order A according to the rule of precedence. After the execution of order E, 100 shares of the market sell order still remain. Orders B, C, and D are each large enough to satisfy the remainder, and thus the rule of parity once again applies; order B, having been placed first, absorbs the remainder of the market sell order.

A sale (purchase) at a price removes all bids (offers) from the floor at that price. These orders, when reinstated, are on parity, subject only to the rule of precedence based on size. Subsequent trades at the price may then be determined by matching (flipping a coin) or by splitting (if the floor members agree to do so).

The secondary priority rules used by the NYSE are a mixture of time and size priorities. Strict time priority applies to the first order (this is the rule of priority); time priority continues to apply if the limit buy order that was placed next in the sequence is large enough to absorb the remainder of the sell order entirely; and size priority applies if the limit buy order that was placed next in the sequence cannot absorb the remainder of the sell order entirely. By combining size and time priorities, the NYSE minimizes the number of separate transactions that a large order can generate, while still adhering to time priority as closely as possible.

The NYSE's procedure facilitates executing on the exchange an order that has been negotiated in the upstairs market. Assume, for example, that a 15,000 share block is negotiated at 42, the price at which the five buy limit orders have been placed. Order A executes against the sell side of the block because of the rule of priority, but the buy side of the negotiated trade executes next because of the rule of precedence.

Special Rules for Order Execution

Short Sell Orders   Every sell order is marked *short* if the seller does not have a long position in the stock, but rather will deliver borrowed shares. Special rules apply to short sales, with the primary one being the *tick-test rule:* a short sale can be executed only on a plus tick or a zero plus tick.[11]

An increase in the price of a stock is called a *plus tick;* a decrease in the price of a stock is called a *minus tick;* a *zero plus tick* is a plus tick followed by a zero tick (two consecutive trades at the same price); and a *zero minus tick* is a minus tick followed by a zero tick. The purpose of the tick-test rule applied to short sales is to prevent public traders from destabilizing the market by selling short while the market price of a stock is falling.

Partial Execution   The rules of priority, parity, and precedence determine the limit orders that execute against a counterpart order, regardless of whether or not the limit orders execute totally (unless the limit order is FOK or AON). For instance, if a limit order is for 400 shares, the arrival of a market order for 100 shares can execute against it, reducing its size to 300 shares. The remaining portion of the limit order does not lose its place on the book.

The Priority of Public Orders   The specialist or any floor trader who handles customer orders as agent and who also trades from his or her own account as principal must give way to public orders at a price. This rule is applied before the rules of priority, parity, and precedence.

The Tick-Test Rule   As noted, the *tick-test rule* specifies that shares can only be sold short on a plus tick or zero plus tick or bought on a minus or zero minus tick.

Ex-Dividend Rules   As noted, on the day a stock goes *ex-dividend,* a specialist reduces the price of certain orders on the book by the amount of the dividend.[12] These orders are limit orders to buy and stop orders to sell.[13]

Block Trades and Odd Lots

The NYSE has established special procedures for handling very large trades (block trades) and very small trades (odd lots). *Block trades* are defined as

---

[11]Some short sales may be exempt from the short sale rules. These orders are marked *short exempt.*

[12]If the per share dividend is not a multiple of $\frac{1}{8}$, it is rounded up to the nearest multiple, and the price per share is reduced by this larger amount. For instance, if the dividend is 70 cents per share (greater than $\frac{5}{8}$), the price per share is reduced by $\frac{3}{4}$.

[13]Prices are not reduced for orders marked DNR, or for sell limit orders and buy stop orders.

any transaction greater than 10,000 shares. *Odd lots* are defined as any transaction less than one round lot (usually 100 shares).

Block Trades   Special block-trading procedures exist because large orders could destabilize the market if they were handled in the usual fashion. Whether or not an order is handled as a block depends on its size in relation to the normal trading volume for the stock, and on the broker's opinion of what the market may absorb without a large price change or time delay.

A client must be qualified for block-handling procedures in order to participate in a block trade. The broker must notify the SEC and obtain the permission of the Exchange.

Odd Lots   Odd lot procedures have been established to economize on the cost of handling very small orders. As noted, an *odd lot* is an order to trade less than one *round lot* (generally 100 shares). An order to buy 50 shares of General Motors (GM) is an odd lot; if the order is for 150 shares of GM, the *odd lot portion* (50 shares) is part of the round lot. The odd lot portion is handled separately, however, when more than 499 shares are involved (an order for 550 shares of GM would be entered as a round lot order for 500 shares and an odd lot order for 50 shares).

A brokerage house may bunch odd lot orders and take them to the Exchange as a round lot order. Odd lots received by the NYSE are handled separately in an electronic system that executes the orders against the specialist's account and sends a report to the specialist. These odd lot transactions are not reported separately on the Consolidated Tape; when they are bunched to form a round lot, the round lot transaction is reported on the tape.

For odd lot market orders, the price of the execution is determined by the first round lot trade (called the *effective trade*) made after the order has been placed. The price for the odd lot transaction is the price of the effective trade plus a price differential for a buy order, and minus a price differential for a sell order. Typically, the odd lot differential is one-eighth of a point.[14] For odd lot limit orders, an execution is achieved after the first round lot trade at or better than the limit price; the execution price is then the price of the limit order plus one-eighth or better for a purchase, or the price of the limit order minus one-eighth or better for a sale.

The Specialist

Specialists, as the key market makers in the U.S. exchange markets, handle much of the order flow for the stocks assigned to them and have the affirma-

---

[14]The odd lot differential is not charged if the order is transmitted before trading begins and is executed at the market's opening; the odd lot is part of a round lot; or the customer has entered multiple odd lots in the same stock for different accounts and these odd lots are bunched together into round lots.

tive obligation to make fair and orderly markets for their stocks.[15] As of December 1985, there were 490 individual specialists on the Exchange, representing 55 different specialist units. Each *unit* is a separate firm that, like the brokerage houses, is a member of the Exchange. Most of the specialist firms are private corporations; a few are subsidiaries of publicly held corporations.[16]

A specialist is subject to rules relating to his or her relationship with the corporation whose stock is traded, to the handling of orders, and to the affirmative obligation to make a fair and orderly market. With regard to a listed corporation whose stock is assigned to a specialist unit:

- The specialist must make at least one annual contact with an official of the corporation.
- Neither the specialist nor anyone associated with the specialist (a partner, clerk, or other) may participate in a proxy contest or in a contest for a change of management of the corporation.
- A specialist may not be an officer or a director of the corporation.
- The specialist may not directly accept orders from officers, directors, or principal stockholders of the corporation or from the corporation itself.

With regard to his or her own trades, the specialist:

- Cannot buy for his or her own account while holding unexecuted market orders to buy, or sell while holding unexecuted market orders to sell, and must always give priority to equally priced limit orders.
- Cannot by his or her own buying or selling activate a customer's stop order on the book.
- May not charge a brokerage commission and be a dealer in the same trade. However, with the permission of a floor official, a specialist can trade with an order he or she is holding on the book.
- May reveal only the highest bid and lowest offer.
- May reveal the number of shares available at the highest bid and lowest offer on the book, but is allowed to open the rest of the book only to an Exchange official for inspection. Accordingly, the specialist determines the orders that have priority, parity, or precedence.
- May not solicit orders in a specialty stock.
- May not accept orders from an institution in a specialty stock (that is, the specialist may not deal directly with an institutional investor).

[15]In 1985, specialists participated in 10.6 percent of shares purchased and sold (see *New York Stock Exchange Fact Book, 1986,* p. 14).

[16]Bear Stearns and Drexel Burnham Lambert own Amex specialty firms. Asiel, Bear Sterns, Pforzheimer, Purcell Graham, and Quick & Reilly own NYSE specialty firms.

With regard to the specialist's affirmative obligation:

- The specialist must intervene in trading to keep price changes acceptably small; what is acceptable has been established by the Exchange with reference to variables such as the price level at which the stock is trading and the stock's trading activity.
- The specialist is restricted in his or her freedom to buy shares at a price higher than the last transaction price, or to sell shares at a price lower than the last transaction price. This tick-test rule prevents the specialist from accentuating a market imbalance by trading against the weak side of the book.

The specialist performs the standard dealership role of supplying immediacy to the market (see Chapter 12), and the standard match maker role of bringing interested buyers and sellers together. In addition, the specialist is an auctioneer, a price stabilizer, and a key participant in the price discovery process.

As auctioneer, the specialist is responsible for seeing that orders are handled in conformity with acceptable auction practice.[17] This involves enforcing the price priority rule; the secondary rules of priority, parity, and precedence; and the tick-test rules. If a public limit order does not execute at a price at which trades have been made, the specialist reports either *stock ahead* (that is, other orders executed first on the basis of priority, parity, or precedence), *matched and lost* (if two orders arrive at the same time, their time sequence is assigned by random selection), or, in the case of a short sale, that a tick-test rule has prevented the execution. As auctioneer, the specialist may stop a stock for a floor broker. *Stopping a stock* is not equivalent to executing a stop order; it means that the specialist has guaranteed a floor broker an execution at the stop price.[18]

As a price stabilizer, the specialist participates in trading when he or she would not otherwise do so as a profit maximizing dealer. There are times, however, of substantial change in market conditions when the specialist is not expected to keep price changes within usual limits. At such times the specialist may, with the permission of a floor official, halt trading. During a *trading halt*, traders have time to digest news and to revise their orders, and the specialist has time to assess market conditions. Specialist intervention, either to make stabilizing trades or to halt trading, prevents

---

[17]Any member may call upon a floor official to make a ruling in the case of a dispute.

[18]The request to stop a stock is initiated at the floor broker's request. Once it is granted, however, the specialist is obliged to honor the request. If the specialist succeeds in finding a better price, the stop is off; if another order is executed in the crowd at the guaranteed price, the specialist must execute the stopped order and inform the floor broker that the stop has been "elected." Only public traders can have stock stopped, and only when the market spread is greater than the minimum tick size of one-eighth.

wide swings in price that might otherwise occur, either because the number of counterpart orders is temporarily sparse or because the market has over-reacted to news.

The specialist plays a key role in the price discovery process. This function is particularly apparent when trading resumes at the opening of the market after the overnight close or after a trading halt. At the opening, the specialist consolidates orders from the book, the crowd, and the Opening Automated Report Service (OARS). In addition, if there is a delayed open-ing, the specialist may send out price indications to test the water more broadly. Then, in a fashion similar to that in a call market, the specialist establishes a price that best reflects the market's aggregate desire to hold shares of the stock. When such a price is found, the market for the stock is opened and trading begins. As trading proceeds during the trading day, the specialist continues to assess market conditions in order to establish prices that best balance buy and sell pressures in the market.

INFORMATION DISSEMINATION

Quotation and recent trade information are reported on CRT screens for the OTC's NASDAQ securities and for exchange listed securities. Current transaction prices and volume are reported for exchange listed securities on the *Consolidated Transaction Tape*.[19] The principal method by which quo-tation information is distributed to brokers and investors is through vendors who provide the quotations and other financial information electronically to terminals throughout the United States and, increasingly, the rest of the world.

NASDAQ Quotations

There are two types of quotations in OTC trading: subject quotes and firm quotes. A *subject quote* (also known as a *workout quote*) is an estimate of the price at which a trade in the process of being worked out may execute. A *firm quote* is posted by a dealer who is willing to buy or sell one round lot at the quote. All NASDAQ quotations are firm. A dealer that does not honor a firm quote (has "backed away") may be censured or fined by the NASD.

Quotes for issues in the NASD's Automated Quotation System are shown on CRT screens in thousands of brokerage offices throughout the country. NASDAQ quotes are given on three levels:

---

[19]For exchange listed stocks, the quotation machines identify by symbol where the trade has occurred: Amex (A), Boston (B), Cincinnati (C), Instinet (O), Midwest (M), NASD (T), NYSE (N), Pacific (P), and Philadelphia (X). *Instinet* (O) is a privately operated system that handles large, institution-to-institution trades.

Level 1 screen: Displays the inside quotes (the highest bid and lowest ask) but does not reveal the origin of the quotes to the registered representative. The level 1 screen is used primarily by smaller, retail oriented brokerage firms.

Level 2 screen: Displays the current quotes and the names of the market makers. The level 2 screen is used by the major brokerage firms.

Level 3 screen: Displays the same information as the level 2 screen but is used by market makers. With the level 3 facility, the market makers are able to enter and to update their quotes in the system when they desire.

The level 2 and level 3 screens for a NASDAQ stock appear as follows:

	CBAB	15⅛	15¾C
XXXX	15⅛		15¾C
YYYY	15		15¾C
ZZZZ	14½		15¾C

The symbol of the stock (CBAB) and the market spread (15⅛ bid, 15¾ ask) are given on the first line. Note that size is not shown in this example (it could be, however, at the dealer's discretion). The next three lines show the quotes of three market makers who are identified by their symbols (XXXX, YYYY, and ZZZZ). The symbol *C* after the quote of 15¾ indicates that this was the closing price for the stock. The symbol is shown after the 4:00 P.M. close until the system opens the next day.

The Consolidated Tape

The *Consolidated Tape* contains two networks:

Network A: NYSE transactions and transactions for NYSE issues executed on the regional exchanges

Network B: Amex transactions, transactions for Amex issues executed on the regional exchanges, and transactions in certain regional issues that meet Amex listing requirements but are not listed on the Amex

A sequence of entries on the Consolidated Tape may appear as follows:

CBS	T	ITT	GM
67⅞	5s66	11,000s40	50.4s50⅛

This is interpreted as follows:

- The transactions occurred in the order shown, reading from left to right (because the tape advances from the right to the left).
- An issue's trading symbol is at the top of the tape; transaction information is at the bottom.
- Only the transaction price is shown if the transaction is for one round lot; for example, the first entry in the sequence shows that one round lot of CBS traded at 67⅞.
- For transactions of two or more but less than 100 round lots, the number of round lots followed by an *s* precedes the price; for example, the second entry in the sequence shows that 500 shares of AT&T (ticker symbol *T*) traded at 66.
- For transactions of 100 round lots or more, the entire volume is shown; for example, the third entry in the sequence shows that 11,000 shares (110 round lots) of ITT traded at 40.
- Information for back-to-back trades in a stock is given sequentially after the symbol, with a decimal point separating the trades; for example, the last entry in the sequence shows that 100 shares of General Motors traded at 50, and then 400 shares traded at 50⅛.

Errors on the Consolidated Tape are corrected in various entries. For instance:

NO.T	WAS
5s66	5s65

indicates that a previous trade in Telephone was at 65, not 66.

CANCEL LAST GM
50⅛

indicates that the reported trade was cancelled, and that it was the most recently reported GM trade.

The Consolidated Tape can print at speeds up to 900 characters a minute; actual speeds depend on the trading activity on the exchange. Current trading information is always available without delay from data vendors connected with the *Consolidated Quotations System* (CQS), and the *Consolidated Transaction System* (CTS), but the Consolidated Tape itself runs late during periods of heavy trading volume (there is a limit to the speed with which the tape can be read). Several delete modes can be activated, however, when heavy trading volume necessitates. For instance, volume and the first digit of reported prices may be deleted, except for opening trades and for prices that are integer multiples of $10 (10, 20, 30, and so on). For example, if the opening trade for GM is 400 at 49⅞, and the ensuing sequence of trades is

100 @ 49¾
200 @ 49⅞
100 @ 50⅛
300 @ 50¼

the tape entries would be

GM	GM	GM	GM	GM
4s49⅞	9¾	9⅞	50⅛	50¼

The tape also contains special entries to convey information concerning inactive stocks, delayed openings, price indications, trading halts, stock splits, and block transactions.

Trading is occasionally halted on the floor of the Exchange, either for individual issues or for all issues (perhaps for environmental reasons such as a snowstorm or for regulatory reasons as when President Kennedy was assassinated on November 22, 1963). In either event, NYSE trading halts need not be followed by other market centers. When trading does continue in other marketplaces, trade reports are not shown on the Consolidated Tape as they occur but are displayed after the NYSE close.

REVENUES AND COSTS

Revenues

Market makers receive revenues from two sources: *commissions* (when they act as brokers) and the *bid-ask spread* (when they act as dealers). For any given trade, OTC dealers and exchange specialists receive either a commission or the return associated with buying low (at their bid) and selling high (at their ask).

The market centers themselves (the exchanges and the NASD) receive revenues from two major sources: the listed companies and their member firms. NYSE revenues for the year ended December 31, 1985, were, in thousands of dollars:[20]

Listing fees	$ 77,534
Trading fees	66,354
Market data fees	44,096
Facility and equipment fees	22,046
Regulatory fees	21,815
Membership fees	9,055
Investment and other income	16,806
Total	$257,706

[20]*New York Stock Exchange Annual Report, 1985*, p. 45.

Labor Costs

Skilled Labor   In the U.S. continuous trading systems:

- Each order that arrives at the market and each trade that is made conveys information to the market maker.
- If the market maker participates in the trade, his or her inventories of cash and of stock are affected.

Consequently, dealers/specialists frequently adjust their quotes while they trade. For the dealer houses, this means that trained personnel must continuously monitor CRT screens and telephones for the stocks for which they are responsible. Likewise, the exchange specialists must stand by their posts and respond to orders as they arrive.

Trading is complex, and mistakes may be extremely costly. A year of training is generally required before a new trader is allowed to handle anything but a "no brainer" (the term used for an order that does not require special handling). The emotional, intellectual, and even physical requirements of trading are demanding. Consequently, the supply of skilled traders is limited, and labor costs are high.

Unskilled Labor   Market making also entails a considerable amount of paper handling and record keeping. This is done in part by clerks who assist the specialists, dealers, and floor traders, and in part by the market makers themselves. For instance, stock exchange specialists enter limit orders on the books and monitor the books. Many of the more clerical aspects of market making are now computerized, as physical capital has been substituted for relatively unskilled labor throughout the industry.

Capital Costs

Physical Capital   Along with the standard need for buildings and equipment, computer technology has substantially increased the investment in physical capital needed for market making. The NASD in 1985–1986, for instance, built a new computer communications facility in Rockville, Maryland, to back up its primary computer complex in Trumbull, Connecticut, at a cost of $17.3 million.

Electronic equipment is being used for monitoring, order routing, information display, record keeping, and, increasingly, for decision making and trade execution. As noted in Chapter 2, electronic display systems, communication systems, and touch screen technology are turning market maker posts into fully automated workstations.

The new technology has increased the number of trading decisions each trader can make and, in so doing, has created a greater demand for highly sophisticated traders. Consequently, taking both the quality and the quantity of the labor input into account, trading has remained labor intensive, despite the increase of physical capital.[21]

Financial Capital   The second capital cost of market making is the financial capital required for the dealership function. Electronic equipment itself has not reduced the financial commitment needed to provide a market in depth, although better intermarket linkages have made it easier for some market makers to rebalance their inventories by interdealer trading. More importantly, the new technology has spurred the growth of markets in futures and options; these instruments are now used by market makers to hedge positions, and thereby to reduce the amount of capital at risk. Nevertheless, for both the dealer oriented OTC markets and the specialist oriented exchange markets, the requisite financial capital remains a major cost of market making in the U.S. continuous trading environment.

Agency Costs

Brokers, as agents, guarantee the validity of orders left with them and are responsible for their trades even if the public traders they represent fail to deliver. Brokers also bear the cost of mistakes made on the trading floor. For instance, if a buyer's agent believes 300 shares had been bought at 50⅛, and a seller's agent on the other side of the trade believes 300 shares had been sold at 50¼ and if both so confirm to their customers, the buyer pays 50⅛ per share, the seller receives 50¼ per share, and their agents absorb the difference.

Risk

Order handling and trade execution involve risk when a dealer firm, in the process of facilitating a trade, acquires an *unbalanced inventory* (buys shares that are not desired, or sells shares that are desired, from the dealer firm's own investment point of view). The risk-related cost of carrying an unbalanced inventory is a major cost to dealer firms; we consider it in greater detail in Chapter 12 ("The Economics of Market Making").

CONTRAST OF THE ALTERNATIVE MARKET CENTERS

The largest firms in the United States are generally listed on the NYSE, although the equity shares of some very large companies are traded in the

---

[21]In microeconomic terminology, the computer is a substitute factor of production for unskilled labor, but a complementary factor of production for skilled labor.

NASDAQ/NMS. Medium size NASDAQ/NMS issues are similar in size to medium size NYSE issues. Both the NASDAQ/NMS and Amex include a substantial number of smaller issues (less than $100 million value of shares outstanding).

Table 3.2 contains data on the overall size of the NYSE, Amex, and NASDAQ markets. Table 3.2(a) shows the number of companies listed in each of the market centers, along with share volume, for the years 1981–86. Table 3.2(b) shows, for 1985 and 1986, the share volume and the dollar volume of trades for these three market centers and for the regional exchanges. The entry ''NASDAQ/OTC Trading in Listed Securities'' in Table 3.2(b) refers to the third market trades.

Many more companies have equity shares traded in the NASDAQ market than are listed on the exchanges. In terms of share volume and the dollar value of trades, the NYSE is the largest market, although the NASDAQ market is indeed substantial. As shown in Table 3.2(a), the NASDAQ market has also grown appreciably from 1981 to 1986, in terms of both the number of companies and the share volume. Share volume has also increased on the NYSE and Amex, but the number of exchange listed companies has actually decreased somewhat.

A growing number of companies that would meet the requirements for an exchange listing have chosen to remain on the NASDAQ market. According to Wall, in 1983, over 600 NASDAQ companies qualified for

Table 3.2   COMPARISON OF NYSE, AMEX, AND NASDAQ EQUITY MARKETS

| | (a) Six year comparison | | | | | |
| | Number of companies | | | Share volume (000,000) | | |
Year	NYSE	Amex	NASDAQ	NYSE	Amex	NASDAQ
1981	1,565	867	3,353	11,854	1,343	7,823
1982	1,526	834	3,264	16,458	1,338	8,432
1983	1,550	822	3,901	21,590	2,081	15,909
1984	1,543	792	4,097	23,071	1,545	15,159
1985	1,540	783	4,136	27,511	2,101	20,699
1986	1,573	796	4,417	35,680	2,979	28,737

| | (b) Comparison of the order flow for 1985 and 1986 | | | |
| | Share volume (000,000) | | Dollar volume ($000,000) | |
Market center	1985	1986	1985	1986
NYSE	27,511	35,680	$ 970,500	$1,374,350
Amex	2,101	2,979	26,710	44,453
Regional exchanges	4,621	6,088	145,666	200,770
NASDAQ	20,699	28,737	233,454	378,216
NASDAQ/OTC trading in listed securities	1,101	1,326	36,757	48,649
Totals	56,033	74,810	$1,413,087	$2,046,438

Sources: National Association of Securities Dealers, Inc., *1986 Fact Book; 1987 Fact Book.*

Table 3.3   OTC MARKETS VERSUS EXCHANGE MARKETS

	OTC markets	Exchange markets
Competition	Dealer market	Agency/auction market
	Multiple dealers	Public order flow
Flexibility	Freedom to select stocks	Stocks are assigned
	Primary and secondary markets	Secondary markets only
	Active interaction with the order flow	Passive interaction with the order flow
Regulation	No obligation	Affirmative obligation
	Much freedom	Surveillance systems
	Relies on competition to limit abuses	Trading restrictions
Information flows	Deal directly with customers	Consolidated order flow and floor information
	Close contact with firms	

an NYSE listing, and over 1600 qualified for an Amex listing.[22] The intensified competition between the NASDAQ and exchange markets is attributable to the markedly improved quality of the OTC market in recent years. Currently, the exchanges and the OTC present very viable alternatives for firms whose shares are traded in secondary markets. In light of this development, it is desirable to consider more carefully the differences between the systems.

Differences between the exchange and OTC markets are summarized in Table 3.3. These differences are classified according to the competitive structure of the markets; the flexibility with which market makers can select the issues for which they make markets, and the freedom with which they can operate in those markets; the regulation of the market makers; and the information flows in the markets.

Competition

The OTC market is a dealer market, and the exchange is an agency/auction market. OTC dealers compete with each other; not surprisingly, these market makers have not accepted additional competition from the public order flow. The OTC depends on interdealer competition to keep markets fair, orderly, and liquid.

The exchanges assign listed issues to single specialist firms, which they regulate. Specialists, as well as OTC dealers, do, however, face competition—in the agency/auction environment of the exchange floor, competition is primarily from the public order flow and from floor traders. Specialists face further competition from upstairs traders, from *third market*

[22]For further discussion, see Wall (1985).

firms (which make off-board markets in listed securities) and from in-house markets for stocks that are not subject to the Exchange's off-board trading restrictions. Exchange specialists also face competition from specialists on other exchanges linked by the ITS.

In addition to the constraints imposed by competition, specialists also face exchange regulation and control with regard to their affirmative obligation to make fair and orderly markets for the stocks assigned to them. Not surprisingly, the specialists have not accepted further competition in the form of competing specialists on the same exchange making markets in the same issue.

Flexibility

OTC dealers are free to select the stocks they make markets in: they face no significant regulatory impediments to becoming market makers for an issue or to ceasing their market maker operations for an issue. Specialist firms, on the other hand, must apply for the right to be the market maker for a newly listed issue, and, once assigned, an issue is rarely taken away from (or given up by) a specialist firm.

OTC dealers are free to participate in the new issues market, although they must temporarily give up being market makers when they act as underwriters. Exchange specialists operate only in the secondary market. OTC dealers are also allowed to take the initiative in finding buyers or sellers, whereas stock exchange specialists must assume a more passive position: they post their quotes and wait for other traders to respond.

Regulation

OTC dealers face fewer regulatory restrictions than exchange specialists, for the following reasons:

- The NASD relies more on the implicit constraints of a competitive market environment to discipline dealer firms.
- Specialist firms handle the public order flow on an agency basis and thus have a fiduciary responsibility to give executions that are consistent with reasonable auction practice.
- Specialist firms have the affirmative obligation to maintain a fair and orderly market.

Accordingly, the rules, regulations, and market surveillance of market maker operations are considerably more elaborate on the exchanges than in the OTC market.[23]

---

[23]By way of illustration: both the Amex and NYSE prohibit short selling by specialists, other floor traders, and the public on a minus or zero minus tick; the NASD has no such restriction for its dealers.

Information Flows

The fourth major distinction between the two systems concerns information flows. Unlike the exchange specialists:

- OTC dealers can receive orders directly from customers, including institutional traders. The orders are generally transmitted by telephone, enabling the dealer houses to sense the motive behind an order (general optimism or pessimism, news concerning the company, and so on).
- OTC dealers may maintain close contact with the firms whose securities they trade and commonly act in an advisory capacity for these firms. Investment banking firms usually make markets in the stocks of their clients.

The direct contact with traders and firms gives the OTC dealers a strong informational advantage that the exchange specialists do not enjoy. Furthermore, the freedom of the OTC dealers (particularly the large brokerage houses that make OTC markets) to participate in the lucrative primary markets gives these houses an incentive that the exchange specialists do not have to make liquid markets.[24]

Exchange specialists, however, have an informational advantage that is not shared by the OTC dealers—specialists see more of the order flow because the order flow is more consolidated in exchange trading.

All told, the exchange and OTC markets represent very different approaches to market making. The differences encompass far more than the simple distinction between multiple, competitive dealers and a single designated market maker (the exchange specialist). Each system has advantages that the other does not enjoy, and it is not possible to determine on the basis of theory alone which may make better markets.

CONCLUSION

The chapter has provided detail concerning the objectives, organization, and operations of the U.S. exchange and OTC markets. Understanding these systems enables one to appreciate the complexity of market operations and to recognize that clear alternatives exist between trading systems. The institutional background provided will also prove valuable when we turn to an analysis of the market process in Part Two.

SUGGESTED READING

Y. Amihud, T. Ho, and R. Schwartz, eds., *Market Making and the Changing Structure of the Securities Industry,* Lexington, Mass.: Lexington Books, 1985.

---

[24]Brokerage houses that make better secondary markets are more likely to be favored by firms issuing new securities in the primary markets.

G. Sanger and J. McConnell, ''Stock Exchange Listings, Firm Value, and Security Market Efficiency: The Impact of NASDAQ,'' *Journal of Financial and Quantitative Analysis,* March 1986.

G. W. Schwert, ''Stock Exchange Seats as Capital Assets,'' *Journal of Financial Economics,* January 1977.

H. Stoll, *The Stock Exchange Specialist System: An Economic Analysis,* Monograph Series in Finance and Economics, Salomon Brothers Center for the Study of Financial Institutions, New York University Graduate School of Business Administration, 1985.

J. Wall, ''The Competitive Environment of the Securities Market,'' in Amihud, Ho, and Schwartz (1985).

R. West and S. Tinic, *The Economics of the Stock Market,* New York: Praeger, 1971.

chapter *4*

The Securities Industry

The securities industry encompasses:

> The securities exchanges and OTC market
>
> Investment banks and brokerage houses
>
> Commercial banks (to the extent that they provide brokerage, trust, custodial, and/or investment management services)
>
> Institutional investors such as insurance companies, mutual funds, and pension funds
>
> The clearance system

The different parts of the industry are interrelated in many ways, and all are integrally involved in or connected with market making and trading.

This chapter takes a broad look at the securities industry. It identifies the firms that the industry comprises and surveys the securities that are traded. The operations of the major investment banking and brokerage houses are set forth. The chapter also focuses on the operations of the trading desks (the upstairs market makers) and describes the clearance system.

THE FIRMS

Securities firms can be classified in several ways. The primary distinctions are between:

> National full line firms and investment banking firms
> Clearing/carrying firms and introducing firms
> NYSE member firms and non-NYSE member firms
> Broker firms and dealer firms

In addition, we make note of special niche and special bracket firms, consider the sizable and growing presence of commercial banks in the securities industry, and identify the major institutional investors.

National Full Line Firms and Investment Banking Firms

The national *full line firms* include:

> Dean Witter Reynolds, Inc.
> Drexel Burnham Lambert, Inc.
> E. F. Hutton & Company, Inc.
> Merrill Lynch & Company, Inc.
> Paine, Webber, Jackson & Curtis, Inc.
> Prudential Bache Securities
> Shearson Lehman Brothers
> Smith Barney, Harris Upham & Co., Inc.
> Thomson McKinnon Securities, Inc.

The full line firms do an extensive retail business through a network of branch offices. In addition to receiving customer orders, these firms transmit orders to the major market centers, are involved in post-trade clearance operations, and carry customer accounts. The full line firms also engage in operations such as investment banking; mergers and acquisitions; investment research; principal trading for their own accounts; real estate; asset management, including the provision of custodial services; and brokerage of life insurance.

The major *investment banking firms* include:

Bear Stearns & Company
Dillon, Read & Company, Inc.

First Boston Corporation

Goldman, Sachs & Company

Kidder, Peabody & Company

Lazard Frères & Company

Morgan Stanley & Company, Inc.

Salomon Brothers, Inc.

These firms are primarily involved in large scale underwriting and trading, rather than in retail operations. In addition, investment banking firms perform broker/dealer transactions in secondary markets, including the handling of block orders in the upstairs markets. As is the case with full line firms, the operations of the investment bankers extend into areas such as real estate, commercial paper, asset management, risk arbitrage, money market trading, bond trading, OTC market making, and mergers and acquisitions.

Clearing/Carrying Firms and Introducing Firms

Clearing/carrying firms clear securities transactions for themselves and/or for other firms and maintain possession of customers' cash and securities. *Introducing firms* neither clear nor carry securities for their customers. Rather, these back-office functions are delegated to a clearing/carrying firm with which the introducing firm is affiliated.

A clearing arrangement may be on a fully disclosed basis or on an omnibus basis. Under the *omnibus* arrangement, the clearing firm does not know the identity of the introducing firm's customer, and it simply executes and settles transactions in the name of the introducing firm, for the introducing firm's account. The introducing firm in turn sends individual confirmations to its customers and carries the customer accounts but does not handle the clearing operation.

The division of functions between introducing and clearing/carrying firms is subject to negotiation. Most important is the allocation of responsibility for holding cash and securities and for margin lending.

Various legal questions concerning clearing arrangements have arisen: which firm (introducing or clearing/carrying) is responsible for transactions that fail to be completed? which firm is responsible for "knowing the customer" (particularly with regard to margin accounts)? which firm should be held responsible for the suitability of transactions, including the existence of account churning? and so on.

In recent years, the relationship between introducing and clearing/carrying firms has been clarified in case law and regulatory changes.[1] Currently:

- Customers must be informed in writing of the allocation of responsibility between introducing and clearing/carrying firms for opening, approval, and monitoring of accounts; credit extension; maintenance of books and records; receipt, delivery, and safeguarding of securities and funds; confirmations and other statements; and acceptance of orders and execution of transactions.
- Carrying/clearing firms do not have the responsibility to "know their customers" and are not required to maintain or examine customer data to determine the existence of churning, the suitability of transactions, and so forth.

NYSE Member Firms and Non-NYSE Member Firms

In 1981, only 453 of 2473 securities firms doing business with the public were members of the NYSE. Not surprisingly, most nonmember firms (1207 out of 1413) were introducing firms.[2] NYSE firms are either New York–based (if their head office is located in New York City) or are NYSE regional firms (if their head office is located outside New York City).

Exchange membership affects a broker/dealer firm's freedom to execute customer orders away from the exchange markets. Although off-board trading restrictions have been relaxed in recent years, member firms are still required to take customer orders for stocks listed before April 26, 1979, to an exchange. This regulation reduces the freedom of member firms to make in-house markets or to operate in the *third market* (OTC transactions for exchange listed issues).

Brokerage Firms and Dealer Firms

As previously discussed, brokers participate in trading as agents, and dealers participate as principals. Although many firms assume both broker and dealer roles (and are referred to as *broker/dealer firms*), some firms are primarily involved with the receipt and transmission of customer orders, and others are primarily concerned with market making.

---

[1]The current regulation was established in 1982, when the SEC approved an amendment of NYSE Rule 382 concerning the regulation of clearing/carrying agreements. For further discussion, see Minnerop and Stoll (1986).

[2]See Bloch (1986).

Since the elimination of fixed brokerage commissions in 1975, some firms have specialized in the provision of discount brokerage services. OTC dealer firms, on the other hand, are primarily concerned with market making in their list of securities. *Professional floor firms* (specialist units in particular) are also dealer firms, although they routinely handle customer orders on an agency basis.

Special Niche Firms and Special Bracket Firms

Special niche firms are companies that have carved out a particular segment of the market. Some special niche dealer firms specialize in foreign securities. Some, such as discount brokers, concentrate on one customer service (execution) and do not provide other customer services (such as research). Drexel Burnham has established a special niche in *junk bonds* (high risk bonds with low credit ratings or bonds that are in default).

The premier full line firms and investment banking firms are sometimes referred to as *special bracket firms* because of their preeminence in the industry. Firms in this group include Merrill Lynch, Goldman Sachs, Salomon Brothers, First Boston, Morgan Stanley, and Shearson Lehman. One or more of these firms typically assumes the leadership position in syndicates formed to float new issues. Given their size, profitability, and reputation, these firms form an elite group in the industry.

Commercial Banks

Commercial banks and investment banks are both conduits for funds flows:

- A *commercial bank* accepts deposits from the suppliers of funds and makes loans to the users of funds.
- An *investment bank* raises funds in a primary market and passes them on to ultimate users.

These two types of banks differ in certain important respects:

- Individual suppliers and users are not matched with each other in commercial banking, and depositors in a commercial bank do not own shares in the firms that have received the funds. Commercial banks, in other words, are financial intermediaries.
- Commercial banks supply only debt capital to the users of funds, whereas investment banks raise both debt and equity capital for the

users of funds, by selling financial claims on the users to the suppliers of funds.
- An investment bank transfers *marketable* securities to the suppliers of funds; a commercial bank opens a nonmarketable deposit for its depositors. Demand deposits (the major component of the money supply) are perfectly liquid; marketable securities are not.

At the beginning of the twentieth century, a broad array of financial services, including both commercial and investment banking, were offered by large integrated trust companies, the "department stores of finance." This joint pursuit of commercial and investment banking by a single firm was disallowed in 1933 with the passage by Congress of the Glass-Steagall Act (formally known as the Banking Act of 1933). Glass-Steagall prohibits commercial banks from underwriting new issues, either directly or through affiliates. Passage of the Act left the securities business exclusively to broker/dealer firms and investment banking firms regulated by the SEC. At the time, houses such as J. P. Morgan & Co. were forced to choose between commercial banking and investment banking. Morgan chose commercial banking; in 1935, however, several partners and staff members resigned to organize Morgan Stanley & Co., the investment banking firm.

The separation between commercial and investment banking has once again started to blur, and commercial banks are emerging in the currrent era of deregulation as a prominent force in the securities industry. Concurrently, securities firms have moved into the more traditional commercial banking area. Merrill Lynch, for instance, has done so with the development of the *Cash Management Account* (CMA).

Commercial banks started to return to investment banking in the 1960s, when they were allowed to underwrite state and local government bonds. Subsequently, other regulatory constraints regarding the freedom of commercial banks to pay interest on deposits and to participate in interstate banking have been relaxed. Currently, the operations of commercial and investment banks encompass activities such as asset management, real estate financing, mergers and acquisitions, research, money market trading, and brokerage.

Glass-Steagall does not (and never did) apply to foreign banking operations. At present, the expanding global operations of the largest commercial banks such as Citicorp are positioning these giant financial institutions so that they may once again integrate a full array of financial services. As the trend continues, the major commercial banks and the major securities firms are once again becoming indistinguishable.

Institutional Investors

Institutional investors include insurance companies, pension funds, trust companies, investment management companies (open- and closed-end mutual funds and unit trust funds), and nonprofit institutions such as foundations.

Institutional investing has grown appreciably in recent years. This is explained by:

1. *Economies of scale in portfolio management:* Economies of scale, which may always have existed in the administration and control of portfolios, are increasingly apparent in today's highly complex environment. Some investment strategies can be implemented efficiently only on a large scale; for instance, a passive investment strategy (buying a representative market portfolio) is most cost effective when used by an index fund.
2. *Economies of scale in trading:* Economies of scale also exist in trading, in that explicit transaction costs (such as commissions) are appreciably lower for larger orders. Economies of scale have traditionally existed in executing orders; since the advent of negotiated commissions in 1975, the economies have been passed on to investors. Institutions, as the largest investors, have benefited most.
3. *Tax law:* Tax laws favored the growth of institutional investing by allowing the postponement of tax payments on income placed in pension funds, IRAs, and Keogh plans.
4. *Complexity of financial instruments:* The development of new financial instruments such as options and futures on market indexes has resulted in the formulation of sophisticated trading strategies that are exploited most effectively by professional management.
5. *Globalization of trading/investing:* The growing opportunities offered by international investing can, for many individuals, be exploited most efficiently by investing in an international fund.
6. *Other social trends:* The growth of institutional investing is in large part accounted for by the growth of pension funds. Growth of the pension funds is in turn the result of a broader set of socioeconomic factors than are encompassed by the preceding five points.

Institutional investing and trading involve three stages: (1) establishment of a fund, (2) management of the fund, and (3) implementation of the fund's trading decisions. For example, pension funds are established by *plan sponsors,* the private firms or public institutions that have pension plans for their employees. These funds may then be managed by the plan sponsors themselves, by professional management firms such as Batterymarch, by the asset management department of brokerage firms such as Morgan Stanley or Merrill Lynch, or by the trust department of a commercial bank such as Citicorp. Finally, fund managers use a brokerage firm to handle their buy/sell orders. Typically, block orders (10,000 shares or more) are transmitted to the trading desk of broker/dealer firms such as Paine Webber, Morgan Stanley, or Drexel Burnham.

One further way of classifying institutional investors and traders is useful:

- *Longer term investors:* Mutual funds, pension funds, and insurance companies
- *Fast money firms:* Hedge funds and securities firms involved in arbitrage operations
- *Proprietary traders:* Trading by investment banking houses and brokerage firms for their own accounts
- *Asset management companies:* Investment advisers hired by funds and paid a fee for their services

THE SECURITIES

This section identifies the securities that are traded in secondary financial markets.

Equities

Equity issues are common stock. The owner of common stock owns a claim on the *residual income* (receipts minus contractual expenses) of a corporation.[3] Because they represent claims on residual income, equity issues are variable income securities.

Equity issues exist for the life of the corporation. Companies typically do not have a stated life horizon, and equity shares are generally evaluated as existing in perpetuity.

A company's equity shares outstanding may be increased by the issuance of additional shares, by a stock split, or by a stock dividend. After the change, new shares are not differentiated from the old. Different categories of equity shares may exist, however. For instance, Class A shares may enjoy voting privileges, whereas Class B shares may not. The number of shares outstanding may also be reduced by share repurchase or by a reverse stock split.

Traders can also effectively change the number of shares outstanding by short selling. The trader who *sells short* sells shares that he or she does not own but rather has borrowed from a brokerage house. The brokerage firm generally lends shares owned by other customers (usually institutional investors). After the short sale, a new buyer receives and owns the shares; but the brokerage firm's customers do not own fewer shares. Consequently, the number of shares outstanding has effectively increased. The issuing corporation does not pay dividends on shares created by short selling, but all share owners do receive dividends. The brokerage firm *charges* the investor who sold short an amount equal to the dividend; therefore, the

---

[3]Stockholders have a similar claim on *net assets* (total assets less all contractual claims) in the advent of bankruptcy or liquidation.

original share owner can be appropriately credited for the payment, as can the investor who bought the borrowed shares.[4]

Fixed Income Securities

Fixed income securities are debt issues for which the income payable to the owner is contractually fixed.[5] Fixed income assets include:

- Savings deposits
- Negotiable certificates of deposit and commercial paper
- U.S. Treasury bills, notes, and bonds[6]
- State and municipal government securities
- Real estate mortgages
- Corporate bonds, foreign bonds, and Eurobonds[7]

Preferred stock is also classified as a fixed income security.[8] The classification is blurred, however, for convertible preferreds because these assets can, under stated conditions, be converted into common stock, a variable income security. Convertible preferreds can be assessed as a combination of two assets: a standard fixed income security and a warrant to buy equity shares. Convertible debentures similarly straddle the fixed and variable income classifications—until converted, they yield a fixed, contractual return (so long as they are not in default); when converted, they yield the variable return of the equity shares for which they are exchanged.

Private versus Government Securities

As noted, *fixed income securities* include both private and government issues. The public/private distinction is important for two reasons: risk considerations and tax considerations.

With regard to *risk,* the debt issues of the federal government are not subject to bankruptcy risk (the federal government has the power to issue new money and thus can always cover its debt service and retire issues as they mature). Investment in the debt issues of the U.S. government is not

---

[4]After the trader who has sold short buys shares in the market and returns them to the brokerage house, the effective number of shares outstanding is reduced to its previous level.

[5]More specifically, the *maximum* income payable is fixed; few assets are totally without risk, and any contractual payment may not be made in full at the agreed upon time.

[6]*Treasury bills* have maturities of one year or less (three months and six months). *Treasury notes* have maturities ranging from one to ten years. *Treasury bonds* have maturities at time of issue greater than ten years.

[7]*Eurobonds* are bonds offered outside the country in whose currency the securities are denominated. A large percentage of Eurobond issues are Eurodollar issues.

[8]Preferred stock need not have a fixed maturity, however, and may provide for the payment of dividends only to the extent that the company has realized earnings.

without risk, however—interest rate fluctuations subject investors to uncertainty whenever future cash flows (interest and principal) are not perfectly synchronized with the future uses to which the funds will be put.

With regard to tax law, interest (but not capital gains) is not subject to taxation for most state, municipal, and municipal agency bonds.[9] In addition, income from U.S. Treasury bills is not subject to state income taxation.

Long Term versus Short Term Securities

Most fixed income securities have a finite life; the exceptions are preferred stock and some government bonds such as British Consols,[10] which have been issued in perpetuity. The existence of a finite horizon at which a fixed income security will mature at a predetermined price (face value) affects the issue's price behavior; the effect becomes increasingly important as the maturity date approaches, because at that date the security must be worth its face value.

Duration is another measure of an issue's longevity. *Duration* is the weighted average time to payment for each cash flow (interest and principal) payable to the security holder, where the present values of the individual cash flows relative to the price of the bond are the weights. The duration of a fixed income security is important to investors for matching the receipt of income with the use of funds. Consequently, issues of similar duration but with different maturity dates are closer substitutes for one another than are issues of similar maturity dates but of different duration.

Other Primary Securities

The securities discussed thus far may be classified as *primary issues:* their initial sale results in the receipt of fresh capital (debt or equity) for the issuer. Two other assets—warrants and rights—fit into the category.

Warrants   A *warrant* conveys the right to purchase a given number of shares (typically one) of stock at a given price (called the *exercise price*) within a given period of time (usually at least several years, and in some cases an unlimited period). The exercise price of a warrant is typically higher than the price of the underlying stock at the time the warrant is issued, but the warrant has value because of the possibility that the stock's price will rise above the exercise price in the future.

---

[9]An issue that is exempt from federal taxation may not be exempt, however, from state and local taxation for out of state residents.

[10]*Consols* are the ''consolidated annuities'' of the British government that were issued between 1750 and 1757 to eliminate a confusing variety of debt instruments that had been incurred by the government. Until the First World War, consols constituted most of the national debt of the government of England.

Warrants are issued by a corporation along with other securities (usually a preferred stock or bond issue) to "sweeten" an offering. Alternatively, warrants may be distributed in place of a cash or stock dividend or may be sold separately as a new issue. As part of a larger package, warrants facilitate raising new capital in the primary markets; as an alternative to paying a cash dividend, warrants enable a company to conserve internally generated equity capital; as a stand-alone issue, warrants bring fresh capital into a company. For these reasons, warrants are classified as primary issues. Warrants are traded both on the exchanges and in the over-the-counter markets.

Rights   *Rights* are similar to warrants in that they convey to the holder the right to purchase shares from a company. Like warrants, rights facilitate raising new funds. Unlike warrants, however, rights are used solely in conjunction with the sale of new common stock, have a very brief life (generally two to ten weeks), and have an exercise price (called *subscription price*) that is generally below the current market value of the stock.

Rights are distributed to current shareholders. Until the day on which a stock goes "ex-rights," ownership (purchase) of a share of stock automatically includes any rights per share that have been declared for the stock. After the rights are issued they can be exercised or traded. By exercising one's rights, a shareholder can maintain his or her proportionate share holdings in the corporation. Rights may be issued explicitly for this purpose. Rights are traded on the exchanges and in the over-the-counter markets.

Repackaged Assets

Financial innovation has resulted in the repackaging of primary, fixed-income securities. Securities can be *repackaged* in two ways: (1) primary securities can be pooled together and new claims on the pool (called *pass-through securities*) issued, and (2) cash flows for a security can be separated and the parts sold individually (called *stripped securities*).

Pass-through Securities   The classic example of assets being pooled together and resold as a standardized contract is the *GNMA pass-throughs* ("Ginnie Maes") issued by mortgage banks and insured by the Government National Mortgage Association, a federally chartered corporation. Ginnie Mae certificates represent claims on a pool of mortgages that have been insured by an agency of the federal government. Cash payments made on Ginnie Mae certificates include interest, amortization of principal, and payments of principal. In addition to creating a standardized contract, the repackaging arrangement also differentiates the financial security bought by an investor from the mortgage agreement made with the primary user of the funds (the homeowner). Consequently, highly marketable securities are substituted for very illiquid mortgage agreements.

Stripped Securities   The cash flows for a fixed income security are the interest payments to maturity and the payment of principal at maturity. As noted, there is no risk of these payments' not being made for securities issued by the federal government, but holders of U.S. government securities are subject to interest rate risk if the cash flows received are not harmonized with the use of funds.[11]

An individual can minimize interest rate risk by appropriately selecting government securities according to their duration. However, the menu of instruments is limited, and a complex pattern of future cash flows may not be easily matched. An attractive possibility was developed to mitigate the problem—repackaging government securities in a process, called *coupon stripping,* that works as follows: shares of a given government issue are purchased by a brokerage firm and placed in trust (a bank typically acts as custodian), and separate receipts are issued and sold for each individual payment of interest and principal. Investors are able to buy the separate receipts according to their own cash flow requirements so as more easily to harmonize their investment income with their need for funds.[12]

Derivative Securities

The securities thus far discussed, whether primary or repackaged, represent claims on an issuer's cash flows. *Derivative securities,* on the other hand, entail agreements to purchase or to sell other assets under stated conditions in the future. Because the purchase/sell agreements can themselves be traded, these agreements are also marketable securities; because their existence and value are based on the assets on which they are written, they are called *derivative securities.*

Agreements concerning trades in the future are made for many different types of assets: individual securities, baskets of securities (market indexes and submarket indexes), foreign currency, commodities, and so on. Two types of agreements can be made: (1) deferred delivery and payment agreements called *forward contracts* when arranged in dealer markets and

---

[11]Consider, for instance, an individual with a known expenditure two years in advance who decides to purchase a one year treasury note and, when it matures, to roll it over in another treasury security that will mature in one year. The risk faced by this individual is that with fluctuating interest rates, the return to be realized when the funds are reinvested for the second year cannot be known with certainty at the present time.

[12]Coupon stripping is done by, for example, Lehman Brothers' *Lehman Investment Opportunity Notes* (LIONs), Salomon Brothers' *Certificates of Accrual on Treasury Securities* (CATs), and Merrill Lynch's *Treasury Investment Growth Receipts* (TIGRs); in honor of the acronyms, these securities are known on the Street as "animals."

futures contracts when entered into on an exchange; and (2) *options* or discretionary contracts by which the seller (writer) of a contract extends to the buyer the right, to be exercised at the buyer's option, to buy or to sell a given number of asset shares at stated terms in the future.

The development of the market for derivative securities illustrates how the design of an effective financial instrument and the institution of an effective trading system can increase market liquidity and expand the size of a market. Deferred delivery contracts and discretionary contracts have existed for centuries; what is new is the standardization of futures and options contracts and the introduction of organized, exchange based trading and clearance procedures. Trading in exchange listed options first began on April 26, 1973, when the Chicago Board Options Exchange (CBOE) began trading in standardized call option contracts. Since that date, the growth of option trading on the CBOE, the American Stock Exchange, and elsewhere has been enormous.

The dazzling array of derivative assets that have been introduced in recent years (options and futures on stock market indexes and submarket indexes, interest-rate futures, options on futures, currency options, commodity options, and so forth) illustrates the integral role that electronic technology plays in modern securities markets, not just for order routing and information dissemination, but also for information processing and decision making.

To appreciate more fully the importance of the computer, consider the following. A liquid market for futures or options on a stock market index cannot exist without a substantial number of traders interacting continuously in the purchase and sale of contracts. A large group of traders does remain in the trading pits on, for example, the CBOE, Chicago Board of Trade (CBOT), Chicago Mercantile Exchange (CME), and New York Futures Exchange (NYFE). They do so because the market indexes they trade change rapidly enough to generate sufficient trading interest. The recorded index values do change rapidly enough because they are updated virtually continuously with the aid of computer technology.[13]

A great deal has been written about the valuation of derivative assets and the uses to which they may be put. In the following discussion, we simply describe the contracts.

Futures Contracts   A standardized *futures contract* specifies the asset on which it is written, the amount of the asset, the standards for "good delivery" of the asset, and the delivery date for the asset. For instance, in May

---

[13]Similarly, option trading involves tracking an option's price, tracking the price of the security on which the option is written, and assessing related variables (such as price volatility) in a complex pricing formula. For these purposes, the computational power of the computer is typically utilized by professional traders.

1986 the CBOT traded contracts for 1000 troy ounces of silver (of a particular type) for delivery in June, August, October, and December of 1986 and for February, April, and June of 1987. The price of the standardized contract is all that traders themselves determine. On May 30, 1986, the settlement price for the June silver contract was 523.0 cents per troy ounce (hence the price for one contract was $5230).

An investor who sells a futures contract is legally obligated to deliver the asset on which the contract is written and is "short" the asset. An investor who buys a futures contract may receive delivery and is "long" the asset. Because there is a seller for every buyer, the net of all long and short positions for a given futures contract must be zero.

A measure of the size of the market for a contract is the number of contracts outstanding, which is called *open interest*. For example, the open interest for the June silver contract on the CBOT reported on May 30, 1986, was 4671.[14] The number of contracts outstanding for the derivative securities depends on the trading interest of investors.[15]

Many futures traders do not care about receipt or delivery of the underlying asset itself. Accordingly, they generally close out their positions with offsetting transactions before the delivery date. If a contract is not closed before the delivery date, the asset on which it is written is delivered. Folk tales are told of the hapless futures trader who, having forgotten to close out a position in red winter wheat, had several truck loads of grain deposited on the front lawn.

Options Contracts   A standardized *option contract* specifies the asset on which it is written, the amount of the asset (a stock option contract is generally for 100 shares), the price at which the option can be exercised (the exercise price), the date at which the option will expire if not exercised (the expiration date), and the type of option that the seller (writer of the option) is extending to the buyer. The option is a *put option* if the right extended by the seller to the buyer is to sell shares; the option is a *call option* if the buyer of the option has the right to buy shares (call the shares) from the seller of the option. More complex options are combinations of puts and calls. For instance, a *straddle* combines one put and one call at the same exercise price; a *strip* combines two puts and one call; a *strap* combines two calls and one put.

Market information pertaining to an option can be illustrated with reference to Disney options, which are traded on the American Stock Ex-

---

[14]Open interest is reported for the previous day.

[15]The supply of derivative securities is determined by the trading interest of investors in the same way that an increase of equity shares attributable to short selling depends on the trading interest of investors (see the preceding discussion).

change. Prices for the standardized Disney options were reported in *The Wall Street Journal* on Friday, May 30, 1986, as follows:[16]

Option & NY Close	Strike Price	Calls-Last			Puts-Last		
		Jun	Jul	Oct	Jun	Jul	Oct
Disney	25	s	r	s	s	$1/16$	s
$47\frac{1}{8}$	30	s	$17\frac{1}{2}$	$18\frac{1}{4}$	s	r	r
$47\frac{1}{8}$	35	r	13	14	r	$1/16$	$3/8$
$47\frac{1}{8}$	$36\frac{1}{4}$	s	r	s	s	$1/8$	s
$47\frac{1}{8}$	40	8	8	$9\frac{1}{4}$	$1/16$	$1/4$	1
$47\frac{1}{8}$	45	$2\frac{3}{4}$	$3\frac{3}{4}$	$6\frac{3}{8}$	$7/16$	$13/16$	$2\frac{3}{4}$
$47\frac{1}{8}$	50	$11/16$	$1\frac{7}{8}$	4	$3\frac{1}{8}$	$4\frac{1}{4}$	5
$47\frac{1}{8}$	55	$1/8$	$11/16$	$2\frac{1}{16}$	r	$7\frac{5}{8}$	r

The table is interpreted as follows: The closing price of Disney stock (on the NYSE) was $47\frac{1}{8}$. The *strike price* is the exercise price of the option. The prices of the option contracts are shown in the columns on the right; prices for the call contracts are shown in the first three columns; and prices for the puts are given in the last three columns. The letter *s* is used when a contract has not yet been introduced; the letter *r* is used when a contract has been introduced but has not traded during the day. The preceding entries show, for instance, that an October 50 call on Disney sold for $4 per share ($400 per contract); the buyer of this contract has the right to buy 100 shares of Disney at $50 a share any time until the close of trading on the third Friday in October.[17]

Whether the option is a put, call, straddle, strip, or strap, it may be written as a European option or as an American option. *European options* can be exercised only on the expiration date. Most standardized options contracts traded in the United States are American options.[18]

Options need not be exercised or allowed to expire by the original buyers, but may instead be traded in the exchange or over-the-counter markets. The buyer of an option who subsequently sells the contract or the seller (writer) of an option who subsequently buys the contract closes out his or her position in a *closing trade*.

Additional options terminology is useful:

At/out/in the money: An option with an exercise price equal to the current price of the stock is said to be "at the money." If the exercise price is above the market price, a call option is "out of the money" and a put option is "in the money"; if the exercise

---

[16]Note that at low values, prices can be stated in one-sixteenths.

[17]Exchange traded stock options expire on the Saturday after the third Friday in the designated month.

[18]The Standard and Poor's 500 Index option, which is traded on the CBOE, and the Institutional Investor Index option, which is traded on the Amex, are European options.

price is below the market price, a call is "in the money" and a put is "out of the money."

Option premium: The price the buyer of an option pays the writer of an option is called the *premium;* the premium is simply the price of the option contract itself.

Intrinsic value: An option's intrinsic value is the dollars it would yield if exercised immediately, evaluated at the market price for the underlying shares (in the case of a stock option). An option's intrinsic value is zero if it is out of or at the money.

Time value: An option's time value is the excess of its current market price over its intrinsic value. The excess reflects the value of holding an option that has time remaining before expiration.

Covered/naked position: A call option is covered if the writer of the call has a long position in the stock. The option is naked if the writer of the call does not own shares of the stock or of a security convertible into the stock.

A number of the securities considered in the preceding discussion may be viewed as options. Warrants and rights, for instance, explicitly extend the option to purchase shares of common stock according to specified terms (the only difference is that the supply of rights and warrants is set by the issuing firm, not by traders, and the exercise of a warrant or right impacts on the capitalization of the issuing firm). Similarly, convertible debentures and convertible preferreds extend the option to convert (buy shares of common) according to specified terms.[19]

Equity shares can also be viewed as call options extended by a firm's creditors to its equity investors. The premium received by creditors (the writers of the option) is the proceeds from the issuance of equity plus retained earnings. The creditors have effectively invested the premium plus their own funds (the proceeds received by the firm from the sale of the debt instrument to the creditors) in the assets of the firm. The *exercise price* (strike price) of the call option is the set of interest and principal payments promised to the creditors, and the *maturity date* of the debt is the expiration date of the option. In the event of bankruptcy, creditors retain the firm's assets, but if the firm remains solvent, the promised payments are made to creditors, and the assets are called away from the creditors by the shareholders.

---

[19]As noted, *convertible issues* are effectively combinations of two issues: a standard fixed income security and a warrant to buy common stock.

Synthetic Securities

The securities thus far considered are created by either a primary issuer, a brokerage-type operation (repackaged securities), or a contractual agreement between traders recorded with a clearing organization (options and futures). In addition, individual traders can combine financial assets so as to create *synthetic securities*, as we show in this subsection.

An *investment position* can be described by the relationship, as of the end of a holding period, between the price of the security on which the position is taken and the profit an investor will have realized from taking the position. For instance, an investor with a long position profits if the price of common shares has increased, as does the buyer of a call option; an investor with a short position profits if the price of common shares has

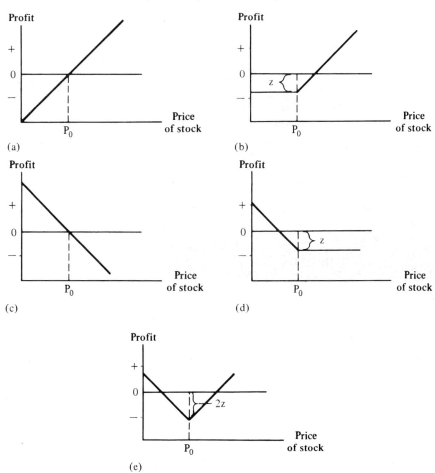

Figure 4.1 Relationships of the profits to a position to the price of a stock. (a) Long the stock. (b) Buy a call. (c) Short the stock. (d) Buy a put. (e) Buy a straddle (a put and a call).

decreased, as does the buyer of a put option; the buyer of a straddle profits if the price of shares has increased *or* decreased sufficiently; and so on.

Five relationships between the profits to a position (as of the end of a holding period or at the expiration of an option) and the price of a stock are displayed in Figure 4.1. The profit (per share) to the holder of a position is shown on the vertical axis, the stock price at the end of the holding period is shown on the horizontal axis, and P_0 is the original purchase/sale price for a long position (Figure 4.1[a]), short position (Figure 4.1[c]), or the exercise price of an option (Figure 4.1[b], [d], and [e]).[20] Assume the put and the call options are priced the same way; then the vertical distance marked z in Figure 4.1(b) and Figure 4.1(d) is the premium (per share) for a put or call option, and the vertical distance marked $2z$ in Figure 4.1(e) is the premium (per share) for the put and call options combined. The upward and downward sloping lines are at 45 degree angles to the axes because, when an option is in the money, profits to the position change dollar-for-dollar with the price of the stock.

Short/long positions and option contracts redistribute returns between investors with opposite positions. Consequently, the stock price, profits-to-position relationships are symmetrical for matched positions, as illustrated in Figure 4.2(a), (b), and (c). Specifically, the relationships shown for the

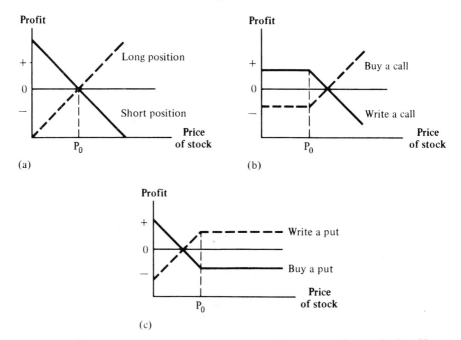

Figure 4.2 Symmetry of stock price, profits-to-position relationships for matched positions. (a) Long/short positions. (b) Buy/write positions for a call. (c) Buy/write positions for a put.

[20]For simplicity, the effect of dividends on the long/short positions is ignored.

"Long/short the stock," "Buy/write a call," and "Buy/write a put" positions are each symmetrical around the horizontal line at the zero profits level. Therefore, ignoring transaction costs, combined profits for a long and short position, for buying and writing a call, and for buying and writing a put are always zero.

Two positions taken in combination (for instance, buy a stock and write a call) also generate a specific relationship between the price of the stock and the profits to the composite position taken by the investor. This is illustrated in Figure 4.3: Figure 4.3(a) is for a "Buy the stock" position; Figure 4.3(b) is for a "Write a call" position; and Figure 4.3(c) is for the composite position. The relationship shown in Figure 4.3(c) is obtained by adding, at each price, the profits (negative or positive) for the long position and the written call position. Observe that the relationship shown in Figure 4.3(c) is the same as that shown by the upward sloping dashed line labeled "Write a put" in Figure 4.2(c).

The conclusion follows that the investor, by simultaneously being long the stock and writing a call, has created his or her own "synthetic" security—a synthetic put option.

Another example is a synthetic futures contract. Futures contracts are not traded for some stock market indexes for which both put and call options are available. The simultaneous purchase of a European call option and sale

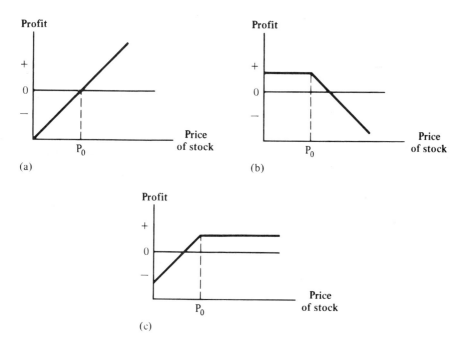

Figure 4.3 Two positions taken in combination generate a specific relationship between the price of the stock and the profits to the composite position taken by the investor. (a) Long the stock. (b) Write a call. (c) Positions shown in (a) and (b) combined.

of a European put option at the same exercise price results in returns, at expiration, that rise or fall, dollar-for-dollar, with the value of the index (if the index increases, profits are realized from the purchase of the call; if the index decreases, losses are realized from having written the put). Therefore, since the options are exercisable only at expiration (that is, they are European options), the created position is equivalent to a long position in a futures contract. Consequently, the investor has obtained the equivalent of a futures contract even though no such contract is traded in the market.

The analytics for the synthetic futures contract are shown in Figure 4.4(a), (b), and (c). As in Figure 4.3, the upward sloping line in Figure 4.4(c) is obtained by summing the profits shown in Figure 4.4(a) and (b) for each of the two positions, at each value of price.

Basket Securities

A stock market *index* measures the average value of securities traded in a market. A portfolio that contains stocks in proportions equal to their weights in an index increases or decreases in value at the same rate as that index. Therefore, by holding such a *basket portfolio,* an investor can obtain the overall market rate of return.

"The index" itself is not a security that can be bought and sold. The best one can do in the *spot market* (that is, the market for immediate delivery) is to replicate the market by holding a basket portfolio or by

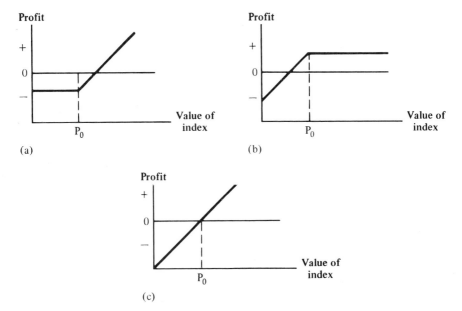

Figure 4.4 Analytics for the synthetic futures contract. (a) Buy a call. (b) Write a put. (c) Positions shown in (a) and (b) combined.

buying shares in an index fund (which does the same thing). An alternative that has become very attractive in recent years exists, however: an investor can buy or sell a futures or an option contract written on a market index. The payment (settlement) on expiration of the contract depends upon how the market index has changed between the contract date and the settlement date.

Futures and option contracts written on a market index differ from similar contracts written on commodities in that they do not specify delivery, but rather are for cash settlement. That is, whereas traders with long positions in a silver contract may expect delivery of silver when the contract expires, traders with long positions in an index future receive only cash settlements (positive or negative) from traders with short positions. The settlements depend on how the index has changed over the life of the contract. As the index rises, traders with long positions are credited and traders with short positions pay the difference; as the index falls, traders with short positions are credited and traders with long positions pay the difference.[21]

Market index trading can be used to hedge a position, to arbitrage pricing discrepancies, or to speculate on future market movements. Index trading also enables an investor to speculate on a stock's (or a group of stocks') returns relative to the market without being affected by aggregate market movements. For instance, an investor who is bullish on a company but who does not want to be exposed to the risk of an aggregate market decline can obtain a long position in the stock of the company and sell off market risk by taking a short position in a market index futures contract.

Standardized options and futures contracts written on market indexes are traded on a number of exchanges. For instance,

- *S&P 500 Stock Price Index:* Futures contracts traded on the Chicago Mercantile Exchange (CME); options contracts traded on the Chicago Board Options Exchange (CBOE)
- *NYSE Composite Index:* Futures contracts traded on the New York Futures Exchange (NYFE); options contracts traded on the NYSE
- *Major Market Index:* Futures contracts traded on the Chicago Board of Trade (CBOT); options contracts traded on the Amex
- *Futures Options:* Contracts for options on futures contracts also traded for the S&P 500 Index and the NYSE Composite Index

The size of futures contracts is typically 500 times an index's value. The size of options contracts is 100 times an index's value.

---

[21]The settlement process is explained in further detail in the section "Clearance and Settlement."

Interest Rate and Currency Swaps

Traditional *swaps* involve the exchange of debt instruments between two investors. For instance, two partners in a bond swap exchange bonds of comparable value and settle the difference in cash. A benefit of asset swapping is that it enables investors to restructure their portfolios in a single transaction, thereby reducing transaction costs. Dealer/brokers who have the capacity to execute bond swaps can give better service to their customers.

Swaps need not involve the debt instruments themselves or the indebtedness obligations of the borrowers. Rather, each borrower may simply agree to pay the debt service of the other. Such an agreement is called an *interest rate swap* when the indebtedness obligations differ because, for example, one instrument has a fixed interest rate and the other instrument has a variable interest rate. The agreement is called a *currency swap* when the indebtedness obligations are written in different currencies (for instance, Swiss francs and U.S. dollars).[22]

Interest rate and currency swaps are made when one firm can borrow in a market that is not easily accessed by the other. The swap agreement has benefits akin to that of a synthetic security discussed earlier. Effectively, the two partners in a swap each sell an issue to the other. Each issue may be valued separately, and any differences in present value can be adjusted for at the beginning or during the life of the swap agreement.[23]

An example of an interest rate swap illustrates what is involved. Assume that (1) a commercial bank that makes short term commercial loans has issued a 12 percent, 10-year bond, and (2) a savings and loan association (S&L) with a fixed-rate mortgage portfolio yielding 14 percent obtains funds from savers at the variable money market rate. The commercial bank borrows long-term to finance short term lending, and the S&L borrows short term to finance long term lending.

The S&L and the commercial bank could become swap partners. The commercial bank would agree to service the S&L's variable money market rate obligation, and the S&L would agree to service the bank's bond obligation. The commercial bank benefits from reducing its interest rate risk by locking in a relatively fixed differential between the short term lending rate and the money market rate the S&L pays depositors. The S&L benefits as long as the spread between its fixed rate mortgage portfolio (14 percent) and the 10 year bond rate (12 percent) remains positive.[24] For both partners,

[22]Swaps can also be made across both currencies and interest rates.

[23]The swap is "clean" if no adjustment is involved.

[24]A cancellation provision can be written into the swap contract so that the agreement may be "rolled up" if a decrease in interest rates results in a prepayment of mortgages decreasing the yield to the S&L on its mortgage portfolio. The S&L may, however, impose a prepayment penalty so as to lock in its portfolio return with greater certainty.

the swap offsets the interest rate risk caused by a mismatching of liability and asset maturities.[25]

Interest rate and currency swaps are typically arranged and valued with the aid of an investment bank. Often a swap is part of a broader financing plan. The swap market has grown immensely in recent years and now comprises swap dealers (typically divisions of giant international banks) who swap a client's loans or other obligations for new loans or obligations, perhaps in a different currency. Each transaction is essentially between the dealer and the client; the dealer, however, tries to maintain a balanced portfolio so as to keep his or her own aggregate position at low risk.

THE OPERATIONS OF A BROKERAGE HOUSE

Scope of Operations

Full line brokerage houses and investment banking firms offer a wide range of financial services. Although these vary somewhat from firm to firm, the following provides a representative view of what is involved:

- *Asset management:* for individuals, firms, and governments (domestic and foreign), retirement plans (IRA, Keogh), pension plans, money market funds, growth funds, bond/debenture funds, and so on
- *Equities:* stocks, options, and futures (both as writer and purchaser); research; principal trading; OTC market making; brokerage; risk arbitrage; and so forth
- *Fixed income securities:* government securities, corporate bonds, municipal bonds, unit investment trusts, mortgage backed securities, money market instruments, commercial paper, foreign exchange, commodities, research, trading and OTC market making, brokerage operations, interest rate and currency swaps, and so on
- *Investment banking:* public and private financings (including initial public offerings), mergers and acquisitions, leveraged buyouts, venture capital, equipment lease financing, sale and leasebacks, recapitalization and reorganization, access to foreign capital markets, new issue valuation and marketing, corporate finance (project finance and valuation), other investment banking services (financial advice, maintaining and developing investment banking relationships), and others
- *Real estate:* public and private syndications, income producing property acquisitions for clients and own account, commercial mortgage brokerage, leasing, management of real estate portfolios, and other services

[25]For further discussion, see Bloch (1986).

- *Commodities:* base and precious metals, "soft" commodities (coffee, cocoa, cotton, oil, and so on), and foreign currency, hedging, advisory services, market making, and so forth
- *Other services:* custody and escrow services, investment advisory services, clearing and settlement (including complex multicurrency transactions), financial advisory, working capital management, insurance (life insurance, annuities, and others), quantitative analysis and financial innovation, data processing, management information systems, administration, and others

The categories listed can be reclassified under five headings:

1. *Investing:* Asset management, investment management, and real estate
2. *Investment banking*
3. *Market making:* OTC market making for equities, fixed income securities, and commodities
4. *Trading:* Principal trading (position trading and arbitrage), brokerage operations, swaps, and commodities
5. *Support, administrative, and other services:* Custody and escrow services, clearance and settlement services, research, advisory, insurance, management information systems, administration, and others

In later sections we focus on market making and trading. In the discussion, market making is differentiated from trading in the following way: (1) *market making* involves establishing quotes, finding the transaction price, and otherwise "creating a two-sided market" so that trades can be made; (2) *trading* (either for the security firm's proprietary account or for customer accounts) involves submitting one-sided orders (buy or sell) so as to rebalance a portfolio or to benefit from short run price movements (such as arbitrage trading).

Investment Banking[26]

Raising equity funds in primary markets is one of the major functions of an investment banking firm. Funds may be raised by an initial public offering (IPO) or by issuing new shares of an existing issue, by selling warrants, or by floating a new issue. In each case, the funding is arranged with the services of an investment banker who, in essence, "makes the market." Our description of market making operations starts with investment banking.

[26]Much of the discussion in this section draws on Bloch (1986).

A company has an initial public offering when it first *goes public,* a decision made in consultation with an investment banking firm. Going public is akin to moving from a closet to a goldfish bowl, with all the attending pressures, problems, and benefits. The disadvantages of going public include (1) increased regulatory requirements and (2) an obligation to release considerably more corporate information (including financial data on corporate insiders). The benefits of going public include (1) broader access to capital markets for raising funds for the firm's operations and (2) increased liquidity for owners. There is also a social benefit to a firm's going public: increasing the marketability of its shares means that its equity can and will be evaluated in the marketplace. This facilitates the assessment of the firm's cost of capital and, consequently, results in a more efficient distribution of funds across firms in the economy.

To go public, a firm must engage legal counsel and investment banking services. Financial and other information has to be assembled, audited, filed with the SEC, and presented in a prospectus. The objective is to enable reasonable valuation of the firm, both for the firm itself and for potential investors.

Along with valuing the firm, the investment banker markets the issue. Marketing efforts encompass four activities:

1. *Formation of a syndicate:* Most large issues are sold by syndicates formed by an investment banking firm that acts as the managing underwriter. The formation of a syndicate spreads the risk of any individual underwriter and enables the investment bankers to diversify their efforts and capital over a larger number of underwritings. The managing underwriter in a syndicate carries the largest single share of risk; risk to other members is distributed according to their participation and the underwriting agreement.

2. *Underwriting:* Underwriting a new issue is similar to underwriting insurance. The underwriter of an insurance policy assumes the risk of an adverse event's occurring (for instance, if the house on which an insurance policy has been written catches fire). The adverse event for new issue underwriting is that the issue will not be fully purchased by the public (because the offering price has been set too high).

3. *The placement of shares:* A sale of new issues in the open market is a *public offering;* a negotiated sale to a small number of individual and institutional investors is a *private placement.* Shares that are presold as a private placement reduce the underwriting risk incurred by the investment banking syndicate at the time of a public offering. After an offering, registered representatives of the syndicate firms join the marketing effort by calling the issue to the attention of their customers.

4. *Price stabilization:* After the offering is effective and during the flotation period, the syndicate manager supports price to facilitate acceptance of the issue in the secondary market. This stabilization against price decreases typically involves considerably more capital and control over price than is provided by stock exchange specialists in secondary markets. Issuing corporations themselves are prohibited at all times from stabilizing their own shares (largely to prevent firms from manipulating their share price).

Valuation is especially difficult for an IPO. Until a firm goes public, its equity shares have not been assessed by the market (as a consequence of their not having been traded in an organized secondary market). The investment banker, therefore, operates as an appraiser when determining the price at which to issue new shares. The *appraisal,* like standard security analysis, involves an investigation of the financial, operational, and managerial capabilities of the firm; a forecast of future cash flows; and an assessment of the industry within which the firm operates. In addition, broad economic conditions are taken into consideration, both to determine current worth in the market and to assess the timing of the offering.

Six major decisions concerning an offering are made:

1. *Total dollar value:* The total dollar value of an issue is determined by relating the corporation's need for funds to the firm's cost of capital (which reflects the willingness of the market to supply funds to the firm); the amount of funds to be raised from other sources (a future debt issue, for instance) is simultaneously taken into account.
2. *Share size of offer:* If a firm has, for instance, decided to raise $100 million and wishes its stock to trade in the $20 to $30 price range, the offer size would be set at about 4 million shares.[27]
3. *Offering price:* The specific price of an offering is set according to the market's expected receptivity to the issue. Setting the exact price at which shares will be sold to the public is one of the most difficult and important steps in an offering.
4. *Gross spread:* The gross spread is the difference between the per share offering price to the public, and the per share proceeds to the company. After the size of the issue, the price to the public, and the gross spread have been established, the issuing company knows exactly how many dollars it will realize from the flotation.

---

[27]Many new stock issues contain a "Green Shoe" option (so called because it was first used by the Green Shoe Co.). This gives the underwriter the option to acquire, from the issuing company, up to 15 percent more shares than are indicated in the prospectus, at the same terms. The underwriter thereby gains some protection if, in stabilizing the new issue price, a short position is taken by the syndicate manager prior to an unforeseen price surge (the short position may be covered, in part at least, by exercising the Green Shoe option).

The risk of this dollar amount's not being raised is borne by the investment bankers. The gross spread paid to investment bankers includes an allowance for selling costs[28] (on the order of 60 percent of the spread), a management fee for the lead underwriter (20 percent of the spread), and an allowance to cover underwriting (20 percent of the spread). The allowance for underwriting is distributed to syndicate participants (including the managing underwriter) in relation to their participation. These payments are designed to cover the underwriter's expenses and to yield a profit.[29]

5. *Timing:* The timing of an offering is crucial and difficult. It takes time to bring a new issue to market, and market conditions are difficult to assess and to predict. After a syndicate has been formed, the offering plan and prospectus completed, and all else prepared, it may take two days for the SEC to give final approval (the *regulatory delay*), and a week or so to float an issue (the *flotation delay*). Because the hoped-for offering price may have been established in advance of these delays, the issuers have in effect set their hopes on a *future* price, not a *spot* price.

6. *The amount existing shareholders sell at an IPO:* Funds raised by an IPO can be used in part to purchase the equity holdings of current shareholders. However, the market may have a negative response if it perceives that the current owners are attempting to ''bail out.'' For this reason, the current owners generally continue to hold an appreciable portion of the new financial package.

In part because a future rather than spot price is involved, the pricing of a new issue, as seen through the eyes of an investment banking firm, is similar to the pricing of an option. The syndicate has effectively purchased the entire issue from the issuing firm at the offering price minus the gross spread and has offered to sell the shares to the public at the offering price. Accordingly:

- The syndicate is long the stock.
- The syndicate has extended (written) an American call option to the public.
- The offering price of the issue is the exercise price of the call option.
- The gross spread is the option premium received by the syndicate for writing the call option.[30]

[28]Selling expenses include SEC listing and transfer agent fees; federal and state revenue stamps, taxes, and fees; and legal, accounting, printing, and other expenses. Roughly 5 percent of the allowance to cover underwriting is for these expenses.

[29]The underwriters, however, are at risk because their returns are lower, dollar for dollar, if the issue does not sell on the market at the hoped-for price.

[30]The investor who obtains (buys) an option typically pays for the instrument. In the current case, the issuing company pays the writer of the option (the syndicate) by giving up the gross spread, and the call option itself is costless to the public. The option pricing analogy is from Bloch (1986).

As discussed, holding a long position in a stock and writing a call create a synthetic put. Therefore:

- If the issue is bought at the price at which it is offered to the public (the *exercise price*), the syndicate earns the gross spread (the *option premium*).
- At higher prices, the syndicate profits from its long position but loses (dollar for dollar) from having written a call; thus the syndicate continues to receive the gross spread, and no more.
- At lower prices, the synthetic put is in the money, and thus the syndicate loses, dollar for dollar; this offsets the profits realized from the gross spread and results in a loss if the realized price is below the price guaranteed to the issuing firm.

Market Making

Like a dealer who operates in the secondary markets, an investment banker raising funds in the primary market is a market maker. A dealer bears the risk of committing capital to market making; an investment banker similarly places capital at risk when underwriting an offering. A dealer plays a key role in the price discovery process; as discussed, investment bankers play a key role in determining the price received by an issuing firm and the price at which the shares are sold to the public. The price paid to the issuing company is the investment banker's bid; the offering price to the public is the investment banker's ask. Like any dealer, the investment banker hopes to earn the difference between the bid and the ask, which in the case of an offering is called the *gross spread*.

Dealers in secondary markets, by establishing bid and ask quotes, effectively extend a free option to public traders:[31] the dealer extends a put option to public sellers, and a call option to public buyers (thereby creating a straddle). As discussed previously, the investment banker effectively writes a synthetic put by buying at the agreed-upon price from the issuing firm, and extending a free call option to public buyers. Viewing the posting of quotes in a secondary market, and the flotation of a new issue in the primary market, in the context of an option pricing model enriches one's understanding of the determinants of market prices and of the market makers' return.

Along with raising large sums of capital in primary markets, investment banks also handle large transactions in secondary markets. The secondary market transaction that most closely resembles a primary market flotation is the registered secondary offering used to facilitate the sale of a

---

[31]Copeland and Galai (1983) first applied option pricing theory to a dealer's pricing decisions.

large block of stock. As with a new issue, a prospectus is required for a registered secondary, and the sale must be announced to the public in advance of the offering period.

Other procedures for the handling of block sales also involve investment bankers in secondary markets. For instance, a spot secondary, which is unregistered and announced without notice, may be used by an institutional trader (or other owner) who wishes to sell large amounts of an issue. Or the investment banker may simply purchase a block and resell the shares to buyers that it itself finds.

Investment bankers are involved in a dealership capacity in secondary markets for the following reasons:

- They transact in the secondary market to stabilize the price of a new issue during its flotation period.
- Participation in the secondary markets is profitable, given the expertise, capital, and other resources the investment bankers have developed with regard to primary market operations.
- The continuing involvement of investment banking firms in secondary market making activities enables them continuously to maintain a feel for the market. This knowledge facilitates the share valuation and pricing decisions they make intermittently in the new issues market.
- Institutional investors participate heavily in both the primary and the secondary markets; relationships investment bankers develop with institutional traders in secondary markets facilitate placing newly issued shares in the primary market.
- Market making is a service to the client; providing this service may help the investment bank to maintain a relationship when no other services are required by the client firm.

Each of the five reasons points to one underlying factor: market making in primary markets and market making in secondary markets are highly complementary operations.

The securities firms have established sizable operations as OTC market makers. In the spring of 1986, for instance, Shearson Lehman made markets in over 2000 securities. At the time, Merrill Lynch made markets in 1250 domestic OTC stocks and had plans to add approximately 50 stocks per month to its market making book until reaching a long term goal of 2000 firms.[32]

The investment banker's reach extends beyond the equity markets and the long term fixed income markets, to real estate, commodities, commercial paper, foreign exchange, and other transactions. This is because ar-

---

[32]The preceding information was reported in *Securities Week,* May 26, 1986.

ranging financing for a corporation does not end with the flotation of a single issue, and market making is not confined to a simple one-on-one exchange of assets. This point can be illustrated in relation to four financings that Goldman Sachs participated in during 1985:[33]

- Assisted Monsanto with its restructuring and acquisition of a pharmaceutical company, G.D. Searle & Co., for $2.8 billion: the financing plan included short term debt (commercial paper in the form of private placement notes), long term debt (including two domestic bond offerings totaling $400 million), and corporate restructuring (the sale of part of Searle and the divestiture of various oil and gas properties).
- Assisted Philips N.V. to increase its equity base by selling 10 million shares of common stock at a total value of $185 million: Goldman sold roughly 50 percent of the issue to more than 100 different accounts. The transaction required expertise in equity trading, in research, in international investment banking, in syndication, and in sales.
- Assisted Owens-Corning Fiberglas Corporation (which had acquired Armco Inc.'s Aerospace and Strategic Materials Group for $418 million) with various aspects of the acquisition and subsequent refinancing arrangements: comanaged a 15-year $50 million debt issue in the Swiss franc market and a 15-year $50 million debt issue in the Deutschemark market and simultaneously swapped both issues into U.S. dollars to hedge Owens-Corning's exposure to foreign currency risk; issued $150 million of commercial paper and arranged commercial paper based interest rate swaps to fix the interest payments for periods up to three years; managed offering of a $100 million five year extendable note callable after three years (the transaction was hedged in the U.S. Treasury market to protect against interest rate fluctuations because the company could not immediately enter the U.S. public markets). Goldman's *Annual Review 1985* (p. 6) states that, "Through the combination of these transactions, the Company's all-in cost of financing was lower than if the entire financing had been done in the U.S. Owens-Corning successfully met its financing objectives and maintained its single A ratings."
- Assisted Walt Disney Productions with a series of transactions to create a low-cost yen liability to hedge the yen cash flows generated by its Tokyo Disneyland: Lead managed a $62 million European Currency Unit (ECU) bond issue with a ten year amortization schedule; used a currency swap to convert the ECU denominated bond obligation into a yen obligation that fit Disney's projected cash flows; and converted the proceeds of the bond issue from ECUs into U.S.

---

[33]See Goldman Sachs's *Annual Review 1985*.

dollars by executing several short forward contracts in the foreign exchange market. Goldman's *Annual Review 1985* (p. 8) states that, "The transaction drew on the expertise of professionals in Capital Markets, Corporate Finance, Investment Banking, London Syndicate and Fixed Income Trading and Sales. . . . The series of transactions in world-wide markets saved Walt Disney 75 basis points per year over the life of the ECU offering as compared to a yen-syndicated loan."

The conclusion is clear: investment banking is a complex, multifaceted business that in many ways revolves about one activity—market making. This broad commitment to market making is clearly stated in Morgan Stanley's fiftieth annual review, its final annual review before itself going public in the spring of 1986:

> In 1971, the firm concluded that in order to maintain its leadership position in the securities industry, it must build a major presence in the securities markets and become an important distributor to the institutional marketplace. These decisions mark the beginning of the second period of our history and set us on a course of expansion and diversification which we continue to follow. . . . We intend to be a leading participant in every major primary and secondary market which is of significance to our clients and customers around the world. [pp. 6 and 7]
>
> *S. Parker Gilbert, chairman*
> *Richard B. Fisher, president*

> We made one decision, and that simple decision led to all the subsequent growth of our firm. Our decision was that we had to earn day-to-day relationships with the suppliers as well as the users of capital. [p. 20]
>
> *Richard B. Fisher, president*

And so the major securities firms, with both the ability and the incentive, have developed operations in commodities markets and money markets, have set up OTC operations, and have established the block trading desks that are to upstairs markets what the specialist posts are to an exchange's trading floor.

Trading

Just as the involvement of investment bankers in the primary markets leads to their participation in secondary markets, so too does the participation of investment bankers in secondary markets *as market makers* lead to their participation in secondary markets *as traders*. There are three categories of principal trades: position trading, arbitrage trading, and program trading.

Position Trading In their capacity as market makers, securities houses routinely take positions to facilitate block transactions for institutional traders. For instance, if an institutional seller wants to dispose of a block of 200,000 shares, and buyers for only 150,000 shares are found, the investment banking or brokerage house may itself buy 50,000 shares to conclude the deal. The firm receives a brokerage commission for both sides of the transaction and may earn a spread on the 50,000 it itself has acquired. However, the securities firm is then at risk: the price of the stock may decrease.

A securities firm may also take a short position if the number of shares sought for purchase is greater than the number of shares offered for sale by other public traders. Again the firm is at risk: the price of the stock may increase.

An investment banking or brokerage firm occasionally accommodates a large trader by taking the entire contra side of a block transaction. The following is an example:[34] In early 1983, Allied Corporation decided to sell 5.4 million shares of RCA Corporation common acquired in a takeover of the Bendix Corporation. One possibility for arranging the sale was an underwriting deal proposed by Lehman Brothers. In the opinion of legal advisers, such a deal would have had to be registered, would have required SEC approval, and would have involved a two day delay. An alternative presented itself, however, and was accepted by Allied: at 3:15 P.M. of March 30, 1983, Salomon Brothers agreed to buy the entire block, apparently without having lined up customers in advance. The transaction crossed the Consolidated Tape, at 3:22 P.M., at $23.75 a share.

After an unwanted long or short position has been acquired, the securities firm can use its sales force to attempt to place the shares or can turn to a position trader to rebalance the inventory position. In the Allied case, the investment banker did not use a position trader because of the size of the purchase. Rather, a Salomon sales force of 300 made "a blaze of phone calls," and all shares were resold by 3:30 P.M. (roughly 90 percent to institutional buyers).[35] For its 15 minutes of phone calls and, far more importantly, because of the risk it took in committing capital to the deal, Salomon is believed to have earned roughly $2 million in commissions and a spread of one-quarter point per share.

The risk the investment banker took was large, the payment it received was large, and the services it provided were substantial. Allied obtained

---

[34]See Bloch (1986).
[35]See "The Story Behind The Deal," *Investment Dealer Digest,* April 12, 1983.

immediate liquidity for a 5.4 million share block, and RCA weathered the sale without its share price being unduly destabilized or its cost of capital being increased.

Ordinarily, a securities firm uses its sales force to line up the contra side of a block during the negotiation process that precedes a transaction and then uses a position trader to work off any position taken by the firm to facilitate the deal. A position trader is not a two-sided market maker but rather, as the name implies, a trader. As a trader, he or she submits sell orders (if the firm has acquired a long position) or buy orders (if the firm has acquired a short position). The position trader may also take an offsetting position in a related security to hedge a position that cannot be quickly unwound.

Arbitrage   *Pure arbitrage* involves buying an asset in one market at a relatively low price and simultaneously selling that same asset in another market at a higher price. There is no market risk in pure arbitrage.

A classic example of virtually riskless arbitrage involves certain stocks (mainly mining issues) that are cross-listed on the Toronto Stock Exchange (TSE) and American Stock Exchange (Amex). Arbitrage firms have stationed agents at positions just off, but in view of, the trading floors of the two exchanges. The TSE and Amex agents maintain telephone contact while continuously monitoring quotes for the cross-listed stocks. When a price discrepancy appears, each agent communicates the appropriate buy or sell response to his or her representative on the trading floor. If the offsetting transactions can be made at the quoted prices, a virtually riskless arbitrage profit can be realized.[36]

Arbitrage is risky when purchase and sale are not simultaneous, when price differentials are not completely locked in, and/or when opposing positions are taken on similar but not identical assets. With regard to the TSE/Amex operation, price discrepancies may not be instantaneously found (there are lags in reporting quotes), the attention of the floor traders cannot always be instantaneously caught (they are not involved exclusively in arbitrage trading), and the TSE and Amex transactions cannot be made at precisely the same moment. Thus the operation is not totally without risk.

The term *risk arbitrage* has come to be used specifically with regard to arbitrage possibilities presented by publicly announced corporate transactions—principally mergers and takeovers, changes in capital structure, and dividend payments. The takeovers have received the most attention.

Sizable premiums are commonly paid in takeover situations. Consequently, takeover bids generally increase the value of the target firm's stock

---

[36]The arb operation avoids currency risk by including the purchase or sale of a five day (the settlement period) forward contract for Canadian dollars.

and decrease the value of the acquiring firm's stock. Accordingly, arbitrageurs ("arbs") take a long position in the target firm, and a short position in the acquiring firm, if the takeover is with stock. The long/short combination allows exploitation of price movements caused by a takeover bid and hedges the arb's position: after acquisition, the short position in the acquiring company is offset because the long position in the target company is converted into a long position in the acquiring company. Therefore, if the takeover is successful, the arb is not affected by a change in the price level of the acquiring company's stock.

The arbitrageur has in effect taken a position in the *takeover deal,* not in the target or acquiring companies per se. The risk to the arb is that the deal will fall through. When a deal does collapse, the arbitrageur who is unable to unwind the long and short positions quickly does become an investor.[37]

By the time a merger agreement between two companies is finalized, the arbitrage possibility has long vanished. Arbitrage profits are realized by attaining hedged positions before the takeover is even a certainty. Hence the term *risk arbitrage.* Successful arbs depend on an extensive information network, rapid decision making, and the ability to move fast. Sam Hunter, one of the leading block traders in the industry, has written, "Risk arbitrage . . . is not for the faint-hearted. . . . On the surface, the arbitrage business appears simple, but it is not. It requires hard work from some of the most dedicated people on Wall Street. The returns can be substantially higher than market returns, but so can the risks."[38]

Risk arbitrage emerged as a consequence of the wave of corporate mergers in the 1960s and continued to grow with the merger activity of the 1980s. In recent years the scope of arbitrage activities has extended beyond risk arbitrage. This is largely explained by the following:

1. A reduction in commission income after the elimination of fixed commission rates in 1975 increased the importance of trading profits as an income source to securities firms.
2. The development of derivative products (options and futures) opened new possibilities for arbitrage and hedging transactions. For instance, the act of shorting a stock and buying a call creates a synthetic put, which can be compared with an actual put trading under the same conditions for the same stock.

---

[37]For additional details concerning the risks involved and further discussion see Wyser-Pratte (1982).

[38]See Hunter (1985, pp. 147 and 149).

3. The more frequent use of *hedged positions* (taking opposite positions in similar instruments) in highly dynamic markets has made traders more aware of arbitrage possibilities.
4. Successful arbitrage operations, when widely used, dry up arbitrage profits and send professionals into new areas.
5. With the increasing globalization of trading, arbitrage possibilities now exist in international markets; for instance, in relation to issues such as Eurodollar convertibles or stocks that trade both ordinary shares and American Depository Receipts (ADRs).

The arbitrage community largely comprises a small number of major brokerage and investment banking firms and some large specialty NYSE member firms. As reported by Hunter (1985, p. 149), "Private money pools, hedge funds, aggressive domestic institutional investors, and selective foreign institutions have all been attracted to the arbitrage business. A number of individual investors have also been attracted, many of them supported by companies such as Bear Stearns and Oppenheimer."

Program Trading In the early 1980s, risky arbitrage developed along an innovative new track. Arbs would create a portfolio of stocks that proxied the S&P 500 index. When an S&P future was high in relation to the proxy portfolio, arbs would buy the portfolio and short the future; when the S&P future was low in relation to the proxy portfolio, arbs would buy the future and short the proxy portfolio. This arbitrage operation is now called *program trading*.

Program trading actually refers more broadly to the buying or selling of large baskets of stocks by brokerage firms, either for their own proprietary accounts or for institutional customers. The programs typically involve computer assisted transaction strategies that, particularly for index arbitrage, are designed to be executed with maximum speed. Hence the term *program trading*.

A program trade may be run for an institutional investor simply to restructure a portfolio. Reasons for doing so include (1) keeping an index fund representative of a market index, (2) changing the industry (or other grouping) composition of stocks in a portfolio, or (3) making pervasive alterations in the portfolio's composition after a change in portfolio management.

Programs to arbitrage a market index are typically run for a securities firm's proprietary account. More recently, however, securities firms have also started to run these programs for institutional investors.

Arbitrage opportunities between futures or options contracts on an index and the underlying stocks exist for the following reason. The markets for individual stocks, for index futures, and for index options are made side by side during the trading day. The price of each stock in an index is set in relation to the order flow (and dealer pricing decisions) for the particular stock. The prices of futures contracts and of options contracts on the index are set in relation to traders' desires to take long or short positions in the contracts. Clearly, the price of a contract for the market index should be related to the average price of the individual stocks that the index comprises. There is no assurance, however, that the established prices will be in alignment, because the prices are literally set in different markets. Consequently, arbitrage profits are possible, and arbitrage is the mechanism that keeps pricing consistent across the markets.

Programs are structured differently by each securities firm, and the specifics of a program are each firm's carefully guarded secret. However, similar decisions are made, and similar procedures are generally followed. These can be illustrated with reference to arbitrage between a representative basket of stocks and a stock index future (the situation is analogous for a stock index option). For this purpose, let:

F = the price of the index future

S = the cash price of the index (that is, the *current value* of the index, which is the average cash price of the stocks in the index)

m = the number of days until the futures contract matures

T = the dollar transaction cost of running a program divided by the current value of the index (T is expressed as a percentage)

r = the annualized risk-free rate of interest over the m-day period

d = the annualized dividend yield for a portfolio that proxies the index, for the m-day period (d is negative for a short position in the proxy portfolio)

The percentage differential between the price of the future and the cash price, $(F - S)/S$, is referred to as *the basis*. F equals S when the future matures on day m, and hence the basis is zero. The basis therefore represents a return that is realized over the m-day period because the cash price must equal the futures price by the end of the m-day period. The annualized value of this return is $[(F - S)/S][365/m]$. If the basis is positive, an investor may obtain the annualized return by a *long arbitrage* (buying the stocks in the index portfolio and shorting the index future); if the basis is negative, the return may be obtained by a *short arbitrage* (shorting the stocks and buying the future).

Both the long arbitrage and the short arbitrage eliminate all risk associated with change in the level of prices (that is, the arb's profits are not affected by proportionate change in F and in S). If, for instance, prices increase, profits realized from a long position in the stocks are offset, dollar for dollar, by losses realized from the short position in the index future. Similarly, losses from a short position in the stocks are offset, dollar for dollar, by profits from the long position in the index future. The hedged position also establishes an equivalent offsetting of profits and losses if prices decrease over the m-day interval. Therefore, because F must equal S when the futures contract matures, the basis is a riskless (gross) return for an investor with the appropriate long or short arbitrage position.

The total gross return (expressed as a rate per annum) is the annualized basis plus the dividend yield (d), which, for the moment, may be taken to be riskless. The dividend yield is an additional return for an investor with a long arbitrage but is subtracted out as a cost (that is, is assessed as $-d$) for an investor with a short arbitrage. If it were riskless, the total gross return must, in the absence of transaction costs, equal the risk-free rate, r (profitable arbitrage would eliminate any difference). Therefore,

$$\left(\frac{(F - S)}{S}\right)\left(\frac{365}{m}\right) + d = r \tag{4.1}$$

For the riskless arbitrage, the equilibrium value of the annualized basis is therefore

$$\left(\frac{F - S}{S}\right)\left(\frac{365}{m}\right) = r - d \tag{4.2}$$

If the basis differs from the value given by equation (4.2), an arbitrage opportunity exists. The difference, however, must be large enough to cover transaction costs (T). For a positive basis, a long arbitrage will be profitable if

$$\left(\frac{F - S}{S}\right)\left(\frac{365}{m}\right) - T\left(\frac{365}{m}\right) > r - d \tag{4.3}$$

For a negative basis, a short arbitrage will be profitable if[39]

$$- \left(\frac{F - S}{S}\right)\left(\frac{365}{m}\right) - T\left(\frac{365}{m}\right) > r - d \tag{4.4}$$

Index arbitrage is not riskless, however, and a program will not be run unless the inequalities shown in equations (4.3) and (4.4) are sufficiently large.[40] The risks involved in index arbitrage include the following:

[39]Recall that d in equation (4.4) is negative because the arb has shorted the stock. Hence for a short arbitrage to be profitable, the positive return from the negative basis, minus transaction costs, must exceed the risk-free rate of interest *plus* the dividend yield declared on the proxy portfolio, $r - (-d)$.

[40]A premium of from 200 to 250 basis points is commonly required to compensate for risk.

- Transaction costs may vary because the cost of achieving rapid executions cannot be known with certainty.
- The realized dividend yield may differ from the expected dividend yield.
- The proxy portfolio may not track the market index perfectly; hence at the close of day m, the futures price may not exactly equal the average cash price for the basket of stocks that comprise the proxy portfolio.
- When the futures contract matures on day m, positions must be unwound and settlements made in cash; if positions are not unwound at the market's closing prices, S generally does not equal F exactly.

A program trader formulates a plan for activating a program in order to exploit the arbitrage possibility as effectively as possible by keeping transaction costs at a minimum and achieving rapid execution of the program. Alternative sets of preprinted orders may be kept in sealed boxes on an exchange floor and certain critical personnel notified of general, but not specific, actions to be taken. When a program is activated, coded instructions are sent to key positions on a stock exchange (often the NYSE) and a futures exchange (often the Chicago Merc). Market orders are used because the window of opportunity is never open for long, and speed is essential. Brokers may also use ''stops'' to attempt to improve the prices at which their orders execute (see the section ''Orders and Order Handling in Chapter 3). If necessary, the size of a program can be varied by the head program trader as it is being carried out. Programs can reportedly be executed in less than 60 seconds (15 to 30 seconds to transmit orders and another 15 to 30 seconds to execute orders).

A number of decisions must be made to set up a program. These entail:

- Selection of the specific market index to use for the arbitrage: the S&P 500 is commonly used; this explains why shares are generally bought/sold on the NYSE and why futures contracts are generally bought/sold on the Chicago Merc.[41]
- Selection of the specific stocks to include in the proxy portfolio used for the arbitrage: purchasing all 500 shares in the S&P 500 would be unnecessary and overly cumbersome (baskets typically contain from 100 to 400 stocks).
- Choice of the appropriate rate of return (r): a short term borrowing or lending rate is commonly employed.
- Computation of the expected dividend yield.

---

[41]A program can be run with maximum success in a liquid market because a program's execution is less apt to result in adverse price movements in a thicker market.

- Determination of the critical value the basis must attain for a program to be activated: the determination of this value involves an assessment of transaction costs, T, and of r and d, and of the premium that must be added to compensate for risk.
- Specification of the size of the program: programs are generally as large as possible; a constraint on size, however, is that larger programs are more likely to result in adverse price effects.

The Costs/Benefits of Arbitrage Trading   Arbitrage trading is, in most respects, desirable. Arbitrage consolidates markets and increases market liquidity. Greater liquidity itself makes it easier for traders to hedge positions (take opposite positions in similar assets). Being better able to hedge, traders (and market makers) are willing to take larger positions, thus further increasing the liquidity of the markets.

As discussed, index trading gives rise to arbitrage possibilities. Index trading also enables investors to hedge against, or to speculate on, aggregate market movements. Each of these opportunities is valued by traders:

- As a hedge, an investor with a long position in a few stocks and a short position in an index future has ''sold off'' market risk and retained the company specific risk.
- By buying a futures contract on a market index, an investor can speculate on the aggregate market while avoiding firm specific risk.
- An investor with an arbitrage position can profit as the futures price and the cash price of the index regain an equilibrium alignment.

Index trading also benefits investors in the aggregate. The cash value of a market index reflects expectations concerning broad market conditions, as does the price of an index futures contract. These are valuable pricing guides for the individual stocks. If the average price of the individual stocks is out of alignment with the price of an index future, an inconsistency is revealed. When this occurs, arbitrageurs step in, drive up the price of the undervalued asset(s), and drive down the price of the overvalued asset(s). This action preserves the desirable consistency in pricing between the markets. While the hedged positions are being established, arbitrage trading also stabilizes the markets and enhances market liquidity.

There is another side to index arbitrage, however: when positions are unwound at the expiration of the futures contracts, the market can be destabilized. Destabilization may occur because index futures contracts are satisfied by cash settlement rather than by the literal delivery of shares.

As noted previously, most futures contracts call for delivery of the asset they are written on. For instance, a silver futures contract that remains open at maturity is satisfied when the seller of the contract delivers silver to the buyer of the contract. If the trader who sold the contract already owns the silver (as is frequently the case with commodities), no market transaction is necessary. With a stock index future, however, actual shares are not delivered (although in principle they could be).

Index futures call for cash settlement. Thus an arb with a long position in a proxy portfolio of stocks and a short position in the corresponding index future sells the stocks to unwind the arbitrage position (instead of delivering shares to the contra party with a long position in the index future). This *forced selling* puts downward pressure on share prices. Alternatively, an arb with a short position in the proxy portfolio and a long position in the index future buys the stocks to unwind the position (instead of receiving shares from the contra party with a short position in the index future). This *forced buying* puts upward pressure on share prices. Thus each arbitrage trade that has helped to stabilize the market when the program was first run results in an *unwinding trade* that can destabilize the market when the futures contract matures.

Until recently, index arbitrage positions have been unwound by placing *market-on-close* orders to sell (buy) shares that have been held long (short) in the proxy portfolios. If these orders execute at the close (that is, at the last price established on the trading day when the futures contract matures), the arb is unaffected by any price impact the unwinding trades may have. If the closing value of the index is pushed down by the sale of the individual stocks (or is pushed up by their purchase), the futures contract will itself be settled at a lower (or at a higher) price. Therefore, the arbs ignore the destabilizing effects their own unwinding trades may have.

The arbs each run their individual programs according to their own decision rules, and different programs are run to arbitrage the index on different dates over the life of a contract. All unwinding trades, however, take place as near as possible to the close of trading on the day the futures contract matures. The aggregate of all unwinding trades made on the same day has the potential to destabilize the market appreciably, to the detriment of other traders. Substantial destabilization occurs if the cumulative sum of all long arbitrage positions and the cumulative sum of all short arbitrage positions do not balance.[42] If the longs exceed the shorts by an appreciable amount, prices are driven down; if the shorts exceed the longs, prices are driven up.

---

[42]If the imbalance of short and long arb positions were known before expiration, the likely price movement the unwinding trades would create could be predicted, and further stabilizing orders would be attracted to the market. Unfortunately, because of the secrecy attending program trading, this imbalance is generally not known with much precision. Furthermore, even if these positions were known, prediction would be difficult because the institutions do not always liquidate their positions (particularly when they are long the stock).

Four days a year, on the third Fridays of March, June, September, and December, three types of contracts—index futures, index options, and stock options—expire. In the colorful language of Wall Street, the closing period for each of these four days is called "the triple witching hour."

Various proposals have been advanced to lessen the perils of the triple witching hour. These include:

- Changing the dates that contracts expire so as to avoid simultaneous expiration
- Requiring that large arbitrage positions be unwound early by imposing successively tighter position limits as the expiration date approaches (this is called *telescoping*)
- Basing settlements on opening rather than closing prices for the last trading day
- Requiring that market-on-close orders be placed earlier than some specified time during the trading day[43]
- Requiring delivery of shares instead of cash settlement

Although the third and fourth proposals have been experimented with with some success, each of these proposals could make it more difficult and/or more expensive for traders to obtain adequately hedged positions and thus would itself impose a cost. The question is whether the cure would be more costly than the disease.

The cure could be costly. As noted, only when contracts mature at the same time can traders obtain properly hedged positions. Increasing the costs and decreasing the benefits of hedging can impair the provision of liquidity to the market.

With regard to the disease, the destabilization may, all said and done, be more dramatic than serious. For one thing, the interval of time during which it is likely to occur is completely predictable. Second, the gyrations appear to be very short-lived—Stoll and Whaley have estimated the interval to be on the order of 15 minutes.[44] Therefore, any market order trader wishing to avoid the turbulence can do so by slightly altering the timing of his or her order.[45]

A further reason for not changing the futures and options contracts

---

[43]The NYSE has in fact requested early notification by traders of their intent to place market-on-close orders so that other market participants may have time to assemble orders on the other side.

[44]For further discussion, see Stoll and Whaley (1986).

[45]A cost might nonetheless be imposed on investors, however, because closing prices are used for various valuations, such as estate held shares or the cash redemption value of certain mutual fund shares.

exists: the triple witching hour phenomenon may simply be a manifestation of the market's unfamiliarity with the new trading instruments. As traders increasingly gain experience with index arbitrage by program trading, the market effects will become better understood and thus more predictable. These pricing aberrations will themselves attract the attention of the arbs; then they too may be eliminated.

THE TRADING DESK

Block Trades

Block trades are typically negotiated in the upstairs market. The negotiation is conducted by institutional sales traders and block positioners seated at the trading desks of the major securities houses. The process requires rapid assessments and decision making, diplomacy and the ability to sell, and sangfroid.

Block trades are transactions involving 10,000 shares or more. In 1986, blocks were executed on the NYSE at a rate of over 6 per minute, for a total of 665,587 for the year and an average of 2631 per trading day. That year, the 10 largest transactions on the NYSE each exceeded 4 million shares. The average size of all blocks was 26,760 shares. In 1986, the average price of shares on the NYSE was $36.89; thus the average block transaction had a value in the neighborhood of $1 million. In total, block transactions accounted for 49.9 percent of NYSE share volume.[46]

On an average day 74,988 trades were made on the NYSE in 1986.[47] Thus, although they represent a substantial portion of total share volume, the 2631 block transactions a day accounted for less than 4 percent of the total number of all transactions. Because of their size and relative infrequency, the blocks are handled differently than smaller, retail orders. The blocks could generate severe, adverse price effects if simply presented to the market, either as market or as limit orders. Consequently, the specialists' limit order books mainly contain smaller orders, and an operative order book does not exist for the blocks.

The largest transactions (100,000 shares and over) are typically block sales rather than block purchases. In part this is because large sellers are more likely than large buyers to initiate transactions. This asymmetry could be explained by portfolio managers' believing that the out-of-pocket cost of not selling shares quickly after bad news is more onerous than the opportunity cost of not buying shares quickly after good news. Therefore, institutional sellers are more likely to pay the execution cost of achieving a fast transaction.

[46]*The New York Stock Exchange Fact Book, 1987,* pp. 12 and 77.
[47]*The New York Stock Exchange Fact Book, 1987,* p. 10.

The preponderance of large block sales over block purchases may also be due to the fact that upstairs position traders, being more reluctant to hold a short position than a long position, are more willing to commit capital to facilitate block sales than block purchases. The reason for this asymmetry may be the fact that the losses to a short position are unlimited because a stock's price can increase without bound, whereas the losses to a long position are limited because a stock's price cannot drop below zero.[48]

Portfolio managers may also be reluctant to take short positions for the same reason. Therefore, although every institutional investor may be a potential buyer, only an institution that holds shares may be a seller. Consequently, it may be easier for large sellers to attract large buyers than for large buyers to find large sellers.

The Negotiation of a Block Transaction

An example conveys a sense of how a large block transaction may be negotiated.[49] Assume that an institutional investor wishes to sell 600,000 shares of XYZ stock at a minimum price of 35. Information concerning the sale, recent trade information, and current floor information is given in Table 4.1.

Some large buy orders may be behind the quotes on the NYSE limit order book, and some orders are being worked on the exchange floor. But the daily trading volume for XYZ is only 700,000 shares, and only a handful of relatively small orders is on the books. Clearly, the market for XYZ stock is not sufficiently liquid to absorb a 600,000 share sell order without a substantial price decrease. Simply dumping the block on the market would result in an unacceptable transaction for the seller.

The seller could, of course, place a huge limit order on the book (perhaps at 35⅜). This, however, is an unacceptable alternative. For one thing, the sell order would be highly visible and, correctly or erroneously, would be interpreted as a signal of informational change. Buyers would respond to the signal by lowering their bids. In addition, the seller's limit order would extend to all other traders a free option to call the stock at the limit price. Because of its size, this call option would, over some time interval, prevent an increase in the stock's price. With this (partial) protection against the opportunity cost of missing an advantageous purchase,

[48]This point can be made more formally. Stock price movements conform to a distribution (the *lognormal distribution,* with mean very close to zero for returns intervals that are very brief, that is, a day or so) for which the probability of price changing by a multiple x equals the probability of price changing by a multiple $1/x$; the dollar loss to a short position if price were to change by a multiple $x > 1$ is greater than the dollar loss to a long position if price were to change (with equal probability) by a multiple $1/x < 1$.

[49]My thanks to Bart Breakstone and Theresa Woolverton for providing source material upon which this example is largely based.

Table 4.1   THE SELLING DECISION OF AN INSTITUTIONAL TRADER

1. Objective: Sell 600,000 shares of XYZ stock at $35 or better

2. Current and recent floor information:

Average daily trading volume	700,000
Last night's close	35⅜
Last trade (15 minutes ago)	35¼
Current quotes	35¼–35½, 1,200 by 2,500
Several floor brokers each bidding for	500 to 2,000 shares
Yesterday Goldman Sachs shorted 50,000 at	35½
Recent trade history: some big blocks at	35¼

3. The Instinet book (buy side)

Buy	Price
10,000	35¼
7,000	35⅛
3,500	35

4. AutEx buy
interest

200,000	35⅛	(Paine Webber)
50,000	35	(Morgan Stanley)

buyers are likely to lower their bids and gamble that selling pressure will decrease the price of the stock.

The institutional seller has a third possibility: convey the order to a broker on the exchange floor. Medium size orders are worked on the exchange to avoid the price impact of a market order or the price impact attributable to the option value of a revealed limit order. This approach is not viable, however, for a 600,000 share order—the contra orders on the floor, whether on the book or held by other floor traders, simply are not large enough to provide the liquidity this institutional trader requires.

There is a fourth possibility: convey the order to Instinet, a privately owned electronic system that routes orders and maintains a book on which institutional limit orders may be placed and against which they may be executed. The Instinet system has a feature of particular interest—a buyer and seller can meet electronically, obtain privacy on the screen, and submit tentative bids and offers to each other in an electronic negotiation. Only when agreement is reached is the trade revealed to other subscribers in the Instinet market.

As shown in Table 4.1, the Instinet book for XYZ stock is not very big at the moment.[50] A fifth alternative would also be considered: break the order up into smaller pieces to be sold over a period of a day or so.

---

[50]Trades of over 1 million shares have, however, executed in the Instinet market.

While large orders are often worked in this way, assume the current seller is impatient for a fast transaction. Therefore, the investor with 600,000 shares to sell turns to a sixth alternative: negotiation of the order in the upstairs market.

The negotiation starts when the trader at the asset management firm seeking to sell the shares contacts a block trader at a large brokerage firm. The determination of which block trader to approach is important—simply making the contact reveals information that a sell order is in the offing. Ideally, the house that receives this information knows of buying interest on the other side and is able to assemble a package that is attractive to the institutional seller. If the wrong house is chosen, one trading desk too many will know of the impending sell order.

For our example, the institutional seller contacts Paine Webber, the brokerage house that has revealed a sizable buying interest on the AutEx screen. *AutEx* (which stands for "automated exchange") is neither an exchange nor even a system that gives automated executions. Rather, it is used to display buying and selling indications by broker/dealers to institutions. Information on the system may be "noisy"; quotes may have been placed on the AutEx by a brokerage house that is simply "fishing" for customers, and several brokerage houses may be indicating an order that has originated from only one customer. Nevertheless, AutEx does help sellers and buyers find each other. In the present case, the seller calls Paine Webber and learns that an institutional buyer is behind the 200,000 share order on AutEx.

On this first contact, the seller reveals as little as possible to the Paine Webber block trader. The seller's objective is to find out whether the buy order does have sufficient size, while divulging only a minimum of detail about his or her own order. On the other hand, the block trader seeks to learn as much as possible about the seller's offer size and minimum acceptable price.

The relationship between the institutional trader and the block trader is crucial. These professionals must have trust and confidence in each other. Information has to be revealed, but the information can be used against the seller. The block trader can make a proprietary bid for some of the shares and then compete with the institutional trader as a seller. The block trader must strike a balance between seeking a better price for the customer and pushing for an execution in order to get commission income.

In the first phase of the negotiation, the institutional trader indicates that the order is for 100,000 shares, and that "there is more behind it." The block trader conveys the impression that demand for the stock does exist and understands that the institutional trader's offer is indeed very large. The block trader asks whether the institutional trader would sell at 35⅛ or better. The seller responds, "Yes, but first offer your buyer the shares at 35¼."

The next phase of the negotiation involves the Paine Webber block trader's obtaining up-to-the-minute market information from the exchange floor and contacting the trader who represents the buyer behind the 200,000 share order on AutEx. In a cat and mouse exchange, the Paine Webber block trader finds out the size of the buy order and the highest price the buyer will pay. The buyer is in fact looking for 300,000 shares and will pay a maximum of 35¼. The Paine Webber block trader also learns through the firm's floor broker that the exchange specialist knows another buyer who is on the scene for 100,000 shares at the 35 level.

The block trader assembles the information to determine a reasonable price for the transaction. The seller will go down to 35⅛ for over 100,000 shares. One buyer will pay up to 35¼ for 300,000, and another will probably go as high as or higher than 35⅛ for 100,000. Goldman had recently shorted 50,000 at 35½ and would likely be a buyer at this level. The Instinet screen is showing a bid for 10,000 shares at 35¼, and a bid for 7,000 shares at 35⅛ (the buyers behind these bids, however, may be the ones behind some of the orders being worked on the exchange floor). The current market bid is for 1,200 shares at 35¼. Price has come down somewhat since last night's close at 35⅜, and the current market for a large seller-initiated trade appears to be around 35¼ or less. The block trader senses that the seller's order is, indeed, very large. Therefore, putting the pieces together, the block trader determines that 35⅛ is a fair price for the trade.

The block trader makes a bid to the institutional seller for 100,000 shares at 35⅛, stating that more could be sold at this price. The institutional trader reveals that the order is in fact for a total of 600,000 shares, and that a sale at 35⅛ would be acceptable.

Paine Webber now has to put the deal together. On the sell side are 600,000 shares. The block trader quickly assembles 460,000 on the buy side as follows: 300,000 from the institutional buyer behind the AutEx message, 100,000 from the institutional buyer known by the specialist, 40,000 from Goldman Sachs, and 20,000 from the book and floor traders (including 10,000 being worked by the Goldman Sachs floor trader).

Now 140,000 additional buy orders have to be lined up. The sales traders at the Paine Webber trading desk place phone calls to institutional customers around the country, informing them of a large two-sided transaction in XYZ at the 35⅛ level.

The phone calls attract three more buyers for another 100,000 shares in total. One buyer will participate *only on a print* (that is, only if all 600,000 shares actually do trade at 35⅛); this is a hedge fund that is attracted to the deal because of the temporary price pressure it is expected to exert on the market.

The block trader has now obtained a commitment to sell 600,000 shares at 35⅛ and commitments to buy 560,000 shares at 35⅛. At this point, Paine Webber decides to take a long position of 40,000 shares to facilitate the trade. The Paine Webber order, however, is to be reduced share for share if in the final moments any other buy orders appear on the NYSE floor.

The package assembled, the brokerage house transmits the buy and sell orders to the specialist post for execution on the exchange floor. The limit bids on the book at 35⅛ and better are protected (included in the transaction) and executed at 35⅛ under a cleanup price rule. The trade is executed, and the print crossing the Consolidated Transaction Tape shows that 600,000 shares of XYZ traded at 35⅛.

The brokerage house receives a commission for the 600,000 shares it bought (from the seller) and for the 560,000 shares it sold (to the buyers). Because Paine Webber put its own capital at risk to facilitate the transaction, the seller is charged a greater commission than the commission charged to the buyers. The position trader at Paine Webber is left with a long position of 40,000 shares to work off.

As a result of the efforts of the block trader a large number of shares have transacted at a price that is reasonable in light of current market conditions. The transaction did put pressure on the market (the trade went through at 35⅛, whereas the current bid was 35¼; however, the negative market impact has been limited by the information gathering, selling, and risk taking activities of the block trader.

Upstairs Traders versus Exchange Specialists

The example points up several differences between the operations of a trading desk and of a specialist:

Freedom to Search for Orders Block traders and sales traders play an active role in searching for customers to take the contra side of a trade. Exchange specialists are required to be more passive in relation to the order flow.

Dealers versus Brokers A brokerage house may act as both broker and dealer in the same block trade, can charge a commission on all shares traded, and may earn a spread while unwinding any position it took to facilitate the transaction. Exchange specialists act either as dealer or as broker in any particular trade; as dealers they expect to earn the spread, and as brokers (but only as brokers) they receive a commission.

The Obligation to Make Two-sided Markets Exchange specialists (and OTC market makers) must continuously make two-sided markets for their stocks. The upstairs block trader, on the other hand, does not deal actively with a stock until contact has been established with another trader. At this point, the block trader makes the other side of the market, by finding other customers and/or by taking a contra position in the trade.

Rules and Regulations   Stock exchange specialists have an affirmative obligation to make a fair and orderly market. The brokerage house is under no obligation to stabilize a market (although it is in the house's own best interest to prevent its trades from being destabilizing). Standard tick size rules do not apply to block transactions. Other rules do, however.

Continuous versus Batched Trading   The U.S. stock exchanges are continuous (as distinct from call) markets. The block trading desk requires time to put a deal together and, in the process of making a market, effectively batches orders for execution at a single price (as in a call market). The batching interval is not fixed, of course, but rather depends on how long the negotiation process lasts for any particular trade. After a transaction, the block positioner works off any long or short position in the continuous market. Large orders are similarly worked in a call back period after market clearing in batched trading regimes such as the Paris Bourse. Upstairs trading, therefore, has characteristics of both a continuous and a batched market.

Information Transfers   Much of the order flow does not, on its own, go to any single trading desk. However, block traders are free to seek customers on the contra side of a large deal. Consequently, upstairs traders have developed extensive networks that they use continuously. Every opportunity is taken by traders to contact their counterparts in other firms; every news bit that is hinted at is noted. News, when it occurs, travels rapidly through the brokerage community. Information networks are important for both exchange specialists and upstairs traders; the specialists, however, no longer have the only privileged view of the market.

The Importance of the Trading Desk

Research is no longer the key factor that differentiates brokerage houses as they compete for the business of institutional investors. Rather, it is the ability to give good executions. Concurrently, the reduction of commission rates for large traders (which followed the elimination of fixed rates in 1975) has increased the importance of trading profits to the brokerage houses. Profits are not realized from the block trades alone, however; as noted, arbitrage trading for the firm's proprietary account is also a major income source.

Richard Falk, who heads the upstairs trading desk at Paine Webber, has summarized the recent change as follows:[51]

> The upstairs-trading room in 1984 is very different from what it was five to seven years ago. It has become the focal point for much of the new electronic hardware, from touch screen data phones and on-line inventory monitoring, to systems allowing constant updating of inter-product arbitrage. . . .
>
> Obviously, none of this has happened without change in staffing and capital commitment. Paine Webber, for example, has grown from two listed block traders in 1977 to fourteen in 1984. These block traders, moreover, are quite different than those of seven years ago. They all trade multiple vehicles; a couple of them are mathematical geniuses; several have been bond traders; two have been arbitrageurs; most are young and many have MBAs. There is also a technical analyst and a number of computer jockeys. Capital commitment has gone from $5 million to $500 million.

The secondary markets of today are characterized by high speed electronic communication and market dominance by large institutional investors. In this environment, the trading desks of the upstairs market makers have become a major force in the price determination/trade execution process. Block traders and exchange specialists continue to benefit from mutual cooperation—specialists depend on block traders for order flow, and the upstairs trading desks use the exchange floor in their search for market information. However, as Falk[52] has noted, "Within the past decade, upstairs trading has moved to center stage in the securities industry. . . . The implications for market structure and investment style are obvious, and represent profound change."

CLEARANCE AND SETTLEMENT

Post-Trade, Back Office Operations

Two dates are relevant for a transaction: the date the trade executes (*trade date*), and the date delivery and settlement are expected (*settlement date*). For listed equity transactions and most OTC transactions, the settlement date is five business days after the trade date. Thus a transaction that takes place on a Tuesday is settled on Tuesday of the following week.

Written contracts are not exchanged on trade dates. Despite the huge sums of money that may be involved, only verbal agreements are made

[51]See Falk (1985).
[52]Ibid., pp. 151 and 153.

between the traders. Specialists report their trades to the exchange and enter the transactions in their own records. OTC dealers report their trades to the NASD and enter the transactions in their own records. Buying and selling brokers report the trades to their respective firms. Then the back offices of the brokerage firms and a clearing corporation take over.

The purchase and sales (P&S) department of each brokerage firm prepares a *blotter*, the firm's worksheet that gives details of its trades each day. The P&S department also prepares comparison tickets to confirm transactions with other brokers. The process of verifying trades with other brokers is called *comparison;* the process of correcting any discrepancies is called *reconcilement*. Comparison tickets are submitted to the National Securities Clearing Corporation (NSCC) or to a regional clearing corporation, where the tickets are compared. Items that match result in *matched trades* on a *contract list*. Items that do not match are researched by the respective firms. Differences are resolved according to rules of the marketplace. Matched trades go on to be settled on the settlement date. Errors are not the responsibility of public traders; they must be resolved or paid for (perhaps according to the flip of a coin) by the brokers and dealers that handled the trades.

Customer records are kept by a brokerage firm's *margin department,* which authorizes all payments and receipts of money and of securities. Special records are also kept (and carefully watched) of all margin transactions; the following rules apply:

- Only customers with approved *margin accounts* may buy on margin; other customers have *cash accounts.*
- Short sales can be made only in margin accounts.
- Margin account customers must leave their shares with the brokerage firm; cash account customers can receive delivery of their securities or leave them with the firm in street name, as they choose.

When opening a margin account, the customer signs a *hypothecation agreement* that allows the broker to use that customer's shares as collateral for the broker's own loans. Brokers themselves must pay full price for shares bought on margin for customers. Thus securities firms typically borrow the difference between a stock's cost and a margin customer's payment from commercial banks and use the shares as collateral for the bank loans.[53]

Another part of back office operations is handled by the cashier's department, which is commonly called "the cage." One part of the cage

---

[53]Cash account customers cannot sign a hypothecation agreement. They own the shares, and thus the shares are not available for use as collateral by the brokerage firm. Fully paid-for securities may not be pledged, but they can be lent to cover short sales with the permission of the customer.

is the *box section,* where securities are stored. Records of the certificates that come into or go out of the box are kept. Other parts of the cage include the receive and deliver section and the stock transfer section. The *stock transfer section* handles the firm's requests to transfer stock and tracks the shares when they are sent out for transfer and when they are returned. Stock transfer itself is usually handled by a bank that has been appointed *transfer agent* by the issuing corporation.

Other back office functions involve the dividend department, stock record department, and proxy department. The *dividend department* tracks and collects dividends for shares held in street name, appropriately credits customer accounts, and makes claims for dividends that customers should have been paid, but have not received. The *stock record department* maintains an inventory of securities held in street name; this entails keeping records of the number of shares each customer owns of each security, where the shares are kept, and so forth. The *proxy department* forwards voting materials and corporate reports to customers who have left their shares in street name and handles proxy forms that the customers have signed and returned to the firm with instructions.

The Clearance System

Trade-for-Trade Settlement Trade settlement may involve either actual delivery of shares in exchange for cash or book entry transfer. Physical delivery on a trade-for-trade basis involves direct contact between the two brokerage firms that were contra parties to a trade. With trade-for-trade settlement, the receiving firm prepares a check, payable on receipt of the security, to the delivery firm. If the delivery firm's record states the proper amount to be paid, the check is released when the shares are delivered; if not, the delivery is returned to the selling firm without payment.

Trade-for-trade comparison and delivery are costly, because each brokerage firm has to contact and deal separately with every other brokerage firm with which it has traded. Furthermore, the cost of each trade depends uniquely on where the two contra parties to the trade are located. A trade, therefore, could be more costly if, for instance, it involves a buyer in San Francisco and a seller in Philadelphia than if both traders are in San Francisco or if both are in Philadelphia. Differences in transaction costs and final settlement prices for different traders are an undesirable aspect of trade-for-trade settlement.

The clearance process became far more efficient with the establishment, in 1976, of the National Securities Clearing Corporation (NSCC). The NSCC was formed from the associated clearing agencies of the NYSE, Amex, and NASD. Currently, NSCC also includes interfaces with various regional clearing agencies. The NSCC has reduced clearance and settlement costs appreciably, and differences in these costs for trades made in different markets are now inconsequential. The NSCC has also made possible inter-market trades between brokers who may not be members of each other's markets; this has facilitated the development of major intermarket linkages, such as the Intermarket Trading System (ITS).

Balance-Order Settlement   All transactions entering the clearing corpo-ration's settlement cycle have previously been compared in the NSCC com-parison operation. Thus, for each security, there is indeed a buyer for every seller, and a seller for every buyer, at an agreed-upon price. Thus the total number of shares recorded as having been purchased equals the total number of shares recorded as having been sold. However, transactions made in the course of a day are generally made at different prices.

Balance-order settlement adjusts for the price differences by the following netting procedure:

1. The difference between the total number of shares bought and sold is computed for each brokerage firm. Firms that bought more shares than they sold are *net buyers;* firms that sold more shares than they bought are *net sellers;* firms that bought and sold an equal number of shares are *flat.*
2. The average price is computed for all trades made for a stock in a given day; this average is called the *settlement price.* For each firm, each transaction is revalued by using the settlement price rather than the actual transaction price; any difference in payment made or received is called an *adjustment.* For instance, if the set-tlement price for a stock is 25 and firm A bought 300 shares at 24, the adjustment is +\$300; if firm B bought 200 shares at 26, the adjustment is −\$200; and vice versa for sales.
3. The adjustments for each firm are summed over all of the firm's transactions in a stock. Firms for which the sum is positive have their account at the clearing corporation credited; firms for which the sum is negative have their account at the clearing corporation debited. Because the settlement price is an average, the total for a stock of all credits and all debits across all firms is zero.
4. The clearing corporation issues balancing orders instructing firms that are net sellers to deliver shares to firms that are net buyers, for payment at the settlement price.

The netting procedure used for balance-order settlement enables a firm to settle one position per security per day. The position is either to receive, to deliver, or to be flat (if the number of shares bought equals the number of shares sold).

Balance-order settlement, like trade-to-trade settlement, calls for physical delivery of securities (although appreciably fewer deliveries are called for). If a delivery cannot be made, it is a *fail:* a *fail to deliver* for the selling firm and a *fail to receive* for the buying firm. Fails are cleaned up when delivery is finally made.

Continuous Net Settlement (CNS)   The delivery and settlement process has been further simplified. Brokerage firms may deposit securities in a central depository, such as the Depository Trust Company.[54] Then, instead of physically transferring shares the firms instruct the depository to move a stated number of shares from one account to another. This enables settlement to be effected by book entry, a considerably more efficient system. Book entry delivery and a central depository do not by themselves, however, eliminate the problem of fails.

Continuous net settlement, which uses the facilities of both a clearing corporation and a depository, simplifies settlement with respect to fails. Brokerage firms settle their accounts on a daily basis, as described for the balance-order procedure. However, when there is a fail, the clearing corporation opens a record of fails to deliver for the net seller, and a record of fails to receive for the net buyer. CNS then alters these fails records on successive days, until they are eliminated:

- The system reduces the fails to deliver record by any net receipt of shares on the next day. Therefore, if firm A has failed to deliver 200 shares on day 1, and is a net buyer of 100 shares on day 2, it is treated as being flat on day 2, and its fails to deliver account is reduced to 100 shares.
- The system reduces the fails to receive record by any net delivery of shares on the next day. Therefore, if firm A has failed to receive 200 shares on day 1, and is a net seller of 100 shares on day 2, it is treated as being flat on day 2, and its fails to receive account is reduced to 100 shares.

The CNS procedure updates a firm's position daily, thus simplifying tracking requirements. With CNS, all money settlements for transactions are made with the clearing corporation. All transactions for each securities firm are netted, for all CNS eligible securities, to one total (either a *money receive* or a *money payment* figure). Payments to, and receipts from, the clearing corporation are controlled and monitored by the brokerage firm's *cashier's department*. This department is also responsible for ensuring that

---

[54]The depository assumes part of the function of a brokerage firm's cashier's department.

the corporation has an adequate number of shares on deposit at the depository.

Clearance and Settlement for Futures and Options Contracts

Clearance and settlement have a unique importance for futures and options contracts. The reason is that these contracts are made between individual traders with regard to actions that will (or may) be taken in the future. The individual traders would, therefore, appear to be dependent on each other's performance in the future.

Does, for instance, the buyer of a call option depend on the writer of the call for delivery of the shares if the option is called? Does the trader with a long position in an index future depend on a trader with a short position for delivery of cash if the index increases in value? Does a bakery with a long position in wheat futures depend on a trader with a short position actually to deliver the wheat? What if trader A writes a put option, trader B buys the put option, and then trader A unwinds his or her position?

Clearance and settlement have been organized so that individual traders are not dependent upon one another for future performance. This can be illustrated with reference to futures contracts.

Each futures exchange is associated with a *clearing corporation,* which intervenes between the seller and the buyer of a futures contract at the point the trade is made. When the clearing corporation steps in, it becomes the buyer for the seller, and the seller for the buyer. Therefore, both the buyer and the seller need look only to the clearing corporation for performance.

The clearing corporation continuously adjusts the accounts of traders with long and short positions so that each position is settled on a day-to-day basis, as the futures contract approaches maturity. The process, called *marking to market,* works as follows.

1. Assume that on Monday, June 2, 1987, trader A contracts to buy, from trader B, 1000 troy ounces of silver for August delivery for 5.30 per ounce, and that neither trader had an opposite position before the trade. This contract increases the open interest in silver by 1000 troy ounces. The clearing corporation separates this open interest into two parts: it assumes the responsibility for delivering 1000 ounces to trader A for a total payment of $5300, and it assumes the responsibility for buying 1000 ounces from trader B for a total payment of $5300.

2. Assume that on Tuesday, June 3, the settlement (closing) price of the August silver futures contract has increased to 5.40 per ounce. If trader A reversed the contract written on June 2 (by contracting

to sell 1000 ounces in August), he or she would have received $.10 an ounce, or 100 dollars in total more for the August sale (contracted June 3) than would be paid for the August purchase (contracted June 2). Consequently, the value of A's position has increased by $100. If the contract is in fact reversed by A, A's position will have been unwound and some other trader C would have assumed A's place vis-à-vis the clearing corporation and, indirectly, vis-à-vis trader B. If A did not in fact reverse the contract, the clearing corporation acts as if the old contract at 5.30 had been terminated and replaced with a new contract at 5.40. Accordingly, the clearing corporation credits A's account with $100, thereby marking A's account to the market.

3. Trader B's account is also marked to market. If B had unwound his or her position on June 3 by a reversing trade at 5.40, B would have had to pay $100 more than he or she had contracted to pay on June 2. Thus B's account at the clearing corporation would have been debited by $100. As in step 2, if B does not actually enter a second contract, the clearing corporation acts as if the first contract had been replaced by a second written at 5.40. Accordingly, the clearing corporation debits B's account by $100 (and thus offsets the credit to A), thereby marking B's account to the market.

4. Because the price of the contract increased on June 3, trader A (who has a long position) is credited with the increase, and trader B (who has a short position) is debited by the increase, and B literally has to pay the $100 to the clearing corporation. The effect of marking the contract to market is inverted when the contract price goes down: A is debited (and has to pay the clearing corporation) and B is credited.

Because the clearing corporation has interjected itself between buyers and sellers, any individual buyer or seller can unwind a position with a reversing trade at any time without affecting any other trader: a new buyer or seller simply replaces the initial buyer or seller in the accounts of the clearing corporation. Or if both the buyer and the seller are unwinding their positions, the open interest decreases. Further, the process of marking to market keeps accounts up-to-date so that unwinding trades need not be assessed to determine settlements. Marking to market also reduces the risk to the clearing corporation: losses to a position are not allowed to accumulate. Risk to the clearing corporation is further reduced by requiring that traders post *margins* with the clearing corporation. Initial margins are imposed when positions are first opened; these may be on the order of 5 to 10 percent of a contract's total value.

The Importance of Clearing Operations

As long as they work smoothly, post-trade clearance and settlement operations are one of the least visible parts of the securities industry. Nevertheless, they are of crucial importance. A sizable part of commission dollars goes to cover clearance and settlement costs. When back office work piles up, mistakes are made, fails accumulate, and successful brokerage operations are threatened. Consequently, an effective trading system must be built around a well functioning clearance system. In this regard, the clearing corporation plays a central role.

In addition to expediting post-trade procedures, the clearing corporation has an even more critical function with regard to options and futures. These derivative assets involve contracts between specific traders regarding future obligations. The clearing corporation, by intervening, separates the traders and "depersonalizes" their agreements. Consequently, neither party to a futures or options contract need be concerned with whether the other will honor the contract. Without this freedom, the futures and options markets would not be able to operate at the levels of activity they have achieved in recent years.

Major changes have occurred in the securities industry, and most of these are reflected in the operations of the clearing corporation. The enormous increase in the order flow has necessitated the change from trade-for-trade settlement to continuous net settlement with a central depository and book entry accounting. The extensive adoption of electronic data processing equipment has also transformed many post-trade operations. Recent examples are the NSCC's *Automated Customer Account Transfer Services,* which facilitates the transfer of customer accounts between broker/dealers, and the NSCC's program to standardize and automate the processing of mutual fund purchases and redemptions. The globalization of trading and development of 24 hour trading are also creating the need for cooperative clearance and settlement systems across countries.

The proliferation of new products, the development of new trading strategies, the expanding sophistication of institutional traders, and the globalization of trading have opened, and will continue to open, new horizons for the securities industry. The new opportunities cannot be effectively exploited, however, unless post-trade clearance and settlement procedures keep pace.

CONCLUSION

This chapter has taken a broad look at the structure and operations of the securities industry. Major attention has been given to the large investment banking and brokerage firms that hold a central position in both the primary and secondary markets. In addition, the securities that are traded have been identified, and post-trade clearance procedures have been described.

One theme has pervaded much of the chapter: the integral involvement of the major securities firms in market making and trading. Investment banking is a market making operation; the big Wall Street houses have sizable OTC dealer operations in both the equity and bond markets; the trading desks of the upstairs market makers are located in the securities firms; and the firms are all involved in proprietary trading, both to facilitate the negotiation of block transactions and to arbitrage pricing discrepancies in the market.

Over a decade ago, investment banking firms were primarily involved in providing standard investment banking services to firms for which they had been bankers and advisers for years, and full line brokerage firms were primarily involved in providing research, brokerage, and other financial services to their retail customers. In the mid-1970s, however, changes started to occur in the industry. Major structural alterations have continued at a remarkable pace up to the current time.

The forces of change have included the deregulation of the industry, an increasingly volatile and global economy, the growing presence of institutional investors in the market, and the advent of computer technology. The result has been a sharp decrease in the importance of commission revenue for the securities firms, a proliferation of new trading instruments, an emerging globalization of trading, the development of complex arbitrage and hedging operations, a breakdown of old line, clublike relationships, and a renewed intensification of competition in the industry.

For the securities firms, one change in particular is striking. The provision of research and other investment services no longer dominates operations. Rather, commitment of the securities firms' own financial capital for underwriting new issues and financing acquisitions, for the provision of execution services, and for proprietary trading has indeed moved to center stage.

SUGGESTED READING

Y. Amihud, T. Ho, and R. Schwartz (eds.), *Market Making and the Changing Structure of the Securities Industry.* Copyright © 1985 by D. C. Heath and Company (Lexington, Mass.: Lexington Books). Reprinted by permission of the publisher.

E. Bloch, *Inside Investment Banking,* Homewood, Ill.: Dow Jones-Irwin, 1986.

T. Copeland and D. Galai, "Information Effects on the Bid-Ask Spread," *Journal of Finance,* December 1983.

J. Cox and M. Rubinstein, *Options Markets,* Englewood Cliffs, N.J.: Prentice-Hall, 1985.

F. Fabozzi and I. Pollack, *The Handbook of Fixed Income Securities,* Homewood, Ill.: Dow Jones-Irwin, 1983.

R. Falk, "Upstairs Trading," in Amihud, Ho, and Schwartz (1985).

S. Figlewski, *Hedging with Financial Futures for Institutional Investors,* Cambridge, Mass.: Ballinger Publishing Company, 1986.

S. Hunter, "Arbitrage Trading," in Amihud, Ho, and Schwartz (1985).

M. Keenan, *Profile of the New York Based Security Industry,* Monograph Series in Finance and Economics, Salomon Brothers Center for the Study of Financial Institutions, New York University Graduate School of Business Administration, 1977.

H. Minnerop and H. Stoll, "Technological Change in the Back Office: Implications for Structure and Regulation of the Securities Industry," in Saunders and White (1986).

A. Saunders and L. White, *Technology and the Regulation of Financial Markets,* Lexington, Mass: Lexington Books, 1986.

M. Stigum, *The Money Market,* Homewood, Ill.: Dow Jones-Irwin, revised edition, 1983.

H. Stoll and R. Whaley, *Expiration Day Effects of Index Options and Futures,* Monograph Series in Finance and Economics, Salomon Brothers Center for the Study of Financial Institutions, New York University Graduate School of Business Administration, 1986.

G. Wyser-Pratte, *Risk Arbitrage II,* Monograph Series in Finance and Economics, Salomon Brothers Center for the Study of Financial Institutions, New York University Graduate School of Business Administration, 1982.

chapter 5

Development of the Markets

This chapter presents an overview of the development of the United States equity markets, starting with the period from the Revolutionary War to the stock market crash of 1929. During these years, the markets acquired organizational form, and much requisite infrastructure was established. The period extending from the Securities Acts of the 1930s to the Securities Acts Amendments of 1975 is treated next. Much of the legislative environment needed to control the industry was developed during these years. The years from 1975 to the present, a period that has been characterized by remarkable technological developments, both of the trading systems and of the securities that are traded, are considered in the final section of the chapter.

THE REVOLUTIONARY WAR TO THE GREAT CRASH OF 1929

Discrimination, Funding, and Assumption

In 1790, the year after Washington was elected president of the United States, the newly formed federal government faced the problem of honoring the Revolutionary War debts incurred by the Continental Congress and the 13 colonies. Three issues had to be settled: discrimination, funding, and assumption. The resolution of each had major implications for the subsequent development of the financial markets.

Discrimination Most of the original recipients of Continental and Colonial paper, many of whom were veterans of the war, had sold their holdings to speculators. The unjustice of having the soldiers who had suffered in battle be denied their due pay while those who had bought the paper at a fraction of its worth profited led James Madison to propose *discrimination:* payment for a Continental bond should be made in part to the current holder, and in part to the original holder. The proposal was widely popular.

The certificates were bearer bonds, however, making the plan illegal, and the cost of finding the original owners would have been prohibitive. Because some of the debt was held in Europe, refusing to honor it in full would have undermined the foreign credit of the country. Alexander Hamilton, the first secretary of the treasury, perceived a further reason for opposing discrimination: distributing the money among a large number of people would result in its disappearance in a large number of small purchases. But in the hands of a small number of investors, the funds could be used to finance enterprise badly needed to strengthen the fragile economy of the new country. The proposal was voted down.

Funding The *funding* of the debt was handled as follows. New bonds were issued for the old paper, and tax revenues were used to pay the interest expense and to retire some of the debt. Most importantly, only 2 percent of the bonds were to be retired per year by the government. The plan had the immediate advantage of reducing the current tax burden and the longer run benefit of creating a liquid asset that could be circulated like money.

Assumption The most difficult issue to resolve was *assumption,* the proposal that the federal government assume responsibility for the unpaid war debts of the individual states. A major problem concerning the proposal was that some states (such as Virginia) had already retired a good part of their debt and were unwilling to share the debt burden of other states (such as Massachusetts) that were waiting for the federal government to take over the obligation. Furthermore, the South resisted because much of the state paper had been bought by northern speculators.

Federal assumption of the debt would unify the financial system and strengthen the union. Furthermore, public creditors would support federal taxation if the federal government were responsible for paying interest and principal on a debt instrument that the creditors owned.

The debate was settled by linking it with another issue that, particularly in the days of primitive transportation and poor communication, was also of considerable importance: the location of the nation's capital, which, at the time, was New York City. In a swap arranged by Madison, Hamilton, and Jefferson, northern votes to move the capital to the South were exchanged for southern votes in favor of assumption. Both proposals passed. The federal government moved to Philadelphia for ten years, while the permanent capital on the Potomac was located and built.

Resolution of the three issues created a pool of liquid capital, strengthened the federal government, and helped pave the way for the economic growth of the country. The debates, themselves, spurred the early development of the securities markets, as trading in government debt was stimulated by the shifting expectations of speculators in Boston, New York, and Philadelphia.

Formation of the Stock Exchanges

Philadelphia was initially the financial center of the country, and the location of the Bank of the United States, founded in 1791. The Philadelphia Stock Exchange was also organized in 1791, and quotes set on this exchange were used as the basis for pricing securities in other markets. However, trading, primarily in the Continental and Colonial war bonds, increased on Wall Street in 1790.

Trading sessions were not held regularly on Wall Street until the Stock Exchange Office was opened in March of 1792. Because of space problems, traders started meeting outdoors on pleasant days, near a buttonwood tree located at what is now 68 Wall Street. These auctions in the open led to a problem, however; outsiders, after following the auctions to learn of current prices, would themselves trade the securities at lower commission rates. The outsiders also continued their dealings after the daily close of the buttonwood trading sessions.

On May 17, 1792, in response to this competition, 24 brokers signed an agreement to give each other preference on stock deals and to trade at a minimum commission rate, which was set at 0.25 percent. This accord, known as the *Buttonwood Agreement,* resulted in off-board trading restrictions and in a fixed minimum commission structure that remained until the 1970s.

During the following winter, the brokers decided to obtain a building of their own. The Tontine Coffee House was built, and the brokers, known as the Tontine Merchants, operated there into the 1880s.

A peripheral group of curbstone traders had also existed since the start of the Stock Exchange Office. By 1815, these traders began cornering the market on some stocks, and customers started to go to them with orders. In 1817, to meet the competition and to attract order flow away from the exchanges in Boston and Philadelphia, the Tontine Merchants adopted a constitution and the name *New York Stock & Exchange Board*. The constitution set provisions regarding membership, procedures, and fines for the purpose of establishing a more orderly, less speculative exchange. On January 29, 1863, the exchange, which had come to be known as "The Board," changed its name to the *New York Stock Exchange*.

Until 1868, each member of the NYSE had a reserved seat on the exchange and the right to hold that seat for life. Initially, there were reserved seats for 1060 members; currently, there are 1366 seats. Seats became salable for the first time on October 23, 1868.

By the 1860s, the decade referred to as the golden age of the curbstone brokers, 11 different exchanges had developed from the curb. One of these, the Open Board of Brokers, not only provided stiff competition for the NYSE, but by 1869 was attracting 5 to 10 times as much business. Trading on the Open Board was conducted in the "Long Room," where traders would shout out their intentions to buy or to sell shares and compete for the other side of trades in dozens of small, simultaneous auctions. Because no one individual could participate in all of the auctions, the brokers began to station themselves at specific locations and to concentrate their dealings in specific issues. It was from this structure that the current specialist system developed.

At its inception, the NYSE was a periodic call market, whereas the Open Board, like the other curbstone exchanges, was a continuous market. As the two systems competed side-by-side, the continuous market proved more efficient at handling a large volume of orders, and the NYSE was faced with its first major challenge. On May 8, 1869, the two exchanges merged, and the NYSE became a continuous market.

In 1885, four smaller organizations combined to form the Consolidated Exchange, which came to be known as the "Little Board." Commodities, pipeline certificates, and mining shares were traded on the Consolidated Exchange. It was on the Consolidated that dealings in odd lots were first introduced. The Consolidated's activities, although supplemental to those of the NYSE, put further competitive pressure on the Big Board, and the NYSE took measures to impede them. The Little Board was known for its speculators and small gamblers. In the 1920s, its officers became involved in shady dealings; some went to prison, and the Consolidated Exchange folded.

During the 1840s and 1850s, volume increased appreciably in the outdoor curb market on Broad Street, where traders known as "curbstone brokers" would meet, regardless of the weather. In the beginning of the twentieth century, Emanuel S. ("Pop") Mendels and a few associates set up operations as an informal screening committee to upgrade brokers and securities in the curb market. Their enforcement methods were simple, but relatively effective—dishonest brokers were shunned, and/or Mendel and his associates would refuse to trade a particular stock, thereby signaling that something was wrong.

At that time a public order was sent to a clerk situated in one of the buildings that lined the street. The clerk would go to a window, lean out, and transmit the order to a broker on Broad Street. The broker would take the order to a specialist's post for execution and then report back to the clerk in the window. Orders and execution reports were transmitted between clerks and brokers by hand signal. The clerks and brokers first had to attract each other's attention, however, and to do so, each team had its own distinctive cry, call, or shout. Trading in the outdoor market was a noisy process.

In 1908, under Mendel's leadership, the New York Curb Market Agency was formed to encourage higher standards in listings and brokerage and to codify existing practices. In 1911, the agency became the New York Curb Market, and more formal requirements for listings and membership were imposed. Starting in 1915, only members of the Curb Market were permitted to trade at the outdoors exchange, and they were allowed to trade only listed shares.

On June 27, 1921, the New York Curb Market moved indoors to a new building at 86 Trinity Place, one block west of Wall Street, and the era of curbstone trading was practically at an end. Circular booths were located on the exchange floor. On top of each booth was an object that resembled the street lamps of the Broad Street market. Curiously, a large number of specialists and brokers developed colds during the first winter of trading after the move. The traders, apparently, did not adjust easily to the change in their trading environment.

The New York Curb Market became the New York Curb Exchange in 1929. In 1953, it changed its name to the *American Stock Exchange*. The Amex is still located at 86 Trinity Place; all vestiges of street lamps, however, have vanished.

Growth of Market Participation and the Crash of 1929

In addition to organizational structure, many developments marked the early growth of the securities markets. Most important among these were improvements in the distribution of current market information to investors. The invention of the telegraph, and the opening of telegraph services between major cities in the 1840s and 1850s, allowed newspapers throughout the country to list Wall Street quotations. The Atlantic cable was completed in 1866. The stock exchange ticker was first introduced on November 15, 1867, and perfected in 1880 by Thomas Edison. The telephone was invented and patented in 1876 and 1877. In 1883, Charles Dow and Edward Jones started publication of a two page leaflet called the *Customers Afternoon Letter;* in July 1889, the leaflet was expanded to four pages and renamed *The Wall Street Journal.*

Security trading in volume started with speculation in Continental and Colonial bonds. To grow, however, the financial markets required the securities of industry. In the 1840s, railroad issues became more prominent; they continued to be a dominant investment vehicle throughout the remainder of the century. Mining stocks gained importance during the period of "gold mania," from the late 1840s to the early 1850s. The scope of the market increased further during the Civil War, in large part because of active trading in government bonds. Utility company securities started to appear around 1890. By the end of the century, local government issues (state and municipal) became more common, and a market for industrial securities began to emerge.

Only the very wealthy participated as investors in the financial markets at the start of the twentieth century. Security analysis at the time was a rudimentary process. Most industrial corporations began as family businesses, and, not surprisingly, the owners did not choose to divulge much information about their operations. The prevailing attitude concerning disclosure was caveat emptor, "let the buyer beware."[1]

The early history of the markets is characterized by much fraud, speculation, and manipulation. People such as Daniel Drew, Jay Gould, and "Jubilee Jim" Fisk were well known for their exploits. For instance, upon learning that Cornelius Vanderbilt was spending a fortune in an attempt to take over the Erie Railroad in 1867 and 1868, Drew printed up and sold Vanderbilt 100,000 shares of Erie stock at a price of $7 million. After this particular stock watering episode, the Open Board and the NYSE both required that shares traded at their auctions be registered.

Speculation was encouraged by the availability of easy margin credit (margin requirements were as low as 10 percent in the late 1920s). During the 1920s, *pools* became a widespread means of manipulating the market: A small number of brokers, dealers, corporate insiders, and/or specialists would unite, either by verbal or written agreement, and time their transactions to rumors that they themselves started, or to inside information, in order to exploit other market participants. Bear pools, for instance, were

---

[1]In 1900, the NYSE first required that earnings statements and balance sheets be released, but the ruling applied only to newly listed firms. In 1899, having been questioned by an ad hoc congressional commission about the public's right to know the earnings power of a public corporation, Henry O. Havermeyer, head of the American Sugar Refining Company, responded, "Let the buyer beware; that covers the whole business. You cannot wet-nurse people from the time they are born until the day they die. They have got to wade in and get stuck and that is the way men are educated and cultivated." The quotation is reported in McCraw (1984).

formed to drive down the price of a stock, so that members might jump in and make a fast profit on the rebound.

Stock trading became more widespread in the United States in the first third of the twentieth century. About half a million people owned shares of stock at the end of the nineteenth century; ten million Americans were shareowners by 1930. The equity markets had become a major part of the economy, and the vicissitudes of the market were linked to fluctuations in the aggregate economy. The years leading up to 1929 were prosperous, and investors in record numbers sought to share the wealth.

The economy, however, was fragile. Holding companies and investment trusts had become part of the corporate structure. Promoters, swindlers, and frauds were free to operate with little restraint. Stockbrokers encouraged frequent trading to earn commission revenue. Many ordinary citizens ignored the risks involved in stock market investments. Public euphoria and the market reached an unsustainable level; when the crash occurred on October 29, 1929, the market started a long, tragic decline.

The Dow Jones Industrial Average reached a high of 358 on October 11, 1929. On the 29th of October, it closed at 230. By December 1930, the Dow closed at a yearly low of 157. A year later it closed at an annual low of 73. The market finally reached its bottom on July 8, 1932, when it fell to 41. As the market declined, trading dropped off. Not until 1963 did the annual volume of transactions on the NYSE reach the level that had been attained in 1929.

THE SECURITIES ACTS OF THE 1930s TO THE SECURITIES ACTS AMENDMENTS OF 1975

The Securities Acts of the 1930s

In the wake of the stock market crash and the depression years that followed, the need to establish the very legitimacy of the markets was felt first and foremost.

State regulation of the securities markets existed in the form of Blue Sky Laws enacted between 1911 and 1933. With the objective of preventing the sale of pieces of the blue sky, laws in every state except Nevada required the registration of securities dealers, and/or required the registration of securities, and/or enacted penalties for various offenses such as fraud. The state laws were not sufficiently comprehensive, however. Furthermore, provisions for enforcing them were inadequate, and jurisdictional problems existed between the states. Considerably more regulatory structure was needed.

Federal regulation of the securities markets began in the 1930s. In all, five major pieces of legislation were enacted by Congress during the decade:

1. The Securities Act of 1933 (The 1933 Act)
   - Mandated disclosure of information about new corporate securities
   - Required that all new corporate securities be registered with the Federal Trade Commission (later with the Securities and Exchange Commission)
   - Demanded that financial information in a registration statement be certified by an independent accountant.
   - Stipulated antifraud provisions
2. The Securities Exchange Act of 1934 (The 1934 Act)
   - Extended disclosure requirements established by the 1933 Act to existing securities
   - Established the Securities and Exchange Commission (SEC)
   - Empowered the SEC to approve commission rate changes proposed by the exchanges and to request commission rate changes
   - Empowered the SEC to change rules, to prohibit stock manipulation, and to formulate additional regulations as necessary
   - Established regulation of the business conduct of broker/dealer members of an exchange
   - Left disciplinary power over its members to the exchanges
   - Empowered the Federal Reserve Board to set minimum margin requirements
3. The Glass-Steagall Banking Act of 1933 (The Glass-Steagall Act)
   - Mandated the separation of investment banking and commercial banking
   - Established the Federal Deposit Insurance Corporation (FDIC) to insure bank accounts
4. The Public Utility Holding Company Act of 1935
   - Required public utility holding companies to register with the SEC
   - Empowered the SEC to oversee the break-up and dissolution of some companies and the simplification of the multilayered corporate structure of others
   - Empowered the SEC to help plan the integration of utilities to improve engineering efficiency and to eliminate exploitation of operating units by profiteering holding companies
5. The Maloney Act of 1938
   - Brought the over-the-counter market under the supervision of the SEC
   - Encouraged the industry to establish private associations to administer new regulations; gave the SEC authority to oversee and to change the rules of the private associations

The 1934 Act and the Maloney Act both established further administrative and regulatory control of the financial markets. The 1934 Act created the SEC; the National Association of Securities Dealers (NASD) was created under the authority of the Maloney Act. The NASD, which was responsible to the SEC, provided an organizational structure for the over-the-counter markets. These markets could not be regulated until this structure was in place.

The relationship between the securities acts and antitrust laws had to be resolved after passage of the 1934 Act and the Maloney Act, because rules of the SEC, the exchanges, and/or the NASD could contravene antitrust laws. Consequently the jurisdiction of the SEC and of the Antitrust Division of the Department of Justice had to be determined. The issue has been resolved in case law. In *Silver* v. *NYSE,*[2] the Supreme Court rejected the exchanges' total immunity from antitrust laws and allowed that immunity is "implied only if necessary to make the Securities Exchange Act work, and even then only to the minimum extent necessary." The SEC itself, however, was granted explicit jurisdiction so that antitrust immunity may be allowed when needed.[3]

The Public Utility Holding Company Act sought to change corporate structures that had been established, not with regard to long run economic efficiency, but to leverage earnings and to exploit operating units.

The Glass-Steagall Act addressed another structural issue: the relationship between commercial banking and investment banking. As discussed in Chapter 4, the operations of commercial and investment banks overlap and are complementary in various important ways. At the time the act was passed, however, bankers could invest depositors' money virtually without control because the operations were merged under one corporate roof. Commercial banks were also known to use their investment affiliates to manipulate prices in the market and to speculate in bank stocks. In addition, a bank that provided underwriting services for a corporation and that, in the process, may have acquired an equity interest in the corporation might make loans that were not otherwise justified to that firm. In the days of speculative excesses, fragile capital structures, widespread fraud, and uncontrolled price manipulation, separating the two banking functions was prudent.

The 1933 Act, sometimes called the "Truth in Securities Act," and the 1934 Act were both responses to the need to increase the dissemination of corporate information to the market. With the passage of these acts, the principle of caveat emptor was no longer unchallenged in the industry. Now sellers, too, had to beware, because the burden of telling the truth resided with the original sellers of shares, the issuing companies.[4]

Investors had lost an estimated $25 billion between 1923 and 1933 through the purchase of worthless securities.[5] This loss was partially attributable to the incompetence of investment banks and investment advisers

---

[2]373 U.S. 341 (1963)

[3]See Stoll (1979).

[4]The 1933 Act called for detailed data release by corporations, including balance sheet and profit and loss statements, the salaries of company officers and directors, and underwriters' commissions.

[5]Fainsod, Gordon, and Palamountain (1959).

and partially to outright fraud. The public lost more than wealth, however; it also lost confidence in the market. The decrease in trading activity was costly to investors, brokers, and listed corporations, and capital formation for the aggregate economy was jeopardized. Passage of the 1933 Act was facilitated by a clear need for the legislation.

Requiring disclosure of information is one thing; ensuring that information is timely and accurate is another. The 1933 Act not only addressed the legislative issue of what should be done, but also the administrative issue of how the goals of the act were to be achieved. Three provisions were of key importance:

- The regulatory commission was empowered to subpoena information, and noncompliance with a legitimate subpoena became a penal offense. The issuance of subpoenas by a regulatory agency was not new; the innovation in the 1933 Act was to change the burden of proof in cases of noncompliance. Making noncompliance an offense placed the burden of proof for not disclosing information on the individuals from whom it was requested, rather than on the commission.
- The act established a 20-day period between the submission of a registration statement and prospectus to the regulatory commission and the time when the securities could be sold to the public.
- The act empowered the regulators to issue a *stop order* that prevented the sale of an issue if anything amiss were discovered in the corporate documents during the 20-day period.

These three provisions enabled the regulatory agency to administer the 1933 Act with a considerably smaller staff than might otherwise have been necessary. The act economized further on the use of government resources by requiring that the issuing corporations have their statements certified by independent auditors. The 1934 Act (which established the SEC) and the Maloney Act (which resulted in the establishment of the NASD) also allowed for indirect governmental regulation: the exchanges and the NASD became *self-regulatory organizations* (SROs) that shared the work of overseeing their members and were responsible to the SEC. With this regulatory machinery, the SEC became one of the most effective governmental agencies in Washington, D.C.

The SEC versus the Exchanges

During its early years the SEC had to establish control over the exchanges. The first chairman of the SEC was Joseph P. Kennedy, a former bank president and Wall Street speculator. Some considered the appointment similar to placing a fox in the chicken coop. Kennedy, however, immediately sought to reassure the investment community. He and a small group of dedicated people attracted first-rate lawyers, accountants, and statisticians to the SEC.[6]

James M. Landis, a Harvard Law School professor and one of the chief architects of the Securities Acts of 1933 and 1934, succeeded Kennedy as chairman of the SEC in 1935. Two years later, Landis was succeeded by William O. Douglas, who subsequently became an associate justice of the Supreme Court of the United States. All three men, Kennedy, Landis, and Douglas, followed the basic strategy of directing private incentives so as to achieve public objectives. And each of them had to deal with Richard Whitney, president of the NYSE.

Whitney was president of the Exchange from 1930 to 1935, and an influential member of the Exchange's powerful governing committee for some time thereafter. He and his colleagues had fought the new legislation because they believed it would reduce their power; now the Exchange's president did little to enforce the new rules.

After Whitney stepped down as president in 1935, Charles Gay, his successor, and other leaders at the NYSE sought to end the Whitney reign totally. To this end, they instituted a series of rules and new disclosure requirements for exchange members. Quite unexpectedly, the reports brought to light improprieties by Richard Whitney: the ex-president had used clients' securities and assets in an exchange fund, as collateral for personal loans to cover losses from various speculative ventures. Within weeks of his exposure, Whitney was convicted of embezzlement. He spent the next three years in prison.

On June 30, 1938, William McChesney Martin, Jr., was elected the first salaried president of the Exchange.[7] At the time he became president, Martin was a 31-year-old broker. He directed an extensive revision of the rules and regulations of the NYSE. This task was accomplished under the close watch of William O. Douglas and his associates at the SEC.

The development of a stronger regulatory environment could not in and of itself spark economic recovery, however. The financial markets failed to regain momentum as the country went directly from the depression years to World War II. In 1942, the year after the United States entered the war, trading volume on the NYSE had decreased to about 125 million shares a year. Despite a considerable number of new listings on the Exchange during the war, trading remained low.

[6]See McCraw (1984).
[7]Martin subsequently became chairman of the Board of Governors of the Federal Reserve System.

The Postwar Period

Two pieces of legislation in the postwar period had major implications for the economy and the financial markets: The *Full Employment Act of 1946* pledged the government to create and maintain conditions under which employment opportunities would be available to those able and willing to work. The *Bretton Woods Agreement* arranged for the creation of the International Monetary Fund and World Bank, and established an international monetary system based on fixed exchange rates and a gold price of $35 an ounce.

The economy stabilized, and the markets revived. The decade of the 1950s was one of substantial economic growth. Car sales soared, major advances were made in medicine and pharmaceuticals, a vast interstate highway system was built, and television sets were bought by households throughout the country. By the late 1950s, institutions started to invest more heavily in equities. The NYSE undertook a public education program to build confidence in the stock market and to encourage participation by small investors. The NYSE's Monthly Investment Plan was launched, with its slogan "Own Your Share of American Business." As the economy surged, the bull market that had started in 1949 became one of the longest in history. In 1959, the Dow reached 600 for the first time.

Additional legislation was passed. The Investment Company Act of 1940 was enacted to regulate investment companies, and the Investment Advisers Act of 1940 was enacted to limit the activities of investment advisers. Concern for public protection also resulted in the passage of the Securities Acts Amendments of 1964. The 1964 Amendments extended the SEC's surveillance to include small OTC companies, lowered brokerage commissions, curtailed some specialist activities, tightened insider trading rules, stopped certain mutual funds from charging exorbitant sales commissions, and introduced more demanding examinations for floor traders.

The Emergence of New Problems

The years 1963–1968 were the go-go years. After a collapse of the market in 1962 (caused in part by President Kennedy's confronting U.S. Steel over a planned price increase), the economy entered one of its strongest expansionary periods ever. As prosperity rose to new heights, annual trading volume soared on the NYSE from 1,351 million shares in 1963 to 3,298 million shares in 1968.[8]

The industry was not prepared for this increase in trading. Back office staffs in the 1960s were small, and procedures were primitive by current

---

[8]*The New York Stock Exchange Fact Book,* annual.

standards. Firms raided one another for experienced personnel and rushed to install electronic data processing systems. However, the number of trained people was insufficient, and the new systems often failed because of installation and programming difficulties. Stock certificates were misplaced and found in the back of filing cabinets, tucked behind water pipes, in trash baskets, and in various other inappropriate places.

Customer complaints multiplied as the back office crisis deepened. The operating expenses of broker/dealer firms mounted, and profits declined. The number of deliveries of stock rejected by recipients because of recording discrepancies rose to an unprecedented high (reportedly between 25 and 40 percent). The number of fails to deliver increased to a record $4.1 billion in December 1968.[9] The fails to deliver were most critical, because a broker/dealer is responsible for paying a selling customer even if it is unable to make delivery of the stock and receive payment. The increase in the number of firms that were thereby driven out of the industry was alarming. Nearly 110 broker/dealer firms were forced into liquidation during 1969 and 1970.[10]

In an attempt to deal with the crisis, the markets were closed on Wednesdays, and daily trading hours were shortened to give back-office staffs time to catch up. These efforts, however, proved insufficient. The brokerage houses could not keep up with the paperwork.

The crisis affected market regulation. The two primary responses were to enforce minimum net capital requirements and to increase the size of special funds for investor protection. These changes were first made by the NYSE in its self-regulatory (SRO) capacity. The NYSE, however, refused to suspend members without first finding insolvency.

The inadequate supervision and control by the SROs were of great concern to the SEC. The SEC also had a net capital rule for broker/dealer firms but had granted the Exchange exemption from it because of the Exchange's own rule. The SEC at first tried to cooperate with the Exchange. The NYSE, however, was reluctant to pass negative judgment on its members and refused to share information on the financial condition of member firms. Consequently, no rule was being enforced. The situation finally ended in June 1975 with the adoption of the SEC's *uniform net capital rule,* which superseded the capital rules of the exchanges and established minimum capital requirements for all broker/dealers, including NASD firms.

By this time, Congress had also been drawn into the situation. Congress first passed the Securities Investor Protection Act of 1970. The act

[9]*The New York Stock Exchange Fact Book,* 1974.

[10]*Staff Study* of Special Subcommittee on Investigations of House Committee on Interstate and Foreign Commerce, ''Review of SEC Records of the Demise of Selected Broker-Dealers,'' 92nd Cong., 1st Sess., 1971, p. 3. For further discussion, see Bloch (1979).

established governmental insurance of customer accounts. Until this point, Congress (and previous congressional legislation) had been concerned with preventing fraud, manipulation, and other abuses of power that primarily hurt individuals. The government's role as an insurer, however, gave rise to its interest in controlling the industry to prevent the continuing failure of broker/dealer firms. Thus Congress became involved in operational issues and in the competitive structure of the markets.

Another impetus also explains the expansion of regulatory attention in the 1970s: commissions for handling large institutional orders had become exorbitant. Furthermore, in attempting to avoid the fixed commissions imposed by the major market centers, institutions were increasingly taking their orders to third market firms.[11] This diversion of the order flow fragmented the market and resulted in a deterioration of the quality of pricing.

Thus regulatory attention turned in the 1970s to the absence of spatial integration among various parts of the industry, to the quasi-monopoly position of various market makers (primarily the stock exchange specialists), and to the restrictions on entry into certain market centers (primarily the two national exchanges).

One of the first moves toward regulating the market with regard to these issues was the undertaking of the Institutional Investor Study ordered by Congress and sponsored by the SEC. The study was filed with the SEC in 1971. It assessed the competitive structure of the markets, the profitability of specialist operations, and the behavior of major market participants such as the institutions. The first reference to a national market system appears to be the mention of a "central market system" in the letter of transmittal for the study. The Institutional Investor Study also inspired the first wave of academic studies of the microstructure of the markets.

In 1975, Congress passed the Securities Acts Amendments. The legislation, a major overhaul of the Securities Exchange Act of 1934, did the following:

1. Obligated the SEC to abrogate exchange rules that were anticompetitive
2. Precluded the securities exchanges from imposing fixed commission rates
3. Clarified the jurisdiction of the courts and the process of judicial review
4. Mandated the development of a national market system (NMS) and charged the SEC with the responsibility for facilitating its establishment

---

[11]Third market firms are not exchange members, but make markets in exchange listed securities.

5. Set forth four broad goals that the NMS was to achieve:
  5.1. Enhance the economic efficiency of transactions (namely, reasonable transaction costs)
  5.2. Ensure fair competition among brokers, dealers, and markets
  5.3. Ensure the broad availability of information on quotations and transactions
  5.4. Provide the opportunity, consistent with efficiency and best execution, for investors' orders to be executed without the participation of a dealer

The 1975 Amendments, as the first major act of deregulation, sought to strengthen the forces of competition in a free market environment. Governmental deregulation was subsequently extended to other industries—banking, airlines, trucking, and telecommunications, in particular.

FROM 1975 TO THE PRESENT

The Design of The National Market System

A few years after the passage of the Securities Acts Amendments of 1975, Donald Stone, a leading NYSE specialist soon to be vice-chairman of the NYSE stated, "The momentum that Congress and the SEC have set in motion has created a tidal wave of change and activity that will leave the equity markets of the United States as unrecognizable as the original thirteen colonies."[12] Stone's prediction was fulfilled within a decade. The industry was transformed by the new governmental legislation. The elimination of fixed commissions had the greatest impact. The rapid development of technology also propelled the industry forward.

Various pieces of a *national market system* (NMS) have been instituted as follows:[13]

- *The Consolidated Tape:* A consolidated reporting system was first proposed by the SEC in 1972. The Consolidated Tape with its unified reporting rules was put into place as early as 1974.[14]
- *The Clearance and Settlement System:* The National Clearance and Settlement System was developed in 1976. The system combined the clearing corporations of the NYSE, Amex, and NASD to form the National Securities Clearing Corporation (NSCC).
- *The Consolidated Quotation System:* The Consolidated Quotation System (CQS) became operational in 1978. CQS sends floor information to data vendors, such as Bunker Ramo and Quotron, for display on cathode-ray tube (CRT) devices.

[12]Stone (1979).
[13]For further detail, see Williams (1985).
[14]See Chapter 3 for details concerning the Consolidated Tape.

- *The Intermarket Trading System:* The Intermarket Trading System (ITS) was established on an experimental basis in April 1978. At first, ITS linked only two exchanges (NYSE and Philadelphia) and was limited to 11 stocks. ITS now connects each of the two national exchanges with the five regional exchanges and the OTC market. By the end of 1986, a total of 1278 issues, which represented most of the stocks traded on more than one exchange, were eligible for trading on the ITS.

The Debate over the National Market System

Congress did not specify in the 1975 Amendments exactly what the national market system was to be. Rather, a National Market Advisory Board (NMAB) was established to work out the design for the SEC. The NMAB, however, reflected all too well the deeply divided industry that it represented. It failed to achieve its objectives in the two years it was given and met for the last time on December 12, 1977. It should be noted, however, that the approach implemented in ITS had its origins in the discussions of the NMAB.

At the time, the SEC had been involved historically with setting rules and with supervising the markets, primarily to prevent undesirable conduct and to ensure the adequate capitalization of member firms. The commission, therefore, was not prepared to undertake, by itself, the difficult task of satisfying the congressional mandate to design a new system. Consequently, the industry witnessed much debate and suffered through much uncertainty during the first years after the 1975 Amendments.

The debate centered on two issues in particular: removal of the long-standing exchange prohibition on off-board trading and consolidation of orders for a security in a single limit order book. Many in the industry felt that if the wrong decisions were made with respect to either of these issues, the exchange system as it was known would be destroyed, much to the detriment of all.

Off-Board Trading Restrictions The debate over off-board trading was particularly protracted and intense.[15] Dating from the Buttonwood Agreement of 1792, the requirement that member firms take their orders to the exchange market had been considered a mainstay of the system. Yet the commission sought to eliminate the off-board trading restrictions to reduce exchange control over the order flow in order to increase competition in the provision of dealer services.

The specific restrictions in question were *NYSE Rule 390* and *Amex Rule 5,* which required that member firms take orders for listed issues to

---

[15]This issue is considered in further detail in Chapters 13 and 14.

an exchange (not necessarily the NYSE or Amex, however) for execution. On June 23, 1977, the SEC announced that NYSE Rule 390 and Amex Rule 5 were to be eliminated by the end of the year. The industry reacted with alarm. In response to this reaction, the SEC backed off in early December by postponing removal of the restrictions. For the next few years, the commission's continuing threat to remove Rule 390 kept the industry moving toward freer competition, and toward adoption of an intermarket linkage system.

On July 18, 1980, the SEC introduced a new rule: SEC Rule 19c.3, which superseded NYSE Rule 390 and Amex Rule 5 and allowed off-board trading by member firms for all stocks listed after April 26, 1979. Rule 19c.3 was enacted on a temporary basis, was applied only to some stocks (newly listed issues), was instituted for the purpose of determining how the market would react, and has been referred to as the "19c.3 experiment."

For a few years, several large brokerage firms such as Merrill Lynch and Bache made in-house markets for 19c.3 stocks. By 1984, listed securities subject to Rule 19c.3 had increased to nearly 600 issues. By the summer of 1983, however, virtually all of the brokerage firms had terminated their 19c.3 operations. In part, the foray into market making was simply unprofitable for the brokerage houses. In part the design of the 19c.3 experiment had doomed it to failure. In part, the exchange specialists had fought the brokerage houses and had won the battle for the order flow.

As stated by Williams (1985, p. 264), "there has been no dramatic effect on the way (19c.3) securities trade in comparison with previously listed securities not subject to Rule 19c.3. Nor is there any evidence that Rule 19c.3 has done anything to encourage effective competition with the primary exchanges or to attract additional capital to regular market making in Rule 19c.3 securities." The issue of off-board trading has never been satisfactorily settled.

A Consolidated Limit Order Book   Discussion concerning the national market system also focused on the need to protect limit orders by consolidating all orders for a security in a single limit order book. The problem is that, without limit order protection, *trade-throughs* can occur: that is, a trade may be made in one market at a price that is inferior to a competitive bid or offer posted in another market.

Various proposals were presented for consolidating limit orders. The acronym commonly used for a facility to do so was *CLOB,* the "consolidated limit order book." The primary advantages of a CLOB are that all orders would be fully exposed to the market, and trading priority rules (both primary and secondary) could be enforced.

General agreement that price priorities should be enforced has always existed. Many have not felt it necessary, however, to maintain a secondary priority rule such as time priority, under which orders that are placed first execute first. The argument was also made that the price priority rule could be enforced without instituting a CLOB. The very notion of a CLOB evoked a negative reaction from many market participants; the prospect of having orders execute in what was viewed as a ''black box'' inspired great concern.

Some in favor of a CLOB argued that a computerized limit order book would best exploit the power of electronic technology. Specifically, an electronic book would:

- Ensure order exposure and preservation of price and of time priorities (as noted previously).
- Allow order handling and trade execution systems to be interfaced electronically with trade reporting and clearance systems.
- Permit traders to obtain instant access to historic trading information and other data bases.
- Enable the limit order book to be opened to all traders. In addition to providing useful information on current market conditions, this would further ensure limit order protection.[16]
- Avoid the inefficiencies, added costs, and unnecessary complexity that would inevitably attend a piecemeal introduction of computer technology.

The first comprehensive computer-based system was the National Book System proposed by J. Peake, M. Mendelson, and R. Williams.[17] The National Book System represented a clear alternative to the current exchange-based system, and the proposal generated much debate. The exchanges, as one might expect, vigorously opposed the plan. Attention focused on three considerations:

1. *Cost:* The Securities Industry Automation Corporation (SIAC) anticipated a minimum cost of $20 million for developing the CLOB and an implementation period of three to six years. Francis Palamara, then executive vice president of the NYSE, responded to the estimate by stating, ''CLOB is rather like goldplated plumbing—very elegant, to be sure, but hardly necessary to do the job that has to be done, and a lot more expensive than we can afford.''[18] The $20 million figure can now be evaluated with the hindsight of history. In its annual report for 1985, the NYSE referred to ''The Exchange's sophisticated *$150 million* network of trading support,

[16]A rationale for not allowing the specialist to disclose orders on the book is that, without a means of disseminating the information widely, the information should not be disseminated at all for reasons of fairness.

[17]Peake, Mendelson, and Williams (1976). More recently, Y. Amihud and H. Mendelson (1985) have presented a blueprint for an integrated, computer based system.

[18]Discussion by F. Palamara, in Bloch and Schwartz (1979, p. 104).

communications and data-processing systems.'' The annual report also noted that, in 1985, ''the Exchange undertook a *$20 million* expansion of the equities trading floor. . . . ''[19]

2. *The specialist's affirmative obligation:* There was widespread agreement that a specialist could not be expected to fulfill the affirmative obligation to make a fair and orderly market if all orders were electronically consolidated in a limit order book that was open to all traders. The debate, therefore, centered on the desirability of retaining the present specialist oriented exchange system. There was widespread reluctance to eliminate the specialist. Stone wrote, ''At such time, when member firms execute against CLOB themselves, exchanges will disappear. If at that time the government chooses to study the continuity and depth of trading in all securities formerly traded on the New York Stock Exchange, the disparity from this day will be quantum dollars.''[20]

3. *''Terra Incognita'':* Peake-Mendelson-Williams referred to the difficulty of introducing a totally new system as '' 'Terra Incognita,' with depictions of sea monsters and other unspeakable horrors, . . . the phrase cartographers of the period of exploration would use to describe the land beyond their ken.''[21] This fear of change, which can always inhibit the introduction of new ideas, has slowly decreased with the industry's growing familiarity with electronic equipment. Nonetheless, in the late 1970s, the concern was deeply felt. Paul Kolton, then chairman of the board of the American Stock Exchange, commented that Peake-Mendelson-Williams's National Book System ''seems not an orderly step but a drastic departure; it is less a measured progression than a giant leap, with the landing place obscure.''[22]

Despite the opposition to the National Book System, an electronic market, the National Securities Trading System (NSTS), was introduced in June 1978. Although it receives only a small fraction of the order flow, NSTS has remained in operation. NSTS was not a response to the governmental mandate to develop a national market system; rather, it was initially created and operated by Weedon and Co., which at the time was a leading third market dealer. NSTS is now owned by the Cincinnati Stock Exchange and is known as the Cincinnati experiment. Initially, the SEC allowed 38 stocks to be eligible for trading in NSTS, then authorized expansion to 200.

Dealers and brokers who participate in NSTS can enter orders (market or limit) through a computer terminal. The market itself is managed by a central computer without an exchange floor. A trade is triggered when a

---

[19]*New York Stock Exchange Annual Report 1985*, pp. 10 and 11, emphasis added.
[20]D. Stone (1979, p. 209).
[21]Mendelson, Peake, and Williams (1979).
[22]In Bloch and Schwartz (1979, p. 107).

bid matches the best (lowest) offer, or when an ask matches the best (highest) bid. Strict price and time priorities are maintained, public agency orders are given precedence over dealer orders at the same price, and the NSTS order book is open to participants. NSTS has an electronic link with the Intermarket Trading System, and much of its order flow (about 40 percent) is accounted for by the ITS.

At its inception in 1978, NSTS's share volume as a percentage of total volume (in all market centers) for NSTS stocks was 2.0 percent, with Merrill Lynch being its largest customer. Merrill Lynch withdrew from the system in April 1983; that year, NSTS share volume fell to 0.6 percent of the composite volume for stocks traded in the system.[23] The failure of this electronic system to capture more of the order flow has been a disappointment to advocates of computerized trading.

Two factors in particular explain why the Cincinnati experiment did not meet with success. First, unlike the Peake-Mendelson-Williams proposal, NSTS is not, and never was, the sole trading system for NSTS listed issues. Rather, it is a satellite system and, as such, has faced all the disadvantages of a small market competing with a large market. Second, the system does not cater to the unique needs of the large upstairs traders, who have remained reluctant to expose their orders in an electronic market.

Failure of the Cincinnati experiment should not be taken as evidence that computerized trading will not work. Rather, the experiment has shown that much remains unknown about the design and implementation of an electronic system.[24]

The Intermarket Trading System   A CLOB has not become part of the national market system. Rather, the industry has followed a more moderate route by developing the Intermarkct Trading System. ITS simply links the markets and facilitates order exposure and preservation of price priority across markets. Orders routed by ITS are commitments to trade a given number of shares at a given price. The commitments include an expiration time of one or two minutes. A broker on the floor of the NYSE, as on any of the other six U.S. stock exchanges, can observe the quotes for an ITS stock on a CRT device by the specialist's post. Then, after obtaining the specialist's own quotes, the broker can choose whether to trade with the specialist or through the ITS. If the broker chooses the ITS, a commitment is sent by the broker to the exchange where the best ITS quote has been posted (for example, the Philadelphia Exchange). This commitment can be accepted by the Philadelphia specialist or rejected if the Philadelphia quote

[23]Davis (1985, p. 275).
[24]See Chapter 13 for further discussion.

has been filled or withdrawn. ITS trades are typically executed in about 26 seconds.[25]

The number of shares executed on the ITS increased from 209.4 million in 1979 (its first complete year in operation) to 1827.2 million in 1986.[26] The NYSE participates in roughly 90 percent of all ITS volume, although the share volume of the NYSE's ITS trades is less than 3 percent of total NYSE share volume.[27]

ITS was initially accepted with much reluctance by the primary exchanges. However, the facility has strengthened (not weakened, as some had expected) the NYSE, and ITS is considered by many to have contributed to the overall liquidity of the markets. Some observers, however, have questioned the success of the ITS. No clear evidence exists that bid-ask spreads have been significantly reduced, or that limit order protection has been appreciably improved, or, in fact, that limit order protection ever was a significant problem. Furthermore, in the opinion of some, the ITS suffers from a design deficiency in that it allows for quote matching.[28]

When a floor broker contrasts a specialist's quote with quotes shown on the ITS screen, the specialist has an opportunity to match the best quote shown in the ITS and thus to capture the order. Therefore, an order initially submitted to the NYSE market is most likely to execute on the NYSE; an order initially submitted to the Philadelphia Stock Exchange is most likely to execute on the Philadelphia Exchange; and so forth. Quote matching is possible because no secondary trading priority rule is enforced in the ITS. As a consequence of quote matching, markets continue to compete for the order flow, larger markets continue to have a competitive advantage because of their size (order flow attracts order flow), and the equities markets remain fragmented.[29]

The Impact of the 1975 Amendments

Enough time has now passed to assess the impact of the 1975 Amendments. The most apparent effect of the deregulation was a sharp decrease in commission rates for large orders (see Chapter 14, Table 14.1). This decrease was followed by a surge of order flow to the markets (see Chapter 1, Table

[25]Stone (1985, p. 114).
[26]*The New York Stock Exchange Fact Book, 1987*, p. 19.
[27]Davis (1985).
[28]See Davis (1985).
[29]Mendelson, Peake, and Williams (1979, p. 69) have argued that competition should be "*for* the security rather than *where* to obtain it." Davis (p. 278) has written, "true linkage eliminates the geographic distinctions between the various marketplaces. In a linked system of marketplaces, it should be irrelevant which marketplace brings an order into the system; this is a mere conduit function."

1.2). The enormous expansion of the order flow has itself led to technological change in trading systems.

Negotiated commissions and the recent structural advances have also altered the distribution of the order flow among the national exchanges, the regional exchanges, and the third market. For the third market, market share decreased sharply, from 6.03 percent in 1972 to 2.46 percent in 1981. Market share for the regional exchanges decreased slightly, from 11.01 percent in 1972 to 10.88 percent in 1981. The NYSE's market share increased appreciably, from 82.56 percent in 1972 to 86.66 percent in 1981.[30]

The changes in market share have been studied by Hamilton (1987), using multiple regression analysis. Hamilton's findings show that negotiated commissions and the ITS both caused order flow to be drawn to the NYSE in substantial proportion from the third market and, to a lesser extent, from the regional exchanges. Hamilton inferred that, in 1981, the impact of ITS alone caused the third market's market share to be at least 41 percent below, and the regional exchanges' market share to be at least 4 percent below, what they otherwise would have been.

The fate of fixed commissions was in fact determined before the 1975 Amendments. In 1968, volume discounts were instituted, at the urging of the SEC, for transactions over 1000 shares. In 1971, the SEC mandated that commissions be negotiated on that portion of an order in excess of $500,000. In 1972, the SEC mandated negotiation for the portion in excess of $300,000. By 1975, the SEC and the Department of Justice were both pushing for further deregulation. It was the SEC, responding in part to pressure from the Department of Justice and Congress, that set May 1 as the deadline for the total elimination of fixed commissions. The date is referred to as "May Day." The 1975 Amendments, which were enacted later that month, ensured that negotiated rates remain.

The structural pieces of the national market system can be individually assessed. Without question, the national clearance and settlement system is of tremendous value (see Chapter 4). But do the 1975 Amendments deserve the credit? Given the clearly perceived economic need, in all likelihood the system would have been developed anyway.

The Consolidated Tape was instituted in 1974, the year before the Amendments.

Quotron Systems, Inc., had started in 1957 and was providing price, trade, and news information to investors. The Consolidated Quotation System (CQS) became operational in 1978. With the advent of CQS, comparable quotes were consolidated from different markets for distribution by the private vendors of market information.

---

[30]Market share for 1972 is reported in the Securities and Exchange Commission, "The Effect of the Absence of Fixed Rates of Commission," Washington D.C.: September 1981. Market share for 1981 is reported in *The New York Stock Exchange Fact Book*.

Although it appears to have largely satisfied the 1975 congressional mandate, the Intermarket Trading System has not blended the exchange markets into a truly integrated system. This is partially attributable to the fact that ITS allows quote-matching, as discussed earlier. Moreover, the equity markets have remained fragmented because of the growth of the upstairs market for institutional orders. Over half of the order flow is currently accounted for by block trades (as shown below in Table 5.1). These trades are handled by block positioners and sales traders at the trading desks of the major brokerage houses. The block trades are negotiated by telephone, increasingly without the participation of the specialist (see Chapter 4). The blocks, however, are nearly always brought to the exchange market and exposed to the mechanism of that market at the time of execution.

Assessed one at a time, the steps taken pursuant to the 1975 Amendments are not impressive. A broader evaluation of the industry's response to the deregulation yields a different impression, however. To see this, consider the state of the markets in the prederegulation days.

Prior to 1975, three factors caused the NYSE to be a very noncompetitive marketplace: (1) the price of its services was fixed (fixed commissions), (2) members were not allowed to trade away from the exchange markets (off-board trading restrictions), and (3) membership in the club was restricted (purchase of a seat was required for access to the trading floor, there were 1366 seats to be held, and only an individual could buy a seat). These restrictions resulted in excess profits that institutional investors could not share in, because the institutions were barred from NYSE membership.

Not surprisingly, market distortions resulted. Prior to December 1968, NYSE member firms were allowed to "give up" (rebate) commission dollars to other NYSE member firms (but not to nonmember firms). The magnitude of give-ups on institutional size orders was on the order of 60 percent.[31] "Soft" (as opposed to "hard") dollars were also directly rebated to investors in the form of research and other investment services. Institutional orders were directed to the third market and, to a lesser extent, to regional exchanges.[32] Thus the barriers to competition—fixed commissions, off-board trading restrictions, and control over exchange membership—were simultaneously generating excess profits and fragmenting the market. In addition, the Exchange, in its semiprotected position, felt little pressure to improve the transactional efficiency of its marketplace.

In 1970, the NYSE did allow member firms to go public; Donaldson, Lufkin, and Jenrette was the first to do so, in April 1970.[33] By 1975, the

---

[31]Stoll (1979).

[32]Order flow was not diverted to regional exchanges because of lower commission rates, but because it allowed for give-ups to firms that were not members of the NYSE.

[33]No longer public, Donaldson, Lufkin, and Jenrette is currently an independently operated subsidiary of The Equitable Life Assurance Society of the United States.

pressure of competitive forces (the market) and of regulatory forces (the SEC) had started to dismantle the other barriers. The 1975 Amendments provided congressional sanction for the process. The total and permanent elimination of fixed commissions was a major structural change. The success of this deregulation encouraged the SEC to honor the congressional order to abrogate other anticompetitive rules by calling for the total removal of off-board trading restrictions. The threat, which was only partially carried out, instigated further change in the industry. The Exchange experimented with a system of competing specialists, and a few stocks were cross-listed on the NYSE and Amex. Neither of these experiments was successful, but they did symbolize a new atmosphere at the Exchange: the NYSE was no longer a club for the privileged few, and it was no longer protected from the forces of competition.

In conclusion, a truly integrated national market system has not been achieved since the Securities Acts Amendments of 1975. The congressional legislation will be better remembered for the old order that it helped to dismantle than for a new system that it mandated.

New Competition, New Technology, and New Markets

The Over-the-Counter Market   Other powerful forces, in addition to governmental regulation, have affected the industry in recent years. One of the most prominent has been the emergence of the over-the-counter market.

In 1986, the volume of trading in the three largest equity markets in the world was, in billions of dollars: NYSE, $1374.3; Tokyo, $958.1; and NASDAQ, $378.2.[34] The OTC became a major marketplace after the introduction in 1971 of NASDAQ.

OTC dealer firms at first feared the competition that the system would introduce and were reluctant to display their quotes on the NASDAQ screen. However, NASDAQ has been of tremendous value to OTC dealers. To do business, a dealer firm must receive orders from brokers. NASDAQ has enabled those firms that make good markets to receive the orders. Furthermore, a dealer firm can now successfully make a market in a stock it has not previously traded, by posting quotes on the NASDAQ screen. With the advent of NASDAQ, OTC firms began making markets in larger numbers of issues. The firms became larger, and some became nationally known for the first time. In 1986, 526 market makers made markets in 5189 NASDAQ securities; on average that year, there were 8.0 market makers per NASDAQ security.[35]

---

[34]NASD, *NASDAQ 1987 Fact Book*. For further comparison of the size of the OTC and NYSE, see Chapter 3, Table 3.2. Also see Wall (1985).

[35]NASD, *NASDAQ 1987 Fact Book*.

The NASD has continued to make improvements in the NASDAQ system. In 1982, the NASDAQ/NMS (national market system) was established for the most prominent NASDAQ issues. Current volume and last-sale price reporting are required for these issues. The NASDAQ/NMS now provides a clear alternative to the stock exchange markets and strong competition for listings and the order flow.

The Upstairs Market Growth in the number and size of block trades of institutional investors started in the late 1960s and has continued to the present time. Upstairs trading has not, as yet, had an appreciable impact on trading systems or on the structure of the market centers, but it has created the potential for such change—the introduction of an electronic trading system that would successfully integrate the upstairs market, as NASDAQ has integrated the OTC dealer market, could divert major order flow from the exchanges.

Table 5.1 shows the number of shares involved in block transactions on the NYSE and their percentage importance in relation to total NYSE volume for the years 1965–1986. The number of shares and the percentage importance of NYSE share volume accounted for by block trades have increased almost every year over the period. In 1965, only 3.1 percent of shares traded on the NYSE were accounted for by the blocks; in 1986, the number was 49.9 percent. The remarkable increase in block trading is explained by the lowering of commission rates for large orders, by the enhanced importance of trading to institutional investors and to large brokerage houses, and by the growth of, in particular, the pension funds.

For the NASDAQ/NMS, block volume in 1986 was 8.2 billion shares, which amounted to 41.8 percent of total NASDAQ/NMS share volume. Block trades have accounted for over 36 percent of NASDAQ/NMS volume since the market was instituted in 1982.[36]

Technology
Striking technological advances have been made in trading systems. Instinet, an electronic trading and order routing system, was developed in 1969 to handle direct institution-to-institution trades. Substantially improved in recent years, it is now gaining appreciable order flow in both exchange listed and OTC securities.[37] Another block trading system is London-based ARIEL, which was started in 1974 by several major institutional investors.

The first exchange based computerized trading system was the Toronto

---

[36]NASD, *NASDAQ 1987 Fact Book*.

[37]A major Instinet innovation is the Instinet Designated Market Makers, who, as specialists on the Pacific and Boston exchanges and OTC market makers, guarantee, for a large number of exchange listed and NASDAQ securities, 30 second execution at best market quotes, for orders up to 1000 shares.

Stock Exchange's *Computer Assisted Trading System* (CATS), introduced in 1977 because the Toronto Exchange was running out of space on its trading floor. In 1982, a modified version of the system was adopted by the Tokyo Stock Exchange for all issues traded in the Second Section of the Tokyo market. In 1985, Tokyo CATS was extended to all but the 250 largest issues in the First Section of the Tokyo Exchange. The Cincinnati Stock Exchange's NSTS was introduced in 1978 (see preceding discussion). The first computerized futures exchange started operations in 1984, Bermuda's *International Futures Exchange* (INTEX), which has a computer in Bermuda with electronic linkages that go through London and Virginia.[38]

Table 5.1   NYSE BLOCK TRANSACTIONS

Year	Shares (000)	Percentage of reported volume	Year	Shares (000)	Percentage of reported volume
1965	48,262	3.1%	1976	1,001,254	18.7%
1966	85,298	4.5	1977	1,183,924	22.4
1967	169,365	6.7	1978	1,646,905	22.9
1968	292,681	10.0	1979	2,164,726	26.5
1969	402,064	14.1	1980	3,311,132	29.2
1970	450,908	15.4	1981	3,771,442	31.8
1971	692,536	17.8	1982	6,742,481	41.0
1972	766,406	18.5	1983	9,842,080	45.6
1973	721,356	17.8	1984	11,492,091	49.8
1974	549,387	15.6	1985	14,222,272	51.7
1975	778,540	16.6	1986	17,811,335	49.9

Source: *The New York Stock Exchange Fact Book*, annual.

A large number of other computerized systems have been introduced in the U.S. equity markets in recent years. These include:

- *COMEX (1976):* The Pacific Stock Exchange's order-routing system.
- *DOT (1976):* The NYSE's designated order turnaround, an order routing system for small orders.
- *PACE (1976):* The Philadelphia Stock Exchange's order routing system.
- *ABS (1977):* The NYSE's automated bond trading system.
- *SCOREX (1979):* The Pacific Stock Exchange's improved COMEX system; market orders in SCOREX are guaranteed execution within 30 seconds at the best ITS quotes; the system automatically reports trades and initiates clearance.
- *CAES (1979):* The NASD's computer assisted execution system; a CAES/ITS electronic linkage was established in 1982, but largely abandoned in 1983.

[38]Thus far, INTEX has captured only a small fraction of the order flow.

- *OARS (1980):* The NYSE's opening automated reporting system.
- *MAX (1980):* The Midwest Stock Exchange's automated execution system.
- *R4 (1980):* The NYSE's registered representative rapid response system; the system allows brokers to give clients immediate execution on market orders up to 599 shares at best ITS quotes.
- *AUTOPER (1983):* The Amex's electronic order routing and display system.
- *AUTO AMOS (1984):* The Amex's adaptation of AUTOPER to options.
- *COLT (1984):* The order execution system of Herzog, Heine, & Geduld, a leading OTC dealer firm.
- *MAX OTC (1984):* The Midwest Stock Exchange's automated execution system for OTC issues.
- *SOES (1984):* The NASD's small order execution system for NASDAQ securities.
- *SUPER-DOT (1984):* The NYSE's improved DOT system; the system allows automated execution when the spread is one-eighth.
- *BEACON (1987):* The Boston Stock Exchange's automated execution system.

New Financial Instruments   A general incorporation law enacted in Connecticut in 1837 and soon followed by other states facilitated the organization of companies and the flotation of stock. This set the stage for an expansion of trading in equity shares in the second half of the nineteenth century. In the 1870s, Russell Sage, a Connecticut grocer, banker, and member of the NYSE, designed and initiated trading in put and call option contracts. The contracts were initially traded outdoors and in offices along Broad Street in lower Manhattan. Until the 1970s, options contracts were only traded in the OTC market.

In 1972, the Chicago Mercantile Exchange began trading in foreign currency futures contracts. In 1973, organized options trading was initiated by the newly formed Chicago Board Options Exchange (CBOE). Call options were introduced on the Amex (1975), the Philadelphia Stock Exchange (1975), the Pacific Stock Exchange (1976), and the Midwest Stock Exchange (1976). Trading in put options began in each of these market centers in 1977. Exchange trading was also established for futures and options on broad stock market indexes, and on submarket indexes. By 1985, more new products had been introduced—interest rate futures, interest rate options, exchange rate options, commodity options, and so forth.

The American Stock Exchange's experience with option trading illustrates the importance of the new financial instruments to the market centers. The Amex options market was launched in January 1975. Initially, 10 call options were traded. Daily volume in the first year averaged 14,352 contracts, which represented 20 percent of the options market. By 1980, the Amex was trading 80 put and 80 call options, and daily volume averaged 114,816 contracts, representing 30 percent of the options market. By 1984, after a decade of trading, average daily volume had increased to 158,516 contracts, or 28 percent of the options market.[39] Options trading has become a major part of the Amex's operations and an important source of revenues, particularly to its floor members.

The new financial instruments are contingent claims on underlying assets. The prices of the contingent claims and of the underlying assets are closely related to each other, but the instruments are traded in different market centers. A necessary link between market centers has been provided by the arbitrage trading of upstairs market makers, who have become an integral part of the price formation process. This linkage is illustrated by the events of September 11 and 12, 1986.

On September 11, on a volume of 237.6 million shares, the Dow Jones Industrial average dropped 86.61 points, to close at 1,792.89. On September 12, the Dow fell another 34.17 points, on a volume of 240.5 million shares, to close at 1,758.72. The two-day decline in the equity markets was reportedly brought about as follows.

On September 11, the price of Treasury bonds fell roughly 2 percent. Uneasy about the economy and worried in particular about rising interest rates, banks, insurance companies, pension funds, and mutual funds started to hedge their long positions in equities by obtaining short positions in S&P futures contracts on the Chicago Mercantile Exchange. The institutional investors had chosen to hedge their long positions rather than to sell equity shares because their expectations concerned the broad market, and transaction costs (commissions and execution costs) are lower for futures trading. Falling prices triggered portfolio insurance programs, which led to further sell pressure on the Chicago Mercantile Exchange.[40]

Thirty-six billion dollars in S&P futures contracts traded on the Chicago Merc on September 11 and 12. Because the institutional investors turned initially to the Chicago market, the selling pressure did not, at first, affect the price of equity shares traded on the NYSE. Consequently, the precipitous decline in the futures market caused the price of the futures contract to fall below the cash value of the equity shares that comprise the index. The price discrepancy then triggered the index arbitrage programs of the large brokerage houses.[41] The arbitrage operations provided price support for the S&P 500 index future contract and pushed prices down on

---

[39]American Stock Exchange annual reports for 1980 and 1984.

[40]The computer driven insurance programs have an effect similar to stop loss orders: a price decrease of sufficient size activates sell orders that reinforce a market decline and can have an explosive effect on price.

[41]*The New York Times* (September 18, 1986, p. D6) reported that Morgan Stanley bought approximately a billion dollars of futures and sold a billion dollars worth of stock on September 11.

the NYSE, until the price of the index future and the average cash price of the stocks were once again in alignment.

Globalization of Trading   In the years following the Securities Acts Amendments of 1975, competition developed between the national and regional stock exchanges; the stock exchanges and the over-the-counter market; the equity markets and the new products markets; dealers/specialists and upstairs market makers; and, increasingly, domestic and foreign trading systems.

Currently, equity shares in foreign firms can be obtained on a foreign exchange, either through a foreign broker or through an international broker such as Merrill Lynch or Nomura Securities. In addition, the equity shares of a large number of international companies have been listed on the U.S. exchanges and are traded in the OTC market. Domestic trading in foreign shares has been facilitated by use of the *American Depository Receipts* (ADRs) (see Chapter 4). However, trading stocks away from their major market centers puts traders at a disadvantage with respect to market information.

Direct intermarket linkages have been developed in recent years, both for trading and for the dissemination of current market quotes. In September 1984, an operational link was instituted between the Chicago Mercantile Exchange and the Singapore International Monetary Exchange. In the fall of 1985, a link was established between the American Stock Exchange and the Toronto Stock Exchange. In 1985, a link for options trading was established between the Sydney, Vancouver, Montreal, and Amsterdam exchanges. Linkages are also being planned between the Midwest Stock Exchange and the Toronto Stock Exchange, between the Boston and the Montreal Exchanges, and between NASDAQ and the London Stock Exchange.

Instinet has expanded internationally, and the system will increasingly provide traders with improved international capabilities. In March 1985, Instinet signed a cooperative agreement with Reuters, a leading supplier of financial news, quotations, and other market data to brokers and banks in Europe. Under the agreement, Instinet is being connected via satellite to Reuter's electronic information network in Europe and England. In May 1987, Instinet became a wholly owned subsidiary of Reuters.

Deregulation, primarily in the United States and England, has lowered the barriers to international investing and trading. Concurrently, the development of new financial instruments has enabled multinational firms to raise money in foreign countries, either in foreign currencies or in dollars, and to swap across currencies and interest rates to hedge positions. Increasingly, large U.S. companies have tapped foreign markets, not only for debt, but also for equity capital. The *Euroequity market,* which was less than $500 million in 1984, exceeded $3 billion in 1985 and in the first six months of

1986.[42] As the primary market becomes more international, so too will the secondary market.

International trading will also increase with the modernization of foreign markets. The English market changed dramatically on October 27, 1986, the day of the "Big Bang" (equivalent to the United States's "May Day" in 1975): fixed commissions were removed, and British market makers were allowed for the first time to operate in the dual capacity of both dealers and brokers.

Financial capital will increasingly flow through the British market. London is situated between the two largest financial markets in the world, the United States and Japan, and its trading day overlaps Tokyo's in the morning and New York's in the afternoon. For many years, London has been a major market for non-British stocks. It also enjoys prominence in the Eurobond market and is a leader in foreign-exchange trading.

The Bank of England, which acts as the equivalent of the SEC, allowed the international financial market in London to develop with a minimum of regulation. The domestic securities market, on the other hand, was tightly controlled until the day of the Big Bang in 1986. Foreign financial institutions are rapidly building up their London offices, now that deregulation has spread throughout the City of London, the mile square financial district that is equivalent to New York's Wall Street. For instance: Deutsche Bank has based its international bond business in London; Salomon Brothers has made London the headquarters of its international operations; Goldman Sachs tripled its London office to 500 employees during 1985 and 1986; Citicorp now owns two British brokers, one of which has seats on both the London and Tokyo exchanges.

For a number of years the Paris Bourse has considered changing from a call market to a continuous auction market. The Milan stock market is now in the process of changing from a once per day call to continuous trading, by instituting a system patterned after the U.S. OTC market.[43] SOFFEX, Switzerland's computerized options and financial futures exchange, is scheduled to begin trading in the spring of 1988. Throughout the world, in Hong Kong, Tokyo, Toronto, and elsewhere, trading systems are being upgraded. The changes will no doubt unfold rapidly. The U.S. markets increasingly will face strong foreign competition.

Current Issues

Commissions in excess of the cost of handling an order and executing a trade still result in soft dollar payments, as they did in the days of fixed

---

[42]*The New York Times,* August 21, 1986, p. D1.
[43]Continuous trading currently takes place on an informal basis in the Italian market.

commissions before 1975. Investment managers and plan sponsors still select brokers (and thus "direct" brokerage commissions) according to the soft dollar services they receive. However, trading costs have attracted increased attention as brokerage firms and institutional investors have become larger, and as trading has gained importance. Interest is now focused on execution costs (the bid-ask spread and market impact effects), and more attention is being given to obtaining good executions for hard-to-handle trades.

New pricing policies are being tested. For example, tiered commissions are being used, with the highest rates applied to hard-to-handle capital commitment trades, intermediate rates applied for discretionary trades that do not require capital commitment, and the lowest rates applied to the "no brainers." Incentive fees are also being considered: investment managers are paid a percentage of assets, plus a percentage of any portion of a portfolio's return that exceeds a predetermined benchmark, such as the return on the S&P 500.

Another change, with implications that are not as yet clear, has also accompanied the events of recent years—economic power has become more concentrated in the industry. In the current environment, market making involves large sums of capital and large securities firms. The large securities firms have expanded their proprietary trading and are increasingly making markets as dealers rather than simply handling orders as brokers. This change of operations involves considerable financial risk. Consequently, one major securities firm after another has gone public and/or has merged with a larger company to obtain the capital that is needed to make markets, and to withstand the risks involved.

Will the increased dealer activities of the brokerage firms lead to conflicts of interest between these firms and their customers? How will portfolio managers respond if dealer spreads widen? Will portfolio managers attempt to bypass the dealers by posting more limit orders on the market?

Upstairs traders are now the dominant source of the order flow to the exchange and NASDAQ markets. These traders are connected by an extensive communications system, and they negotiate their own trades, often without the participation of the exchange specialists or OTC dealers. The advent of an electronic system to which the upstairs traders would be willing to submit their orders could substantially reduce the order flow to existing market centers. What implications would this have for the stability of prices and the fairness of the market?

Many observers of the market believe that security prices are now more volatile. Are the underlying determinants of share value less stable than they once were? Has the increased speed of information dissemination, order transmission, and trade execution destabilized the market? Does program trading result in explosive price movements? Or is the increased volatility only an illusion?

Computerized trading has caused considerable apprehension in certain segments of the industry and in the financial press. In the late 1970s, the industry almost uniformly opposed the development of a computerized consolidated limit order book. Block traders are still unwilling to expose their orders in a computerized trading system. Currently, the market is believed to be destabilized by upstairs traders who use the computer to run arbitrage programs, to perform insurance programs (for hedging), and to implement other trading strategies. On September 13, 1986, after the precipitous two-day market drop on September 11 and 12, the headline of a front page article in *The New York Times* read: ''Volatility Tied to Wide Use of Computers to Set Trading Patterns.''

The article went on to state that ''The stock market's plunge this week was as much a product of computer technology and Wall Street inventiveness as it was a reflection of new worries over the economy.'' Is this impression correct? If the price move had resulted from technical aspects relating to trading rather than a real change in investor expectations, one might expect that the Dow would soon have regained its previous level. It did not. One week later, on Friday, September 19, the Dow closed at 1762.65, only four points higher than its close at 1758.72 on September 12, after it had dropped 120.78 points in two days.

The advent of new machinery generated fear over a century ago, during the industrial revolution. Is the current reaction to the computer a similar expression of people's fear of change and of the unknown?

Trading is rapidly becoming international. But problems continue to exist. Requirements for information disclosure differ across countries and exchanges. Trading activity (for instance, insider trading) that is legal in one country may be considered fraudulent in another. Trading is conducted in strikingly different ways in markets around the world, and interfaces between dissimilar systems are not easily arranged. Systems for international settlement are just beginning to be developed. In addition to various technical problems, concern exists about the economic effects of large pools of funds being transferred with electronic speed across market centers and national boundaries. Funds, of course, have no particular loyalty, not to geographic area, economy, or firm, and their sudden flight from one market to another can have major economic consequences.

CONCLUSION

In 1985, Henry Kaufman, vice chairman of Phibro-Salomon, wrote, ''If a modern-day Rip Van Winkle had fallen asleep twenty years ago, or for that matter even ten years back, on awakening today, he would be astonished as to what has happened in the financial markets. Instead of a world of isolated national capital markets and a preponderance of fixed-rate financing, he would discover a world of highly integrated capital markets, an extensive array of financing instruments and new methods of addressing market risk.''[44]

What would be the thoughts today of a colonial Rip Van Winkle? Two hundred years ago, securities were traded outdoors, on the streets of Boston, New York, and Philadelphia. Communications were rudimentary, and financial instruments simple and few in number. Investment analysis was an intuitive process. Traders and speculators learned about the market by shouting, pushing, and maneuvering on the curb and on the exchange floors. The self-imposed rules of exchange members constituted the only regulation of the markets. Neither traders nor issues were registered; fraud and manipulation were rife. Initially, only the very wealthy invested in the market, and only the physically strong traded.

A loud voice and a large frame can still be an advantage. But the financial maturity of the economy, an extensive regulatory system, and sophisticated technology have transformed the industry. The marketplace is now multinational. Settlements in foreign currencies are common, and trading occurs 24 hours a day. Complex instruments such as futures and options contracts on broad market indexes and submarket indexes are bought and sold by traders using highly sophisticated strategies. Regulators are committed to preventing fraud, manipulation, and other abuses of power that hurt individuals. The scope of regulation has also expanded to encompass the financial health of institutions, the competitive vitality of markets, and the economic efficiency of market centers.

Computer technology has permeated the industry. Order routing and information dissemination are handled electronically, and a growing number of market centers, both national and international, are linked by computer. Institutional traders, with instantaneous access to large data bases and easy access to a large number of other traders and markets, have become a dominant force in the marketplace. News travels fast, orders are executed almost instantly, and prices adjust quickly to the changing expectations of investors.

Many now believe that the 1975 congressional mandate for a national market system has been satisfied. Nevertheless, the period of evolution for the securities markets has not ended. The process of innovation and change in market design is now endogenous to the system and self-perpetuating.

The attitude of the industry has also evolved since the contentious days that followed the passage of the 1975 Amendments. According to William Lupien, president and chairman of the board of Instinet,

[44]*Phibro-Salomon 1985 annual report*, p. 15.

"Ten years ago we used to fight fiercely over our own turf because everyone was afraid of being gored economically. Today, people have adjusted to the changes and are willing to look at new ideas. For instance, many people who fought the concept of automated trading are now strong advocates of it. Ten years ago we had tremendous doubts. Now the problem we all face is simply adjusting fast enough to the various technological and structural changes that are taking place, regardless of the debates."[45]

The securities industry in the United States has changed as much in the last 20 years as it had in the first 175 years of its history, and the current pace of change has not yet slackened. As one looks to the future, one can safely predict that trading will be increasingly computerized, that more markets will be interlinked, and that proprietary trading will become even more important to the leading brokerage houses. Economic power will be more concentrated on the national scale, although increased international competition will keep markets competitive. Foreign market centers will undoubtedly gain in importance. The London market in particular has benefited and will continue to benefit from the deregulation of October 1986, much as the U.S. markets were strengthened by the Securities Acts Amendments of 1975.

In discussing the extensive change that has occurred in the industry and in attitudes toward the industry, John Phelan, Jr., chairman and chief executive officer of the New York Stock Exchange, recently wrote,

"the academic world once regarded most of us in the financial services industries as nonintellectuals who might know our own business, but not much else. What has happened over the past ten years or so is that those same people—in brokerage, banking, insurance—have turned the financial world upside down and brought on a national and international revolution in which everybody is both learning and getting into everybody else's business."[46]

To emphasize his point, Phelan told a story about Albert Einstein. Einstein, who was having a terrible time getting on with people, was advised by a psychiatrist to go outside, sit on a park bench, and start a conversation with the first person to come along. When the first person passed, Einstein introduced himself and inquired about the stranger's IQ. It was 190, and the two gentlemen started to talk about space and time relationships and other mathematical formulas. They had a wonderful time.

[45]Lupien (1985).
[46]Phelan (1985).

The second person to come along had an IQ of 140, and the conversation turned to government, politics, and world affairs. Again, Einstein had a wonderful time. A third person arrived. "What is your IQ?" the mathematician inquired. "Sixty," was the reply. "Hmm," Einstein responded, "what do you think the market will do today?" Given the complexity of today's markets, one can afford to chuckle.

SUGGESTED READING

Y. Amihud, T. Ho, and R. Schwartz (eds.), *Market Making and the Changing Structure of the Securities Industry.* Copyright © 1985 by D. C. Heath and Company (Lexington, Mass.: Lexington Books). Reprinted by permission of the publisher.

Y. Amihud and H. Mendelson, "An Integrated Computerized Trading System," in Amihud, Ho, and Schwartz (1985).

E. Bloch, "Securities Markets Under Stress: 1967 to 1976," in Bloch and Schwartz (1979).

E. Bloch and R. Schwartz (eds.), *Impending Changes for Securities Markets: What Role for the Exchange?,* Greenwich, Conn.: JAI Press, 1979.

J. Davis, "The Intermarket Trading System and the Cincinnati Experiment," in Amihud, Ho, and Schwartz (1985).

M. Fainsod, L. Gordon, and J. Palamountain, Jr., *Government and the American Economy,* New York: Norton, 1959.

J. Hamilton, "Off-Board Trading of NYSE-Listed Stocks: The Effects of Deregulation and the National Market System," *Journal of Finance,* December 1987.

W. Lupien, "Star Wars Technology in Trading," in Amihud, Ho, and Schwartz (1985).

T. McCraw, *Prophets of Regulation,* London, England: Belknap Press, 1984.

M. Mendelson, J. Peake, and R. Williams, "Toward a Modern Exchange: The Peake-Mendelson-Williams Proposal for an Electronically Assisted Auction Market," in Bloch and Schwartz (1979).

J. Peake, M. Mendelson, and R. Williams, "The National Book System: An Electronically Assisted Auction Market," R. Shreiber Associates, Parsippany, N.J., April 1976.

J. Phelan, Jr., "An Era of Opportunity and Challenge for the Securities Industry," in Amihud, Ho, and Schwartz (1985).

R. Sobel, *The Big Board: A History of the New York Stock Market,* New York: Free Press, 1965.

R. Sobel, *The Curbstone Brokers,* New York: Macmillan, 1970.

H. Stoll, *Regulation of Securities Markets: An Examination of the Effects of Increased Competition,* Monograph Series in Finance and Economics, Salomon Brothers Center for the Study of Financial Institutions, New York University Graduate School of Business Administration, 1979.

D. Stone, "Future Shock Is Here," in Bloch and Schwartz (1979).

D. Stone, "The View From the Trading Floor," in Amihud, Ho, and Schwartz (1985).

J. Wall, "The Competitive Environment of the Securities Market," in Amihud, Ho, and Schwartz (1985).

S. Williams, "The Evolving National Market System," in Amihud, Ho, and Schwartz (1985).

two

ANALYSIS

chapter 6

Microeconomic Foundations

This chapter considers how microeconomic analysis can be used to gain insight into the workings of the equity markets. Microeconomics is concerned with the theory of choice: what action to take, how much to buy or to sell, what price to offer to pay, and so on. This theory of choice has much relevance to decisions concerning investing and trading.

The chapter begins by discussing theoretical analysis in relation to four other approaches: institutional description, empirical analysis, experimentation, and analysis of institutional/legal history. Three extensions that have substantially advanced the usefulness of the discipline for our purpose are highlighted: (1) the analysis of decision making under uncertainty, (2) the analysis of how imperfect information affects the behavior of decision makers and market outcomes, and (3) the more restricted analysis of auction pricing that has considered the effect of the rules of an auction on market outcomes. An overview of the recent literature on the microstructure of security markets is then presented. This literature, which considers the impact of the trading process on trading decisions and market outcomes, provides the analytical foundation used in this book.

A review of the individual choice model starts with a discussion of utility functions, proceeds to the decision maker's indifference curves and budget constraint, and then depicts an individual's optimal demand propensities. Two concepts related to the demand curve are next established: *consumer surplus* and *reservation prices*. Following this discussion, the supply curve is identified. We next show how individual demand/supply propensities are aggregated to obtain market clearing values for the price and size of trades. The market clearing results are then assessed to show how trade benefits participants in the market process. The section concludes by identifying the concept of Walrasian *tâtonnement*.

The final section of this chapter deals with a technical issue: the time dimension used for measuring a variable. We explain the difference between a *flow variable* (which is measured as a rate per unit of time) and a *stock variable* (which is measured at some specific point in time). The stock dimensioned demand curve, which is germane to the investor's portfolio decision of how many shares of an asset *to hold*, is then distinguished from the more commonly used flow dimensioned curve, which depicts the decision maker's time rate of consumption.

UNDERSTANDING THE OPERATIONS OF A TRADING SYSTEM

Institutional Description

Part One of this book considers the current structure and development of the markets. Much of this information is of interest in its own right. However, several questions cannot be immediately answered in relation to the preceding discussion: (1) How perfectly or imperfectly do the markets operate? (2) Why might the markets operate imperfectly? (3) How might public participants in the marketplace respond to operational inefficiencies? (4) How might professional market makers improve (or impair) the efficiency of market operations? (5) How might a trading system be designed and regulated so as to enhance its efficiency? Institutional description alone cannot answer these questions.

Theoretical Modeling

Having observed the marketplace, the next step is to analyze it. To some extent observations can be interpreted with verbal logic. There is a more satisfactory alternative, however: theoretical modeling. Microeconomic analysis provides a language, a conceptual framework, and a methodology that are essential.

A fundamental principle in microeconomics is that, as the price of a resource falls, a decision maker's demand for the resource rises. The relevance of a downward sloping demand curve for asset shares can, of course, be questioned. Would an investor, for instance, consider holding more shares of a particular stock if, at a given moment in time, the stock's price were lower?[1]

No real world trader has a downward sloping, continuous demand curve to hold shares of an asset. Some traders (primarily the larger ones) do submit multiple orders. However, many investors simply stay out of the market until price decreases to a critical value, at which point they purchase just one quantity (for example, 100 shares), regardless of how far below their critical value price might decrease.

Nevertheless, the decisions of an investor can be modeled as if that person had a demand curve that shows quantity continuously increasing as price continuously falls. This is the methodology of microeconomics. Whether the product is shares of an asset or quarts of orange juice bought in a supermarket, it is assumed that consumers make continuous adjustments to price changes. This may be an unrealistic description of the behavior of any specific individual, but it is a good representation of the average behavior of a group of individuals. Accordingly, it is a good depiction of how a market operates in the aggregate.

Empirical Analysis

A theoretical model's validity should, if possible, be tested by empirical analysis. However, verification is not a simple matter, even when available data are reasonably good. The reason is that many events happen simultaneously in the marketplace, and this obscures the pure relationships to which theory points. Consider, for instance, the theoretical statement "Taller people make better basketball players." The statement would not be correct if it implied "always." But theoretical statements rarely mean "always," and the hypothesis should be interpreted differently: "*Ceteris paribus,* taller people make better basketball players."

The Latin phrase *ceteris paribus* means "all else equal." The concept of *ceteris paribus* was introduced into the preceding statement because height alone does not determine a person's ability to play the game. Other factors include speed, spirit, intelligence, accuracy, and jumping ability. Some of these factors are independent of height (taller people are neither more nor less intelligent than shorter people); some are positively related to height (one can hit the hoop more accurately if one is closer to it); and some may be negatively related to height (it is more difficult for big people to make quick moves). Nevertheless, it is still a valid theoretical proposition that, *ceteris paribus,* "Taller people make better basketball players."

---

[1]For now, assume a decreasing price does not suggest that something undesirable has happened to the company (that is, that price changes do not signal informational change). Price signaling is considered in Chapters 7 and 9.

Empirical analysis is used to examine data so as to infer *ceteris paribus* relationships. The process is not simple, however, when multiple relationships are simultaneously involved. Furthermore, relevant data are not always available. Fortunately, the securities industry has generated an enormous amount of data, and computer technology has greatly facilitated its collection and processing in recent years. Asset prices recorded over very brief time intervals (that is, intraday prices) are increasingly becoming available on magnetic tape, and a truly unique opportunity to study market processes in action is now being realized.

Experimentation

There is an alternative to standard empirical analysis that has been used to test propositions concerning the operations of the securities markets: generating data by running an experiment. This has been done with regard to electronic trading (the computerized Cincinnati Exchange has been called the *Cincinnati experiment*), and with regard to in-house trading (Securities and Exchange Commission Rule 19c.3, which allows in-house trading, has been adopted on an experimental basis).[2]

There is, however, a problem with applying this real world approach to economic experimentation. The Cincinnati Exchange, for instance, does not exist as an isolated entity—stocks traded in that market are also traded on the NYSE. Therefore, conclusions derived from the Cincinnati experiment might not remain valid if the NYSE were to be dissolved and *all* orders were routed to the computerized market.

The same applies to in-house trading. In the 19c.3 experiment, only some stocks are allowed to trade in-house (all stocks listed on the NYSE after April 26, 1979). Conclusions concerning the impact of in-house executions on the overall resiliency of the market might not be valid if the large brokerage houses were allowed to extend their market making operations to large volume issues such as IBM and General Motors, which were listed before April 26, 1979.

It is a virtual necessity that economic experimentation with systems design violate some *ceteris paribus* conditions. The reason is that, in experimenting with new systems (such as the Cincinnati Exchange), existing systems (such as the NYSE) should not be torn down. Nevertheless, experiments can still be run. They should be designed carefully, and the results must be interpreted with caution.

In recent years the methodology of laboratory research has been applied to economics, and a rapidly increasing literature called *experimental economics* has resulted. The research uses controlled laboratory experiments

---

[2]See Chapter 5 for further discussion.

to study aspects of market behavior that cannot otherwise be tested empirically. In the typical experimental economics laboratory, people trade shares of an anonymous asset. The participants are given an incentive to trade rationally by being allowed to keep the profits they make.

The initial objective of experimental economics was to study the convergence of transaction prices to an equilibrium price in an oral double auction market.[3] Particular attention has been given to the effect of the form of market organization on price convergence to an equilibrium value.[4] Experimental economics has also focused on issues concerning information and market efficiency: for example, the speed with which information is reflected in market prices and the impact of simultaneous versus sequential information arrival in a double auction market.[5]

The flow of orders to a market may be viewed as the input into a process that generates trades and transaction prices. Empirical analyses of the equity markets have thus far been limited because the order flow to the markets is unobservable (only the best market quotes, transaction prices, and volume are currently available in machine readable form). Therefore, the development of a laboratory where the strategic decisions of traders can be observed and analyzed offers much promise for furthering our understanding of the effect of transaction costs, transaction price uncertainty, and market design on the behavior of market participants. It is hoped that, in the future, experimental economics will make an appreciable contribution to the microstructure literature.

Institutional/Legal History

One further approach to understanding the operations of the equity markets is to consider their institutional and legal history. Much of what exists today is not the product of discretionary planning based upon economic analysis, but rather is explained by legal considerations, by economic exigencies of the past, and, to a not inconsequential degree, by chance.

What exists today, however, establishes constraints within which the market must operate. These constraints affect both the participants in trading and those who are concerned with the regulation of the markets and with the design and implementation of new systems. One must take historical realities into account in order to understand these constraints.

---

[3] This research includes Smith (1962), Isaac and Plott (1981), and Smith and Williams (1981).

[4] This research includes Plott and Smith (1978) and Hong and Plott (1982).

[5] This research includes Friedman, Harrison, and Salmon (1984); Plott and Sunder (1982); and Copeland and Friedman (1987). Comprehensive reviews of the academic literature on experimental economics have been provided by Plott (1982, 1986) and Smith (1982).

Recapitulation

Five approaches have been identified to understanding the operations of a trading system. Each has its role to play. However, for one purpose—predicting the effect of a change in system design or in the regulatory environment—theoretical analysis should play the major role. When the rules of the game are changed, relevant data may not be available (data, of course, are always collected from events of the past); adequate experimentation may not be feasible; and experience from the past, though meaningful, may be misleading as well. In other words, when debating structural change, one often has to fly blind. In such an event, theory must be the primary guide.

RECENT DEVELOPMENTS IN ECONOMIC ANALYSIS

Therefore, theory is needed. However, the applicability of traditional analysis for our purpose must be questioned. The reason is that in traditional microeconomic analysis "a market" is an abstract concept far removed from the equity markets this book focuses on.

As discussed in Chapter 1, a major limitation of traditional analysis is that, by and large, it assumes trading is a frictionless (that is, costless) process. Consequently, the connection between institutional arrangements (the design of actual trading systems) and market outcomes (prices and the size of trades) has not been made in formal analysis. *Friction* refers to various costs and other impediments that interfere with the free interaction of traders (buyers and sellers) in the marketplace. Included are taxes and commissions; the cost of information, order handling, clearance, and record keeping; and impediments such as trading halts, restrictions, and other blockages. These aspects of the market process can have a substantial impact on the trading decisions of market participants.

Nevertheless, much as frictionless physics provides underpinnings for nonfrictionless physics, traditional theory provides a foundation upon which to build. Furthermore, economic analysis has expanded well beyond its traditional bounds in recent years. Major developments relevant to our needs have been made in the economics of uncertainty and the economics of information. In addition, questions concerning the impact of institutional design on market outcomes have been raised in the auction pricing literature. Each of these areas is considered in this section. The section that follows then focuses on a fourth area, security market microstructure, the subfield of financial economics into which this book fits.

The Economics of Uncertainty

Analytical tools now exist for analyzing decision making when outcomes are subject to uncertainty. The uncertain outcomes may pertain to the price that a firm will receive for its product, to the productivity of inputs for a firm, to the quality of resources purchased by a household, to the value of financial assets at some time in the future for an investor, and so on.

Many of the problems related to trading stem from the fact that investors do not know what price they will receive in the marketplace when they write their orders, or what price they could have received if they had changed the price, size, or timing of their orders. We will show that this uncertainty concerning current market outcomes exists because trading is not a costless process, and because investors are uncertain about each other's buy/sell propensities, which are subject to rapid variation. Recognizing how institutional arrangements affect the magnitude and impact of transaction price uncertainty, and how transaction price uncertainty affects the behavior of traders, gives insight into institutional arrangements that have been developed to facilitate the operations of a marketplace.

The Economics of Information

The economics of information considers informational activities that reduce the uncertainty of future outcomes. The activities include the production, purchase, exchange, and dissemination of information. Once it is explicitly recognized that market participants do not have complete information, it is natural to consider what happens when some participants are better informed than others. Of key importance in the economics of information is the effect of informational asymmetries (that is, market participants' not possessing equal amounts of information) on individual behavior and market results. Asymmetries exist, for instance, between buyers and sellers, between principals and agents, between professional and nonprofessional traders, and, in general, between informed and uninformed traders.

Two broad findings of particular interest have been developed in the information literature with regard to asymmetries. The first is that the asymmetry of information between buyers and sellers can cause a market to fail completely (that is, there will be no trades) even if potential trades that would make both buyers and sellers better off exist.[6] The second is that with asymmetric information, it may be profitable for market participants with better information to transmit this information to the relatively uninformed by an action that carries conviction. For instance, a firm might signal its profitability to investors by increasing its dividend or by increasing the proportion of debt in its capital structure.

Imperfect information (which is attributable to information's not being a free good) is itself an expression of the fact that operating in the marketplace is not costless. In view of this, it is interesting to recognize that when economic analysis is extended beyond the traditional confines of the

[6]Akerlof (1970).

frictionless market assumption, it generates implications that explain institutional arrangements. This is seen in the *signaling literature*, which, as just noted, provides justification for dividend policy and capital structure, decisions that do not matter in a perfect-information world.

The Auction Pricing Literature

One branch of economic analysis has considered the effect of institutional design on price setting: the *auction pricing literature*. This literature has focused primarily on the specific situation where a number of buyers compete in a simultaneous auction for the purchase of a fixed quantity of a good being sold by one seller. The analysis considers the effect that the auction procedure has on the expectation and variance of price received by the seller.

Alternative procedures considered include the *Dutch auction* (where the auctioneer first calls out a high price and then lowers it until some buyer first cries out, ''I will take it''), and the *English auction* (where price starts at a low level and interested buyers bid the price up until only one trader is left in the bidding). It has been demonstrated in the auction pricing literature that the rules of the auction do not affect the price that the seller expects to receive, although they do affect the variance of price.

The auction pricing literature assumes a market that in a number of ways resembles the primary auction market for treasury bonds, but that differs in several important respects from the secondary equity markets. For one thing, the stock exchanges are two-sided auctions—not only do buyers compete with buyers, but sellers also compete with sellers. Second, each trader is not necessarily a buyer or a seller in the market—he or she is either, depending on the price of shares. Third, the size of a trade is not fixed for any individual trader—rather, the number of shares that a trader wishes to buy or to sell depends on the share price of an asset. Fourth, in many secondary markets, orders are not batched for simultaneous execution at a *market call* (when the auction is held); rather, trades occur in the continuous market at any time during the trading day that two opposing orders cross.

Additionally, we are concerned with rules that apply to issues other than the way price is called out at an auction. Other issues include whether the market is a continuous trading system or a call, the extent to which orders are spatially consolidated, the role of dealers and specialists, the computerization of trading, the provision of price stabilization, the disclosure of price information, the handling of the limit order book, and so on. Thus, although the auction pricing literature has addressed an issue that is related to our interest, it is too narrow for our purposes. Fortunately, a broader literature now exists. That literature is referred to as *security market microstructure*.

Price

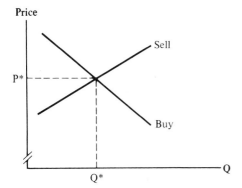

Figure 6.1 How much people (in aggregate) wish to buy from and sell to a market.

MICROSTRUCTURE ANALYSIS

Microstructure analysis focuses on the details of the trading process. The major elements of this process include the generation and dissemination of information, the arrival of orders, and the rules, institutions, and other design features of a market that determine how orders are transformed into trades. Microstructure analysis could, in principle, be applied to any market. Thus far, it has been developed almost exclusively in relation to securities markets.

Although the term *microstructure* was not coined until a decade later, the first microstructure papers to appear in the literature are Stigler's[7] and Demsetz's[8] papers on the role of the dealer as a market maker. Both Stigler and Demsetz considered the dealer as a supplier of immediacy to the market and viewed the bid-ask spread as the price charged for the dealer's services. Much of the microstructure literature has continued to focus on the dealership function and on the bid-ask spread. These issues are briefly discussed here so as to give a specific illustration of the microstructure literature.

A dealer sets his or her own bid-ask quotes and so sets his or her own spread. When just one dealer posts bid and ask quotes on the market and has a monopoly position with regard to the order flow, the market spread is the same as that individual dealer's spread. An investor buys from a dealer at the dealer's asking price and sells to a dealer at the dealer's bid.

Why do investors allow the dealer this spread? Because the dealer provides them with a service. The specific service identified by Stigler and Demsetz is the supply of immediacy. By considering what that supply entails, microstructure analysis treats an issue that has not been taken into account by traditional economic analysis.

The curves labeled *Buy* and *Sell* in Figure 6.1 show, respectively, how

[7]Stigler (1964).
[8]Demsetz (1968).

much people (in aggregate) wish to buy from and sell to a market. The negatively inclined buy curve shows that people buy more at lower prices, and the upward sloping sell curve shows that they sell more at higher prices. Given these two curves, the market price is expected to settle at a value of P*. At P*, people in aggregate buy the same amount they wish to sell: the amount labeled Q*.

Assume that an asset's share price is indeed P*, and that at this price a trader wishes to sell 200 shares. Since this desire to sell is reflected in the aggregate sell curve, one might expect that the trader would have no difficulty in selling the 200 shares at P*. However, this is not necessarily true. Q* is the number of shares (to buy and to sell) that are expected to arrive at the market within some interval of time. But the buy orders generally do not arrive at precisely the same moment that the sell orders arrive.

Nonsynchronous order arrival creates a problem for traders: how do buyers and sellers literally meet each other in time? Do some traders wait for other traders to appear? Is a mechanism available for storing and displaying orders on the market? Is some other kind of system needed? The fact is, if no arrangements are made, buyers might not meet sellers even if, in a frictionless world, Q* shares would trade at the price P*.

Problems such as this and the institutional arrangements that have been developed to deal with them are the subject of microstructure analysis. With regard to the problem of nonsynchronous order arrival, one of the institutional arrangements that has evolved is the *dealer*. Rather than buyers' and sellers' waiting for each other at the market, the dealer alone stands continuously available, and traders trade indirectly with each other by trading with the dealer. This is how Stigler and Demsetz viewed the dealer as a provider of immediacy to the market. As Demsetz showed, in providing immediacy, the dealer establishes an ask price that is generally above P*, and a bid price that is generally below P*.

An ever-growing literature has built on the early papers on the dealership function, and microstructure analysis has now been applied to a considerably broader spectrum of subjects pertaining to the securities markets. The major analytical issues, which are the subject of subsequent chapters of this book, can be classified under the following headings: (1) decisions of individual participants in the trading process; (2) advent, dissemination, and impact of information; (3) returns generation and price behavior of securities; (4) measures of market performance (price volatility, size of bid-ask spreads, and correlation patterns in a security's returns); (5) design features of a trading system; and (6) regulation of the markets.

THE INDIVIDUAL CHOICE MODEL

The chapter has thus far provided an overview of how microeconomic theory can be used to analyze the workings of the secondary asset markets.

We next turn to the specific concepts needed to analyze trading in equity markets.

Utility Functions

Utility is an abstract concept economists use to represent an individual's preference ordering. It is assumed that an individual seeks to maximize utility when he or she makes decisions that involve choice. The individual does this, given tastes and the set of resources over which he or she has command.

Utility cannot be measured directly. We can, however, construct utility rankings. That is, we can say that some alternative, A, contains more utility than some other alternative, B, if A is picked rather than B when both are available. Under certain conditions, we can go further and actually construct index numbers to represent the levels of utility achieved for differing quantities of a resource (good, service, or activity).

A *utility function* shows the relationship between the quantity of some resource obtained and the level of utility achieved. For the moment, let X stand for the resource. Then, write the utility function for X as

$$U = U(X) \tag{6.1}$$

where   U = the index of utility
        X = the quantity of the resource.

This function is illustrated graphically in Figure 6.2.

Note four points about the function:

1. $U(0) = 0$ (that is, $U = 0$ for $X = 0$). This is allowable regardless of the decision maker's unique tastes for X because, with utility being measured by index numbers, we are free to scale the function as we wish. That is, we can assign index values to any two arbitrarily selected values of X; then, the index values for all other X are uniquely given by the tastes of the decision maker. Thus we arbitrarily select $X = 0$ and assign it a value $U = 0$.

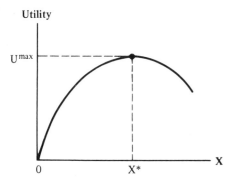

Figure 6.2 Utility function: the relationship between the quantity of a resource and the level of utility achieved.

2. The curve is positively inclined for the smaller values of X. That is, the first derivative of the function, dU/dX (= U′(X)), is positive. This means that, initially at least, additional increments of X add to utility. Hence X is a desired resource (that is, X is a "good," not a "bad").

3. The curve is concave from below. That is, the second derivative of the function, dU′(X)/dX (= U″(X)), is negative. This means that successive additional increments of X result in successively smaller additions to the decision maker's utility. In other words, the decision maker has decreasing marginal utility with respect to X.

4. The curve reaches a maximum at X*, at which point utility becomes a decreasing function of X. At X*, marginal utility is zero (U′(X*) = 0), and for X > X*, marginal utility is negative (U′(X) < 0).

If X is free and hence the decision maker's choice of X is not constrained, we see from Figure 6.2 that the specific quantity, X = X* will be the optimal choice. That is, setting X = X* results in the maximization of utility (U = U^{max}). However, if X can be obtained only at a price (that is, if something else that yields utility must be given up to get X), then some value of X less than X* will be the optimal choice. At this point we would have

$$U'(X) = \lambda P_x \tag{6.2}$$

where P$_x$ = the dollar denominated cost per unit of obtaining X

  λ = a factor that converts this dollar value into a utility denominated measure

In the theory of consumer choice, λ is the marginal utility of income.[9]

λ and P$_x$ are both positive, and thus the marginal utility of X is positive at the optimal quantity of X selected. This means that we need not be concerned with the function at or to the right of its maximum at X*. Consequently, neither need we be concerned with whether or not the function has a maximum.

This lack of concern is important: for many uses to which it is put, it is unrealistic to expect that the utility function would reach a maximum. This is because a maximum implies satiation with respect to X. Although any of us may be satiated by sufficient quantities of most specific products (refrigerators, Broadway plays, or chocolate ice cream sodas), our desire for broad product groups (consumer durables, entertainment, consumption

---

[9]See the discussion in the section "Optimality".

goods, or a well diversified portfolio of financial assets) is generally thought to be unlimited.

The concavity of the curve in Figure 6.2 shows that the consumer has diminishing marginal utility with regard to X. The property of diminishing marginal utility was used by classical economists to explain why demand curves are negatively inclined. The modern theory of consumer choice does not require the assumption. However, a brief look at the classical argument (using current notation) is useful. At any value of P_x, the consumer selects the quantity of X that satisfies equation (6.2). Thus, write equation (6.2) for two separate price/quantity sets $<P_0, X_0>$ and $<P_1, X_1>$ that satisfy

$$U'(X_0) = \lambda P_0 \qquad (6.3)$$
$$U'(X_1) = \lambda P_1$$

Let P_1 be less than P_0; then, assuming λ constant,[10] we must have $U'(X_1) < U'(X_0)$. To attain this with diminishing marginal utility, we must have $X_1 > X_0$. A negatively inclined demand curve for X follows.

X could, on the one hand, stand for the quantity of a specific good such as chocolate ice cream sodas, or it could represent a more inclusive measure of an individual's consumption. For our purposes, it is convenient to treat utility as a function of income or of wealth (the all-inclusive measure of consumption). Interpreted as a utility function for wealth, equation (6.1) would more conventionally be written as $U = f(W)$. This function is of central importance to theories of investing and trading. Several points should be noted with regard to it:

1. Consistent with Figure 6.2, we can arbitrarily set $U(W = 0) = 0$.
2. Consistent with Figure 6.2, we would, for small W, require that $U'(W) > 0$.
3. Contrary to Figure 6.2, we should, over at least some values of W, allow that *increasing* marginal utility with regard to wealth $(U''(W) > 0)$ is a possibility.
4. Contrary to Figure 6.2, we do not expect the utility function defined on wealth to reach a maximum, because satiation with regard to the broadest possible definition of the economic resource does not appear likely.

A decision maker's attitude toward risk can be specified with reference to the utility (of wealth) function. Let the decision maker be offered the following fair bet: h dollars may be won with probability equal to .5, or h dollars may be lost with probability equal to .5. Using the utility function

---

[10]λ (the marginal utility of income) in general changes with income but can be assumed to be constant with respect to the price of X if X is taken to be a sufficiently small part of the individual's consumption basket.

and assuming a starting wealth of W, the decision maker's utility would be $U(W + h)$ if the bet were won, or would be $U(W - h)$ if the bet were lost. Given these utility values and the probabilities of a win and a loss, the decision maker's expected utility if the bet is accepted is

$$E(U) = .5U(W + h) + .5U(W - h) \qquad (6.4)$$

If the bet is not accepted, the decision maker's expected utility is

$$E(U) = U(W) \qquad (6.5)$$

Assume that the act of betting provides no utility (positive or negative), and that the decision maker selects the alternative that yields maximum expected utility. Therefore, if the decision maker does not accept the bet, we must have

$$U(W) > .5U(W + h) + .5U(W - h) \qquad (6.6)$$

Multiplying equation (6.6) by 2, and subtracting $[U(W) + U(W - h)]$ from both sides gives

$$U(W) - U(W - h) > U(W + h) - U(W) \qquad (6.7)$$

Equation (6.7) shows that the increase in the decision maker's utility, as wealth increases by h from $W - h$ to W, is greater than the increase in the decision maker's utility as wealth increases by h from W to $W + h$. Therefore, the decision maker who does not accept a fair bet must have diminishing marginal utility of wealth. Accordingly, we associate risk aversion with diminishing marginal utility. In similar fashion, risk neutrality can be associated with constant marginal utility (of wealth), and risk seeking behavior can be associated with increasing marginal utility (of wealth).

Utility as a function of wealth can be transformed into a function of the rate of return (r) or of income (I). For certain purposes, these are useful transformations to make. The transformations are made by specifying an initial wealth position (W_0), and by writing the rate of return as

$$r_T = \frac{W_T - W_0}{W_0} \qquad (6.8)$$

and income as

$$I = r_T W_0 \qquad (6.9)$$

where the subscript T identifies the future point in time at which the new level of wealth will be attained.

Equations (6.8) and (6.9) show that, given W_0, r_T and I are each linear transformations of W_T. Because transforming these variables in this way is equivalent to rescaling the original function, utility can be written as a function of either a rate of return or income, once we know utility as a function of wealth.

Indifference Curves

Indifference curves, like the utility function, are a representation of the decision maker's tastes. Indifference curves, however, give a clearer picture of the alternatives involved. The curve labeled U_0 in Figure 6.3 is an *indifference curve*. The curve is so named because the decision maker is indifferent about the various combinations of two goods (X and Y) that lie along the curve. The consumer, for instance, is indifferent between the two bundles labeled A and B. Any bundle above and to the right of U_0 is preferred to any bundle on U_0, and any bundle to the left and below U_0 is inferior to any bundle on U_0. For instance, bundle C is preferred to A and B, and bundle D is inferior to A and B.

To see more precisely what is involved, write utility as a function of the quantities of the two goods, X and Y:

$$U = g(X, Y) \tag{6.10}$$

The marginal utility of each good is the change in utility with respect to the change in the quantity of that good. That is,

$$MU_x = \frac{\partial U}{\partial X}$$
$$\tag{6.11}$$
$$MU_y = \frac{\partial U}{\partial Y}$$

Assume that MU_x and MU_y are both positive. It follows that some addition of X will make the decision maker better off, that some subtraction of Y will make the decision maker worse off, and that some combination of more X and less Y will leave the person's utility unaffected. Equivalently, some combination of less X and more Y will also leave the person's utility unaffected. This can be seen in Figure 6.3.

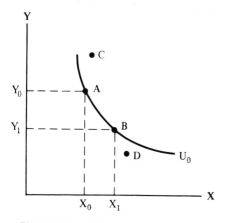

Figure 6.3 Indifference curve.

In Figure 6.3, bundle A is defined by the combination $<X_0, Y_0>$, and bundle B is defined by the combination $<X_1, Y_1>$. Comparing B to A, increasing X by $X_1 - X_0$ adds to the decision maker's utility exactly what decreasing Y by $Y_0 - Y_1$ subtracts. Thus the decision maker is indifferent between the two bundles. An indifference curve is the locus of all such points.

The utility function, equation (6.10), is associated with a family of indifference curves. That is, equation (6.10) shows the utility rating for any combination of X and Y, and each indifference curve is a contour that connects all X, Y combinations that yield the same utility.[11]

Every combination of X and Y has a utility rating, and hence every combination of X and Y must lie on an indifference curve; and so, therefore, must bundles C and D in Figure 6.3. Indifference curves could be drawn through the points C and D. These curves would also be downward sloping (because we have assumed MU_x and MU_y positive). Also, the curves would not cross (intersecting indifference curves imply contradictory utility statements). Finally, each curve would be convex throughout; convexity is consistent with (but does not strictly require) diminishing marginal utility.[12]

Note the following about a family of indifference curves:

1. The mapping is unique to the decision maker. That is, the specific addition of X that has to be made to compensate for any subtraction of Y (or vice versa) depends on the person's unique tastes for the two resources.
2. If X and Y are both desired goods (that is, if for each of them more is preferred to less), the indifference curves are negatively inclined and, throughout the mapping, preferred points lie to the northeast of less preferred points. However, if either X or Y is a bad (that is, less is preferred to more), then the indifference curves are positively inclined; the line of increasing utility slopes toward the northwest (if X is the bad) or to the southeast (if Y is the bad).
3. The objective of the decision maker is to reach the indifference curve with the highest utility rating obtainable. Finding this curve and the optimal values of X and Y is a constrained maximization problem (choice is constrained by scarcity).

The Constraint

The constraint limits the amount of utility the decision maker can attain and, by forcing the decision maker to choose among alternatives, gives rise to the economic problem. In microeconomic theory, the constraint is typ-

---

[11]Equation (6.10) is assumed to be a continuous function.

[12]See any standard microeconomics text for a discussion of these three properties of indifference curves (negatively inclined, nonintersecting, and convex to the origin).

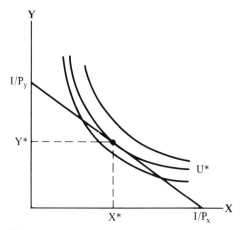

Figure 6.4 Budget constraint and indifference curves.

ically called the *budget constraint*. The budget constraint is most easily defined with respect to two goods (X and Y) that can be obtained at fixed unit prices (P_x and P_y). Assuming the decision maker allocates his or her income (I) entirely between these two goods, we have

$$I = P_xX + P_yY \tag{6.12}$$

Solving for Y gives

$$Y = \frac{I}{P_y} - \frac{P_x}{P_y}X \tag{6.13}$$

Equation (6.13) shows the maximum amount of Y that can be consumed for any amount of X selected. Because I, P_x, and P_y are constant, the constraint is linear. The constraint is presented graphically in Figure 6.4.

Optimality

A set of indifference curves is also shown in Figure 6.4. One of the curves is tangent to the budget constraint. The point of tangency shows the optimal bundle of X and Y to select. The optimal quantities of X and of Y (which define the bundle) are labeled X* and Y*. The tangency solution also shows the maximum utility attainable; the highest indifference curve reached is labeled U*.

The optimal solution can also be obtained analytically. The objective is to maximize $U = g(X, Y)$ subject to the constraint, $I - P_xX - P_yY = 0$. To do so, write the function

$$L = g(X, Y) + \lambda (I - P_xX - P_yY) \tag{6.14}$$

where λ = the Lagrangian multiplier[13]

[13]The Lagrangian multiplier is interpreted later.

Taking the partial derivatives of equation (6.14) with respect to X and Y, equating the derivatives with zero, and using equation (6.11) gives[14]

$$MU_x - \lambda P_x = 0 \qquad (6.15)$$
$$MU_y - \lambda P_y = 0$$

which is consistent with equation (6.2). Rearranging (6.15) gives

$$\frac{MU_x}{MU_y} = \frac{P_x}{P_y} \qquad (6.16)$$

The left-hand side of equation (6.16) can be interpreted. The change in utility caused by any small change in X equal to dX, and small change in Y equal to dY, is

$$dU = \frac{\partial U}{\partial X}dX + \frac{\partial U}{\partial Y}dY \qquad (6.17)$$
$$= MU_x dX + MU_y dY$$

If the associated changes in X and Y leave total utility unchanged, the consumer remains on the same indifference curve, and thus dU = 0, which gives

$$MU_x dX + MU_y dY = 0 \qquad (6.18)$$

Rearranging equation (6.18) gives

$$\frac{dY}{dX} = -\frac{MU_x}{MU_y} \qquad (6.19)$$

where dY/dX is the slope of an indifference curve.[15] Therefore, the left-hand side of equation (6.16) is the negative of the slope of the highest indifference curve the consumer reaches, at the point of optimality.

The right-hand side of equation (6.16) can also be interpreted. The change in expenditures (E) caused by any small change in X equal to dX, and small change in Y equal to dY, is

$$dE = P_x dX + P_y dY \qquad (6.20)$$

When utility is maximized, expenditures equal income, and income is constant; thus dE = 0, which gives

$$P_x dX + P_y dY = 0 \qquad (6.21)$$

Rearranging equation (6.21) gives

$$\frac{dY}{dX} = -\frac{P_x}{P_y} \qquad (6.22)$$

---

[14]We assume the second order conditions for a maximum are satisfied. See any standard microeconomics text for further discussion.

[15]Note that with MU_x, $MU_y > 0$, the indifference curve is negatively inclined, as shown in Figure 6.2.

which is the slope of the constraint described algebraically by equation (6.13) and shown graphically in Figure 6.4. Therefore, the right-hand side of equation (6.16) is the negative of the slope of the consumer's budget constraint.

We therefore see that the solution obtained analytically is consistent with the solution shown graphically in Figure 6.4: the consumer equates the ratio of marginal utilities (MU_x/MU_y) with the ratio of prices (P_x/P_y) by selecting the specific combination $<X^*, Y^*>$ where the indifference curve labeled U^* is tangent to the budget constraint.

The Lagrangian multiplier (λ) in equation (6.14) can also be interpreted. The *Lagrangian multiplier* shows how the maximum realization of the objective is increased for a slight relaxation of the constraint. Here, the objective is to obtain as much utility as possible, and the constraint is relaxed by increasing income a small amount. Hence λ is the marginal utility of income. The interpretation can also be seen by rearranging (6.15) to write $\lambda = MU_x/P_x = MU_y/P_y$. Therefore, when utility is maximized, λ equals the marginal utility per dollar spent on X, equals the marginal utility per dollar spent on Y, equals the marginal utility of a dollar of income.

The Individual's Demand Curve for X

The optimal solution, X^* and Y^*, shows how much X (and Y) the decision maker will select given the price of X (as well as the price of Y and income). Conceptually, it is a simple matter to specify some different value of P_x (keeping P_y and I constant) and to obtain a new utility maximizing solution for the quantity of X demanded. Figure 6.5(a) shows the utility maximizing solution for X for two different prices of X (P_1 and P_2), with P_1 being greater than P_2. The information contained in Figure 6.5(a) is then restated in Figure 6.5(b), where the price of X is shown explicitly as the variable on the vertical axis. Figure 6.5(b) shows that, when the price of X is P_1, X_1 units are demanded, and that when the price is P_2, X_2 units are demanded. With P_2 less than P_1, X_2 is greater than X_1.

The downward sloping line in Figure 6.5(b) is the consumer's demand curve for X; for simplicity, we have taken the curve to be linear. The demand curve is the relationship between the price of X and the optimal selection of X, other relevant variables (other prices, income, and tastes) being constant. To keep terms clear, we refer to this demand curve as the *normal* demand curve.

Consumer Surplus

It is apparent from Figure 6.5 that the decision maker is better off when the price of X is P_2 rather than P_1. The reason is that lowering this one price, other prices and income constant, enables the decision maker to

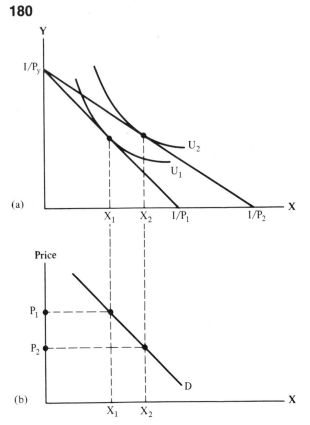

Figure 6.5 Derivation of the decision maker's demand curve for X. (a) Indifference curves and budget constraints. (b) Demand curve.

consume more of all goods (here, X and Y). This can be seen graphically in Figure 6.5(a) by contrasting the two budget constraints. Decreasing the price of X has shifted the X intercept to the right from I/P_1 to I/P_2; since the Y intercept, I/P_y, has not changed, the budget constraint has rotated in a counterclockwise direction around a fixed point on the Y axis. As a result, the options available to the decision maker have increased, and that person can reach a higher level of utility. This is shown in Figure 6.5(a) by the decision maker's moving from the indifference curve labeled U_1 to the higher indifference curve labeled U_2.

The utility gained from moving along the demand curve from $<P_1$, $X_1>$ to $<P_2, X_2>$ is related to the concept of consumer surplus. In fact, what we have just shown is the *change* of consumer surplus that occurs when price decreases in the marketplace. *Consumer surplus* itself is defined as a monetary measure of the *total* gains from trade.

Consumer surplus can be defined precisely with reference to Figure 6.6. Consider Y to be a composite commodity that might be called "money," and let the decision maker start with an initial endowment of Y and no X.

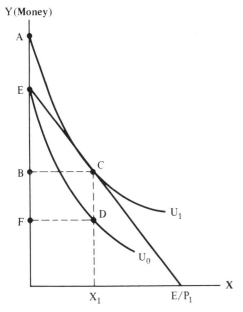

Figure 6.6 Consumer surplus.

This point is labeled E on the diagram. Assume indifference curves originate from the Y axis so that point E has a utility rating: E is on the indifference curve labeled U_0.

When the price of X is P_1, the consumer demands X_1 units, maximizing utility subject to the budget constraint shown graphically by the line from E to E/P_1. In total, the decision maker gives up EB units of Y to get the X_1 units of X and, in the process, increases utility from U_0 to U_1. Utility is not subject to direct measurement, and so $U_1 - U_0$ cannot be taken as a measure of the gains of trade. Nevertheless, the gain can be reflected by a dollar measure.

To obtain this dollar measure, we have drawn the two indifference curves shown in Figure 6.6 so that the vertical distance between them is the same at all values of X.[16] Accordingly, the line segment $\overline{AE}$ equals the line segment $\overline{CD}$. This equality is desirable because each segment has an interpretation that we wish to be consistent with the other. $\overline{AE}$ is a monetary measure of the compensatory increase in the composite commodity, money, that the decision maker would require in order to achieve the utility level U_1 without trading for X. CD is a monetary measure of the amount of the composite commodity that would have to be taken away to restore the decision maker to the initial level of utility (U_0) if that person were to trade $\overline{EB}$ units of Y for X_1 units of X. For $\overline{AE} = \overline{CD}$, each of these magnitudes

[16]The assumption behind this construction is that the ratio of the marginal utilities of the two goods is, at a given value of X, the same for all Y.

is an unambiguous monetary measure of the gains of trade. The measure is called *consumer surplus*.

Reservation Prices

We have thus far focused on how much X the decision maker will demand given the price of X. We now consider the maximum amount the decision maker would be willing to pay for some specific quantity of X (for example, X_1 units). This maximum price per unit is called the *reservation price*.

To obtain the reservation price, the decision maker must be forced to choose between exactly X_1 units, and no X at all. The reason is that if a little bit less of X could be bought, the quantity of X demanded would stray from X_1. Thus, the reservation price is the highest unit price that will be paid for a quantity when the only alternative to that quantity is nothing at all. For this reason, the reservation price is sometimes referred to as an *all-or-nothing price*.

Figure 6.6 shows that, if the price of X is P_1, the decision maker will demand X_1 units. The decision maker pays $\overline{EB}$ units of Y and gains a consumer surplus that is equivalent, in monetary terms, to $\overline{CD}$ units of Y. It is therefore clear that, at most, the decision maker would be willing to pay $\overline{EF} = \overline{EB} + \overline{CD}$ for X_1 units of X. A total expenditure of $\overline{EB} + \overline{CD}$ for X_1 units would keep the consumer on the same indifference curve (that is, would leave that person's total utility unaffected). Therefore, the reservation price per unit for X_1 units is

$$P_1^R = \frac{\overline{EB} + \overline{CD}}{X_1}$$

Clearly, P_1^R is greater than P_1.

The Normal Demand Curve and the Reservation Demand Curve

When a consumer buys an optimal amount of a good at a given price, that price reflects the marginal value of the good to the consumer [see equation (6.2)]. On the other hand, when a reservation price is paid, the consumer realizes no consumer surplus from the trade; this means that the reservation price reflects the average value of the good to the consumer. Recognizing this, we can identify the reservation demand curve and relate it to the normal demand curve defined previously.

First write the normal demand function as[17]

---

[17]X is typically written as a function of P. The exposition is simplified here by writing the inverse function, $P = g(X)$.

$$P = a - bX \qquad (6.23)$$

From equation (6.2), $P_X = U'(X)/\lambda$. Making the substitution and integrating, we get

$$U(X)/\lambda = aX - \tfrac{1}{2}bX^2 \qquad (6.24)$$

where $U(X)/\lambda$ is the monetary value of the total quantity of X consumed. We get the average monetary value for any quantity of X, and thereby obtain the reservation demand curve, by dividing equation (6.24) by X. Thus we have

$$P^R = a - \tfrac{1}{2}bX \qquad (6.25)$$

When the normal demand curve is linear, the reservation demand curve is also linear, and the slope of the normal demand curve (dP/dX) is twice that of the reservation price demand curve, as can be seen by comparing equations (6.23) and (6.25). Both of these curves are shown in Figure 6.7, where the normal demand curve is labeled D^N and the reservation demand curve is labeled D^R.

The two demand curves can be used to derive the consumer surplus realized when the decision maker obtains X_1 units at the price P_1. In Figure 6.6, the consumer surplus associated with this purchase is shown to be the distance $\overline{CD}$. This is because consumer surplus is the difference between the maximum total amount a consumer would be willing to pay in an all-or-nothing situation and the total amount actually paid when quantity is freely adjustable. Given the definition of the reservation price, the consumer in an all-or-nothing situation would be willing to pay $P^R X_1$ for X_1 units. But when the unit price is P_1, the total expenditure is $P_1 X_1$. Therefore, the consumer surplus shown by the distance $\overline{CD}$ in Figure 6.6 is also given in Figure 6.7 by the area

$$P_1 P^R bc = 0P^R bX_1 - 0P_1 cX_1$$

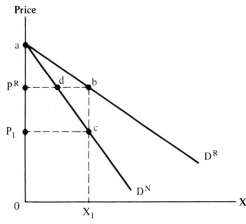

Figure 6.7 Normal (D^N) and reservation (D^R) demand curves.

We can go one step further. Because the slope of D^N is twice that of D^R, the point d is at the midpoint of the line segment P^Rb. Consequently, the triangle P^Rad is equal to the triangle dbc, and so the area of the triangle P_1ac equals the area of the rectangle P_1P^Rbc. Therefore, the triangular area P_1ac under the normal demand curve is also a measure of consumer surplus.

The triangular measure of consumer surplus is useful for showing how consumer surplus changes as price changes and the decision maker moves to a new point along his or her demand curve. To see this, identify consumer surplus by the triangular area under the demand curve for two different prices. The triangular area is larger for the lower price than for the higher price; the difference in the two triangular areas is the increase in consumer surplus that results from the decrease in price.

Supply Curves

When individuals supply their labor services or their income (in the form of interest bearing loans or equity investments) to the market, their supply decisions are made with reference to utility functions in much the same way that consumption decisions are made. The individual's supply curve is a statement of how much of a resource he or she will offer to the market as a function of price (all else constant). The major difference between the supply curve and the demand curve is that the supply curve is usually taken to be upward sloping, whereas we have shown that the demand curve is generally a downward sloping function of price.

Given a supply curve, we can also define the concepts of *producer surplus* (it is analogous to consumer surplus) and *reservation sell price* (it is analogous to a reservation buy price). Further, we can distinguish between a normal supply curve and a reservation supply curve. These curves, along with producer surplus, are shown in Figure 6.8, where the normal

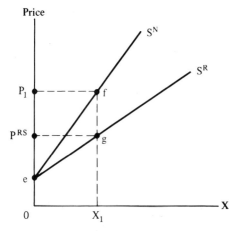

Figure 6.8   Normal supply curve (S^N), reservation supply curve (S^R), and reservation sell price (P^{RS}).

supply curve is labeled S^N, the reservation supply curve is labeled S^R, and the reservation sell price is identified as P^{RS}. In Figure 6.8, the rectangular area $P^{RS}P_1fg$ and the triangular area eP_1f are both equal to producer surplus.

AGGREGATION AND MARKET CLEARING

Aggregation from Individual to Market Demand-Supply Curves

Assume that N buyers and M sellers constitute the market for X. For each ith buyer, let the demand function for X be

$$X_i = D_i(P) \tag{6.26}$$

For each jth seller, let the supply function for X be

$$X_j = S_j(P) \tag{6.27}$$

The *aggregate quantity* demanded and supplied at each price is the summation of all individual quantities demanded and supplied. Thus the market demand function is

$$D(P) = \sum_{i=1}^{N} X_i = \sum_{i=1}^{N} D_i(P) \tag{6.28}$$

and the market supply function is

$$S(P) = \sum_{j=1}^{M} X_j = \sum_{j=1}^{M} S_j(P) \tag{6.29}$$

The summation is shown graphically in Figure 6.9 for the aggregate demand curve. For simplicity, we have taken the number of buyers to be two. At prices greater than a_2, aggregate demand is zero. Individual 2 enters the market at a price of a_2 and is the sole market participant until price drops to a_1. At the price a_1, individual 1 also enters the market (note the kink in the market demand curve at a_1). Below a_1 market demand is the aggregate of both individuals' demands. Equation (6.28) is illustrated in Figure 6.9 at the arbitrarily selected price P_0. At P_0:

$$D_1(P_0) = X_1$$
$$D_2(P_0) = X_2$$
$$D(P_0) = X_1 + X_2$$

Market Clearing

A market *clears* when the price is such that the total number of units demanded in the market by buyers equals the total number of units supplied

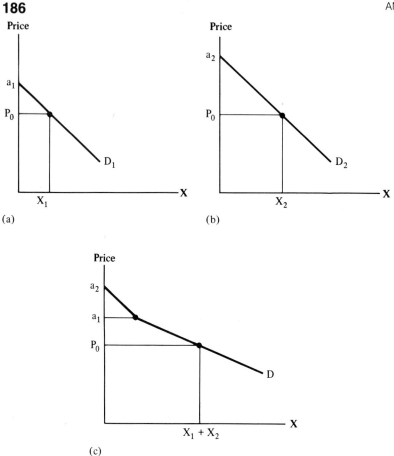

Figure 6.9 Derivation of the aggregate demand curve. (a) Demand curve of buyer 1. (b) Demand curve of buyer 2. (c) Combined demand curve for buyer 1 and buyer 2.

by sellers. The price that clears the market is a stable equilibrium price if a higher price would induce an excess of supply (which exerts downward pressure on price), and if a lower price would induce an excess of demand (which exerts upward pressure on price). With the demand curve downward sloping and the supply curve upward sloping, this condition is satisfied and the clearing price is a stable equilibrium price.

However, a second condition must also be fulfilled in order that the market clearing price be an equilibrium price: all buy and sell desires at the price must be fully and simultaneously expressed in the market. This condition is implicit in standard economic analysis, because demand and supply propensities are assumed to be fully revealed to the market. The reason is that economic theory typically assumes a frictionless world (that is, that trading in the market is a costless process). For the remainder of this chapter, we assume this condition is satisfied.

To obtain the market clearing price, let the number of buyers (N) and the number of sellers (M) be large enough so that no individual participant has significant market power; that is, assume all participants are price takers. Price takers simply "accept" the market determined price and adjust their own demand or supply to it (price takers are too small to have a perceptible impact on the clearing price). The market clearing price is then solved for by setting equation (6.28) equal to equation (6.29). Thus the market clearing equation is

$$D(P^*) = S(P^*) \qquad\qquad 6.30)$$

where the symbol * indicates that P is the equilibrium solution for price. Having used equation (6.30) to solve for P*, we can substitute P* into either equation (6.28) or (6.29) and solve for X*, the equilibrium value of X.

The determination of P* and X* is illustrated graphically in Figure 6.10. The solution for these variables is given by the intersection of the market demand curve (D) and the market supply curve (S). When D is downward sloping and S is upward sloping, P*, X* is a stable equilibrium solution: as shown in Figure 6.10, at any price P' greater than P*, supply exceeds demand (which causes price to fall toward P*), and at any price P'' less than P*, demand exceeds supply (which causes price to rise toward P*).

Pareto Optimality

We assess the market clearing solution (P*, Q*) by focusing initially on the demand side of the market. The purpose of the assessment is to show that the frictionless market achieves an efficient distribution of resources.

When P* is established as the market price for X, each ith buyer demands the specific quantity of X given by equation (6.26) assessed at

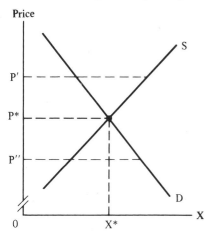

Figure 6.10 Determination of equilibrium price (P*) and equilibrium value of X (X*).

$P = P^*$. In equilibrium, the price (P^*) reflects the marginal value of X to the ith buyer. Assume that N buyers each allocates income over two goods, X and Y, and that the market for Y has also achieved an equilibrium solution, P_y^*, Y^*.

Equation (6.16) shows that when any i^{th} buyer optimally allocates his or her income, the ratio of the marginal utility of the two goods is equal to the ratio of the prices. Since P_x^* and P_y^* are the same for all buyers, the ratio of marginal utilities must be the same for all buyers. That is, we must have

$$\left(\frac{MU_x}{MU_y}\right)_i = \frac{P_x^*}{P_y^*} \qquad \text{for each buyer, } i = 1, \ldots, N \qquad (6.31)$$

Equation (6.31) shows that when X and Y are distributed across the N buyers according to the consumer choice and market equilibrium models shown previously, it would not be possible to redistribute these resources so as to make at least one buyer better off without making at least one other buyer worse off. This concept stated in economic terminology is, the distribution of X and Y across the N buyers is Pareto optimal. *Pareto optimal* means that no one individual can be made better off without at least one other individual being made worse off.

An opportunity to trade exists whenever a distribution of resources is not Pareto optimal (assuming a market structure to handle the trade). For instance, consider two individuals (A and B) and two goods (X and Y) and let

$$\left(\frac{MU_x}{MU_y}\right)_A > \left(\frac{MU_x}{MU_y}\right)_B \qquad (6.32)$$

Because on the margin the first individual values X relative to Y more than does the second individual, there is some (marginal) exchange of X and Y between A and B that will enable both to achieve a higher level of utility. Thus, with the inequality shown in (6.32), the distribution of X and Y across individuals A and B is not Pareto optimal. Conversely, when equality holds, the distribution is Pareto optimal.[18]

The concept can be clarified with the graph shown in Figure 6.11. The width of the box in Figure 6.11 shows the total amount of good X available to the two traders (A and B), and the height of the box shows the total amount of good Y available to the two traders. The lower left-hand

---

[18]To see this, reverse the process: if an exchange is made given that (6.32) is initially in equality, equality cannot hold after the trade. Then, for one of the traders to have been made better off, the other trader must have been made worse off. Since no exchange exists that could make both traders better off, the equality of (6.32) implies a Pareto optimal distribution.

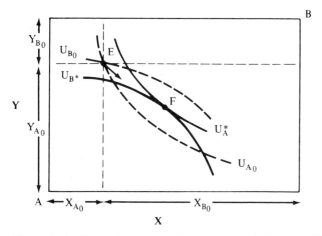

Figure 6.11 Determination of a Pareto optimal distribution of X and Y among traders A and B.

corner of the box represents the origin for trader A, and the upper right-hand corner represents the origin for trader B. Let the starting allocation of resources between A and B be given by point E.

Because A and B both gain utility from both goods, A seeks to move as far as possible to the northeast, and B seeks to move as far as possible to the southwest. Note, however, that a move in the southeasterly direction toward the point labeled F will make both individuals better off (both can reach higher indifference curves than the curves drawn through point E). At point F, further trade would be undesirable. This is because for one trader to reach a higher indifference curve, the other must be forced to a lower indifference curve. The distribution represented by point F is, there-fore, Pareto optimal.[19] The distribution represented by point E is not.

The concept of Pareto optimality also applies to the quantities of X and Y that are being produced, given the cost to suppliers and the benefits to buyers. It can be shown by using the microeconomic theory of the firm that, in the competitive equilibrium we have described, each firm produces at a rate that equates the marginal cost of production with the market price of the resource produced. Thus for resources X and Y,

$$P_x^* = MC_x \qquad \text{for each } j^{th} \text{ seller of X} \qquad (6.33)$$

and

$$P_y^* = MC_y \qquad \text{for each } j^{th} \text{ seller of Y} \qquad (6.34)$$

[19]Notice that, at point F, the ratio of marginal utilities is the same for the two traders (because their indifference curves are tangent and thus have the same slope).

Dividing equation (6.33) by equation (6.34) gives

$$\frac{P_x^*}{P_y^*} = \frac{MC_x}{MC_y} \tag{6.35}$$

Equations (6.31) and (6.35) together imply

$$\left(\frac{MU_x}{MU_y}\right)_i = \frac{MC_x}{MC_y} \qquad \text{for each buyer, i} = 1 \ldots \text{N.} \tag{6.36}$$

Equation (6.36) shows that, in equilibrium, X and Y are valued on the margin in the same proportion by all consumers, and that this proportion is equal to the cost on the margin of producing X, relative to the cost on the margin of producing Y. Hence both the distribution of resources in the production of X and Y, and the distribution of X and Y across buyers, are Pareto optimal.

We have described the efficiency of allocating resources according to the individual choice model and the market equilibrium model described in this chapter. When resources are so allocated, the market has accomplished its job of effecting all desired trades. When these trades have been made, there is no unsatisfied desire among market participants to trade further or to recontract. The allocation of resources is Pareto optimal; the market price is a Pareto optimal price; and we have achieved all that could be expected from a trading system. For this reason, the Pareto optimal solutions provide the ideal against which to assess solutions attained in a less than perfect trading environment.

Walrasian *Tâtonnement*

The Pareto optimal values of P_x^* and X^* were obtained by solving two simultaneous equations: the demand equation (6.28) and the supply equation (6.29). Prices and quantities, of course, are not found this way in actual markets, but rather are the result of real world processes. It is of interest, however, to consider how market clearing might be achieved if trading were a costless activity.

The French economist Leon Walras (1834–1910) envisaged buyers and sellers of a resource (X) being brought together by an auctioneer who calls out tentative prices. The process of finding a solution by a series of tentative trials is known as a *Walrasian tâtonnement*. Assume that the prices of other resources have been established and that we can focus separately on the market for X. At any price at which the demand for X exceeds supply, a higher price is called out; or, if supply exceeds demand, a lower price is called out. The *tâtonnement* process is continued until the clearing price is found. When that price is found, buyers and sellers trade optimally.

As a result of the Walrasian *tâtonnement* process, X* units are traded at a price of P*, the solution to the two simultaneous equations.

THE TIME DIMENSION

Stocks versus Flows

Stock refers to one way of measuring quantity, *flow* to another way. *Stocks* are quantities measured at some moment of time—the stockpile of raw materials in a warehouse, the number of loaves of bread on a supermarket shelf, the amount of money in one's pocket, the value of assets/liabilities on a balance sheet, the quantity of water in a reservoir, and so on. *Flows*, on the other hand, are quantities that are measured over some period of time—the hourly flow of water out of a reservoir, a monthly earnings figure, the number of cans of beer consumed per quarter, one's annual income, and so on.

We have been discussing two variables, quantity (X) and X's unit price (P). Is the quantity of X stock or flow dimensioned?

For many resources, quantity can be measured as either a stock or a flow, depending on the specific purpose of the study. That is, one could refer to car sales per year (a flow), to the total number of cars in existence at any moment in time (a stock), to the relationship between the price of cars and the frequency with which a household might buy a new car (a flow), or to the relationship between the price of cars and the number of one car families, the number of two car families, and so on (a stock).

Most microeconomic models treat quantity as a flow variable, and we have implicitly done so in our discussion thus far. For instance, equation (6.12), which is used to obtain the budget constraint, equates income (I) with total expenditures ($P_xX + P_yY$). Since income is a flow variable, then so too must be expenditures; because price in this context has no time dimension, X and Y must themselves be flow variables. For this reason, a statement such as "The quantity of X demanded is 12 units when the price per unit is $5" means that the time *rate* of consumption is 12 (for example, per day, per month, or per year, depending on the interval used to express income and consumption).

With regard to investing and trading, quantity is stock, not flow dimensioned. That is, at a given price per share, the investor decides how many shares of an asset to *hold*, not how many to buy, as a rate per unit of time. Suppose, for instance, that at a price of $50 per share the investor would like to hold 150 shares, and that the investor currently has 200 shares in his or her portfolio. The decision then is simply to sell 50 shares, not to keep on selling 50 shares per day, per month, or whatever. Therefore, just as the decision to hold 150 shares is stock dimensioned, so too is the decision to adjust the portfolio holdings by 50 shares.

The Stock Dimensioned Demand Curve to Hold Shares

Figure 6.12(a) shows the demand curve (labeled D) of an investor to hold shares of an asset. This curve resembles the curve labeled D^N in Figure 6.7, and with minor exceptions it is the same. In Figure 6.12(a), the quantity variable (the number of shares held) is denoted by the symbol N. N_0 identifies the number of shares currently held. For this demand curve, the investor would want to hold the N_0 shares at a price per share of P_0.

Given the demand to hold shares (D) and the current share holdings (N_0), we can determine the number of shares the investor would want to buy or to sell as price varies from P_0. This information is shown in Figure 6.12(b) by the downward sloping curve labeled *Buy*, and by the upward sloping curve labeled *Sell*.

The symbol Q in Figure 6.12 denotes the number of shares the investor would like to add to or subtract from his or her portfolio. Sell orders can be graphed as positive values of Q because the upward sloping function is labeled *Sell* (in other words, a negative buy order is equivalent to a positive sell). For instance, if the share price is P_2, Figure 6.12(a) shows that the investor would want to hold $N_0 - Q_2$ shares. Accordingly, Figure 6.12(b) shows that, at price P_2, he or she will seek to sell a positive number, Q_2. Alternatively, if price is P_1, the investor's optimal holdings will be $N_0 + Q_1$ shares, and the investor will want to buy Q_1 shares.

Generalizing over all values of P gives the buy and sell curves in Figure 6.12(b). These can be found geometrically from the demand curve in Figure 6.12(a): place a mirror on the vertical line at N_0, project the segment of the demand curve to the left of N_0 onto the quadrant to the right of N_0 (note that the mirror image is positively inclined), and change the origin from zero shares to N_0 shares.

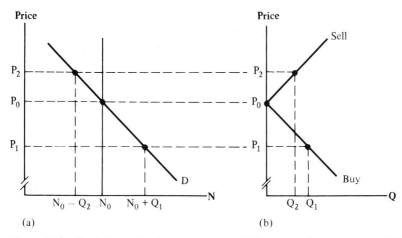

Figure 6.12 Stock dimensional demand curves. (a) Investor's demand curve to hold shares. (b) Investor's buy and sell curves.

Recapitulation

1. Like any demand curve, the stock dimensioned demand curve can be derived from a utility function. For this derivation, we may treat utility as a function of wealth.

2. An investor gains consumer surplus by trading in relation to this demand curve. Referring to Figure 6.12, utility will be greater if an investor is able to buy at a price less than P_0, or sell at a price greater than P_0.

3. We could label the demand curve in Figure 6.12 D^N and then obtain the reservation demand curve associated with it. The reservation curve would pass through $<P_0, N_0>$, but would have half the slope (dP/dN).

4. There is no *supply* curve associated with the market's aggregate demand to hold shares. With a given aggregate number of shares outstanding for an asset, investors simply trade the fixed number of shares among themselves.

5. Each trader has a demand curve to hold shares; given this curve, each specific trader will be either a buyer or a seller depending on the asset's price and his or her initial share holdings.

6. Aggregate market buy and sell curves can be obtained from the individual buy/sell curves illustrated in Figure 6.12(b) according to the aggregation process described by equations (6.28) and (6.29).

7. The market clearing price can be obtained according to the market clearing process described by equation (6.30).

8. If the market is frictionless, the aggregation and market clearing processes result in a Pareto optimal share price and distribution of shares across investors.

9. The procedure for finding the clearing price in a frictionless environment can be considered a Walrasian *tâtonnement*. Interestingly, for traders actually present on the trading floor of the Paris Bourse or in other call markets, the trading system does resemble a Walrasian *tâtonnement*, except for the fact that the markets for different issues are not called simultaneously.

CONCLUSION

There are five approaches to understanding the workings of the security markets: institutional description, theoretical analysis, empirical analysis, experimentation, and examination of institutional and legal history. All five approaches are relevant and, with the exception of the fourth (experimentation), all are used in this book.

For the most part, however, our examination is structured around a theoretical framework. The reason is threefold. First, theory is precise: it provides a specific vocabulary and a rigorous methodology. Second, theory gives a conceptualization of the problems that affect the equity markets and of the forces that drive market events. Third, a theoretical formulation may enable one to predict the impact of structural change, and hence to assess the potential effectiveness of a new and untried trading system, or of a new and untried regulatory change.

Having established the central role that theory must play, the chapter next considered the relevance of standard microeconomic analysis for our purposes. We noted one major limitation—that traditional microeconomic analysis is based on the assumption that markets are frictionless (that is, that trading is a costless process). Nevertheless, despite this limitation, the standard tools of microeconomic analysis are essential. Furthermore, recent developments have provided the foundation needed for this book. These developments have occurred in the economics of uncertainty, the economics of information, and the auction pricing literature. Most importantly, a sizable body of material now exists on the microstructure of the security markets.

The review of microeconomic theory presented in this chapter has focused primarily on the consumer choice model, on market clearing, and on an assessment of the market clearing results. We have defined reservation prices and have distinguished reservation demand and supply curves from normal demand and supply curves. We have also given special emphasis to the concept of consumer surplus, to the Walrasian *tâtonnement* process, and to the Pareto optimality of market clearing in a frictionless environment. These concepts will be used in subsequent chapters of the book.

The stock dimensioned demand curve to hold shares, along with the related buy and sell curves, is discussed more fully in later chapters. Chapter 7 shows how this demand curve may be obtained in the context of portfolio analysis and establishes the negative slope of the curve. Chapter 8 shows how an individual investor might specify a buy or sell order to transmit to the market, given this demand curve to hold shares; the investor's expectation of what the market clearing price will be; and the design of the trading system that determines how the order will be handled and the rules by which it will be executed. Chapter 9 considers the aggregation of buy and sell orders over investors and the determination of market clearing prices in a nonfrictionless market.

Trading can in theory generate an efficient distribution of resources among market participants. Knowledge of the process and its benefits is essential to understanding the equity markets. Microeconomics, the study of resource allocation, provides a vocabulary and a methodology we could not do without. In addition, we have used microeconomic analysis to establish the theoretical ideal against which the performance of actual markets can be assessed.

SUGGESTED READING

G. Akerlof, "The Market for 'Lemons': Quality Uncertainty and the Market Mechanism," *Quarterly Journal of Economics,* August 1970.

T. Copeland and D. Friedman, "The Effect of Sequential Information Arrival on Asset Prices: An Experimental Study," *Journal of Finance,* June 1987.

H. Demsetz, "The Cost of Transacting," *Quarterly Journal of Economics,* October 1968.

R. Engelbrecht-Wiggans, "Auctions and Bidding Models: A Survey," *Management Science,* February 1980.

D. Friedman, G. Harrison, and H. Salmon, "The Informational Efficiency of Experimental Asset Markets," *Journal of Political Economy,* June 1984.

J. Henderson and R. Quandt, *Microeconomic Theory: A Mathematical Approach,* New York: McGraw-Hill, third edition, 1980.

J. Hirshleifer and J. Riley, "The Analytics of Uncertainty and Information: An Expository Survey," *Journal of Economic Literature,* December 1979.

J. Hong and C. Plott, "Rate Filing Policies for Inland Water Transportation: An Experimental Approach," *Bell Journal of Economics,* Spring 1982.

R. Isaac and C. Plott, "Price Control and the Behavior of Auction Markets: An Experimental Examination," *American Economic Review,* June 1981.

M. Machina, "Choice Under Uncertainty: Problems Solved and Unsolved," *Journal of Economic Perspectives,* Summer 1987.

R. P. McAfee and J. McMillan, "Auctions and Bidding," *Journal of Economic Literature,* June 1987.

C. Plott, "Industrial Organization Theory and Experimental Economics," *Journal of Economic Literature,* December 1982.

C. Plott, "Laboratory Experiments in Economics: The Implications of Posted-Price Institutions," *Science,* 1986.

C. Plott and V. Smith, "An Experimental Examination of Two Exchange Institutions," *Review of Economic Studies,* February 1978.

C. Plott and S. Sunder, "Efficiency of Experimental Security Markets with Insider Information: An Application of Rational Expectations Models," *Journal of Political Economy,* August 1982.

P. Schoemaker, "The Expected Utility Model: Its Variants, Purposes, Evidence and Limitations," *Journal of Economic Literature,* June 1982.

V. Smith, "An Experimental Study of Competitive Market Behavior," *Journal of Political Economy,* April 1962.

V. Smith, "Microeconomic Systems as an Experimental Science," *American Economic Review,* December 1982.

V. Smith and A. Williams, "On Nonbinding Price Controls in a Competitive Market," *American Economic Review,* June 1981.

G. Stigler, "Public Regulation of the Securities Markets," *Journal of Business,* April 1964.

chapter 7

The Pricing of Risky Assets

Equity shares are evaluated according to their risk, return, and liquidity. This chapter abstracts from liquidity and establishes a framework for pricing risky assets in relation to risk and return parameters.

The chapter serves three functions. First, it develops the link between trading and traditional portfolio analysis. Second, it presents the demand curve of an investor to hold shares of a risky asset. Third, it shows how investment decisions are made and equity prices are established in a frictionless securities market. As in Chapter 6, the frictionless market formulation is an ideal against which to contrast actual market results.

The chapter discusses optimal portfolio selection as a constrained maximization problem. We begin by establishing the maximization of the expected utility of wealth as the goal of the investor. Next we show how the mean and variance of portfolio returns are related to the means, variances, and covariances of individual stock returns. We then derive the constraint that in portfolio theory plays the role that the budget constraint plays in the standard consumer choice model. The section concludes with a discussion of the optimal portfolio decision.

Next the analysis is extended to show how the prices of risky assets would be determined in a "perfect world" described by zero transaction costs, no taxes, homogeneous expectations, and unlimited borrowing and lending at a risk-free rate of interest. The model presented is the *capital asset pricing model*.

Then the market model, a more general relationship between the return on an asset and the return on the market, is set forth. The market model is used to distinguish between two types of risk: *systematic risk* (also called *undiversifiable risk*) and *unsystematic risk* (also called *diversifiable risk*).

The following section derives the investor's demand curve to hold shares of the market portfolio in an environment where the individual allocates his or her wealth between shares of the market portfolio and the risk-free asset. This derivation is used to obtain the normal and reservation demand curves discussed in Chapter 6 and to show how, in a perfect world, equilibrium prices are established for the market portfolio and the risk-free asset.

The demand to hold shares of a risky asset when the strict assumptions of the capital asset pricing model are relaxed is analyzed. Three possible outcomes are considered: (1) that the demand curve is infinitely elastic because different assets are sufficiently close substitutes for one another, (2) that the demand curve for a risky asset is positively inclined because of a wealth effect, and (3) that the demand curve is positively inclined because current prices convey informational signals and hence generate an expectations effect. We show that none of these three possibilities is likely to prevail.

PORTFOLIO SELECTION

The Objective

Let three points in time, $T = 0, 1, 2$, identify two time periods: (1) the period from 0 to 1 is a brief trading period (for example, one day), and the period from 1 to 2 is an individual's holding (investment) period (for instance, one year). The individual seeks to maximize the expected utility of wealth that will be realized at the end of the investment period, $T = 2$. Following our discussion in Chapter 6, write that person's utility function for wealth as

$$U = U(W_2)$$

where the subscript 2 denotes wealth at $T = 2$.

The decision maker's portfolio at the start of the investment period, $T = 1$, is described by the share holdings N_{i1}, $i = 1, \ldots, M$ assets. Assume that the portfolio's composition is not altered over the holding period (this is the standard assumption of single period analysis). Thus for each ith asset, $N_{i1} = N_{i2}$. Therefore we can suppress the time identification on share holdings and write

$$W_2 = \sum_{i=1}^{M} P_{i2}N_i$$

where P_{i2} is the price of the ith asset at time $T = 2$.

The investor controls the value of W_2 by his or her selection of the N_i. However, because the change of share value for each security is subject to variation, the investor does not have total control over the future value of the portfolio, but rather is faced with a set of uncertain outcomes. For this reason, the investor is not able simply to maximize utility, as discussed in Chapter 6. Rather, decisions are made with reference to *expected* utility.

Following the standard Von Neumann-Morgenstern approach, we take the investor's objective to be the maximization of the expected utility of wealth.[1] Specifically, the investor seeks to

$$\underset{N_i}{\text{Max}} \ E[U(W_2)] = \underset{N_i}{\text{Max}} \int U(W)f(W) \ dW \qquad (7.1)$$

where E is the *expectations operator* and f(W) is a *probability density function*. The utility function itself $[U(W_2)]$ has the properties discussed in Chapter 6. The maximization is with respect to the specification of the N_i.[2]

The investor obtains the N_i, $i = 1, \ldots, M$, which maximize the expected utility of W_2 by optimally combining assets according to their risk and return characteristics. Accordingly, we will consider how the risk/return characteristics of individual stocks are related to the risk/return characteristics of a portfolio.

With initial wealth (W_0) given, first write utility as a function of the portfolio return, r_P. That is, rewrite $U(W_2)$ as $v(r_P)$.[3] An advantage of dealing with r_P rather than with W_2 is that the parameters of the returns distribution relate to a portfolio's composition and are independent of an individual decision maker's own wealth position.

For theoretical analysis, we assume r_P to be normally distributed. This is convenient, because it enables two parameters alone (mean and variance)

---

[1]This objective is not directly assumed in the Von Neumann-Morgenstern formulation, but rather is implied by a more basic set of assumptions. See Baumol (1977) for further discussion.

[2]There are alternatives to the maximization of expected utility: the maximization of the geometric mean return and various safety first criteria. For further discussion, see Elton and Gruber (1986).

[3]We showed in Chapter 6 that $v(r_P)$ is a linear transformation of U(W).

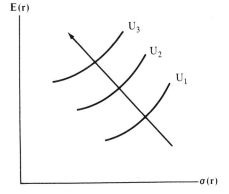

E(r)

$\sigma(r)$

Figure 7.1 Risk averse investors realize higher expected utility with a greater expected return (variance constant), or with a lower variance of returns (expected return constant).

to describe the returns distribution.[4] Therefore, for normally distributed returns, we rewrite $v(r_P)$ as[5]

$$U(W_2) = f[E(r_P), Var(r_P)] \tag{7.2}$$

where $E(r_P)$ is the *mean return* and $Var(r_P)$ is the *variance of returns* over the investment period.

From equation (7.2), it can be shown (and it is easy to accept intuitively) that risk averse investors realize higher expected utility with a greater expected return (variance constant) or with a lower variance of returns (expected return constant). This is shown in Figure 7.1, where we display a family of mean-variance indifference curves. The investor maximizes expected utility by attaining the highest possible indifference curve in mean-variance (of returns) space. The arrow pointing to the northwest in Figure 7.1 shows the direction of increasing utility.

The Mean and Variance of Portfolio Returns

Like the consumer choice problem modeled in Chapter 6, optimal portfolio selection is a constrained maximization problem. For portfolio selection, however, the constraint is not the budget constraint, but rather is given by the set of risk/return combinations available in the marketplace. To derive this constraint, it is necessary to compute portfolio mean and variance from

[4]The third moment of the returns distribution, *skewness,* has also been considered in some portfolio selection models. For further discussion, see Elton and Gruber (1986).

[5]There are two other conditions under which utility can be written as a function of mean and variance: (1) quadratic utility and (2) lognormally distributed returns. Economists differ in their willingness to assume quadratic utility. The empirical evidence suggests that returns distributions are approximately lognormal, however, and the assumption of lognormality is widely accepted. To simplify the discussion here, we assume that returns are distributed normally.

the means, variances, and covariances of individual assets. This is done as follows:

The return on the ith asset in the portfolio is[6]

$$R_i = \frac{P_{i2}}{P_{i1}} = \frac{P_{i1} + \Delta P_i}{P_{i1}} = 1 + r_i \qquad (7.3)$$

where R_i is a *price relative;* $\Delta P_i = P_{i2} - P_{i1}$; and r_i has the standard returns dimension with which most people are more accustomed.[7] The change in the value of a portfolio over the investment period is

$$\Delta W = \sum_{i=1}^{M} \Delta P_i N_i, \qquad (7.4)$$

The return on the portfolio is

$$r_P = \frac{\Delta W}{W_1}$$

$$= \frac{\sum_{i=1}^{M} \Delta P_i N_i}{W_1} \qquad (7.5)$$

Rewrite equation (7.5) as

$$r_P = \sum_{i=1}^{M} \left(\frac{P_{i1} N_i}{W_1}\right)\left(\frac{\Delta P_i}{P_{i1}}\right) \qquad (7.6)$$

The dollar weight of the ith stock in the portfolio is

$$k_i = \frac{P_{i1} N_i}{W_1} \qquad (7.7)$$

Substituting equation (7.7) into (7.6) and using the definition of r_i gives

$$r_P = \sum_{i=1}^{M} k_i r_i \qquad (7.8)$$

Taking expectations of equation (7.8) gives the expected (mean) return,

$$E[r_P] = \sum_{i=1}^{M} k_i E[r_i] \qquad (7.9)$$

---

[6]Any dividend paid during the period is assumed to be paid at time $T = 2$, and P_{i2} is the actual price plus the dividend per share.

[7]R is used in some places in the text and r in others, depending on which is simpler in context to treat mathematically.

Taking variances gives

$$\text{Var } (r_P) = \sum_{i=1}^{M} \sum_{j=1}^{M} k_i k_j \sigma_i \sigma_j \rho_{ij} \tag{7.10}$$

where σ_i is the standard deviation of returns on the ith asset, and ρ_{ij} is the correlation between the return on the ith and the jth assets.[8] Equations (7.9) and (7.10) show how the means, variances, and covariances for a set of stocks combined in a specific way (that is, a specific set of portfolio weights) result in specific values for the mean and variance of the portfolio's return.

The Constraint

Different assets can be combined in a portfolio in many different ways, and a set of alternative portfolios is available to the decision maker. This set is called *the feasible set*. The decision maker balances the portfolio weights so as to obtain the one portfolio in the feasible set that maximizes his or her expected utility.

   The methodology used here differs from that used in Chapter 6 in two respects. First, the constraint with respect to which expected utility is maximized is not defined by income (or wealth) and current prices, but rather is given by the set of available risk/return combinations. Second, because of the positive slope of the risk/return indifference curves, a positively inclined portion of the boundary of the feasible set is identified as the constraint.

   Equation (7.9) shows that the portfolio's expected return is an average of the individual stock returns, with each return weighted by the stock's dollar importance in the portfolio. Equation (7.10) shows that the relationship between the returns variance for the portfolio and the returns variances for the stocks is more complicated. To analyze the stock/portfolio variance relationship, write equation (7.10) for two stocks (A and B):

$$\text{Var } (r_P) = k_A^2 \text{ Var } (r_A) + k_B^2 \text{ Var } (r_B) + 2k_A k_B \sigma_A \sigma_B \rho_{AB} \tag{7.11}$$

[8]The Var (r_P) equation follows the rule that the *variance* of a sum is equal to the sum of the variances plus twice the sum of the covariances. To see this, consider the case where there are only two assets (asset 1 and asset 2):

$$\sigma_1 \sigma_1 \rho_{11} = \sigma_1^2 \qquad \text{for } i, j = 1, \text{ since } \rho_{11} = 1$$
$$\sigma_2 \sigma_2 \rho_{22} = \sigma_2^2 \qquad \text{for } i, j = 2, \text{ since } \rho_{22} = 1$$
$$\sigma_1 \sigma_2 \rho_{12} = \sigma_2 \sigma_1 \rho_{21} \qquad \text{for } i = 1, j = 2 \text{ and } i = 2, \quad j = 1$$

Substituting into the variance equation gives

$$\sigma_p^2 = k_1^2 \sigma_1^2$$
$$+ k_2^2 \sigma_2^2$$
$$+ 2k_1 k_2 \sigma_1 \sigma_2 \rho_{12}$$

where $\sigma_1 \sigma_2 \rho_{12} = \text{Cov}_{12}$

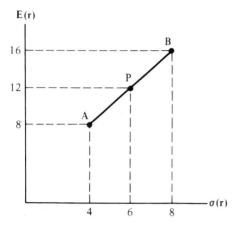

Figure 7.2 Mean and standard deviation parameters for a two stock (A and B) portfolio, $P_{AB} = 1$.

If the returns on the two stocks are perfectly correlated ($\rho_{AB} = 1$), equation (7.11) is a perfect square. Thus we have

$$\text{Var}(r_P) = (k_A\sigma_A + k_B\sigma_B)^2 \qquad \text{for } \rho_{AB} = 1 \qquad (7.12a)$$

$$\text{Var}(r_P) < (k_A\sigma_A + k_B\sigma_B)^2 \qquad \text{for } \rho_{AB} < 1 \qquad (7.12b)$$

Taking square roots of (7.12) gives

$$\sigma_P = k_A\sigma_A + k_B\sigma_B \qquad \text{for } \rho_{AB} = 1 \qquad (7.13a)$$

$$\sigma_P < k_A\sigma_A + k_B\sigma_B \qquad \text{for } \rho_{AB} < 1 \qquad (7.13b)$$

We see that the portfolio return's *standard deviation* is the weighted average of the *standard deviations* of the individual stock returns if the stock returns are perfectly correlated with each other. Thus we generally deal with means and standard deviations, even though the term *mean-variance analysis* is commonly used.[9]

---

[8]The Var (r_P) equation follows the rule that the *variance* of a sum is equal to the sum of the variances plus twice the sum of the covariances. To see this, consider the case where there are only two assets (asset 1 and asset 2):

$$\sigma_1\sigma_1\rho_{11} = \sigma_1^2 \qquad \text{for } i, j = 1, \text{ since } \rho_{11} = 1$$

$$\sigma_2\sigma_2\rho_{22} = \sigma_2^2 \qquad \text{for } i, j = 2, \text{ since } \rho_{22} = 1$$

$$\sigma_1\sigma_2\rho_{12} = \sigma_2\sigma_1\rho_{21} \qquad \text{for } i = 1, j = 2 \text{ and } i = 2, \ j = 1$$

Substituting into the variance equation gives

$$\begin{aligned} \sigma_P^2 = \ &k_1^2\sigma_1^2 \\ &+ k_2^2\sigma_2^2 \\ &+ 2k_1k_2\sigma_1\sigma_2\rho_{12} \end{aligned}$$

where $\sigma_1\sigma_2\rho_{12} = \text{Cov}_{12}$

[9]Notice that the horizontal axis of Figure 7.1 is labeled $\sigma(r)$. Mean-standard deviation indifference curves are also simpler to deal with on the utility side of the analysis, although here too the term *mean-variance* is commonly used.

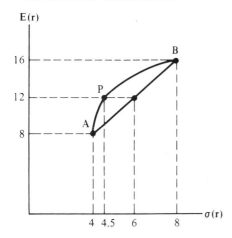

Figure 7.3 Mean and standard deviation parameters for a two stock (A and B) portfolio, $P_{AB} < 1$.

in ρ (all else constant) reduces Var (r_P). Therefore, since equation (7.13a) holds for $\rho = 1$, for $\rho < 1$ we must have

$$\sigma_P < k_A\sigma_A + k_B\sigma_B \qquad (7.14)$$

the result shown by equation (7.13b). For a given set of weights (k_A, k_B), the difference between σ_P and the weighted average of the standard deviations of the individual stocks depends on how far the correlation coefficient, ρ, is below unity. At the lower limit $(\rho = -1)$, Var$(r_P) = (k_A\sigma_A - k_B\sigma_B)^2$, from which it follows that Var(r_P) will be zero if $k_A/k_B = \sigma_B/\sigma_A$.

Note the direction of the inequality in equation (7.14). The effect of this inequality is shown graphically in Figure 7.3. For the particular case where $k_A = 0.5$, $k_B = 0.5$, we have $E(r_P) = 12$ and $\sigma_P = 4.5 < 6$. More generally, the locus of all $E(r_P)$, σ_P points (for differing values of k_A and k_B) is a concave arc from A to B. The concavity of the arc reflects the fact that, for $\rho < 1$, portfolio diversification reduces the variance of portfolio returns.

Let a third stock (C) be introduced. As shown in Figure 7.4, we now

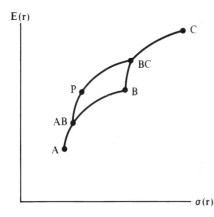

Figure 7.4 Mean and standard deviation parameters for a three stock (A, B, and C) portfolio.

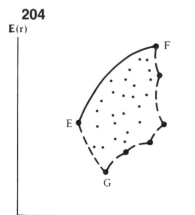

E(r)

F

E

G

σ(r) **Figure 7.5** Feasible set and constraint.

have a positively inclined concave arc between A and B and a second such arc between B and C. The point labeled *AB* on the first arc shows the mean-variance parameters of a two-stock portfolio defined by $k_A = 0.5$, $k_B = 0.5$. The point labeled *BC* on the second arc shows the mean-variance parameters of a two-stock portfolio defined by $k_B = 0.5$, $k_C = 0.5$. What if the decision maker's wealth were divided between an AB-type portfolio and a BC-type portfolio?

Replication of the preceding discussion would show that the mean-variance parameters of this three-stock portfolio are given by the coordinates of a point on the concave arc from AB to BC. For instance, the weights $k_{AB} = 0.5$, $k_{BC} = 0.5$ (which are equivalent to $k_A = 0.25$, $k_B = 0.5$, $k_C = 0.25$) would identify a point such as the one labeled *P* in Figure 7.4.

The *positively* inclined mean-variance indifference curves in Figure 7.1 reflect the fact that risk averters value expected returns but dislike returns variance. Therefore, given the existence of point P in Figure 7.4, the risk averse decision maker would not place all of his or her wealth in asset B. The reason is that the point labeled B lies below and to the right of the arc between AB and BC and thus is dominated by multistock portfolios such as P, which give both a higher expected return and a lower returns variance.[10] Less than perfect returns correlation explains the variance reduction associated with portfolio diversification, and this in turn explains why risk averters generally hold diversified portfolios.

The feasible set and the constraint can now be identified. These are illustrated in Figure 7.5. Each dot in Figure 7.5 shows the mean-standard deviation parameters for each asset the decision maker considers for inclusion in his or her portfolio. The dashed and solid lines on the outer border delimit the set of all feasible mean-standard deviation combinations, given the means, variances, and covariances for the individual stocks. For the

[10]Stock B, of course, is not dominated out. B enters the multistock portfolios; it is only dominated out as a single-stock portfolio.

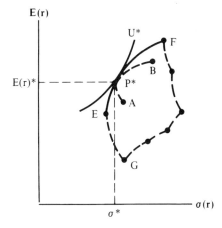

Figure 7.6 Tangency solution identifying optimal mean-variance combination.

most part, multiple-stock portfolios lie along the left-hand segment that passes through points G, E, and F, for reasons discussed in relation to Figure 7.4. The constraint itself is the positively inclined, solid line segment between E and F. This is because, when the investor has achieved a portfolio along the EF arc, greater expected returns can be obtained only at the cost of higher variance, and lower variance can be realized only at the expense of lower expected returns. Accordingly, this arc is called the *efficient frontier*.[11] The efficient frontier is the constraint.

The Optimal Portfolio Decision

The optimal portfolio is given by the point of tangency between the efficient frontier and the highest indifference curve the investor can reach. The tangency solution identifies the optimal mean-variance combination, given the alternatives that are available and the investor's utility function. The solution is illustrated in Figure 7.6 by the point labeled P^*. When portfolio P^* is selected, the decision maker achieves an expected return of $E(r)^*$, a standard deviation of σ^*, and an indifference curve labeled U^*.

In Figure 7.6, the optimal portfolio lies on the arc between point A and point B. Assume that point A is associated with a single stock. Point B may represent either a single stock or a multistock portfolio; if the latter, assume that stock A does not enter portfolio B. We can consider the specific equation that shows how A and B are combined to get portfolio P^* and may thereby determine stock A's weight (k_A^*) in P^*. In similar fashion, we can obtain the weight (k_i^*) for any other i^{th} stock in the portfolio. The weights express the investment decision.

---

[11]Note that the investor is an efficient decision maker only if he or she has achieved a position where a trade-off is necessary to get more of a "good" or less of a "bad." Alternatively stated, the ability to improve one's position at no cost indicates a suboptimal solution, and hence inefficiency.

Note the following about the optimal investment decision:

- Because for each ith asset $k_i = (P_i N_i)/W_1$, and since W_1 is given, determining optimal weights is equivalent to determining optimal dollar holdings in each asset. Therefore, for given market prices (the P_i), the individual's investment decision reduces to determining how many shares to hold of each stock (the N_i).
- The investment decision is implemented by buying or selling the appropriate number of shares of each asset, given the solution for the optimal weights, initial portfolio holdings, and share prices.
- Just as the portfolio decision is *stock dimensioned,* so too is the trading decision. That is, if the decision maker wants to hold N_i^* shares of the ith asset and currently holds N_0 shares, then he or she will seek to trade $N_i^* - N_0$ shares.
- There is no fundamental distinction between buyers and sellers in the securities market. Any trader is either a buyer or a seller, depending on his or her desired portfolio adjustment. $N_i^* - N_0 > 0$ indicates a buy decision, and $N_i^* - N_0 < 0$ indicates a sell decision.
- The desired share holding for an asset depends upon the price at which shares of the asset can be bought or sold. There are two reasons for this: (1) Expected returns, variances, and covariances all depend on the relationship between initial prices (the P_{i1}) and end of period prices (the P_{i2}); hence the optimal investment decision also depends on the initial prices. (2) The decision concerning the total dollar investment in a security is translated into the number of shares to hold (N_i^*) *given* the price per share (P_i).

THE CAPITAL ASSET PRICING MODEL

This section shows how the portfolio selection model may be extended to obtain an equilibrium pricing model for risky assets. The formulation is the *Capital Asset Pricing Model* (CAPM).[12] Assume:

1. Each investor has a single investment period, from T_1 to T_2.
2. Each investor makes his or her portfolio decision with regard to the mean and variance of portfolio returns.
3. Investors agree on the mean, variance, and covariance characteristics of individual securities; that is, investors have *homogeneous expectations*.
4. Each investor can borrow or lend unlimited amounts of a risk-free asset at a risk-free rate of interest, r_f.

---

[12]The CAPM was first developed by Sharpe (1964), Lintner (1965a), and Mossin (1966). A recent alternative to explaining asset prices is arbitrage pricing theory (APT). See Ross (1976), and Elton and Gruber (1986) for further discussion.

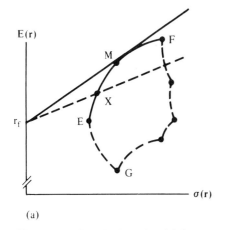

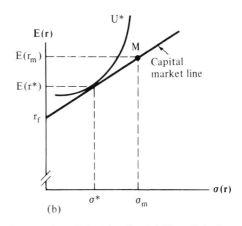

Figure 7.7 Introduction of a risk-free asset changes the efficient frontier. (a) The efficient frontier. (b) The capital market line and an investor's indifference curve.

5. There are no taxes, transaction costs, short selling restrictions, or other frictions in the market.
6. Price and quantity (of share holdings) are continuous variables.
7. No individual has the economic power to affect any price by his or her trading (that is, the market is perfectly competitive).

The Capital Market Line

Introduction of a risk-free asset changes the efficient frontier (the arc from E to F in Figures 7.5 and 7.6). To see how, select a point on the EF arc, such as the point labeled X in Figure 7.7(a). The risk/return parameters for combinations of the risky portfolio X, and the risk-free asset, are given by the dashed line from r_f through X.[13] The dashed line is above the EF arc in the region to the left of X. Hence, over this region, higher mean returns and/or lower returns variance can be obtained by combining the risky portfolio X and the risk-free asset.

Next consider the point labeled M along the EF arc. The risk/return parameters for combinations of the risky portfolio M, and the risk-free asset, are given by the solid line from r_f through M. Because the solid line is above the dashed line, the portfolio combinations it describes dominate the portfolio combinations described by the dashed line. That is, higher expected returns and/or lower returns variance can be obtained from portfolios on the solid line, than on the dashed line. Because the solid line through

[13]Return variance for the risk-free asset is zero, and there is no covariance of return between the risk-free and the risky assets. Therefore, the locus of mean, standard deviation values for the combined portfolio is a straight line, with the standard deviation for the combined portfolio being equal to $k_x\sigma_x$, where k_x is the weight of the risky portfolio in the combined portfolio.

M is tangent to the EF arc, no other line from r_f to any other point along the EF arc lies above the solid line through point M. Therefore, the efficient frontier with unlimited borrowing and lending at the riskless rate is the straight line that passes through r_f and M. This line is called the *capital market line*. Because investors have homogeneous expectations, they all make decisions with respect to this capital market line.

Each investor selects the specific risk/return combination given by the point of tangency between the capital market line and the highest indifference curve he or she can attain, as illustrated in Figure 7.7(b). For each investor, the specific combination of the risky portfolio (M) and the riskless asset depends on the tastes of the individual. If (with reference to Figure 7.7) the point of tangency is to the right of M, the investor borrows the risk-free asset and pays the rate r_f; if the point of tangency is to the left of M, the investor lends the risk-free asset and receives the rate r_f [as shown by the tangency solution depicted in Figure 7.7(b)]. The combination of risky stocks, however, is the same for all investors—it is the portfolio M.

When the market is in equilibrium, all shares of all issues must be held by investors; accordingly, M must be the market portfolio of all stocks. The capital asset pricing model shows how equilibrium share prices are determined for each security in the market portfolio. To obtain the equilibrium pricing relationships, first write the equation for the capital market line. From Figure 7.7(b), it is clear that the intercept parameter is r_f, and that the slope parameter is $[E(r_m) - r_f]/\sigma_m$. Accordingly, the equation for the capital market line is

$$E(r) = r_f + \left[\frac{E(r_m) - r_f}{\sigma_m} \right] \sigma \qquad (7.15)$$

Equation (7.15) shows that the return on an equilibrium portfolio can be decomposed into two parts: (1) r_f compensates the investor for postponing the receipt of income (waiting), and (2) $\{[E(r_m) - r_f]/\sigma_m\}\sigma$ compensates the investor for risk. $[E(r_m) - r_f]$ may be viewed as the price of risk (that is, what the market will pay the investor for accepting risk). In equation (7.15), the total compensation for risk taking is, therefore, the price per standard deviation of the market portfolio, which is $[(E(r_m) - r_f]/\sigma_m$, times the amount of risk accepted, which is σ.

The Security Market Line

The capital market line shows the risk/return relationship to which an equilibrium portfolio must conform, given the assumptions of CAPM. Individual securities, however, are not generally equilibrium portfolios, and thus they do not generally lie on the capital market line. An equation equivalent to equation (7.15), to which the risky securities must conform, is obtained by identifying the relevant measure of risk for each asset in the market portfolio.

The relevant measure of risk for the ith asset is the increase in the risk of the market portfolio caused by a small increase in the ith asset's weight in the market portfolio. That is, in keeping with the standard microeconomic pricing model, the compensation for risk bearing with regard to the ith asset equals the price of risk times the marginal increase in portfolio risk attributable to an increased investment in the ith asset. The change in portfolio risk is therefore obtained by differentiating the standard deviation of the market portfolio with respect to the portfolio weight of the ith asset. The derivation is shown in the Appendix to this chapter; the derivative equals σ_{im}/σ_m.

Replacing σ in equation (7.15) with σ_{im}/σ_m, the measure of the ith stock's contribution *on the margin* to overall market risk, gives

$$E(r_i) = r_f + \left[\frac{E(r_m) - r_f}{\sigma_m}\right]\left(\frac{\sigma_{im}}{\sigma_m}\right) \qquad (7.16)$$

Equation (7.16) can be rewritten as

$$E(r_i) = r_f + \beta_i[E(r_m) - r_f] \qquad (7.17)$$

where

$$\beta_i = \frac{\sigma_{im}}{\sigma_m^2}.$$

Equation (7.17) is the equation for the *security market line,* shown graphically in Figure 7.8. The expected return/beta (β) characteristics of

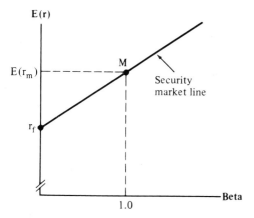

Figure 7.8   The security market line.

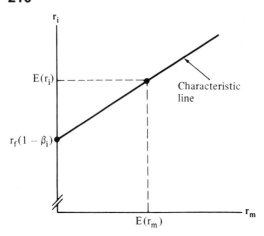

Figure 7.9   The characteristic line.

all efficiently priced securities (and portfolio combinations of securities) must lie on the security market line, given the CAPM assumptions. Consequently, the market portfolio must also lie on the security market line, as shown in Figure 7.8 by the point labeled *M*, with coordinates $E(r) = E(r_m)$ and $\beta = 1.0$.

The Characteristic Line

The equation for a security's *characteristic line* is

$$r_i = r_f(1 - \beta_i) + \beta_i(r_m) \qquad (7.18)$$

This equation is shown graphically in Figure 7.9. The line can be estimated by regressing the returns for the ith security on the returns for the market portfolio.[14] The regression line passes through the *point of means* [the point in Figure 7.9 with coordinates $E(r_i)$ and $E(r_m)$], and the slope parameter of the regression equation equals the security's returns covariance with the market return, divided by the variance of the market return.[15] Therefore, equation (7.18) assessed at the point of means can be rewritten as equation (7.17).

[14]Tests for the CAPM typically regress excess returns for the stock on excess returns for the market, using an equation of the form

$$r_i - r_f = a + b[E(r_m) - r_f]$$

where the parameter a is expected to be zero, and the parameter b is the estimate of beta.

[15]The slope parameter, b, of any regression equation $y = a + bx$ is equal to Cov(y, x)/Var(x).

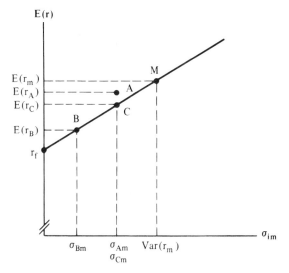

Figure 7.10 The relationship between the expected return on an asset or portfolio and its covariance with the market.

Equilibrium Prices for Individual Assets

Equation (7.17) can also be written as

$$\frac{E(r_i) - r_f}{E(r_m) - r_f} = \beta_i \tag{7.19}$$

The numerator of the left-hand side of equation (7.19) is the excess expected return (over the risk-free rate) for the ith security, and the denominator is the excess expected return for the market portfolio. Equation (7.19) shows that, in equilibrium, the excess return for the asset in relation to the excess return to the market must be proportionate to the systematic risk of the stock.

The *equilibrium price* for the ith asset in the market portfolio is the value that equates the expected return for the asset with the expected return shown by the security market line, given the value of the asset's beta coefficient. As is next discussed, an arbitrage argument supports this equilibrium condition.

Figure 7.10 restates the *security market line* as a relationship between the expected return on an asset (or portfolio) and the asset's covariance, $Cov(r_i, r_m)$.[16] Figure 7.10 also shows the expected return, covariance relationship for two different assets (A and B) and for two different portfolios, the market portfolio (M) and a portfolio C. Portfolio C is selected so that $Cov(r_C, r_m)$ equals $Cov(r_A, r_m)$.

[16]That is, the horizontal axis in Figure 7.10 is beta (β), the horizontal axis in Figure 7.8, times $Var(r_m)$.

Given asset B and the market portfolio, a portfolio such as C must exist. The reason is that portfolio C can be formed by combining asset B and the market portfolio in proportions k_B and k_m that satisfy

$$Cov(r_C, r_m) = k_B Cov(r_B, r_m) + k_m Var(r_m)$$
$$= Cov(r_A, r_m) \qquad (7.20)$$

with

$$E(r_C) = k_B E(r_B) + k_m E(r_m) \qquad (7.21)$$

The simultaneous existence of asset A and portfolio C presents an attractive investment opportunity. By simultaneously obtaining a long position in asset A and an offsetting short position in portfolio C, an investor can receive an expected return of $E(r_A) - E(r_C) > 0$. This is because, for any return on the market, the return for the long position (using equation [7.18] and adjusting the intercept parameter to reflect the additional expected return) is

$$r_{+A} = [r_f(1 - \beta) + E(r_A) - E(r_C)] + \beta(r_m) \qquad (7.22)$$

The return on the short position is

$$r_{-C} = -r_f(1 - \beta) - \beta(r_m) \qquad (7.23)$$

Hence, adding equations (7.22) and (7.23) we have that, whatever the return on the market, the expected return to the hedged position is $E(r_A) - E(r_C)$, and the beta for the hedged position is equal to zero. Because unrestricted short selling and zero transactions costs have been assumed, the investor can attain the hedged position by using the proceeds from selling C short to finance the long position in A. Hence, the return r_f is not required to compensate for the delayed receipt of income and, given the market price of risk, the hedged position would be taken by the investor.

If, alternatively, asset A were to map directly below point C in Figure 7.10, a long position in portfolio C and an offsetting short position in asset A would yield a positive expected return of $E(r_C) - E(r_A)$. Again beta for the position would be zero, the return r_f would not be required, and the hedged position would be taken by the investor.

In general, if the expected return/beta characteristics of a risky asset do not describe a point on the security market line, a profitable arbitrage opportunity exists. This is because any point off the line implies the simultaneous existence of two investments with identical risk (beta), but different expected returns. Arbitrage trading will lead investors to acquire a long position in the underpriced asset and a short position in the overpriced asset.

Arbitrage is the process by which the prices of otherwise identical resources are brought into alignment with each other. The increased demand for a security with an expected return that is too high (given its beta) increases the asset's share price and lowers its expected return. Short selling a security with an expected return that is too low (given its beta) decreases the asset's share price and raises its expected return. The price changes brought about by the arbitrage trading continue until the expected return for each asset, given its beta coefficient, is brought into harmony with the relationship described by the security market line.

For the capital asset pricing model, the market demand curve to hold shares of each risky asset is infinitely elastic at the equilibrium price. The reason is that the different assets and/or portfolios are perfect substitutes for one another, and being perfect substitutes, they must trade at the same price. Thus the price of each asset is determined, given its market risk (beta), the risk-free rate of interest, and the market price of risk.

THE MARKET MODEL

The Market Model Equation

The return on a risky asset is a linear function of the return on the market under the strict assumptions of the capital asset pricing model. The intercept parameter of the linear equation equals the risk-free rate of interest times one minus the asset's beta coefficient [see equation (7.18) for the asset's characteristic line].

The *market model* also relates the return on a risky asset to the return on the market portfolio. The equation for the market model is

$$r_{it} = a_i + b_i r_{mt} + e_{it} \tag{7.24}$$

where b_i is the stock's beta coefficient as in equation (7.18), and e_{it} is the market model residual. The *residual* is that part of the price change for the stock that is not related to the return on the market. If the strict form of CAPM is satisfied, a_i in equation (7.24) will equal $r_f(1 - b_i)$.

Informational Change

The capital asset pricing model provides a theoretical foundation for the market model. The relationship between the stock return and the return on the market portfolio described by equation (7.24) may also be attributable to informational change that affects a broad spectrum of stocks and to portfolio rebalancing.

Informational change that affects many assets generates price changes that are cross-sectionally correlated. This is clearly true for changes in aggregate economic indicators (such as unemployment or inflation), because these indicators have a pervasive impact on the market.

Informational change need not and indeed does not affect the price of all assets identically. Rather, it differs across assets according to the market model parameters. Stocks with high beta coefficients have percentage price changes that on average are greater than the market; stocks with beta coefficients between zero and unity have percentage price changes that on average are less than the market; and negative beta stocks have price changes that on average counter broad market movements.

Portfolio Rebalancing

Portfolio rebalancing is the readjustment of portfolio weights by investors that occurs when price changes in the market cause the weights to stray from their optimal values. Assume, for instance, that Liquidity Inc. strikes oil, and that the price of the stock rises. *Ceteris paribus,* four changes will occur as the new equilibrium value of price is attained: (1) the weight of Liquidity Inc. in investor portfolios will be greater; (2) the expected return on the stock will be greater (to compensate for the larger portfolio weight); (3) investors will be wealthier (because of the increased value of this asset); and (4) the equilibrium price of other stocks will be higher.

One reason for the increased price of other shares is the increased demand due to greater investor wealth. But there is a more important reason: if the relative portfolio weight for Liquidity Inc. is to be greater, other weights must be less; the inducement for the other weights to be less is a reduction in the expected returns for the other assets, and this reduction occurs as *ceteris paribus,* the share prices of the other assets rise.

The realignment of share prices is the effect of portfolio rebalancing. As can be seen from the preceding discussion, after the process is complete, the price of Liquidity Inc. and of all other stocks will be higher.[17] Because portfolio rebalancing causes the prices of different assets to move in harmony with one another, it generates systematic market movements. Of course, the broader market movements will not be apparent when an issue as small as Liquidity Inc. is the sole recipient of informational change. Nevertheless, the relationship is there. Moreover, the relationship is important when the informational change relates to a significant proportion of firms.

---

[17]The increased average value of equities can, of course, be supported only by additional funds being committed to the market. In the context of the CAPM, this would be attributable to a decreased demand to hold the risk-free asset.

Because of portfolio rebalancing, informational change need not affect all stocks for all stocks to exhibit reasonably consistent, cross-sectionally correlated price movements.

Systematic (Undiversifiable) versus Unsystematic (Diversifiable) Risk

The market model can be used to distinguish two types of risk: *systematic risk* and *unsystematic risk*. To see this, take variances of equation (7.24):

$$\text{Var}(r_{it}) = b_i^2 \, \text{Var}(r_{mt}) + \text{Var}(e_{it}) \qquad (7.25)$$

Because the return on the stock is partially explained by the return on the market index, part of the riskiness of the stock is explained by the underlying riskiness of all stocks. The first term on the right-hand side of equation (7.25) is the stock's *systematic risk*. Because the market related component of a stock's return is perfectly correlated with the market, the systematic variance cannot be reduced by portfolio diversification. For this reason, systematic variance is often called *undiversifiable risk*. It is clear from equation (7.25) that if a stock's beta coefficient is greater than unity, the systematic variability of the stock's return is greater than that of the market. On the other hand, the systematic component of the stock's return is more stable than the return on the market portfolio if the stock's beta coefficient is positive but less than unity.

The second term on the right-hand side of equation (7.25) is the stock's *unsystematic risk*. Because the price movements for the stock are in part independent of general market movements, part of the riskiness of the stock is independent of the riskiness of the market. Because the residual return for one stock is uncorrelated with (1) the residual return on other stocks and (2) the return on the market index, unsystematic risk can be reduced by portfolio diversification. For this reason, it is often called *diversifiable risk*. In a frictionless environment, the risk averse decision maker will hold a well diversified portfolio so as to eliminate diversifiable risk.

THE MARKET PORTFOLIO

The Investor's Demand Curve

This section shows how the value of the market portfolio is determined. Assuming the market portfolio is traded as if it were a single risky asset, we first show how an individual investor's demand curve to hold shares of the market portfolio can be derived from his or her utility (of wealth) function. The procedure used here differs from that described in Chapter 6. Rather than maximizing utility subject to a constraint, we restate the utility function to make explicit the price at which shares of the market portfolio may currently be traded, and the mean and variance of future share prices.[18] The demand curve to hold shares of the market portfolio may then be obtained directly from the utility function, as shown later.[19]

Assume:

1. The investor's portfolio comprises a risk-free asset and one risky asset (shares of the market portfolio).
2. Share price and share holdings are continuous variables.
3. Short selling is unrestricted.
4. The existence of a brief trading period, T_0 to T_1, which is followed by a single investment period, T_1 to T_2.
5. All transactions made during the trading period are settled at point in time T_1.
6. The investor seeks a portfolio at the beginning of the investment period (at time T_1) that will maximize the expected utility of wealth to be realized at the end of the investment period (at time T_2).
7. Investor expectations with respect to the share price at the end of the investment period (at time T_2) are exogenously determined (expectations are independent of the current price of shares).
8. All investors are risk averse.

The following variables are used:

C_0 = holdings of the risk-free asset at the beginning of the trading period (T_0)

C_1 = holdings of the risk-free asset at the beginning of the investment period (T_1)

N_0 = number of shares of the market portfolio held at the beginning of the trading period (T_0)

N_1 = number of shares of the market portfolio held at the beginning of the investment period (T_1)

$R_0 - 1$ = risk-free rate of interest over the trading period

$R_1 - 1$ = risk-free rate of interest over the investment period

P_1 = price at which shares of the market portfolio are purchased or sold during the trading period

---

[18]The manipulation of the utility function involves a procedure called Taylor expansion. We state the results later. See, for example, R. G. D. Allen (1960) for a discussion of the Taylor procedure.

[19]The derivation of the demand curve follows Ho, Schwartz, and Whitcomb (1985).

P_2 = price at which shares of the market portfolio can be sold at the end of the investment period (T_2)

Q = number of shares traded by the investor at the beginning of the investment period (T_1); $Q > 0$ indicates a purchase; $Q < 0$ indicates a sale

The Model   The decision maker starts the *investment period* with C_1 dollars of the risk-free asset and N_1 shares of the market portfolio (the risky asset). Therefore, wealth at T_2 is given by $C_1R_1 + N_1P_2$. As of T_1, this wealth is uncertain because P_2 is uncertain. As of T_1, the expected utility of end of period wealth can be written as

$$EU(C_1R_1 + N_1P_2) \qquad (7.26)$$

The decision maker starts the *trading period* with C_0 dollars of the risk-free asset and N_0 shares of the risky asset. If during the trading period the decision maker were to exchange holdings of the risk-free asset for Q shares of the risky asset at a price of P_1, the *expected utility of end of period wealth*, written as a function of P_1 and Q, given N_0 and C_0, would be[20]

$$h(P_1, Q|N_0, C_0) = EU[(C_0R_0 - QP_1)R_1 + (N_0 + Q)P_2] \quad (7.27)$$

where $C_0R_0 - QP_1 = C_1$ and $N_0 + Q = N_1$. Equation (7.27) can be rewritten as[21]

$$h(P_1, Q|N_0, C_0) = c + gQ(a - bQ - P_1) \qquad (7.28)$$

where $\quad c = U(W) - \pi N_0^2\, U'(W)/R_1$
$\qquad g = U'(W)R_1$
$\qquad a = [E(P_2) - 2\pi N_0]/R_1$
$\qquad b = \pi/R_1$
$\qquad \pi = -\frac{1}{2}[U''(W)/U'(W)]\,\text{Var}(P)$

Measures of Risk Aversion   Before analyzing equation (7.28), we first identify two measures of an investor's risk aversion and define an investor's risk premium. The two measures of risk aversion are: (1) $R_A =$

---

[20]The vertical line in the parenthesized expression on the left-hand side of equation (7.27) means "given."

[21]The step from equation (7.27) to equation (7.28) involves expanding (Taylor expansion) the investor's utility around the expected value of wealth if the investor does not trade. The procedure is a convenient way of introducing the variance term into the utility function. Two further assumptions are required to obtain equation (7.28): (1) the third derivative of utility with respect to wealth is small enough to ignore; and (2) the squared deviation of the expected rate of return on the risky asset from the risk-free rate is small enough to ignore.

$-U''(W)/U'(W)$ is a measure of absolute risk aversion; and (2) $R_R = WR_A$ is a measure of relative risk aversion. Because we have $U'' < 0$ for a risk averse decision maker, we have R_A, $R_R > 0$ for risk aversion. Larger values of R_A and R_R indicate higher degrees of risk aversion. R_A is a measure of *absolute* risk aversion because it reflects the decision maker's reaction to uncertainty in relation to the *absolute* (dollar) gains/losses in an uncertain situation. R_R is a measure of *relative* risk aversion because it reflects the decision maker's reaction to uncertainty in relation to the *percentage* gains/losses in an uncertain situation.[22]

Risk Premiums   A *risk premium* is the minimum dollar compensation a decision maker would require to hold a risky asset in place of an alternative that involves no risk. Specifically, a decision maker would be indifferent between a riskless investment with a certain return of D dollars, and a risky investment with an expected dollar return of E(Z) equal to D plus the investor's risk premium. In general, the investor's risk premium depends upon his or her utility function and initial wealth, and on the distribution of Z.

Pi (π) in equation (7.28) is a risk premium: π equals one-half of R_A (the measure of the investor's absolute risk aversion) times $Var(P_2)$, which measures the absolute (dollar) risk attributable to holding one share of the market portfolio. The uncertainty associated with holding N shares of the risky asset is $Var(NP_2) = N^2 Var(P_2)$; thus the total risk premium for holding N shares is

$$\pi_T = \pi N_1^2 \tag{7.29}$$

Dividing equation (7.29) by N_1 ($= N_0 + Q$) gives the risk premium per share (the average risk premium):

$$\pi_A = \pi N_1 \tag{7.30}$$

Differentiating equation (7.29) with respect to N_1 gives the risk premium for a marginal share (the *marginal risk premium*):

$$\pi_M = 2\pi N_1 \tag{7.31}$$

Dividing equation (7.31) by P_1 expresses the marginal risk premium as a percentage of current price:

$$\pi_{M\%} = \frac{\pi_M}{P_1} = \frac{2\pi N_1}{P_1} \tag{7.32}$$

The return on the combined portfolio of N_1 shares of the market

[22]For further discussion, see Pratt (1964).

portfolio and C_1 dollars of the risk-free asset is

$$r_P = \left(\frac{P_2}{P_1} - 1\right)\left(\frac{P_1 N_1}{W}\right) + \left(1 - \frac{P_1 N_1}{W}\right) r_f \qquad (7.33)$$

and the variance of the return on the combined portfolio is

$$\text{Var}\left[\left(\frac{P_2}{P_1}\right)\left(\frac{P_1 N_1}{W}\right)\right] = \left(\frac{N_1}{W}\right)^2 \text{Var}(P_2) \qquad (7.34)$$

Thus the investor's risk premium associated with the uncertain return realized from the combined portfolio is

$$\pi_{rp} = \left(\frac{N_1}{W}\right)^2 \pi \qquad (7.35)$$

The various risk premiums identified here are used in the subsection "Interpretation" that follows.

The Reservation Demand Curve   Equation (7.28) can be used to obtain both a reservation price demand curve and an ordinary demand curve. We consider the *reservation demand curve* first. The maximum price at which the decision maker would be willing to buy any given number of shares, $Q > 0$, or the minimum price at which the decision maker would be willing to sell any given number of shares, $Q < 0$, is the *reservation price* for the purchase or sale. Equation (7.28) shows that, if no trade is made (that is, if $Q = 0$), the decision maker's expected utility is equal to c. The reservation price for any value of Q is the price that equates the expected utility $[h(P_1, Q|N_0, C_0)]$ if the trade were made, with the expected utility (c) if no trade were made. Thus the reservation price for any value of Q is given by

$$h(P^R, Q|N_0, C_0) = c \qquad (7.36)$$

where P^R is the reservation price associated with the trade of Q shares. For equation (7.36) to be satisfied, we must have a $- bQ - P_1 = 0$. Hence the reservation price demand curve is

$$P^R = a - bQ \qquad (7.37)$$

The Ordinary Demand Curve   Using equation (7.28), we can also obtain the ordinary demand curve. At any value of P_1, the decision maker selects the value of Q that maximizes expected utility. Hence, the ordinary price demand curve is given by

$$\frac{\partial h}{\partial Q}(P^o, Q|N_0, C_0) = 0 \qquad (7.38)$$

where P^o is the "ordinary" price associated with the trade of Q shares. Therefore, differentiating h in equation (7.28) with respect to Q, setting the derivative equal to zero, and rearranging gives

$$P^o = a - 2bQ \qquad (7.39)$$

D^R, the reservation curve given by equation (7.37), and D^o, the ordinary curve given by equation (7.39), are shown graphically in Figure 7.11. Note the following about the two curves:

1. For both curves, the parameter a shows the price at which Q is zero, and hence the price at which the initial number of shares (N_0) will be held.
2. The price intercept for the reservation and ordinary demand curves can be obtained by substituting $Q = -N_0$ into equations (7.37) and (7.39), respectively. The intercept for the ordinary demand curve is $E(P_2)/R_1$, the present value (at the risk-free rate) of the price expected for point in time T_2. The intercept for the reservation demand curve is $[E(P_2) - N_0]/R_1$.
3. The location of D^R depends on initial share holdings; the location of D^o does not.
4. Both curves are linear. Linearity is a consequence of an assumption made to simplify the derivation: the squared deviation of the expected rate of return on the risky asset from the risk-free rate is small enough to be ignored (see footnote 21). The assumption is reasonable for the neighborhood of $E(P_2)/R_1$, but is not acceptable for prices sufficiently different from $E(P_2)/R_1$. Consequently, linearity is a reasonable approximation only as long as the price (P_1)

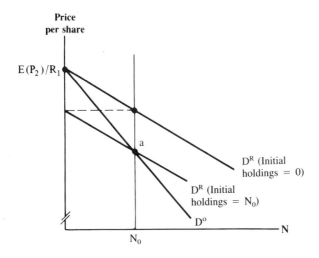

Figure 7.11 D^R, the reservation curve in equation (7.37), and D^o, the ordinary curve in equation (7.39).

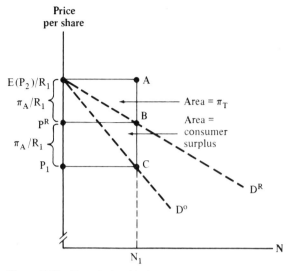

Figure 7.12 The relationship between the reservation curve, ordinary curve, total and average risk premium, and consumer surplus.

of the risky asset does not deviate too far from the present value of the expected future price.[23]

5. The slope (dP/dQ) of the reservation demand curve given by equation (7.37) is half that of the ordinary demand curve given by equation (7.39). This is consistent with the analysis in Chapter 6.

6. The slope of the demand curve would be zero (the price elasticity of demand would be infinite) if the risk premium were zero (that is, if the investor were risk neutral), in which case the market portfolio and the risk-free asset would be perfect substitutes.

Interpretation

The previous subsection shows how the demand curve to hold shares of the market portfolio can be obtained for a representative investor, given the risk-free rate of interest, expectations of P_2, and the investor's utility function. Figure 7.12, which reproduces part of Fig. 7.11, shows that:

- If the price per share of the market portfolio is P_1, the investor will hold N_1 shares.

[23]One might expect the demand curve to hold shares of the market portfolio to be convex from below, such that it does not intersect the quantity axis. This is because, with zero storage cost, the investor would hold an unlimited number of shares at a sufficiently low price per share.

- The reservation price for the N_1 shares equals $E(P_2)/R_1$ minus the present value of the risk premium per share, π_A/R_1.[24]
- Because the slope (dP/dN) of the ordinary demand curve is twice that of the reservation curve, $[E(P_2)/R_1] - P_1 = 2\pi_A/R_1$.
- The present value of the total risk premium π_T/R_1 equals the area of the rectangle $[E(P_2)/R_1]ABP^R$, which, consistent with equation (7.29), equals $\pi(N_1)^2/R_1$.
- Consumer surplus equals the area of the rectangle P^RBCP_1, which equals the area of the triangle $[E(P_2)/R_1]CP_1$.

The Risk Premium and the Market Price of Risk   When the investor has traded the optimal number of shares of the market portfolio at the market determined price per share, his or her risk premium can be related to the market price of risk. To see how, assess the ordinary demand curve at $P^o = P_1$:

$$P_1 = \frac{E(P_2)}{R_1} - \frac{2\pi N_1}{R_1} \qquad (7.40)$$

Multiplying by R_1/P_1, rearranging, and recognizing that $[E(P_2)/P_1] - 1 = E(r_m)$ and $R_1 - 1 = r_f$, we get

$$\frac{2\pi N_1}{P_1} = E(r_m) - r_f \qquad (7.41)$$

Therefore, using equation (7.32) we have

$$\pi_{M\%} = E(r_m) - r_f \qquad (7.42)$$

As discussed in the previous section, the right-hand side of equation (7.42) is the price of risk. We thus see that the investor achieves an optimal holding of the risky asset by obtaining the number of shares that equates the marginal risk premium with the market price of risk. This result is consistent with the consumer choice model: price is equated with marginal value. Here, the price is the additional expected return the investor receives as compensation for accepting risk, and the marginal value is the marginal risk premium required by the investor.

It is apparent from equation (7.31) that the marginal risk premium increases with N. For a given price of risk, if the investor holds fewer shares than the value given by the ordinary demand curve, the marginal risk premium will be less than $E(r_m) - r_f$; consequently, the investor will *increase* his or her share holdings until his or her marginal risk premium has risen to equality with the market determined price of risk. Alternatively, if the investor holds more shares than the value given by the ordinary

---

[24]The equation for D^R when $N_0 = 0$ is $[E(P_2)/R_1] - bN_1$, and $bN_1 = \pi_A/R_1$ [from the definition of b and equation (7.30)].

demand curve, the marginal risk premium will be greater than $E(r_m) - r_f$; consequently, the investor will *reduce* his or her share holdings until the marginal risk premium has fallen to equality with the market determined price of risk.

The Investor's Optimal Point on the Capital Market Line   The demand model can be assessed to show the determination of the investor's optimal point on the capital market line [equation (7.15)]. From equation (7.35) we have

$$\pi = \pi_{rp}\left(\frac{W}{N_1}\right)^2$$

which, using $R_A = -U''(W)/U'(W)$, the measure of absolute risk aversion, can be written as

$$\pi = \tfrac{1}{2} R_A \text{ Var}(r_p)\left(\frac{W}{N_1}\right)^2 \tag{7.43}$$

Because $\sigma_p = (NP/W)\sigma_m$, we have $\text{Var }(r_p) = \sigma_p(NP/W)\sigma_m$, and can write equation (7.43) as

$$\pi = \tfrac{1}{2} R_A \sigma_p\left(\frac{PW}{N_1}\right)\sigma_m \tag{7.44}$$

Substituting (7.44) into (7.41) and simplifying gives

$$R_R\sigma_p = \frac{E(r_m) - r_f}{\sigma_m} \tag{7.45}$$

where R_R $(= WR_A)$ is the measure of relative risk aversion.

Equation (7.45) shows that for the investor to hold an optimal portfolio, the market price of risk per standard deviation of the market portfolio must be equal to the investor's coefficient of relative risk aversion times the standard deviation of the combined portfolio's return.

Letting $k = N_1P_1/W$, substituting $k\sigma_m = \sigma_p$ into equation (7.45), and rearranging gives

$$k = \frac{E(r_m) - r_f}{\text{Var}(r_m)R_R} \tag{7.46}$$

Equation (7.46) shows that the percentage of wealth that the risk averse investor invests in the market portfolio is positively related to the expected return $E(r_m)$, and negatively related to r_f, $\text{Var}(r_m)$, and R_R. Investors all face the same values of $E(r_m)$, $\text{Var}(r_m)$, and r_f; the investors are assumed to differ, however, according to their degree of risk aversion. More risk averse investors (larger R_R) have smaller optimal values of k and hence are more apt to lend at the risk-free rate (which implies $k < 1$); less risk averse investors (smaller R_R) have larger optimal values of k and hence are more likely to borrow at the risk-free rate (which implies $k > 1$).

The right-hand side of equation (7.45) is the market price of risk per standard deviation of the market portfolio. As discussed in the section on the capital asset pricing model, the total compensation for risk taking is the price of risk times the number of standard deviations the investor accepts (here, the standard deviation of the combined portfolio). Thus, multiplying both sides of equation (7.45) by σ_p, we obtain

$$R_R \, \text{Var}(r_p) \; = \; \left[\frac{E(r_m) \; - \; r_f}{\sigma_m} \right] \sigma_p \qquad (7.47)$$

Adding r_f to both sides of equation (7.47) gives the investor's total compensation for waiting and for risk taking:

$$\begin{aligned} E(r_p) \; &= \; r_f \; + \; R_R \, \text{Var}(r_p) \\ &= \; r_f \; + \; \left[\frac{E(r_m) \; - \; r_f}{\sigma_m} \right] \sigma_p \end{aligned} \qquad (7.48)$$

Equation (7.48) shows that the location of the investor's optimal point on the capital market line [equation (7.15)] depends on his or her measure of relative risk aversion (R_R).

The ith Risky Asset's Point on the Security Market Line   The demand model can also be assessed to show the location of a risky asset on the security market line [equation (7.17)]. Equation (7.42) shows that the marginal risk premium for each investor, as a percentage of P_1, will equal $E(r_m) \; - \; r_f$. Therefore, for each investor,

$$\frac{R_A \, \text{Var}(P_2)N_1}{P_1} \; = \; E(r_m) \; - \; r_f \qquad (7.49)$$

where $R_A N_1$ is constant across investors.[25] Because $r_m \; = \; (P_2/P_1) \; - \; 1$, $\text{Var}(r_m) \; = \; \text{Var}(P_2)/P_1^2$. Substituting $\text{Var}(r_m)P_1^2 \; = \; \text{Var}(P_2)$ into equation (7.49) and simplifying gives,

$$R_A \, \text{Var}(r_m)P_1 N_1 \; = \; E(r_m) \; - \; r_f \qquad (7.50)$$

Using $P_1 N_1 \; = \; kW$ we obtain

$$k R_R \, \text{Var}(r_m) \; = \; E(r_m) \; - \; r_f \qquad (7.51)$$

---

[25]It follows from the equation for the ordinary demand curve [equation (7.39)] that investors with lower values of R_A hold a larger number of shares, such that the product $R_A N_1$ is the same for all investors.

Equation (7.51) can be interpreted as an equilibrium condition for each investor. Because $R_R k = R_A N_1 P_1$, and because the product $R_A N_1$ is constant across investors, $R_R k$ is constant across all investors.[26]

The equilibrium condition for each investor with respect to the market portfolio implies an equilibrium condition for each investor with respect to any i^{th} risky asset in the market portfolio. The CAPM showed that the relevant measure of risk for the ith risky asset is $\beta_i = \sigma_{im}/Var(r_m)$. Therefore, writing $Var(r_m) = \sigma_{im}/\beta_i$, substituting into equation (7.51), and multiplying both sides by β_i we get

$$k R_R \sigma_{im} = \beta_i [E(r_m) - r_f] \qquad (7.52)$$

Adding r_f to both sides of equation (7.52) gives

$$\begin{aligned} E(r_i) &= r_f + k R_R \sigma_{im} \\ &= r_f + \beta_i [E(r_m) - r_f] \end{aligned} \qquad (7.53)$$

Equation (7.53), assessed at $k = 1$, shows that the expected return for the ith risky asset depends on its covariance with the market return, and on the measure of relative risk aversion for an investor whose optimal combined portfolio contains the market portfolio only. The equation also shows that the ith risky asset's specific location on the security market line (equation [7.17]) depends on the covariance of the asset's return with the return on the market portfolio, as discussed in the section about the CAPM.

Market Equilibrium

Determination of the *equilibrium market price* of risk can be visualized as follows. Arbitrarily select a value of $E(r_m) - r_f$, and consider the number of shares of the market portfolio that investors in aggregate will seek to hold, as each attempts to obtain the specific number of shares given by his or her ordinary demand curve at the particular value of $E(r_m) - r_f$. If the total number of shares demanded exceeds the total number of shares available, excessive buying pressure will increase the price of a share of the market portfolio, and $E(r_m) - r_f$ will decrease. Alternatively, if the total number of shares demanded is less than the total number of shares available, excessive selling pressure will decrease the price of a share of the market portfolio, and $E(r_m) - r_f$ will increase. The equilibrium value of the price of risk, $[E(r_m) - r_f]^*$, is the price that equates the aggregate desire to hold shares of the market portfolio with the total number of shares available to be held.

For the capital markets to achieve equilibrium, an equilibrium value

---

[26]It is also clear from equation (7.46) that the product $R_R k$ must be constant across all investors [because $E(r_m)$, r_f, and $Var(r_m)$ are the same for all].

for the risk-free rate, r_f, must also be attained. If r_f is below its equilibrium value, investors in aggregate will seek to borrow more of the risk-free asset than they are willing to lend, thus putting upward pressure on r_f. Alternatively, if r_f is above its equilibrium value, investors in aggregate will seek to lend more of the risk-free asset than they are willing to borrow, putting downward pressure on r_f. The equilibrium value of the risk-free rate, r_f^*, is the rate which equates the aggregate desire to borrow the risk-free asset and the aggregate desire to lend the risk-free asset.

Therefore, when the capital markets are in equilibrium: (1) the number of shares investors in aggregate wish to hold of the market portfolio equals the number of shares available, and (2) the amount of the risk-free asset they wish in aggregate to lend equals the amount they wish in aggregate to borrow. When the market has achieved this equilibrium, each investor will hold the specific number of shares that equates his or her own marginal risk premium with the equilibrium market price of risk, $E(r_m)^* - r_f^*$.

The capital market equilibrium is described graphically by Figure 7.13. The expected return on the market portfolio is shown on the vertical axis, and the *number of shares outstanding* (NSO) of the market portfolio is shown on the horizontal axis. Each of the upward sloping r_f-curves shows the relationship between the expected return on the market portfolio and NSO, for the associated value of r_f. $E(r_m)$ is determined given NSO and r_f because (1) the marginal risk premium is established by the aggregate demand curve evaluated at NSO, and (2) the marginal risk premium equals $E(r_m) - r_f$. For a given value of r_f, $E(r_m)$ is an increasing function of NSO because the marginal risk premium is an increasing function of NSO.

Let r_{f2} be greater than r_{f1}. The upward sloping line labeled r_{f2} is above

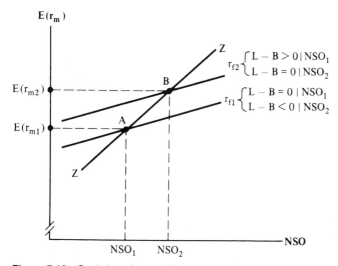

Figure 7.13   Capital market equilibrium.

the line labeled r_{f1} because (1) the equilibrium value of the risk premium is determined for a given value of NSO, and (2) the higher the risk-free rate, the higher must be the expected return on the market portfolio for the risk premium to equal its equilibrium value.

Let $L - B$ (aggregate lending minus aggregate borrowing) stand for investors' net aggregate desire to lend at the risk-free rate. For a given value of NSO, the higher the risk-free rate, the larger $L - B$ is. Information concerning the net desire to lend is given in Figure 7.13 by the labels shown for the two r_f curves. The upper curve shows, for the rate r_{f2}, that $L - B > 0$ when the number of shares outstanding is NSO_1, and that $L - B = 0$ when the number of shares outstanding is NSO_2. The lower curve shows, for the rate r_{f1}, that $L - B = 0$ for $NSO = NSO_1$, and $L - B < 0$ for $NSO = NSO_2$.

Given a value for NSO, the capital market is in equilibrium if $L - B = 0$, and if the market price of risk equals each investor's marginal risk premium. Such an equilibrium is shown in Figure 7.13 by point A for $NSO = NSO_1$, and by point B for $NSO = NSO_2$.

$$\text{At point A:} \quad L - B = 0 \quad \text{with } r_f = r_{f1}$$

Given that $r_f = r_{f1}$, the marginal risk premium for NSO_1 equals the price of risk with $E(r_m) = E(r_{m1})$.

$$\text{At point B:} \quad L - B = 0 \quad \text{with } r_f = r_{f2}$$

Given that $r_f = r_{f2}$, the marginal risk premium for NSO_2 equals the price of risk with $E(r_m) = E(r_{m2})$.

Notice that the equilibrium value for the risk-free rate is shown to be higher if the number of shares of the market portfolio is $NSO_2 > NSO_1$. This is because (1) as NSO increases, the risk premium increases; (2) r_f constant, the risk premium increases by $E(r_m)$ increasing; but (3) if $E(r_m)$ were to increase r_f constant, $L - B$ would become negative; and hence (4) r_f must also increase to maintain $L - B = 0$.

Because r_f increases with NSO, capital market equilibrium will lie on the more steeply inclined line labeled ZZ, which passes through points A and B. The intersection of ZZ and the vertical line at the exogenously determined value of NSO identifies the equilibrium values of the expected return to the market portfolio and the risk-free rate of interest. For example, if $NSO = NSO_1$, $E(r_m)^* = E(r_{m1})$, and $r_f^* = r_{f1}$. Alternatively, if $NSO = NSO_2$, $E(r_m)^* = E(r_{m2})$ and $r_f^* = r_{f2}$.

THE DEMAND TO HOLD SHARES OF A SINGLE ASSET

The determination of asset prices is less straightforward when the assumptions of the capital asset pricing model are relaxed. Nonstandard forms of the CAPM do allow for modifications of the assumptions concerning risk-less borrowing and lending rates, and the absence of taxes, transaction costs, and other trading restrictions.[27] One of the most critical assumptions of the CAPM, and one of the most troublesome to relax, is that investors have homogeneous expectations concerning the risk, return, and covariance characteristics of individual securities. When this assumption is relaxed, we can no longer obtain a unique market portfolio in relation to which individual asset prices may be established, given their covariances with the market.

This section discusses the pricing of an individual risky asset in a multi-asset environment. A formal derivation of the demand curve for a single asset along the lines followed in the previous section will not be attempted, because of the complexity of the multiasset context. Rather, we consider more broadly whether such a demand curve would be negatively inclined, upward sloping, or infinitely elastic. Following the standard practice in microstructure theory, we conclude by assuming the existence of a negatively inclined market demand curve to hold shares of a single risky asset. This demand curve is important for much of the analysis that follows in the book.

A Technical Issue

We first clarify a technical issue concerning the demand to hold shares of a financial asset. The investment decision concerns how much of one's wealth to invest in a particular asset. However, implementation of the investment decision involves the decision to buy or to sell shares. In other words, investors trade shares but derive utility from the dollar value of their investments. This condition differs from that of most markets, in which the resources that are traded are themselves the source of utility. Because it is shares that are traded, market equilibrium must be analyzed with regard to the demand to hold shares.

The individual's propensity to invest in an asset can be expressed as[28]

$$V = V(P) \tag{7.54}$$

where $V = NP$, P is the price per share, and N is the number of shares of the asset that are held.[29] Dividing both sides of equation (7.54) by P gives the demand to hold shares,

---

[27]See Elton and Gruber (1986) for further discussion.

[28]V(P) is a general functional form; it is not V times P.

[29]The analysis presented in this section applies to an individual asset, and so we can, for notational simplicity, suppress the subscript i. We also suppress the time identification on P when it is clear in context that we are referring to value as of point in time 1. Note that $V/W = k$, the asset's portfolio weight.

$$N = \frac{V(P)}{P} \qquad (7.55)$$

To explore whether equation (7.55) is downward sloping, first differentiate it with respect to P:

$$\frac{dN}{dP} = [V'(P)P - V(P)]P^{-2}$$

$$= \left[\left(\frac{dV}{dP} \right) P - V \right] P^{-2} \qquad (7.56)$$

Then multiply both sides of equation (7.56) by P/N, use V = NP, and simplify:

$$\frac{dN}{dP} \frac{P}{N} = \frac{dV}{dP} \frac{P}{V} - 1 \qquad (7.57)$$

The term on the left-hand side of equation (7.57) and the first term on the right-hand side are both *elasticities,* the economist's measure of responsiveness. The first is the elasticity of N with respect to P, and the second is the elasticity of V with respect to P. Therefore, equation (7.57) can be rewritten as

$$\eta_{N,P} = \eta_{V,P} - 1 \qquad (7.58)$$

where η is the symbol for elasticity.[30] Equation (7.58) shows the relationship between the number of shares held (N) as a function of P and the value of holdings (V) as a function of P. With this equation, we can reason in terms of the relationship between value and price and then draw conclusions concerning the relationship between the number of shares and price (which is the demand curve to hold shares).

Before proceeding, let us assess equation (7.58):

Case 1: $\eta_{V,P} < 0$ implies $\eta_{N,P} < -1$; here, the demand to hold shares is a negative and elastic function.

Case 2: $\eta_{V,P} = 0$ implies $\eta_{N,P} = -1$; here, the demand to hold shares is a negative function of unitary elasticity.

Case 3: $0 < \eta_{V,P} < 1$ implies $-1 < \eta_{N,P} < 0$; here, the demand to hold shares is a negative and inelastic function.

---

[30]For any function, y = f(x), the elasticity of y with respect to x is defined as the percentage change in y that results from a percentage change in x. Thus, writing the percentage change in y as dy/y and the percentage change in x as dx/x, elasticity (η) is (dy/y)/(dx/x). The expression can be rewritten in the form used in equation (7.57), (dy/dx)(x/y). Writing the elasticity as $\eta_{y,x}$ shows explicitly that the elasticity of y is with respect to x. y = f(x) is considered elastic if (in absolute value) $\eta > 1$, of unitary elasticity if $\eta = 1$, and inelastic if $\eta < 1$.

Case 4: $\eta_{V,P} > 1$ implies $\eta_{N,P} > 0$; here, an increase in the price of an asset would result in the investor's wanting to hold more shares (the demand curve is upward sloping).

The Availability of Substitutes

It is well established in microeconomics that demand elasticities depend on the availability of substitutes, that elasticities are greater the closer the substitutes are, and that demand elasticities are infinite in the presence of perfect substitutes.

Under the assumptions of the capital asset pricing model, perfect substitutes exist for individual securities. For the CAPM, the equilibrium prices of the individual risky assets that the market portfolio comprises are determined given (1) the risk-free rate of interest, (2) the investors' (homogeneous) expectations concerning future prices, (3) the investors' tastes for risk, and (4) the number of shares of the market portfolio to be held. In this context, the market demand to hold shares of any i^{th} risky asset is infinitely elastic at a price established by the ith asset's contribution to aggregate market risk, and by the market price of risk.[31]

This result is perturbed when the assumptions of homogeneous expectations and unrestricted borrowing and lending at the risk-free rate are relaxed. Even if some investors view certain assets as having perfect substitutes, the market in aggregate may not, because different investors may not agree on what the perfect substitutes are. If an individual investor believes a perfect substitute exists for an individual risky asset, that investor's demand for that risky asset will be infinitely elastic over some range; however, in the absence of unrestricted borrowing and lending, the range of infinite elasticity will be bounded. In this event, the market demand for the individual risky asset will be downward sloping.

For instance, assume two assets (A and B) and two investors. Let each investor believe that A and B are perfect substitutes. This belief is reflected in each investor's having A, B indifference curves that are negatively inclined, straight lines in the space of A, B shares.[32] The slope of each investor's linear indifference curve reflects both the rate at which that investor would be willing to substitute shares of B for shares of A and the price at which he or she would switch from including only A in his or her portfolio to only B.

Now let the slope of the A, B indifference curves be different for the two investors (because they do not agree about the comparative riskiness of the two securities). It is clear in this case that the price change that will

[31]Note that $\eta_{V,P} = \infty$ implies $\eta_{N,P} = \infty$.
[32]Note that these are not risk/return indifference curves, but rather indifference curves that relate two assets given the mean and variance parameters for each.

cause one of the investors to switch between the assets will not cause the other investor to switch. Therefore, the two investors do not switch at the same price. Accordingly, the market in aggregate will not move entirely into or out of the two assets at a single price.

The analysis of the substitution effect shows that two conditions must be satisfied for the market to have an infinitely elastic demand to hold shares of an asset:

1. Each investor must view the asset as having perfect substitutes.
2. The set of investors must have homogeneous expectations.

These are extreme conditions, and they are unlikely to prevail. Therefore, we continue to adhere to the primary law of choice: demand will be greater (but not infinitely greater) when price is lower.

The Income/Wealth Effect

Demand theory distinguishes between a substitution effect and an income or wealth effect.[33] These are as follows:

The Substitution Effect   When the price of a good falls *in relation to* other prices, that good is substituted for others in the consumer's budget. The substitution effect is never positive. Specifically, if in a two-good universe, X becomes cheaper in relation to Y, more of X is always consumed in relation to Y, except in the extreme case of perfect complementarity.

The Income Effect   The consumer's *nominal* income and other prices constant, a decrease in the price of a resource will expand the consumer's command over *all* resources, thereby increasing *real* income. Because the demand for most goods is positively related to real income, the income effect will generally reinforce the substitution effect, assuring negative inclination of the demand curve.

The Wealth Effect   When an investor's share holdings and all other asset prices are constant, a decrease in the price of one asset will cause both an increase of wealth (additional shares of the asset can be purchased at a lower price) and a reduction of wealth (the shares an investor already owns are worth less). The net change in wealth will affect the individual's investment decision. This is called the *wealth effect*.

---

[33]The income effect is primarily relevant for flow dimensioned demand curves, and the wealth effect is primarily relevant for stock dimensioned demand curves. It is the wealth effect that we are concerned with here.

In general, assuming the investor's demand to hold asset shares is positively related to wealth, for a perverse wealth effect to reverse the slope of the demand curve:

- The negative change in wealth due to the reduced value of shares already owned must exceed the positive change of wealth associated with the investor's ability to buy additional shares at a lower price.
- The *response* to the net reduction in wealth must more than offset the substitution effect associated with the share price being lower.
- The perverse wealth effect must offset the substitution effect *by enough* to make $\eta_{V,P} > 1$ [see equation (7.58)].[34]

In the preceding section, however, the derivation of an individual's demand to hold shares of the market portfolio showed that, under risk aversion, the individual's demand is a downward sloping function, regardless of initial share holdings. Furthermore, the wealth effect must be weaker for any i^{th} asset than for the portfolio of assets because the change in wealth resulting from an x percent (x%) change in the share price of the ith asset is $k_i x\% < x\%$, where $k_i < 1$ is the portfolio weight for that asset.

Therefore, we discount the possibility of a perverse wealth effect and continue to adhere to the primary law of choice: demand will be greater when price is lower.

Expectations

An investor's expected utility is positively related to expected returns, and if the return an investor expects to realize from an asset increases (*ceteris paribus*), the dollar importance of that asset in his or her portfolio should be increased. We now assess the effect of P_1 on expected returns. This effect depends on the relationship between P_1 and $E(P_2)$. When the assumption of homogeneous expectations is relaxed, change in P_1 can cause change in $E(P_2)$ because current prices may signal information that would alter the expectations of relatively uninformed investors (see the discussion in Chapter 9).

To analyze the expectations effect, write the expected return for the asset as $E(R) = E(P_2)/P_1$, and consider the relationship between $E(P_2)$ and P_1 for four categories of investors:

1. *The rugged individualists:* Such people conduct their own security analysis, develop their own assessment of how a stock might per-

---

[34]This requirement is more severe than its counterpart in ordinary demand theory, where all that is required to reverse the slope of the demand curve is that the perverse income effect outweigh the substitution effect.

form in the future, and are totally unaffected by what others might think. For these people, the elasticity of $E(P_2)$ with respect to P_1 is zero.

2. *The sheep:* These investors exercise no independent judgment; rather, they simply assume that the price set on the market is the correct price. This being the case, any price change is interpreted as signaling new information on the future value share price will attain, but does not change expected returns. For these people, the elasticity of $E(P_2)$ with respect to P_1 is unity.

3. *The exaggerators:* These people assume that current price changes understate the impact of informational change. Thus they believe that any percentage increase or decrease in current price is associated with a greater percentage increase or decrease in $E(P_2)$.

4. *The rest of us:* Decision makers in this category think for themselves and come to their own conclusions, but also respect the market's collective judgment as this is reflected in security prices. These people revise their expectations on P_2 after a change in P_1, but do so less than proportionately. Consequently, for this category, the elasticity of $E(P_2)$ with respect to P_1 is between zero and unity.

To illustrate, consider a company called Liquidity Inc. (tape symbol LIQ). Suppose that LIQ has been trading at 50, that a 20 percent expected annual rate of return is reasonable for the stock given its riskiness, and that the rugged individualists, the sheep, the exaggerators, and the rest of us happen to expect that one year from now the stock will be worth 60. Now suppose the price decreases to 45.

The rugged individualists still expect a future price of 60; hence, for them, $E[R] = {}^{60}\!/_{45} = 1.33$. The sheep still expect a return of 20 percent; hence, for them, $E[R] = E(P_2)/45 = 1.20$, which implies $E(P_2) = 54$. What about the exaggerators and the rest of us? The answer depends on how each individual's expectation is adjusted, given that price is now 45, not 50. A representative answer for a member of the rest of us category can be given. Write the individual's expectation of price one year from now, given the price today as $E(P_2 \mid P_1)$.[35] Note that $E(P_2 \mid P_1)$ has a one-to-one correspondence with $E(R \mid P_1)$, the return that is expected given today's price. For a representative member of the rest of us set, assume

$$E(P_2 \mid P_1 = 50) = 60 \quad \text{which implies } E(R \mid P_1 = 50) = 1.20$$
$$E(P_2 \mid P_1 = 45) = 58 \quad \text{which implies } E(R \mid P_1 = 45) = 1.29$$

---

[35]The expectation of P_2 could be written more explicitly as $E(P_2 \mid P_1, \theta)$ where θ stands for all prior price history upon which current expectations might be based. This allows, for instance, for P_1 to transmit a different signal if the last preceding price were some $P' < P_1$, or if alternatively it were some $P'' > P_1$. Because θ reflects information concerning past events, it is a constant in the analysis and need not be expressed explicitly.

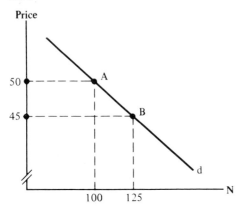

Figure 7.14   The demand curve with price signalling.

The investor's portfolio decision can now be made, on the basis of the returns that are expected. For instance, we might have:[36]

Hold 100 shares at 50 [because $E(R \mid P_1 = 50) = 1.20$]

Hold 125 shares at 45 [because $E(R \mid P_1 = 45) = 1.29$]

These two demand propensities are shown by points A and B in Figure 7.14.

We could in principle determine other demand points in a similar way and so obtain the complete demand function. Such a function is represented by the line labeled d in Figure 7.14. Thus, even though expectations of the price at the end of the investment period $[E(P_2)]$ vary along the curve, desired share holdings are uniquely determined at each price. In other words, we have an unambiguous specification of the *ex ante* demand propensities and hence of the demand curve.

We may now consider whether or not the dependence of expectations on the current value of price could cause the demand curve to be positively inclined. To this end, we first show how change in an asset's expected return $E(R)$ with respect to the asset's current price (P_1) is related to the change in $E(P_2)$ with respect to P_1. The relationship is obtained as follows: Differentiate $E(R) = E(P_2)/P_1$ with respect to P_1:

$$\frac{dE(R)}{dP_1} = \frac{[dE(P_2)/dP_1]P_1 - E(P_2)}{P_1^2} \tag{7.59}$$

[36]For simplicity and with no loss of generality, we here ignore the variance term. As the example has been structured, an increase of the variance term could not reverse the slope of the demand curve. This is because any price decrease would shift all points of the returns distribution to the right, causing the new distribution to dominate the old.

Multiply both sides by $P_1/E(R)$ and rearrange:

$$\left[\frac{dE(R)}{dP_1}\right]\left[\frac{P_1}{E(R)}\right] = \left[\frac{dE(P_2)}{dP_1}\right]\left[\frac{1}{E(R)}\right] - \left[\frac{E(P_2)}{P_1}\right]\left[\frac{1}{E(R)}\right] \qquad (7.60)$$

Use $E(R) = E(P_2)/P_1$ and write in elasticity form:

$$\eta_{E(R),P_1} = \eta_{E(P_2),P_1} - 1 \qquad (7.61)$$

The relationship expressed by equation (7.61) reflects the following:

- *For the sheep:* The expectation of the future price changes at precisely the same rate as does the current price ($\eta_{E(P_2),P_1} = 1$). Hence the expected return is independent of the current price. With the expected return constant, the portfolio decision (V) will remain constant (that is, $\eta_{V,P_1} = 0$, as in Case 2 in subsection 1). Thus, given equation (7.58), the demand curve for an investor in the sheep class will be downward sloping.
- *For the rugged individualists:* $\eta_{E(P_2),P_1} = 0$, and thus by equation (7.61), $\eta_{E(R),P_1} = -1$. When E(R) changes because P_1 changes, the portfolio decision (V) will change in the same direction as E(R) [see footnote [(36)]]. Therefore, as P_1 decreases, E(R) and V both increase as in Case 1, and hence, by equation (7.58), the demand curve for the rugged individualist will be downward sloping.
- *For the rest of us:* It is clear from equation (7.61) that with the response of the expected price to the current price positive and inelastic, the response of the expected return to the current price is negative (although inelastic). Again, by equation (7.58), the demand to hold shares will be downward sloping (this is likely to fit Case 3).
- *For the exaggerators:* $\eta_{E(P_2),P_1} > 1$ for the exaggerators, and hence, from equation (7.61), we have $\eta_{E(R),P_1} > 0$. As a consequence, the demand curve for these people may not be downward sloping (as in Case 4).

It follows that, for an individual's demand curve to be positively inclined because of the expectations effect:

1. The expectations elasticity ($\eta_{E(P_2),P_1}$) must be greater than unity (which holds only for the exaggerators).
2. The response to the change in expected returns must be *great enough* to make $\eta_{V,P} > 1$ [see equation (7.58)].

The analysis of the expectations effect shows that the response necessary for the slope of the demand curve to be perturbed is conceivable but unlikely. Therefore, we discount the possibility and continue to adhere to the primary law of choice: demand will be greater when price is lower.

Recapitulation

Having considered the possibilities for substitution, the wealth effect, and the expectations effect, we conclude that the representative investor's demand to hold shares of a single risky asset, as well as the market demand curve, will be an inverse function of price. The downward sloping demand curve represents the individual's investment decision; it is of key importance to the analysis that follows.

CONCLUSION

The chapter has considered how the investor determines the optimal number of shares of an asset to include in his or her portfolio and how this decision varies as the price of the asset changes. In so doing, we have obtained the investor's demand curve to hold shares of a risky asset.

The capital asset pricing model was presented to show how the prices of risky assets would be determined in a frictionless environment characterized by homogeneous expectations and the existence of a risk-free asset. When the assumptions of CAPM hold, all investors hold shares of the market portfolio of risky assets, and each borrows or lends at the risk-free rate, according to his or her degree of risk aversion.

Because the composition of the market portfolio of risky assets is the same for all investors, we analyzed an individual investor's demand to hold shares of the market portfolio as if it were a single risky asset. The demand curve was found to be negatively inclined for a risk averse investor, with the slope (dP/dN) being greater, the greater the risk aversion of the investor.

With regard to any i^{th} risky asset in the market portfolio, we considered whether or not the existence of highly substitutable investment alternatives might cause the demand curve for that asset to be horizontal (infinitely elastic). Although this would be the case under the CAPM assumptions, we dismissed the possibility when the assumptions of homogeneous expectations and unlimited borrowing and lending at the risk-free rate were relaxed. Some individuals may view different assets as being very close substitutes for one another; however, the set of investors would have to agree on what the substitutes are for the market demand curves to be infinitely elastic. In a world where investors do not have identical information, such agreement is not likely.

The chapter also considered the possibility that either a wealth effect and/or an expectations effect would cause the curve to be upward sloping.

An unlikely set of events would have to occur for these effects to cause a slope reversal, and we accordingly choose to ignore the possibility.

We therefore conclude that the market demand to hold shares of an asset is a negative function of price. With a downward sloping demand curve established for the investor, we proceed to Chapter 8 for an examination of that investor's trading decision.

APPENDIX

The appendix shows that the derivative of the market portfolio with respect to the portfolio weight of the ith asset equals σ_{im}/σ_m. The derivative is obtained as follows. Since

$$\sigma_m = [\text{Var } (r_m)]^{1/2}$$

where $\text{Var } (r_m) = \sum_{i=1}^{M} k_i^2\sigma_i^2 + \sum_{i=1}^{M} \sum_{j=1}^{M} k_{ij}\sigma_{ij},$

$$i \neq j$$

the derivative of σ_m with respect to k_i is

$$\frac{d\sigma_m}{dk_i} = \frac{1}{2} [\text{Var } (r_m)]^{-1/2} \left[\frac{d[\text{Var } (r_m)]}{dk_i} \right] \qquad (7.A1)$$

with

$$\frac{d[\text{Var } (r_m)]}{dk_i} = 2k_i\sigma_i^2 + 2\sum_{j=1}^{M} k_j\sigma_{ij} \qquad (7.A2)$$

Therefore

$$\frac{d\sigma_m}{dk_i} = \frac{k_i\sigma_i^2 + \sum_{j=1}^{M} k_j\sigma_{ij}}{\sigma_m} \qquad (7.A3)$$

Since $r_m = \sum_{j=1}^{M} k_j r_j$, and because[1] $\text{Cov}(r_i, k_j r_j) = k_j\sigma_{ij}$ and $\text{Cov}(r_i, \sum_{j=1}^{M} k_j r_j) = \sum_{j=1}^{M} k_j\sigma_{ij}$, we have

---

[1]The covariance of a variable (x) with the weighted sum of two other variables $(k_y y + k_z z)$, is equal to the weighted sum of the covariance between x and y, and the covariance between x and z. The proof is

$$\begin{aligned}
\text{Cov}(x, k_y y + k_z z) &= E[(x - \bar{x})(k_y y + k_z z - k_y \bar{y} - k_z \bar{z})] \\
&= k_y E[(x - \bar{x})(y - \bar{y})] + k_z E[(x - \bar{x})(z - \bar{z})] \\
&= k_y \text{ Cov}(x, y) + k_z \text{ Cov}(x, z)
\end{aligned}$$

$$\sigma_{im} = \text{Cov}\left(r_i, \sum_{j=1}^{M} k_j r_j\right) = \sum_{i=1}^{M} k_i \sigma_{ij}$$

$$= k_i \sigma_i^2 + \sum_{j=1}^{M} k_j \sigma_{ij} \tag{7.A4}$$

Hence the numerator of (7.A3) is σ_{im}, and

$$\frac{d\sigma_m}{dk_i} = \frac{\sigma_{im}}{\sigma_m} \tag{7.A5}$$

Q.E.D.

SUGGESTED READING

R. G. D. Allen, *Mathematical Analysis for Economists,* London, England: Macmillan, 1960.

W. Baumol, *Economic Theory and Operations Analysis,* fourth edition, Englewood Cliffs, N.J.: Prentice-Hall, 1977.

E. Elton and M. Gruber, *Modern Portfolio Theory and Investment Analysis,* third edition, New York: Wiley, 1986.

T. Ho, R. Schwartz, and D. Whitcomb, "The Trading Decision and Market Clearing Under Transaction Price Uncertainty," *Journal of Finance,* March 1985.

J. Lintner, "The Valuation of Risk Assets and the Selection of Risky Investments in Stock Portfolios and Capital Budgets," *Review of Economics and Statistics,* February 1965a.

J. Lintner, "Security Prices, Risk, and Maximal Gains from Diversification," *Journal of Finance,* December 1965b.

J. Lintner, "The Aggregation of Investor's Diverse Judgments and Preferences in Purely Competitive Security Markets," *Journal of Financial and Quantitative Analysis,* December 1969.

J. Mossin, "Equilibrium in a Capital Asset Market," *Econometrica,* October 1966.

J. Pratt, "Risk Aversion in the Small and in the Large," *Econometrica,* January 1964.

S. Ross, "The Arbitrage Theory of Capital Asset Pricing," *Journal of Economic Theory,* December 1976.

W. Sharpe, "Capital Asset Prices: A Theory of Market Equilibrium Under Conditions of Risk," *Journal of Finance,* September 1964.

W. Sharpe, *Investments,* third edition, Englewood Cliffs, N.J.: Prentice-Hall, 1985.

chapter 8

Trading

The discussion in Part One emphasized the complexity of trading in the equity markets. In large part, trading is complex because individual orders can affect market prices. A price effect may be attributable to various factors:

1. A large order submitted to a relatively thin market can have a temporary market impact effect (a large buy order may drive price up, and a large sell order may drive price down).
2. The orders of some traders may signal information to other traders (a large buy order may be viewed as a signal of positive informational change, and a large sell order may be viewed as a signal of negative informational change).
3. A limit order, because it extends a free option to other traders,[1] gives counterpart sellers an incentive to place their orders at higher prices, or counterpart buyers an incentive to place their orders at lower prices.

The market impact, information, and options effects are more pronounced, the larger the size of a trader's order. Consequently, large investors in general, and institutional investors in particular, are especially cau-

---

[1]The placement of a buy limit order is in effect the writing of a put, and the placement of a sell limit order is in effect the writing of a call (see Chapter 4).

tious about revealing their buy and sell intentions to the market. As discussed in Chapter 4, large orders are typically worked by a trader on an exchange floor, and institutional block transactions are typically negotiated in the upstairs market by the trading desks of the major brokerage houses.

The particular problems faced by the larger traders, however, may cause one to overlook a more fundamental factor that is shared by all traders, regardless of size—the optimal specification of an order in an environment where transaction prices are uncertain, and where the act of trading is itself costly, is a complex process. Consequently, in an uncertain, nonfrictionless environment, the proper specification of the price, size, type (for example, market or limit), and timing of an order is a strategic decision that calls for separate analysis.

This chapter examines the investor's trading decision. In order to address the issues of transaction price uncertainty and costly trading in their purest form, we assume the investor is not large enough to have an appreciable impact on prices established in the market. That is, we assume a *perfectly competitive environment*. An analysis of the trading decision in this context should provide insight into the strategic decisions that all traders, both large and small, make as they approach the market to implement their investment decisions.

The investor's demand curve for an asset is analyzed in Chapter 7. This curve shows how many shares of an asset the investor would want to hold at alternative prices. As noted, however, information, decision, and order handling costs impede the ease with which an investor can implement an investment decision in the marketplace. In addition, trading under transaction price uncertainty involves *opportunity costs:* (1) the opportunity cost of trading at inferior prices (buying at prices that are unnecessarily high or selling at prices that are unnecessarily low) and (2) the opportunity cost of missing a trade because a buy order was priced too low, or because a sell order was priced too high.

In analyzing the reaction of investors to transaction price uncertainty and to the costs of trading, we continue to consider the actions of a decision maker who is assumed to know his or her demand curve and who could transmit a complete order function to the market, if desired. Studying such an individual enables us to identify the factors that give rise to the trading decision and to understand better how a real world investor, as trader, will behave. Perhaps the most important insight to be gained is that, even if a price taker, such a trader will not fully reveal his or her investment desires to the market.

The second section of the chapter considers a frictionless market. Various technical details concerning the stock dimensioned demand curve and the associated buy/sell order functions are first clarified. The main features of the analytic context are set forth, and the aggregation of the buy/sell order functions of individual traders and the determination of market equilibrium are analyzed.

Next, the discussion turns to the nonfrictionless market. The impact of explicit costs on the trading decision is first considered, and then the interpretation of an investor's buy/sell order functions as a set of instructions that may be submitted to the market is discussed. This analysis paves the way for a discussion of the opportunity costs of trading. The section concludes by establishing that, even if a trader were able to specify a complete buy/sell order function, he or she would transmit only discrete order points to the market. For the remainder of the chapter, we assume that the investor submits only one order to buy and one order to sell to the market. The submission of a single order reflects both the explicit and the opportunity costs of trading.

The trader's optimal order placement strategy is then examined. The objective of the trading decision, maximization of the expected value of consumer surplus, is first established. We then show how this goal is achieved when the trader is restricted to placing just one *order point* (one price and one quantity) in relation to his or her buy order function. The analysis for a call market and that for a continuous market are presented. It is clear from the ensuing discussion that orders written in a nonfrictionless environment reflect three elements: (1) the location of the investor's demand curve to hold shares of the risky asset, (2) the investor's expectation of what the clearing price will be, and (3) the institutional design of the market that determines how orders are translated into trades.

THE FRICTIONLESS MARKET

The Investor's Demand Curve

The demand curve of the representative investor is shown in Figure 8.1(a). The individual's current holdings are identified in the figure by the vertical

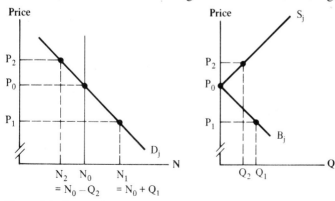

Figure 8.1 Investor's demand curve and buy and sell curves. (a) The demand curve. (b) The buy and sell curves.

line at N_0.[2] P_0 is the price at which the investor would be willing to hold N_0 shares. At any price greater than P_0, the decision maker would like to hold fewer shares; at any price lower than P_0, he or she would like to hold more shares. Chapter 6 shows how the buy and sell curves can be identified from the demand curve to hold shares. For convenience, the geometry is replicated in Figure 8.1(b).

The analysis in this section assumes a costless trading environment. In this environment the investor transmits continuous buy/sell order functions to the market and trades the appropriate amount at whatever price is established on the market. The investor will do so even if, as discussed in Chapter 7, the price established on the market signals information. This is because the order functions describe a set of *ex ante* propensities, and hence the market price does not have to be known *ex ante* in the frictionless environment.

For instance, if the price in the frictionless market turns out to be P_1, the investor will want to hold N_1 shares (because of the price and the signal that it conveys), and he or she will in fact achieve this by buying Q_1 shares. If, instead, the price turns out to be P_2, the investor will want to hold N_2 shares (because of the alternative value of price and the alternative signal that is conveyed), and he or she will in fact achieve this by selling Q_2 shares, and so forth. In general, the *ex post* result will harmonize the *ex ante* propensity with the price established on the market. This being the case, the trading decision is trivial in a frictionless environment, even with transaction price uncertainty: all the investor need do is submit his or her buy/sell order functions to the market.

Note the following about the demand curve to hold shares and the associated buy/sell order curves:

1. We have suppressed the i subscript that denotes the ith asset, because the discussion in this chapter relates to the demand to hold shares of *one* particular asset. However, because we now consider the full set of participants in the market for a stock, the subscript j has been introduced to identify the jth investor/trader, j = 1, . . . , $\mathcal{J}$.
2. The buy/sell functions for the individual trader branch off the price axis at a value determined by the intersection of the investor's demand curve (D_j) and the vertical line at N_0 that denotes the number of shares the jth investor holds.

---

[2]The subscript 0 here refers to an initial share holding; alternative share holdings will be denoted by subscripts 1 and 2. Similar subscripts will be used for the price variable. These subscripts should not be confused with those used to time date variables in Chapter 7.

3. N_0 constant, the point of intersection depends on the location of the demand curve. Accordingly, shifts in D_j are associated with shifts in the buy/sell order curves shown in Figure 8.1(b).

4. D_j constant, the point of intersection depends on the size of share holdings. Therefore, each trade is accompanied by a shift of the buy/sell order curves (the curves shift down with a purchase and up with a sale).

5. An investor's wealth changes with each purchase or sale of shares. An investor's risk aversion measure (either absolute and/or relative) is, in general, dependent on his or her wealth, and thus the slope of the demand curve derived in Chapter 7 in general changes as the investor trades. This is a second order (of importance) effect, however, and to simplify the exposition we ignore it in the discussion that follows. Thus the investor's demand curve (D_j) is assumed not to shift because of a trade.

The Analytic Context

This subsection sets forth the *modeling specifications* that define the analytic context. These are the following:

1. As in Chapter 7, there are two distinct time spans: a trading period and an investment period. The two periods are demarcated by three points in time: point in time T_0 is the *start of the trading period;* point in time T_1 is the *end of the trading period and the beginning of the investment period;* point in time T_2 is the *end of the investment period.* The span between T_0 and T_1 is brief (for instance, one day), and the same for all traders. The span between T_1 and T_2 is considerably longer, and may be unique to the specific investor.

2. Participants in the market convey their orders to the market during the trading period. All trades are *settled* (shares traded are delivered and cash payments are made) at point in time T_1, the end of the trading period.

3. Each investor writes his or her order without knowing the other investors' orders. Therefore, when writing their orders, all investors face transaction price uncertainty.

4. Each trader anticipates what the transaction price will be. This anticipation is described by two parameters: an expected transaction price and the variance of the transaction price around its mean.

5. As in Chapter 7, traders make their investment decisions at point in time T_0. They do so by projecting their thoughts forward to point in time T_1 and considering the optimal share holdings for the investment period in relation to the share prices that may be established during the trading period.

6. The decision maker implements the investment decision at T_0 by making a trading decision: the specification of the specific order,

set of orders, or continuous order function to convey to the market.
7. For the frictionless market all orders are batched for simultaneous execution at a single price during the trading period, as in the call market environment described in Chapter 2.

Market Equilibrium

Given (1) each investor's order functions (the S_j and B_j trade curves), (2) an environment where trading is costless, and (3) a call market trading arrangement, each investor submits his or her complete trade curves to the market. The reason is twofold. First, the order size associated with each price along the trade curves will have been accurately written *given that* that price is in fact set on the market. Second, the call market system guarantees that the investor realizes only one execution in the trading session. The importance of this second consideration is shown later in relation to the opportunity costs of trading.

With each decision maker submitting his or her complete order function, the market clearing values of price (P^M) and the number of shares traded (Q^M) are determined in the standard way discussed in Chapter 6. That is, for

$$B_j = f_j(P) \tag{8.1}$$
$$S_j = g_j(P) \tag{8.2}$$

the aggregate buy and sell functions are

$$B = \sum_{j=1}^{\mathcal{S}} f_j(P) \tag{8.3}$$

$$S = \sum_{j=1}^{\mathcal{S}} g_j(P) \tag{8.4}$$

The aggregate functions are shown graphically in Figure 8.2. Unlike

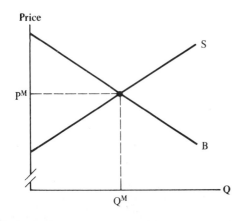

Figure 8.2 Aggregate buy and sell curves.

the B_j and S_j curves for an investor, the market curves, B and S, can intersect each other, because the locations of D_j and of the vertical line at N_0 vary across investors. When the trade curves of different investors do branch off the price axis at different values, the aggregate buy and sell curves intersect in the positive quadrant, as shown in Figure 8.2.

When the aggregate buy and sell trade curves intersect, prices exist at or below which some investors are willing to sell, and at or above which other investors are willing to buy. Hence, trades occur. For the configuration shown in Figure 8.2, Q^M shares will trade at a price of P^M.

Trading eliminates orders from the B and S curves. After the subtraction of Q^M shares from both the B and S curves, the trade curves will have shifted to the left until the intersection point shown in Figure 8.2 is at the price axis, as shown in Figure 8.3(a).

The process of trading harmonizes the jth decision maker's investment desires with the market. As shown in Figure 8.3(b), the trade curves the

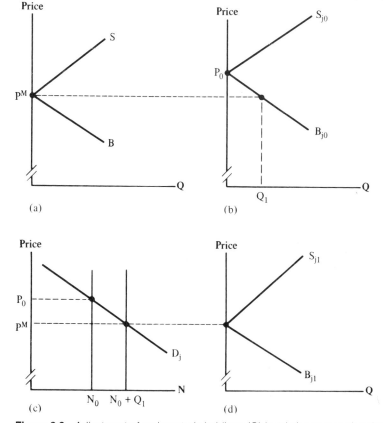

Figure 8.3 Adjustment of an investor's holdings (Q) in relation to a market determined price (P^M). (a) Aggregate buy and sell curves after trades have eliminated all crossing orders. (b)The jth investor's initial trade curves result in the purchase of Q_1 shares, at the price P^M. (c) After the purchase of Q_1 shares, the vertical line intersects the jth investor's demand curve at $N_0 + Q_1$ shares. (d) The jth investor's buy and sell curves immediately after the purchase of Q_1 shares.

j^{th} investor submitted to the market will have resulted in the purchase of Q_1 shares at the price P^M. Figure 8.3(c) shows that, after the trade, the vertical line that denotes that investor's holdings has shifted from N_0 to $N_0 + Q_1$. Consequently, the vertical line now intersects D_j at the market price, P^M. Thus after the trade, the jth investor is holding exactly the number of shares that he or she would like to hold at the current market price.

If the investor were to submit a new set of trade curves to the market after the trade, the curves would appear as shown in Figure 8.3(d). Note that the new trade curves necessarily branch off the price axis at P^M. Because this is true for each trader, mutually profitable trading opportunities do not exist immediately after a trading session for any pairing of market participants. Therefore, one round of trading in a frictionless call market environment harmonizes the trading propensities of all investors and leaves no desire to recontract. In this equilibrium, the distribution of asset shares across investors is Pareto optimal (see Chapter 6).

The market's aggregate demand curve to hold shares of the risky asset can now be identified: it is the curve labeled D in Figure 8.4(b). The relationship between the market's trade curves, B and S [as shown in Figure 8.4(a)], and the market's demand curve, D, is the same as that which relates B_j and S_j to D_j (as shown in Figure 8.1).

Unlike the case for an individual, the market in aggregate must hold a *given* number of shares—the aggregate *number of shares outstanding* (NSO). Thus we take the vertical line at NSO as fixed and locate the aggregate demand curve, D, in relation to it. In equilibrium, D crosses the vertical line at P^M, the price that has been established on the market. Alternatively stated, the equilibrium price for the market can be obtained by assessing $D = D(P)$ (the market demand equation) at $D = $ NSO. Because the market in aggregate must hold the number of shares outstanding, and

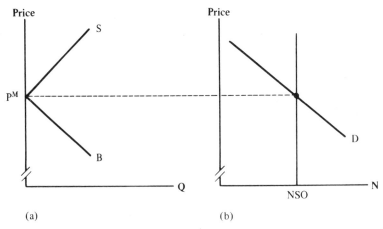

Figure 8.4 Market buy and sell curves and demand curve. (a) The buy and sell curves (b) The demand curve.

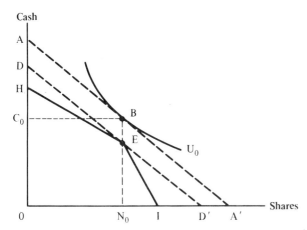

Figure 8.5 Effect of explicit costs on the cash/shares budget constraint.

because this number is given, a separate supply equation is not needed to obtain a solution.[3]

The vertical line at NSO is not a supply curve. If total corporate earnings, dividends, growth, and so on, are unaffected by the number of shares outstanding, then any change in NSO due, for example, to a stock split or stock dividend, would be associated with an equal but opposite percentage change in share price (for instance, a 2 for 1 stock split would result in the share price being halved). This being the case, with demand propensities constant, shifts of the vertical line at NSO would trace out a locus of equilibrium prices that is a negatively inclined, convex curve of unitary elasticity. It would be misleading to consider this curve the market demand curve for an asset. Therefore, NSO should not be interpreted as a supply curve.

THE NONFRICTIONLESS MARKET

Explicit Trading Costs

We begin our analysis of the nonfrictionless market by considering the explicit costs of trading (commissions, taxes, communication expenses, and so forth). These costs comprise both a *fixed* (lump sum) *component* (F) and a *variable* (per share) *component* (V). The effect of the fixed and variable costs on the trading decision is most easily considered with a *two asset model:* cash and the risky asset. To focus on explicit costs only, we here assume no transaction price uncertainty. The opportunity costs associated with transaction price uncertainty are discussed in the section "The Opportunity Costs of Trading."

Figure 8.5 shows how explicit costs affect the cash/shares budget

[3]There are two equations, D = D(P) and D = NSO, and two unknowns, D and P.

constraint. Point B in the figure identifies the initial holdings of cash (C_0) and of the risky asset (N_0). For a given cash price of shares and with costless trading, the budget constraint is the dashed line from A to A', which passes through B.[4]

The fixed cost of trading lowers the budget constraint by the dollar amount F = AD = BE. Hence, with fixed costs alone, the budget constraint is the dashed line from D to D', which passes through E. In addition, the point B is also a part of the constraint, because the investor can remain at point B by not trading at all.[5]

The addition of variable costs pushes the constraint farther down and to the left, to the kinked line labeled *HEI*. Thus the budget constraint with both fixed and variable costs is the solid line segments HE and EI and the point B. Because of the variable costs of trading, HE is flatter then DD' (fewer additional dollars are obtained when shares are traded for cash), and EI is steeper than DD' (fewer additional shares are obtained when cash is traded for shares).

The curve labeled U_0 in Figure 8.5 is the cash-shares indifference curve that passes through point B. Let U_0 be tangent to AA' at the point B. Thus the investor would want to trade only if the indifference curve were to change its slope and/or if the budget constraint were to shift because of a change in the share price of the risky asset. With the frictionless market budget constraint (AA'), any change in tastes, expectations, or share price induces the investor to seek a trade.

This is not the case, however, with transaction costs, because, as Figure 8.5 shows, nonzero fixed and/or variable transaction costs cause point B to be a corner solution. Therefore, a larger (discrete) change in either tastes or in price is required to motivate a trade. Furthermore, when the investor does seek to trade, the order size will be smaller than it would be in the absence of transaction costs (budget constraint HEI defines a more restricted feasible set than does budget constraint AA').

The effect of variable transaction costs on price and on the quantity of shares traded can also be seen for the aggregate market by application

---

[4]Cash is the *numeraire asset,* and hence its unit price is 1. Therefore, the cash price per share for the risky asset is given in Figure 8.5 by the ratio of the line segment 0A to the line segment 0A'.

[5]An X, Y budget constraint shows the *maximum* quantity of X that can be obtained given Y. Therefore, the existence of point B causes part of the dashed line from D to D' not to be a part of the constraint. To see this, draw a horizontal and a vertical line through point B so as to identify four quadrants; the section of the line DD' that passes through the quadrant to the southwest of B is not, strictly speaking, part of the budget constraint (vis-à-vis any point along this part of the line, B contains more of both cash and shares, and so must dominate). We simplify the exposition, however, by not taking further account of this technical consideration in the following diagrams or the discussion. Nothing essential is lost by the simplification, because it would never be optimal to move from B to any point that is southwest of B.

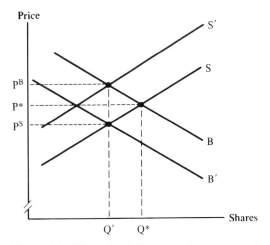

Figure 8.6 Effect of variable transaction costs on the market buy and sell curves.

of the sales tax model, a standard formulation in microeconomics.[6] To see the effect, consider Figure 8.6.

The curves labeled B and S in Figure 8.6 describe the aggregate trading desires of buyers and sellers, respectively. If trading were costless, the intersection of B and S would establish P* and Q* as the equilibrium price and quantity for the market. The impact of transaction costs can be seen in relation to this frictionless market result. We proceed as follows.

Write the market buy and sell equations, expressing P as a function of Q:

$$P = B(Q)$$
$$P = S(Q)$$ (8.5)

Let V be a buyer's and a seller's combined transaction cost per share traded.[7] Thus buyers would have to pay $P^B = S(Q) + V$ per share to purchase Q shares. As far as they are concerned, the sell curve is the curve labeled S' in Figure 8.6. Alternatively viewed, sellers would receive $P^S = B(Q) - V$ per share for the sale of Q shares. As far as they are concerned, the buy curve is the curve labeled B' in Figure 8.6.

---

[6]The sales tax, like any other transaction cost, is a payment made by a buyer that is not received by a seller. If the difference between the payment made and the payment received is collected by the government, it is a *sales tax;* if the difference is collected by the post office, a shipping company or a taxi driver, it is a *transportation charge;* if it is collected by a broker who brings the buyer and seller together, it is a *commission;* if it is collected by a dealer quoting a higher selling price than buying price, it is a *bid-ask spread.* And so on. Whatever it is called, the transaction cost has the same effect.

[7]The division of V between buyers and sellers is not relevant for the analysis that follows.

Equilibrium in this nonfrictionless market is given by the intersection of S' and B (from the viewpoint of buyers) or equivalently by the intersection of S and B' (from the viewpoint of sellers). Either way, the optimal exchange is now Q', buyers pay a price of P^B, and sellers receive a price of P^S. In summary, the effect of the variable transaction cost on the market is given by the following comparisons:

$$P^B > P*$$
$$P^S < P*$$
$$V = P^B - P^S$$
$$Q' < Q*$$

Therefore, when it costs something to transact, buyers pay more, sellers receive less, and the aggregate number of shares traded is decreased.

Order Functions

The remainder of the chapter makes extensive use of a trader's buy and sell functions. We here show how these functions can be interpreted as instructions (orders) that might be submitted to the market. The discussion treats only buy orders (the analysis is symmetric for sell orders).

Figure 8.7 presents five alternative sets of instructions. Three different markings are used in the figure: (1) solid lines indicate that the continuous order function is operative over the range shown; (2) dashed lines indicate that the underlying propensities are not to be implemented over the range shown; (3) circles identify discrete order points along an otherwise inoperative (dashed-line) order function. In addition, it should be understood that when a sequence of orders is executed in relation to these functions, the number of shares to be bought at a price is the *difference* between the number identified on the quantity axis and the number of shares previously purchased in the sequence.

Specifically, each of the five orders illustrated in Figure 8.7 is interpreted as follows:

Figure 8.7(a): The solid line labeled B is the ordinary buy curve that was identified in relation to the individual's demand curve in Figure 8.1. Since any point along the curve is operative, the investor's instructions are to buy Q_1 shares if the price is P_1, or Q_2 shares if the price is P_2, and so on, for any arbitrarily selected price. However, if Q_1 shares are bought at P_1 and the price jumps down to P_2, then the order at P_2 is for $(Q_2 - Q_1)$ shares.

Figure 8.7(b): The solid line labeled *MB* is related to the dashed line labeled B in the same way that a marginal revenue curve is related to a demand curve. As an order function, MB is to be

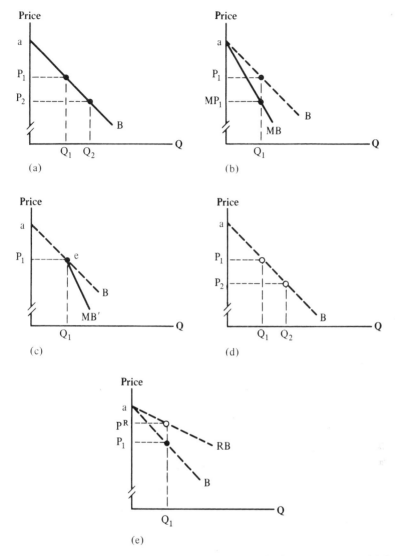

Figure 8.7 Buyer order curves. (a) Order function B. (b) Order function MB. (c) Order function MB'. (d) Discrete order points on function B. (e) Discrete order point on function RB.

implemented in the same way as the solid line labeled *B* in Figure 8.7(a). The MB order function may be used when price can descend by infinitesimal steps, thereby triggering a continuous succession of executions. For this reason, MB shows, at each quantity, the price the investor is willing to pay for a marginal share, given that the number of shares shown on the quantity axis has already been bought.

Figure 8.7(c): The instruction given by the order function shown in Figure 8.7(c) is that no purchases are to be made until price falls to P_1. At P_1, Q_1 shares are to be bought. If price continues to decrease, marginal shares are to be bought in accordance with the solid line labeled MB'.

Figure 8.7(d): The instruction given by the order function shown in Figure 8.7(d) is either (1) buy Q_1 shares at P_1, (2) buy Q_2 shares at P_2 (if the first order has not been executed), or (3) buy Q_1 shares at P_1 and $Q_2 - Q_1$ shares at P_2.[8]

Figure 8.7(e): The dashed line labeled RB is related to the dashed line labeled B in the same way as a reservation demand curve is related to a normal demand curve (see Chapter 6). The instruction given by the single order point shown along the dashed line RB is to buy Q_1 shares at the price P^R *or less*. An order of this type is relevant for the discussion of the periodic call market in the section "The Optimal Trading Decision."

Writing P as a function of Q, the relationships among the curves labeled B, RB, and MB are as follows:

The equation for the curve labeled B is [see equation (7.39)]

$$P = a - 2bQ \tag{8.6}$$

The equation for the curve labeled RB is [see equation (7.37)]

$$P = a - bQ \tag{8.7}$$

The equation for the curve labeled MB is

$$P = a - 4bQ \tag{8.8}$$

The curve labeled B is linear because we have assumed the investor's demand function to hold shares to be linear. We showed in Chapter 6 that the slope (dP/dQ) of the RB curve is half that of the linear demand curve B. Equivalently, the slope of the MB curve is twice that of the B curve. To see this, first multiply equation (8.6) by Q to obtain total expenditure as a function of Q:

$$PQ = aQ - 2bQ^2 \tag{8.9}$$

Then differentiate with respect to Q to obtain the marginal expenditure as a function of Q:

$$\frac{d(PQ)}{dQ} = a - 4bQ \tag{8.10}$$

The *marginal expenditure* is the price the decision maker would be willing to pay for an incremental share, given that Q shares have already been

---

[8]The preference ordering for the three alternatives is (2), (3), (1).

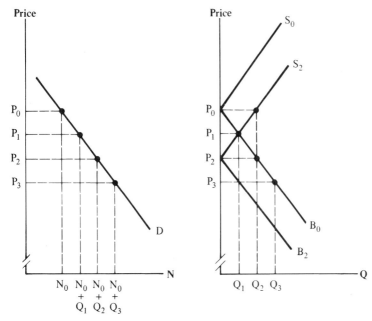

Figure 8.8 Adjustment of an order curve after a price reversal. (a) Trades result in movements along the investor's demand curve to hold shares. (b) Purchases shift the investor's sell order function and sales shift the investor's buy order function.

bought. Therefore, equation (8.10) is the equation for the curve labeled *MB* (equation [8.8]), and for the linear case its slope (2b) is twice that of the curve labeled *B* [equation (8.6)].

The buy orders just identified can remain operative through a sequence of price continuations but must be adjusted after a price reversal.[9] This can be demonstrated with reference to Figure 8.8. Let the solid line B_0 in Figure 8.8(b) be the trader's order function [as in Figure 8.7(a)], and assume a sequence of two negative price jumps, from P_0 to P_1 and then from P_1 to P_2. In accordance with the instruction given by the line B_0, the trader will buy Q_1 shares at P_1, and $Q_2 - Q_1$ shares at P_2. If price continues to jump down to some $P_3 < P_2$, a third purchase $(Q_3 - Q_2)$ will be appropriately identified from the order curve labeled B_0.

However, suppose a reversal occurs before the third negative price change, and that price jumps back to P_0. Then, in accordance with the sell order curve labeled S_2, the decision maker will sell Q_2 shares. If price now jumps down to P_3, the desired purchase is Q_3, not $Q_3 - Q_2$. Generalizing, we see that the buy order curve shifts after each sale (and, symmetrically, the sell order curve shifts after each purchase). Because the price reversal

[9]In a *price continuation* a price change is followed by another price change of the same sign (a decrease is followed by a decrease, or an increase is followed by an increase). In a *price reversal* the change in price reverses direction from one transaction to the next (price goes up after a decrease or declines after an increase).

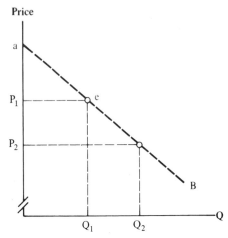

Figure 8.9 Identification of the opportunity cost of an intramarginal purchase, and of the loss of consumer surplus from a trade that was missed.

in the sequence of negative jumps triggers a sale, it also causes a shift of the buy order function.[10]

The shifting of order functions that occurs because of a purchase or a sale means that the decision maker must transmit a considerably more detailed set of instructions to the market. Higher explicit costs are incurred because of the added complexity involved. However, the problem is technical and in principle it can be handled.

The Opportunity Costs of Trading

This subsection takes the explicit costs of trading to be zero and analyzes two opportunity costs of trading that are attributable to transaction price uncertainty. One opportunity cost relates to trades that have been made, and the other relates to trading opportunities that have been missed. Even in the absence of the explicit cost of trading, the opportunity costs affect the flow of orders to a market. Our analysis of these costs assumes a continuous market environment.

The opportunity cost of trades made is the loss of consumer surplus that occurs when a trader has more than one buy or sell order execute in sequence. The loss is the extra amount paid per share for the higher priced buy orders in a sequence or the extra price per share not received for the lower priced sell orders in a sequence. This loss can be identified precisely with reference to Figure 8.9.

Figure 8.9 shows the order set described in Figure 8.7(d): buy Q_1 shares at P_1; Q_2 at P_2; or Q_1 at P_1 and $(Q_2 - Q_1)$ at P_2. Suppose that the orders at both prices execute. Then the $\langle P_2, (Q_2 - Q_1) \rangle$ order is the *mar-*

[10]Notice that the direction of the shifts illustrated in Figure 8.8(b) depends on whether the transactions are buys or sells, and that the magnitude of the shifts depends upon the size of the price changes. Therefore, the revision of the order functions after any transaction depends on what the realized transaction has turned out to be.

ginal order (it just executed), and the $\langle P_1, Q_1 \rangle$ order is the *intramarginal* order (the market price could have been somewhat higher than P_2, and the order would still have executed).

The consumer surplus lost (the extra amount paid) as a result of the intramarginal order's executing is $(P_1 - P_2)Q_1$. Because of this cost, one might question why the intramarginal order was written in the first place. The reason is that the decision maker does not know in advance what the transaction price will be. If the price does not fall enough to trigger the execution at P_2, the order at P_1 will be the marginal order. In such an event, its execution will yield the consumer surplus shown by the area of the triangle aP_1e, which is equal to $(a - P_1)Q_1/2$. Accordingly, if the order had not been written at P_1, this consumer surplus would have been lost. This loss of consumer surplus is the second opportunity cost of trading. It is the opportunity cost of missing a trade.

Recognition of the two opportunity costs (the extra payment made for intramarginal executions and the consumer surplus lost when a marginal order is not written) is key to understanding the trader's decision problem. These costs exist because of the very factor that distinguishes the trading decision from the investment decision: transaction prices are not known when the buy/sell orders are specified. Analyzing the trader's response to these opportunity costs shows why proper specification of an order is a strategic decision.

The two opportunity costs of trading can be analyzed by using the alternative order sets the decision maker can submit to the market. As in the discussion of order functions, we need consider only the buy orders (the analysis on the sell side is symmetric).

Because we have assumed that the environment is perfectly competitive (any individual trader is too small to affect a market price) and that price and quantity are continuous variables, it is not necessary to take account of the possibility of partial execution of an order. That is, an individual may enter an order of discrete size at a specific price, but that order, being insignificant in relation to the market, will execute totally if the transaction price on the market reaches the order's price.[11] Neither need we take account of a secondary trading priority rule, such as the time priority rule that the first order placed at a price is the first to execute.

---

[11]The analog in the theory of the firm under competition is that, if the market price for the resource supplied by the firm reaches a level equal to the minimum point on the firm's average cost curve, the firm will enter the market, producing a (discrete) amount given by the minimum point on the firm's average cost curve. The firm, being insignificant in relation to the market, will always be able to sell the entire (discrete) amount it produces at its entry price. If the firms are continuously distributed according to the height of their cost curves, the supply curve of the industry will be a continuous, everywhere differentiable function, even though the entry quantity of each firm is not infinitesimal on the micro level.

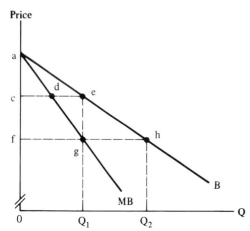

Figure 8.10 Analysis of the MB order curve.

Order Function B   If the decision maker were to submit the complete buy order function labeled *B* in Figure 8.7(a), then with price continuations he or she would buy at a succession of points while moving down the order curve. This would eliminate much of the trader's consumer surplus if price were to change by discrete jumps and would eliminate *all* of the decision maker's consumer surplus if price were to change by infinitesimal jumps.

Order Function MB   The trader can avoid the total loss of consumer surplus by submitting the curve labeled *MB* in Figure 8.7(b), which is reproduced in Figure 8.10. Referring to Figure 8.10, assume price drops in infinitesimal steps from $\overline{oa}$ to $\overline{of}$.[12] In such a case, the investor purchases Q_1 shares at a total cost equal to the area $oagQ_1$. Since the slope (dP/dQ) of the curve MB is twice that of the curve B, it can be shown that adc and deg are equal triangles, and therefore are of equal area. Thus the area $oagQ_1$ equals the area $oceQ_1$. Accordingly, the investor will have purchased the Q_1 shares at an average price of $\overline{oc}$.

One can now see why the investor would prefer to submit the curve MB rather than the curve B to the market. Submitting the marginal order function reduces the opportunity cost of intramarginal orders executing at higher prices. Therefore, if the price decreases to $\overline{of}$ as discussed previously, the investor receives the consumer surplus associated with buying Q_1 shares at an average price of $\overline{oc}$, rather than no consumer surplus at all. This consumer surplus equals the area of the triangle ace, which equals the area of the triangle age.

[12]The bar indicates that *oa* is the line segment o to a, and that *of* is the line segment o to f.

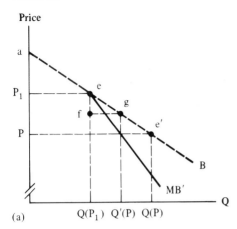
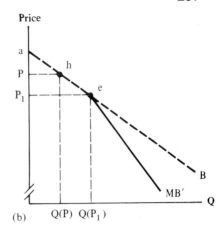

Figure 8.11 Analysis of the MB' order curve. (a) The opportunity cost of intramarginal purchases. (b) The opportunity cost of not transacting.

Furthermore, by submitting the marginal order curve MB, the decision maker automatically enjoys more consumer surplus, the further the market price falls in the trading period. That is, as point g moves down the line MB, the associated point e (which shows the average price at which the shares are bought) moves down the line B, and the area of the triangle ace increases.

Order Function MB'   Note, however, that for the trader to benefit from buying at an average price of $\overline{oc}$, the price on the market has to fall to the lower value, of. This suggests that although the second strategy (submit the MB curve) is better than the first (submit the B curve), some other strategy may be even better. The alternative we next consider is the following order: buy Q_1 shares at P_1 and buy additional shares at lower prices according to the order function labeled *MB'*. This order can be analyzed with reference to Figure 8.11. Note that the order function labeled *MB'* in Figure 8.11 has the same slope as the order function labeled *MB* in Figure 8.10 and has twice the slope (dP/dQ) of the order function labeled *B*.

Figure 8.11(a) shows that, given the MB' order, if the market price decreases in infinitesimal steps to a value P, the decision maker's consumer surplus equals the area of the triangle aP_1e plus the area of the triangle efg.[13] If, alternatively, the decision maker's order had been to buy Q(P) shares at the price P, his or her consumer surplus would have equaled the area of the larger triangle, aPe'. Therefore, the opportunity cost of the

---

[13]Note that the average price paid for $Q(P_1)$ shares is P_1, and that the average price paid for $Q'(P) - Q(P_1)$ shares is given by the vertical distance $gQ'(P)$ [which is why the incremental consumer surplus for $Q'(P) - Q(P_1)$ shares is given by the area of the triangle, efg]. The argument is analogous to that used previously with respect to the MB order function.

intramarginal purchases equals the area $aPe' - aP_1e - efg$. Note that the line segment $\overline{ef}$ divided by the line segment $\overline{fg}$ equals b, where $-b$ is the slope of order function B. Therefore, $(\overline{ef}) = (b)(\overline{fg}) = (b)[Q'(P) - Q(P_1)]$, and hence the area of the triangle efg equals $(b)[Q'(P) - Q(P_1)]^2(\frac{1}{2})$.

Assume, alternatively, that the decision maker submits the same order described in the preceding paragraph, but that the price on the market does not decrease as far as P_1. Figure 8.11(b) shows that, in this case, the opportunity cost of not transacting at all equals the area of the triangle defined by the intercept parameter (a), the market price (P), and the point h.

Because the trader does not know what the transaction price will be when the order is placed, he or she cannot react to a specific opportunity cost. Rather, the trader assesses the *expected opportunity cost* (EOC) associated with an order. The change in the EOC realized by submitting order function MB′ rather than order function MB is the possible loss of consumer surplus in the range P_1 to a (in Figure 8.11) if a transaction is missed, minus the possible gain of consumer surplus in the range 0 to P_1 if the intramarginal purchases between P_1 and a are avoided. The Appendix to this chapter shows that this difference in the expected opportunity cost can be expressed analytically as

$$\Delta EOC = \frac{1}{2}b\left\{ \int_{P_1}^{a} [Q'(P)]^2 f(P)\ dP - \int_{0}^{P_1} [Q(P_1)]^2 f(P)\ dP \right\} \quad (8.11)$$

Note in equation (8.11) that $Q(P_1)$ is greater than $Q'(P)$ for P in the range between P_1 and a. This suggests that, *ceteris paribus,* the change in the expected opportunity cost will be negative. Nevertheless, the sign of equation (8.11) depends on the probability function, $f(P)$, and on how close P_1 is to a. For the difference in the expected opportunity cost to be positive, $f(P)$ would have to be sufficiently small over the region 0 to P_1, compared to its value over the region P_1 to a.[14] This is unlikely, however, for P_1 close to a. Therefore, we anticipate that the expected opportunity cost is less if P_1 is set in the neighborhood immediately below a. Consequently, it will be preferable for the decision maker to specify an order starting at a point such as e (in Figure 8.11), where e is a discrete distance below the intercept, a.

Discrete Order Points   The trader can do even better by following a fourth strategy that necessarily dominates the third, and hence the first two as well: convey only discrete order points to the market. Such a strategy is illustrated

---

[14]A necessary but not sufficient condition is

$$\int_{0}^{P} f(P)\ dP < \int_{P_1}^{a} f(P)\ dP$$

by the two order points shown in Figure 8.7(d). The dominance of this strategy for prices less than P_1 can be established by replicating the argument just presented with respect to the MB′ order function. To replicate the proof, simply change the origin in Figure 8.11 from 0 to $Q(P_1)$ and the intercept from a to P_1.

A Partially Collapsed Order Function   The trader has one more alternative: reduce the order size at each price (P) in the neighborhood below the intercept a, and submit a continuous order function. To assess this alternative, consider the purchase of Q shares at an arbitrarily selected price P′ that is greater than P_1 but less than a. The consumer surplus per unit purchased at this price decreases linearly from (a − P′) to 0, as Q increases from 0 to $Q(P′)$. On the other hand, if the price on the market decreases to the value $P_1 < P′$, the additional opportunity cost per share of the intramarginal purchase equals $P′ − P_1$ regardless of the number of shares purchased at the price P′. Therefore, setting Q less than $Q(P)$ reduces the opportunity cost of missing a transaction by more than the opportunity cost of intramarginal purchases is increased, and it may be optimal for the trader to specify an order at the value P′.

Therefore, in the final analysis, the trader facing opportunity costs but not explicit costs may still submit a continuous order function to the market. That function, however, will be *partially collapsed* toward the price axis [that is, at each price we will have $0 < Q < Q(P)$]. The smaller is the probability f(P) dP in the neighborhood below a, the closer the order function is to the price axis in the neighborhood below a.

Recapitulation

This section has shown that both the explicit costs and the opportunity costs of trading reduce the size of buy/sell orders. The opportunity costs cause the order function to collapse toward the price axis, and the explicit costs make it undesirable to submit orders of small size. We therefore conclude that, with costly trading and transaction price uncertainty, a trader with a continuous demand curve to hold shares will submit only *discrete* order points to the market. We next analyze the order placement strategy of a market participant who is restricted to placing *just one* order to buy and one order to sell during a trading session. The restriction to a single point order simplifies the analysis with no substantive loss of generality.

THE OPTIMAL TRADING DECISION

This section considers the optimal placement of a point order (a specific price and size) for two alternative market environments: a call market and a continuous market. In neither case is the investor forced to pick a point from his or her demand curve. Rather, an optimal order is determined, given: (1) the location of the investor's demand curve to hold shares, (2) the investor's expectation of what the transaction price will be, and (3) the design of the trading system (whether it is a call or continuous market). We begin by establishing the goal of the decision maker as trader.

The Trader's Objective: The Maximization of Expected Consumer Surplus

The goal of the trader is the maximization of expected consumer surplus. This goal is consistent with the maximization of the expected utility of wealth (the ultimate objective of the decision maker). Consistency can be established as follows.[15]

Chapter 7 shows for a two asset universe (a risk-free asset and one risky asset) how the investor's demand function to hold shares of the risky asset can be obtained from the utility function defined on wealth. A key equation in the derivation is[16]

$$h(P, Q \mid N_0, C_0) = c + gQ(a - bQ - P) \qquad (8.12)$$

Using $P^R = a - bQ$, the equation for the reservation buy/sell function, equation (8.12) can be rewritten as

$$h(P, Q \mid N_0, C_0) = c + gQ(P^R - P) \qquad (8.13)$$

Because c and g are parameters, the decision maker maximizes his or her expected utility, $E(h)$, by maximizing the expected value of $Q(P^R - P)$. This term, however, is the expression for consumer surplus. Therefore, the decision maker maximizes the *expected* utility of wealth by maximizing the *expected* value of consumer surplus.

The maximization of expected consumer surplus is an intuitively appealing objective. Consumer surplus is a monetary measure of the gains of trading any given number of shares at any given price. The uncertainty for the trader is what the specific execution will be, and thus what the specific value of consumer surplus will be. That is why the trader is concerned with the *expected* value of consumer surplus; it is the probability weighted average of the possible outcomes. The decision maker's risk aversion is reflected in the demand curve to hold shares, which is used to determine consumer

---

[15]Note that the maximization of expected consumer surplus is identical to the minimization of the expected opportunity cost referred to in the previous section. The following analysis is based on Ho, Schwartz, and Whitcomb (1985).

[16]Equation (7.28) (in Chapter 7) includes a subscript 1 on the variable P to show explicitly that the price applies as of point in time T_1. This time identification is clear in context in the current chapter and thus is suppressed for simplicity.

surplus and need not be taken account of again. Thus we need not take account of the variance of consumer surplus.

The logic involved may be better appreciated with reference to a specific example. Consider the trader's choice between two alternative sets of instructions:

$$A: \quad \text{Buy 150 shares at \$50}$$
$$B: \quad \text{Buy 225 shares at \$45}$$

Let the outcomes associated with alternative A be:[17]

Transaction	Probability	Consumer surplus
1. No purchase is made	.10	–0–
2. 150 shares bought at 50	.90	$(55 - 50)150/2 = 375$

Let the outcomes associated with alternative B be:

Transaction	Probability	Consumer surplus
1. No purchase is made	.50	–0–
2. 225 shares bought at 45	.50	$(55 - 45)225/2 = 1125$

The expected consumer surplus for alternative A is .9(375) = 337.5. The expected consumer surplus for alternative B is .5(1125) = 562.5. The expected consumer surplus maximizing trader selects the alternative with the highest value. Therefore, alternative B is chosen over alternative A.

The Optimal Trading Decision in a Call Market Environment[18]

All orders that transact at a trading session in a call market are executed at the same market clearing price (P^c). An investor's buy order executes if it is placed at a price equal to or greater than P^c; an investor's sell order executes if it is placed at a price equal to or less than P^c. We continue to treat buy orders only; as in preceding sections, the analysis for the specification of a sell order is symmetrical.

---

[17] We assume for the computation of consumer surplus that the order function intersects the price axis at a value of $55.

[18] The following model was presented by Ho, Schwartz, and Whitcomb (1985).

Let $G(x)$ be the investor's subjective probability of the clearing price being less than some value x. Assume the clearing price is normally distributed, with mean $E(P^c)$ and variance $Var(P^c)$. As established in the previous subsection, the investor maximizes his or her expected utility $[E(h)]$ by specifying a buy order price (P) and an order size (Q) that maximize the expected value of his or her consumer surplus. Because there is no purchase for $x > P$, the objective is

$$\max_{P,Q} \int_{-\infty}^{P} Q[P^R(Q) - x]G'(x)\, dx \tag{8.14}$$

where $G'(x)\, dx$ is the probability of the clearing price equaling x, and $P^R(Q)$ is the reservation price for a buy order of size Q.

Equation (8.14) may be more easily understood with reference to Figure 8.12. Assume that an investor with the reservation buy curve RB submits an order to buy Q_1 shares at a limit price of P_1. The order will execute if P^c is equal to or less than P_1. In Figure 8.12(a), $x < P_1$, and the order would execute if P^c equaled this value. In Figure 8.12(b), $x > P_1$, and the order would not execute. If the investor's order does execute, the consumer surplus received is $Q_1(P^R - x)$. Equation (8.14) shows that the investor's *expected* consumer surplus for the P_1, Q_1 order is the probability weighted average over all x up to P_1, of the consumer surplus at each value of x.

The P_1, Q_1 order illustrated in Figure 8.12 is not an optimal order. Referring to Figure 8.12(b), we see that the investor would have received consumer surplus if his or her order had executed at the higher value of x [because $Q_1(P^R - x)$ is positive]. In general, the investor's expected consumer surplus is reduced if the limit price (P) for Q shares is less than

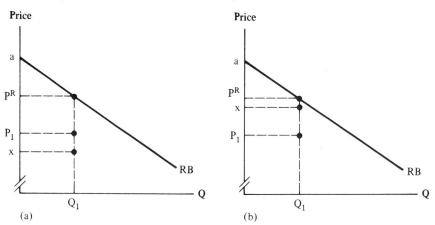

Figure 8.12 Relationship between a market clearing price, and a trader's order price and consumer surplus in a call market environment. (a) The clearing price x is less than the order price P_1. (b) The clearing price x is greater than the order price P_1.

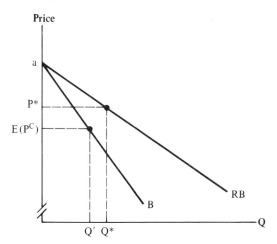

Figure 8.13 A trader's optimal buy order in a call market evironment.

$P^R(Q)$ (because a transaction that would yield positive consumer surplus may not be realized). Therefore, the limit price for Q_1 shares will be $P^R(Q_1)$ (the reservation price for an order of size Q_1),[19] and the objective (equation [8.14]) becomes

$$\max_{Q} \int_{-\infty}^{P^R(Q)} Q[P^R(Q) - x]G'(x) \, dx \qquad (8.15)$$

Ho, Schwartz, and Whitcomb (1985) use equation (8.15) to obtain an explicit solution for an individual's optimal order. The solution, which is illustrated in Figure 8.13, depends on the mean and variance of the clearing price, and on the parameters of the investor's order function.[20] Figure 8.13 shows that, in the absence of transaction price uncertainty, if the price at the call is a known value equal to $E(P^c)$, the investor will place an order for Q' shares. Ho, Schwartz, and Whitcomb show that, with transaction price uncertainty and an *expected* clearing price of $E(P^c)$, the investor's optimal order price is a value P^* greater than $E(P^c)$, and that his or her optimal order size is a value Q^* greater than Q'. The reason is as follows.

The trader's order executes only if the price of the order is equal to or greater than P^c and, if it executes, it does so at the clearing price, not at its own price. Therefore, the investor obtains protection from transaction

[19]Referring to equation (8.14), this is because each integrand is positive for $P < P^R$. Each integrand is also negative for $P > P^R$.

[20]The specific order is obtained by setting the derivative of equation (8.15) with respect to Q equal to zero. The solution requires solving two simultaneous equations that involve the mean and standard deviation of the clearing price, and the slope and intercept parameters of the investor's order function. See Ho, Schwartz, and Whitcomb (1985, Appendix B).

price uncertainty by specifying his or her reservation price for the order size submitted; thus we have $P^* > E(P^c)$. With this protection, the trader gambles on receiving the larger consumer surplus associated with an execution farther down and to the right, along the ordinary buy curve. The trader does so by increasing the order size somewhat ($Q^* > Q'$), and by lowering the order price somewhat (P^* is less than the reservation buy price for Q' shares).

The Optimal Trading Decision in a Continuous Market Environment

An order executes in a continuous market whenever it crosses, or is crossed by, a counterpart order. For our purpose, the continuous market can be modeled in three ways:[21]

1. *Limit order model:* All limit orders are executed or cancelled by the end of each trading session, and the trader whose decision we are analyzing is the first to submit an order in a new trading session. Therefore, this trader can submit only a limit order (there are no other limit orders for a market order to execute against), and, if the order executes, it will do so at its own price. This model specification, which is most pertinent to the decision of a monopoly dealer, enables us to focus on only one type of order (the limit order).

2. *Hybrid model:* The trader specifies the price and size of an order before the start of a trading session, and the order is received by the market some time during the trading session. If the order price is sufficient to trigger a transaction upon its arrival, it executes as a market order at the price established by the limit order it transacts against. If the order price is not sufficient to trigger a transaction upon arrival, it is placed on the order book. If the order subsequently executes, it does so at its own limit price, as in the preceding model. This model specification, which is most pertinent for an individual who is at a distance from the trading floor, combines elements of the limit order model (the trader's order may execute at its own price) and the call market (the trader's order may execute at a price set on the market).

3. *Discretionary model:* The trader writes an order during the trading day, after learning the current bid and ask quotations. In this model, which is most pertinent to the decision of a floor trader, the trader can submit a market order or a limit order, at his or her own discretion.

The Limit Order Model We consider the limit order model first. By itself, this model is artificial, but it provides a foundation for analyzing the

[21]The models are further analyzed by Bronfman (1988).

two that follow. To obtain a *ceteris paribus* contrast with the call market, assume the trader has the same demand curve to hold shares, and let $G(x)$ describe his or her subjective probability of the transaction price decreasing to some value x in the course of a trading day. This structures the analysis so that the only difference between the two markets is that the limit order submitted to the continuous market executes at the price of the order, not at a common market clearing price as in the call market described previously.

Because in this model the order executes at its own price, its price and size are determined by the ordinary buy function, not the reservation buy function. That is, if the order is written at the price P_1 and if it does execute, the trader wishes to purchase $Q_1 = Q(P_1)$ shares, the associated number of shares on the ordinary buy function. Therefore, the trader does not seek protection from transaction price uncertainty by submitting an order from his or her reservation curve.

Given his or her subjective probability distribution $G(x)$, let $E(P)$ be a value such that an order at a price above $E(P)$ has a greater than 50 percent chance of transacting, and an order at a price below $E(P)$ has a less than 50 percent chance of transacting during a trading session. Figure 8.14(a) shows that, in the absence of transaction price uncertainty, if the price in the continuous market decreases to a known value equal to $E(P)$, the investor places an order for Q' shares.

With transaction price uncertainty, the trader's optimal order may be placed above or below $E(P)$, depending on the location of the order function in relation to $E(P)$. Given the slope of the order function, the higher is the intercept parameter (a) in relation to $E(P)$, the greater would be the decision

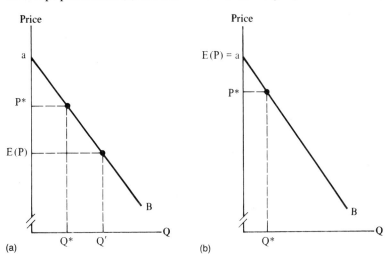

Figure 8.14 A trader's optimal buy order in a continuous market environment. (a) For a − E(P) large (a relatively intense desire to trade), the optimal buy order price P* is greater than the expected price E(P). (b) For a = E(P) (a trade would not be sought at the expected price), the optimal buy order price P* is less than the expected price E(P).

maker's consumer surplus from trading Q′ shares at the price E(P), and the larger would be his or her opportunity cost of missing such a trade. Consequently, when the value of a − E(P) is large, the trader is likely to increase the probability of realizing an execution by placing an order at a price above E(P). This is shown by the P*, Q* order along the ordinary buy function in Figure 8.14(a).

On the other hand, if a − E(P) is small, the trader would receive little consumer surplus from buying at a price equal to or greater than E(P), and therefore is likely to place an order at a price below E(P). The trader's optimal order for this second case is shown by the P*, Q* order along the ordinary buy function in Figure 8.14(b), where we have set the expected price [E(P)] equal to the intercept parameter, a. The order placed at a price below E(P) is not expected to execute, but is optimal nevertheless because of the greater consumer surplus that would be received in the event the lower price is attained.

We conclude the following from the limit order model:

1. The trader submits an order from his or her ordinary buy function.
2. The price and size of the order depend on the mean and variance of the transaction price over the trading session.
3. If at E(P) the decision maker has a strong incentive to trade [a − E(P) is large], the order price will be above E(P); if at E(P) the decision maker does not have a strong incentive to trade [a − E(P) is small], the order price will be below E(P).
4. The order transmitted to the continuous market differs from the order that would have been transmitted to a call market.

The Hybrid Model The hybrid model is similar to the limit order model, except that it takes account of the possibility of the order executing as a market order. If it transacts as a market order, the order executes at a price below its limit price, in which event the trader would want to buy a larger number of shares. The trader takes account of the possibility of the order executing at a lower price by specifying a larger number of shares (Q) for any given limit price or, equivalently, by specifying a higher limit price for any given number of shares. Therefore, in the hybrid model, the trader picks an order above and to the right of the ordinary buy curve.

However, because the order may not execute at a market determined price but rather at its own limit price, the trader picks a point below and to the left of his or her reservation buy curve. Therefore, in the hybrid model the trader picks an order between the ordinary buy curve (that would apply in the limit order model) and the reservation buy curve (that would apply for the call market).

The Discretionary Model   In the discretionary model, the trader knows whether the order will execute as a market order or will be placed on the book as a limit order. In this case, the limit order is a point picked from the ordinary buy function, as in the limit order model. The size (Q) of the market order is set equal to the value given by the ordinary buy function assessed at the price of the counterpart market quote. The trader selects the greater of (a) the known consumer surplus that would be realized from the market order or (b) the expected consumer surplus that would be realized from the limit order.

The option to submit a market order affects the placement of the limit order. As discussed further in Chapter 10, the limit order is not placed infinitesimally close to the price at which the market order would execute. This is because the uncertainty associated with the limit order strategy is justified only if the expected consumer surplus of the limit order is greater than the specific consumer surplus of the market order. However, (1) the probability of the market order executing is unity, (2) the probability of the limit order executing is a discrete amount less than unity no matter how close its price is to the price at which the market order would execute, and thus (3) the expected consumer surplus for the limit order must be less than the known consumer surplus for the market order if the price of the limit order is infinitesimally close to the price of the market order.

CONCLUSION

This chapter has analyzed the decision maker's implementation of the investment decision formulated in Chapter 7. Traders approach a nonfrictionless market with caution—they do not want to pay more than necessary for a purchase or accept less for a sale. At the same time, however, they do not want to miss a trade because they have bid too low or offered too high.

Thus trading in a nonfrictionless market involves strategy. Orders written in the nonfrictionless market depend on the location of the investor's demand curve to hold shares of the risky asset, on his or her expectation of what the market clearing price will be, and on the design of the trading system. With regard to the trading system, the chapter has shown that the price and size of orders transmitted to a continuous market differ from those of orders transmitted to a call market. Thus we see that, for nonfrictionless markets, the design of the trading system affects individual trading decisions.

We have assumed that no trader has the ability to affect market prices by his or her trading decision. This simplification has enabled us to focus on the pure effect of transaction costs and transaction price uncertainty. Actual traders make more complex decisions. A larger variety of order types than we have considered exists (see Chapter 3), the frequency with which trades are to be sought is itself a decision variable, and the price impact of orders must be taken into account (large orders are commonly negotiated or broken up and worked over time). For these reasons, further analysis of the trading decision would be desirable. Unfortunately, much remains to be learned about the subject by financial economists.

Investors perturb the market price by the strategic games they play. For this reason, clearing prices that are observed in actual markets generally differ from values that would be attained if trading were a frictionless process. This point is of critical importance in our analysis of the equity markets; we return to it in the next chapter.

APPENDIX

Equation (8.11) may be derived more formally as follows. Given the MB' order function, the opportunity cost associated with any market price (P) less than P_1 is $\frac{1}{2}[(a - P)Q(P) - (a - P_1)Q(P_1)b[Q'(P) - Q_1]^2]$, and the opportunity cost associated with any market price between P_1 and the intercept parameter (a) is $\frac{1}{2}(a - P)Q(P)$. Therefore, the *expected opportunity cost* (EOC) is

$$\text{EOC} = \int_0^{P_1} [(a - P)Q(P) - (a - P_1)Q(P_1) - b(Q'(P) - Q_1)^2]\frac{1}{2}\, f(P)\, dP$$

$$+ \int_{P_1}^a (a - P)Q(P)\frac{1}{2}\, f(P)\, dP \tag{8.A1}$$

where P is the price of the lowest priced buy order that executes, and $f(P)$ is the probability that an order at P is the marginal order to execute. From equation (8.A1), as P_1 is increased to the value a,

$$\lim_{P_1 \to a} \text{EOC} = \int_0^a [(a - P)Q(P) - b[Q'(P)]^2]\,\frac{1}{2}\, f(P)\, dP \tag{8.A2}$$

In the limit, as P_1 goes to a, the order strategy described by the MB' order function becomes the order strategy described by the MB function. Note that $(a - P)Q(P) = b[Q(P)]^2$ and $Q(P) > Q'(P)$; thus $(a - P)Q(P)b[Q'(P)]^2 > 0$, and hence the limit is positive.

If the decision maker sets P_1 some discrete distance below the intercept, a, the expected opportunity cost associated with intramarginal purchases is less, but the EOC associated with not transacting at all is introduced. The EOC for $P_1 < a$, as compared with $P_1 = a$, can be assessed by subtracting equation (8.A2) from equation (8.A1), and by integrating by parts:

$$\Delta \text{ EOC} = \frac{1}{2} \left[\int_0^{P_1} (a - P)Q(P)f(P) \, dP - \int_0^{P_1} (a - P_1)Q(P_1)f(P) \, dP \right.$$

$$- \int_0^{P_1} b[Q'(P) - Q_1]^2 f(P) \, dP + \int_{P_1}^a (a - P)Q(P)f(P) \, dP$$

$$\left. - \int_0^a (a - P)Q(P)f(P) \, dP + \int_0^a b[Q'(P)]^2 f(P) \, dP \right] \qquad (8.A3)$$

The first, fourth, and fifth terms on the right-hand side of equation (8.A3) sum to zero. For P_1 close to a, Q_1 is close to zero, and thus the third term on the right-hand side of equation (8.A3) is approximately

$$- \int_0^{P_1} b[Q'(P)]^2 f(P) \, dP$$

Cancelling the first, fourth, and fifth terms; combining the third and sixth terms; and using $a - P_1 = bQ(P_1)$, gives equation (8.11).

SUGGESTED READING

C. Bronfman, "The Informational Content of Frequently Changing Prices: Implications for the Structural Organization of a Securities Market," Doctoral dissertation in process, Graduate School of Business Administration, New York University, 1988.

K. Cohen, S. Maier, R. Schwartz, and D. Whitcomb, "Transaction Costs, Order Placement Strategy, and Existence of the Bid-Ask Spread," *Journal of Political Economy,* April 1981.

T. Ho, R. Schwartz, and D. Whitcomb, "The Trading Decision and Market Clearing Under Transaction Price Uncertainty," *Journal of Finance,* March 1985.

R. Schwartz and D. Whitcomb, "Trading Strategies for Institutional Investors," Monograph Series in Finance and Economics, Salomon Brothers Center for the Study of Financial Institutions, New York University Graduate School of Business Administration, forthcoming, 1988.

chapter 9

Information and Prices

Information changes almost continuously in the equity markets. But information gathering and processing are not costless, and investors are never perfectly informed. This chapter focuses on the use of information, the impact of information on prices, the role of the marketplace as an aggregator of the diverse opinions of traders, and the informational efficiency of markets. The analysis provides a link between the investment and trading decisions of individuals and the behavior of security prices, a topic we turn to in Chapter 10.

This chapter first considers the relationships among information, expectations, and prices. We start with the definition and classification of information. Next we consider why, in relation to the information set, investors have heterogeneous rather than homogeneous expectations. Then, in light of the heterogeneity of investor expectations, we clarify that security prices are not determined by intrinsic values that are independent of market forces, but rather are established in the marketplace by the interaction of investor demand propensities. The section then discusses the relationship between investor expectations and market determined prices and presents a model of expectations formation.

The next section defines informational efficiency. The five parts of the discussion reflect five dimensions of the issue: (1) the efficiency with which a given information set is exploited, (2) the efficiency with which information gathering and processing activities are pursued, (3) the accuracy with which the aggregation of investor demand reflects the information set,

(4) the accuracy with which clearing prices reflect the information set, and (5) the dynamic efficiency of information dissemination in the market.

Then evidence on the informational efficiency of markets is considered. Three subsections discuss three levels of informational efficiency: (1) *weak form efficiency* (the information contained in past price movements is reflected in current prices), (2) *semistrong form efficiency* (all publicly available information is reflected in current prices), and (3) *strong form efficiency* (all information, both public and private, is reflected in current prices). We then return to the issue of heterogeneous expectations and show that informational efficiency does not imply that investor expectations will be homogeneous in equilibrium, even in a frictionless market.

INFORMATION, EXPECTATIONS, AND PRICES

What Is Information?

Information can be classified into two broad categories: (1) the information set that relates to the investment decision (the basic determinants of share value) and (2) floor information.

Floor information includes knowledge of the current quotes, last transaction prices, and transaction volume. In addition, some traders take account of recent high-low prices, the daily opening price, and the previous day's close. Furthermore, it would be of value to have information on orders that have not yet executed, including knowledge of the limit order book (orders on the specialist's book are not, however, disclosed to traders), knowledge of orders held by traders in the crowd (which are partially revealed), and statements of buying or selling interest by block, institutional, and other large traders (which are partially available on systems such as AutEx).

Information relevant to the investment decision pertains to the determinants of future share value. The most useful form for information to take would be a direct statement of the means, variances, and covariances of security returns (as discussed in Chapter 7). However, one can at best form expectations on means, variances, and covariances, given the information that is available:

> *Recent share price history:* for example, knowledge of the historic values of the means, variances, and covariances of returns.

> *Current financial information:* for example, information concerning current capital structure and earnings forecasts.

> *Current economic information:* for example, information concerning the firm's product market, the firm's competitors, and national economic conditions.

Structural change: for example, knowledge of recent acquisitions, divestitures, discoveries, and regulatory change.

Organizational efficiency: for example, knowledge of corporate structure and managerial ability.

The five categories of information pertain to the environment and to the firm whose security is being evaluated. One might view information even more broadly, however. The relevant set encompasses attributes of the decision maker—the technical knowledge and experience[1] that allow a proper assessment of relevant facts. This information varies from formal knowledge of portfolio theory and the capital asset pricing model to the decision maker's experience and skill at assessing intangibles such as managerial ability. Information of this type may be nothing more than enlightened intuition; nevertheless, it is a key input into decision making.

Homogeneous Versus Heterogeneous Expectations

Expectations are formed of future returns, given the current information set. Much formal analysis assumes that different investors have the same (homogeneous) expectations concerning security returns. The assumption of homogeneous expectations, for instance, underlies formulations such as the standard capital asset pricing model (see Chapter 7). Even though the assumption is known to be unrealistic, models based upon it give much insight into how the market prices various assets according to their risk and return characteristics.

Rational decision making may seem to imply the homogeneity of expectations. This is because such decision making considers what a rational person would conclude, given "the facts," and what one rational person would conclude, all rational people should conclude. However, having considered the elements that the information set comprises, one may better understand why homogeneous expectations is an unrealistic assumption.

Expectations are heterogeneous because information is costly and investors do not have perfect information.[2] Each investor obtains that quantity of information that is deemed to be optimal, given his or her cost of

[1]"Experience" includes events and bits of past information that have been analyzed and remembered.

[2]It is plausible for a group of investors to have homogeneous expectations only if they have perfect information. In the CAPM, the assumption of homogeneous expectations is equivalent to the assumption that decision makers have perfect information concerning the mean and variance of returns.

acquiring it and efficiency as an information processor.[3] The costs of obtaining and the benefits of having information differ appreciably across investors. In particular, the cost of an information bit is likely to be relatively low for large institutional investors with established information gathering systems. Moreover, the return on an information bit is larger, the larger the dollar sum that will be invested in relationship to it.[4] Therefore, all else equal, one would expect larger investors to be better informed investors.

Furthermore, because information is imperfect, it must be evaluated. Each investor analyzes informational inputs according to his or her past experience and knowledge. Thus assessments differ from one investor to the next, and consequently even expectations based upon commonly shared information may differ from decision maker to decision maker.

Most people agree that the world is characterized by heterogeneous expectations. The homogeneous expectations assumption has pervaded the formal literature, however, and it has the potential of causing one to believe that "*the* information set" is a compilation of objective facts about which we might all agree. Unfortunately, the real world is not so transparent.

Intrinsic Values Versus Market Determined Prices

Security analysis involves the assessment of share value, given fundamental determinants such as expected earnings, operating and financial risk, and the expected level of interest rates. Good analysts make good assessments in relation to these variables. Might these assessments be considered intrinsic values?

Whether or not a security has an intrinsic value depends on whether or not perfect substitutes for it exist in the eyes of the market. If perfect substitutes do exist, the market demand curve for the asset is infinitely elastic. With infinitely elastic market demand, the share price of the asset is given by the height of the demand curve (*the price intercept*). A price that is determined by the intercept parameter alone can be considered an intrinsic value.

The price of most resources is not determined by an intrinsic value, however, but rather is set in the marketplace by the forces of supply and demand (see Chapter 6). This is also the case for asset prices if analysts do

[3]For expositional simplicity we refer to the *quantity* of information as a decision variable, although the speed with which information is obtained is also of concern. The timeliness of information affects the quality of the information, and a complete analysis should treat quantity and quality simultaneously.

[4]That is, the cost of an information bit depends on the difficulty of getting it, but the benefit depends on the dollar magnitude of the decision to be made.

not agree about the risk/return characteristics of different securities, and if they do not view securities as having perfect substitutes. Generally the prices of risky assets are not obtained by solving evaluation equations about which all decision makers agree, and different securities cannot be grouped in identical risk/return categories.

Security analysts do, of course, assess the value of a stock for their own portfolios. This does not imply, however, that they undertake a treasure hunt to find a golden number that one might call an "intrinsic value." Rather, share prices are set the way they are for most resources—in the marketplace, in relation to the forces of demand and supply.[5]

The Beauty Contest

Keynes (1958, p. 156) drew a colorful parallel between stock selection and a beauty contest:

> . . . professional investment may be likened to those newspaper competitions in which the competitors have to pick out the six prettiest faces from a hundred photographs, the prize being awarded to the competitor whose choice most nearly corresponds to the average preferences of the competitors as a whole; so that each competitor has to pick, not those faces which he himself finds prettiest, but those which he thinks likeliest to catch the fancy of the other competitors, all of whom are looking at the problem from the same point of view. It is not a case of choosing those which, to the best of one's judgment, are really the prettiest, nor even those which average opinion genuinely thinks the prettiest. We have reached the third degree where we devote our intelligences to anticipating what average opinion expects the average opinion to bc. And there are some, I believe, who practise the fourth, fifth and higher degrees.

Keynes's analogy suggests one way of relating share prices to expectations. An investor hopes that the price of the shares he or she owns will rise in the future, so that the shares might then be sold at a profit. Whether it is because other investors in the future *think* the shares are worth more or because fundamental economic change has actually *caused* the shares to be worth more is irrelevant. What matters is only that the price does, indeed, rise. If some investors anticipate that other market participants will expect

[5]There are some exceptions. Some prices are used for trading or valuation purposes outside the market in which they are established. When so used, the price can be viewed as an intrinsic value. This is commonly referred to as *derivative pricing* or as *price basing*. Derivative pricing applies when one market (such as the Cincinnati Exchange) operates within a context provided by another market (such as the NYSE). Price basing is used in relation to futures trading—the price determined in the futures market is used to set price in the related cash market.

a price increase, they will buy shares and the current market price of the stock will be bid up.

The beauty contest analogy is inadequate, however, as an expectational model. For one thing, share evaluation, unlike the assessment of beauty, is not a purely subjective matter; objective information is also taken into account. Furthermore, Keynes's analogy does not allow that the judges in the stock market contest can, over time, learn how the process works, and that learned judges do not make systematic mistakes.

Expectations are the link between the market value of shares and current information. This link can be considered within the context of a specific model of expectation formation: a *rational expectations* model. The model is structured as follows:

1. The stock market contest is played repetitively in consecutive periods. The outcome of each contest is given by the share assessments established at the end of each period. Each assessment reflects what investors, at the time, anticipate shares will be worth at the end of subsequent periods.
2. Investor assessments of share values are based, in part at least, on expectations concerning the future dividend payments they will receive, and the expected stream of future dividend payments depends on the future worth of the firm.
3. At the start of each period, investors can, at a cost, obtain additional information pertaining to the economic worth of the corporation as of the end of the period. Uncertainty is not eliminated, but investors who obtain the information do form more accurate expectations than uninformed investors of the future value of share price.

There still is a beauty contest. All investors do not become informed each period (information is not costless), the uninformed still guess what the informed may have learned, and the informed anticipate that the uninformed will do so. However, with informed investors, the current value of shares is linked to future economic worth. In addition, the uninformed investors learn with experience how the contest works, and learned judges do not make systematic mistakes.

The presence of a meaningful informational signal and the absence of systematic mistakes are the essence of a rational expectations model.

A Grossman-Stiglitz Rational Expectations Model[6]

A rational expectations model can be used to show how market prices are determined in an environment where trading is frictionless, but where in-

---

[6]The exposition that follows draws on Grossman and Stiglitz (1976).

formation gathering is costly. For this purpose, assume the following:

1. A succession of investment periods of length T that are identical for all decision makers; each investment period may be considered a contest period.
2. All informed investors at the start of each contest period possess an information set that applies to that single period.
3. All informed investors assess the information set the same way (homogeneous expectations). When assessed, the information is given a dollar dimension, the expected value of share price as of the end of the period.
4. Uninformed investors may have publicly available information but do not know part of the current information set possessed by informed investors.
5. The coefficient of absolute risk aversion for each investor decreases with increases in the investor's wealth.
6. Share prices at the end of each contest period are determined by the information set and by other changes that the informed traders are not themselves able to predict (such as additional informational change or changing liquidity needs).
7. Trades are made and share prices set in a frictionless Walrasian call market.

These assumptions and the investor's ordinary demand equation [see Chapter 7, equation (7.40)] may be used to present the *Grossman-Stiglitz model*.[7] Write the demand equation as

$$P = \frac{E(P_T)}{R_f} - 2bN \qquad (9.1)$$

where P is the share price of the risky asset at the beginning of a contest period, $E(P_T)$ is the expected value of price at the end of the contest period, $R_f - 1$ is the risk-free rate of interest, b is the present value of the investor's risk premium, and N is the number of shares the investor wishes to hold.

Equation (9.1) shows that two parametric changes affect the location of the investor's demand curve. First, change in the expectation of the end of period price alters the height of the curve. Second, change in the investor's risk premium alters the slope of the curve. The investor's risk premium depends on his or her coefficient of absolute risk aversion, and this in turn depends on the investor's wealth (we have assumed diminishing absolute risk aversion). Hence, given the parameters of the utility function, the

---

[7]Our formulation differs in that (1) we specifically assume a call market environment (Grossman and Stiglitz are silent on the point), and (2) we let liquidity trading cause the market price to be a noisy signal (Grossman and Stiglitz alternatively assume that change in the number of shares outstanding for an issue causes its price to be a noisy signal).

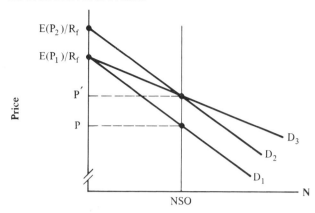

Figure 9.1   Effect of informational change and liquidity change on the market demand curve.

investor's demand curve depends upon his or her expectations and wealth.

To facilitate the exposition of the individual decision model, assume that all market participants but one have obtained the current information set and thus are informed traders, and consider what a single uninformed trader may be able to infer from a market determined price. Figure 9.1 shows three alternative market demand curves. The demand curves labeled D_1 and D_2 describe identical aggregate demand conditions, except that D_1 applies when the expected value of the end of period price for the informed traders is $E(P_1)$, and D_2 applies when the expected value of the end of period price is $E(P_2)$. The third curve, D_3, reflects the same expectation of the end of period price $[E(P_1)]$ as does D_1, but a lower risk premium for the informed traders.

The risk premium for each informed trader changes because of cash flows (liquidity changes) that are unique to each trader. Cash inflows increase a trader's wealth and so decrease his or her coefficient of absolute risk aversion [thereby decreasing the slope (dP/dN) of his or her demand curve]. Cash outflows decrease a trader's wealth and so increase his or her coefficient of absolute risk aversion (thereby increasing the slope of his or her demand curve). Because the price intercept of the demand curve is the same for all informed traders and given that each has linear demand, the slope of the market demand curve reflects the *average* risk premium of the traders.[8]

Returning to Figure 9.1, assume for the moment that the market demand curve shifts only because of change in the information set. Therefore, if the informed traders' assessment of the information set leads them to expect a price of $E(P_1)$ for the end of the contest period, their aggregate demand is D_1. Thus, given the number of shares outstanding (NSO), the

[8]Specifically, the slope of the market demand curve equals the negative of twice the average risk premium, divided by the number of traders.

current equilibrium price established at the Walrasian call is P. Alternatively, if the informed traders expect a price of $E(P_2)$ for the end of the contest period, their aggregate demand is D_2, and the current equilibrium price is P′. If, in the repetitive environment of the game, information alternates between the set that underlies the curve D_1 and the set that underlies the curve D_2, the uninformed trader soon learns, by relating beginning period prices to end of period results, that:

1. Whenever the current market clearing price is P, the informed traders must be anticipating an end of period price of $E(P_1)$.
2. Whenever the current market clearing price is P′, the informed traders must be anticipating an end of period price of $E(P_2)$.

In general, if market demand were to shift in the way described, the uninformed trader would learn to infer the current information set perfectly from the current market clearing price. If so, and given that the current price is established in a Walrasian-type call market, there would be no advantage to being an informed trader.

If no trader were to become informed, the market price would lose its informational content. This situation is avoided, however, because the uninformed trader cannot infer the information perfectly from the current market price. The reason is that, as noted, liquidity changes that are not related to information changes also shift the market demand curve. For instance, as shown in Figure 9.1, the clearing price may change from P to P′ because (information constant) the aggregate demand curve has shifted from D_1 to D_3 for liquidity reasons. Thus the uninformed investor, knowing neither the information set nor the wealth of other traders, cannot determine upon observing the price P′ whether curve D_2 or curve D_3 applies. Thus the uninformed investor does not know whether the expected end of period price is $E(P_2)$ or $E(P_1)$.

The market price, therefore, is a noisy signal. With a *noisy signal*, the uninformed trader can at best guess that the expected end of period price is $E(P_1)$ if the current price is P, or that it is $E(P_2)$ if the current price is P′, and so on.

In the rational expectations model, the uninformed trader forms unbiased expectations of $E(P)$. That is, over a sufficiently large number of contest periods, the uninformed trader is correct in that the informed traders do in fact, *on average,* expect an end of period price of $E(P_1)$ when the current price is P, an end of period price of $E(P_2)$ when the current price is P′, and so on. Thus the uninformed trader can infer information from the market determined price.

The information inferred by the uninformed trader is not as precise as that obtained by the informed traders. Therefore, being informed does give

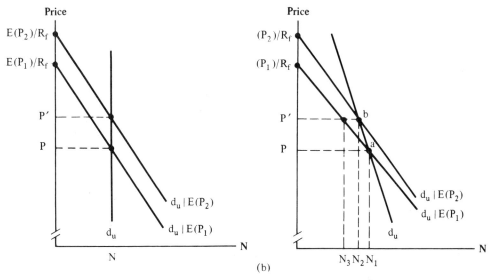

Figure 9.2 Uninformed trader's demand curve with price signaling. (a) The variance of end of period price is not related to the level of prices. (b) The variance of end of period price increases with the level of prices.

traders an advantage in the marketplace. This advantage, in equilibrium, just compensates the informed traders for the additional cost of being informed.

And so we see how the market price conveys an informational signal to the uninformed trader. The discussion in Chapter 7 of the expectations effect establishes that the investor's demand curve is less price elastic with price signaling than without price signaling.[9] The relative inelasticity of the uninformed trader's demand curve is also implied by the current analysis.

Figure 9.2(a) shows (1) the demand of the uninformed trader if he or she were to obtain the information that implies an expected end of period price of $E(P_1)$ [this curve is labeled $d_u \mid E(P_1)$] and (2) the demand of the uninformed trader if he or she were to obtain the information that implies an expected end of period price of $E(P_2)$ [this curve is labeled $d_u \mid E(P_2)$]. We see that the uninformed trader, upon observing a market price of P and *inferring* an expected end of period price of $E(P_1)$, would wish to hold N shares. This same trader, upon observing a market price of P′ and inferring an expected end of period price of $E(P_2)$, would also wish to hold N shares.

[9]Equation (7.61) (in Chapter 7) shows that the elasticity of expected returns with respect to the current price is minus 1 if the elasticity of the expected end of period price with respect to the current price is zero. The elasticity is closer to zero if the elasticity of the expected end of period price with respect to the current price is greater than zero, as is the case with price signaling. Therefore, price signaling decreases the elasticity of the expected return with respect to the current price [if the current price goes up (down), the expected end of period return does not fall (rise) as much as it would without price signaling]. As a consequence, the investor's demand curve to hold shares is less elastic.

Generalizing, the demand curve of the uninformed trader is the infinitely inelastic curve labeled d_u.

The uninformed trader's demand curve is infinitely inelastic because of the strict form of the model presented. We have assumed that the variance of the end of period price does not change as price increases from P to P′, and thus that the trader's risk premium does not change. In this case, the change of the present value of the expected price equals the change of the current price {the two demand curves [$d_u \mid E(P_2)$ and $d_u \mid E(P_1)$] are parallel}.

It is plausible that the uninformed investor expects the variance of the end of period price to be greater when E(P) is greater. If so, the uninformed investor's risk premium is positively related to E(P), and the demand curve labeled $d_u \mid E(P_2)$ is steeper than the demand curve labeled $d_u \mid E(P_1)$. In this case, the change of the present value of the expected price is greater than the change of the current price {the two demand curves [$d_u \mid E(P_2)$ and $d_u \mid E(P_1)$] are not parallel}. As shown in Figure 9.2(b), the uninformed investor, upon observing a market price of P, would wish to hold N_1 shares as indicated by point a or, upon observing a market price of P′, would wish to hold N_2 shares as indicated by point b. The demand curve of the uninformed trader is now the relatively inelastic curve, d_u, that passes through points a and b.[10]

The intuition behind the relative inelasticity of the demand curve d_u for the uninformed trader is the following. Assume that the trader initially holds N_1 shares, that price is initially P, and that the price then increases to P′. If the trader knew that the information set was unchanged (and that, therefore, the price increase was due to liquidity induced buying), he or she would seek to sell $N_1 - N_3$ shares to take advantage of the price increase. However, if the trader does not know whether or not information has changed, he or she will sell a smaller amount ($N_1 - N_2$ shares) because of the possibility that the price increase is attributable to bullish economic news. Generalizing, the uninformed trader's response to the price signal reduces the size of a sale for a price increase, reduces the size of a purchase for a price decrease, and hence reduces the elasticity of the trader's demand curve.

In a frictionless Walrasian call market, the uninformed trader would transmit to the market the buy and sell order functions associated with the demand curve labeled d_u in Figure 9.2(b). The trader in this environment would trade the appropriate number of shares at the market determined price, given his or her demand propensities and the information signal that the market price conveys. In addition, the model implies that:

---

[10]The demand curve labeled D_2 in Figure 9.1 may also be more steeply inclined than the curve labeled D_1, for the same reason. More generally, for d_u to be downward sloping, the curves labeled $d_u \mid E(P_2)$ and $d_u \mid E(P_1)$ in Figure 9.2 must converge more rapidly than the curves labeled D_2 and D_1 in Figure 9.1.

1. End of period price uncertainty is greater for the uninformed trader than for the informed traders (the uninformed trader is not able to condition his or her expectations directly on the information set).
2. The uninformed trader faces less uncertainty than if there were no informed traders (the market price does convey a meaningful informational signal).
3. Current prices are unbiased reflections of the information set (the uninformed trader does not systematically over- or underestimate the expected end of period price from the signal conveyed by the current price).

Recapitulation

Investors have heterogeneous expectations because information is costly. Because investors have heterogeneous expectations, risky assets do not have intrinsic values; rather, equilibrium prices are established in the marketplace.

The market price of a stock at the start of each period depends on the information set informed traders have observed. If the information is favorable, the current market price is higher because of the increased demand of the informed traders; if the news is unfavorable, the current market price is lower because of the decreased demand of the informed traders. The information set is eventually revealed publicly. The outcome of the contest depends in part on the disclosure (otherwise the information would not have value). Thus the information set establishes an association between the current and future values of price. In the repetitive environment of the contest, uninformed investors observe the association. Thus the uninformed investors learn to infer from the current market price the import that the information must have for future share value. The uninformed accordingly take account of the current price when forming their expectations, and they face less uncertainty than they would if there were no informed traders.

The inferences of the uninformed are not perfect, however. The changing liquidity needs of some traders cause current prices to have a less than perfect association with the current information set. The less than perfect association is important: if the uninformed could infer information without error from the current price, no one would become informed (information is not costless).

Informed traders invest optimally in the risky asset given their information, and uninformed traders invest optimally in the risky asset given the signal they infer from the current market price. The two groups together simultaneously set the market price in a frictionless Walrasian auction. In the repetitive environment of the market, the uninformed have learned the process by which information is reflected in market prices, and they are not on average wrong in their expectations. That is, although their anticipations are less accurate than those of the informed, the uninformed do not systematically over- or underestimate the future values that share prices are expected to attain.

We have just described an equilibrium. In this equilibrium, each investor realizes a rate of return that is optimal, given the riskiness of the investment and the benefits and cost of information. With a rational expectations equilibrium, all investors (both informed and uninformed) do not make systematic errors in their anticipations of future price changes, because repetitive errors of forecasting are discovered and eliminated by the players in the contest.

Rational expectations is a very useful modeling device. It gives valuable insight into necessary equilibrium conditions for a frictionless market environment, and it provides a benchmark against which to assess real world results. Furthermore, it is the best (and only truly rigorous) model of expectations formation that we have. However, the model should not be retained as an untarnished description of reality in actual markets. The truth concerning each information bit reveals itself over time, and, as this occurs, some anticipations at least are revised. The process by which heterogeneous anticipations are revised and ultimately approach unanimity may not be random, and current prices may not be unbiased reflections of current information. Most importantly, the equity markets are not a repetitive environment, and market participants do not have the opportunity to learn perfectly the parameters of the price determination process. Consequently, the rational expectations results may be perturbed.

Where do we stand now with regard to a theory of expectations? Somewhere between Keynes and rational expectations. The literature on the subject is extensive, but much still remains to be learned. The task of modeling expectations is indeed a challenge.

INFORMATIONAL EFFICIENCY

This section considers five conditions for informational efficiency:

1. The existing information set cannot be exploited in order to make abnormally high returns on the margin.
2. Additional information gathering and processing activities do not generate abnormal profits.
3. Equilibrium prices accurately reflect the information set.
4. Clearing prices accurately reflect the aggregation of investor demand propensities.[11]
5. The process by which information is disseminated does not consistently favor some investors over others.

[11] We use the term *equilibrium price* for the price at which the aggregate buy order function equals the aggregate sell order function, and the term *clearing price* for the price at which the aggregate of all buy orders equals the aggregate of all sell orders.

Efficiency with Regard to the Existing Information Set

Investors make decisions in relation to the information set in two ways. First, they search for situations in which they think the market has mispriced an asset given the asset's risk/return characteristics. When such a situation is found, an investor takes a position in relation to it that enables him or her to realize profits if and when prices are appropriately adjusted in the market. Second, even if all assets are appropriately priced on the market, a selection of alternative mean-variance efficient portfolios exists, and the investor uses information concerning the risk/return characteristics of securities to select an optimal portfolio (given his or her unique tastes for risk and return). The discussion that follows focuses on the first use to which information may be put and abstracts from the second.

The decision maker formulates returns expectations by assessing publicly available information, his or her own private information, and current market prices. If, on the basis of the assessment, the risk adjusted return expected on an asset seems abnormally high, the decision maker seeks to buy additional shares. Alternatively, if the return seems abnormally low, the decision maker seeks to sell shares (if he or she is long in the asset), to short the stock, or simply to ignore the stock (if short selling is restricted).[12]

Buying pressure increases current prices and thus decreases expected returns. Selling pressure decreases prices and thus increases expected returns. Unlimited buying or short selling unbalances the investor's portfolio, thus increasing the variance of the portfolio's returns. Therefore, appropriate buying and selling bring risk adjusted returns into harmony with normal values for the investor. When harmony is achieved, the information set cannot be further exploited by the individual investor. Thus individual optimizing behavior leads the market to an informationally efficient outcome.

The thought can be stated somewhat differently. *Abnormal returns* on an investment are, by definition, returns that are either higher than an investor would require or lower than the investor must receive to make the investment. Therefore, abnormally high returns are "bought" (by buying the shares or shorting the stock), and abnormally low returns are "sold" (by selling shares or covering a short position). Because of the effect of purchases and sales on current prices and on portfolio diversification, transactions that exploit the abnormal returns also eliminate them. It follows that abnormal expected returns are eliminated when investors achieve portfolios that are optimal, given the information set.

Therefore, the first condition for informational efficiency—that ab-

---

[12]A negative return on the stock is a positive return to the investor with a short position. Therefore, by shorting a stock, a trader who is bearish in relation to the market may also anticipate positive returns.

normally high returns cannot be realized by exploiting the existing information set—is equivalent to the requirement that investors maximize utility by obtaining efficient portfolios, given the information that they possess.

Efficiency with Regard to Information Gathering Activities

Tradeoffs   Assume the investor anticipates a particular mean and variance of returns, given the level of price at which the stock is currently trading. Also assume that, on the basis of logic and past experience, the investor has some understanding of how a new bit of information would alter the stock's price. At a cost, the investor can attempt to obtain that information before its impact is fully reflected in market prices. If successful, he or she benefits from the price adjustment the news will trigger.

With heterogeneous expectations, an individual may also profit from information that has already been widely distributed. For instance, let there be some information bit that an individual would interpret differently than the market in the short term. If that individual were indeed more astute in his or her assessment of the information, then in the longer term that person would realize a return from it even if the news had already been assessed by others and had had its impact on market prices.

As time goes by, truth reveals itself. As it does, some investors find that their anticipations were correct, and others find that they were wrong. Therefore, the return to information includes the profits one can achieve by being more correct than the market. This is, of course, a difficult game to play, and few believe they can consistently play it with success. Nevertheless, security analysis is potentially valuable, even to decision makers who cannot beat the market by being among the first to receive news.

One need not, however, only attempt to obtain information directly—along the lines discussed previously, the investor can *infer* informational change from market prices. That is, on the basis of past experience, the investor can interpret price changes as signals (albeit noisy signals) that some new information bit has been released. Therefore, rather than directly looking for the information, the investor may decide to let the price change signal the information. This person would be a member of the "sheep" category defined in Chapter 7. In his or her opinion, a change in the stock's share price may not imply a change of the stock's risk/return characteristics.

What value might price signaling have to a member of the sheep category? From time to time new funds are invested in the market and old funds are withdrawn; knowledge (or the belief) that the risk/return characteristics of a security have not changed is relevant for portfolio decisions made in relation to these liquidity changes. In addition, the realization (or belief) that the risk/return characteristics of a security regain their previous values after the stock has adjusted to news may prevent the investor from mistakenly buying or selling after an opportunity has passed (note that nonaction itself implies a decision). In this regard, it may be advisable to act as sheep if one does not have a preferential position vis-à-vis the information flow or special insight into information's meaning. Finally, the investor may in fact benefit from signals inferred from price changes. For instance, if prices do not adjust instantly and accurately to new equilibrium values, the investor may profit from quickly entering market orders or stop loss orders (in continuous trading) or limit orders (in call market trading).[13]

Chartists in particular believe that profitable trading rules can be formulated on the basis of patterns exhibited by past price movements. Although chartism is not accepted by many, the belief that the ebb and flow of investor reactions, psychology, and so on, introduce predictable, repetitive patterns is not, per se, erroneous. The reason for questioning the premise of the chartists is that in an informationally efficient environment, the exploitation of such price patterns would eliminate the patterns. This point is clarified later in the chapter, in the section "The Efficient Market Hypothesis."

In conclusion, information is valuable whether received directly or inferred from prices, and whether received before or after the market has had a chance to adjust to it. However, when it is received sooner and directly (rather than later and inferred), it is (1) more valuable and (2) more costly to obtain. This is why tradeoffs exist in information gathering.

Individual Optimality Consider one individual's decision of whether or not to purchase a single bit of information concerning a corporation. As discussed previously, the alternative for an investor who does not purchase the information is to make a portfolio decision regarding the corporation's stock on the basis of the stock's market price and other available information.

The value of the information bit to any specific decision maker depends upon the quality of the anticipations he or she can formulate given that information, in relation to the quality of the market's anticipations (which are reflected in the current price of the asset). The faster (in relation to other market participants) the specific individual can obtain the information bit and the better he or she is as an information processor (in relation to other market participants), the greater is the value of the information.[14]

---

[13]Tests using filter rules have shown that trading strategies based on past price changes do in fact generate excess gross returns (although transaction costs make them, on net, unprofitable). A *filter rule* is a decision to buy if price goes up x percent and to sell if price goes down x percent, where the value of x sets the strength of the filter. See Alexander (1961).

[14]The investor should look for information not yet gathered by others, and for information that is not highly correlated with existing information.

Suppose a specific investor is moderately efficient at obtaining and assessing information. The larger the number of other investors who are informed and the more efficient they are as information gatherers and processors, the less likely it is that that investor would realize a competitive advantage by obtaining the information bit. If the decision maker's abilities were low enough in relation to the market, then he or she might do better to let others obtain and process the information and simply to turn to price as an unbiased signal of the information.

The second condition for informational efficiency—that additional information gathering and processing activities do not generate abnormal profits—is equivalent to the requirement that an investor does indeed obtain information directly if its incremental value is greater than its incremental cost, or infer it from market prices if its incremental value is less than its incremental cost (including the opportunity cost of time).

Market Equilibrium[15]   We have established that the value of additional information to each individual depends, not just on the information itself, but also on that individual's efficiency vis-à-vis others at information gathering and processing. The market is in equilibrium with respect to a piece of information if all individuals for whom that information's value exceeds its cost do obtain it, and if all individuals for whom that information's value is less than its cost infer it from the market price of the asset. In such an equilibrium, the information gathering activities that are undertaken are on net profitable, but additional information gathering does not yield positive returns.

To establish the existence of an equilibrium amount of information gathering for the market, first consider a situation in which no one actively seeks additional information directly, but rather all participants base their expectations entirely on current market prices and on whatever information was publicly available in the past. The informational content of security prices declines, and prices soon convey *very* noisy signals. In such a market, an investor with even the smallest amount of additional information is able to spot some extraordinary situations—a stock paying a $15 dividend, offering much promise of dividend growth, and trading at $20 a share; some other stock trading at $75 a share although the company has slashed the dividend and is about to collapse. In such an environment, additional information gathering activities clearly are profitable.

What would the situation be if many investors were informed? The informational content of security prices would then be high, and prices would convey a far less noisy signal. In this case, all but the most efficient

---

[15]The discussion concerning market equilibrium draws heavily on Grossman and Stiglitz (1976).

information processors might find that the quality of prices set in the market is too good to beat. Accordingly, rather than attempting to outguess the market, most people might simply follow the crowd. In the limit, if all share prices were to reflect all information fully and were not noisy signals, there would be no return to additional information gathering.

This may seem to imply a paradox: on the one hand, if stock prices were to reflect all information fully, no one would undertake security analysis; on the other hand, if no one were to undertake security analysis, stocks could not be appropriately priced.

There is no paradox. An equilibrium amount of information gathering exists. At one extreme, if virtually no one looks for information, the net returns to information gathering are likely to be positive for at least the most efficient information gatherers and processors. At the other extreme, if nearly everyone looks for information, the net returns to information gathering are likely to be negative for at least the most inefficient information gatherers and processors. In equilibrium, an equilibrium number of investors is informed. Those who are informed are those who are the most efficient at the process and/or those for whom information has the greatest value. For the marginal information gatherer, the value of the information just equals the cost of obtaining it. Those for whom the value of information is less than the cost of obtaining it infer the information from prices. A market that has achieved such an equilibrium is *informationally efficient* with regard to the intensity with which information gathering activities are pursued.

The Informational Accuracy of Equilibrium Prices[16]

Prices act as constraints that lead individuals to use resources optimally, given supply and demand conditions (see Chapter 6). *Nonstochastic prices,* however, convey no information about the resources themselves—market participants are assumed to have complete information to begin with. On the other hand, when outcomes are uncertain and information is incomplete, prices play an important informational role. Prices are a mechanism for information transfer (from the informed to the uninformed) and for the aggregation of diverse information bits (for both informed and uninformed traders). This section considers the efficiency with which prices perform these two functions.

With a diversity of expectations in the market, a security's price reflects a weighted average opinion of all investors in the market. The more weight the market gives to the opinions of those who are better informed,

---

[16]The discussion in this section draws heavily on Figlewski (1978).

the greater is the informational accuracy of the equilibrium prices. Therefore, whose expectations might the equilibrium prices reflect?

People who believe themselves to be the most efficient at information gathering and processing are those most likely to become informed traders (as noted, others will simply let price be their signal). With regard to the distribution of the informed, two factors affect the dollar strength of each person's opinion,[17] and hence the weight of his or her conviction in the market: (1) the accuracy of the decision maker's opinion and (2) the decision maker's wealth.

The dollar strength of an anticipation is correlated with the accuracy of that anticipation, to the extent that truth carries its own conviction. However, the presence of some bull- (or bear-) headed fools in the market makes the association between truth and conviction somewhat less than perfect.

The wealth an individual has realized in the financial markets is his or her reward for having invested successfully in the past, and to an extent, the quality of a decision maker's earlier anticipations is correlated with his or her current abilities as a forecaster. Therefore, current wealth should be positively related to the accuracy of current opinion. However, this association is also less than perfect. Few are able to predict consistently well over time. Furthermore, some inefficient information processors may be richly rewarded by chance, and some efficient information processors may not do well—also by chance.

With regard to the informational efficiency of equilibrium prices, we conclude that even in a market that is informationally efficient in other respects, prices are noisy signals. We may never be sure who the most efficient information processors are by spotting the consistent winners; in a large population of investors, some may win often, only by chance. Thus expectations remain heterogeneous and the market does not completely achieve informationally accurate prices.

The Informational Accuracy of Market Clearing Prices[18]

The preceding section considered the informational accuracy of equilibrium prices. As previously defined, *equilibrium prices* are values determined by the intersection of the aggregate buy and sell *order functions* of all traders. We now consider the informational accuracy of market clearing prices. *Market clearing prices* are values that clear all crossing buy and sell *orders* that have been written in relation to the underlying order functions (see

---

[17]The *dollar strength* of an investor's opinion is the funds he or she commits to a position in light of the strength of his or her conviction.

[18]The discussion in this section draws heavily on Ho, Schwartz, and Whitcomb (1985).

Chapter 8). The difference between an equilibrium price and a clearing price is shown in Figure 9.3.

The downward sloping line labeled B_j in Figure 9.3(a) is the buy order function of the jth trader. The trader's anticipations of the clearing price are shown by the bell shaped curve drawn on the vertical axis. E(P) is the expected clearing price. Let the trader submit just one order point (a single price and a single quantity) to the market, as discussed in Chapter 8. Assume a call market trading environment. Then, given the buy order function (B_j), expectations of the clearing price (as described by the bell shaped curve), and the call market arrangement, the optimal order for the jth trader to submit is P_j, Q_j, as shown by the point labeled a on the curve RB_j.

The *equilibrium price* for the asset and for the trading session is shown

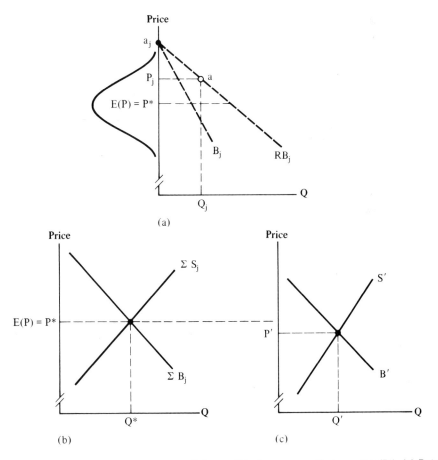

Figure 9.3 A market clearing price (P′) can differ from an equilibrium price (P*). (a) Determination of the optimal buy order point of the jth trader. (b) Determination of the equilibrium market price P* by aggregating investor buy and sell order functions. (c) Determination of the market clearing price P′ by aggregating investor buy and sell order points.

in Figure 9.3(b) by the intersection of the aggregate buy and sell order functions. P* is the equilibrium price, and Q* is the equilibrium number of shares traded. In the case depicted in Figure 9.3(b), we have set P* equal to E(P). In other words, the representative investor has been assumed to have an unbiased, rational expectation of the clearing price. This accuracy of expectations need not be satisfied in any given trading session, however.

The asset's *clearing price* for the trading session is shown in Figure 9.3(c) by the intersection of the curves labeled B' and S'. B' and S' are not aggregates of the individual order functions, but rather of the individual order points [such as the single point a, in Figure 9.3(a)]. In the case depicted in Figure 9.3(c), the market clearing price is P', and the number of shares traded is Q'.

Under transaction price uncertainty, P', in general, differs from P*, as shown in the figure. Likewise, Q', in general, differs from Q*. We will demonstrate this for the call market environment. Our discussion focuses on the price variable.

The simplest way to show that P' and P* generally differ is to show the special conditions under which they will be the same. There are two conditions that must both hold: (1) buyers and sellers must all expect a clearing price of P* (the equilibrium price), and (2) the distribution of buyers and the distribution of sellers must be symmetric. These two conditions hold in any given trading session only by chance. Let us consider the matter further.

Figure 9.4 shows the reservation buy and sell order curves RB_1, RB_2,

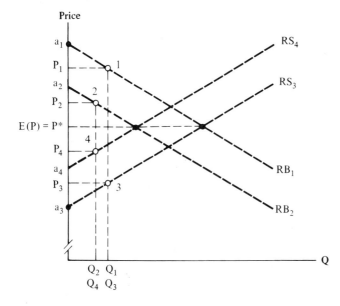

Figure 9.4   Reservation buy and sell curves of four symmetrically distributed traders.

RS_3, and RS_4 of four traders. All of the traders have identical and unbiased expectations of the clearing price, as reflected by the fact that each places his or her order with reference to the same expected price, E(P), with E(P) being equal to P*. The symmetry of the distribution of buyers and sellers is reflected by the symmetry between the curves labeled RB_1 and RS_3, and between the curves labeled RB_2 and RS_4. To see these symmetries, place a mirror on the horizontal line at E(P) = P* and note that the buy curves are parallel to each other, the sell curves are parallel to each other, the slopes of the sell curves are equal to the inverse of the slopes of the buy curves, $a_1 - P^* = P^* - a_3$, and $a_2 - P^* = P^* - a_4$.

Given the individual order functions, the expectations on the clearing price, and the call market environment, the specific orders that are written by the two buyers and the two sellers can be solved for analytically as discussed in Chapter 8. These orders are shown in Figure 9.4 by the circles labeled 1, 2, 3, and 4, respectively. Because the order functions are symmetrically distributed around P*, the optimal solutions for the individual orders are symmetrically distributed around P*.

If additional buy and sell order functions were to be drawn in Figure 9.4 with symmetry preserved, the additional order points would also be symmetrically distributed about P*. If a large number of these order points were then aggregated to get market buy and sell order curves [such as those labeled B' and S' in Figure 9.3(c)], the symmetry of the orders would be reflected in the two aggregate curves being symmetric around P*. Hence, the aggregate curves would intersect at P*. Thus the market clearing price (P') would equal the equilibrium price (P*).

There is, however, no reason to expect that investors will be symmetrically distributed at any given trading session (although on average they may be over a large number of trading sessions), and there is no reason to expect that at any given session they will all have unbiased expectations of the clearing price (although, on average, over a large number of sessions they may have unbiased expectations). When symmetry is perturbed *at any specific trading session*, P' does not equal P* for that session.[19] This can be seen by relaxing the assumption that the distribution of the price intercept terms for the sellers is symmetric with that of the buyers.

All traders may expect the same clearing price, but they all face transaction price uncertainty. Accordingly they all submit orders that protect them optimally in relation to that uncertainty. If the price intercept terms are not symmetrically distributed, the intensity with which some traders wish to buy shares is not balanced by the intensity with which other traders wish to sell shares. Therefore, the intensity with which some buyers react to transaction price uncertainty is not balanced by the reaction of some

---

[19]Ho, Schwartz, and Whitcomb (1985) show this result analytically. Here we give only an intuitive explanation.

sellers. This alters the relationship between the buy and sell orders that are revealed at the market call. The order functions twist, and equality between the clearing price and the equilibrium price is lost. Depending upon the specific situation, the realized clearing price could be above or below the expected clearing price, and thus above or below the equilibrium price.[20]

Because the clearing price can (and in general does) differ from the equilibrium price, the informational accuracy of the market clearing price is impaired. That is why the accuracy of price discovery is an important consideration from a market's operational viewpoint. We return to this thought in subsequent chapters of the book (see Chapter 15 in particular).

The Dynamic Efficiency of Information Dissemination

The four efficiency criteria thus far considered concern static efficiency. We now turn to the dynamic efficiency with which information is disseminated in the investment community.

The efficiency of information dissemination has two dimensions: (1) the time needed for new information to be fully reflected in market prices and (2) the sequential order in which the information is disseminated among investors. After change has occurred in a company's fortunes, investors should learn of it quickly, and the change should be quickly reflected in market prices. This is true for both equity and efficiency: market prices provide better signals to decision makers if they reflect current, rather than outdated, information. But because information dissemination is not instantaneous, some investors are bound to receive news before others.

On June 18, 1815, Napoleon was defeated at Waterloo. A carrier pigeon took news of the British victory to Nathan Rothschild in London. In a single day, Rothschild reaped a fortune by buying shares from uninformed, and quite frightened traders (he was also credited with having saved the London Stock Exchange). Rothschild's profit was not due to the news. It was due to his having received the news first.

A tremendous amount of information is disseminated in today's markets, and only minutes may separate many investors in the receipt of news. Nonetheless, certain investors still receive information before others, and some may do so consistently. Thus we should continue to question the informational dynamic efficiency of the markets.

Investors receive information at different times for two reasons: (1) they are not equally efficient and aggressive as information gatherers, and (2) some people have a preferential position vis-à-vis the information flow. The efficiency and aggressiveness of investors should be rewarded, and they are. The returns to these people are the profits they receive from the

---

[20]The deviation of the market clearing price from the equilibrium price may represent the fourth degree in Keynes's beauty contest analogy: market prices are not even accurate reflections of the average opinion about what the average opinion is.

price adjustments which occur when others lag behind them in the receipt of news. In part, it is the scramble to benefit from the price adjustments that accounts for the informational static efficiency of a market.

For some people, however, information is a by-product of a service they provide that has no relation to information gathering. The proofreader in a securities firm, the typesetter in the print shop, or the lawyer in a merger case, for instance, may receive information that has not yet been released to the public. When these people profit from their prior receipt of information, we may observe certain proofreaders, typesetters, and lawyers being grossly overpaid for their services. No economic function is served by this overpayment. On the contrary, the feelings of inequity it can engender may have harmful repercussions.

Insiders are deemed to have a preferential and unfair advantage vis-à-vis the information flow. Accordingly, these people are restricted in their freedom to trade shares of their corporation's stock. Insiders must file with the SEC after trading, and they are not allowed to trade on news that has not yet been made public.

A tradeoff exists between the dynamic efficiency and the static efficiency of a market. The greater the flow of information in the market, the more accurate are the prices that are set and hence the more static efficient is the market. But the flow of information is positively related to the return to information, and the return to information is in large part the price adjustments an informed trader profits from when he or she receives the news first. Therefore, *dynamic inefficiency* motivates the informational gathering activities that make a market static-efficient.

That such a tradeoff exists is not surprising. Information gathering, like trading, is a manifestation of disequilibrium behavior. Also, as with trading, information gathering helps to repair imbalance in the market and to bring prices back to equilibrium values. It is too much to expect that the dynamic process by which equilibrium is regained will generate no undesired side effects. If we want prices that are the best possible signals of information, we must let those who have the best information (insiders included) trade with a minimum of restrictions. Alternatively, if we do not want insiders consistently to exploit the uninformed public, we must settle for prices that are noisier reflections of the information set. Making wise decisions in relation to this tradeoff is indeed difficult. We return to this public policy issue in Chapter 14.

EVIDENCE ON THE INFORMATIONAL EFFICIENCY OF MARKETS

The discussion thus far has pointed up a factor of paramount importance: an investor cannot realize superior risk adjusted returns merely by having informed expectations about future returns. To enjoy excess profits, the investor must be *more* correct than the market. Consistently winning the guessing game, however, is extremely difficult in informationally efficient markets. An understanding of this leads to the following realization: the informational efficiency of a market can be tested by examining whether or not traders in it can realize excess returns.

The *null hypothesis* is that prices set in the marketplace are informationally efficient. This hypothesis is referred to as the *efficient market hypothesis* (EMH). The EMH is articulated in three forms:

1. *Weak form:* The information contained in the past sequence of price movements is reflected in current prices.
2. *Semistrong form:* All public information is reflected in current prices.
3. *Strong form:* All information is reflected in current prices.

Weak Form Tests

Weak form tests of the EMH focus on the informational content of the previous sequence of stock price movements. How much information should these movements contain for a market to be informationally efficient? If the market is a frictionless environment, the answer is *none*. Alternatively stated, in informationally efficient markets, above normal returns cannot be realized by using trading rules based upon past price movements.

Weak form efficiency does not require that price changes (returns) be strictly independent over time. Rather, price changes are expected to exhibit upward drift, because risk averse investors demand a positive expected return. Weak form efficiency requires only that past price changes cannot be used to improve predictions concerning the expected value of future price changes. Price changes that follow a *martingale process* satisfy this requirement.

The upward drift in stock price movements would be slight in short period (for instance, daily) intervals, and we ignore it to simplify the discussion. When the expected value of a stock's price change is zero, and when successive price changes are statistically independent and identically distributed, the security's price follows a random walk over time.[21] The *random walk* process is in essence a random number generator. The term *random walk,* and what it implies, has an interesting history.

Assume one were to leave a drunk in the middle of a large field, let him stumble around for a while and then, after some time has passed, go back and look for him. Where is the most efficient place to start looking? Because the drunk follows a random walk, knowledge of the direction of

---

[21]Price changes, on the other hand, can follow a martingale process even if they are statistically dependent and not identically distributed.

his last observed steps contains no useful information, and the best place to start looking is where the drunk was last seen.

Random walk was never the domain of the drunk alone. Bachelier (1900) reported evidence that the current price of a commodity is an unbiased estimate of the future price of the commodity. Subsequently, other students of asset price movements have reported that prices change randomly over time.[22] The curious point is that the early findings presented evidence of random walk, but an understanding of why price changes would be uncorrelated in a frictionless, informationally efficient market was not forthcoming for many years.[23]

That prices are expected to follow a random walk in informationally efficient and operationally efficient markets is most important in light of the subject of this book. Following the empirical demonstration that, by and large, the markets are informationally efficient, we can focus on deviations from random walk as evidence of operational inefficiency in nonfrictionless markets. Therefore, it is important first to understand why random walk would be evidence of informational efficiency.

To some extent a stock's price is expected to drift up over time because, as noted, shareholders expect a positive return that is commensurate with the riskiness of the stock. This drift, however, would not be very apparent in short period price movements.[24] Accordingly, we ignore price drift in the following discussion. Instead, what is of interest are those price changes that result from changes in investor desires, information, and expectations. The question addressed is whether these price changes can be predicted or whether they are random.

Assume some investors know that in one week other investors will discover something about a stock that will drive its price up 20 percent. Those who are currently in the know have an opportunity to capture the 20 percent increase for themselves and so can make excess profits. They do this by buying the stock at the lower price.

But as the knowledgeable investors transmit their buy orders to the market, the price of the stock is bid up until these people no longer expect a further, abnormal price increase. Consequently, the price increase that was expected in a week will have been realized in the current period.

The current adjustment of price to change that is anticipated for the future means that, in equilibrium, *all* expectations are reflected in the current value of price. Accordingly, it is not possible to predict when, how,

---

[22]See, for instance, Kendel (1953), Roberts (1959), Osborne (1959), Granger and Morgenstern (1963), and Alexander (1964). The most comprehensive review of this literature is that of Fama (1970).

[23]See Samuelson (1965), Mandelbrot (1966), and Fama (1965, 1970).

[24]A return of 36 percent a year is associated with a price change of less than 0.1 percent per day.

or by how much an equilibrium price will change in the future. This is because something that is *unanticipated* must occur in order for the equilibrium price to change. Therefore, in a market that is efficient in the sense that equilibrium prices are attained, market prices follow a "random walk" over time.

The random walk can be pictured for a call market environment with reference to Figure 9.5. Let the market be in the initial equilibrium position shown in Figure 9.5(a), with the aggregate demand curve being D_0, and the market price being P_0. Then, the associated trade curves will be B_0 and S_0, as shown in Figure 9.5(b). Until the demand curve shifts for at least some trader, the market price will remain P_0.

Assume that after a short period of time has passed, some individual demand curves do shift. Perhaps there has been a change in expectations, or in the willingness of some investors to undertake risk, or in liquidity. Let the aggregate trade curves change to the lines labeled S_1 and B_1 in

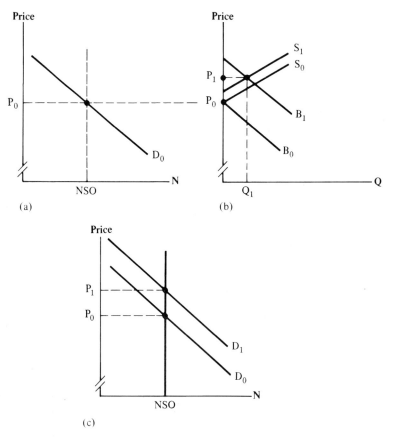

Figure 9.5   Effect of a market demand shift on the price of an asset. (a) Determination of the initial equilibrium price P_0. (b) Shifts in the aggregate trade curves change the market price. (c) Contrast of the initial equilibrium price P_0 and the new equilibrium price P_1.

Figure 9.5(b). This shift causes the sell and buy curves to cross and results in Q_1 shares trading at a price of P_1. After the trade, market demand is the curve labeled D_1 in Figure 9.5(c), and the market clearing price is P_1. Once again, the market will have achieved equilibrium. In summary, this is what happens:

1. The price change is $\Delta P = P_1 - P_0$.
2. The return is $r_1 = \Delta P/P_0$.
3. After the price change, the market is in equilibrium, as it was before demand shifted.

What will the next price change be? For the reasons just discussed, this cannot be predicted. Perhaps the next shift will change price from P_1 to some new value, P_2. The next return will then be $r_2 = (P_2 - P_1)/P_1$. Because the second return (r_2) cannot be predicted before it occurs, it must be independent of everything that preceded it. Hence, r_2 must be independent of r_1. That is,

$$r_2 \neq f(r_1) \tag{9.2}$$

Nonetheless, might not the economic environment be such that information changes in a correlated fashion such that successive changes in the equilibrium prices are correlated? Abstracting from issues of operational inefficiency in a nonfrictionless market, the answer is no. The reason is as follows:

1. Aside from drift, if the sequence of price changes is not independent, knowledge of past price changes would enable investors to predict future price changes.
2. However, for these profitable predictions to be fulfilled in the future, investors could not act on them in the present. The reason is that, as is generally true with arbitrage trading, the very act of trading eliminates price patterns that can be profitably exploited.
3. It follows that a correlated sequence of price movements would suggest that investors are inept at spotting profitable price patterns.

Random walk is not caused by the pattern of information arrival, but rather by investor responses to information. Aside from long-run drift, a random walk is expected in a frictionless market that is informationally efficient.

Semistrong Form Tests

Semistrong form tests focus on the speed with which specific pieces of public information are reflected in stock prices. The announcement of a piece of information is considered an *event,* and the studies are commonly referred to as *event studies.*

One early event study established the methodology that has subsequently been used by many others: Fama, Fisher, Jensen, and Roll's (1969) analysis of the effect of stock splits on share price. Stock splits are expected to increase the total value of shares because they convey a bullish signal to shareholders (since stock splits have historically been associated with strong earnings growth and increased dividends). Fama, Fisher, Jensen and Roll (FFJR) report that, for 940 splits for NYSE stocks between 1927 and 1959, over two-thirds were followed by the announcement of a dividend increase.

FFJR examined the pattern of price changes observed in the months preceding and following splits. Specifically, they considered the difference between the actual return on a stock and the return expected, given the return on the market.[25] This difference is referred to as the *abnormal return.* They found for a sample of 622 stocks that abnormal returns tend to be considerably higher in the months preceding a stock split, that these returns continue to be somewhat higher in the months following a split for companies that do increase their dividends, and that they are somewhat lower in the months following a split for companies that do not increase their dividends.

FFJR captured these effects with the following procedure. For each stock in their sample, the month of the split was defined as month zero,[26] the last month before the split as month -1, the first month after the split as month $+1$, and so on, for a time span extending from month -29 to month $+30$. The abnormal return was then computed for each stock for each month. The month -29 abnormal returns were then averaged across the stocks, as were the month -28 abnormal returns, and so forth. The average abnormal returns were then cumulated, starting at month -29 and extending to month $+30$. The resulting cumulative average for all stocks is shown in Figure 9.6.

Notice that the cumulative average rises in the months preceding the split and is flat in the months following the split. FFJR also reported that the cumulative average rises somewhat after month zero for firms that do increase their dividends, and that it falls for firms that do not increase their dividends. These deviations of actual returns from expected values are evidence of the following adjustment pattern.

The considerably greater than expected returns before the split dates show that prices are adjusted upward on the basis of the optimistic signals

[25]The relationship between the return on a stock and the return on the market is discussed in Chapter 7.

[26]Month zero is not, therefore, the same calendar month for the different stocks in the sample.

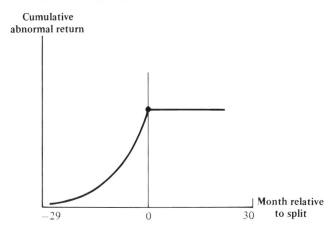

Figure 9.6 Abnormal price changes before and after stock splits.

that the stock splits convey.[27] The somewhat greater than expected returns after the split dates for companies that increased their dividends show the positive price responses that result when the bullish signal is confirmed. The lower than expected returns after the split dates for companies that do not increase their dividends are evidence of the negative price adjustments that occur when a bullish expectation turns out to have been unjustified.

For a large sample of stocks, the FFJR findings show that prices adjust to news before an event (for instance, before the dates of the stock splits) has occurred. Therefore, profitable trading strategies cannot be developed in relation to an event after it has occurred. A sizable number of other event studies in addition to that of Fama, Fisher, Jensen and Roll have substantiated the informational efficiency of the market in the semistrong form of the hypothesis.

The tests of semistrong form efficiency have not, however, addressed the question of dynamic efficiency. As discussed previously, information may be quickly reflected in prices, but some investors may nevertheless have a preferential position vis-à-vis the information flow. If so, these investors might receive and act upon information first and may receive excess profits.

Dynamic efficiency is particularly difficult to test, largely because price adjustments do occur rapidly. One would not expect to observe dynamic inefficiency in monthly price data as were used by FFJR and in many other studies. Rather, intraday prices could reveal a far more telling story. Dann, Mayers, and Raab (1977), in their examination of the effect of block sales on transaction-to-transaction price movements, for instance, found that

---

[27]It is also likely that the companies were enjoying above average and unsustainable prosperity in the two years before the split, and that the effect of this is also observed in the pattern of the residuals.

the price pressure caused by these sales does allow the formulation of profitable trading rules. To earn a profit, however, an investor must make a purchase within *5 minutes* of the block transaction; within *15 minutes* of the transaction, prices appear to have adjusted completely to their previous levels. Given the speed with which price adjustments are made in the equity markets, one might question the inferences concerning market efficiency that have been drawn from studies based on monthly prices. If the studies had shown evidence of inefficiency, the results would have been striking. Unfortunately, the failure to demonstrate inefficiency does not carry as much conviction.

Strong Form Tests

The semistrong form of the EMH refers to news that is publicly available, the weak form refers to information that is contained in prior stock price movements, and the *strong form* refers to what remains: inside information, and that which can be "dug out" by superior security analysis. Unfortunately, academic researchers are not as a rule privy to such information. Therefore, researchers have attempted to draw inferences concerning strong form efficiency by testing whether or not investors who are most apt to enjoy this informational advantage do in fact realize excess returns.

Finding that the better informed do not make excess profits would be evidence in support of the EMH. On the other hand, observing that certain classes of investors make excess profits net of information costs may not be evidence against the EMH. The reason is twofold:

1. As discussed previously, informational efficiency requires that the marginal return to information equals the marginal cost of obtaining it. However, decreasing average and marginal returns and increasing average and marginal costs, result in average returns exceeding average costs when marginal returns equal marginal costs.[28] Hence excess profits[29] can be realized by some decision makers.[30]
2. As indicated previously, some investors do better than others simply because of luck. Therefore, larger realized returns *ex post* do not necessarily indicate that better decisions were made *ex ante*. For this reason, excess *ex post* returns are not themselves evidence against the strong form of the EMH. Rather, to reject the hypothesis, one must demonstrate that excess returns accrue to one individual persistently (and thus are not explained by chance).

---

[28]The reason is that a marginal value is less (greater) than an associated average value for a decreasing (increasing) average value function.

[29]Such profits are sometimes referred to as *economic rent*.

[30]Decision makers who undertake their own research are both producers and consumers of information. As producers they may face increasing average costs, and as consumers they may realize decreasing average returns.

The empirical evidence shows that professional investment managers do not consistently realize superior portfolio returns. Mutual funds have been the most frequently studied of the institutions. Some of the best known studies that have shown that the funds do not outperform the market include those of Friend, Brown, Herman, and Vickers (1962), Sharpe (1966), and Jensen (1969).

With regard to inside information, the evidence is quite clear that insiders do realize abnormally high returns from their trading. See, for instance, Jaffe (1974), Neiderhoffer and Osborne (1966), Lorie and Neiderhoffer (1968), and Givoli and Palmon (1985).

Heterogeneous Expectations Revisited

We have shown how the orders placed and trades made in a frictionless market harmonize the investment desires of all traders (Chapter 8). In such an environment (1) all orders are executed in one round of trading, (2) there is no desire among traders to recontract immediately after the market call, (3) market prices appropriately reflect all information, and (4) market prices follow a random walk. In light of these results, we return to an issue addressed earlier in this chapter and again question whether or not the *expectations* of all traders may be heterogeneous in the equilibrium configuration just described.

To answer this question, assume a situation in which some investors obtain information that suggests that a stock's price will rise 20 percent within the week and, on the basis of this information, buy more shares. Consider two investors, j and k. Assume these two individuals are identical in all respects (same wealth, same tastes for risk, and so on) except that j is not informed about the likely price change, and k is informed. The demand curves of the two investors are shown in Figure 9.7. Because k

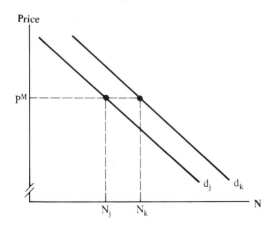

Figure 9.7 Demand curves of two traders with heterogeneous expectations.

has received the bullish information and j has not, k's demand curve (d_k) is above and to the right of j's demand curve (d_j). Assume the price P^M clears the market for the asset in one round of trading and that, as a consequence of their trades, j now holds N_j shares and k now holds N_k shares. We thus have the following results:

1. The value weight of the stock is greater in k's portfolio than in j's portfolio (both started with the same wealth).
2. j has obtained an optimal portfolio (given j's expectations) that, compared to k's, yields a lower expected return and a lower returns variance.
3. k has obtained an optimal portfolio (given k's expectations) that has a higher expected return (in k's opinion) and a higher returns variance. The higher expected return is accounted for by the differential information. The higher variance is explained by the fact that, with a greater value weight for the stock, k does not enjoy as fully the benefit of portfolio diversification.
4. Trade between k-type (informed) and j-type (uninformed) individuals has harmonized the trading propensities of these two investors.
5. Trading has not harmonized the expectations of these investors: k still expects a higher return for the stock than does j.
6. Frictionless trading, random walk, and substantiation of the efficient market hypothesis do not imply that, in equilibrium, investor expectations will be homogeneous.

The existence of heterogeneous expectations in equilibrium carries an important implication: once it is allowed that investors can have different expectations, it must also be allowed that some investors have *more accurate* expectations than others. That is, some people may be better security analysts and better decision makers than others. In equilibrium, therefore, we would expect these people to realize higher returns.

It also follows that good security analysis can be a profitable activity even in informationally efficient markets. Once an equilibrium configuration is obtained with regard to information gathering and processing activities, it is only *additional* analysis that would not yield returns over and above the marginal cost involved.

CONCLUSION

Information is the input that drives trading, and security prices are an output of the system. In efficient markets, the information should be reflected in prices with an accuracy that leaves no investor an incentive to search for additional information, or to trade. This concept may appear straightforward; it is in fact subtle:

1. Informational efficiency is multifaceted. Involved are the efficient exploitation of the existing information set and the optimal allocation of resources to expand the information set. Also involved are the accuracy of the signals that prices convey and the fair and efficient dissemination of information to investors.

2. Prices are both the result of information and a signal by which information is transmitted. That is, with costly information, some investors undertake research, and other investors infer information from market prices.

3. The relationship between information and prices involves concepts that at first may appear paradoxical. For instance, pricing securities properly in relation to the information set eliminates the ''chaos'' that characterizes sloppy pricing; in frictionless markets, however, equilibrium prices change randomly over time. Securities picked by random selection would yield appropriate risk adjusted returns if prices accurately reflect all information; but how can prices accurately reflect all information if securities are selected randomly?

4. Expectation formation, decision making, and market equilibrium under uncertainty and imperfect information are only partially understood by financial economists; they remain complex subjects.

5. An investor cannot achieve superior returns in the market by having good information. Rather, he or she must have *better* anticipations than the market. This feat is extremely difficult to accomplish consistently in informationally efficient markets. But it is not impossible.

6. Even with frictionless trading and complete substantiation of the efficient market hypothesis, investor expectations need not be homogeneous in equilibrium. The existence of heterogeneous expectations in equilibrium carries an important implication: once it is allowed that investors can have different expectations, it must be allowed that some investors may have *more accurate* expectations than others.

7. Security analysis can be a profitable activity even in an informationally efficient market. Over time, the truth regarding the import of any given bit of information reveals itself. As it does, some investors are shown to have been more correct than others, and, on average, we expect these people to realize higher returns. Accordingly, good security analysis can be profitable. Once an equilibrium configuration is obtained with regard to information gathering and processing, it is only *additional* analysis that would not yield sufficient returns to compensate for the marginal costs involved.

Our analysis of the relationship between information and prices points up another factor. In a world of heterogeneous expectations, market demand curves to hold shares of risky assets are negatively inclined, and hence share prices can be found only by buyers and sellers meeting in the marketplace. The share prices that are established reflect, not intrinsic values, but rather the investment desires of the traders, as these are based on available information. In such an environment, a primary function of the securities markets is to find the prices that best represent the market's aggregate assessment of the information set.

The quality of prices established in a market should be assessed in two ways:

1. In terms of *informational efficiency,* given the information set, the information gathering and dissemination procedures, and the design of the trading system
2. In terms of *operational efficiency,* given informational efficiency

The chapter has discussed three approaches to testing informational efficiency: *weak form tests* (whether or not information contained in past price movements is reflected in current prices), *semistrong form tests* (whether or not all public information is reflected in prices), and *strong form tests* (whether or not all information, both public and private, is reflected in prices). The strong form tests show that insiders do enjoy excess returns. With this single exception, tests of the efficient market hypothesis have not found evidence that markets are informationally inefficient.

Understanding how the information set is reflected in the structure of security prices enables one to appreciate more fully the meaning of equilibrium prices. With this understanding, we can proceed to a consideration of how, in a nonfrictionless environment, operational inefficiency causes market clearing prices to deviate from the equilibrium values.

SUGGESTED READING

S. Alexander, "Price Movements in Speculative Markets: Trends or Random Walks," *Industrial Management Review,* May 1961.

S. Alexander, "Price Movements in Speculative Markets: Trends or Random Walks No. 2," *Industrial Management Review,* Spring 1964.

L. Bachelier, *Théorie de la Spéculation,* Paris, France: Gauthier-Villars, 1900.

A. Beja and N. Hakansson, "Dynamic Market Processes and the Rewards to Up-to-Date Information," *Journal of Finance,* May 1977.

A. Beja and N. Hakansson, "On the Dynamic Behavior of Prices in Disequilibrium," *Journal of Finance,* May 1980.

P. Cootner, *The Random Character of Stock Market Prices,* Cambridge, Mass.: The M.I.T. Press, 1964.

T. Copeland, "A Model of Asset Trading Under the Assumption of Sequential Information Arrival," *Journal of Finance,* September 1976.

L. Dann, D. Mayers, and R. Raab, "Trading Rules, Large Blocks and the Speed of Price Adjustments," *Journal of Financial Economics,* January 1977.

E. Fama, "The Behavior of Stock-Market Prices," *Journal of Business,* January 1965.

E. Fama, "Efficient Capital Markets: A Review of Theory and Empirical Work," *Journal of Finance,* May 1970.

E. Fama, L. Fisher, M. Jensen, and R. Roll, "The Adjustment of Stock Prices to New Information," *International Economic Review,* February 1969.

S. Figlewski, "Market 'Efficiency' in a Market with Heterogeneous Information," *The Journal of Political Economy,* August 1978.

K. French and R. Roll, "Stock Return Variances: The Arrival of Information and the Reaction of Traders," *Journal of Financial Economics,* September 1986.

I. Friend, F. Brown, E. Herman, and D. Vickers, *A Study of Mutual Funds,* Government Printing Office, 1962.

K. Garbade and Z. Lieber, "On the Independence of Transactions on the New York Stock Exchange," *Journal of Banking and Finance,* October 1977.

K. Garbade, J. Pomrenze, and W. Silber, "On the Information Content of Prices," *American Economic Review,* March 1979.

D. Givoli and D. Palmon, "Insider Trading and the Exploitation of Inside Information: Some Empirical Evidence," *Journal of Business,* January 1985.

M. B. Goldman and H. Sossin, "Information Dissemination, Market Efficiency and the Frequency of Transactions," *Journal of Financial Economics,* March 1979.

C. Granger and O. Morgenstern, "Spectral Analysis of New York Stock Market Prices," *Kyklos,* January 1963.

S. Grossman, "An Introduction to the Theory of Rational Expectations Under Asymmetric Information," *Review of Economic Studies,* October 1981.

S. Grossman and J. Stiglitz, "Information and Competitive Price Systems," *American Economic Review,* May 1976.

S. Grossman and J. Stiglitz, "On the Impossibility of Informationally Efficient Markets," *American Economic Review,* June 1980.

R. Hellwig, "Rational Expectations Equilibrium with Conditioning on Past Prices: A Mean-Variance Example," *Journal of Economic Theory,* April 1982.

S. Hillmer and P. Yu, "The Market Speed of Adjustment to New Information," *Journal of Financial Economics,* December 1979.

T. Ho, R. Schwartz, and D. Whitcomb, "The Trading Decision and Market Clearing Under Transaction Price Uncertainty," *Journal of Finance,* March 1985.

J. Jaffe, "The Effect of Regulation Changes on Insider Trading," *Bell Journal of Economics and Management Science,* Spring 1974.

M. Jensen, "Risk, the Pricing of Capital Assets, and the Evaluation of Investment Portfolios," *Journal of Business,* April 1969.

M. Jensen, "Capital Markets, Theory and Evidence," *Bell Journal of Economics and Management Science,* Autumn 1972.

O. M. Joy and C. Jones, "Should We Believe Tests of Market Efficiency?" *Journal of Portfolio Management,* Summer 1986.

M. Kendel, "The Analysis of Economic Time Series," *Journal of the Royal Statistical Society,* Series A, 1953.

J. M. Keynes, *The General Theory of Employment Interest and Money,* New York: Harcourt, Brace, 1958.

J. Lorie, P. Dodd, and M. H. Kimpton, *The Stock Market: Theories and Evidence,* second edition, Homewood, Ill.: Richard D. Irwin, 1985.

J. Lorie and V. Neiderhoffer, "Predictive and Statistical Properties of Insider Trading," *Journal of Law and Economics,* April 1968.

B. Malkiel, *A Random Walk Down Wall Street,* fourth edition, New York: W. W. Norton, 1985.

B. Mandelbrot, "Forecasts of Future Prices, Unbiased Markets, and 'Martingale' Models," *Journal of Business,* January 1966.

V. Neiderhoffer and M. F. Osborne, "Market Making and Reversal on the Stock Exchange," *Journal of the American Statistical Association,* December 1966.

M. F. Osborne, "Brownian Motion in the Stock Market," *Operations Research,* March-April 1959.

H. Roberts, "Stock Market 'Patterns' and Financial Analysis: Methodological Suggestions," *Journal of Finance,* March 1959.

P. Samuelson, "Proof That Properly Anticipated Prices Fluctuate Randomly," *Industrial Management Review,* Spring 1965.

W. Sharpe, "Mutual Fund Performance," *Journal of Business,* Supplement, January 1966.

L. Summers, "Does the Stock Market Rationally Reflect Fundamental Values?" *Journal of Finance,* July 1986.

chapter 10

Prices and Returns[1]

The investment and trading decisions considered in Chapters 7 and 8 take into account the expected prices at which asset shares can be currently traded and the means, variances, and covariances of future returns. Our analysis of these decisions has thus far paid scant attention either to the way the marketplace translates orders into transaction prices or to the relationship between prices and returns. By and large, "a return" has been an abstract concept.

Each transaction price in a continuous market reflects the interaction of at least two orders—a buy order and a sell order. Each return that is established reflects two separate transaction prices, the price at the beginning of the period over which the return is measured and the price at the end of the period. All told, prices and returns are complex results of informational change, liquidity change, and the mechanics of the market.

The insights to be gained from studying the price determination and returns generation processes are essential for understanding the operations of the equity markets. This chapter considers the issues involved. The analysis also establishes the requisite foundation for empirically assessing the operational efficiency of a marketplace, a topic we turn to in the next chapter.

---

[1]This chapter draws heavily on Cohen, Hawawini, Maier, Schwartz, and Whitcomb (1983) and on Cohen, Maier, Schwartz and Whitcomb (1978, 1981, and 1986).

This chapter first focuses on the measurement of returns. We clarify the various ways in which the time dimension pertains to returns measurement, define *price,* define *returns,* and identify the *intervalling effect* (how measures of returns behavior change as the interval of time over which returns are measured is altered).

Next the factors that cause prices to change are considered. We first distinguish between broad market movements and idiosyncratic change in traders' demand propensities to hold shares of an asset. The section then shows how broad market shifts of the demand curve generate price movements and hence returns, how idiosyncratic shifts generate price movements and hence returns, and how these changes combine to produce the return over a measurement interval of given length. The section then shows how the returns generation process is affected by the mechanics of the market: the procedures that determine how orders are handled and translated into trades and the fact that traders periodically (rather than continuously) transmit discrete (rather than continuous) order functions to the market. After this discussion, we consider how the mechanics of the market affect the market model relationship and how market realities may perturb the random walk of stock prices.

The following section examines the mean and variance of a security's returns. We begin by modeling the impact of informational change and idiosyncratic order arrival on security prices, next set forth the equation for the return measured over a time interval of given length, and then obtain expressions for the mean and variance of this return. The independent variables in the variance equation are next assessed, and consideration is then given to the effect of the market's mechanics on returns variance.

The next topic is the bid-ask spread. The bid-ask spread model presented shows that investor trading strategies explain the existence of spreads in markets comprising many participants who post quotes on the market. The model is then assessed (1) to establish that spreads exist because of transaction costs, (2) to identify the concept of an equilibrium spread, (3) to show that the equilibrium spread is expected to be larger in thinner markets, and (4) to show that the effective spread is expected to be larger for larger orders.

The final section analyzes intertemporal correlation in security returns. We first establish the concept of an intertemporal portfolio and contrast the intertemporal portfolio with a conventional (cross-sectional) portfolio of risky assets. The section then considers, in turn, positive intertemporal correlation, negative intertemporal correlation, and serial cross-correlation (the terms are defined in the section). Serial cross-correlation is shown to account for biased measurements of the market model beta, when the beta coefficient is estimated by using short period returns. We conclude by again considering the intervalling effects identified earlier in the chapter. As will be seen here and in Chapter 11, inflated short period returns variance, negative serial returns correlation, and biased estimates of the market model beta coefficient are all explained by the fact that equilibrium prices are rarely achieved in the equity markets.

THE MEASUREMENT OF RETURNS

A market's microstructure is manifest in the returns that are generated as an asset's price changes over time. To see this, it is necessary first to understand various technical factors concerning returns generation. The relevant analysis is contained in this section. We start with the time dimension used to measure returns.

The Time Dimension

The time dimension enters the measurement of returns in a number of ways. $T + 1$ points in time establish T time intervals; t identifies the tth interval, $t = 1, \ldots, T$. The return for an interval is given an index that corresponds to the index for the interval. Thus r_t is the return over the interval $(t - 1)$ to (t). If the length of the interval is changed, then the index on the return corresponds to the point in time that demarcates the end of the longer period. That is, R_T denotes the return from 0 to T if the full span is referred to, and r_T denotes the return from $(T - 1)$ to (T) if the Tth (last) short interval is referred to. Using this notation, the relevant time dimensions are as follows:

- *Points in time:* The $T + 1$ points in time extend from the first (0) to the last (T).
- *Time intervals:* The T time intervals are indexed $t = 1, \ldots, T$, with the index on each interval corresponding to the count on the price observation at the end of that interval.
- *Time span:* The overall time span is of length T, and it comprises T short intervals.
- *Interval length:* The length of each interval is point in time t, minus point in time $t - 1$.
- *Unit period:* Both the overall time span and the shorter time intervals are measured as multiples of a *unit period of time*. For instance, if the unit period is one day, then both the time interval $t - 1$ to t and the overall time span, T, are measured in days.
- *Common period:* A return measured for one interval of time (such as a week) can be expressed as a rate per some other interval (for instance, per year). Converting all time rates into a common period sometimes facilitates analysis and evaluation.

- *Compounding frequency:* Interest can be compounded once per time interval, more frequently, or, in the limit, continuously.
- *Calendar time:* For theoretical analysis, time can be treated as an abstract concept. For empirical analysis, actual price observations are located in *calendar time.* With seasonal variability, secular trends, and/or nonstationary returns distributions, the exact location of the span $t = 0, \ldots, T$ in calendar time will affect the observed price behavior. Location in calendar time may be altered *in the large* by, for example, using 1985 prices instead of 1975 prices, or *in the small* by using daily opening prices instead of daily closing prices.

Prices

The term *price* can refer either to a transaction price or to a bid-ask quotation price. *Transaction prices* are prices that have been established for trades already made. *Quotation prices* are *ex ante* expressions of the willingness of buyers and sellers to trade. We generally restrict the use of the term *price* to transaction prices and refer to bid-ask prices as *quotes.* The behavior of prices and quotes is studied by analyzing their change from one point in time to another.

Price changes are *returns.* Price changes computed by using points of time that are separated by an interval of specified length (such as one day) are identified as pertaining to that period (for instance, *daily returns*). Price changes computed for a sequence of prices recorded at the points of time that trades occur are *transaction-to-transaction returns.* For the most part, we deal with returns measured for specified time intervals.

In empirical work, prices are adjusted for stock and cash dividends paid during an interval so that the return measured for the interval is the total return—capital gains plus dividends. Therefore, if the closing price of a stock at time $t - 1$ is 50, the recorded closing price at t is 49, a dividend of \$.25 a share is paid, and t is the ex-dividend date, the adjusted price at t is $49\frac{1}{4}$, and the price change from $t - 1$ to t is $50 - 49\frac{1}{4} = -\frac{3}{4}$.

Returns

Let P_0 be the value of price at some initial moment in time, and P_T be the value of price at some final moment of time. Divide this time span into T equal intervals, and let $P_1, \ldots, P_T$ denote the value of price at the end of each of the intervals. Price changes (returns) can be measured as price relatives, as dollar amounts, or as percentages. Arithmetic percentages can be converted into logarithmic values or into growth rates.

The *price relatives* are

$$\frac{P_T}{P_0} = \left(\frac{P_1}{P_0}\right)\left(\frac{P_2}{P_1}\right) \cdots \left(\frac{P_T}{P_{T-1}}\right) \tag{10.1}$$

For the time interval 0, 1 we can write

$$P_1 = P_0 + \Delta P_1 \tag{10.2a}$$
$$P_1 = P_0(1 + r_1) \tag{10.2b}$$
$$P_1 = P_0 e^{g_1} \tag{10.2c}$$

Accordingly:

The *dollar return* is

$$\Delta P_1 = P_1 - P_0 \tag{10.3}$$

The *percentage return* is

$$r_1 = \frac{\Delta P_1}{P_0} = \frac{P_0 + \Delta P_1}{P_0} - 1 = \frac{P_1}{P_0} - 1 \tag{10.4}$$

The *logarithmic return* is

$$r_1^* = \ln(1 + r_1) \tag{10.5}$$

The *growth rate* is

$$g_1 = \ln\left(\frac{P_1}{P_0}\right) \tag{10.6}$$

where ln indicates a logarithm to the base e ($e = 2.7182 \ldots$).
Generalizing for a succession of periods, $t = 1, \ldots, T$,

$$P_T = P_0 + \Delta P_1 + \cdots + \Delta P_T = P_0 + \sum_{t=1}^{T} \Delta P_t \tag{10.7a}$$

$$P_T = P_0(1 + r_1) \ldots (1 + r_T) = P_0 \prod_{t=1}^{T} (1 + r_t) \tag{10.7b}$$

$$P_T = P_0 e^{g_1} \ldots e^{g_T} = P_0 \prod_{t=1}^{T} e^{g_t} \tag{10.7c}$$

For the overall time span we can also write

$$P_T = P_0 + \Delta P_T \tag{10.8a}$$
$$P_T = P_0(1 + R_T) \tag{10.8b}$$
$$P_T = P_0 e^{g_T} \tag{10.8c}$$

Equations (10.7) and (10.8) give

$$\Delta P_T = \sum_{t=1}^{T} \Delta P_t \tag{10.9a}$$

$$1 + R_T = \prod_{t=1}^{T} (1 + r_t) \tag{10.9b}$$

$$e^{g_T} = \prod_{t=1}^{T} e^{g_t} \tag{10.9c}$$

Taking logarithms of (10.9c) gives

$$g_T = \sum_{t=1}^{T} g_t \tag{10.9d}$$

It follows from equations (10.9a)–(10.9d) that

- The average price change over the time span of length T is the arithmetic average of the price changes over the T short intervals that comprise it.
- $(1 + R_T)^{1/T}$ is the geometric mean of the $(1 + r_t)$.[2]
- g_T is T times the arithmetic mean of the g_t.

Let $R_T^* = \ln (1 + R_T)$ and $r_t^* = \ln (1 + r_t)$. Then, from (10.7b) and (10.8b), we have

$$\ln \left(\frac{P_T}{P_0}\right) = R_T^* = \sum_{t=1}^{T} r_t^* \tag{10.10}$$

From (10.8b) and (10.8c) we have

$$(1 + R_T) = e^{g_T} \tag{10.11}$$

Taking logarithms of (10.11) gives

$$R_T^* = g_T \tag{10.12}$$

The growth rate g_T is, therefore, a logarithmic return.

As seen in equation (10.7b), the $(1 + r_t)$ are multiplicative returns; it follows from equation (10.9b) that $(1 + R_T)^{1/T}$ is a geometric mean return. Multiplicative returns, geometric means, and especially the variance of multiplicative returns are cumbersome to deal with; additive returns, arithmetic means, and the variance of additive returns are not. For this

---

[2]The geometric mean of n observations is the nth root of the product of the n observations.

reason, microstructure analysis frequently uses logarithmic returns (r*) instead of arithmetic returns (r); the r_t^* are additive, and we can treat their arithmetic mean and variance.

Additional relationships between the arithmetic returns, logarithmic returns, and growth rates are given in the appendix to this chapter.

The Intervalling Effect

The *intervalling effect* is the way in which measures of returns behavior change as the measurement interval is varied. The relevant return measures for our purposes are

- Mean return (stock and index)
- The variance of returns (stock and index)
- Market model beta
- The variance of residual returns
- Market model R^2

Following the previous discussion, taking logarithms of

$$\frac{P_T}{P_0} = \left(\frac{P_1}{P_0}\right), \ldots, \left(\frac{P_T}{P_{T-1}}\right)$$

gives

$$R_T^* = \sum_{t=1}^{T} r_t^* \tag{10.13}$$

Let the short time span (t − 1 to t) be the unit period; the intervalling effect is the effect on each of the five measures of increasing the interval T over which the long period return, R_T^* in equation (10.13), is measured.

Mean Return (Stock and Index)   Taking means of equation (10.13) and, assuming the returns distribution is stationary, gives

$$E(R_T^*) = \sum_{t=1}^{T} E(r_t^*)$$

$$= TE(r^*) \tag{10.14}$$

It is clear from equation (10.14) that the mean logarithmic return increases linearly with T. For instance, the average weekly logarithmic return expressed as a rate per week is five times the average daily logarithmic return expressed as a rate per day.

The Variance of Returns (Stock and Index)   Taking the variance of equation (10.13) gives

$$\text{Var}(R_T^*) = \sum_{t=1}^{T} \sum_{u=1}^{T} \sigma_t \sigma_u \rho_{t,u} \tag{10.15}$$

where σ_t (σ_u) is the standard deviation of returns in the tth (u^{th}) short period and $\rho_{t,u}$ is the correlation between the tth short period return and the uth short period return, t, u = 1, . . . , T.

The correlation between returns affects the relationship between the variance of the long period return and the variances of the short period returns. Because of this, the intervalling effect on variance depends on the correlation pattern in security returns.[3]

To simplify the analysis assume:

1. The returns distribution is stationary ($\sigma_t = \sigma_u$ for all short periods t, u = 1, . . . , T).
2. $\rho_{t,u}$ is the same for all $|t - u|$.[4]

From assumption (1) we have

$$\sigma_t \sigma_u = \text{Var}(r^*) \qquad \text{for all } t, u = 1, \ldots, T \tag{10.16}$$

From assumption (2) we can write[5]

$$\rho_{t,u} = \rho_{1,1+s} \qquad \text{for } s = |t - u|, s = 1, \ldots, T - 1 \tag{10.17}$$

How many $\rho_{t,u}$ are there in the series t, u = 1, . . . , T that are equal to $\rho_{1,1+s}$ for any s = 1, . . . , T − 1? Consider the case where T = 8 and s = 3. The pairs of returns that are three periods apart in the set of eight returns are

1, 4
2, 5
3, 6
4, 7
5, 8

There are 8 − 3 = T − s pairings. Generalizing for all T and s, and substituting equations (10.16) and (10.17) into equation (10.15) gives

[3]The correlation referred to here is *serial correlation:* the correlation between the returns in the time series $r_1, \ldots, r_T$.

[4]That is, for instance, if t = 8, u = 5, and thus the returns are three short periods apart, the correlation between these two returns is identical to the correlation between any other pair of returns that are three short periods apart (the 9th return and the 12th return, the 7th and the 4th, and so on).

[5]To illustrate, consider the following. Let the correlation between the return for t = 4 and the return for u = 6 be $\rho_{4,6}$. Because $|4 - 6| = 2$, the correlation is, by assumption (2), the same as the correlation between return 1 and return 3. Using the notation in equation (10.17), the correlation between return 1 and return 3 is $\rho_{1,1+2}$ (that is, s = 2 in this case). Equation (10.17) shows that $\rho_{4,6} = \rho_{1,3}$, an equality that follows from assumption (2).

$$\mathrm{Var}(R_T^*) = T \, \mathrm{Var}(r^*) + 2 \, \mathrm{Var}(r^*) \sum_{s=1}^{T-1} (T - s)\rho_{1,1+s} \quad (10.18)$$

Equation (10.18) shows that the variance of logarithmic returns increases linearly with T if there is no intertemporal correlation in the returns (that is, if $\rho_{t,u} = 0$ for all $t \neq u$). It also follows that, for any value of $\mathrm{Var}(r^*)$, the long period variance $\mathrm{Var}(R_T^*)$ will be larger if the intertemporal correlations are predominantly positive and will be smaller if the intertemporal correlations are predominantly negative. As will be seen in Chapter 11, the negative correlation patterns are of particular interest.

Market Model Beta   The market model beta for a stock can be written as

$$\beta_i = \frac{\mathrm{Cov}(R_i^*, R_m^*)}{\mathrm{Var}(R_m^*)} \quad (10.19)$$

From the intervalling relations defined previously for the variance term, and given that

$$\mathrm{Cov}(R_i^*, R_m^*) = \sigma_i \sigma_m \rho_{i,m}$$

it is clear that a stock's beta will be independent of the differencing interval if there is no intertemporal correlation in security returns [that is, if $\mathrm{Var}(R_{iT}^*)$ and $\mathrm{Var}(R_{mT}^*)$ increase linearly with T, and if the cross-correlation $\rho_{i,m}$ is the same for all T]. On the other hand, intertemporal correlation in returns will introduce an intervalling effect on the beta coefficient. As noted later, the use of short period returns causes beta estimates to be lower for relatively thin issues and higher for the largest issues.[6]

The Variance of Residual Returns   The *variance of residual returns* behaves in the same way as the variance of returns—it increases linearly with T in the absence of serial correlation, at a faster rate in the presence of positive serial correlation, and at a slower rate if the serial correlations are predominantly negative.[7]

The Market Model R²   The squared coefficient of correlation for a regression equation shows the percentage of the variation in the dependent variable that is explained by change in the independent variable. For the market model regression,

[6]For a rigorous derivation of the intervalling effect bias in beta, see Cohen, Hawawini, Maier, Schwartz, and Whitcomb (1983) and Cohen, Maier, Schwartz, and Whitcomb (1986, chapters 6 and 7).

[7]Residual variance is further affected if beta itself is dependent on T, with the effect depending upon the impact that the intervalling effect on beta has on the average absolute size of the residual term.

$$R^2 = \frac{\beta_i^2 \, Var(R_m^*)}{Var(R_i^*)} \qquad (10.20)$$

There will be no intervalling effect on R^2 if there are no intertemporal correlation patterns in security returns. This is because, in the absence of such correlation, beta is independent of T, and $Var(R_m^*)$ and $Var(R_i^*)$ both change linearly with T. On the other hand, intertemporal correlations cause an intervalling effect on R^2; the effect depends upon the intervalling effect on beta, and on the intervalling effect on the variance of R_m^* in relation to the intervalling effect on the variance of R_i^*.

The Empirical Evidence on the Intervalling Effects As discussed, the mean return increases linearly with T regardless of the serial correlation that may exist in stock specific or market index returns. However, the intervalling effect associated with each of the other four measures of returns behavior is affected by serial correlation. Consequently, analysis of the intervalling effects is an effective way of obtaining evidence on such correlation in security returns. We return to this thought in Chapter 11. In brief, the empirical evidence shows that:

1. R_{iT}^*: The variance of R_{iT}^* increases less than proportionately with T as the differencing interval is increased from one-half hour to two days. This is clear indication of negative serial correlation in very brief period returns for individual securities.
2. R_{mT}^*: The variance of market index returns increases more than proportionately with T as the differencing interval is increased from one day to somewhat larger values. This indicates positive autocorrelation in market index returns.
3. *Beta:* Daily betas, compared to their longer period values, are clearly lower for relatively thin stocks; essentially unchanged for intermediate sized stocks; and larger for a few very large stocks. This indicates that an intricate pattern of serial cross-correlation exists in stock returns.[8]
4. *Residual returns:* The variance of residual returns increases less than proportionately with T as the differencing interval is increased from one day to larger values. This indicates the presence of negative serial correlation in the residual returns.
5. *Market model R^2:* The regression statistic, R^2, increases as the differencing interval is increased from one day to larger values. This further indicates that an intricate pattern of serial and serial-cross correlation exists in stock returns. The evidence is consistent

[8]Serial cross-correlation exists when the return for stock i in some period t is correlated with the return for another stock j in some other period u (see the discussion of intertemporal correlation later in the chapter).

with that suggested by the negative autocorrelation in stock returns and residual returns, by the positive autocorrelation in market index returns, and by the observed intervalling effect on market model beta coefficients.

FACTORS THAT ACCOUNT FOR STOCK PRICE CHANGES

Broad Market Movements and Idiosyncratic Change

A stock's price changes (and hence returns) reflect shifts in the location of investor demand curves to hold shares of the stock. These shifts are due to informational change, to investor reassessments of information, and/or to the changing liquidity and liquidity needs of individual investors. The demand shifts may reflect broad-based market movements in the stock, or they may be uncorrelated across investors.

The broad market shifts are due to informational change. Such change may pertain to one stock in particular, to a group of stocks, or to all stocks in aggregate. For instance:

- News that an infallible electronic proofreader has been developed by IMB will increase the price of that company's shares.
- News that the government is going to increase the tax credit for the purchase of office equipment will increase the share price for all securities in the office equipment industry.
- News that the Federal Reserve has learned how to stabilize interest rates while lowering inflation, reducing unemployment, and accelerating economic growth will increase the price of all shares.

The demand shifts that are uncorrelated across investors are called *idiosyncratic change*. For instance:

- Upon further reflection, investor j decides that the home market for electronic proofreaders is overrated; accordingly, he calls his broker and submits an order to sell 100 shares of IMB at market.
- Upon inheriting $20,000, investor i acquires more shares of her favorite stock (Liquidity Inc.).
- Upon the receipt of a $15,000 tuition bill, Mr. Pere de Student liquidates his position in Podunk Mines.

Shifts in the Market Demand for a Stock

To consider in its pure (frictionless) form how market shifts in the demand for a stock affect share price, we make the extreme (and clearly unrealistic) assumption that all investors react identically and simultaneously to informational change. This being the case, such change will shift the market demand curve, but no trades will be made. To see this, consider Figure 10.1.

The curve labeled D_0 in Figure 10.1(a) reflects the initial market demand propensities. With NSO shares outstanding, the location of D_0 establishes P_0 as the equilibrium price of the stock. Figure 10.1(b) shows that the associated buy and sell curves are, respectively, the negatively inclined line labeled B_0 and the positively inclined line labeled S_0. Then, due to the receipt of news, let the demand curve shift to D_1, and let the associated buy and sell curves shift to B_1 and S_1. Because all investors adjust their orders simultaneously, no trades occur. However, the new equilibrium price is P_1.

Idiosyncratic Shifts

Figure 10.2 shows the impact of an idiosyncratic order on the market price of a stock. As in Figure 10.1, market demand is initially shown by the line labeled D_0, and the associated buy and sell order functions are the curves labeled B_0 and S_0.

Assume the idiosyncratic arrival of a market order to sell Q_1 shares. This order will execute against the Q_1 shares along the curve B_0, and price will decrease to P_1 (given the order function B_0, price has to decrease to this value for the Q_1 shares to be absorbed by the market). The return generated by this idiosyncratic order is, therefore, $(P_1 - P_0)/P_0$.

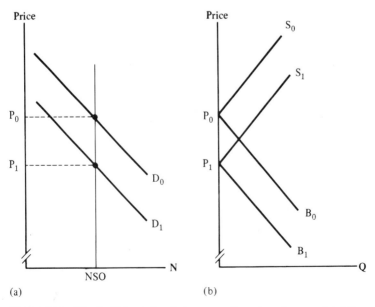

(a)   (b)

Figure 10.1 Effect of informational change on the price of an asset. (a) The market demand curves. (b) The market buy and sell curves.

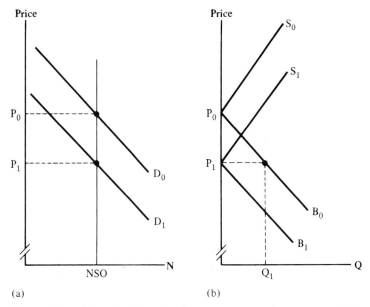

Figure 10.2 Effect of an idiosyncratic order on the price of an asset. (a) The market demand curves. (b) The market buy and sell curves.

After the execution of the idiosyncratic order, the market demand curve has shifted down to the curve labeled D_1, and the market buy and sell order functions are the curves labeled, respectively, B_1 and S_1. As was not true with the aggregate shift, a trade has occurred as a result of the idiosyncratic order.

From Transaction-to-Transaction Returns to Periodic Returns

We have described the return that results from one aggregate demand shift or from the arrival of one idiosyncratic order. These returns occur at the points in time that something happens (that is, the aggregate demand shifts, or the idiosyncratic order arrives). Therefore, these are transaction-to-transaction returns.[9] Over any given interval of time (such as a trading day), a sequence of transaction-to-transaction returns is expected, and the return for the interval shows the combined impact of the individual returns that the sequence comprises. The return over a time interval of given length is, therefore,

$$r_t = \prod_{s=1}^{N_A} (1 + r_s) \prod_{k=1}^{N_I} (1 + r_k) - 1 \qquad (10.21)$$

[9] It may be more accurate to call these "event-to-event" returns, especially since the aggregate demand shift has not triggered any transaction. This is unusual terminology, however; thus we retain the term *transaction-to-transaction return*.

where:

r_s = the percentage price change generated by the sth aggregate demand shift.

N_A = the number of aggregate demand shifts that occurred in the interval.

r_k = the percentage price change generated by the kth idiosyncratic order.

N_I = the number of idiosyncratic orders that arrived during the interval.

Because of the commutative property of multiplication ($xy = yx$), the return over the interval is unaffected by the sequence in which the individual percentage price changes actually occur. Therefore, the ordering of the aggregate demand shifts and the idiosyncratic order arrivals does not matter (the events are, of course, generally interspersed).

The last event (demand shift or idiosyncratic order arrival) will in all likelihood occur before the literal end of the time interval. The reason is that these events occur sporadically rather than continuously and therefore are unlikely to happen in any brief instant of time (such as at the market close). This does not affect the computation of the return for the interval. The closing price is P_t, and the return over the interval is the percentage difference between this price and the price at the start of the interval (P_{t-1}).

The Mechanics of the Market

The preceding analysis does not take account of the mechanics of the marketplace. Neither does it recognize that traders transmit order points rather than continuous order functions, or that traders do not revise their orders continuously. We here consider how the mechanics of the market affect the returns generation process. Our discussion refers to a continuous market trading regime and assumes a system in which public orders are stored on a limit order book.[10]

Figure 10.3 shows how the buy/sell order functions might appear at any moment in time when point orders rather than continuous order functions are submitted to the market. The lengths of the horizontal line segments in Figure 10.3 show the total number of shares sought for purchase or offered for sale at each price. Thus the length of the line at P^A shows the number of shares offered at the market ask, and the length of the line at P^B shows the number of shares sought at the market bid.

The height of each vertical line segment shows the price change between orders. The minimum tick size for most stocks is one-eighth of a

[10] The discussion might seem more relevant for an exchange system than for a pure dealer market system because of our reference to a limit order book. Although this is true to some extent, the basic principles involved are applicable to both systems.

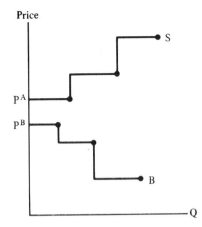

Price

pA

pB

Q

Figure 10.3 Buy and sell order curves when point orders rather than continuous order functions are submitted to the market.

dollar, and therefore the minimum vertical length is one-eighth. Gaps (air pockets) in the limit order book, however, can cause price jumps of more than one-eighth. The bid-ask spread itself is the vertical distance between P^A and P^B.

The orders on the limit order book have arrived during a preceding period. Because of the cost of continuously monitoring the market and updating orders, these orders reflect decisions made in relation to an earlier information set. Therefore, if the orders had been written in light of current news and current market conditions, they would have differed somewhat. Because orders on the book are not continuously updated, the limit order book is "sticky." Quotes that are grossly out of line with current information are called *stale orders*.

The mechanics of the market include the rules by which orders are executed when multiple orders are tied at a price on the limit order book (see Chapters 2 and 3). The priority rule may be time (the first orders entered are the first to execute), size (the largest orders execute first), combinations of time and size (the New York Stock Exchange uses this procedure), or random selection. When orders are tied at a price, some traders may not realize a transaction, even if transactions are made at the prices at which their orders have been placed.

Another aspect of the market is the sequential arrival of orders following informational change. Order arrival is *sequential* when transaction costs and information costs cause delays in the dissemination of news, in investor reactions to news, and in order handling itself. The reason is that when orders are delayed, they are generally nonsynchronous with each other.[11] With sequential order arrival, the demand curve does not shift as depicted in the discussion of shifts in market demand for stock; rather, the first orders to arrive on the basis of new information will interact with orders

[11]The orders of course arrive in quick succession in highly efficient markets, and the impact of news is quickly reflected in share prices. Nonetheless, the returns generation process is affected.

that do not reflect the news. As the informational orders arrive, trades can occur, as we showed for the idiosyncratic orders. The difference between sequential order arrival based on news and that based on idiosyncratic change is that the sequential informationally motivated orders are not independent events, whereas the idiosyncratic orders are.

The mechanics of the market also include the operations of dealers and specialists, the market makers who facilitate the process of trading. As we discuss in Chapter 12, market maker quotes reflect considerations in addition to the underlying information set. That is, a dealer or specialist buys or sells shares from a public trader simply to accommodate the public trader's demand to transact. In the process, transaction prices and quotes are affected.[12]

In summary, order functions in actual markets are discontinuous; price is a discontinuous variable (one-eighth of a point is generally the minimum tick size); orders arrive on the market and are revised periodically rather than continuously; the limit order book is "sticky"; quotes get "stale"; informationally motivated orders arrive sequentially rather than simultaneously; and market makers intervene in trading. These realities of the marketplace also affect the returns series that are observed. For instance, with a bid-ask spread, transaction prices may move from the bid to the ask or from the ask to the bid, simply because of the sequence in which market orders happened to arrive on the market. With a sticky limit order book and the sequential arrival of informationally motivated orders, trades that are triggered by new information may reveal outdated prices.

To understand further the extent to which returns based on either quotation prices or transaction prices may misrepresent the underlying change in market conditions, consider the following. Assume that at 3:35 P.M. on a given trading day, an order to buy 500 shares of Liquidity Inc. at $50 sets the market bid, and that this order had been placed at 10:05 A.M. on that day. Suppose further that a market order to sell 200 shares hits this bid at 3:52 P.M., and that no further orders arrive before the market's 4:00 P.M. close. In this case, both the last transaction price and the closing market bid quotation have been affected by an order that was placed a few minutes after the market opened. More than likely, information changed during the trading day, but presumably the change was not enough to induce the writer of the 500-share buy order to revise the order. Therefore, to an extent, the closing price and the return for the day have been affected by an earlier information set.

---

[12]In the process of accommodating public traders, the dealer/specialist attains a portfolio that is not optimal from an investment point of view. The dealer's subsequent attempts to rebalance the portfolio also have an impact on the stock's price movements.

The Market Model Revisited

Having considered the returns generation process as it relates to information arrival, idiosyncratic trading, and the mechanics of the market, we return to the market model [equation (7.24) in Chapter 7] and again consider the dichotomization of returns into a market related component ($b_i r_{mt}$) and a stock unique component (e_{it}).

1. *Informational change:* Informational change is the factor that accounts for the market related component. If such change affects all listed securities, then it directly causes the cross-sectionally correlated market movements. If the informational change relates to one or a subset of stocks, it can in principle generate broad-based, cross-sectionally correlated returns because of portfolio rebalancing.
2. *Sequential information arrival:* Sequential information arrival means that informationally generated orders arrive nonsynchronously, not only for individual stocks, but across stocks. For this reason, even broad-based informational change generates only weakly correlated interstock price movements over very brief time intervals (we return to this thought in Chapter 11).
3. *Stock specific information:* Stock specific information generates stock unique returns if the price movements for an individual stock do not result in an appreciable amount of portfolio rebalancing.
4. *Idiosyncratic orders:* Idiosyncratic orders also generate stock unique returns.
5. *Mechanics of the market:* The mechanics of the market primarily have an impact on residual returns. However, there are exceptions. A wave of buy orders for different stocks causes many ask prices to be hit; a wave of sell orders causes many bid prices to be hit; and a cross-sectionally correlated jump of transaction prices across bid-ask spreads gives rise to a broad market movement. In such an event, the price discontinuity represented by the spread exaggerates the market related component of returns.

Random Walk Revisited

Having analyzed the returns generation process, we again consider the feasibility of examining the efficiency of a market by testing for serial correlation in stock returns. As discussed in Chapter 9, the inferences to be drawn from such tests are the following: (1) significant autocorrelation in returns would suggest the existence of profitable and unexploited trading opportunities, and (2) the existence of such opportunities would suggest that the market is informationally inefficient.

Assume the following price series:

Point in time:	0	1	2	3	4
Transaction price:	50	51	52	54	56
Return:		$\frac{1}{50}$	$\frac{1}{51}$	$\frac{2}{52}$	$\frac{3}{54}$

The profitability of this series would appear to be the return one could realize from exploiting the positively autocorrelated series of returns. Alternatively assume:

Point in time:	0	1	2	3	4
Transaction price:	50	52	49	51	48
Return:		$\frac{2}{50}$	$-\frac{3}{52}$	$\frac{2}{49}$	$-\frac{3}{51}$

The profitability of this series would appear to be the return one could realize from the negatively autocorrelated series of returns.[13] The random walk hypothesis is that, by appropriately buying and selling so as to exploit these return patterns, traders alter the price series (increase prices by their purchases and decrease prices by their sales) and so eliminate the patterns.

But how might the trader appropriately buy and sell so as to realize excess profits from either of the preceding returns series? Even if the trader were reasonably certain about what the price movements would be, could he or she have actually obtained any or all of the returns in the sequence? The fact is, the observed returns are the result of a process that involves market orders hitting limit orders, limit orders being stored on the limit order book, and limit orders tied at a price executing according to priority rules. Consequently, no individual trader can enter the system and, even with perfect foresight over a brief interval of time, simply realize the pattern of returns that will be measured for a stock.

The conclusion follows that deviations from random walk are not necessarily evidence against informational efficiency. The random walk test is too strict; returns autocorrelation need not imply the existence of profitable but unexploited trading opportunities because the returns that are tested for autocorrelation may be associated with price sequences at which no individual trader could have traded.

The bid-ask spread is one reason why a historic pattern of transaction price changes may not be exploited by a trader. The transactions that generate the observed price changes are triggered by orders to buy at market hitting the ask and by orders to sell at market hitting the bid. The trader who uses market orders, however, pays the spread as an execution cost,

---

[13]The second and fourth returns, $-\frac{3}{52}$ and $-\frac{3}{51}$, would be exploited by short sales.

whereas the trader who uses limit orders must accept the probability that his or her limit orders will not execute.

Trading will not eliminate all autocorrelation in returns. This understanding is reflected in the random walk literature but is not typically explained in terms of the returns generation process itself. Rather, the hypothesis is stated more generally—because of the *transaction costs* involved, traders are not able to realize above normal returns by exploiting the information contained in past price movements.

THE MEAN AND VARIANCE OF RETURNS

This section analyzes the determinants of the mean, E(r), and variance, Var(r), of returns. The analysis builds on the foundation developed in the preceding section. Six assumptions establish the analytical context:

1. The market comprises many traders who post quotes and who can therefore trade with each other without the services of a dealer.
2. The trading arena is a continuous market system.
3. Public limit orders are stored on a limit order book.
4. Market orders arrive sporadically during the trading day and execute against limit orders on the book.
5. The market's demand to hold shares of an asset is a linear function of price.
6. Price and quantity are continuous (rather than discrete) variables.

We begin the analysis by modeling the effect of informational change and idiosyncratic order arrival.

Informational Change

We made the extreme (and clearly unrealistic) assumption in the preceding section that investors react identically and simultaneously to informational change. We retain that assumption here to simplify the discussion, because it enables us to identify and to measure informational change as shifts in the location of the market's demand curve to hold shares [Figure 10.1(a)]. That is, instead of assuming news bits arrive in the form of statements such as "Podunk Mines is now pumping oil from its Dunkpo well," we assume news arrives in the form "the market demand curve to hold shares of Podunk Mines now crosses the vertical line at NSO at a price that is 2 percent higher than its previous value." The 2 percent figure is thus the informational change, stated as a rate of return.

This treatment is consistent with the analysis in Chapters 7 and 9, where, for a single holding period model, the intercept parameter of the linear demand curve is shown to be the present value of the expected price at the end of the period. In the context of that model, informational change would be represented by the percentage change in the intercept parameter.

Let the variable U be the returns dimensioned value of the information bits that arrive on the market. $U > 0$ indicates a shift up of the demand curve, and $U < 0$ indicates a shift down of the demand curve. Therefore, the return generated by the arrival of one information bit is

$$\frac{\Delta P}{P} = r = U \tag{10.22}$$

Idiosyncratic Order Arrival

Assume that one sell order of size Q_1 arrives on the market. Figure 10.2 shows the price change that this one order generates. Given the buy order function labeled B_0, price has to fall from P_0 to P_1 for the Q_1 shares to be absorbed by the market. The sale eliminates Q_1 shares from the buy order function. Therefore, the market buy order function shifts to the line labeled B_1, the market sell order function shifts to the line labeled S_1, and the market demand curve to hold shares shifts to the line labeled D_1.

The size of the order (Q_1) is related to the size of the return it generates, $(P_1 - P_0)/P_0$. The return is a percentage price change. Therefore, by expressing the order size (Q_1) as a percentage of the total number of shares outstanding (NSO), we can use the standard definition of elasticity to relate the two percentage changes to each other. In Figure 10.2, the appropriate elasticity is the elasticity of D_0 at the point $\langle P_0, \text{NSO} \rangle$:

$$\eta = \frac{dN}{dP} \frac{P_0}{N}$$

where, for notational simplicity, $N = \text{NSO}$. Because D_0 is linear, the slope of the curve (dN/dP) at the point $\langle P_0, N \rangle$ equals the slope of the curve over a discrete interval. Hence

$$\frac{dN}{dP} = \frac{\Delta N}{\Delta P} \tag{10.23}$$

Because the slope of D_0 equals the slope of B_0 (and because Q is the size of the order),

$$\frac{\Delta N}{\Delta P} = \frac{Q}{\Delta P} \tag{10.24}$$

Thus, substituting equation (10.24) into (10.23), and (10.23) into the expression for elasticity gives

$$\eta = \frac{Q}{\Delta P} \frac{P}{N} \tag{10.25}$$

Rewriting equation (10.25) shows the return generated by the sell order:

$$r = \frac{\Delta P}{P_0} = \frac{1}{\eta} \frac{Q}{N} \tag{10.26}$$

Translating the share size of the order into the dollar value of the order shows how the return (r) is related to the investment decision that triggered the trade. Assume the investor has decided to alter his or her portfolio weights by selling $Y worth of the asset and uses the initial price, P_0, to determine the size of his or her order. Thus,

$$Q_1 = -\frac{Y}{P_0} \tag{10.27}$$

where the minus sign shows that the order is to *sell* Q_1 shares.[14] Substituting equation (10.27) into (10.26) gives

$$r = -\frac{1}{\eta} \frac{Y}{NP_0} \tag{10.28}$$

where NP_0 is the total value of shares outstanding for the stock. Therefore, letting $V = NP_0$, we have

$$r = -\frac{1}{\eta} \frac{Y}{V} \tag{10.29}$$

Equation (10.29) shows the return that is triggered by the arrival of one idiosyncratic order.

The Return over a Period of Length T

Equations (10.22) and (10.29) can be used to obtain an expression for the sequence of returns that is generated by the sequence of orders that arrive over a time interval of length T. With such an expression, we can obtain the mean and variance of returns for the time interval. Assume that informational change and idiosyncratic order arrival occur sporadically according to statistical processes with known parameters.[15] Then, the returns for any

---

[14]Treating positive Q as a purchase and negative Q as a sale avoids the need to label separately the buy and sell transactions.

[15]The most reasonable process to use is the Poisson arrival process.

time interval are given by equation (10.21). Substituting equations (10.22) and (10.29) into (10.21) and rearranging gives

$$1 + r_t = \prod_{s=1}^{N_A} (1 + U_s) \prod_{k=1}^{N_I} \left(\frac{1 + Y_k}{\eta V} \right) \qquad (10.30)$$

Taking logarithms of equation (10.30) gives

$$r^* = \sum_{s=1}^{N_A} \ln (1 + U_s) + \sum_{k=1}^{N_I} \ln \left(\frac{1 + Y_k}{\eta V} \right) \qquad (10.31)$$

The Expected Return

By applying the logarithmic approximation[16] $\ln (1 + x) \cong x$ to equation (10.31), we can more easily assess the mean and variance of returns in relation to the parameters of the right-hand side variables. From equation (10.31), the mean return is[17]

$$E(R_T) = T\gamma(2p - 1)E(U) \qquad (10.32)$$

where T is the length of the time span over which r is measured, γ is the arrival rate parameter for the statistical process that describes the arrival of news over the interval of length T, p is the probability that any given value of U is positive, and E(U) is the average absolute value of U. If new information is as likely to shift the aggregate demand curve up as it is to shift it down, $p = .5$ and the expected return is zero. If new information is more likely to shift the aggregate demand curve up, $p > .5$ and $E(R_T)$ is positive. $E(R_T)$ positive implies an upward drift in the security's price; such a drift may be consistent with an informationally efficient equity market in which the price sequence is described by a martingale process rather than by a random walk (see Chapter 9).

Note that $E(R_T)$ in equation (10.32) increases linearly with T. This is consistent with the intervalling relationship for the expected return shown in the section "The Measurement of Returns."

Returns Variance

Taking variances of equation (10.31) gives[18]

---

[16]See the Appendix for a discussion of the logarithmic approximation. The approximation is reasonable for values of x where x^2 is sufficiently less than unity. The values of r_s and r_k are expected to be well below unity for transaction-to-transaction returns.

[17]See Cohen, Maier, Schwartz, and Whitcomb (1986, chapter 4) for the derivation.

[18]η and V are assumed constant over the interval. See Cohen, Maier, Schwartz, and Whitcomb (1986, chapter 4) for the derivation.

$$\text{Var(r)} = T\gamma E(U^2) + \frac{T\mu E(Y^2)}{\eta^2 V} \tag{10.33}$$

where μ is the arrival rate parameter for the statistical process that describes the arrival of idiosyncratic market orders over the interval of length T.

More specifically, μ is the total number of buy and sell market orders that are expected for the trading day, divided by the value of shares outstanding, V. Because the flow of idiosyncratic orders for an issue should be roughly proportionate to the issue's size, the mean arrival rate of such orders *per dollar value* of shares outstanding should, all else equal, be the same for different securities. That is, if IBM is 100 times the size of Podunk Mines, IBM should have roughly 100 times as many shareholders, and hence the total number of idiosyncratic orders that are expected to arrive in any interval of time should be roughly 100 times as large for IBM as for Podunk Mines.[19] Therefore, the parameter μ should tend to be the same for IBM as for Podunk Mines.

Assessment of the Variance Equation

The first term on the right-hand side of equation (10.33) shows that returns variance is greater, the greater the frequency with which information changes (as reflected in the parameter γ), and the greater the price impact of the information [as measured by the variable $E(U^2)$].

The second term on the right-hand side of equation (10.33) shows the determinants of price volatility that are related to idiosyncratic order arrival, but that are not directly related to the arrival of news. We consider each variable in that term in order:

> *T:* Var(r) increases linearly with the length of the measurement interval, T. The linear relationship is consistent with the inter-valling effect discussed earlier for the case of no serial correlation of the returns. This case is relevant here because we have assumed a random order arrival process, a zero bid-ask spread, and instantaneous and accurate price adjustments to new equilibrium values.
>
> μ: All else equal, larger μ results in larger returns variance. Rather than the direction of causality running from μ to variance, however, we expect the variance to affect μ. This is because investors who anticipate trading more frequently for liquidity needs include less volatile stocks in their portfolios (all else equal). Thus the presence of μ in the numerator of equation (10.33) actually mitigates the effect of the other right-hand-side varia-

---

[19]As discussed later, this simple relationship will be perturbed if larger firms attract larger shareholders.

bles. For instance, looking at the numerator, we see that an increase of the variable $E(Y^2)$ increases $Var(r)$. This means that μ, in response, tends to be lower (all else equal) for large $E(Y^2)$ stocks. However, the negative response of μ could not be strong enough to cause $Var(r)$ actually to be *lower* for large $E(Y^2)$ stocks, because lower $Var(r)$ would then itself result in *higher* μ (which would be contradictory).[20]

$E(Y^2)$: As one might expect, an increase in the size of investor orders in relation to the size of the issue (V) and the demand elasticity (η) increases the variance of returns. The derivation shows specifically that $Var(r)$ changes linearly with $E(Y^2)$, not $E(Y)$ or $[E(Y)]^2$. The intuition behind this result is that $E(Y)$ is expected to be close to zero for all stocks (the distribution of Y spans both negative and positive values), variance cannot be a negative number, and the variable Y^2 is a reasonable reflection of what is relevant: the absolute size of the buy and sell orders.[21] $E(Y^2)$ is expected to differ across stocks because of differences in the investors who select different stocks. Most importantly, institutional investors in particular tend to concentrate in large V issues, and the orders of these investors are, indeed, large.

η: All else equal, returns variance is less if the demand to hold shares of the stock is more elastic. A larger elasticity means, of course, that any given percentage change in quantity is associated with a smaller percentage change in price. With regard to the case at hand, a larger elasticity means that price does not have to change as much for an order of given size to be absorbed by the market. Note that, as is the case with order size, it is η^2, not η, that enters the equation.[22]

V: All else equal, price is less volatile for larger issues. The derivation shows that the value of shares *outstanding,* not the value of shares *traded,* the number of shareholders, or some other proxy for market size is the relevant measure. Because of this derivation, we generally take V to be an inverse measure of the thinness of a market.

The appearance of V in the denominator of equation (10.33) may lead one to expect that returns variance will be lower for large V securities. We cannot be sure of this result, however—the other right-hand side variables may also be related to V. For instance, as suggested previously, $E(Y^2)$ is

---

[20]Similarly, if $Var(r)$ is less for large V (or large η) securities, μ tends to be larger for large V (or large η) securities, which to some extent offsets the effect of V or η on $Var(r)$.

[21]$E|Y|$ would also be intuitively reasonable; the math, however, shows that the appropriate measure is $E(Y^2)$.

[22]Demand elasticity is negative and variance must be a positive number. η enters the derivation of equation (10.33) as a multiplicative constant; for any multiplicative constant (c) and random variable (x), $Var(cx) = c^2 Var(x)$.

likely to be larger for large V securities. η is also likely to be larger for large V securities. The reason is that security analysis is more intensive for bigger issues, more intensive security analysis is likely to make traders' expectations more homogeneous, and, as discussed in Chapters 7 and 9, greater homogeneity of expectations causes the market demand curve to be more elastic. Thus we conclude the following with regard to V. A negative relationship between Var(r) and V (1) can be mitigated but not reversed by a positive relationship between μ and V, (2) can be reversed by a sufficiently strong and positive relationship between $E(Y^2)$ and V, and (3) can be reinforced by a positive relationship between η and V.

The Effect of the Market's Mechanics on a Security's Price Behavior

Having assessed the *ceteris paribus* impact of the individual determinants of the mean and variance of returns, we now derive various insights concerning the effect of the market's mechanics on a security's price behavior.

1. Transaction costs (commissions, taxes, the opportunity costs of trading with transaction price uncertainty, and so forth) decrease expected returns and reduce the flow of orders to the market. Accordingly, these costs decrease the elasticity of the market demand curve. We see from equation (10.33) that transaction costs therefore also increase the variance of returns.
2. Dealers and stock exchange specialists have the function of "making a market" by posting buy and sell quotes. Stock exchange specialists further have the "affirmative obligation" to post buy and sell quotes at those times when the sparsity of public orders would result in "unacceptably" large transaction-to-transaction price changes. The posting of quotes by dealers and specialists makes the market demand curve more elastic and thereby decreases returns variance. The affirmative obligation of the stock exchange specialists *forces* these market makers to enter their quotes more frequently for the thinner issues; this dampens any inverse relationship between Var(r) and V that might otherwise exist in an unregulated market.
3. The appearance of V in the denominator of equation (10.33), and therefore the possibility of an inverse relationship between variance and V, suggests that the marketplace may give corporations a financial economy of scale; that is, a greater price stability enjoyed by larger companies simply because of their size would enable these firms to raise funds at lower cost in the new issues market.
4. The capital asset pricing model suggests that, in a frictionless environment, all investors would hold some fraction of the market portfolio, and that the composition of that portfolio would be the same for all investors. Therefore, when buying or selling for their

own idiosyncratic reasons, investors in this frictionless environment would buy or sell shares of all stocks in proportion to each stock's weight in the market portfolio. The following would result: μV, $E(Y^2)/V^2$, and η would be the same for all stocks.[23] Therefore, given equation (10.33) we have that, in a frictionless environment, returns variance would not differ across stocks because of the idiosyncratic arrival of orders in the market, but rather would depend only on differential change in the information set. For this reason, evidence that returns variance is related to the size of issues would further show the impact that friction has on price behavior in the equity markets.

Our analysis of a security's price behavior is to this point incomplete. We have thus far assumed a zero bid-ask spread and, as is implicit in the order arrival process and price determination model used, we have assumed that equilibrium price determination is an instantaneous process. We deal with the bid-ask spread and with noninstantaneous price discovery in the next two sections of the chapter.

THE BID-ASK SPREAD

A market's mechanics also affect a security's return through the bid-ask spread. An investor who buys at market pays the asking price; an investor who sells at market receives the bid price. For this reason, the spread is the cost of a round-trip (buying and then selling a given number of shares). Even if the investor buys at market and holds the shares for a long period of time, the spread is a cost of transacting.[24] To be properly assessed, the shares held in a portfolio should be evaluated at the price at which they could be sold—the bid price. If, for example, the quotes for a stock are 50 bid, $50\frac{1}{4}$ ask and an investor has bought at the ask, the bid must rise $\frac{1}{4}/50 = 0.5$ percent in order for the investor to break even on the purchase.

The spread and the variability of the spread both increase the variance of returns. Because spreads tend to be larger for thinner issues, the effect of the spread on price volatility reinforces the variance-thinness relationship discussed in the previous section.

A public investor need not pay the spread for securities traded on an

---

[23]To see this, recall that μ is the arrival rate per V, and therefore μV is the actual rate of order arrival for a stock. Further, when each investor holds a given fraction of the market portfolio he or she always changes his or her holdings in different assets in equal proportion ($Y_i/V_i = Y_j/V_j$ for any i^{th} and j^{th} assets). Finally, in this environment the elasticity of the demand curve to hold shares in any asset is equal to the elasticity of the demand curve to hold shares of the market portfolio. See Cohen, Maier, Schwartz and Whitcomb (1986, appendix A) for further discussion.

[24]Specifically, one-half of the spread is taken to be the cost of the purchase, and one-half is viewed as the cost of the sale.

Buy	44	Sell		Buy	44	Sell
100	$44\frac{1}{8}$			300	$44\frac{1}{8}$	
	$44\frac{1}{4}$			100	$44\frac{1}{4}$	
300	$44\frac{3}{8}$			500	$44\frac{3}{8}$	
	$44\frac{1}{2}$				$44\frac{1}{2}$	
	$44\frac{5}{8}$	200			$44\frac{5}{8}$	400
	$44\frac{3}{4}$	100			$44\frac{3}{4}$	100
	$44\frac{7}{8}$				$44\frac{7}{8}$	
	45	300			45	400
(a)				(b)		

Figure 10.4 Depiction of a limit order book. (a) A relatively thin book. (b) The book after additional orders have been entered.

exchange. There is an alternative: submit a limit order to the market.[25] For instance, if the quotes for a stock are 50 bid, $50\frac{1}{4}$ ask, and the investor enters a limit order to buy at 50, he or she saves the spread if the order in fact executes at 50.

As previously noted, however, placing a limit order entails the risk that the market will move away from the limit price and that the limit order will not execute. The trader, therefore, faces the dilemma of choosing between paying the spread and running the risk of not achieving an execution. The tighter the spread, the more likely the trader will be to write a market order, and the less costly will be the transaction.

The Bid-Ask Spread Model

Consider the limit order book displayed in Figure 10.4(a). The book shows buy orders from $44\frac{1}{8}$ to $44\frac{3}{8}$ and sell orders from $44\frac{5}{8}$ to 45. The inside market is $44\frac{3}{8}$ bid, $44\frac{5}{8}$ ask. There are no orders on the book at prices of $44\frac{1}{4}$, $44\frac{1}{2}$, and $44\frac{7}{8}$. The inside spread is larger than one-eighth because there is no buy or sell order at $44\frac{1}{2}$.[26] The absence of orders at $44\frac{1}{4}$ and $44\frac{7}{8}$ are "air pockets" in the limit order book.

The air pockets in the limit order book are likely to disappear if the book fills with the arrival of more orders, as shown in Figure 10.4(b). Contrasting Figure 10.4(b) with Figure 10.4(a) shows additional orders at some of the prices at which orders previously existed and the elimination

---

[25]Limit orders can also be handled by OTC dealers. The OTC dealers, however, are not required to expose public limit orders to the market, and such orders are rarely used in OTC trading.

[26]The market spread must, of course, be at least as large as the minimum allowable price change (which is one-eighth of a point for most stocks). If, for instance, the ask quotation for a stock is $50\frac{1}{4}$, a bid of $50\frac{1}{4}$ or higher transacts. Therefore, with one-eighth pricing and an ask at $50\frac{1}{4}$, the highest allowable bid that does not transact is $50\frac{1}{8}$.

of the air pocket at $44\frac{1}{4}$ on the buy side of the market. If enough additional orders were placed on the book, one would also expect the air pocket at $44\frac{7}{8}$ on the sell side of the market to be eliminated.

The absence of a limit order at $44\frac{1}{2}$, on the other hand, is apt to persist. Just why is not obvious, however, for markets comprising a very large number of traders. It is for this reason that we first establish the existence of the spread and then analyze the determinants of its size.

Seven assumptions facilitate modeling the existence of the gap between the buy and sell orders:

1. The trading arena is a continuous market system.
2. Public limit orders are stored on a limit order book.
3. Public limit and market orders arrive randomly during the trading day.
4. The dissemination of floor information and order transmission are instantaneous.
5. Investors specify their trading decision for one trading period.
6. Price is a continuous (rather than discrete) variable.
7. Each investor submits an order for just one round lot (100 shares).

Assumptions 4 through 7 require explanation. Instantaneous dissemination of floor information and order transmission are assumed so that market orders can be taken to execute with certainty at the posted quotes. Investors are assumed to specify their trading decision for just one trading period so that the probability of a limit order executing can be defined precisely as the probability that the order will execute within the trading period. Price is assumed to be a continuous variable to facilitate the mathematical derivation; a proof that the spread is noninfinitesimal when price is continuous suggests that spreads may indeed be greater than the minimum price change when price is discrete. Each investor is assumed to submit just one round lot order so that we need not be concerned with the probability of an order partially executing.

The spread remains (with continuous pricing) if when we consolidate the orders of an arbitrarily large but finite number of traders, no buyer or seller places a limit order at a price infinitesimally close to a price already established by a counterpart order (a sell or a buy). To see that no trader would in fact write such an order, return to the situation described in Figure 10.4(b) and consider the decision that might be made by a representative buyer. Assume the trader's reservation price for the purchase is $50 per share.

The buyer can either place a limit order at any price below the market ask of $44\frac{5}{8}$ or can submit a market order that would execute at the market ask of $44\frac{5}{8}$. The decision involves resolving a tradeoff between the desirability of buying at a lower price and the desirability of transacting with certainty.

The trader's objective is to maximize the expected value of his or her consumer surplus from trading (see Chapter 8). The optimal order placement strategy can be determined with this objective in mind. As discussed in Chapter 8, the *consumer surplus* from the purchase is the difference between the reservation price and the actual purchase price times the number of shares bought. For the case at hand, the purchase of $Q = 100$ shares at a price P gives a consumer surplus of

$$CS = Q \times 50 - Q \times P = 5000 - 100P \qquad (10.34)$$

The graph of equation (10.34) is shown in Figure 10.5(a).

The buyer's expected consumer surplus is obtained by multiplying equation (10.34) by the probability that the order at price P will execute. Let F(P) be the probability of the market ask being equal to or less than P during the trading session; the expected consumer surplus of an order placed at the price P is therefore

$$ECS = (5000 - 100P)F(P) \qquad (10.35)$$

where F(P) is an increasing function of P. We examine this function before considering the expected consumer surplus equation itself.

The probability of the buy order executing is shown as a function of price in Figure 10.5(b). Of particular interest are the two jumps in the curve: one jump is at the market bid ($44\frac{3}{8}$), and the other is at the market ask ($44\frac{5}{8}$). The limit order of some other buyer has already set the bid and so has priority over any order placed below that price. The probability jump at the bid occurs because by placing an order at a slightly higher price than the established bid, the trader both increases the probability that a market sell order will hit the limit bid (since the new buy order decreases the spread) and gains priority in the queue.

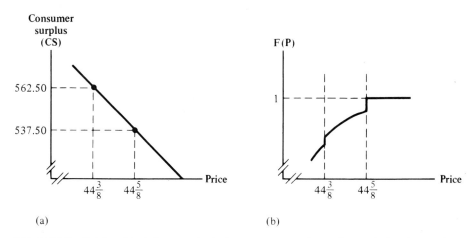

(a) (b)

Figure 10.5 Relationship between a trader's consumer surplus and an order's price, and between the probability of order execution and an order's price, for a buy order. (a) Consumer surplus. (b) The probability of order execution.

The probability jump at the market ask occurs for the following reason. A limit buy price equal to or greater than the ask quote established on the market executes with certainty at the ask, as shown in Figure 10.5(b) by the probability being unity at $44\frac{5}{8}$ and above.[27] However, for any limit buy price less than the ask (but no matter how close to it), there is a finite probability that the market will move away from the buyer and that the investor's order will not execute within the trading period. Therefore, there must be a discrete probability jump to unity as the price of the buy order is increased to equal the market ask.

The thought can be stated differently. Consider the following question: Can a buyer make the probability of execution infinitesimally close to unity by writing the buy order at a price infinitesimally close to, but still below, the market ask? No, he or she cannot; a noninfinitesimal probability will remain that the ask price will increase, and that the buy limit that had been infinitesimally close to it will not be hit in the trading period. Therefore, as the buy is placed ever closer to the market ask, the probability of execution rises, but to a value that is discretely less than unity, as shown in Figure 10.5(b).

This argument can be proved mathematically for a discrete order arrival process (such as the Poisson process assumed in the analysis in the preceding section).[28] There is, however, an exception to the argument— for a continuous order arrival process, the probability of execution does go continuously to unity as the price of the buy order becomes infinitesimally close to the established ask.[29] In a moment we will note why this exception is of interest; first, however, consider the significance of the probability jump to unity at the market ask.

Equation (10.35) shows that the expected consumer surplus function is obtained by multiplying the *consumer surplus* (CS) function depicted in Figure 10.5(a) by the probability function [F(P)] depicted in Figure 10.5(b). Figure 10.6 displays two alternative expected consumer surplus functions for a buy order. With CS a negative function of price (for a buy order) and F(P) a positive function of price (for a buy order), *expected consumer surplus* (ECS) is shown in both parts of the diagram as initially rising [the effect of F(P) increasing initially dominates], reaching a maximum, and then falling (the effect of CS falling eventually dominates).

The price at which the buyer should write his or her order is given by

---

[27]This is strictly true if the specialist has "stopped the stock" (see Chapter 3) or if there is no delay in order transmission (which, for simplicity, we have assumed here).

[28]See Cohen, Maier, Schwartz, and Whitcomb (1986, Chapter 5).

[29]The Wiener process is one such continuous time process. The price movements associated with that process are so rapid that, if change in the market quotes were to be generated by it, and if at any instant in time the market quote were to be infinitesimally close to some value, the probability that the quote would hit that value would be infinitesimally close to unity.

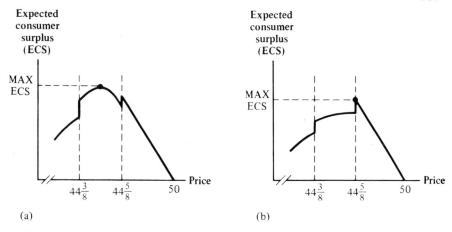

Figure 10.6 Relationship between a trader's expected consumer surplus and an order's price, for a buy order. (a) Case where a limit order strategy is optimal. (b) Case where a market order strategy is optimal.

the value at which ECS reaches a maximum. Figure 10.6(a) depicts a case in which the optimal strategy is to place a limit order above the market bid of $44\frac{3}{8}$. Figure 10.6(b) depicts another case in which the optimal strategy is to hit the market ask of $44\frac{5}{8}$ with a market order. The strategy that is optimal for any specific trader depends on that trader's demand function, and on his or her subjective expectation that the limit order will execute.

Having analyzed the order placement strategy of the trader, we can now see why the market spread will persist when the market comprises a very large number of traders: (1) There are no jumps in the CS function, and the F(P) function jumps to unity at the market ask; hence the ECS function must also jump a discrete amount at the market ask. (2) Because ECS does jump a discrete amount at the market ask, the function cannot reach a maximum in the neighborhood immediately to the left of the market ask. (3) Consequently, no trader will post a buy limit at a price infinitesimally close to the price of the market ask, and therefore a noninfinitesimal market spread is preserved under aggregation.

Our formal analysis has assumed continuous pricing and has shown that the market spread is not infinitesimal. We can apply this result to understand intuitively why, with one-eighth pricing, the market spread may be greater than the minimum allowable pricing change of one-eighth of a point. The trader's selection between a limit order and a market order involves a tradeoff between more consumer surplus and the certainty of execution. When the limit price of the buy order is close enough to the market ask, the incremental consumer surplus that would be lost by instead trading at the ask is relatively small, and the attractiveness of trading with certainty at the ask is relatively large. Therefore, rather than risking losing the trade in an attempt to buy at a price slightly below the ask, the buyer increases his or her price and trades with certainty at the market ask.

Alternatively viewed, it is as though the market ask exerts a gravitational pull on the new buy order, if the new buy order is sufficiently close to it. After all, if a prospective trader would very much like to buy 100 shares of a stock at a market ask of $44\frac{5}{8}$, why would he or she place a limit buy at $44\frac{1}{2}$ and chance not getting the shares?[30]

A symmetrical situation faces a prospective seller who is choosing between placing a limit order and selling at the bid. If the limit price being considered is close enough to the market bid, the seller simply drops his or her price and hits the bid with a market order. Thus, for both buyers and sellers, the presence of quotes already posted on the market exerts on incoming orders a gravitational pull that prevents counterpart limit orders from being placed within a sufficiently narrow range of one another. Therefore, the spread between the buys and the sells remains as the book gets thicker, despite the elimination of air pockets on either side of the book.

Assessment of the Model

Existence of the spread having been explained, four objectives remain: (1) to show that the spread results from the transaction costs of trading, (2) to establish the concept of an equilibrium spread for a security, (3) to analyze the size of a security's equilibrium spread, and (4) to show that the effective spread for larger orders is greater than for smaller orders.

The Market Spread and the Transaction Costs of Trading   As we have seen, the bid-ask spread is a transaction cost of trading. However, the spread exists because of other costs of trading (information and decision making costs, opportunity costs, commissions, taxes, and so on). If trading were costless, investors would transmit complete buy and sell order functions to the market; accordingly, the individual spreads would vanish, and so too would the market spread. Therefore, transaction costs account for the market spread because they cause individual investors to transmit point orders (rather than complete order functions) to the market.

In addition, with costly trading, investors do not continuously revise their orders or continuously submit new orders to the market. Therefore, with a finite population of investors, orders arrive on the market at discrete points in time, rather than continuously. We have noted that the probability jumps at the market quotes occur because order arrival is a discrete time process. It follows that the probability jumps occur because trading is not costless.

---

[30]The logic applies equally to the example of a one-on-one buyer/seller negotiation. Suppose, for instance, that the asset being traded is a house in the $200,000 range. If the buyer and seller get close enough in price (say within $1000), they typically agree to split the difference and consummate the deal.

In summary: Market spreads exist because of the probability jumps, the probability jumps exist because order arrival is discrete rather than continuous, and order arrival is a discrete time process because of transaction costs. Therefore, the factor that explains the existence of bid-ask spreads in markets comprising many traders is the factor that ultimately drives all of microstructure analysis: trading is not a frictionless process.

The Equilibrium Spread   We have established that the market spread exists because no trader will place a limit order infinitesimally close to a counterpart quote already posted on the market. The actual size of the market spread for a security depends on the actual distribution of buy and sell limit orders that have been placed on the book. Furthermore, the actual market spread varies over time—new limit orders may be placed between the quotes so as to narrow the spread, and market orders may execute against the quotes so as to widen the spread. For any given stock, the wider the spread, the more likely is the next order that arrives on the market to be a limit order; conversely, the tighter the spread, the more likely is the next order that arrives on the market to be a market order.[31]

The *equilibrium spread* for a stock is that spread for which the probability of the spread next increasing (because of the arrival of a market order) is equal to the probability of the spread next decreasing (because of the arrival of a limit order within the quotes).

The Size of the Equilibrium Market Spread   The major determinant of the equilibrium spread for a security is the security's order flow. All else equal, a larger order flow is associated with a higher probability that the limit orders that set the quotes will execute. This increases the proportion of investors who will choose to place limit orders rather than market orders for any given size of the spread. This in turn implies that, when the order flow is greater, the spread must be smaller for the pressures that widen it and tighten it to be in balance.

Therefore, a major determinant of the size of spreads is the size of the market. We reached a similar conclusion with regard to price volatility, although price volatility is affected by market size in a more complex way. Furthermore, whereas the value of shares outstanding is the appropriate measure of market size in the price volatility model, the size of the order flow is what matters in the bid-ask model.

---

[31]This follows from our previous discussion—the cost of trading by market order is greater the larger the spread (which makes investors more likely to select the limit order strategy). On the other hand, the tighter the spread, the more likely it is that the next investor to place an order will select the market order strategy.

The Size of Orders and the Size of the Spread   We now relax the assumption that each investor submits an order for just one round lot (100 shares), and consider the relationship between the size of the spread and the size of orders. It is commonly believed by professional traders that the *effective spread* is larger for large orders than for small orders.

For a 100-share order, the effective spread is the inside market, because the limit orders that are posted on the market must be for at least one round lot. The trader who typically buys and sells in the neighborhood of 5000 shares, however, does not care about the inside market if only 100 shares are posted at the bid and the ask. The effective spread for the 5000-share trader is the difference between the price at which 5000 shares can be bought (the effective ask for this trader) and the price at which 5000 shares can be sold (the effective bid).

The effective spread will be larger for a larger trader for a trivial reason: a market order that is large in relation to limit orders on the book may have to transact against limit orders at more than one price if it is to execute totally. More interesting is the fact that large limit orders tend to be placed on the book at prices further from the counterpart market quotes than small limit orders. That is, the equilibrium spread between large orders is greater than the equilibrium spread between small orders. The reason for this is that the gravitational pull is stronger for larger orders.

The gravitational pull is stronger for larger orders because the probability of, for example, a 5000-share order executing totally at any price is smaller than the probability of, for example, a 100-share order executing totally at the price. This is because the arrival of any counterpart order at the price results in the 100-share limit order executing totally; however, the counterpart order must be for at least 5000 shares for the 5000-share limit order to execute totally. In other words, the market is effectively thinner for larger orders.

With the probability of execution being lower, the larger order is more likely to be submitted as a market order than to be placed as a limit order at a price in the neighborhood of a large counterpart order. Therefore, a large limit order is entered at a price further from the counterpart quotes than is a smaller order. Hence the spread between the larger orders is greater than the spread between the smaller orders.

The positive relationship between the effective spread and order size explains the market impact effect observed by professional traders—a trader who wishes to execute a large order quickly may have to pay an additional price concession to have the order execute totally. Larger traders, in other words, expect to incur higher execution costs (*ceteris paribus*). We return to this point in Chapter 11.

INTERTEMPORAL CORRELATION

The term *intertemporal* refers to events that occur in different time periods. For instance, if the price change for a stock in one period of time is correlated with the price change for that same stock in another period (for example, one day later), the stock's returns are said to be *intertemporally correlated*. When the return is for the same stock, this intertemporal correlation is referred to as *autocorrelation,* or as *serial correlation.*

Returns are positively autocorrelated when positive returns are more likely to be followed by other returns that are positive, and when negative returns are more likely to be followed by other returns that are negative. Therefore, if returns are positively autocorrelated, a series of price changes includes a larger number of *price continuations* (an uptick followed by other upticks, or a downtick followed by other downticks) than would be expected in a random sequence of price changes. If, on the other hand, returns are negatively autocorrelated, a series of price changes includes a larger number of *price reversals* (an uptick followed by a downtick or a downtick followed by an uptick) than would be expected in a random sequence of price changes.

The intertemporal correlation need not be between adjacent returns. With delayed price adjustments, for instance, the return in one period may be correlated with the return several periods later. The correlation between adjacent returns is called *serial correlation,* or *first order autocorrelation.* The correlation between nonadjacent returns is called *higher order autocorrelation.* The term *autocorrelation* simply means that the returns for an issue are autocorrelated, although not necessarily of first order.

The return on one stock in one period of time may also be correlated with the return on another stock in another period of time. This is *serial cross-correlation.* Serial cross-correlation exists when different stocks do not adjust simultaneously to common informational change.

The Intertemporal Portfolio

The section ''The Measurement of Returns'' shows how the return over a time span of length T is related to the returns for the T short intervals that compose it. Conceptually, the long period return is related to the short period returns, much as the return on a portfolio is related to the return on the individual securities that constitute the portfolio. The standard portfolio return is a cross-sectional average of the individual stock returns; the long period return is an intertemporal average of the returns for the individual periods. For this reason, the long period return may be considered the return on an intertemporal portfolio. Increasing T and hence including more short period returns in the intertemporal portfolio is similar to increasing the number of stocks in a cross-sectional portfolio.

The intertemporal portfolio, however, differs from the cross-sectional portfolio in certain respects:

- The return $(1 + R_T)$ on the intertemporal portfolio is the geometric mean of the returns [the $(1 + r_t)$] for the individual periods. In contrast, the return on the cross-sectional portfolio (R_p) is the arithmetic mean of the returns (the r_i) on the individual securities.
- All short periods have the same weight in the intertemporal portfolio. In contrast, the weights for the individual issues in a cross-sectional portfolio are specified by the decision maker.
- The size of the intertemporal portfolio (the value of T) is likely to be exogenously determined for the investor (T is no doubt larger for younger people who are just starting to accumulate wealth than for older people who are approaching retirement). In contrast, the number of shares to include in a cross-sectional portfolio is specified by the decision maker.
- The point of reference for the intercorrelation between short interval returns in an intertemporal portfolio is zero. In contrast, the point of reference for the intercorrelation between individual stock returns in a cross-sectional portfolio is unity. The reason is that if the intertemporal correlations are zero, returns variance increases linearly with T, whereas if the cross-sectional correlations are unity, the standard deviation of the portfolio return is a linear combination of the standard deviations for the individual securities.
- As T increases sufficiently for an intertemporal portfolio, the average covariance between short period returns is expected to go to zero (the correlation between distant returns is likely to be weaker than the correlation between nearby and, in particular, adjacent returns). In contrast, as additional securities are added to a randomly selected cross-sectional portfolio, there is no reason to expect a change in the average covariance between securities.

Understanding these technical differences may help one to understand better the intervalling effect discussed earlier. There is another reason for considering the properties of the intertemporal portfolio. The value of portfolio diversification can be understood only in terms of the variance reduction attributable to stock returns not being perfectly intercorrelated; likewise, the effect of measurement interval length on returns variance can be understood only when one recognizes the implications of return not being perfectly independently distributed over time.

The diversification of an intertemporal portfolio can be contrasted with the diversification of a cross-sectional portfolio.[32] Assume that each security

---

[32]Diversification of a cross-sectional portfolio reduces portfolio variance by eliminating nonsystematic (diversifiable) risk (see Chapter 7).

has the same weight in the cross-sectional portfolio (that is, that $k_i = 1/N$ for each ith stock, where N is the number of stocks in the portfolio). Thus the variance of the cross-sectional portfolio can be written as

$$Var(r_P) = \left(\frac{1}{N}\right)^2 \left[\sum_{i=1}^{N} Var(r_i) + \sum_{i=1}^{N}\sum_{\substack{j=1 \\ i \neq j}}^{N} \sigma_i\sigma_j\rho_{ij}\right] \qquad (10.36)$$

By writing the single sum on the right-hand side of equation (10.36) as the average variance times the number of terms in the sum (N), and the double summation as the average covariance times the number of terms in the double summation ($N^2 - N$), equation (10.36) can be rewritten as

$$Var(R_P) = \left(\frac{1}{N}\right)\overline{Var}(r) + \left(\frac{N-1}{N}\right)\overline{Cov}(r_i, r_j) \qquad (10.37)$$

Equation (10.37) shows that, as N increases, $Var(R_P)$ decreases asymptotically to the average covariance, which is the systematic market risk.

The effect of T on the intertemporal portfolio can be most easily assessed for the case in which all intertemporal correlations are zero. We then have, from equation (10.18),

$$Var(R_T^*) = T\ Var(r_t^*) \qquad (10.38)$$

As previously noted, variance increases linearly with T in the absence of returns autocorrelation. The mean return also increases linearly with T [see equation (10.14)]. The reason is that the return R_T is expressed as a rate per T.

The period for which returns are expressed can be made explicit. Let $R_{T/T}^*$ identify the logarithmic return for period T expressed as a rate per T, and $R_{T/t}^*$ identify the logarithmic return for period T expressed as a rate per t. Then[33]

$$R_{T/T}^* = TR_{T/t}^* \qquad (10.39)$$

Substituting equation (10.39) into equation (10.38) and rearranging gives

$$Var(R_{T/t}^*) = \left(\frac{1}{T}\right)Var(r_{t/t}^*) \qquad (10.40)$$

where $Var(r_{t/t}^*)$ is the variance of the short period (logarithmic) return expressed as a rate per t.

Equation (10.40) shows variance falling with T, much as equation (10.37) shows variance falling with N. The only difference between the

---

[33]Equation (10.39) is consistent with equation (10.A12) in the Appendix to this chapter.

equations [equation (10.37) has a positive asymptote whereas equation (10.40) does not] is attributable to the different intercorrelation patterns between cross-sectional and intertemporal returns. The relationships among equations (10.37), (10.38), and (10.40) are shown graphically by Figure 10.7(a), (b), and (c).

Equation (10.40) may seem to suggest that an investor with a longer time horizon faces lower returns variance than does an investor with a shorter time horizon (*ceteris paribus*). Equation (10.38), on the other hand, appears to suggest that an investor with a longer time horizon faces greater returns variance. Which impression is correct? The apparent contradiction can only be resolved by rephrasing the issue: *ceteris paribus,* would an investor with a longer time horizon hold a portfolio that has greater short period variance than would an investor with a shorter time horizon?

The effect of holding period length on an investor's optimal portfolio decision is itself a complex issue, with the answer's depending on the form of the investor's utility function. We will not pursue the matter here; the issue has been raised only to show the formal relationship between the

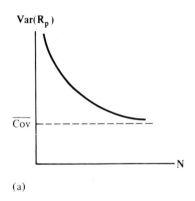

(a)

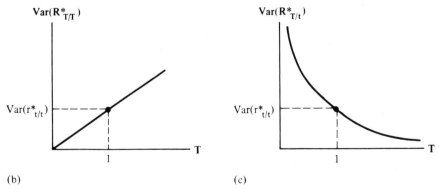

(b)   (c)

Figure 10.7   Effect of portfolio diversification (N) and of holding period length (T) on the variance of portfolio returns. (a) As N increases, $Var(R_P)$ decreases asymptotically to $\overline{Cov}$. (b) As T increases, $Var(R_{T/T})$ increases linearly. (c) As T increases, $Var(R_{T/t})$ decreases asymptotically to zero.

intertemporal portfolio and the cross-sectional portfolio. We now proceed to analyze the intertemporal portfolio because of the insights into the returns generation process for a nonfrictionless market that may be gained. In the discussion that follows, we refer to the variance of returns expressed as a rate per T.

Positive Intertemporal Correlation

Four factors may cause the returns for a security to be positively autocorrelated: sequential information arrival, the limit order book, market maker intervention in trading, and noninstantaneous price discovery after change in investor demand.

Sequential Information Arrival   Copeland (1976) has shown that the sequential arrival of information (or, equivalently, the sequential adjustment of expectations) can cause a security's returns to be positively autocorrelated.

The Limit Order Book   If orders on the book are not quickly revised after informational change, new orders based on the information transact at prices set by existing limit orders. As a series of such transactions eliminates the older orders seriatim from the book, a security's transaction price rises or falls in increments to a new equilibrium value.

Market Maker Intervention   The affirmative obligation of stock exchange specialists leads these market makers to intervene in trading when transaction-to-transaction price changes would otherwise be unacceptably large. This can cause a security's price to adjust in increments to a new equilibrium value after the advent of news.

Inaccurate Price Discovery   The term *price discovery* identifies the process by which the market finds a new equilibrium after a change in investor demand. Price discovery is inaccurate when new equilibrium values are not instantaneously achieved. Price discovery is inaccurate because investors do not instantaneously transmit their orders to the market, because orders left on the market are not continuously revised, and because, when they write their orders, investors do not know what the equilibrium prices are or will be. With inaccurate price determination, actual prices differ from equilibrium values. Some price changes are too small (they underadjust to news), and other price changes are too large (they overadjust to news). *Ceteris paribus,* if inaccurate price determination that involves partial adjustment (undershooting) predominates, returns will be positively autocorrelated.

The positive serial correlation resulting from informational change will not be very apparent in informationally efficient markets. The limit order book and specialist intervention apply to the exchanges, but not to OTC trading. Even for the exchanges, the effects of both should be apparent only in very brief period returns. This is true in part because the arrival of informationally motivated orders quickly eliminates stale orders from the book, and in part because trading is halted if informational change is substantial (so that existing orders may be revised and new, more appropriate transaction prices determined).

Negative Intertemporal Correlation

Four factors may cause negative intertemporal correlation in security returns: (1) the temporary market impact exerted by large orders, (2) the bid-ask spread, (3) price rounding, and (4) noninstantaneous price discovery after change in investor demand propensities.

Market Impact Effects   The section analyzing the mean and variance of returns shows how the arrival of one sell order changes a security's price as it interacts with the market's buy order function. Equation (10.29) demonstrates that the price change generated by the sell order is greater, the larger the relative size of the order (Y/V) and the lower the elasticity (η) of the market demand curve. An analogous effect would be observed for a buy order. The section treating the bid-ask spread shows that the effective spread is expected to be greater for larger orders. In general, relatively large orders exert price pressure, and the pressure is greatest when the short run market demand is not very price responsive.[34] Assume the arrival of a large sell order, for instance. If the book is relatively sparse and the effective spread large at the time of the order's arrival, the transaction price will be depressed so that the order may be absorbed by the relatively thin market. In this case, the lower price itself attracts new buy orders to the market (assuming the underlying demand is indeed more elastic), and price once again rises. Therefore, the initial price decrease is followed by a reversal (an increase), and the successive price changes are negatively autocorrelated.

The Bid-Ask Spread   With a spread, orders to sell at market execute against the bid, and orders to buy at market execute against the ask. In the process, the transaction price moves between the bid and the ask. The bid

[34]The price effect of an order may, however, be an equilibrium change (as we assumed it to be in the analysis of the mean and variance of returns). If so, one would have no way of predicting, on the basis of the change, what the next price change would be, and hence the successive price movements would be uncorrelated.

and ask quotes themselves change over time with the arrival of new limit and market orders. Nonetheless, the bouncing of the transaction price between the quotes causes transaction-to-transaction price returns to be negatively autocorrelated. To see this, assume the quotes are fixed. Then if at some moment in time the last transaction in a particular stock is at the bid, the next transaction that generates a nonzero return must be at the ask, and a positive return is recorded. If the quotes remain unchanged, the next nonzero return must be negative (when a market sell once again executes at the bid). Price reversals thus occur as the transaction price moves back and forth between the bid and the ask. Even if the quotes change randomly over time, the price reversals attributed to the spread introduce negative intertemporal correlation in transaction price returns.[35]

Price Rounding   Assume that the equilibrium price of a security is a continuous variable, but that each transaction price is rounded to the nearest one-eighth of a point. Rounding to one-eighth of a point establishes a minimum tick size (price cannot change by less than one-eighth of a point) and a minimum bid-ask spread (the spread cannot be less than one-eighth of a point). Like the spread, price rounding introduces negative serial correlation in security returns. To see this, assume that the upward drift of prices is small enough to be ignored and that the equilibrium price follows a random walk. Then, if the recorded price at point in time $t - 1$ has been rounded up, the transaction price at point in time t is likely to produce a downtick (because the transaction price at $t - 1$ was above the equilibrium price). Alternatively, if the price at $t - 1$ has been rounded down, the transaction price at t is likely to produce an uptick (because the transaction price at $t - 1$ was below the equilibrium price). Hence, with price rounding, positive returns are more likely to be followed by negative returns, and vice versa. The negative correlation introduced by price rounding is expected to be more pronounced for a low price stock (for which a one-eighth price change is a substantial return) than for a high price stock (for which a one-eighth price change is not a substantial return), for a low variance stock, and for returns measured over relatively short time periods. Evidence on the effect of price rounding on returns variance is presented in Table 10.1.[36]

---

[35]For further discussion, see Chapter 11 and Roll (1984).

[36]Results reported in Table 10.1 are based on a simulation analysis performed by Schwartz and Whitcomb (1977b). In the study, 20 series of unrounded prices were generated for various combinations of price levels and standard deviations, using a normal returns distribution with a mean of zero. Each price was then rounded to the nearest eighth; variances were computed for each rounded series; and ratios of the matched variances were taken. Table 10.1 shows the 20-iteration averages of these ratios for each price level and standard deviation.

Inaccurate Price Discovery As noted, with inaccurate price discovery, actual prices wander about their equilibrium values. If inaccurate price determination that involves overreaction to news (overshooting) predominates, returns are negatively autocorrelated. Further, Goldman and Beja (1979) have shown that returns are negatively autocorrelated if the equilibrium price changes randomly over time and if the transaction price wanders randomly about its equilibrium value. The intuition behind this result is that the equilibrium price pulls the transaction price back to itself whenever the transaction price wanders away. Thus, even if the equilibrium price is following a random walk, the price discovery process causes reversals and hence negative correlation in transaction price returns.[37]

Table 10.1 RATIO OF THE VARIANCE OF ROUNDED RETURNS TO THE VARIANCE OF UNROUNDED RETURNS

Standard deviation of unrounded returns	Price	Differencing interval ("days")					
		1	2	5	10	20	50
.002	2	12.16	8.30	5.12	3.68	2.66	1.56
	10	4.02	2.73	1.81	1.44	1.20	1.07
	50	1.26	1.21	1.03	1.00	.96	.95
	100	1.07	1.02	1.00	.99	.97	.95
.01	2	2.47	1.77	1.29	1.14	1.04	.98
	10	1.15	1.07	1.01	.99	.96	.96
	50	1.01	1.00	.99	.98	.95	.96
	100	1.00	1.00	.99	.98	.95	.96
.05	2	1.27	1.13	1.04	1.00	.97	.96
	10	1.01	1.00	.99	.98	.95	.95
	50	1.00	.99	.98	.98	.95	.96
	100	1.00	.99	.98	.98	.95	.96

Source: Schwartz and Whitcomb (1977b).

Serial Cross-Correlation

The returns for two different securities are serially cross-correlated if the price adjustments generated by a causal factor (for example, the advent of a new industrywide regulation) do not occur at the same moment in time (that is, if they are nonsynchronous).

If all price adjustments were instantaneous for all securities (as would be the case in a frictionless market), the price adjustments for different securities would be synchronous. However, the factors we have discussed

---

[37]Picture a man walking his dog on a leash across a field, with the dog racing randomly about the man, but never straying too far because of the leash. If the man follows a random path, the leash causes reversals in the dog's path, and thus the animal's movements are negatively autocorrelated.

in relation to returns autocorrelation also cause price adjustment delays and hence serial cross-correlation. Assume, for instance, a news bit arrives that implies a 2 percent upward revision in the price of two stocks, Podunk Mines and Liquidity Inc. In the very short run any or all of the following may happen, thereby causing the short run price movements to be different for the two securities:

1. A large investor in Liquidity Inc. has been trying to liquidate her position for strictly personal reasons. On the other hand, a large buyer has suddenly, and for reasons known only to himself, decided that Podunk shares must be included in a well structured portfolio.
2. The last trade in Podunk occurred at the bid; the last trade in Liquidity occurred at the ask.
3. The book in Podunk happens, by chance, to be unusually deep; the book in Liquidity is relatively sparse.
4. Investors in Liquidity Inc. are relatively conservative; initially they believe the news will induce only a 1.5 percent appreciation in the share price. Investors in Podunk Mines are more optimistic; initially they anticipate a price change of 2.5 percent.
5. Many investors in Liquidity Inc. are otherwise occupied when the news bit arrives; many investors in Podunk Mines happen to be watching the broad tape when the news is publicly announced.

After the dust has settled, the prices of the two stocks are once again realigned. However, the paths the price adjustments follow are disparate and, in fact, largely uncorrelated.

The prices of some securities tend to adjust faster than others to changing market conditions. One would expect the large, intensely watched issues on average to lead the market and the smaller issues to lag behind. This gives rise to a pattern of serial cross-correlation where price adjustments for securities such as IBM and Exxon precede price adjustments for thinner issues such as Liquidity Inc. and Podunk Mines.

Serial cross-correlation patterns, however, are no doubt diffuse, complex, and not readily subject to exploitation by a clever trader. The reason is twofold: the time lags involved are not stable, and imperfect price discovery for the thinner issues may entail both overshooting and undershooting.

Intervalling Effects Revisited

Market impact effects, the bid-ask spread, price rounding, and inaccurate price discovery cause negative intertemporal correlation in security returns. These four factors are expected to have a greater effect on thinner issues.

This pattern of serial correlation suggests the following intervalling effect for a security's returns variance: short period variances are inflated in relation to longer period variances, and hence $Var(R_T^*)$ increases less than proportionately with T, especially for thinner issues. The relative inflation of short period variances may be offset by the factors that introduce positive correlation in short period returns, but on net the negative correlation is expected to predominate.

The pattern of price adjustments for different securities should be nonsynchronous, with the prices of larger issues generally adjusting before the prices of thinner issues. This pattern of intertemporal cross-serial correlation suggests the following intervalling effect in estimates of a stock's beta coefficient: short period betas are expected to be reduced for smaller securities (because their price adjustments tend to lag the market) and are expected to be increased for the largest companies (because their price adjustments tend to lead the market).[38]

The relationships suggested in the two preceding paragraphs are examined empirically in Chapter 11.

CONCLUSION

Transaction prices generally deviate from equilibrium values in the equity markets. Therefore, the behavior of price must be analyzed in light of the microstructure of the markets. We have done so in this chapter, paying primary attention to price volatility, the bid-ask spread, and intertemporal correlation in security returns.

The market impact effect, the bid-ask spread, price rounding, and imperfect price discovery all result in three related phenomena—negative intertemporal returns correlation, inflated short period returns variance, and serial cross-correlation in returns. Each is evidence of one reality: transaction prices generally differ from equilibrium values that would be achieved in a frictionless marketplace. It is important, therefore, to evaluate price behavior in a market center. Accordingly, the next chapter turns to an empirical assessment of our premier trading systems.

APPENDIX

The appendix further considers the relationship between arithmetic returns, logarithmic returns, and growth rates. The difference between the *arithmetic return*, R_T, and the *logarithmic return*, $R_T^* = g_T$, is that R_T is the single

---

[38]Knowledge of these intervalling effects is necessary for the development of a corrective procedure that allows unbiased beta estimates to be obtained from short period data. See Cohen, Maier, Schwartz and Whitcomb (1986, chapter 7) and Cohen, Hawawini, Maier, Schwartz, and Whitcomb (1983) for further discussion.

period return without compounding, whereas g_T is the return for the period with *continuous* compounding. This can be seen by writing

$$P_T = P_0\left(1 + \frac{r}{m}\right)^m = P_0\left(1 + \frac{r}{m}\right)^{(m/r)r} \tag{10.A1}$$

where m is the frequency with which returns are compounded over the period T. Since

$$\lim_{x \to \infty} \left(1 + \frac{1}{x}\right)^x = e \tag{10.A2}$$

where $e = 2.7182 \ldots$ is the base of natural logarithms, the limit of equation (10.A1) as m goes to infinity (continuous compounding) is

$$P_T = P_0 e^g \tag{10.A3}$$

where g is used in place of r as a convention to indicate continuous compounding. In practice, g is computed by taking the log of 1 plus a rate of return.

The effect of compounding is seen by setting $T = 2$:

$$(1 + R_{T=2}) = (1 + r_1)(1 + r_2) \tag{10.A4}$$

Expand the right-hand side and subtract 1 from both sides:

$$R_{T=2} = r_1 + r_2 + r_1 r_2 \tag{10.A5}$$

The term $r_1 r_2$ captures the effect of compounding.

It is helpful to see specifically how the return for any period (such as 1 year) is related to the returns for the shorter intervals (for example, 12 months) that it comprises. Write R_{yr} to designate the return for the year, and $\bar{r}_{mth}$ to designate the average monthly return. Following equations (10.8b), (10.7b), and (10.8c), respectively, the price change from P_0 to $P_{T=12}$ can be written as

$$P_{12} = P_0(1 + R_{yr}) \tag{10.A6}$$

$$P_{12} = P_0 \prod_{t=1}^{12} (1 + r_{t(mth)}) \tag{10.A7}$$

or as

$$P_{12} = P_0 e^{g(yr)} \tag{10.A8}$$

We could also write

$$P_{12} = P_0(1 + \bar{r}_{mth})^{12} \tag{10.A9}$$

From equations (10.A7) and (10.A9) we can obtain

$$\ln (1 + \bar{r}_{mth}) = \frac{1}{12} \sum_{t=1}^{12} \ln (1 + r_{t(mth)}) \qquad (10.A10)$$

Equation (10.A10) shows that one plus the average monthly return is the *geometric mean* of the 12 individual monthly returns, plus one.

Now equate the right-hand sides of equations (10.A6) and (10.A9):

$$1 + R_{yr} = (1 + \bar{r}_{mth})^{12} \qquad (10.A11)$$

Taking logarithms of equation (10.A11) gives

$$\ln (1 + R_{yr}) = 12 \ln (1 + \bar{r}_{mth}) \qquad (10.A12)$$

We thus see that the log of 1 plus the annual return expressed as a rate per year is 12 times the log of 1 plus the average monthly return expressed as a rate per month. Therefore, 1 plus the monthly return is annualized by multiplying its logarithmic value by 12 and then taking the antilog.

Now apply the logarithmic approximation, $\ln (1 + x) \cong x$, to equation (10.A12):[1]

$$R_{yr} = 12\bar{r}_{mth} \qquad (10.A13)$$

As might be expected, the annual return is approximately 12 times the arithmetic mean monthly return. The reason equation (10.A13) is not a strict equality is that annualizing a monthly return by simply multiplying by 12 ignores the fact that returns generate returns (that is, that returns are compounded). Because of compounding, the arithmetic return over the time span T is not an arithmetic average of the arithmetic returns in each of the T short intervals that it comprises. Rather, the short period returns are multiplicative, and their appropriate average is the geometric mean. This is shown in equation (10.9b).

When the arithmetic returns are multiplicative, the logarithmic returns are additive [as shown in equation (10.10)]. Therefore, the logarithmic return over the time span T is an arithmetic average of the logarithmic returns in each of the T short intervals that it comprises. This is shown in equation (10.A10). The results are consistent: the geometric mean of arithmetic returns is the antilogarithmic value of the arithmetic mean of the logarithmic returns.

SUGGESTED READING

Y. Amihud and H. Mendelson, "Trading Mechanisms and Stock Returns: An Empirical Investigation," *Journal of Finance*, July 1987.

---

[1]The approximation is generally acceptable for x^2 sufficiently less than 1. For instance, if $x = 0.1$, $x^2 = 0.01$ (which is substantially less than 1) and the log of 1.10 is 0.1125 (which is approximately equal to x).

M. Atchison, K. Butler, and R. Simonds, "Nonsynchronous Security Trading and Market Index Autocorrelation," *Journal of Finance,* March 1987.

C. Ball, "Security Price Estimation Bias Induced by Discrete Observations," University of Michigan working paper, 1986.

F. Black, "Noise," *Journal of Finance,* July 1986.

M. Blume and R. Stambaugh, "Biases in Computed Returns: An Application to the Size Effect," *Journal of Financial Economics,* November 1983.

K. Cohen, G. Hawawini, S. Maier, R. Schwartz, and D. Whitcomb, "Friction in the Trading Process and the Estimation of Systematic Risk" *Journal of Financial Economics,* August 1983.

K. Cohen, S. Maier, W. Ness, H. Okuda, R. Schwartz, and D. Whitcomb, "The Impact of Designated Marketmakers on Security Prices: I, Empirical Evidence," *Journal of Banking and Finance,* December 1977.

K. Cohen, S. Maier, R. Schwartz, and D. Whitcomb, "The Returns Generation Process, Returns Variance, and the Effect of Thinness in Securities Markets," *Journal of Finance,* March 1978.

K. Cohen, S. Maier, R. Schwartz, and D. Whitcomb, "Transaction Costs, Order Placement Strategy, and Existence of the Bid-Ask Spread," *Journal of Political Economy,* April 1981.

K. Cohen, S. Maier, R. Schwartz, and D. Whitcomb, *The Microstructure of Securities Markets,* Englewood Cliffs, N.J.: Prentice-Hall, 1986.

T. Copeland, "A Model of Asset Trading Under the Assumption of Sequential Information Arrival," *Journal of Finance,* September 1976.

E. Dimson, "Risk Management When Shares Are Subject to Infrequent Trading," *Journal of Financial Economics,* June 1979.

F. Fabozzi and C. Ma, "Third Market Activities During NYSE Trading Halts: A Note," working paper, Massachusetts Institute of Technology, 1987.

L. Fisher, "Some New Stock Market Indexes," *Journal of Business,* January 1966.

D. Fowler and C. H. Rorke, "Risk Management When Shares Are Subject to Infrequent Trading: Comment," *Journal of Financial Economics,* August 1983.

D. Fowler, C. H. Rorke, and V. Jog, "Thin Trading and Beta Estimation Problems on the Toronto Stock Exchange," *Journal of Business Administration,* Fall 1980.

K. French and R. Roll, "Stock Return Variances: The Arrival of Information and the Reaction of Traders," *Journal of Financial Economics,* September 1986.

W. Fung and A. Rudd, "Pricing New Corporate Bond Issues: An Analysis of Issue Costs and Seasoning Effects," *Journal of Finance,* July 1986.

M. B. Goldman and A. Beja, "Market Prices vs. Equilibrium Prices: Returns Variance, Serial Correlation, and the Role of the Specialist," *Journal of Finance,* June 1979.

G. Gottlieb and A. Kalay, "Implications of the Discreteness of Observed Stock Prices," *Journal of Finance,* March 1985.

L. Harris, "Estimation of 'True' Stock Price Variances and Bid-Ask Spreads from Discrete Observations," working paper, University of Southern California, 1985.

L. Harris, "A Day-End Transaction Price Anomaly," working paper. University of Southern California, 1986a.

L. Harris, "A Transaction Data Study of Weekly and Intradaily Patterns in Stock Returns," *Journal of Financial Economics,* May 1986b.

J. Hasbrouck and T. Ho, "Order Arrival, Quote Behavior, and the Return Generating Process," *Journal of Finance,* September 1987.

S. Hillmer and P. Yu, "The Market Speed of Adjustment to New Information," *Journal of Financial Economics,* December 1979.

J. Karpoff, "A Theory of Trading Volume," *Journal of Finance,* December 1986.

B. King, "Market and Industry Factors in Stock Price Behavior," *Journal of Business,* September 1966.

T. Marsh and E. Rosenfeld, "Non-Trading, Market Making, and Estimates of Stock Price Volatility," *Journal of Financial Economics,* March 1986.

T. McInish and R. Wood, "Proxies for Nonsynchronous Trading," *Financial Review,* May 1983.

T. McInish and R. Wood, "Intraday and Overnight Returns and Day-of-the-Week Effects," *Journal of Financial Research,* Summer 1985.

T. McInish and R. Wood, "Adjusting for Beta Bias: An Assessment of Alternate Techniques: A Note," *Journal of Finance,* March 1986.

W. Mikkelson and M. M. Partch, "Stock Price Effects and Costs of Secondary Distributions," *Journal of Financial Economics,* June 1985.

G. Oldfield and R. Rogalski, "A Theory of Common Stock Returns over Trading and Non-trading Periods," *Journal of Finance,* June 1980.

G. Oldfield, R. Rogalski, and R. Jarrow, "An Autoregressive Jump Process for Common Stock Returns," *Journal of Financial Economics,* December 1977.

P. Perry, "Portfolio Serial Correlation and Nonsynchronous Trading," *Journal of Financial and Quantitative Analysis,* December 1985.

R. Roll, "A Simple Implicit Measure of the Effective Bid-Ask Spread in an Efficient Market," *The Journal of Finance,* September 1984.

M. Scholes and J. Williams, "Estimating Betas from Nonsynchronous Data," *Journal of Financial Economics,* December 1977.

R. Schwartz and D. Whitcomb, "The Time-Variance Relationship: Evidence on Autocorrelation in Common Stock Returns," *The Journal of Finance,* March 1977a.

R. Schwartz and D. Whitcomb," Evidence on the Presence and Causes of Serial Correlation in Market Model Residuals," *Journal of Financial and Quantitative Analysis,* June 1977b.

W. Silber, "Thinness in Capital Markets: The Case of the Tel Aviv Stock Exchange," *Journal of Financial and Quantitative Analysis,* March 1975.

S. Smidt, "Continuous vs. Intermittent Trading on Auction Markets," *Journal of Financial and Quantitative Analysis,* November 1979.

M. Theobald, "The Analytic Relationship Between Intervalling and Nontrading Effects in Continuous Time," *Journal of Financial and Quantitative Analysis,* June 1983.

M. Theobald and V. Price, "Seasonality Estimation in Thin Markets," *Journal of Finance.* June 1984.

chapter 11

Liquidity, Execution Costs, and the Volatility of Security Prices

Investment decisions in a nonfrictionless environment are based on three considerations: expected returns, returns variance, and liquidity. This chapter considers the meaning of liquidity and provides a method to measure it. We demonstrate that prices are more volatile because of execution costs, estimate the size of execution costs, and present evidence of adjustment lags in security prices.

The chapter first considers the meaning of liquidity and discusses various misconceptions about the term. Then it shows how execution costs can be estimated. To this end, the intervalling analysis discussed in Chapter 10 is used to obtain a *market efficiency coefficient* (MEC) that relates short period (half-hour) to longer period (two-day) price volatility for specific stocks. The MEC is scaled so that a value of unity would be expected in a frictionless market. The MEC is related to execution costs (C), and the determinants of MEC and of C are discussed.

Empirical evidence on the size and behavior of MEC and of C for stocks traded in the NYSE, Amex, and NASDAQ/NMS market centers is then presented. The final section sets forth evidence of lagged price adjustments for NYSE issues for measurement intervals of a day and longer.

LIQUIDITY: MEANING AND MISCONCEPTIONS

Consider the following three concepts:

1. *The liquidity of a marketplace:* The ability of individuals to trade quickly at prices that are reasonable in light of underlying demand/supply conditions.
2. *Execution costs:* The hidden costs of transacting—buying at prices that are high and selling at prices that are low. Unlike commission charges that are explicit, the execution costs of transacting are not clearly perceived by traders.
3. *Disequilibrium prices:* Observed market prices that do not equal theoretically desirable, frictionless market values.

The illiquidity of a market, execution costs, and disequilibrium prices are all manifestations of friction in trading. Liquidity is the broader concept; execution costs and disequilibrium prices characterize an illiquid market.

Misconceptions

Traders consider a market liquid when they can place large orders in it without adversely affecting market prices. In keeping with this view, measures of liquidity have generally related the number or value of shares traded during a short interval of time to the absolute value of the percentage price change over the interval. The larger the ratio of shares traded to the percentage price change, the more liquid the market is presumed to be.[1]

How meaningful is the measure? This subsection considers the question, along with various misconceptions about liquidity.

***Ceteris Paribus* Considerations**   All else equal, orders should have a smaller impact on market prices in more liquid markets. There is a problem, however, with measuring liquidity by simply relating the number of shares traded to the size of accompanying price changes. Other factors, primarily the advent of news, also cause prices to change (see Chapter 10). Unless these factors are separately accounted for, a large trading volume associated with small price changes is not evidence of a liquid market.

---

[1]This view underlies various measures of specialist performance that have been used by the stock exchanges and characterizes the approach taken by some researchers to measure and to contrast the liquidity of different market centers. See Cooper, Groth, and Avera (1985) and Hui and Heubel (1984).

Price Changes and Trading Volume   A bid that is too high attracts market orders to sell, and an ask that is too low attracts market orders to buy. Therefore, the more rapid the adjustment of the quotes after news, the smaller the number of shares that will trade during the adjustment process. Consequently, to the extent that trading is triggered by informational change, the ratio of shares traded to the absolute value of the percentage price change is smaller (not larger) in more efficient markets.

Eliminating the Impact of Informational Change   The price change over a long interval of time primarily reflects informational change. The price change over a short interval reflects, in addition, idiosyncratic change in individual investor liquidity needs and expectations, and the mechanics of the marketplace. Accordingly, it may be tempting to believe that liquidity can be measured by using very short period price movements without separately accounting for the impact of news. This is not correct; news also affects short period price behavior (see footnote 7).

The Market Power of Large Traders[2]   Institutional and other investors who are large enough to affect the price of a security may consider the market for that security to be illiquid for them. A market is illiquid, however, only if, because of trading friction, orders execute at disequilibrium prices in the *short run*. If, for example, a 20 percent shareholder (or if a subset of shareholders who in aggregate hold 20 percent of shares outstanding) decides to sell, the equilibrium price of a stock changes, regardless of the efficiency of the marketplace (unless the market demand curve to hold shares of the stock is perfectly elastic). Such a price change is not a manifestation of illiquidity.

Uncertainty   Traders may consider the market for a security to be illiquid if they do not know the price at which shares of an asset may be transformed into cash at some future date. This view, however, confuses illiquidity with uncertainty. Price uncertainty can be an attribute of a frictionless market; illiquidity is a property only of a nonfrictionless market.[3]

---

[2]*Market power* in economics is generally attributed to a seller who faces a downward sloping long run demand curve or to a buyer who faces an upward sloping long run supply curve. This should not be confused with *market impact*, which indicates that large orders cause temporary price changes because of market thinness.

[3]The concept of *illiquidity* is distinct from the concept of risk, and an investor's distaste for illiquidity (referred to as *liquidity preference*) is distinguishable from an investor's distaste for risk (referred to as *risk aversion*).

Illiquidity Reconsidered

Because of transaction costs, a price concession has to be paid in *illiquid* markets to execute an order quickly. No concession would be necessary in a frictionless environment in which all markets and all assets are equally and perfectly liquid. This is true regardless of the impact of informational change, of the market power of some traders, or of the uncertainty of security prices.

The cost of illiquidity is that buyers pay higher prices and sellers receive lower prices at the specific points in time when they trade. The manifestation of illiquidity is larger price changes over brief intervals as transaction prices bounce between the higher values paid by buyers who initiate transactions, and the lower values received by sellers who initiate transactions. The exaggerated price changes are a very short run phenomenon; consequently, to observe the evidence of illiquidity, returns must be analyzed over very brief intervals.

EXECUTION COSTS AND THE MARKET EFFICIENCY COEFFICIENT

Execution Costs (C)[4]

Let P_t^e be the unobservable frictionless market price at time t, and let P_t^r be the realized transaction price at point in time t. With regard to the determination of P_t^r assume:

A1: A continuous market trading regime.

A2: All orders are for the same size (one round lot).

A3: A transaction is triggered when a market order to buy hits an ask quotation or when a market order to sell hits a bid quotation.

A4: The market ask always exceeds the frictionless market price by the percentage amount C, and the market bid is always less than the frictionless market price by the percentage amount C.

A5: P_t^e follows a random walk over time.

A6: $\sigma_t = \sigma_u$ for all short periods t, u = 1, . . . , T.

A7: $\rho_{t,u}$ is the same for all $|t - u|$.

C is the execution cost of trading by market orders. From assumptions A3 and A4, the realized price at time t is

$$P_t^r = \begin{cases} P_t^e(1 + C) & \text{for a market order purchase} \\ P_t^e(1 - C) & \text{for a market order sale} \end{cases} \qquad (11.1)$$

[4]The subsection is based on Roll (1984).

where $C > 0$.

This simple framework can be used to show how an estimate of C might be obtained from a measure of the autocovariance of short period returns. Using the relationship $\text{Cov}(x,y) = E(xy) - E(x)E(y)$, the covariance between r_{t-1} and r_t is

$$\text{Cov}(r_{t-1}, r_t) = E(r_{t-1}r_t) - E(r_{t-1})E(r_t) \quad (11.2)$$

The expected return in any period that is attributable to the transaction price changing randomly between the bid and the ask quotations can be obtained from the following tableau:

P_{t-1}	P_t	r_t	Probability
Ask	Ask	0	$\frac{1}{4}$
Ask	Bid	$-2C$	$\frac{1}{4}$
Bid	Ask	$+2C$	$\frac{1}{4}$
Bid	Bid	0	$\frac{1}{4}$

Multiplying the returns by their associated probabilities and summing gives

$$E(r_t) = \tfrac{1}{4}(-2C) + \tfrac{1}{4}(2C) + \tfrac{1}{2}(0) = 0 \quad (11.3)$$

Therefore, equation (11.2) becomes

$$\text{Cov}(r_{t-1}, r_t) = E(r_{t-1}r_t) \quad (11.4)$$

The adjacent returns r_{t-1} and r_t are given by three prices: P_{t-2}, P_{t-1}, and P_t. Each of these prices could, with equal probability, be equal to a bid or to an ask quotation. Therefore, the adjacent returns could result from any of the sequences shown in the following tableau, with each sequence having an equal probability of occurring.[5] The tableau also shows the alternative pairings of adjacent returns, their associated probabilities of occurrence (pr), and the product $(r_{t-1})(r_t)(\text{pr})$:

(1) P_{t-2}	(2) P_{t-1}	(3) P_t	(4) r_{t-1}	(5) r_t	(6) pr	(7) (4)(5)(6)
Ask	Bid	Bid	$-2C$	0	$\frac{1}{8}$	0
Ask	Bid	Ask	$-2C$	$+2C$	$\frac{1}{8}$	$-\frac{1}{2}C^2$
Ask	Ask	Bid	0	$-2C$	$\frac{1}{8}$	0
Ask	Ask	Ask	0	0	$\frac{1}{8}$	0
Bid	Bid	Bid	0	0	$\frac{1}{8}$	0
Bid	Bid	Ask	0	$+2C$	$\frac{1}{8}$	0
Bid	Ask	Bid	$+2C$	$-2C$	$\frac{1}{8}$	$-\frac{1}{2}C^2$
Bid	Ask	Ask	$+2C$	0	$\frac{1}{8}$	0

[5]Because P_t^e is assumed to follow a random walk, only those price changes that are attributable to the realized transaction price moving between the bid and the ask quotations need be considered to compute the autocovariance term.

Summing column (7) gives the expected value of the product of adjacent returns,

$$E(r_{t-1}r_t) = -C^2 \qquad (11.5)$$

Substituting into equation (11.4) gives

$$Cov(r_{t-1}, r_t) = -C^2 \qquad (11.6)$$

The Market Efficiency Coefficient (MEC)[6]

Equation (11.6) can be used to estimate execution costs, C. However, direct estimation of the covariance term would not reflect the complex pattern of first and higher order correlation that execution costs can introduce into security returns. Consequently, to estimate C, we obtain a more comprehensive assessment of the impact of execution costs on price. This is done by defining a *market efficiency coefficient* (MEC).

The MEC measures the impact of execution costs on a stock's short period price volatility. A measure of C based on an estimate of MEC is an average value of execution costs. The average is interpreted as the value that would itself account for a security's short period price volatility (given its long period volatility) if realized prices were in fact generated by the process described by equation (11.1).

Rather than directly contrasting P_t^r to an unobservable P_t^e, the MEC relates the volatility of P_t^r to an estimate of the volatility of P_t^e. The MEC is scaled so that values different from unity are evidence that realized prices, P_t^r, do not equal frictionless market values, P_t^e. We can estimate the volatility of P_t^e over short time intervals even though frictionless market prices are not observable because:

1. The change in P_t^r over long intervals is a reasonably good measure of the change in P_t^e over long intervals.
2. Therefore, the volatility of P_t^r over long intervals approximates the volatility of P_t^e over long intervals.
3. Change in P_t^e is uncorrelated in informationally efficient markets (Chapter 9). Therefore, the volatility of P_t^e (measured by the variance of the logarithm of price relatives) changes linearly with the length of the interval over which returns are measured (Chapter 10). Consequently, the volatility of P_t^e over shorter intervals can be inferred from the variance of logarithmic returns over longer intervals.

---

[6]The analysis in the remainder of this section and in the following section is based on Hasbrouck and Schwartz (1988).

To obtain the MEC, we follow the steps taken in Chapter 10 in the analysis of the measurement of returns. First write[7]

$$\frac{P_T}{P_0} = \left(\frac{P_1}{P_0}\right), \ldots, \left(\frac{P_T}{P_{T-1}}\right) \tag{11.7}$$

Taking logarithms of the price relatives in equation (11.7) gives

$$R_T^* = \sum_{t=1}^{T} r_t^* \tag{11.8}$$

where
$$\begin{aligned} R_T^* &= \ln(1 + R_T) \\ r_t^* &= \ln(1 + r_t) \\ R_T &= P_T/P_0 - 1 \\ r_t &= P_t/P_{t-1} - 1 \end{aligned}$$

Taking the variance of equation (11.8) and using assumptions A6 and A7 give

$$\text{Var}(R_T^*) = T\,\text{Var}(r_t^*) + 2\,\text{Var}(r_t^*) \sum_{s=1}^{T-1} (T - s)\rho_{1,1+s} \tag{11.9}$$

Dividing both sides of equation (11.9) by $T[\text{Var}(r_t^*)]$ we have

$$\frac{\text{Var}(R_T^*)}{T\,\text{Var}(r_t^*)} = 1 + 2 \sum_{s=1}^{T-1} \frac{T - s}{T} \rho_{1,1+s} \tag{11.10}$$

Equation (11.10) shows that the ratio of $\text{Var}(R_T^*)$ to $T[\text{Var}(r_t^*)]$ is greater than unity if the intertemporal correlations are predominantly positive, and less than unity if the intertemporal correlations are predominantly negative.

To assess the variance ratio, write

$$\begin{aligned} \text{MEC} &= \frac{\text{Var}(R_T^*)}{T[\text{Var}(r_t^*)]} \\ &= 1 + 2 \sum_{s=1}^{T-1} \frac{T - s}{T} \rho_{1,1+s} \end{aligned} \tag{11.11}$$

where MEC is the market efficiency coefficient.

For a sufficiently long interval of length T, $\text{Var}(R_T^*)$ in equation (11.11) is an estimate of the volatility of P_T^e. Since P_T^e is assumed to follow a random

---

[7]A statement made in the preceding section of the chapter can easily be seen with reference to equation (11.7): informational change that is reflected in long run price changes is also reflected in short run price changes. That is, the news that accounts for the long period price relative on the left-hand side of equation (11.7) is reflected in the price relative(s) on the right-hand side of equation (11.7) for the specific shorter interval(s) when the news came onto the market.

walk (assumption A5), $\mathrm{Var}(R_t^*)/T$ on the right-hand side of equation (11.11) is an estimate of the volatility of P_t^e for the shorter interval of length t. $\mathrm{Var}(r_t^*)$ itself measures the volatility of the observed price, P_t^r, over the shorter interval. Hence the MEC relates the estimated volatility of the unobservable equilibrium price to the observed volatility of the realized price over brief time intervals. Negative serial returns correlation and inflated short period variance result in MECs less than unity; positive serial returns correlation and dampened short period variance result in MECs greater than unity.

The MEC is unaffected by informational change, price uncertainty, and long run market power effects. This is because these three factors affect long and short interval returns variance proportionately, and MEC assesses short period returns variance *in relation* to long period returns variance. MEC differs from unity only if returns are serially correlated (see the discussion of intertemporal correlation in Chapter 10). Such correlation, however, would be attributable to execution costs, not to informational change, or to price uncertainty, or to market power. The larger the execution cost, C, the greater the volatility of P_t^r in relation to the volatility of P_t^e, and hence the lower is the MEC.

MEC can be measured for a stock by using different time intervals. In the empirical analysis reported in this chapter, returns variance was measured for half-hour (hh), day (d), and two day (2d) intervals. The shorter period (half-hour to two-day) MEC is[8]

$$\mathrm{MEC}_S = \frac{\mathrm{Var}(r_{2d}^*)}{24[\mathrm{Var}(r_{hh}^*)]} \tag{11.12}$$

The longer period (day to two day) MEC is

$$\mathrm{MEC}_L = \frac{\mathrm{Var}(r_{2d}^*)}{2[\mathrm{Var}(r_d^*)]} \tag{11.13}$$

The Relationship Between MEC and C

Estimates of MEC_S can be translated into measures of C. If realized transaction prices (P_t^r) were related to underlying equilibrium prices (P_t^e) according to equation (11.1), only first order correlation ($\rho_{1,2}$) would be present in the returns series. Thus, for $\rho_{1,1+s}$ equal to zero for all $s > 1$, equation (11.11) becomes

$$\mathrm{MEC}_S = 1 + \frac{2(T-1)}{T}\rho_{1,2} \tag{11.14}$$

---

[8]$T = 24$ in equation (11.12) reflects the fact that, for the empirical study reported in the following section, the trading day comprised six hours.

Multiplying both sides of equation (11.14) by $\mathrm{Var}(r_{hh}^*)$ gives

$$\mathrm{MEC_S}\ \mathrm{Var}(r_{hh}^*)\ =\ \mathrm{Var}(r_{hh}^*)\ +\ 2\left(\frac{T\ -\ 1}{T}\right)\mathrm{Cov}(r_{hh}^*)\qquad(11.15)$$

where $\mathrm{Cov}(r_{hh}^*)$ is the autocovariance of the half-hour returns.

Using equation (11.11), the left-hand side of equation (11.15) can be written as $\mathrm{Var}(r_{2d}^*)/24$, which is an estimate of the volatility of P_t^e over half-hour intervals. Using this relationship and rearranging equation (11.15) gives

$$\mathrm{Var}(r_{hh(r)}^*)\ =\ \mathrm{Var}(r_{hh(e)}^*)\ -\ 2\left(\frac{T\ -\ 1}{T}\right)\mathrm{Cov}(r_{hh}^*)\qquad(11.16)$$

where $\mathrm{Var}(r_{hh(r)}^*)$ and $\mathrm{Var}(r_{hh(e)}^*)$ are, respectively, the observed variance of half-hour returns and the inferred variance of half-hour returns for a frictionless environment. The second term on the right-hand side of equation (11.16) is the component of observed returns variance that is attributable to execution costs. Because of the price reversals and negative serial correlation introduced by $C > 0$, $\mathrm{Cov}(r_{hh}^*)$ is expected to be negative, thus the second term on the right-hand side of equation (11.16) is expected to be positive, and hence the variance of half-hour returns is expected to be greater than it would be in a frictionless market.

The difference between the volatility of P_t^e and the volatility of P_t^r can be analyzed by taking T to be long enough so that the term $T/(T - 1)$ can be ignored, and by solving equation (11.15) for $\mathrm{Cov}(r_{hh}^*)$:

$$\mathrm{Cov}(r_{hh}^*)\ =\ \tfrac{1}{2}[\mathrm{Var}(r_{hh}^*)(\mathrm{MEC_S}\ -\ 1)]\qquad(11.17)$$

Given assumption (A2) (all orders are the same size), the autocovariance term can be related to the execution cost, C.

For C Positive Substituting equation (11.6) into (11.17) and solving for C give

$$C\ =\ \sigma(r_{hh}^*)(\tfrac{1}{2}\ -\ \tfrac{1}{2}\mathrm{MEC_S})^{1/2}\qquad(11.18)$$

where $\sigma(r_{hh}^*)$ is the standard deviation of half-hour returns.

For C Negative The relationship between MEC and C is not as readily derived for the case in which execution costs are negative (which implies $\mathrm{MEC} > 1$). Equation (11.1) has to be respecified [see equation (11.20) later] and equation (11.18) cannot be used (because $\mathrm{MEC} > 1$ on the right-hand side calls for taking the square root of a negative number). The equation used by Hasbrouck and Schwartz for estimating C for $\mathrm{MEC} > 1$ is

$$C = -\sigma(r^*_{hh})(\tfrac{1}{2}MEC_S - \tfrac{1}{2})^{1/2} < 0 \qquad (11.19)$$

Determinants of MEC and of C

If a market were frictionless, one would expect to observe MECs that fluctuate randomly about unity, and estimates of C that fluctuate randomly about zero. In nonfrictionless markets, the following factors could cause MEC to differ from unity and C to differ from zero:

1. The market impact effect
2. The bid-ask spread
3. Price rounding
4. Inaccurate price determination that involves overreaction to news (overshooting)
5. Sequential information arrival
6. The limit order book
7. Market maker intervention
8. Inaccurate price determination that involves partial adjustment to news (undershooting)

Each of these factors is discussed in Chapter 10 in relation to intertemporal returns correlation. As noted, the first four cause negative intertemporal correlation, and the last four cause positive intertemporal correlation. The last four require further consideration in the current context.

Each of the factors that cause positive returns correlation implies that a market order trader may be able to purchase shares at a price below P^e_t or may be able to sell shares at a price above P^e_t. This can be seen in relation to market maker intervention. Assume, for instance, that a transaction has occurred at some point in time $t - 1$ because a market order to sell has executed at the bid, and that the bid was below the equilibrium price. Then let the equilibrium price and the market ask rise one-half point or more by time t, let there be no intermediate transaction, and assume the arrival of a market order to buy at time t. If the specialist does not intervene, and if the ask is above the equilibrium price, the new order would cause the realized transaction price to increase by more than one-half point from the transaction at $t - 1$ to the transaction at t.

If a one-half point transaction-to-transaction price change is unacceptable to the exchange, the specialist intervenes by executing the market order to buy at a price that is closer to (for example, only one-quarter point above) the previous transaction price. This means that the market order buyer has realized an execution at a price that is less than the frictionless market price.

The case just considered implies a wealth transfer to the market order buyer. This transfer can be considered a negative execution cost. A negative execution cost is also implied by the ability of a market order buyer (seller) to obtain a price that is lower (higher) than P_t^e because of either sequential information dissemination (the market order trader receives the news before the quotes have fully adjusted), the presence of a stale limit order on the book, or inaccurate price determination that involves partial adjustment to news.

The following rule for transaction price determination is consistent with the negative cost interpretation:

$$P_t^r = \begin{cases} P_t^e(1 + C) & \text{if market order purchase and } P_t^e > P_{t-1}^e \\ P_t^e(1 - C) & \text{if market order sale and } P_t^e < P_{t-1}^e \end{cases} \quad (11.20)$$

where $C < 0$.

A market maker, of course, cannot realize a profit by giving transactions at negative C. This does not imply, however, that market making in MEC > 1, C < 0 stocks is unprofitable. Stabilizing trades (which are costly to the specialist) need be for only 100 shares, whereas larger orders generally execute at prices that allow the specialist a return and that do imply a positive execution cost for the public market order trader.[9]

Recapitulation

MEC reflects the pattern of first and of higher order autocorrelation in security returns. Whatever causes correlation in short period price changes (whether in adjacent returns or in nonadjacent returns) also changes short period variance in relation to long period variance, thereby causing MEC to differ from unity.

On net, the four factors that cause negative autocorrelation are expected to be stronger than the four factors that cause positive autocorrelation. Consequently, it is expected that price reversals predominate in short interval returns, that MEC generally is less than unity, and that C generally is positive.

As an average, however, C could be refined. The most meaningful adjustment to make would be to disaggregate the order flow and to compute separate MECs and Cs for large and for small trades. A contrast of MEC and of C for large and small trades would give more direct evidence of the market impact effect. However, such an analysis has not, thus far, been undertaken along the lines discussed in this chapter.

Several studies have attempted to isolate and to assess directly the

[9]C, being an average that does not give more weight to larger trades, is best accepted as a conservative estimate of execution costs. The specialist's profits from large trades may in fact more than offset the specialist's losses from small trades and, consequently, market making may on net be profitable for negative C stocks.

price impact of block trades[10] and to measure execution costs for large orders.[11] The evidence is that price impact effects and hence execution costs are appreciable, but that the price effects vanish quickly—within approximately 15 minutes, according to Dann, Mayers, and Raab (1977).

EMPIRICAL ANALYSIS OF MEC AND OF C

The Test Sample

This section reports the results of an analysis of the market efficiency coefficient and of execution costs that was based on a transaction record for 1209 NYSE, 200 Amex, and 651 NASDAQ/NMS issues.[12] The transaction records used comprise all trades and bid-ask quotations for all listed issues for the 42 trading days[13] in March and April 1985.[14] Excluded from the analysis were issues that (1) had fewer than 200 transactions during the period, (2) had stock splits or stock dividends during the period, (3) had an average price under $10, and/or (4) did not pass a 10 percent price reversal filter.[15]

The largest firms in the study are listed on the NYSE, although some very large issues are traded in the NASDAQ/NMS market. Medium size issues in the NASDAQ/NMS are similar in size to medium size NYSE issues. A disproportionate number of issues in the smallest size category (less than $100 million) are traded in the NASDAQ/NMS and Amex markets.

The NYSE and the Amex are clearly different in terms of issue size. The two exchanges, however, are very similar structurally and differ considerably from the OTC market (see Chapter 3). Therefore, an observation that the MECs and execution costs are similar for the two exchange markets but are different for the exchange and the OTC markets would suggest a significant difference in the liquidity provided by the exchange and the OTC markets.

---

[10]For instance, Kraus and Stoll (1972) and Dann, Mayers, and Raab (1977).

[11]For instance, Beebower, Kamath, and Surz (1985).

[12]The study was conducted by Hasbrouck and Schwartz (1988).

[13]Only 41 days of prices were available for Amex issues because of collection errors.

[14]The data were collected electronically by a firm under contract to the American Stock Exchange; essentially, they constitute a transcription of the ticker tapes. All quotes are immediately posted to the tape whenever a revision occurs.

[15]The 10 percent price reversal filter screened for price increases (decreases) of 10 percent or more that were immediately followed by price decreases (increases) of 10 percent or more. Reversals of this magnitude are assumed to have resulted from recording errors. For instance, a price sequence such as 53, 35, 53, where the entry 35 is a single transcription error in the price record, causes two spurious adjacent returns of opposite sign. These errors would cause price reversals and negative serial returns correlation and hence would have depressed the value of the MEC.

The Measurement of MEC

The trading day during the sample period extended from 10:00 A.M. to 4:00 P.M.[16] Half-hour returns were computed by dividing the trading day into 12 periods: 11 half-hour periods from 10:30 A.M. to 4:00 P.M. and the period from 4:00 P.M. to 10:30 A.M. on the following day. The 10:00 A.M. to 10:30 A.M. period was merged with the overnight period (which excludes the opening trade) because the overnight period is sufficiently inactive, and because markets for individual stocks do not open (that is, trading does not start) precisely at 10:00 A.M. Trading usually starts at some time during the first half-hour after the opening bell has sounded.

Returns were computed as the logarithm of price relatives. Returns variances were computed assuming the mean return to be zero: for intervals as brief as those examined in the study, the expected return is so close to zero that estimation errors would cause sample averages to be less reliable estimates than a value of zero of the true mean return. MECs were computed from the variance estimates for the half-hour, day, and two day intervals according to equations (11.12) and (11.13).

MECs computed for different issues are assumed to be independent observations of the relationship between long and short period returns variance. This assumption could be violated, however: a common factor (for instance, the return on a market index) could influence the observed returns behavior across issues. This does not appear to be a problem, however, in the current case. As discussed in the next section, the explanatory power of the market index in the market model regression equation decreases markedly as the return interval is shortened to a day. Consequently, the cross-sectional correlation in intraday returns that is attributable to a common market factor is small.

MEC estimates may be affected by infrequent trading. Returns are measured over fixed intervals so that the intervalling effect on variance can be analyzed by systematically changing the measurement interval. Transactions, however, do not occur continuously but sporadically, and they do not occur at fixed intervals but at any point in continuous time that counterpart orders cross. Consequently, returns measured over half-hour intervals are not, strictly speaking, half-hour returns.[17] Furthermore, the less frequent the transaction rate for an issue, the more a recorded half-hour return may differ from a true half-hour return.

---

[16]The trading day currently is from 9:30 A.M. to 4:00 P.M.

[17]If, for instance, the last transaction in a 10:30 to 11:00 interval occurs at 10:44, and the last transaction in the next half-hour interval occurs at 11:29, the recorded price change reflects a 45 minute return (from 10:44 to 11:29), but is treated as a 30 minute return (from 11:00 to 11:30).

Whether or not infrequent trading biases the MEC estimates is a complex issue. It can be shown that, if the expected return for a stock is zero, MEC estimates are not biased because of infrequent trading. Therefore, because the expected return is indeed very small for the brief measurement intervals used, the MEC computations should not be seriously biased by infrequent trading.[18]

The stability of the MEC estimates over time was examined in the Hasbrouck-Schwartz study by computing MECs for the months of March and April and then regressing the March MECs on the April MECs. The correlation coefficients for the March and April values are

$$\rho = .498 \quad \text{for MEC}_S$$
$$\rho = .163 \quad \text{for MEC}_L$$

The MEC_S are appreciably more stable between the two months than are the MEC_L. This is most likely because (1) the average value of MEC_L is close to unity for each of the market centers (see Table 11.1), (2) the individual MEC_L estimates are not appreciably affected by the illiquidity of the markets (because they are based on longer measurement intervals), and hence (3) fluctuations in the MEC_L estimates are more likely to reflect random sampling error.

Hypotheses Tested

Five hypotheses were tested empirically:

Hypothesis 1:   MECs based on short period returns variances are predominantly less than unity.

Reason: Price reversals are expected to outweigh continuations for most issues.

Hypothesis 2:   The values of MEC in each market center are negatively related to average percentage bid-ask spreads.

Reason: Price reversals are expected to have a lessened effect when spreads are smaller, *ceteris paribus.*

---

[18]To guard against the possibility of bias, issues with fewer than 200 transactions during the two month period were excluded from the sample, as noted previously. As a further check on the possibility of bias, the number of transactions for an issue was included in alternative regression estimates; no meaningful effect was found.

Hypothesis 3:   The values of MEC in each market center are positively related to share prices.

Reason: Price rounding effects are expected to be weaker for higher priced issues, *ceteris paribus.*

Hypothesis 4:   The values of MEC in each market center are positively related to the value of shares outstanding.

Reason: Market impact effects are expected to be weaker for issues with a large value of shares outstanding.

Hypothesis 5:   For all issues and market centers, values of MEC approach unity as the shorter period returns interval on which they are based is increased.

Reason: Serial correlation patterns are expected to decay as the measurement interval is lengthened.

Five independent variables were included in a multiple regression analysis; the first three test hypotheses 2 to 4, and the last two test for a market center effect:

1. *LVSO:* The logarithm of the value of shares outstanding for an issue in millions of dollars
2. *ABAS:* The average bid-ask spread for an issue measured as the average over all quote records of the logarithm of the ask price minus the logarithm of the bid price
3. *LP:* The logarithm of the average transaction price of an issue over the sample period
4. *DNYSE:* An intercept dummy variable that is assigned a value of 1 for all NYSE issues and a value of 0 for all other issues
5. *DAmex:* An intercept dummy variable that is assigned a value of 1 for all Amex issues and a value of 0 for all other issues

Hypothesis 1 was tested by contrasting sample averages, and hypothesis 5 was tested by contrasting MEC_S regression results with MEC_L regression results.

Test Results

Table 11.1 presents summary statistics for MECs, execution costs (C), and other variables for the total sample and for the three market center subsamples. Transactions per issue are greatest on the NYSE, then the NASDAQ/NMS, and then the Amex. Average issue size as measured by LVSO is comparable for the Amex and NASDAQ/NMS samples and is substantially higher for the NYSE. The average price of an issue is highest on the NYSE, followed by the NASDAQ/NMS and the Amex. The markets differ with respect to the average bid-ask spread, with ABAS being the lowest, on average, on the NYSE and the highest, on average, on the NASDAQ/NMS.

Table 11.1   DESCRIPTIVE STATISTICS[a]

Variable	Total sample	Amex	NYSE	NASDAQ/NMS
Number of issues	2060	200	1209	651
Number of transactions	1274	608	1593	909
per issue	(1753)	(963)	(1970)	(1355)
MEC_S	0.683	0.862	0.764	0.488
	(0.386)	(0.463)	(0.381)	(0.258)
MEC_L	1.015	1.005	1.027	0.995
	(0.209)	(0.200)	(0.199)	(0.226)
C (percent)	0.240	0.123	0.148	0.438
	(0.303)	(0.295)	(0.254)	(0.289)
LP	3.158	2.940	3.289	2.990
	(0.517)	(0.497)	(0.515)	(0.453)
LVSO	12.539	11.453	13.129	11.778
	(1.421)	(1.065)	(1.361)	(1.006)
Average bid-ask spread	1.375	1.342	1.065	1.933
($\times 100$)	(0.769)	(0.449)	(0.468)	(0.938)

[a]Standard deviations are given in parentheses.

Average values of MEC_S are less than unity for all market subsamples. The average MEC_S is substantially lower for the NASDAQ/NMS than for either of the exchange markets, and somewhat higher for the Amex than for the NYSE. The distribution of the MEC_S is indicated in Table 11.2. For the NASDAQ/NMS distribution, 60 percent of the issues are in the less than 0.5 category, whereas only 23 percent of the Amex and 27 percent of the NYSE issues are in this group. A substantial proportion of the exchange stocks have MEC_S greater than unity: 30 percent for the Amex and 24 percent for the NYSE, versus 7 percent for the NASDAQ/NMS.

Table 11.2   THE PERCENTAGE DISTRIBUTION OF MEC_S

Sample	Range of MEC_S^a			
	<0.5	0.5–0.75	0.75–1	>1
Total	38	25	18	19
Amex	23	22	25	30
NYSE	27	27	22	24
NASDAQ/NMS	60	22	11	7

[a]Values in table are percentages based on MEC_S classification within each indicated sample; horizontal totals are 100 percent.
Source: Hasbrouck and Schwartz (1988).

The distribution of the MEC_S, for all three market centers, confirms hypothesis 1: the MEC measurements based on short period returns variances are predominantly less than unity. As shown in Table 11.1, the MEC_L averages, on the other hand, are distributed closely about unity, and differences in the MEC_L averages among the three market centers are not statistically significant. This confirms hypothesis 5: values of MEC approach unity as the shorter period returns interval on which the measure is based is increased.

Values of the execution cost (C) for the three market centers are also reported in Table 11.1. These costs were computed for each issue according to equation (11.18) (for MEC < 1) and equation (11.19) (for MEC > 1), using estimates of the standard deviation of half-hour returns and of MEC_S. Values of C were averaged across firms to obtain the values shown in the table. The execution costs are lowest on the Amex, followed by the NYSE and the NASDAQ/NMS. Execution costs do not differ significantly between the two exchanges, but are significantly higher for the NASDAQ/NMS market than for either of the exchange markets.

The dollar magnitude of execution costs can be assessed by applying the values of C reported in Table 11.1 to a stock trading at the $20 level, roughly the average price for the entire sample. The dollar costs are as follows:

Sample	Dollar cost
Total	$.050
Amex	.025
NYSE	.030
NASDAQ/NMS	.090

Bivariate correlations are reported in Table 11.3. These results support hypotheses 2 through 5: the MECs are negatively related to the *average bid-ask spread* (ABAS), positively related to the *logarithmic value of share price* (LP), and positively related to the *logarithmic value of shares outstanding* (LVSO). Further, each of these relationships is appreciably stronger for the shorter interval MEC_S than for the longer interval MEC_L.

Table 11.3 BIVARIATE CORRELATIONS (TOTAL SAMPLE)

	MEC$_L$	C	LP	LVSO	ABAS
MEC$_S$	.537	− .800	.422	.241	− .400
MEC$_L$		− .426	.247	.189	− .274
C			− .485	− .353	.614
LP				.662	− .685
LVSO					− .704

Source: Hasbrouck and Schwartz (1988).

Table 11.4 REGRESSIONS WITH MEC$_S$ AS DEPENDENT VARIABLE[a]

Eq.	Const.	LVSO	ABAS	LP	DNYSE	DAmex	R^2
1.	−.102	.040			.214	.394	.156
	(−1.34)	(7.80)			(11.06)	(13.68)	
2.	.789		−.156		.141	.282	.202
	(30.73)		(−13.68)		(7.34)	(9.94)	
3.	−.384			.291	.189	.389	.269
	(−8.46)			(19.99)	(11.60)	(14.74)	
4.	−.307		−.016	.277	.180	.379	.270
	(−3.75)		(−1.12)	(14.01)	(9.67)	(13.51)	

[a]2060 observations; t-statistics are given in parentheses; R^2 is corrected for degrees of freedom.
Source: Hasbrouck and Schwartz (1988).

Table 11.4 gives the results of the multivariate regression analysis used to assess the MEC$_S$ relationships. Equations 1 through 3 show that the simple relationships reported in Table 11.3 for LVSO, ABAS, and LP persist when market center dummy variables are included in the regression equation. The coefficients for the intercept dummy variables can be used to rank the values of MEC for the three market centers with LVSO, ABAS, and/or LP held constant. For instance, the intercept value of 0.789 in equation 2 shows that, for ABAS = 0, DNYSE = 0, and DAmex = 0, MEC$_S$ for the NASDAQ/NMS market is 0.789. Adding DNYSE = 0.141 to 0.789 shows that, ABAS = 0, MEC$_S$ for the NYSE market is 0.930. Adding DAmex = 0.282 to 0.789 shows that, ABAS = 0, MEC$_S$ for the Amex market is 1.071.

The coefficients for the exchange dummy variables in all four equations in Table 11.4 indicate that the *ceteris paribus* rankings of the three market centers by MEC$_S$ are the same as those observed in the raw averages: the Amex is the highest, followed by the NYSE, and then by the NASDAQ/NMS. Hypotheses 2 through 4 are also confirmed.

LP is the most significant explanatory variable. Inclusion of LP in the regression equations significantly alters the coefficients of ABAS and LVSO: inclusion of LP with ABAS (equation 4) causes the ABAS coefficient to be insignificantly different from zero (though still negative); inclusion of LP with LVSO (results not reported here) causes the coefficient of LVSO to be negative. The LP variable, however, changes neither the sign nor the significance of the market center dummy coefficients.

Table 11.5 reports the results of the multivariate regression analysis used to assess the MEC$_L$ relationships. The overall pattern of relationships is similar to that reported in Table 11.4 for the MEC$_S$ tests, but the values of the market center dummy coefficients are considerably more variable, the rank order relationships implied by the coefficients of the dummy variables are unstable, and the overall explanatory power of the MEC$_L$ regressions is considerably below that of the MEC$_S$ regressions. These results support hypothesis 5; they suggest that the serial correlation in daily returns

Table 11.5 REGRESSIONS WITH MEC$_L$ AS DEPENDENT VARIABLE[a]

Eq.	Const.	LVSO	ABAS	LP	DNYSE	DAmex	R²
1.	.657	.028			−.003	.022	.035
	(14.88)	(7.71)			(−.25)	(1.30)	
2.	1.165		−8.817		−.044	−.042	.082
	(78.06)		(−13.28)		(−3.96)	(−2.55)	
3.	.694			.101	.002	.015	.062
	(24.90)			(11.24)	(.22)	(.93)	
4.	1.010		−6.842	.039	−.039	−.028	.087
	(20.31)		(−7.63)	(3.27)	(−3.44)	(−1.67)	

[a]t-statistics are given in parentheses. R^2 is corrected for degrees of freedom.

is less pronounced than in half-hourly returns and, consequently, that the manifestation of market illiquidity is not detected by the variance analysis when price changes over daily and longer periods represent the shorter measurement interval.

Table 11.6 reports the results of the multivariate regression analysis used to assess the behavior of C. Equations 1 through 4 parallel their counterparts in Tables 11.4 and 11.5. The overall pattern of results is consistent with that shown in Tables 11.4 and 11.5. ABAS, however, appears to be considerably more significant in the C regressions than in the MEC regressions. Nevertheless, the significance of DNYSE, DAmex, and LP in the equations that include ABAS suggests that the bid-ask spread, by itself, is not a comprehensive measure of execution costs.

Interpretation

The analyses of MEC and of C suggest that the market process does cause prices to deviate from frictionless market values, that the MEC$_S$ measure is sensitive to these deviations, and that execution costs are appreciable.

Five hypotheses were examined in relation to MEC, and each was substantiated by the test results—short period MEC measurements (1) are predominantly less than unity, (2) are negatively related to an issue's aver-

Table 11.6 REGRESSIONS WITH C (× 100) AS DEPENDENT VARIABLE[a]

Eq.	Const.	LVSO	ABAS	LP	DNYSE	DAmex	R²
1.	2.174	−.055			−.213	−.331	.257
	(19.55)	(−11.90)			(−15.22)	(−15.73)	
2.	.072		.208		−.110	−.192	.412
	(2.08)		(26.99)		(−8.46)	(−10.04)	
3.	2.363			−.249	−.216	−.328	.372
	(35.76)			(−23.43)	(−18.12)	(−17.03)	
4.	.971		.151	−.114	−.126	−.232	.430
	(8.53)		(14.67)	(−8.28)	(−9.73)	(−11.92)	

Source: Hasbrouck and Schwartz (1988)
[a]t-statistics are given in parentheses. R^2 is corrected for degrees of freedom.

age percentage bid-ask spread, (3) are positively related to an issue's share price, (4) are positively related to the value of an issue's shares outstanding, and (5) approach unity as the measurement interval for the shorter period return is increased (from a half-hour to one day).

Confirmation of these hypotheses gives confidence that the statistically significant market center effect on the MEC_S does indeed reflect the operational efficiencies of the three market centers examined in the study. As might be expected from the discussion in Chapter 3, price behavior is similar on the two exchange markets, but appears to differ appreciably between the exchanges and the NASDAQ/NMS market.

Because MEC is a net measure of positive and negative autocorrelation, the higher exchange values implied by the dummy coefficients could be consistent with either (1) substantial negative autocorrelation for some lag periods coexisting with, and being offset by, substantial positive autocorrelation for other lag periods, or (2) generally weaker negative autocorrelation for exchange issues compared to NASDAQ/NMS issues. For the following reason, the second possibility appears to be more plausible.

First order correlation in short period returns is predominantly negative because of the bid-ask spread, market impact, and price rounding effects.[19] Of the four factors that may account for positive autocorrelation in returns, sequential information arrival is not expected to differ significantly across market centers, and market maker intervention and the limit order book are not likely to introduce higher orders of positive autocorrelation in half-hour returns. Therefore, for the first possibility to hold, negative autocorrelation in half-hour returns would have to be offset by positive autocorrelation of higher orders due to inaccurate price determination. This would be unlikely, however, in part because inaccurate price determination includes overshooting (which introduces reversals) as well as partial adjustment (which introduces continuations). Rather, the positive exchange dummy coefficients in the MEC_S regressions are more likely to be attributable to the exchanges' having (in relation to the NASDAQ/NMS) lower effective spreads, weaker market impact effects, better price determination, and/or specialist stabilization.

Further analysis is called for. Most important would be an assessment of execution costs for larger transactions. One would expect that values of MEC would be lower, and values of C would be higher in all market centers, if smaller trades were screened out of the transactions record.

EVIDENCE ON LAGGED PRICE ADJUSTMENTS

The regression results presented in the preceding section suggest that inflated short period returns variance and execution costs are attributable to

---

[19]For further empirical evidence, see Hasbrouck and Ho (1987).

the bid-ask spread, to price rounding, and to market impact effects. However, these three factors account for only part of the variation in the MECs across stocks, suggesting that another factor also has an influence. The most plausible possibility is inaccurate price discovery. We can test for a price discovery effect by using the market model to examine the relationship between the return on a stock and the return on a market index.

When prices for monthly or longer intervals are used to measure returns, it has been widely observed that returns for individual securities are related to change in the market index. The relationship weakens, however, when shorter intervals are used for computing returns, and the relationship deteriorates markedly when very short periods (for instance, daily intervals) are used. This deterioration is explained by the prices of different stocks adjusting nonsynchronously to informational change. Nonsynchronous adjustments imply lagged price adjustments. Therefore, by analyzing the deterioration of the accuracy with which the returns generation relationships can be measured in very short period data, it is possible to obtain evidence of the accuracy of pricing for a stock.

The biased short period relationship between stock price movements and change in a market index is measured by the intervalling effect on the market model beta coefficient. As discussed in Chapter 10, beta is not subject to an intervalling effect in the absence of intertemporal correlations in security returns. However, serial cross-correlation causes beta estimates obtained from short period returns to be biased downward for stocks that lag the market and to be biased upward for stocks that lead the market. Furthermore, the serial correlation causes R^2 (the square of the correlation coefficient of the market model regression equation) to be less for all stocks when shorter period returns are used for the estimation equation.[20] Therefore, we can obtain evidence on the accuracy of price determination by examining the intervalling effect on beta.

This section reports the findings of an analysis of the returns for 50 NYSE common stocks and for the Standard & Poor's 500 Stock Index, for the four year period January 1, 1970, to December 31, 1973.[21] The 50 stocks were selected as follows. The NYSE issues that had been listed on the Exchange throughout the four year period were ranked according to the market value of shares outstanding as of the last trading day of 1971 (the midpoint of the sample period). The array was then divided into deciles, and a random sample of five stocks was picked from each decile. Firms that did not have shares publicly held since 1965 were excluded and replaced by alternates randomly selected from the same decile.

---

[20]For further discussion, see Cohen, Hawawini, Maier, Schwartz, and Whitcomb (1983b) and Cohen, Maier, Schwartz, and Whitcomb (1986).

[21]The study was undertaken by Cohen, Hawawini, Maier, Schwartz, and Whitcomb (1983a). The findings are further discussed in Cohen, Maier, Schwartz, and Whitcomb (1986). Compatible findings are also found in Fung, Schwartz, and Whitcomb (1985).

For each of the 50 firms in the final sample, a series of 960 daily returns was used to estimate and to assess the intervalling effect on beta. A three pass regression design was employed for the study. In the first pass tests, returns for each stock were regressed on returns to the market index, for 14 alternative differencing intervals ranging from 1 day to 20 days (700 first pass regressions were run). In the second pass tests, the first pass slope coefficients (beta) were regressed on differencing interval length for each stock (50 second pass regressions were run, with each based on 14 observations). In the third pass test, the second pass slope coefficients were regressed, across stocks, on the value of shares outstanding for each stock (one third pass regression was run, based on 50 observations).

First Pass Results

The first pass tests estimated beta coefficients for each of the 50 stocks (indexed by j) for each of 14 different measurement intervals (indexed by L). The market model regression equations were of the form

$$R^*_{jLt} = {}_1a_{jL} + {}_1b_{jL}R^*_{MLt} + e_{jLt} \tag{11.21}$$

$$j = 1, \ldots, 50 \text{ NYSE common stocks}$$
$$L = 1, \ldots, 6, 8, 10, 12, 14, 15, 16, 18, 20 \text{ days}$$
$$t = 1, \ldots, 960/L$$

where R^* is the logarithm of price relatives, R^*_{jLt} is the tth (log) return of length L for stock j, R^*_{MLt} is the corresponding return on the market index, e_{jLt} is the associated regression residual, and ${}_1a_{jL}$ and ${}_1b_{jL}$ are first pass regression coefficients.

The weaker explanatory power of the market model for shorter measurement intervals is shown by the deterioration in R^2 for the first pass regressions as the measurement interval, L, is shortened. Maximum, average, and minimum values of R^2, for the 50 stock sample, for select values of L are as follows:[22]

L	1	2	3	4	5	10	15	20
Max R^2:	.392	.486	.498	.517	.508	.525	.596	.697
Avg R^2:	.109	.164	.175	.202	.236	.305	.328	.404
Min R^2:	.020	.046	.056	.065	.077	.095	.070	.171

[22]Cohen, Maier, Schwartz, and Whitcomb (1986, p. 136).

Second Pass Results

In the second pass tests, the 14 estimated values of beta for each stock were regressed on an inverse of the length of the differencing interval, L.[23] The regression equations were of the form

$$_1b_{jL} = {_2}a_j + {_2}b_j(L)^{-.8} + e_{jL} \tag{11.22}$$

where $_1b_{jL}$ is the first pass beta coefficient for the jth stock estimated for the Lth differencing interval, L is the length of the differencing interval, e_{jL} is the associated second pass regression residual, and $_2a_j$ and $_2b_j$ are the second pass regression parameters.

As noted, the beta coefficient estimated by using short differencing interval returns is expected to be biased downward for stocks that lag the market and biased upward for stocks that lead the market. Therefore, since the second pass tests regressed beta on an inverse of L (specifically $L^{-.8}$), the second pass slope coefficient ($_2b_j$) is expected to be negative for stocks that lag the market and positive for stocks that lead the market.[24]

Table 11.7 shows the results of the second pass test. In the table, firms are ranked according to size (measured by the value of shares outstanding) from the smallest (firm 1) to the largest (firm 50). The column labeled R^2 gives the squared values of the correlation coefficients for the second pass regressions.

The slopes of the second pass regressions are negative for all but the largest issues, those of firms 44 and 48–50. This suggests that price changes lagged the market for almost all of the stocks in the sample. This is not surprising because the stratified random sampling procedure resulted in the inclusion of many small and medium size firms, whereas the market is represented by the S&P 500 index, an index of relatively large firms. The values reported in Table 11.7 suggest that the second pass regression slope parameter is more highly negative and generally more significant for the smallest companies than for the largest companies. This relationship is more rigorously assessed by the third pass test.

Third Pass Results

In the third pass test the 50 estimates of the intervalling effect as reflected by $_2b_j$, the slope parameters of the second pass regressions, were regressed

---

[23]The term *differencing interval* is commonly used to denote the length of the interval over which returns are measured. In this context, it has the same meaning as *measurement interval*. Because $_1b_{jL}$ is expected to approach its true value asymptotically as L increases, it cannot be a linear function of L, but may be a linear function of an inverse of L.

[24]The exponent $-.8$ was selected as the value that, among several alternatives, produced the best second pass regression fit.

Table 11.7 SUMMARY STATISTICS FOR SECOND PASS REGRESSIONS

$$_1b_{jL} = {}_2a_j + {}_2b_j(L)^{-.8} + e_{jL}$$

Firm	$_2b_j$	R^2	Firm	$_2b_j$	R^2
1	−0.936	0.607	26	−0.621	0.598
2	−0.897	0.575	27	−0.858	0.542
3	−0.738	0.710	28	−0.685	0.650
4	−0.839	0.579	29	−0.414	0.597
5	−1.150	0.496	30	−0.079*	0.047
6	−0.659	0.432	31	−0.191*	0.029
7	−0.612	0.690	32	−0.289	0.583
8	−1.296	0.671	33	−0.276*	0.188
9	−0.869	0.614	34	−0.319*	0.217
10	−0.380	0.339	35	−0.714	0.553
11	−0.313*ᵃ	0.141	36	−0.105*	0.021
12	−0.483	0.460	37	−0.312	0.522
13	−0.706	0.573	38	−0.087*	0.049
14	−0.759	0.326	39	−0.041*	0.003
15	−0.405	0.572	40	−0.117*	0.224
16	−0.476*	0.173	41	−0.350	0.352
17	−0.486	0.273	42	−0.286	0.672
18	−0.384	0.692	43	−0.010	0.271
19	−0.617	0.524	44	+0.050*	0.017
20	−0.520	0.494	45	−0.125	0.612
21	−0.367	0.413	46	−0.131	0.345
22	−0.789	0.654	47	−0.206*	0.225
23	−0.454*	0.091	48	+0.053*	0.111
24	−0.268	0.393	49	+0.122*	0.004
25	−0.429*	0.219	50	+0.432	0.712

Source: Cohen, Hawawini, Maier, Schwartz, and Whitcomb (1983a, pp. 137–138).
ᵃAsterisks indicate coefficients *not* significantly different from zero at the .05 significance level.

on the logarithm of the value of shares outstanding for each issue. Issue size should proxy the extent to which a stock leads or lags the market: larger companies are more intensively followed by security analysts, and hence share prices for larger companies should respond more rapidly to informational change.[25]

The regression equation used for the third pass test was

$$_2b_j = {}_3a + {}_3b \, LVSO_j + e_j \qquad (11.23)$$

where $_2b_j$ is the slope of the second pass regression for firm j, $LVSO_j$ is the logarithm of the value of shares outstanding for firm j, e_j is the associated third pass regression residual, and $_3a$ and $_3b$ are the third pass regression parameters.

Similar three pass regression tests were also run by Fung, Schwartz, and Whitcomb (1985). This latter study was based on a sample of 52 issues traded on the Paris Bourse for the period January 3, 1977 to April 3, 1980.

---

[25]The size of the market for a stock is also an important variable in the analysis of price volatility and the size of bid-ask spreads (see Chapter 10).

Third pass regression results for both studies are shown in Table 11.8 (where CHMSW identifies the Cohen, Hawawini, Maier, Schwartz and Whitcomb findings, and FSW identifies the Fung, Schwartz, and Whitcomb findings).

Table 11.8   RESULTS OF THIRD PASS REGRESSION TESTS[a]

	CHMSW	FSW
$_3a$	− 2.637	− 3.442
	(− 11.46)	(− 3.60)
$_3b$	+0.181	+0.162
	(+9.67)	(+3.23)
R^2	0.661	0.173

[a]t-statistics given in parentheses.

The similarities between the two studies are striking. Despite variations in methodology used, in the time periods covered, and in the market centers considered, the third pass regressions show that the intervalling effect is, as expected, significantly positively related to the value of shares outstanding. The finding does not appear to be a statistical artifact or a manifestation of noise in security returns. For the CHMSW sample, variation in the value of shares outstanding explains 66 percent of the variation of the second pass regression slope parameter. It would be highly unlikely that the third pass equation would have such a high explanatory power if a lead/lag pattern of the type posited did not exist in security returns. The evidence that this pattern does exist supports the hypothesis that, in the short run, stock price movements are excessively volatile because price determination in the equity markets is inaccurate.

The relationship between the value of shares outstanding and the strength of the intervalling effect is very similar but statistically weaker for Paris Bourse issues than for NYSE issues. The explanation may be that the value of shares outstanding is a poorer proxy of price adjustment delays for French stocks than for U.S. stocks. The difference may also be accounted for by the difference in the market architecture of the U.S. and French systems— the French market is a call system with no dealers/specialists, and the U.S. exchange markets are continuous trading systems with specialists (see Chapters 2 and 3).[26]

[26]For a comprehensive discussion of empirical tests of price behavior in European markets, see Hawawini (1984).

CONCLUSION

Illiquidity is an attribute of nonfrictionless markets. The manifestation of illiquidity is execution costs: traders who buy at market generally pay higher prices, and traders who sell at market generally receive lower prices.

Execution costs are the difference between realized transaction prices and frictionless market values. Frictionless market values are not observable, however, and thus execution costs cannot be directly measured. Rather, they must be inferred from the dynamic behavior of prices. We have done so by relating the short period volatility of prices (which reflects execution costs) to the long period volatility of prices (which more closely proxies the variability of equilibrium prices) and by assessing the relationship between the return on a stock and the return on a market index.

The *market efficiency coefficient* (MEC) measures the long period/short period volatility relationship. Execution costs generally cause short period price reversals and negative serial correlation in short period returns; consequently, execution costs cause excessive short period (versus long period) price volatility. The MECs are scaled so that values less than unity are evidence of inflated short period volatility.

The execution cost for a stock can be inferred from the stock's MEC. The inferred cost is interpreted as an average difference between reported prices and equilibrium values that would itself explain the observed excessive short period variance.

The analysis reported of the MECs and of execution costs was based on a study of the transaction record for March and April 1985 for stocks traded in the NYSE, Amex, and NASDAQ/NMS markets. For all three market centers, the average MECs are less than unity, and the corresponding values of transaction costs are, on average, positive. Empirically, MECs are explained in part by the average size of bid-ask spreads, by price rounding effects, and by market impact effects. However, the amount of unexplained variance in multiple regression tests of the MECs suggests that an additional factor may also be involved. This factor is likely to be lagged short run price adjustments.

Evidence of lagged price adjustments was obtained by examining the market model, a returns generation equation that relates the return on a stock to the return on the market. It has been widely observed that, over relatively long periods of time (several weeks or more), prices for individual stocks move in harmony with broad market movements. It has also been observed that the explanatory power of the market model is low when returns are measured over short intervals (a few days or less). This would not be the case if equilibrium prices were instantaneously attained. The estimates of beta are biased because of price adjustment delays caused by trading friction. Price adjustment delays in a dynamic environment imply that prices generally differ from equilibrium values.

The accuracy of pricing has therefore been analyzed by measuring the intervalling effect on the market model beta coefficient. Results reported for tests of NYSE and Paris Bourse stocks using intervals of between 1 day and 20 days consistently show that very short period betas are biased and that the bias is related to the size of a security. Short period beta estimates are lower for issues that are relatively thin and are inflated for a few large issues.

Analyses of both the MECs and the beta biases thus indicate the illiquidity of the markets. Illiquidity is in part explained by factors specific to the individual issues: the price level of shares, the value of shares outstanding, and the average size of an issue's percentage bid-ask spread. The findings also suggest that the liquidity of the market for a stock is affected by the market center in which the stock is traded. MECs are observed to be significantly higher, and execution costs significantly lower, for the two exchange markets than for the NASDAQ/NMS. The difference is in part explained by bid-ask spreads' being lower for exchange listed securities, and by the fact that traders commonly achieve executions between the quotes on the NYSE and Amex.[27]

The tighter spreads on the exchanges may themselves be explained, in part, by market architecture. The consolidation of the order flow on the exchange floor, the dissemination of floor information within the exchange system, the affirmative obligation of the stock exchange specialists, and the direct interaction of public orders on the exchanges appear to narrow spreads, to facilitate price discovery, and therefore to increase the liquidity of the NYSE and Amex markets.

The empirical findings reported in this chapter underscore the importance of the architectural design of a market center. Accordingly, the next three chapters of the book deal with the structure of a trading system. Chapter 12 focuses on one critical feature of systems design, the role of dealers and specialists. Chapter 13 turns to three additional design features: the spatial consolidation of orders, the temporal consolidation of orders, and procedures for order handling and trade execution. Chapter 14 then considers the role of the regulatory system in guiding and controlling the development of the markets.

---

[27]During March and April of 1986, for instance, roughly 38 percent of all transactions for frequently traded NYSE issues were executed at prices between the most recently posted bid and ask quotations.

SUGGESTED READING

G. Beebower, V. Kamath, and R. Surz, "Commission and Transaction Costs of Stock Market Trading," working paper, SEI Corporation, July 1985.

P. Bernstein, "Liquidity, Stock Markets, and Market Makers," *Financial Management,* Summer 1987.

J. Campbell and A. Kyle, "Smart Money, Noise, Trading, and Stock Price Behavior," working paper, Princeton University, 1986.

K. Cohen, G. Hawawini, S. Maier, R. Schwartz, and D. Whitcomb, "Estimating and Adjusting for the Intervalling-Effect Bias in Beta," *Management Science,* January 1983a.

K. Cohen, G. Hawawini, S. Maier, R. Schwartz, and D. Whitcomb, "Friction in the Trading Process and the Estimation of Systematic Risk," *Journal of Financial Economics,* August 1983b.

K. Cohen, S. Maier, R. Schwartz, and D. Whitcomb, *The Microstructure of Securities Markets,* Englewood Cliffs, N.J.: Prentice-Hall, 1986.

K. Cooper, J. Groth, and W. Avera, "Liquidity, Exchange Listing, and Common Stock Performance," *Journal of Economics and Business,* February 1985.

L. Dann, D. Mayers, and R. Raab, "Trading Rules, Large Blocks and the Speed of Price Adjustment," *Journal of Financial Economics,* January 1977.

E. Dimson, "Risk Management When Shares Are Subject to Infrequent Trading," *Journal of Financial Economics,* June 1979.

W. Fung, R. Schwartz, and D. Whitcomb, "Adjusting the Intervalling Effect Bias in Beta: A Test Using Paris Bourse Prices," *Journal of Banking and Finance,* September 1985.

J. Gilster, "Intertemporal Cross-Covariances Among Securities Which Trade Daily," working paper, Michigan State University, 1987.

S. Grossman and M. Miller, "The Determinants of Market Liquidity," working paper, Princeton University, 1987.

J. Hasbrouck and T. Ho, "Order Arrival, Quote Behavior, and the Return Generating Process," *Journal of Finance,* forthcoming 1987.

J. Hasbrouck and R. Schwartz, "Liquidity and Execution Costs in Equity Markets," *Journal of Portfolio Management,* Spring 1988, forthcoming.

G. Hawawini, *European Equity Markets: Price Behavior and Efficiency,* Monograph Series in Finance and Economics, Salomon Brothers Center for the Study of Financial Institutions, New York University Graduate School of Business Administration, 1984.

B. Hui and B. Heubel, "Comparative Liquidity Advantages Among Major U.S. Stock Markets," DRI Financial Information Group Study Series no. 84081, 1984.

A. Kraus and H. Stoll, "Price Impacts of Block Trading on the New York Stock Exchange," *Journal of Finance,* June 1972.

S. Lippman and J. McCall, "An Operational Measure of Liquidity," *American Economic Review,* March 1986.

T. Marsh and K. Rock, "Exchange Listing and Liquidity: A Comparison of the American Stock Exchange with the NASDAQ National Market System,"

American Stock Exchange Transactions Data Research Project Report Number 2, January 1986.

T. McInish and R. Wood, "Adjusting for Beta Bias: An Assessment of Alternate Techniques: A Note," *Journal of Finance,* March 1986.

R. Roll, "A Simple Implicit Measure of the Effective Bid-Ask Spread in an Efficient Market," *Journal of Finance,* September 1984.

M. Scholes and J. Williams, "Estimating Betas from Nonsynchronous Data," *Journal of Financial Economics,* December 1977.

R. Schwartz and D. Whitcomb, "Trading Strategies for Institutional Investors," Monograph series in Finance and Economics, Salomon Brokers Center for the Study of Financial Institutions, New York University Graduate School of Business Administration, 1988, forthcoming.

J. Shanken, "Nonsynchronous Data and the Covariance-Factor Structure of Returns," *Journal of Finance,* June 1987.

R. Wood, T. McInish, and J. Ord, "An Investigation of Transaction Data for NYSE Stocks, *Journal of Finance,* July 1985.

three

MARKET STRUCTURE

chapter 12

The Economics
of Market Making

We have shown that (1) prices established in the equity markets differ from equilibrium values that would be attained if trading were a frictionless process, and (2) price behavior depends on the design of the trading system. Consequently, a market's architecture is a matter of paramount importance. Accordingly, we now turn to the effect of the trading system on market performance.

This chapter considers the market makers—the dealers and specialists who play a central role in the U.S. equity markets. Theoretical interest in the operations of the securities markets first focused on the role of the dealer, and much of the academic literature on market making continues to explore this topic. Demsetz drew attention to the dealer as a provider of immediacy, and to the bid-ask spread as the price traders must pay to obtain a dealer's marketability services. Dealers and specialists have subsequently been viewed as price stabilizers, as the premier participants in the price discovery process, and as auctioneers who ensure that trading is fair and orderly. Dealers also fulfill the role of match makers in that their knowledge of the market enables them to bring together buyers and sellers.

Of major interest in the dealer literature have been the factors that affect dealer/specialist costs, the effect of competition and market design on dealer costs, and the presence or absence of economies of scale in market making. Researchers have analyzed cost determining factors such as the level of trading activity in a security and a security's price volatility. Tinic and West (1974) presented one of the first comparative analyses of spreads in different market centers (their empirical investigation covered the NYSE, the over-the-counter market, and the Toronto Stock Exchange). Interest has more recently focused on the development of formal dealer pricing models. As will be seen in this chapter, these analyses have shed much light on the operations of the dealer firm.

This chapter first sets forth the services a dealer/specialist supplies to the market: (1) supply of immediacy, (2) price stabilization, (3) price discovery, and (4) services of an auctioneer who brings order and fairness to a market.

The next section turns to the costs of, and returns to, market making. It identifies the costs, considers the existence of economies of scale in market making, and shows that the costs of market making are minimized when securities dealers follow a dynamic pricing policy whereby their bid and ask quotes change as trading progresses. Then the chapter examines the association between the dealer firm's dynamic pricing policy and its inventory policy (which places bounds on the long and short positions the firm will accept). The discussion shows that with dynamic pricing, the dealer's returns are derived from a *realized spread* that is less than the *quoted spread*. Finally the section considers the effect on the size of dealer spreads of interdealer competition in OTC-type trading.

The last section analyzes the supply of dealer services for the monopoly dealer and for the competitive dealer market. We show that economies of scale for individual dealer firms restrict the number of market makers for any specific stock, but that these are limited in scope and that the potential entry of additional dealer firms keeps market maker prices competitive. We further show that economies of scale that are external to individual dealer firms (1) result in the long run supply curve of dealer services to a market being downward sloping,[1] (2) cause dealer spreads to be tighter for more heavily traded issues, and (3) explain why the number of dealer firms in a market increases less than proportionately to trading activity in the issue. The section concludes with an overview of the determinants of dealer spreads.

---

[1]Throughout this chapter, the term *market* applies to the market for a specific security, not to a market center such as the NYSE or OTC.

MARKETABILITY SERVICES

The Supply of Immediacy

The dealer is most easily understood as a supplier of immediacy to a market. *Immediacy* denotes the ability of buyers and sellers to transact promptly. For instance, consider buyers and sellers in the secondhand car market.

Somebody decides to sell an old jalopy. From time to time, someone else enters the market, looking for an inexpensive, secondhand car. How do the buyer and seller find each other? The traders have to meet in two ways—in time and in place. The used car dealer, as an intermediary, solves both problems. First, the intermediary has an established place of business that both traders can find in the telephone book (this handles the geographic dimension of the problem). Second, the intermediary can hold the car for the seller until the buyer arrives (this handles the temporal dimension of the problem).

The intermediary can hold the car for the seller in either of two ways. First, the car can be left on consignment. In this case the intermediary acts as the seller's agent and remits funds to the seller after the buyer has arrived and the transaction has been completed. The intermediary as agent is a *broker*. Second, the intermediary can *buy* the car from the seller and resell it to the buyer. The intermediary as principal in the trade is a *dealer*. This is the dealership function we are interested in.[2]

As discussed in Chapter 3, an important structural difference between trading systems for the equity markets is whether intermediaries act as brokers/agents or as dealers/principals. The OTC market makers are dealers; the exchange market makers (specialists) are both dealers and brokers.

The exchange specialists can be brokers because of another design feature of the exchange market: the public limit order book, in which buy and sell orders are stored. Public traders have a choice: (1) they can transact with the exchange specialist or against the book at a stated price (buy at the ask, sell at the bid), or (2) they can leave their own limit orders with the specialist.

Gas guzzlers are sold to the used car dealer at low prices; they are bought from the used car dealer at prices that may seem dismayingly high. So too in the securities markets—ask quotes are always higher than the bids. The spread, commonly called "the dealer's turn," is the dealer's compensation.[3]

As discussed in Chapter 6, Demsetz (1968) considered the dealer as

---

[2]Intermediaries are typically dealers in the used car market. This is because each car is unique, it may take a long time to sell any specific car, and sellers are typically eager to receive their money.

[3]Market makers also receive commission revenue from handling orders when they do not participate in the trades.

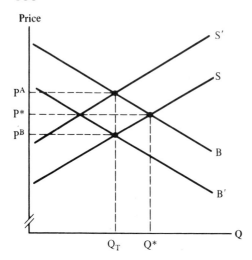

Figure 12.1 Market buy and sell curves with and without the provision of immediacy.

a supplier of immediacy and, in so doing, showed why individual dealer spreads exist. Assume a large number of traders in the market for a security. The curves labeled B and S in Figure 12.1 show, respectively, the traders' aggregate buy and sell propensities.[4] Assume the trading system comprises only a monopoly dealer, and that buyers and sellers meet each other by trading through this dealer. Consider what happens when the dealer knows the buy/sell propensities of the traders, sets prices accordingly, and intermediates in the trades.

Figure 12.1 shows that at P* the number of shares traders in aggregate would wish to buy equals the number they wish to sell. Accordingly, in a frictionless market, Q* shares would trade at the price P*. It is not a simple matter, however, for buyers and sellers to find each other in time and in space. The dealer provides a solution by continuously standing ready to buy and to sell. But the service is not free; the dealer sells to buyers at higher prices and buys from sellers at lower prices. The curves labeled S' and B' in Figure 12.1 reflect this reality. S' is the supply curve of immediately available shares; B' is the demand curve for shares that will be immediately bought. Hence S' and B' reflect the dealer's sale of immediacy.

At each quantity, the vertical distance between S and S' and between B and B' shows the charge imposed by the dealer. For simplicity, let this distance be the same at all Q, and for both sets of curves.[5] Equilibrium is

---

[4]These curves can be interpreted in the same way as the buy and sell functions presented in Chapter 8, Figure 8.6. However, they are not actually order functions, because we have assumed nothing as yet about a market mechanism that would allow for the collection and handling of orders.

[5]The model structure is equivalent to that used to show the effects of transaction costs on prices and volume (see Figure 8.6 in Chapter 8).

given by the intersection of S′ and B and, equivalently, by the intersection of S and B′. The intersection of S′ and B establishes the market ask (P^A), and the intersection of B′ and S establishes the market bid (P^B). The transaction volume at both the bid and the ask is Q_T.

We thus have the following. Buyers and sellers arrive sporadically at the market and generally do not find each other "in time." Traders cannot leave orders on the market because no mechanism exists (by assumption) for handling the orders. Therefore, despite the fact that the market should clear at P* with Q* shares transacting, the market, by itself, cannot operate. The market forms because the dealer posts an ask of P^A and, at this price, sells Q_T shares to the market (given the buy curve labeled B, Q_T is the number of shares the market wishes to purchase at P^A). The dealer also posts a bid of P^B and at this price buys Q_T shares from the market (given the sell curve labeled S, this is the number of shares the market wishes to sell at P^B). Accordingly, Q_T shares pass via the dealer, from public sellers to public buyers. The dealer has accommodated the public's demand for immediacy by selling from inventory and by buying for inventory. The dealer is compensated for providing this service by buying at a relatively low price (the bid) and by selling at a relatively high price (the ask). Note that, because transacting in the market is not costless, the actual number of shares traded, Q_T, is less than the frictionless market number, Q*.

The existence of a dealer is not necessary for immediacy to be provided to a market: (1) intermediaries may be brokers and they can be compensated by a commission, (2) public limit orders can be stored on a public limit order book, and (3) newly arriving public orders can execute immediately by transacting against public orders previously placed on the book. On the other hand, immediacy is not the only marketability service provided by a dealer.

Price Stabilization

The second service provided by a market maker is the stabilization of short period price fluctuations. To simplify the discussion of price stabilization, assume a system that includes brokers and a public limit order book. If the book is thick, market orders can execute at reasonably stable prices; if the book is thin, market orders may have a sizable price impact.[6] Transaction prices are less volatile, therefore, the thicker the limit order book.

Participants in the securities markets prefer prices that, all else equal, are less volatile. They care about this as investors because investors are generally assumed to be risk averse (see Chapter 7). They care about this as traders because they are averse to transaction price uncertainty (see Chap-

---

[6]See the discussion in Chapters 10 and 11.

ter 8). Therefore, it is desirable to have thicker limit order books and the greater price stability that such books imply.

Public limit order traders are not separately compensated for the stability their orders provide, however, because price stability is an "externality" that attends the placement of limit orders.[7] Like any other externality, it is not separately charged for in the free market and therefore is not supplied in optimal amounts by market participants.[8]

Because stabilization is undersupplied in a market composed of public traders alone, inclusion of a professional market maker can make the market better. The improved quality of the market in turn increases trader participation in the market (because traders tend to avoid operationally inefficient, volatile markets). The increased order flow itself increases the dealer's returns because, for a given size of the spread and commissions, gross revenues are larger the greater the transaction rate.

Stabilizing the market with respect to temporary price changes may be profitable for the market makers. When a stock's price is low, they buy; when the price is high, they sell. In so doing, they narrow the bid-ask spread, stabilize the market, and attract investors to the market. The more market makers transact by buying low and selling high with the idiosyncratic arrival of orders, the more profitable their operations are. Accordingly, of their own free will, dealers supply a certain amount of stability to the market.

Professional market makers, however, may not supply the socially optimal amount of stability. *Competitive dealers* supply less than the socially optimal amount because the increased order flow that would result from any one market maker's stabilization activities would be shared by them all.[9] A *monopoly dealer* internalizes the benefits that are external to the competitive dealers but, like any monopolist, realizes greater profits by restricting supply and raising price.

In an attempt to achieve the socially optimal provision of stabilization services, stock exchange regulations include the specialist's "affirmative obligation" to maintain a "fair and orderly market." That is, exchange regulation requires specialists to stabilize prices more than specialists would on their own. A specialist provides this additional stability to the market by entering quotes and transacting when transaction-to-transaction price

---

[7] For further discussion, see Cohen, Maier, Schwartz, and Whitcomb (1977).

[8] To clarify, an example of another positive (desirable) externality is the benefits a homeowner conveys on a community by planting trees that serve as a windbreak in the winter, a coolant in the summer, and a source of beauty all year round. A negative (undesirable) externality is the soot generated in production that filters through the air to dirty one's clothes and to muck up one's lungs. In general, positive externalities are undersupplied and negative externalities are oversupplied.

[9] There are still externalities involved—market makers can free ride on each other's efforts, and individual dealers only take their private benefits into account.

changes would otherwise be unacceptably large.[10] When the market is moving down, the exchange regulation forces the market maker to buy; when the market is moving up, the specialist must sell. These transactions that serve to counter market trends are not profitable. Rather than buying low and selling high, the specialist may buy low and subsequently sell lower, or sell high and subsequently buy higher.

Specialists, however, also have a privileged position vis-à-vis the market. As previously discussed (see Chapter 3), each stock is assigned to just one specialist unit on the floor of an exchange, and the flow of orders to the exchange, for that stock, is all directed to a particular specialist's post. No other single trader has an equivalent view of, or power over, the order flow. Successful specialists realize profits from this privileged position. This is how the system compensates specialists for taking positions that serve more nearly to achieve a socially optimal amount of stabilization.

No market maker, however, can have an appreciable impact on price movements over long periods of time. If, for instance, a stock goes from $32 to $132 in a year, it does so regardless of the specialist's intervention, as it should. Price changes of this magnitude reflect informational change, and there is no reason to perturb the market's assessment of the change. Specialists do not even try; rather, their intervention is intended only to make the movements of price from one level to another more orderly.

How is it that specialists can reduce price volatility without affecting the eventual adjustment of prices to new equilibrium levels? Chapter 11 presents empirical evidence on the relationship between long period and short period price volatility. Short period price movements typically show excessive volatility in relation to the volatility of longer period movements (because the short period price movements are negatively autocorrelated). Consequently, making an orderly market and eliminating excessive short period volatility are consistent objectives, and satisfaction of the specialist's affirmative obligation need not interfere with longer run adjustments.

Two other procedures, in addition to specialist intervention, are also used by the exchanges to stabilize a market: time batching (bunching) orders and imposition of trading halts when news causes a major price adjustment. In brief, the time batching of orders eliminates some of the short period volatility that results from sequential order arrival in a continuous market (see Chapter 13 for further discussion).

The U.S. exchanges are, of course, continuous market systems. Nonetheless, they operate as a call market at one critical point in the trading day—at the market opening. The specialist, before opening the market,

---

[10]Transaction-to-transaction price changes can be unacceptably large if the book is sparse, if the equilibrium spread is not sufficiently tight, and if the advent of large orders exerts undue pressure on the market (see Chapters 10 and 11).

examines the orders that have been transmitted to the post.[11] The market maker may further test the water by sending out indications (potential opening prices) to which traders can react. This special procedure has been instituted to find opening prices that better reflect current market conditions. Accordingly, subsequent price adjustments are not as large as they otherwise would be.

The imposition of trading halts after the advent of major news acts in much the same way as the organized opening procedures. During a trading halt the market is given time to digest the news, and the market maker has time to find a price that is reasonable in light of the new demand conditions. The orderliness of the procedure should impart greater stability to the market at these times of particular stress.[12]

Other exchanges have other approaches to stabilizing the market. For instance, maximum allowable price change limits are typically imposed in call market trading.[13] The reason for this is similar to the reason for the imposition of trading halts in a continuous market: large price changes are associated with major informational change. After such change, traders should be given an opportunity to reassess, and to write their orders in light of current market conditions.

Price Discovery

Chapter 8 shows how investors make their trading decisions in light of (1) their demand curves, (2) their knowledge of how orders are handled and translated into trades, and (3) their expectations of what clearing prices will be. The third factor is of particular interest here. When investors submit their orders, they do not know what the transaction price will be or would have been if they had changed the price, size, type, or timing of their orders. Because of this uncertainty, the aggregation of orders gives a clearing price that in general differs from the equilibrium value that would result if, rather than submitting order points, investors conveyed complete demand curves to the market (see Chapter 9). Accordingly, the third function of the

---

[11]The exchange opens at 9:30 A.M.; the market for a particular stock opens when the first trade is made (at some time after 9:30 A.M.).

[12]The specialist's affirmative obligation does not apply to the price jump that occurs when the market reopens.

[13]The following illustrates a typical price limit rule: If the clearing price determined at any market call differs from the price at the previous call by more than x percent, trading is not allowed for that session, and the price plus or minus x percent is reported as the established price for the session; in the next session, trading again is not allowed if the price differs from this reported price by more than y percent (greater than x percent); by the third trading session, no price limits are imposed.

market maker is to facilitate the market process of finding reasonably accurate prices.

Market makers do not, of course, have a perfect view of the market—they have a *better* view than most traders because of their privileged position vis-à-vis the order flow. Specialists, for instance, have a sense of the orders being held in the crowd by their trading posts, are in frequent communication with the upstairs traders, and alone know the orders on the limit order book. Specialists remain at the center of the market, and, given their familiarity with the order flow for the stocks they handle, these market makers are in an excellent position to sense current market conditions. This feel for the market enables them to improve the quality of prices established on the market.[14]

Market makers affect the quality of price formation in three ways. First, their own quotes directly set market prices. Second, the quotes specialists/dealers post on the market are signals that public traders react to in writing their own orders; therefore, market makers indirectly affect market prices by influencing the public order flow. Third, exchange specialists search for market clearing prices at the start of the trading day and during trading halts caused by the advent of news.

Errors in price discovery tend to increase the variance of short period returns, and accurate price discovery may help to stabilize short period price movements. Furthermore, price stabilization and price discovery are both consistent with the provision of immediacy. This is because *immediacy* is the ability not only to trade promptly, but also to trade at prices that are reasonable in light of current market conditions.[15] Consequently immediacy, reasonable price stability, and accurate price discovery are all attributes of prices that are "fair and orderly."

There are three alternatives to specialist intervention for improving the efficiency of price discovery: (1) superior dissemination of floor information, (2) geographic consolidation of orders, and (3) time batching of orders. These aspects of system design are briefly noted here and are discussed in greater detail in Chapter 13.

The Dissemination of Floor Information   Providing traders with better information when they write their orders enables market participants to

---

[14]With the expansion of the upstairs market and the introduction of information systems such as AutEx and Instinet, specialists do not, however, have as much of an informational advantage as they once enjoyed.

[15]Smidt's (1971) analysis of the market maker emphasizes the supply of liquidity *in depth*, namely the ability of investors to trade quickly and in size, at the market maker's quotes.

harmonize their orders with current market conditions. By so affecting the order flow, floor information improves the accuracy of the clearing prices found on the market. Such information may encompass not only the best market quotes, but also the full set of orders on the limit order books (which in the current system are not open to the public).

Geographic Consolidation of the Order Flow   The information that is inherent in the order flow can best be discovered when the order flow is consolidated geographically. The congregation of traders on the floor of an exchange and the consolidation of orders on the specialists' books give the exchanges an informational advantage that may result in the determination of more accurate prices.

Time Batching Orders   Transaction prices are set in continuous markets whenever two counterpart orders (a buy and a sell) cross in price. Therefore, in the delicate area that separates the larger mass of buyers and sellers, transaction prices may be set by just two traders (a buyer and a seller) whose orders happen to cross. In contrast, when orders are batched for simultaneous execution at a periodic call, prices are set by the interaction of many orders. Therefore, time batching conveys some of the advantages of the geographic consolidation of orders. If properly designed, the call procedure may result in prices that are closer to desired Walrasian equilibrium values.

The Market Maker as Auctioneer

The market maker's fourth function is that of auctioneer. As an auctioneer, the market maker organizes and oversees trading and participates in trades to facilitate the market process.

The Organization of Trading   Exchange specialists (and their clerks) organize trading by maintaining the limit order books and by assuring that trading priority rules (price, time, and size) are honored. Exchange officials in call market trading call the market in a stock, tabulate the buy and sell orders, and announce clearing prices. These functions are primarily clerical, and their burden is increasingly being reduced by automated order handling procedures.

Overseeing Trading   Exchange specialists oversee trading to ensure that various exchange rules are not violated. In particular, destabilizing trades are not allowed; for instance, short sales (with exceptions) may only be executed on plus ticks or on zero plus ticks. In this capacity, the specialist is supported by the surveillance and stock watch systems of the exchanges. On some exchanges (such as the Tokyo Stock Exchange), exchange officials act only in the clerical bookkeeping and regulatory oversight capacities and are not allowed to trade the stocks assigned to them.

Participation in Trading   One aspect of market operations may involve the auctioneer as a participant in trading: share price and order size are discontinuous variables. The role of the auctioneer in relation to these discontinuities is seen in call market trading. The auctioneer at a call searches for the price that will balance buy and sell orders. With discontinuities, however, no price that exactly equates the orders may be found. For instance, at a price of $45\frac{3}{8}$, sell orders for a stock may exceed buy orders by 400 shares; at the next lower price of $45\frac{1}{4}$, buy orders for that stock may exceed sell orders by 300 shares. How might these discrepancies be resolved? One alternative is for an auctioneer to enter his or her own orders so as to fill out the light side of the market. Thus the dealer as auctioneer may buy 400 shares at $45\frac{3}{8}$ or else sell 300 shares at $45\frac{1}{4}$.[16]

The auctioneer does not, however, have to participate in trading to resolve the problem caused by discontinuities. Three alternatives exist: (1) give *pro rata,* partial execution on the heavy side of the book; (2) give execution according to time, size, or some other priority rule on the heavy side of the book; and (3) allow no trading unless public traders voluntarily enter balancing orders that enable the market to clear exactly.[17]

DEALER COSTS AND REVENUES

This section focuses on the costs of, and returns to, market making. We first identify the costs and then consider the existence of economies of scale in market making (that is, that average costs for a dealer are lower at larger trading volumes). We then turn to the price dealers receive for their services. After examining the dynamic behavior of dealer quotes, we distinguish between the *quoted spread* and the *realized spread*. Finally, the section considers the impact of interdealer competition on the average size of a dealer's spread.

---

[16]For further discussion, see Hakansson, Beja, and Kale (1985).

[17]The third approach is used on the Tokyo Stock Exchange for its call market system. That exchange allows no shares to be traded at calls that are used to open and close trading for a small number of large issues, unless the aggregate of all buy orders exactly equals the aggregate of all sell orders at the market clearing price. Because the brokers realize commissions only when they achieve transactions for their clients, these floor traders voluntarily enter balancing orders when needed so as to assure that trading will take place.

Dealer Costs

Order Processing Costs   Order processing costs are straightforward. They comprise the usual assortment of fixed (for example, equipment) and variable (for example, labor) costs of doing business. These costs are the same for dealer firms as for other firms and need not be analyzed in particular.

The Cost of Risk Bearing   Risk bearing is central to the dealership function. Dealers, unlike brokers, acquire ownership in the assets they trade. The dealer, of course, trades to make a market rather than to satisfy his or her own investment motives. As a result, this market maker generally acquires an unbalanced portfolio with respect to the asset in question. Securities dealers maintain separate investment and trading accounts. The desired portfolio weight for the investment account is determined in the same way as for any investor (see Chapter 7). The preferred amount for the trading account is close to zero.[18]

A dealer is subject to uncertainty concerning (1) the future price of an asset and (2) the future transactions volume in the asset. The second source of uncertainty matters because, not knowing when future transactions will be made, the dealer does not know how long an unbalanced inventory position will have to be maintained.

As discussed in Chapter 7, the literature has distinguished between a stock's *systematic risk* (as measured by its market model beta coefficient) and *unsystematic risk* (as measured by residual variation). Ordinary investors should be concerned about systematic risk but not about unsystematic risk, because the latter can be eliminated by portfolio diversification. Interestingly, Ho and Stoll (1981) have shown that unsystematic risk is relevant to a dealer. The intuitive explanation is that, in performing the dealership function, the market maker acquires inventory that is not in and of itself desired and, as a by-product, accepts risk that could have (but has not) been diversified away. The market maker must therefore be compensated for the cost of bearing this risk.

The Cost of Ignorance   The *cost of ignorance* is the cost to the dealer of trading with better informed investors. The discussion in Chapter 9 considers the fact that information is not disseminated instantly and that different traders have differential advantages vis-à-vis the information flow. Dealers

---

[18]The Street has a saying that captures the dealer's desire to be neither long nor short in an asset: dealers wish "to trade down to a sleeping position." However, market makers must allow their trading accounts to vary from zero. If buyers come along, a dealer must be willing to assume a short position; if sellers appear, a dealer must be willing to assume a long position.

and specialists may have an advantage over many public traders; they do not, however, have an advantage over *all* traders. Some public traders receive news and transmit orders to the market before the dealer has learned of the informational change. When this happens, the public trader profits at the dealer's expense.[19]

The dealer controls the cost of ignorance by adjusting his or her quotes. To see how, first assume that all trading is triggered by idiosyncratic liquidity motives and that the dealer, accordingly, is never at a disadvantage because of an asymmetric distribution of information. In such a situation, the dealer profits from the random occurrence of liquidity transactions at the bid and the ask.

What happens when traders who are better informed than the dealer enter the market? When an order to buy or to sell arrives, the dealer does not know whether it is from an informed trader or from a liquidity trader. If it is from an informed trader, the transaction is not profitable from the dealer's point of view. The dealer therefore takes the defensive action of increasing the ask quote and lowering the bid. To see the protection this widening of the spread offers, consider the ask, and the possibility that bullish news triggers the arrival of a buy order. The higher the dealer's ask, the more reasonable the quote may be, *ex post,* vis-à-vis an informationally motivated order. Therefore, by selling to the buyer at the higher ask, the dealer does not lose as much because of his or her relative ignorance.[20]

The dealer cannot, however, achieve total protection by sufficiently widening the spread. Regardless of how much the ask is raised and the bid is lowered, any informationally motivated trade, if it occurs, is at the dealer's expense because an informed public investor does not seek to trade unless he or she profits from the transaction.

Furthermore, the dealer's defensive maneuver is not costless—in the process of increasing the ask and lowering the bid to guard against informational traders, the dealer loses other customers, the liquidity traders. That is, by widening the spread, the dealer transmits some of the cost of ignorance to the liquidity traders, and the liquidity traders transact at lower rates when the cost of transacting is greater. The extent to which the spread can be widened is, therefore, limited.

The dealer, in other words, faces a tradeoff. A tighter spread encourages more liquidity trading (which increases the dealer's revenue), but also results in the dealer being exploited more often by informational traders (which increases the dealer's costs). As the spread widens, the dealer gains more protection against informational traders, but increasingly loses revenue from transacting with liquidity traders. The tradeoff is resolved by

[19]For further discussion, see Bagehot (1971) and Copeland and Galai (1983).

[20]This is consistent with the discussion in Chapter 9, where price is viewed as a signal of information. For further discussion, see Glosten (1987) and Glosten and Harris (1987).

setting a spread that is optimal in that it just balances the marginal cost of accommodating more informational traders, with the marginal revenue realized by servicing more liquidity traders. Note that because the dealer always loses when trading with better informed investors, some investors must trade for noninformational reasons if the dealer is to survive as a supplier of marketability services.[21]

Economies of Scale in Market Making

Interest in economies of scale in market making goes back to Stigler (1964), who first raised the issue. Stigler observed that ''The performance of the main function of the exchange as a market place is subject to economies of scale. The greater the number of transactions in a security concentrated in one exchange, the smaller the discontinuities in trading. . . . As a result the price of a security will almost invariably be 'made' in one exchange.'' Demsetz (1968) estimated the relationship between a stock's spread and its transaction volume and observed that these two variables are negatively correlated for a sample of NYSE stocks.[22] The finding has subsequently been substantiated by many other studies. Demsetz interpreted his observation as evidence of economies of scale in market making.

The existence of scale economies is important for one reason in particular: if average production costs decrease as a firm becomes ever larger, the largest firm in an industry has a cost advantage over its competitors that will eventually drive the other firms out of business. Sufficient economies of scale in market making would therefore mean that market making is a natural monopoly. Such a finding would have major implications for the structure of the equity markets.

On the OTC, multiple dealers typically make markets in a stock. Furthermore, where we observe a single dealer (on the stock exchanges), it is the affirmative obligation of that dealer to provide a ''fair and orderly market'' that makes it uneconomical for the exchanges to assign listed issues to more than one specialist unit.[23] And stock exchange specialists are not,

---

[21]The dealer faces an adverse selection problem vis-à-vis the informational traders. This is because the only time these traders seek to trade with the dealer is when they have superior information. Accordingly, the dealer cannot operate profitably by dealing with these traders alone. Without liquidity traders, a dealer market would collapse.

[22]Transactions volume has generally been taken as the output measure for the quantity of dealer services produced. The value of shares outstanding for an issue, which is highly correlated with transactions volume, has also been used as an alternative measure of the size of a market.

[23]As discussed earlier in the chapter, the stabilization activities of one market maker benefit all. Accordingly, individual market makers have little incentive to supply stability to the market in a competitive environment (rather, each would prefer to free ride on the stabilization provided by others). In addition, the exchange in its surveillance and regulation of specialists would find it impossible in a competitive environment to assess and to regulate specialist responsibility for the provision of stabilization services beyond that which they would freely provide.

strictly speaking, monopolists—as noted, they face competition from the limit order book, from floor traders, from upstairs market makers, and (for cross-listed stocks) from competing market centers. Two questions therefore arise: (1) is evidence of a negative spread/transactions volume relationship evidence of economies of scale and (2), if it is not, what then accounts for the negative relationship?

After Demsetz's original paper, researchers began to doubt that market making is a natural monopoly, and various alternative hypotheses concerning the cause of pervasive empirical evidence that spreads are tighter for thicker issues have been advanced. Two lines of approach are particularly interesting: (1) the bid-ask spread (the *price* received by the market maker for supplying his or her services) is not exactly equal to the cost of providing the service, and (2) dealer spreads are not the same as market spreads.

The Price-Cost Relationship   Spreads would clearly differ from the cost of supplying dealer services if market making were a natural monopoly, because positive profits are realized when average revenue (price) is greater than average cost.[24] With price not equal to average cost, observing that spreads are less for stocks with larger transactions volume does not necessarily imply that the cost of supplying marketability services is less for these stocks.

Smidt (1971) has hypothesized that the negative price-volume relationship is due to greater competition for larger issues. With regard to exchange listed securities, Smidt notes (p. 64) that "specialists face more competition in high volume issues than in low volume issues, and that they therefore quote more nearly competitive bid-ask spreads in these issues.[25]

In long run competitive equilibrium with zero economic profits, price does equal average cost. Allowing for this, Benston and Hagerman (1974) and Hamilton (1976) consider another factor that can keep spreads equal to the cost of market making and still generate a negative spread-transactions volume relationship: industry economies of scale that are external to individual dealer/specialist firms. With external economies, average costs for an individual dealer firm can rise with the firm's own transaction volume, but the *height* of the firm's cost curve is lower when the total transactions volume in the market is greater.

Economies of scale may be realized as trading increases for a security because (1) a superior information flow attends a larger aggregate order flow (even if it is divided across dealer firms), (2) an enhanced opportunity

---

[24]A monopolist maximizes profits by equating marginal revenue and marginal cost, not average revenue and average cost.

[25]Smidt, as does Logue (1975), further differentiates spreads from the cost of providing immediacy by suggesting that the cost of immediacy is, more precisely, the difference between actual transaction prices and frictionless (theoretical) market equilibrium prices. This view has subsequently been incorporated in various formal models of the pricing of dealer services [see, for instance, Ho and Stoll (1981)].

for interdealer trading makes it easier for individual dealers to rebalance their portfolios (and so reduce the cost of risk), and (3) an increased proportion of idiosyncratic orders in relation to informationally motivated orders may characterize a larger market. We consider the issue of external economies further in the next section.

Dealer Spreads Versus Market Spreads   A number of studies of the spread-trading volume relationship have used market spreads, not individual dealer spreads, in empirical tests.[26] In the absence of monopoly dealers, market spreads generally differ from individual dealer spreads (see Chapter 10). Demsetz (1968, p. 39) himself pointed out that on the NYSE, "the spread is determined by persons acting individually, by specialists, by floor traders, or by outsiders submitting market or limit orders." Tinic and West (1974, pp. 732–733) were among the first to recognize explicitly that in the Toronto Stock Exchange (TSE), "bid-ask prices are not necessarily those quoted by a dealer: the reported prices in the TSE simply represent the highest bid and the lowest ask prices that are available at any point in time; it is quite possible that at any given moment, neither will have originated from the floor of the exchange."

Consider the relationship between the market spread and individual spreads in an OTC-type market comprising many dealers who post quotes that, in general, vary from dealer to dealer.[27] Figure 12.2 shows the bid and ask quotes of four dealers. Dealer 1 has the lowest of the asks (A_1), and dealer 3 has the highest of the bids (B_3). Accordingly, dealers 1 and 3 between them set the market spread $(A_1 - B_3)$. Consider the spread that would be set by any other dealer or pairing of dealers (for instance, $A_3 - B_3$, the spread of dealer 3, or $A_1 - B_4$, the spread that would be set by dealers 1 and 4). Among all these alternative spreads, the market spread $(A_1 - B_3)$ is the smallest. Therefore, we can identify the market spread more generally as follows. Let

$$S_{ij} = \min(A_i, A_j) - \max(B_i, B_j) \qquad (12.1)$$

be the spread that would be given by a pairing of the ith and j^{th} dealers. The market spread equals the smallest element in the set of all S_{ij}, namely $\min (S_{ij})$. Let us therefore consider how $\min (S_{ij})$ behaves as the number of dealers (N) in a market increases.

We must, of course, have S_{ij} positive for all i, j because crossing quotes trigger trades (which eliminate the crossing quotes). However, if we ignore the interaction between dealers in the setting of quotes (that is, if

---

[26]These include the studies of Demsetz (1968), Tinic (1972), Tinic and West (1974), Barnea and Logue (1975), and Branch and Freed (1977).
[27]The following discussion is based on Cohen, Maier, Schwartz, and Whitcomb (1979).

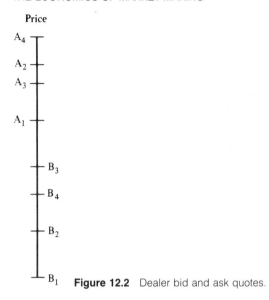

Figure 12.2 Dealer bid and ask quotes.

we assume that each dealer firm sets its own quotes myopically without reference to the quotes of others), it would seem that there is no lower bound on S_{ij} other than zero. For simplicity, suppose the S_{ij} are distributed uniformly in the interval 0 to max (S_i).[28] Then the expected value of the market spread is given by

$$E[\min S_{ij}] = \frac{\max (S_i)}{C_2^N} \tag{12.2}$$

where C_2^N is the number of combinations of N items taken two at a time. $E[\min S_{ij}]$ clearly goes to zero as N, and hence C_2^N, increases.[29] We thus see that, *ceteris paribus,* market spreads are tighter in markets where more dealers post quotes on the market.

This demonstration might lead one to expect that the market spread would vanish if the number of dealers were sufficiently large. The preceding discussion, however, has not taken account of the interaction between dealers in the setting of quotes. Chapter 10 showed that the spread endures in very large markets because, with nonfrictionless trading and hence sporadic order arrival, no trader or dealer posts a quote infinitesimally close to a counterpart quote already established on the market. Rather, if the price at which a dealer is willing to trade is close enough to a counterpart market quote, the dealer "jumps" his or her price and transacts with another dealer

[28]S_i is the spread for i = j (that is, it is the ith dealer's individual spread), and max(S_i), the largest individual dealer spread, equals max(S_{ij}).
[29]Similar proofs could be constructed for any other probability distribution on S_{ij} that satisfies the condition that the probability of S_{ij} being less than any value, epsilon, is positive for all positive values of epsilon.

at that dealer's quote. Therefore, the lower bound on S_{ij} is some value greater than zero.

The factor that preserves the market spread is the "gravitational pull effect." With reference to this effect, Chapter 10 shows than an equilibrium spread exists for a stock, and that the equilibrium spread is, all else equal, smaller for larger issues. This further explains the negative spread-transactions volume relationship that has been observed in studies based upon market spreads rather than individual dealer spreads.

Recapitulation   Economies of scale exist for three reasons. (1) Dealers may individually realize economies over some range of output. However, the existence of multiple dealers in most markets suggests that these economies are not strong enough to cause market making to be a natural monopoly. (2) Dealer costs are lower when the total market for a stock is larger. This is because of the informational benefits associated with larger markets, the benefits to dealers of interdealer trading, and the inclusion of a larger proportion of idiosyncratic orders in the order flow. (3) The price of marketability services is measured by the inside spread (rather than by the size of average dealer spreads), and the dynamics of the market process cause the inside spread to be tighter in a bigger market.

The Dynamic Behavior of Dealer Prices

Dealers in many industries do not adjust their quotes as they trade, but only when they believe market conditions have changed sufficiently. This is not the case with securities dealers, because for them trading and price determination are concomitant processes. Traders in the securities markets are continually searching for a clearing price that is continuously changing with news, with shifts in investor expectations, and with change in investor liquidity needs. Consequently, securities dealers generally alter their quotes as they trade in order to reduce their cost of risk bearing and of ignorance.

Consider the relationship between a dealer's quotes (A and B) and the underlying market clearing price (W), as depicted in Figure 12.3. The smaller A − W is in relation to W − B, the more likely it is that the next

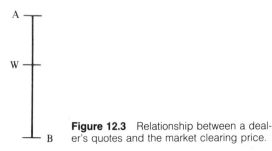

Figure 12.3   Relationship between a dealer's quotes and the market clearing price.

transaction will be at the ask. Or, the higher the quotes are in relation to W, the more likely it is that the next transaction will be at the bid. A public purchase at the dealer's ask lowers the dealer's inventory, and a public sale at the dealer's bid increases the dealer's inventory. Therefore, the dealer firm can control its inventory and hence its inventory costs by properly adjusting its quotes (A and B) in relation to the underlying clearing price (W).[30] Recognizing this, we can now see that dealers generally increase their quotes after a sale and lower their quotes after a purchase.

For simplicity, let the dealer's desired inventory position be zero, and assume the firm starts a trading session with this desired position. Then, after a public purchase at the ask, the dealer is short the stock. This undesired (negative) inventory can be worked off by raising both the bid and the ask (the increase in A − W discourages further public purchases; the decrease in W − B encourages public sales to the dealer). Alternatively, after starting with a zero inventory position and realizing a public sale at the bid, the dealer has a long position in the stock; this undesired inventory can be worked off by lowering the bid (which will discourage further public sales) and by lowering the ask (which will encourage public purchases).

A dynamic pricing policy also decreases the cost of ignorance. To see this, let a public order arrive to buy at the dealer's ask. The dealer, as we have noted, does not know whether the order is motivated by idiosyncratic reasons unique to the trader or by news. In other words, the arrival of the buy order conveys a noisy signal. The arrival of a *second* buy in succession should strengthen the signal. Accordingly, the dealer's optimal sales price (ask) for the second buy order is higher than for the first. Therefore, given the possibility of a second buy order's arriving in succession, the dealer increases the ask and so maintains optimal protection against the better informed traders.[31]

Therefore, in relation to the costs of both risk bearing and ignorance, the dealer increases the quotes after a sale and decreases the quotes after a purchase. This dynamic pricing policy has been modeled in the dealer pricing literature.[32] The approach taken is to assume that the arrival of orders and the behavior of an underlying clearing price can be described by statistical processes, and that the dealer makes pricing decisions in re-

[30]In Ho and Stoll's (1980) model (which assumes the maximization of the expected utility of profits as the objective function), the dealers primarily adjust the position of A and B in relation to W, rather than the size of the spread (A − B) itself. In contrast, in Amihud and Mendelson's (1980) model (which assumes the maximization of expected profits), the size of the spread also changes in response to the dealer's inventory fluctuations.

[31]Amihud and Mendelson also consider how a market maker can infer shifts in the market's buy/sell order functions (due to informational change) from change in the *rates* at which new orders arrive at old prices.

[32]See, for instance, Amihud and Mendelson (1980), Ho and Stoll (1980), and Mildenstein and Schleef (1983).

lation to the anticipated order flow in a multiperiod context. That is, rather than setting quotes at the start of a single decision period and maintaining them until the end of the period, the dealer makes a sequence of decisions through time. The dealer firm accordingly sets its quotes in the current period in relation to the pricing paths that may subsequently be followed.

The future path price will follow depends in part on the current quotes. The current quotes determine the next trade, which affects the next inventory position and the quotes that will be set in the following period. The quotes set in the next period in turn affect future trades, future inventory positions, and hence future quotes. Therefore, the dealer firm's final wealth position depends in part upon the initial bid and ask quotes that are set.

In the theoretical literature on dealer pricing, the optimal value of the current quotes is given by the solution to a dynamic programming model. Dynamic programming reasons in reverse: it first considers the dealer's wealth as of some future point in time and the quotes at the last decision point that will maximize the expected utility of this wealth. The dynamic programming model then considers the second to last decision point and solves for the quotes that will put the dealer in the best possible position as of the last decision point.[33] Continuing to work backward through time, the dynamic program finally solves for the optimal value of the quotes as of the starting decision point. This solution satisfies the ultimate objective— maximization of the expected utility of final wealth.

The dealer accordingly sets the current quotes and sees what happens. As trading actually occurs with the passage of time, the dealer firm remakes its decisions, always considering how the situation may look as of the last point in time, and then working backward to the current moment.

The Dealer's Inventory Policy

Hand in hand with the dealer's dynamic pricing policy is the dealer's inventory policy. The dynamic pricing policy is largely motivated by a desire to maintain reasonable bounds on inventory fluctuations. To see what is involved, we here ignore informational change and focus on the dealer firm as it services the random receipt of buy and sell orders.

Assume the dealer starts with a desired inventory position of zero and sets bid and ask quotes so that the rate at which sell orders are expected to arrive equals the rate at which buy orders are expected to arrive. Assume the expected time rates of order arrival remain constant over time if the bid and ask quotations remain constant. As buy orders actually arrive, the dealer firm sells shares of the risky asset, and its inventory of shares is depleted;

---

[33]The best decision as of the second to last decision point is that which leads to the greatest expected utility of wealth as of the last decision point (assuming that the last decision is an optimal, expected utility maximizing decision).

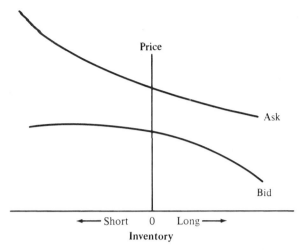

Figure 12.4 Relationship between a dealer firm's quotes and its inventory position.

as sell orders arrive, the dealer firm buys shares, and its inventory of shares grows. If the bid and ask quotes are maintained (and if the expected order arrival rates remain constant), the dealer's inventory, by the law of large numbers, fluctuates between ever increasing bounds.[34] The inventory fluctuations eventually result in a portfolio imbalance (either long or short) that forces the dealer firm into bankruptcy.

The dealer firm therefore controls its inventory by placing a bound on the long position and on the short position that it will accept. When the maximum long position is reached, the dealer ceases to buy; when the maximum short position is reached, the dealer ceases to sell. Furthermore, as the bounds are approached, the firm adjusts its quotes to reduce the probability that moves further from the desired inventory position will occur. These associated price adjustments and inventory fluctuations have been modeled by Amihud and Mendelson (1980).[35]

Amihud and Mendelson show how the dealer firm controls its inventory by using an inventory based pricing policy. The policy is illustrated by Figure 12.4, where price is shown on the vertical axis and the dealer's inventory position is shown on the horizontal axis. The negatively inclined curve labeled *Ask* in the figure shows how the dealer's asking price changes with the inventory position; the negatively inclined curve labeled *Bid* shows

[34]To see this, assume the dealer flips a coin and acquires a share of stock whenever the coin lands heads up and loses a share whenever the coin lands tails up. With a fair coin, the proportion of heads approaches 50 percent as the number of flips increases; however, the absolute *difference* between the number of heads and the number of tails can get ever larger. If the coin is flipped an unlimited number of times, the dealer is certain of either acquiring or losing any given number of shares, no matter how large that number may be.

[35]For a clear assessment and interpretation of the model, also see Amihud and Mendelson (1982).

how the dealer's bid price changes with the inventory position. Note that the ask and the bid decrease as the dealer's inventory increases above the preferred value (which we have assumed to be zero) and that the ask and the bid increase as the inventory falls below the preferred value (that is, when the dealer has a short position). Note also that the spread widens as the inventory moves further (in either direction) from zero.

The logic behind the dynamic adjustment of the quotes is as follows. When the dealer's inventory position is large, he or she seeks to reduce it. The dealer does so by inducing some traders to increase their buying and by inducing other traders to reduce their selling. By lowering the ask price, the dealer encourages buyers; by lowering the bid price, the dealer discourages sellers. Conversely, when the inventory position is too low, the dealer encourages traders to sell by raising the bid and discourages further buying by raising the ask. Consistent with the previous discussion, we thus see that when the dealer firm is short the stock, its bid is high (to encourage public sales) and its ask is high (to discourage public purchases); when the dealer firm has a long position in the stock, its bid and ask are lower (to increase the rate of public purchases and to decrease the rate of public sales).

The tighter the bounds placed on allowable inventory fluctuations, the steeper will be the ask and bid curves in Figure 12.4, and the larger will be the spread at each inventory level. Tighter (looser) inventory bounds imply less (more) willingness of the dealer firm to supply marketability services. Therefore, the willingness of the dealer firm to make a market in a stock is reflected by the slope of the two curves, and by the vertical distance between them. Flatter curves and smaller spreads result in less volatile transaction prices. Therefore, a dealer firm that is willing to commit more capital to market making makes a better, more orderly market.

The Price of Marketability Services

Stoll (1985b) has noted that the continual changing of quotes after transactions differentiates the *realized spread* from the *quoted spread* and thus changes the price of dealer services. As discussed, a dealer's quotes tend to fall after a dealer purchase and to rise after a dealer sale. Therefore, rather than buying at a bid quotation and then selling at the ask, the dealer sells at some *lower* ask. Similarly, rather than selling at an ask quotation and then buying at the bid, the dealer buys at some *higher* bid. Adjusting the quotes in this manner reduces the size of what Stoll calls the *realized spread*. That is, the dynamic behavior of the quotes implies that dealers generally buy and sell at prices that are closer to one another than the bid and ask quotations posted on the market at any one point in time.

The dealer's revenue is derived from the realized spread, not from the quoted spread. Therefore, because the realized spread is smaller than the quoted spread, the dealer's defensive actions in response to inventory risk and ignorance are not costless for the dealer. Stoll estimates that the realized spread (expressed as a percentage of the bid price) is on average roughly 50 percent of the quoted spread for NYSE stocks.[36]

Interdealer Competition[37]

We now consider the effect of interdealer competition on the size of dealer spreads. Assume a set of competitive dealers who are identical in all respects (wealth, risk aversion, expectations, ability, and so on) except their inventory position. Being identical, they would generally set identical spreads; only different inventory positions would cause differences in their quotes.

Further, following Amihud and Mendelson (1980, 1982), assume that the dealers each adhere to an inventory policy that sets limits on the long and short positions they assume. As indicated in the discussion of the dealer's inventory policy, when a dealer firm hits an inventory constraint, it ceases to post an ask (if the maximum short position has been reached) or a bid (if the maximum long position has been reached). To see most simply what this implies for the dealer's average revenue, let the inventory constraints be plus and minus one round lot.

At each inventory position, each dealer firm can determine (1) the profit maximizing quotes that would be set if it had a monopoly position and (2) the quotes that would leave the firm as well off as it would have been had it not traded. This second set of values is the *reservation quotes* of the dealer.

Assume all dealers start with a zero inventory and thus post both bids and asks. Customers shop around to find the dealers with the best quotes. The dealer firms compete with each other by bettering their quotes until no incentive exists to better them further. The interdealer competition forces all dealers to their reservation quotes, because each dealer would profit by servicing the first transaction at a wider spread and so competes to get it. Since all dealers are identical (and start with identical inventory positions), the process drives the quotes to the reservation values.

Now let the trading begin. Since all dealers have identical quotes,

---

[36]Stoll (1985b). Also see Glosten and Harris (1987). The magnitude of the percentage reduction may be somewhat overstated, however, because specialists do give transactions "between the quotes" when the arrival of a market order would otherwise cause an unacceptably large transaction-to-transaction price change (given the affirmative obligation of the specialist).

[37]The discussion in this section draws on Ho and Stoll (1983) and Ho and Macris (1985).

orders arrive randomly at the different dealer houses. After each transaction, the dealer that serviced it is either long one round lot or short one round lot. As trading progresses, a situation in which all dealers but one have a long position or all but one have a short position occasionally arises. These occurrences generate an interesting result: all dealers but one will have reached an identical inventory constraint (either long or short), and thus all but one will cease posting a quote on one side of the market. When this occurs, the one remaining dealer has a temporary monopoly position. The dealer firm with the monopoly position will not be driven to post a reservation quote, but instead will post the quote of a monopolist and will realize a monopoly profit if an execution is achieved at the quote.

Interdealer competition, of course, prevents dealers from enjoying monopoly profits in the long run. However, the dynamic process of competition in a competitive dealer industry affects the average spread realized by the dealers. For simplicity, assume the spreads between the reservation quotes and between the monopoly quotes are constant over time. Then the expected spread (the price of dealer services) is

$$E(P) = pr^A(A^M - B^R) + pr^B(A^R - B^M) + (1 - pr^A - pr^B)(A^R - B^R)$$
$$(12.3)$$

where A^R and B^R are the reservation ask and bid quotations, A^M and B^M are the monopoly ask and bid quotations, pr^A is the proportion of round-trips that are made with the dealer firm's being the only firm to post an ask, pr^B is the proportion of round-trips that are made with the dealer firm's being the only firm to post a bid, and $(1 - pr^A - pr^B)$ is the proportion of round-trips that are made under competitive conditions.[38]

THE SUPPLY OF MARKET MAKER SERVICES

Having considered the dealer's costs and revenue, we now analyze the supply of market maker services. We consider this supply in two alternative contexts: (1) a monopoly dealer market and (2) a competitive dealer market.

The Monopoly Dealer Model

Garman (1976) presented the first formal model of the determination of a monopoly dealer's quotes. Like Demsetz, Garman structured the dealer function in relation to the sporadic arrival of orders for a stock in a continuous market in which trades can be made at any time that two counterpart orders cross. Buyers and sellers meet in this market through Garman's monopoly dealer. By assuming that all orders are for one round lot, the

---

[38]See Ho (1984) for further discussion.

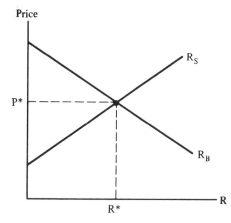

Price

R_S

P*

R_B

R*

R

Figure 12.5 Relationship between share price and the arrival rates of buy and sell orders.

buy and sell propensities of traders can be described by the number of 100 share orders that arrive at the market over an interval of time.

Let R_B and R_S be the arrival rates for, respectively, the buy and sell orders. Figure 12.5 shows that R_B and R_S are both functions of the stock's share price, P. The negatively inclined curve labeled R_B reflects the fact that, as the share price is lowered, more investors want to buy one round lot; the positively inclined curve labeled R_S reflects the fact that, as the share price is raised, more investors want to sell one round lot. Figure 12.5 shows that at a price of P*, arrival rates for buy and sell orders both equal R*.

The time rates show the number of orders that are *expected* to arrive over some period of time (for example, a trading day); the actual order arrival is an uncertain (stochastic) process.[39] Because of the sporadic nature of order arrival, the counterpart buys and sells generally do not meet each other in time. Therefore, in the absence of any other market mechanism, the dealer firm must exist to make the market.

Garman's dealer firm sets quotes to maximize its expected profits from trading per period of time.[40] Because all investors trade with the single dealer, the dealer is a monopolist vis-à-vis the buy curve, and a monopsonist vis-à-vis the sell curve. Accordingly, the dealer firm achieves maximum (expected) profits by equating the marginal cost of buying shares with the marginal revenue obtained from selling shares.[41] In Figure 12.6, the marginal cost function is the upward sloping straight line labeled R_S', and the

[39]Garman assumes a Poisson order arrival process, and R_S and R_B are arrival rate parameters for the process. Garman's analysis goes beyond Demsetz's in taking account of the stochastic variation in the number of orders that will be placed in any interval of time.

[40]Note that "quantity" is measured by the *expected* rates of order arrival at a price of P, and that the dollar volume of both sales and purchases is uncertain.

[41]Garman's model is simplified by the assumption that the market maker has no transaction costs of doing business (that is, the only cost of selling shares is the cost of buying shares).

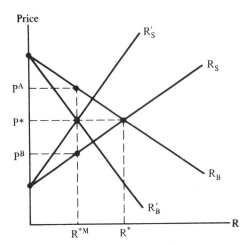

Figure 12.6 Determination of the optimal supply of dealer services in a monopoly dealer market.

marginal revenue function is the downward sloping straight line labeled R'_B. The intersection of these two lines establishes R^{*M} as the equilibrium expected rate of transactions for the monopoly dealer. Accordingly, the dealer firm's optimal ask is given by P^A, and its optimal bid is given by P^B. These prices and the associated quantity (R^{*M}) identify the expected profit maximizing supply of dealer services in the monopoly dealer market.

The role of dealer inventories can be reviewed in the context of Garman's model. As with the Demsetz market maker, the Garman dealer has to accept nonzero inventory positions as trading progresses. In part, this is because of the *asynchronous pattern* with which buy and sell orders arrive.[42] But, unlike in the Demsetz model, there is a second factor in the Garman model that also accounts for inventory fluctuations: the order flow is *stochastic,* and R^{*M} is the *expected* rate of buy and sell arrivals. After the fact, it may turn out, for the trading session, that more buy orders in total have arrived at the dealer's ask (P^A) than sell orders have arrived at the dealer's bid (P^B). In such an event, the dealer firm, on net, has reduced its inventory of the stock. Or perhaps more sell orders have arrived given the dealer's bid than buy orders have arrived given the dealer's ask; in this event, the dealer, on net, has added to its inventory. These are the inventory fluctuations considered in the analysis of the dealer's inventory policy.

[42]If, for instance, the dealer starts with a zero inventory position in the stock and the first order to arrive is a sell, the dealer has to accept a long position in the stock; if two or more buy orders happen to arrive next, the dealer then has to accept a short position in the stock. Therefore, the dealer's inventory fluctuations depend on the specific sequence in which the buy and sell orders happen, *ex post,* to arrive on the market during the trading day.

The dynamic dealer pricing models have extended Garman's model[43] by showing how the dealer firm changes its quotes over time so as to keep its inventory within reasonable bounds. The wider the allowable inventory bounds, the smaller is the spread and the more stable are the quotes. We see again that the dealer firm's willingness to supply marketability services is an expression of its willingness to accept an unbalanced inventory position.

The Competitive Dealer Model

On average, there were 8.0 market makers per security in the NASDAQ market in 1986.[44] Is this number too small to suggest the empirical realism of the perfectly competitive model of standard microeconomic theory?

In 1986, 526 market makers in total made markets for 5189 securities in the NASDAQ system. The provision of marketability services for one stock is a close substitute in production for the provision of marketability services for other stocks. Dealers are free to pick the stocks they make markets in virtually at will. The elasticity of supply for these services is, therefore, large for all stocks, and the potential entry of additional dealer firms in each of the markets keeps prices competitive. If excess profits are being made in some stocks, additional dealers appear to compete the profits away.

The costs and revenues of the dealer firm were considered in the section "Dealer Costs and Revenues." We now show how these interact to give the expected profit maximizing output solution for the competitive dealer firm and an equilibrium output for the market in aggregate. The analysis yields insight into two empirical observations of particular interest: (1) the number of dealers making markets in most individual stocks is relatively small, and (2) the number of dealer firms increases less than proportionately with the size of the aggregate market for a stock.

The following describes our analytical context:

1. We consider long run analysis only (and therefore avoid the need to distinguish between fixed and variable cost).
2. Although each dealer makes markets in many different securities, we simplify the analysis by considering the cost curve of the dealer firm as it applies to one market alone.
3. Although the realized bid-ask spread of individual dealer firms varies over time, we simplify the analysis by assuming that, at all times, the dealer makes decisions in relation to an expected price

---

[43]Amihud and Mendelson (1980), Ho and Stoll (1980), and Mildenstein and Schleef (1983).
[44]NASDAQ 1987 *Fact Book*, National Association of Securities Dealers.

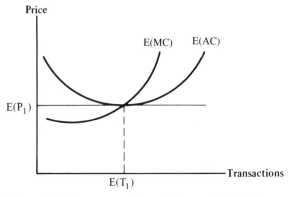

Figure 12.7 Long run profit maximizing solution for the competitive dealer firm.

of dealer services given by

$$
\begin{aligned}
E(P) = \; & pr^A(A^M - B^R) + pr^B(A^R - B^M) \\
& + (1 - pr^A - pr^B)(A^R - B^R)
\end{aligned}
$$

as discussed previously. The competitive dealer firm is, strictly speaking, a price taker with respect to $E(P)$.[45]

4. The dealer firm's objective is to maximize expected profits.

Figure 12.7 shows the long run profit maximizing solution for the competitive dealer firm. The output of the firm is measured by the expected number of transactions in which the dealer participates. The figure shows that, at an expected price of $E(P_1)$, the optimal expected output per trading session is $E(T_1)$. We first consider what this means and then explain how the solution was obtained.

Because order arrival is stochastic, the dealer firm does not know *ex ante* how many transactions per trading session it will actually participate in at the price $E(P_1)$. Rather, given $E(P_1)$, the firm adopts an inventory policy that implies an expected number of transactions equal to $E(T_1)$. That is, the dealer firm places bounds on the magnitude of the inventory fluctuations it will accept, and when the maximum long or short inventory position is reached the dealer firm does not service additional public sell or buy orders. Given these bounds and the expected arrival rate of orders, the firm expects to participate in $E(T_1)$ transactions.

Ex post, the dealer firm will realize a particular transaction rate and will have experienced a specific pattern of inventory adjustments. If by chance buy and sell orders happen to have arrived in a well interspersed pattern, the inventory fluctuations required to service the order flow will have been small and the dealer will participate in more than $E(T_1)$ trans-

---

[45]Ho and Stoll (1980) show that the *size* of the dealer spread is only weakly dependent upon the dealer's inventory (although the *location* of the spread vis-à-vis the frictionless market clearing price is dependent on the inventory position).

actions. Or if, by chance, the buy and sell orders happen to have arrived in clusters (either because of the vagaries of order arrival or because of the pattern of adjustment to informational change), the inventory fluctuations required to service the order flow will have been large, the inventory bounds will have been hit more frequently than anticipated, and the dealer will have participated in fewer than $E(T_1)$ transactions. Nevertheless, the firm sets the maximum inventory limits *ex ante* and, having set these limits, anticipates that it will participate in $E(T_1)$ transactions during the next trading session.

Along with being uncertain as to what its actual transaction volume will be, the dealer firm is uncertain as to what its average revenue will be. Price uncertainty exists because the firm does not know *ex ante* the number of times it will be alone on one side of the market and hence will charge the monopoly price for the next transaction. The dealer firm's output decision, however, is not affected per se by the frequency with which it realizes the monopoly price (excess profits are in any event eliminated by competition). If the dealer firm realizes the monopoly price more often (that is, if there are fewer competing dealers), then it will be willing to supply market maker services with a tighter spread in the reservation quotes.[46]

The competitive firm knows the number of competing dealers in the market and the proportion of transactions it can expect to make under monopolistic conditions. Thus the firm also knows the average price to expect. The competitive dealer solves for the optimal expected number of transactions by equating expected marginal cost with expected price, as shown in Figure 12.7. For this equality to exist and to give a maximum, the expected average cost curve must be increasing over at least some range of output, as shown in Figure 12.7.[47]

The decrease in average cost over smaller ranges of output is reasonable for the dealer firm. Regardless of the transaction volume it may sustain, a firm can make the market in a stock only if it is willing to commit at least a minimum amount of labor and financial capital to posting quotes (so as to be known as a market maker), to staying informed about the company in question (to control the cost of ignorance), and to gaining some understanding of the behavior of the order flow for the security. This expenditure does not increase proportionately as the firm expands its market making activities in the stock. Therefore, economies of scale are expected over relatively small values of output.

---

[46]Dealer firms cannot enjoy the occasional receipt of the monopoly price unless they continually post quotes in the market, because they do not receive order flow unless they do so. Therefore, they are willing to sustain a slight loss from the competitive quotes if they are occasionally compensated by the realization of a monopoly return. The uncertain mix between the two prices, however, keeps the average price uncertain.

[47]Note that we refer to the *expected* value of costs because, with inventory fluctuations uncertain *ex ante,* the exact cost of maintaining any given trading volume is uncertain.

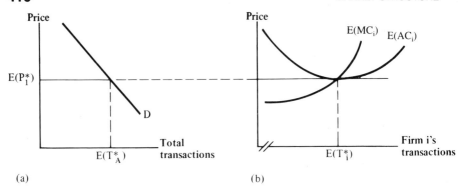

Figure 12.8   Determination of the optimal supply of dealer services in a competitive dealer market. (a) Industry equilibrium. (b) Equilibrium for the ith dealer firm.

As the firm's market making activities in a stock continue to increase, however, the firm must accept ever greater inventory fluctuations in its trading portfolio (as discussed previously). These fluctuations become increasingly costly as they become larger (see the discussion of the costs of risk bearing and of ignorance in the section on dealer costs and revenues). Thus diseconomies of scale are expected beyond a certain transaction volume, and average costs will rise.

Having identified the optimal output solution for the competitive dealer firm, we next consider the aggregate output for all firms making a market in the stock. Figure 12.8 illustrates the output equilibrium that exists when the demand for marketability services is given by the negatively inclined curve labeled *D* in Figure 12.8(a) and when all dealer firms have the same average cost curve labeled $E(AC_i)$ in Figure 12.8(b).[48]

The value of average cost at the minimum point on the firm's average cost curve establishes $E(P_i^*)$ as the no profit, long run, competitive equilibrium price of marketability services. Given the demand curve, D, the aggregate expected transactions volume at $E(P_i^*)$ is $E(T_A^*)$. Given $E(T_A^*)$ and the optimal expected transaction volume for each firm [shown to be $E(T_i^*)$ in Figure 12.8(b)], the equilibrium number of dealer firms, N*, is given by

$$N^* = \frac{E(T_A^*)}{E(T_i^*)} \qquad (12.4)$$

Given N*, the expected price $E(P_i^*)$ is the appropriately weighted average of the competitive spread (that is, the spread of the reservation quotes) and of the noncompetitive spread that is realized when the dealer firm is isolated on one side of the market. E(P*) is given by the height of the average cost curve $E(AC_i)$, N* is given by equation (12.4), and the monopoly quotes

---

[48]The assumption that all firms have identical cost curves simplifies the exposition. Most importantly, the height of the average cost curves is typically taken by theoretical economists to be the same in competitive markets. See Cohen and Cyert (1975).

can be separately determined; therefore, the competitive quotes can be obtained from equation (12.3).

As noted, relatively few dealer firms make a market for most OTC stocks; this implies that the optimal transaction volume for a firm, $E(T_i^*)$, is large in relation to the total transaction volume for the issue, $E(T_A^*)$. The optimal value of $E(T_i^*)$ is given by the dealer firm's cost curve, whereas the demand for marketability services is related to the size of the company whose stock is being traded. If demand is too small in relation to the cost of making a market, the asset is not publicly traded.[49] If a stock does just meet the minimum requirements for public issue, its relatively small trading volume attracts the interest of only one or two dealer firms. Then, if the stock's trading volume increases, more dealer firms start to make a market in the stock.

As noted previously, however, the number of dealer firms making a market in a stock increases less than proportionately with increases in the stock's trading volume. This is because each dealer's average cost curve shifts with the increase in total trading volume, and the minimum point of the curve is lower and further to the right. This shift is explained, along the lines suggested by Hamilton (1976) and Benston and Hagerman (1974), by economies of scale that are external to the individual dealer firms.

As noted earlier, economies that are external to the individual dealer firms result from the following: (1) As the size of an issue increases, the total flow of information concerning the issue to the market increases (the corporation itself releases more information and a larger number of financial analysts pay attention to the stock). (2) As the aggregate order flow increases, dealers can more quickly work off an unbalanced inventory position, both by trading with the public at an increased rate and by trading with each other. (3) As the aggregate market for a stock increases (all else equal), the amount of liquidity trading may increase in relation to informational trading, reducing the risk associated with any given inventory imbalance (which induces the dealer firm to devote more financial capital to making a market in the stock).[50]

Figure 12.9 shows the long run supply curve of dealer services [the curve labeled S in Figure 12.9(a)] with economies of scale that are external to the individual dealer firms. When the market demand for dealer services is given by the curve labeled D_1 in Figure 12.9(a), N_1^* firms make a market

---

[49]There are substantial costs to dealers of making a market in a stock, of remaining informed about a company, and of staying attuned to the trading characteristics of the company's stock.

[50]The discussion in Chapter 10 suggests that price volatility is less for larger issues, and that the arrival rate parameter for idiosyncratic orders is greater when price volatility is less.

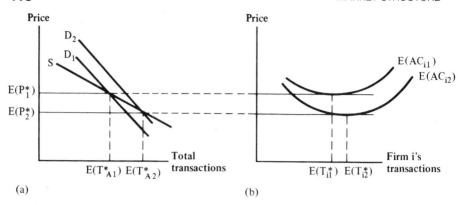

Figure 12.9 Derivation of the long run supply curve of dealer services. (a) Market demand and supply. (b) Equilibria for the ith dealer firm.

in the stock, each firm receives the expected price $E(P_i^*)$, each expects to transact at rate $E(T_i^*)$, and the expected aggregate number of market transactions is $E(T_{A1}^*)$. Underlying this solution is the fact that, when the expected aggregate number of market transactions is $E(T_{A1}^*)$, the expected average cost curve for each firm is the curve labeled $E(AC_1)$.

If the market demand shifts to the curve labeled D_2 in Figure 12.9(a), equilibrium is again achieved for the industry and for each of the individual dealer firms that it comprises. This new solution gives an expected aggregate transaction rate $E(T_{A2}^*) > E(T_{A1}^*)$. Because the expected transaction rate is greater (and recalling the economies of scale that are external to the individual dealer firms), the expected average cost curve for each firm is lower, with its minimum point further to the right [as shown in Figure 12.9(b) by the relationship between $E(AC_{i1})$ and $E(AC_{i2})$]. Because the $E(AC_i)$ curve is lower in the second situation, the market clearing price is also lower—$E(P_2^*) < E(P_1^*)$. Because the minimum point on the firm's average cost curve is further to the right, $E(T_{i2}^*) > E(T_{i1}^*)$. Because the output of each firm has increased, the number of firms in the market has increased less than proportionately with the aggregate transactions volume—$N_2^*/N_1^* < E(T_{A2}^*)/E(T_{A1}^*)$.

Note the following about the long run solution just attained. The individual dealer firms realize no excess expected profits from their market making operations—free entry into an industry ensures that, in the long run, the price of the service just equals its minimum average cost of production. The external economies of scale, nevertheless, produce a result of major import: the long run supply curve of dealer services to the market for a stock is negatively inclined. Therefore, we should expect to observe smaller dealer spreads in larger markets, and we do.[51]

---

[51]Recall that E(P) is the size of the average dealer spread in a competitive market.

The Determinants of Dealer Bid-Ask Spreads

We conclude this discussion of the supply of marketability services by reviewing the determinants of dealer bid-ask spreads. The analysis has highlighted four classes of variables: (1) an activity variable, (2) a risk variable, (3) an information variable, and (4) a measure of interdealer competition. In analyzing these variables, researchers have generally considered the spread as a percentage of the bid price, rather than as an absolute value. Percentage spreads are more meaningful because they should, aside from the effect of price discontinuity, be independent of price (that is, the percentage spread for a $120 stock should be roughly the same as the percentage spread for a $15 stock).[52]

Activity.   All else equal, the greater the trading activity in a stock, the lower the spread a market maker quotes. The reason follows from the economies of scale in market making that attend a larger order flow. The common measure of trading activity is the average number or value of shares traded per period. The empirical evidence is that, all else constant, the percentage spread is less, the greater the normal trading activity in a stock.[53]

Risk.   The normal transaction volume for a stock is related to the length of time a dealer expects to hold any unwanted inventory position; the variance of returns measures the risk to the dealer of holding the inventory over this period. The relevant measure of risk for a market maker is unsystematic risk, rather than total risk or the market model beta. The empirical evidence is that, all else constant, the percentage spread is greater for riskier securities. Furthermore, residual risk does appear to be a major factor in the relationship.

Information   The market maker does not expect to be the *first* to receive news; therefore, it is likely that the spread widens at times of substantial informational change. One way to test this by regression analysis would be to consider the effect of current trading volume on the spread, while taking separate account of a stock's normal trading volume. Another way might be to contrast the size of the spread after the market opening (when uncertainty concerning the market is greater after the overnight close) with the

---

[52]Price discontinuity increases the average percentage spread for the $15 dollar stock because, with one-eighth pricing, the minimum absolute price change of one-eighth is a more substantial percentage of $15 than of $120.

[53]See Cohen, Maier, Schwartz, and Whitcomb (1979) for a review of this literature and the empirical evidence.

size of the spread later in the trading day, or at the market close. Unfortunately, empirical tests along these lines have yet to be performed.

Competition   Competition brings spreads into line with costs (see the discussion of the price of marketability services). The standard measure of competition used in the literature has been the number of market makers. The empirical evidence clearly shows that percentage dealer spreads are narrower, the larger the number of dealers making a market in a stock.[54] It is not clear, however, whether this is the result of competition eliminating excess returns or of the supply curve of dealer services being downward sloping.

The activity variable and interdealer competition should also affect market spreads. That is, the *inside spread* should be smaller, the larger the average trading activity in a stock, and the larger the number of dealers making a market in a stock. This is because the thickness of a market stabilizes price, mitigates the gravitational pull effect, and thereby results in traders' posting new quotes (bids or asks) closer to counterpart quotes (asks or bids) already established on the market.

Short run variations in trading activity, however, are positively related to the size of the market spread, because these variations cause the spread to fluctuate around its equilibrium value: temporary increases in transactions volume clear limit orders off the book, thereby widening the spread; temporary decreases in transactions volume may allow more orders to accumulate on the book, thereby narrowing the spread.

CONCLUSION

Market makers play a key role in the U.S. equity markets. The dealers are center stage in the OTC markets, as are the specialists in the exchange markets. By and large, dealers and specialists operate in similar ways. However, there are differences in emphasis, in the regulatory environment, and in other aspects of systems design that define the market makers' modus operandi.

All dealers (including specialists) provide immediacy to the market in the sense of enabling buyers and sellers to meet each other in time and in space. The quotes dealers post on the market further help to stabilize prices and to keep them reasonable in relation to the market's underlying demand propensities. Furthermore, OTC dealers and exchange specialists, as auctioneers, enforce various trading rules that bring order and fairness to a market.

[54]A percentage spread is the ask minus the bid divided by the bid.

Dealers, as intermediaries, are common in many markets; the operations of securities dealers, however, are unique. In part, this is because of the functions they perform (which include price stabilization and price discovery, along with the more common provision of immediacy and the services of an auctioneer). In part, this is also due to the costs they incur in their willingness to acquire an unbalanced inventory position and in their vulnerability to trading with investors who may be better informed than they are. Understanding how the dealer operates in light of the costs of risk and of ignorance gives much insight into the provision of marketability services.

An important aspect of dealer operations is the dynamic pricing policies used. We have seen how market makers continually adjust their quotes as trading progresses, both to respond to the informational content implicit in the order flow and to control their inventory fluctuations.

A major input into the provision of marketability services is the willingness of the dealer firm to commit capital to service a public sell order when it has a long position or to service a public buy order when it is short the stock. No dealer firm, however, allows inventories to fluctuate without bound. Therefore, the degree to which the firm is willing to make a market is expressed by the magnitude of the inventory fluctuations it accepts. The larger the inventory fluctuations the firm allows, the more it transacts with the public and the greater is its provision of marketability services.

A further point of interest about the economics of market making is the way in which inventory costs, the order flow, and the information flow interact to generate economies of scale, both for individual dealer firms and for all dealers in aggregate. Economies of scale are large enough for individual firms so that only a relatively small number of firms actually makes a market for most stocks.[55] Beyond a certain transaction volume, dealer costs do, however, rise (largely because of the risk of accepting an unbalanced inventory position). Therefore, one firm does not grow in size to monopolize the market for a specific stock. Furthermore, because market making in one stock is a close substitute in production for market making in other stocks, markets remain competitive even if only a few dealer firms operate in each market (potential entry is as effective as actual entry for keeping prices competitive).

Economies of scale also exist, to an appreciable extent, for dealer firms as a group. This is due to the greater informational content of a larger aggregate order flow, to the enhanced opportunities for interdealer trading

---

[55]As noted, if a stock does not generate enough order flow to justify the supply of market making services, the company does not go public.

(to rebalance portfolios), and to the changing composition of the order flow (liquidity motivated trading in particular may be more prevalent, the larger the aggregate order flow).

Economies of scale for the industry (1) cause the optimal size of individual dealer firms' operations to increase with the aggregate order flow for a stock, (2) explain why the number of dealers making a market in a stock increases less than proportionately with the aggregate order flow, (3) cause the long run market supply curve of dealer services to be downward sloping, and therefore (4) result in dealer spreads being tighter, the larger the market for a stock.

Dealers play a critical role in the U.S. equity markets, and it would be difficult to envision these markets without them. However, alternative market structures exist, and dealers do not play an important role in many of the secondary equity markets around the world. Therefore, the next chapter turns to an examination of other structural characteristics of a trading system that also affect the provision of marketability services and the quality of prices set in the marketplace.

SUGGESTED READING

Y. Amihud, T. Ho, and R. Schwartz, eds., *Market Making and the Changing Structure of the Securities Industry,* Lexington, Mass.: Lexington Books, 1985.

Y. Amihud and H. Mendelson, ''Dealership Market: Market-Making with Inventory,'' *Journal of Financial Economics,* March 1980.

Y. Amihud and H. Mendelson, ''Asset Price Behavior in a Dealership Market,'' *Financial Analysts Journal,* May/June 1982.

W. Bagehot, ''The Only Game in Town,'' *Financial Analysts Journal,* March/April 1971.

A. Barnea and D. Logue, ''The Effect of Risk on the Market Maker's Spread,'' *Financial Analysts Journal,* November/December 1975.

G. Benston and R. Hagerman, ''Determinants of Bid-Asked Spreads in the Over-the-Counter Market,'' *Journal of Financial Economics,* December 1974.

B. Branch and W. Freed, ''Bid-Ask Spreads on the Amex and the Big Board,'' *Journal of Finance,* March 1977.

K. Cohen and R. Cyert, *Theory of the Firm,* second edition, Englewood Cliffs, N.J.: Prentice-Hall, 1975.

K. Cohen, S. Maier, R. Schwartz, and D. Whitcomb, ''The Impact of Designated Market Makers on Security Prices: II, Policy Proposals,'' *Journal of Banking and Finance,* November 1977.

K. Cohen, S. Maier, R. Schwartz, and D. Whitcomb, ''Market Makers and the Market Spread: A Review of Recent Literature,'' *Journal of Financial and Quantitative Analysis,* November 1979.

R. Conroy and R. Winkler, "Informational Differences Between Limit and Market Orders for a Market Maker," *Journal of Financial and Quantitative Analysis,* December 1981.

T. Copeland and D. Galai, "Information Effects on the Bid-Ask Spread," *Journal of Finance,* December 1983.

H. Demsetz, "The Cost of Transacting," *Quarterly Journal of Economics,* February 1968.

M. Garman, "Market Microstructure," *Journal of Financial Economics,* June 1976.

L. Glosten, "Components of the Bid-Ask Spread and the Statistical Properties of Transaction Prices," *Journal of Finance,* December 1987.

L. Glosten and L. Harris, "Estimating the Components of the Bid/Ask Spread," working paper, Northwestern University and University of Southern California, 1987.

L. Glosten and P. Milgrom, "Bid, Ask, and Transaction Prices in a Specialist Market with Heterogeneously Informed Traders," *Journal of Financial Economics,* March 1985.

N. Hakansson, A. Beja, and J. Kale, "On the Feasibility of Automated Market Making by a Programmed Specialist," *Journal of Finance,* March 1985.

J. Hamilton, "Competition, Scale Economies, and Transaction Cost in the Stock Market," *Journal of Financial and Quantitative Analysis,* December 1976.

T. Ho, "Dealer Market Structure: A Dynamic Competitive Equilibrium Model," working paper, New York University Graduate School of Business Administration, March 1984.

T. Ho and R. Macris, "Dealer Market Structure and Performance," in Amihud, Ho, and Schwartz (1985).

T. Ho and H. Stoll, "On Dealer Markets Under Competition," *Journal of Finance,* May 1980.

T. Ho and H. Stoll, "Optimal Dealer Pricing Under Transaction and Return Uncertainty," *Journal of Financial Economics,* March 1981.

T. Ho and H. Stoll, "The Dynamics of Dealer Markets Under Competition," *Journal of Finance,* September 1983.

D. Logue, "Market Making and the Assessment of Market Efficiency," *Journal of Finance,* March 1975.

E. Mildenstein and H. Schleef, "The Optimal Pricing Policy of a Monopolistic Marketmaker in the Equity Market," *Journal of Finance,* March 1983.

S. Smidt, "Which Road to an Efficient Stock Market: Free Competition or Regulated Monopoly?" *Financial Analysts Journal,* September/October 1971.

G. Stigler, "Public Regulation of the Securities Markets," *Journal of Business,* April 1964.

H. Stoll, "The Supply of Dealer Services in Security Markets," *Journal of Finance,* September 1978a.

H. Stoll, "The Pricing of Security Dealer Services: An Empirical Study of NASDAQ Stocks," *Journal of Finance,* September 1978b.

H. Stoll, "Alternative Views of Market Making," in Amihud, Ho, and Schwartz (1985).

H. Stoll, *The New York Stock Exchange Specialist System,* Monograph Series in Finance and Economics, Salomon Brothers Center for the Study of Financial Institutions, New York University Graduate School of Business Administration, 1985b.

H. Stoll, "Inferring the Components of the Bid-Ask Spread: Theory and Empirical Tests," working paper, Owen Graduate School of Management. Vanderbilt University, 1987.

S. Tinic, "The Economics of Liquidity Services," *Quarterly Journal of Economics,* February 1972.

S. Tinic and R. West, "Competition and the Pricing of Dealer Services in the Over-the-Counter Stock Market," *Journal of Financial and Quantitative Analysis,* June 1972.

S. Tinic and R. West, "Marketability of Common Stocks in Canada and the USA: A Comparison of Agent Versus Dealer Dominated Markets," *Journal of Finance,* June 1974.

P. Venkatesh and R. Chiang, "Information Asymmetry and the Dealer's Bid-Ask Spread: A Case Study of Earnings and Dividend Announcements," *Journal of Finance,* December 1986.

chapter *13*

Market Architecture

This chapter continues our investigation into the effect of the trading system on market performance. It considers (1) the spatial consolidation of orders, (2) the temporal consolidation of orders, (3) the technology used to display orders and to execute trades, and (4) price stabilization.

Analysis of these market design features underscores the functions of an equity market: the provision of immediacy, price stabilization, and price discovery. It also calls attention to the complexity of the markets. Again we see that trading involves the use of strategy by market participants. We find that the provision of marketability services involves the supply of public goods–type services. We establish that market structure does not involve a simple choice between a monopoly model and a competitive model, but rather that complex tradeoffs are involved. Also of concern is the *static efficiency* of the market (which is reflected in the relationship between the price of marketability services and the cost of providing the services) and the *dynamic efficiency* of the market (which is manifest in the development and implementation of new trading technologies).

First the chapter deals with the spatial consolidation of the order flow for exchange based trading. We define the issue and its relationship to interdealer and intermarket competition. The juxtaposition of two types of markets is next considered: the market for the securities that are traded and the market for marketability services. After discussing the price priority trading rule and order exposure, we examine the consolidation of the order flow in relation to five considerations: (1) the maintenance of secondary priority rules, (2) the consolidation of information concerning the order flow, (3) the public goods nature of various services provided by a securities exchange, (4) the diverse needs of diverse traders, and (5) fairness. The section ends with an overview of the issues involved.

The next section analyzes the temporal consolidation (time batching) of orders. The benefits of temporal consolidation are (1) reduction of operating costs, (2) advantages for price discovery, (3) advantages for price stabilization, (4) mitigation of market impact effects, (5) insurance against transaction price uncertainty, and (6) advantages to traders of transacting at the same price in a given trading session. The costs of temporal consolidation are (1) limited accessibility to the market, (2) informational disadvantages, (3) transaction uncertainty, and (4) increased price volatility that can attend the use of reservation prices in trading. The section ends with an overview of the issues involved.

The third section turns to the display of orders, the execution of trades, and the development of an electronic system to facilitate these processes. A scenario for an electronic market is presented, and the advantages of such a system are considered. The final section then considers the stabilization of prices, both under normal conditions and when the market is under stress.

SPATIAL CONSOLIDATION OF THE ORDER FLOW

The Issue

The term *interdealer competition* applies when the order flow for an individual stock is split between two or more dealers in OTC-type trading, or between two or more market centers (a national and/or regional exchange, the in-house market of a broker/dealer firm, an electronic trading system such as Instinet, and so on). The term *intermarket competition* applies to the broader competition between market centers (for listing, for trading in different products, and so forth). This section contrasts the advantages of interdealer competition with the benefits obtained from spatially consolidating the order flow for exchange listed securities.[1]

Spatial consolidation is not an all-or-nothing feature of an exchange based system; rather, a continuum of possibilities exists. At one extreme, a highly fragmented system may consist of a number of separate market centers linked only by the profit motivated behavior of arbitrageurs. At the other extreme, a highly consolidated system may be based on a single limit order book to which all orders must be directed.

---

[1]The OTC-type competitive dealer market is, by its very nature, a fragmented trading system.

The U.S. equity markets lie between the two extremes. An order transmitted to an exchange is directed to the post of the specialist firm to which the stock has been assigned. The order may be placed on the book, or execute against the book, or execute against the specialist's own quotes. It may also execute against a counterpart order held by a floor trader in the crowd by the specialist's post, or it may be directed to a specialist's post on another exchange if the stock is cross-listed. The order may also be executed in the third market (by being sent to a dealer firm that is not a member of a stock exchange). Or, if it is a large order, it may be negotiated off-board in the upstairs market and then brought to the trading floor as a put through. Large orders are also transacted in the fourth market on systems such as Instinet. If the stock was listed on an exchange after April 26, 1979, it can also be executed in-house by a broker/dealer firm that is a member of an exchange.

In the years following the Securities Acts Amendments of 1975, there was much debate about the extent to which the order flow should be consolidated. Some voices were raised in support of a *consolidated limit order book* (CLOB). Others, who focused on competition in the provision of dealer services, called for a move in the opposite direction—a relaxation of the off-board trading prohibition rules that force the order flow to the exchanges.[2]

The off-board rule that drew most of the attention is *NYSE Rule 390*, which requires that exchange members execute customer orders for exchange listed stocks on an exchange. On July 18, 1980, coverage of Rule 390 was restricted by the institution of SEC Rule 19c-3, which freed member firms to make off-board markets in issues listed on an exchange after April 26, 1979. The legislative history is discussed further in Chapter 14; here we consider the economic issues involved in the consolidation/fragmentation debate.

The Two Markets Conundrum

Most people favor competition in the provision of dealer services, and between the buyers and sellers of a stock. Therefore, why the debate? The reason is that the two types of competition are, to a large extent, incompatible. If all orders for a stock are consolidated in one market so as to maximize the competitive interaction of traders in the stock, there cannot simultaneously be adequate competition between dealers in the provision of marketability services for that stock. Alternatively, if there is interdealer competition, the order flow must be fragmented to some extent.

---

[2]For a discussion of the issues involved, see Sametz (1979).

The root of the problem is that there is not one market, but two—the market for the security that is traded and the market for the provision of dealer services. Consequently, two different prices are of concern—the price of the stock that is traded and the price of marketability services. A tradeoff exists because enhancing the competitive interaction of participants in one of these markets necessarily weakens the competitive interaction of participants in the other market.

In the past, the fragmentation/consolidation debate has primarily focused on the desirability of having multiple dealers make markets for a single security. An alternative exists, however, for resolving the two markets conundrum: allow the order flow for individual stocks on the exchanges to remain consolidated, and rely on intermarket competition to keep the price of dealer services competitive. This alternative has become more apparent in recent years, particularly in the battle between the exchanges and the OTC for new listings.

The typical progression of a public corporation in the past has been for it first to trade OTC as it grew and matured, then for it to list on the Amex as it gained greater strength and visibility, and finally for it to list on the NYSE as it attained full stature and acceptability. Now, an increasing number of firms are remaining on the OTC in the belief that the competitive dealer market is a good market for their stocks and that the services provided by the exchanges are not worth the listing costs involved. How did this situation develop?

The NASD has directly confronted the exchange markets. It has done so by improving the quality of its NASDAQ system and by increasing the visibility of the stocks on its NASDAQ/NMS list.[3] Furthermore, as the quality of the NASDAQ/NMS stocks has become more widely recognized, the relative luster of an exchange listing has dimmed somewhat. Currently, the OTC market makers are giving the exchanges stiff competition.

How have the exchanges reacted? By developing new products and new trading technologies. The exchanges have also opened their doors to new members, lengthened trading hours, tightened their regulation of the specialists, and greatly improved their intermarket linkage systems. In short, the quality of the exchange markets has itself improved.

The exchanges, however, have reacted to a broader competitive challenge than that provided by the OTC alone. The regional and national exchanges compete with each other. New approaches to market making have been developed, as illustrated by the emergence of *Instinet,* the electronic information dissemination and trading system. The globalization of trading has also strengthened competition in the marketplace. This has all had a profound impact on the provision of marketability services. The new

---

[3]See the discussion in Chapter 3.

intermarket competition has helped to keep the price of marketability services in line with the cost of providing the services. The benefits of intermarket competition do not end with price, however—competition has also motivated much of the technological change and innovation of recent years.

Thus interdealer competition may be recognized as being not the only way, or even the best way, of achieving a vigorous, efficient, and improving market system. Interdealer competition for the order flow of a specific security is of course desirable, all else equal; but, as is often the case in economics, all else is not equal.

The Effects of Consolidating the Order Flow

Price Priority and Order Exposure   Two major concerns about a fragmented order flow have been (1) that the price priority trading rule will be violated and (2) that orders will not be fully exposed to the market. The violation of the price priority rule is called *overreaching*. Overreaching may occur if all orders are not exposed to the market and thus if a new order cannot find the best counterpart order against which to execute. Overreaching may also occur if dealers/brokers provide in-house executions at inferior prices without their customers' knowing what the best prices are.

Price priority and order exposure are desirable from the viewpoint of both market efficiency and fairness. Cohen, Conroy, and Maier (1985) have shown analytically that the violation of price priority in a fragmented system increases the thinness of the market and hence results in greater price volatility and larger bid-ask spreads. The exposure of orders in the market not only helps to prevent overreaching, but also encourages competing traders to improve their quotes.

The extent to which overreaching may occur in a fragmented market depends on the quality of intermarket linkages, on the existence of a reasonable order exposure rule, and on the effectiveness of market surveillance. Given today's electronic technology, there is no reason why price priority cannot be maintained in a fragmented system and, indeed, it does not appear that overreaching is currently a problem. Instead, the arguments for and against market fragmentation are more subtle. We turn next to five additional issues that are involved.

Secondary Priority Rules   A secondary priority trading rule specifies the sequence in which orders execute when they have been written at the same price (see Chapter 3). The most common secondary priority rule is *time priority* (the order which has been placed first, executes first). Other possible rules include *partial execution according to time priority* (for instance, after 200 shares of an order have executed, the remainder of the order goes to the end of the queue), *size priority* (the largest order executes first), and *random selection* (the particular order to transact next is selected by chance).

When quotes are posted at the same price in two or more market centers, the next order to execute depends on the market center to which a new counterpart market order happens to be transmitted. If it is not possible to predict which the next market will be, then the secondary priority rule implicitly imposed is one of random selection. If the market center can be predicted, then some other secondary priority rule is implicit in the prediction rule. The implicit rule may not be desirable, however. An advantage of having a consolidated trading system is that it enables the secondary priority rule to be specified explicitly.

Surprisingly, the desirability of imposing an orderly secondary priority rule has received little attention, either in its own right or in relation to the consolidation/fragmentation debate. One might expect, however, that such a rule would be important. It is desirable for a trading system to encourage market participants to place their orders on the books, rather than having them worked in the crowd or otherwise kept hidden as part of a gaming strategy. Larger limit order books are associated with bigger markets, and spreads are tighter and prices less volatile in bigger markets. If realistic prices are to be found, traders must come forth and state their trading propensities. The institution of an orderly secondary priority trading rule could increase the willingness of traders to do so.

No one has thus far shown analytically, however, what the best secondary trading priority rule might be. Not surprisingly, the most widely used rule is time priority. There may be advantages in a gaming situation to letting other players go first, and use of a time priority rule can help to counteract the undesirable tendency of traders to hold their orders back.[4] Furthermore, a trader who knows that the queue of orders at a price will be executed according to the time priority rule may try to beat the queue by increasing the order's bid price (if it is a buy order) or decreasing its ask (if it is a sell order). Without a time priority rule, the trader may be less likely to better the order's price and instead simply hope to get a lucky draw in the random selection when the next order arrives.

Cohen, Conroy, and Maier (1985) used computer simulation to analyze the relative desirability of a time priority rule vis-à-vis random selection. They found that time priority causes a reduction of the bid-ask spread and an increase in the probability that a limit order will execute within a given period of time. These authors concluded that adoption of a time priority rule improves the thickness and the quality of a market.

More extensive analysis is needed. It does appear, however, that some

---

[4]An offsetting incentive to trade quickly, of course, is when the order is motivated by informational change that the trader believes has not yet been fully reflected in market prices.

secondary priority rule is desirable. Such a rule can be instituted only if orders are consolidated in the trading system.

Consolidation of Floor Information   This book has emphasized that a major function of a trading system is to discover prices that are reasonable in relation to the underlying demand propensities of traders. Several major design features of a trading system are best understood in relation to the price discovery process—the special opening procedures of the exchanges, the imposition of trading halts after major informational change, market maker operations, and the extensive systems that have been instituted to provide rapid transmission of transaction prices, volume, and current quotes to market participants.

Floor information is disseminated on the consolidated transaction tape and consolidated quotations system. The physical gathering of orders in a market center and the congregation of traders on a trading floor also contribute to the consolidation of information. Geographic proximity helps traders sense the existence of orders away from the market quotes (for instance, there are indications of trading interest from the crowd by the specialist's post). Further, some information on market conditions may not be conveyed by current prices alone—the moods, facial expressions, and strength of voices of traders also signal a bullish or a bearish spirit.

The value of consolidating floor information may in part explain the well-known adage in the equity markets that "order flow attracts order flow." Traders receive more accurate price indications on which to base their orders from larger markets. Traders also receive better executions in consolidated markets because of the tighter spreads, less volatile prices, and more accurate prices that are set in larger markets.

The consolidation/fragmentation debate has, in the past, paid little attention to the fact that the consolidation of information affects the efficiency of the price discovery process. In part this may be explained by a failure to appreciate adequately that price discovery is indeed a major function of an equity market. Whatever the reason, the omission is critical. Fragmentation of the order flow to bolster interdealer competition could impair the quality of the market by obscuring the informational content of the order flow.

The Public Goods Aspect of Marketability Services   Loaves of bread purchased in a supermarket are private goods. To consume the bread, one has to buy it, and one gets what one pays for. Further, the bread one person consumes is not available for another's consumption. This is not the case with public goods. With a public good, the quantity available for one person is available for all. Consumption of the public good by one person does not preclude others from consuming it. Further, the public good is available to an individual, regardless of the individual's willingness to pay for it.

Goods are *public goods* for the reason that the market technology does not exist (or else is too expensive to use) to prevent people who do not pay for a good from consuming it. The lighthouse in a harbor is a classic example of a public good—all passing ships can see it and receive the information that its presence signals.[5] A city park is another example of a public good—everyone can enter the park free of charge.[6]

The marketability services of an exchange based trading system include both private and public goods. Immediacy is a private good; price stabilization and price discovery are public goods. The trader (and only that trader) who demands immediacy obtains it and pays for it by buying at the higher ask price or by selling at the lower bid. Price stabilization and discovery differ from the provision of immediacy, because neither of these marketability services relates to the execution of one trade per se. If price movements are stabilized, they are stabilized for all traders. If prices closer to theoretically desirable equilibrium values are found by the system, all traders benefit from the accuracy of the information that is thereby conveyed.

Protection against exploitation, fraud, manipulation, and other violations of the rules of the game is another public good–type service. This service is provided by the exchanges' stock watch and market surveillance systems. Like military defense, market surveillance protects investors as a group. Whether surveillance is paid for by a commission based on trading activity or by a listing fee, consumers of the service cannot individually buy a little more or a little less as they wish. The exchange provides just one amount of market surveillance, and that amount is for the benefit of all.

Individual traders do not take the public goods aspects of marketability services into account when making their private trading decisions. If an individual believes his or her order will receive a better execution in some market center B than in some other market center A, the order will be transmitted to market center B even if provision of the public goods–type services is superior in market center A. Problems could arise, however: if enough individuals were to transmit orders to market center B instead of A, the flow of orders to market center A would decline, and the quality of the public goods–type services would deteriorate, to the detriment of all.

Consider the following to see how this situation might occur. Let market center A be the major trading arena for a stock, and let market center B be a small system that bases its prices on the prices set in market center A. Assume that the two market centers are equally efficient in the

---

[5]A transmitter and a jamming device could be used in place of the lighthouse, however, and the signal could be sold as a private good to ships that paid a subscription fee.

[6]A wall could be put around the park, and entrance tickets sold at a gate. This alternative, which would make the park a private good, is generally not acceptable to the body politic.

production of the private good (immediacy), that market center A is producing an optimal amount of the public good (price stabilization, price discovery, and market protection), and that market center B does not attempt to produce the public good.

Let market center B extend the following guarantee to traders: a market order will execute in market center B at the best price established in market center A, and a limit order will execute whenever an order at the limit price executes in market center A. Several electronic trading systems now offer comparable guarantees. A market center must, of course, be willing to commit capital to the provision of dealer services to support the offer.

The customer who directs an order to market B benefits from the accuracy of the price established in market A, and from the protection offered by the stock watch and market surveillance systems of market A. In addition, the limit order trader in market center B has the opportunity for faster execution (because the queue of orders may be shorter than in market A). Furthermore, because market B does not provide the public goods–type services that A provides, it may be able to operate at lower cost and accordingly may charge lower commissions than market A.

Because of market center B's offer, traders individually have a private incentive to send their orders to that market. Collectively, however, traders cannot benefit. We have assumed that market A is as efficient as B in the production of the private good, and traders cannot on average achieve faster execution of their limit orders by jumping to a shorter queue.[7] On the contrary, traders collectively pay a price for directing their orders to market center B: market center A provides less of the public good because it receives less revenue as a consequence of its reduced order flow.

No thought has thus far been given to how decisions regarding the public goods aspects of marketability services might be made in a fragmented system. Indeed, only scant recognition has even been taken of the fact that, if the market were to fragment, the provision of the public goods aspects of marketability would be impaired. Unfortunately, a public good will not be supplied in socially optimal amounts unless a collective decision is made by the body politic concerning how much of it to produce and how much to charge for it.

The Diverse Needs of Different Traders   A market system may have to be fragmented to some extent because different traders operate differently in the marketplace. Size is the primary distinction between traders in this regard:

---

[7]Yogi Berra is quoted as having once said, "No one goes there anymore; it's too crowded." A corollary to Berra's law is of equivalent validity: everyone is now on the new queue; it's shorter.

1. Small retail customers are most likely to leave their limit orders on the order book or to have their market orders executed as quickly and inexpensively as possible through electronic systems such as OARS, DOT, SCOREX, and AUTOPER.
2. Intermediate size orders are commonly worked by traders on the exchange floor.
3. Very large orders are typically negotiated off the floor in the upstairs market.

Market fragmentation is a cost that, to some extent, must be incurred to obtain the operational flexibility a system should have. At present, achieving an effective integration of the diverse needs of diverse traders is a challenge the designers of a trading system must continue to face.

Fairness   A trading system must be viewed as fair by the traders who participate in the market. This largely matters from the viewpoint of equity, but the importance of the issue extends further. A disgruntled subset of traders might shy away from a market if they believe that others consistently obtain superior executions. As a consequence, the price of shares would be depressed, trading volume would be reduced, and the manifestations of a thin market (wider spreads, more volatile prices, and less accurate prices) would become more apparent. These effects could then cause other traders to reduce their participation in the market, and a further decline in the quality of the marketplace would then ensue.

Does the consolidation of orders result in a fairer, more orderly system? For the most part (1) rules that cannot be imposed in a fragmented system may be enforced in a consolidated system, (2) market surveillance is more effective (and less costly) in a consolidated system, and (3) consolidation of the order flow facilitates the access of all participants to market information and ensures the broad market exposure of all orders.

Putting the Pieces Together

The arguments for and against market consolidation fall into three groups:

1. The effect of consolidation on the maintenance of price priority and on order exposure
2. The effect of consolidation on the orderliness, efficiency, and fairness of the system in aggregate
3. The effect of consolidation on interdealer and intermarket competition

The first set of arguments (price priority and order exposure) are essentially nonissues. There is no reason, given computer technology, why price priorities could not be maintained and orders effectively exposed to the market in a fragmented system.

The second set of arguments (orderliness, efficiency, and fairness) pertain to the desirability of consolidating the order flow for a specific security. Of the five factors considered in this regard, consolidation is desirable for four (institution of an orderly secondary priority trading rule, consolidation of floor information, the public goods nature of marketability services, and fairness), and fragmentation is desirable for one (servicing the diverse needs of different traders). The weight of the arguments in this set would seem to favor consolidation of the order flow.

The third set of arguments (interdealer and intermarket competition) is crucial. Interdealer competition is, all else equal, of value. However, such competition requires fragmentation of the order flow for a stock, and fragmentation is not desirable in light of the second set of arguments. For this reason, we should look as much as possible to *intermarket* competition to keep the price of marketability services in line with the cost of providing the services. Furthermore, intermarket competition is an effective spur for technological change, whereas interdealer competition, for the most part, is not.

Intermarket competition has emerged in recent years as the primary force behind the increased efficiency of the equity markets. It may, however, be most effective when combined with interdealer competition. Such is the case when the order flow, for instance, is divided between the national and regional exchanges for cross-listed stocks. If so, the fragmented order flow that is a necessary part of interdealer competition may be justified by the technological change that attends effective intermarket competition. Dividing the order flow between the NYSE and the Pacific Stock Exchange (PSE), for instance, may have reduced spreads somewhat (because a specialist on the PSE is making a market in a stock along with a specialist on the NYSE). More importantly, the institution of the SCOREX automated order handling system on the PSE prodded the NYSE to develop its SuperDot automated small order routing system.

TEMPORAL CONSOLIDATION OF THE ORDER FLOW

Call Market Versus Continuous Market Trading

We now turn to the temporal consolidation of the order flow in call market–type trading. Call markets are not well known in the United States but are prevalent in Europe and in some countries such as Israel that have patterned their systems after the European exchanges.

Temporal consolidation, like spatial consolidation, is not an all-or-nothing feature of a trading system. The Paris Bourse and the Brussels

Bourse have pure call market systems. Markets such as the Frankfurt and Vienna stock exchanges are call market systems that allow continuous trading in a *call back* period that follows the call. The NYSE is a continuous trading system, but its opening procedure resembles a call market. The Tokyo Stock Exchange is a continuous trading system, but both a morning and an afternoon session are opened and closed with call market trading for the largest stocks on that exchange.

Call markets typically have one or two "calls" per stock, per daily trading session. In principle, however, calls could occur several times a day, one per hour, or even more frequently if desired. Some consider a continuous market the limiting case of a periodic call because, if the order flow is taken to be exogenously given, continuous trading is approached as the calls become increasingly frequent.

Behaviorally, however, a call market operates very differently than a continuous market, and traders write their orders differently in a call (see Chapter 8). The salient feature of a call market is that orders are batched over time for periodic execution and then are all executed at the same price. The batching procedure itself arranges for buyers and sellers to meet in time. A designated market maker (dealer or specialist) has not, therefore, been included in the call market systems currently in existence.

Quotes to give traders guidance as to what market conditions might be are generally not posted before the call. This means that traders have to write their orders with less knowledge of market conditions (which may change appreciably from call to call). The lack of quotes (and hence the absence of a bid-ask spread) in call market trading also means that traders cannot purchase transactions certainty by paying the bid-ask spread.[8] That is, traders must accept some probability that their orders will not execute (a maximum or minimum price limit may be hit), and they must accept the uncertainty of not knowing the price at which they will transact until the market is called.

Effects of the Trading System on the Order Flow

The order placement decision of a trader in a call market environment is contrasted with the trader's decision in a continuous market environment in Chapter 8. We begin here by reviewing the analysis. Each order submitted to the call is written in ignorance of what the clearing price will be, but in recognition of the fact that the order will execute at the clearing price

---

[8]Call markets do accept orders that are referred to as *market orders*. These orders execute at the call market price, as long as trades are achieved at the call. Because trading is typically suspended in call markets if a price limit is hit (as discussed in Chapter 12, the price limits are the previous call price plus and minus x percent), a market order in the system is equivalent to a limit order written at the maximum or minimum price limit.

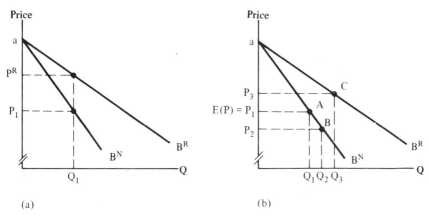

Figure 13.1   Contrast of an investor's order placement decision in call market and continuous market environments. (a) At the price P_1 the investor wants to buy Q_1 shares; the reservation price for Q_1 shares is P^R. (b) The optimal limit order to submit to a call market is illustrated by point C; the optimal limit order to submit to a continuous market is illustrated by point B.

as long as the order price is better than the clearing price. Investors therefore reduce the chance of their orders' not executing by writing their orders at reservation prices. This system contrasts with the continuous market, in which traders price their orders in accordance with their normal demand curves.

The downward sloping curves labeled B^N and B^R in Figure 13.1(a) show, respectively, the normal buy curve and the reservation buy curve of the investor. The normal curve shows that if the investor knows the market clearing price will be P_1, he or she will want to buy Q_1 shares. The reservation curve shows that the reservation price for Q_1 shares is P^R. To structure the call and continuous systems so as to obtain a meaningful *ceteris paribus* comparison under transaction price uncertainty:

1. Let the individual's buy curves and the clearing price he or she expects be the same for the two market regimes.
2. Let the expected price be E(P) with E(P) = P_1, and allow for a small variance of price around E(P).
3. Assume that the order submitted to the continuous market is placed on a limit order book, as in the *limit order only* model discussed in Chapter 8.

Thus we can take transaction price uncertainty to be the same in the two trading regimes in the sense that the probability of the clearing price achieving any particular value or better in the call market equals the probability of a limit order executing at that price in the continuous market.[9]

[9]Recall that the investor in the continuous market realizes an execution if price falls enough in the market for his or her order to set the market quote and if a counterpart market order then arrives.

For this scenario, a point such as B on the normal buy curve in Figure 13.1(b) represents an optimal limit order to submit to the continuous market, and a point such as C on the reservation buy curve represents an optimal limit order to submit to the call market.

Contrasting points A and B, we see that transaction price uncertainty in the continuous market has caused the investor to increase the size of the order and to lower the order's price somewhat. This occurs because with transaction price uncertainty, the investor may submit an order to buy at a lower price solely on the chance that price will be less than E(P) and that a desirable execution will be realized. Or, in continuous trading, the investor may under different circumstances decrease the order size and increase its price. If the intercept parameter is sufficiently above E(P), the investor is eager to trade. In this case, rather than gambling on the price being better than expected, he or she will raise the price of the order (and decrease the order's size) to increase the probability that the order will indeed execute.

Contrasting points A and C, we see that transaction price uncertainty in a call market has caused the investor to increase both the size and the price of the order. Unlike the continuous market, this is always the case. The price increase is attributable to the order being picked from the reservation buy curve rather than from the normal buy curve. The intuitive explanation for the increased size of the order is the following. The protection the investor gains against transaction price uncertainty by placing the order at the (higher) reservation price allows the order to be moved down the reservation buy curve (price is lowered somewhat and the share size increased), so as to yield more consumer surplus if the clearing price turns out to be lower than expected.[10]

Having contrasted the orders an individual would alternatively submit to a continuous market and to a call market, we can now show how temporally consolidating the order flow affects the market's aggregate buy and sell order curves. The process of aggregating orders to obtain the market buy curve is illustrated in Figure 13.2 with reference to the normal buy curve.[11] Figure 13.2(a) shows the normal buy order curves for three different traders. The point identified on each of the curves shows the limit order that each individual would write given the expected clearing price, the variance around the price, and a continuous market regime. Figure 13.2(b) shows the aggregation of these orders. At P_1, only the first trader's order executes and the size of that order is Q_1. At P_2, the second trader's

[10]For further discussion, see Ho, Schwartz, and Whitcomb (1985).

[11]The individual orders, of course, execute sequentially as they arrive at the continuous market, and for that reason aggregating these orders is not of interest in and of itself. The aggregation shows the price and transaction volume that would be established in a call market if the change in the trading system had no effect on the order flow.

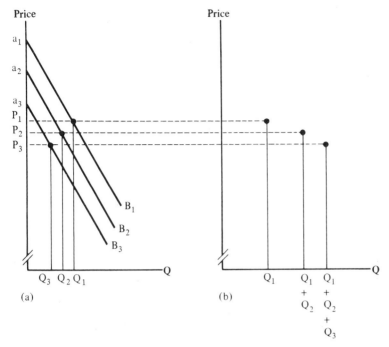

Figure 13.2 Aggregation of individual orders to obtain the market buy curve. (a) Individual buy order curves and order points. (b) Aggregation of individual order points.

order also executes and the aggregate order quantity is $Q_1 + Q_2$. At P_3, the third trader's order executes as well, and the aggregate order quantity is $Q_1 + Q_2 + Q_3$. Individual sell orders are aggregated by a similar process. When the aggregation is done for a large number of traders, the process results in a set of market buy and sell order curves.

Now consider the aggregation of buy orders submitted to the call regime. To highlight the effect of the system, we accentuate the impact it has on the order flow by taking the variance of the transaction price about its mean to be very small. The aggregation process is the same, but the buy orders themselves are different. Specifically, (1) the buy prices are greater than $E(P)$, and (2) orders written at prices in the neighborhood immediately above $E(P)$ are for only a small number of shares.

Buy orders are not submitted to the call market at a price less than $E(P)$ because we have assumed the transaction price is distributed sufficiently tightly around $E(P)$. An order is submitted at a price close to $E(P)$ only if the vertical difference between B^N and B^R is small at $E(P)$. Visual inspection of Figure 13.1 shows that this vertical distance is less, the closer $E(P)$ is to the price intercept a of the demand curves. Consequently, an

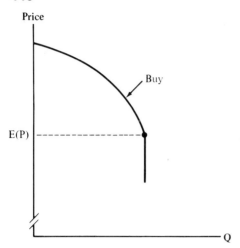

Figure 13.3 Buy order function for a call market.

investor who submits an order at a reservation price only slightly above E(P) submits an order for a small number of shares.[12]

Now assume a large (but bounded) set of buyers, all of whom view the same mean and variance of the transaction price. Let the buyers be distributed according to the price intercept parameter, a, of their buy curves.[13] Let each buyer submit one order. Buyers for whom $a_i - E(P)$ is large write an order at a relatively high price and for a relatively large number of shares; buyers for whom $a_i - E(P)$ is small write an order at a price close to E(P), and the order is for a relatively small number of shares. Aggregating these buy orders according to the procedure depicted by Figure 13.2 gives the buy order function for the call market. This is the curve labeled *Buy* in Figure 13.3.

The important characteristic of the market buy curve is that it becomes increasingly inelastic as price decreases in the neighborhood immediately above E(P). As the price is lowered, more investors' orders are included in the aggregate demand for shares, but, as we have seen, the share size of the marginal orders becomes very small.[14]

Assume that the distribution of sellers is symmetric with the distribution of buyers. That is, for every i^{th} buyer with a specific $a_i - E(P)$, there exists a jth seller with an $E(P) - a_j$ of identical magnitude. The resulting market buy and sell curves are labeled *Buy* and *Sell* in Figure 13.4. Placing a mirror on the horizontal line at E(P) shows that the sell

---

[12]This assumes, of course, that the buy curves are not highly elastic.

[13]For simplicity, assume the slope of the buy order curve is the same for all buyers.

[14]With a *bounded* distribution of investors, the number of investors submitting buy orders as price falls in the range above E(P) cannot increase rapidly enough to reverse the effect of the size of each trader's order becoming smaller. See Ho, Schwartz, and Whitcomb (1985).

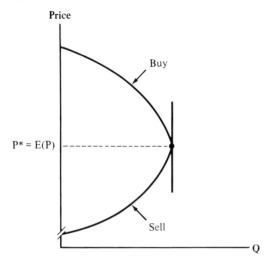

Figure 13.4 For symmetrical distributions of buy and sell orders, the call market clearing price P* equals the expected clearing price E(P).

curve is a mirror image of the buy curve around the line at E(P). This is because in this example the distributions of buyers and sellers are symmetric.

For the symmetrical distributions, the market clearing price, P*, equals E(P), as shown in Figure 13.4. There is, however, no reason for the distributions of buyers and sellers to be symmetric. Figure 13.5 shows an alternative configuration in which the buy orders more than offset the comparable sell orders [because the values of $a_i - E(P)$ tend to be larger than the counterpart values of $E(P) - a_j$]. In Figure 13.5, the clearing price,

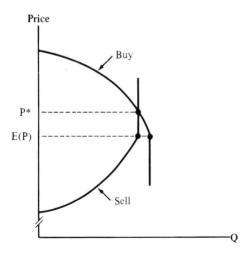

Figure 13.5 For asymmetrical distributions of buy and sell orders, the call market clearing price P* does not equal the expected clearing price E(P).

P*, is greater than E(P). If buyers and sellers are alternatively distributed so that the sell orders more than offset the buy orders, then P* is less than E(P). This demonstration is also made in Chapter 9 (where the relationship between a clearing price and an equilibrium price is considered).

The call market system affects the individual orders, but not the clearing price if buyers and sellers are symmetrically distributed (with regard to the intercept parameter of their buy/sell curves) and if the traders have homogeneous and unbiased expectations of the clearing price [that is, if E(P) is indeed the equilibrium price]. Because these conditions do not generally hold, the clearing price generally differs from its theoretical Walrasian value in the call market, as indeed it does in continuous trading. Further, the fact that the market's aggregate buy and sell order functions are inelastic in the neighborhood of E(P) has an interesting implication that is discussed later.

Having sketched the broad differences between call market and continuous market trading, we can now consider the advantages and disadvantages of time batched trading vis-à-vis a continuous market regime. We do this in the next two subsections.

The Benefits of Temporal Consolidation

Operating Costs   Substantial economies can be realized from batching orders and clearing them out at the same price, and a call market is considerably less expensive to operate than a continuous market system.

- The call process takes less time. The clearing price can typically be found for a stock in a matter of minutes, after which traders turn their attention to the next stock. In contrast, trading continues for a stock as long as the market is open in a continuous trading system.
- All orders are executed simultaneously in call market trading, and the cost of doing so is not appreciably affected by the size of the order flow per se. In continuous trading, counterpart orders are executed as they cross, and operating costs do increase with the size of the order flow.
- All trades are made at the same price at a call, and a specific counterparty to each trade does not exist. Brokerage houses, therefore, need clear only net transactions, not gross transactions, on a trade-by-trade basis.
- Because all trades are at the same price, fewer errors are made; this further facilitates subsequent clearing and settlement processes.

Immediacy   Because the time of each call is predetermined, the orders of counterpart traders can meet in time without the services of a dealer or the posting of limit orders. There is no bid-ask spread in call market trading.

Price Discovery   A third advantage of temporally batching orders concerns price discovery. Price discovery is more efficient when orders are consolidated spatially and may be more efficient when they are consolidated temporally. That is, if the information set is sufficiently constant over a trading interval, underlying demand propensities and market conditions are best assessed by aggregating all orders rather than by dealing with them one at a time as they arrive on the market.

Price Stabilization   The fourth advantage is that time batching orders also stabilizes price (for a given order flow). To see this, assume a set of traders write their orders before the start of a trading session. If the orders are executed sequentially as they arrive in a continuous market regime, the transaction price fluctuates according to the specific sequence in which the orders happen to arrive. If a series of buys happen to arrive in succession, the prices of the last trades in the sequence are relatively high (the sellers are happy but the buyers are not). Alternatively, if a series of sells happens to arrive in succession, the prices of the last trades are relatively low (the buyers are happy, but the sellers are not). Consequently, the price realized by any trader depends not only on the underlying market conditions, but also on when in the sequence of orders the trader's order happens to arrive. Sequencing risk, as a source of price instability, is partially eliminated in call market trading.

The Market Impact Effect   No trader wants to be large in relation to the other side of the market. The reason, as we have seen in Chapter 10, is related to the *market impact effect*—a big buyer facing a thin market on the sell side can push price up, and a big seller facing a thin market on the buy side can push price down. The fifth advantage of call market trading is that time batching reduces the market impact of individual orders, because an order of any given size is less significant when it is temporally consolidated with other orders.

Insurance Against Transaction Price Uncertainty   The sixth benefit of time batching orders is that an investor can obtain protection from transaction price uncertainty by submitting reservation prices to the market. The higher reservation buy prices and lower reservation sell prices give investors more assurance that their orders will indeed execute. Because each investor transacts at the call price, not at the price of his or her own order, the assurance is obtained at minimal personal cost.

One Price for All   Chapter 9 suggests that stocks do not have intrinsic values, but rather that prices are set in the marketplace. As such, prices should reflect broad market conditions, and these conditions are the same for all traders. Therefore, given the information set, price should be the same for all traders.[15] This is not the case in a continuous market regime. With continuous trading, traders can do little about the random sequencing of orders (except to understand that every price change is not attributable to news). Nevertheless, the trader who happens to have bought at the high for the trading session or to have sold at the low will not be pleased with the outcome. The seventh benefit of call market trading is that all trades are made at the same price.

The Disadvantages of Temporal Consolidation

Accessibility to the Market   Investors can trade in a continuous market whenever they wish during the trading day. In a call market, they can trade only at those times when the market is called (typically once or twice per day). Therefore, access to the call market is limited.[16]

Time is of the essence in trading when (1) the trade is motivated by informational change, (2) the trader is attempting to arbitrage price movements in the same stock or for related securities, and (3) the trading decision made with respect to one security is related to an execution that has been, or may be, realized for another security.

With regard to informational change, the early recipients of news are clearly disadvantaged by the call market arrangement. Nevertheless, trading might be fairer and more orderly if traders were not given continuous (and therefore instantaneous) access to the market. The early recipients of news profit at the expense of the uninformed. To protect themselves from being exploited by informed traders, dealers and specialists set wider quotes than they otherwise would (see Chapter 12). Further, concern about the inequitable dissemination of news has resulted in various restrictions on insider trading. And, when informational change is substantial, trading is commonly halted in a continuous market.

With regard to arbitrage trading, floor traders and other professionals might believe that profits can be made by exploiting short period price movements in continuous trading. If so, these professionals would be disadvantaged by a change to time batched trading. The short period price

---

[15]The only justification for price differing for different traders as their orders execute sequentially in a continuous trading regime would be if such a process itself enables more accurate prices to be discovered. But this is not necessarily the case (order flow constant, better prices may be discovered with batched trading).

[16]Accessibility is different from immediacy. Traders do not always have access to a continuous trading system (the market is closed overnight, on weekends, and for holidays). Immediacy refers to the ability of buyers and sellers to meet quickly when the market is open.

movements themselves, however, underscore the inefficiency of continuous trading, which argues in favor of time batching.

Arbitrage between securities is not riskless when transactions cannot be made instantaneously, and with limited access to the market, transactions cannot be made in quick succession in two different stocks. Because arbitrage transactions between securities improve the quality of pricing in the markets, the extent to which these transactions are curtailed by limited accessibility in call market trading is indeed a disadvantage of the system.

Limited accessibility to the market is, for the same reason, costly with regard to other interdependent trading decisions. Call markets trade the list of stocks sequentially (typically in alphabetical order). It is therefore not possible for a buy or a sell decision for a stock higher on the list to be based on the result of trading in a stock lower on the list. For instance, if an investor wants to sell Xerox and buy American Airlines and the market for American Airlines shares is called first, the size of the investor's purchase cannot be related to the price realized from the sale in one round of trading.

The Dissemination of Floor Information Traders present on the floor of a call market hear prices called out and have an opportunity to state the specific number of shares they wish to transact at each price. Consequently, they buy or sell the precise number of shares desired. For such traders call markets imply no informational disadvantage vis-à-vis continuous trading.

This is not the case for traders who are not present on the exchange floor. These traders give their instructions to brokers. Typically they submit a single order (one price and one quantity) rather than a complete demand curve, as discussed here and in Chapter 8. For these traders, the problem associated with call market trading is that they have no advance indication of what the next price will be because quotes are not posted in call market trading.

The most difficult part of trading is finding the price at which to open a market after it has been closed for a period of time. It is then easier to track the price as trading progresses and new quotes and transaction prices are recorded. This is what the continuous market does: it finds an opening price and then allows trading to continue. Traders still have to shoot at a moving target, but at least they have a target to shoot at. In call markets, traders off the floor have far less knowledge of current market conditions. To date, this limitation has remained one of the most fundamental problems with the call market system.

Transaction Uncertainty The posting of quotes in continuous trading gives traders more than information. The posted quotes of some traders give other traders an option that does not exist in call market trading: trades can be made with a high degree of certainty at the market quotes.[17] The inability to provide this service is a disadvantage of call market trading.

The Reservation Price Effect The submission of reservation prices to the market has an aggregate effect that no individual trader takes into account: if any price uncertainty at all exists in the market, this order placement strategy itself contributes to the volatility of the transaction price. To see this, consider whether or not it is possible for the variance of price around its mean, $E(P)$, to be arbitrarily small.

Allowing for any amount of uncertainty (no matter how small) about the clearing price provides all the incentive investors in a call market need to write their orders in relation to reservation buy and sell curves (as discussed in relation to spatial consolidation of the order flow, and as reflected in Figures 13.4 and 13.5). When orders are so written, the market buy and sell curves are inelastic in the neighborhood of the clearing price.

The inelasticity of the market curves implies that any slight asymmetry between the buy and sell order functions has a magnified effect on the clearing price. Therefore, as the configuration of the buy and sell functions changes from call to call, the clearing price exhibits magnified fluctuations from call to call. Accordingly, investors do not expect the transaction price to be distributed tightly around $E(P)$.

Therefore, our supposition of minimal (but not nonexistent) variance for the transaction price is inconsistent with the transaction price behavior that such minimal variance would imply. The conclusion that a nonnegligible amount of price uncertainty must exist in call market trading when traders submit single orders to the market before the call follows. This volatility results from the order flow being endogenous to the trading system, and from the particular effect that existing call market arrangements have on the trading decision.

Balancing the Arguments

The temporal consolidation of the order flow in a call market has advantages that cannot be duplicated in a continuous system. This is particularly true with regard to operating costs and the fairness of all trades executing at the same price at any given market call. Time batching a given set of orders can also provide immediacy, stabilize price, mitigate the market impact of

---

[17]Order transmission is not instantaneous, and the quotes can change while the investor is communicating his or her market order to the exchange. However, the change is not likely to be large, because order transmission is rapid, and the affirmative obligation of the specialists keeps prices relatively stable for brief periods of time.

large orders, and facilitate the discovery of prices that are closer to Walrasian equilibrium values.

Furthermore, for an individual trader, the call market arrangement allows protection against transaction price uncertainty, because the trader can submit an order at a reservation price and trade at whatever clearing price is established on the market. If the order price is good enough (high enough for a buy or low enough for a sell), the order transacts and the trader receives some consumer surplus; if the order price is not good enough, the order does not transact (and at the market clearing price, the trader does not wish to transact).

Call market systems currently in operation are not, however, without their problems. Accessibility to the market is limited, there is no dissemination of floor information to traders away from the exchange, investors cannot purchase transactional certainty by submitting a market order and paying the spread, and the call market's impact on the order flow increases the volatility of the clearing price.

It may, however, be possible to reduce or even to eliminate the undesirable effects by proper design of a time batched trading system. Modern electronic technology in particular may contribute significantly to the efficiency of call market trading. The call market arrangement most closely approximates the theoretical Walrasian auction, and it is likely that desired Walrasian prices would be most successfully found in actual markets if the order flow were to be temporally consolidated. The next section discusses the possibility of overcoming the current disadvantages of call market trading with electronic technology.

THE USE OF ELECTRONIC TECHNOLOGY

The display of orders and execution of trades are interrelated design features of critical importance. There are two dimensions to order display: (1) the amount of information that is made available and (2) the way in which orders are displayed. Orders can be executed (1) by a matching process, (2) by an auction process, or (3) by negotiation. All of the processes involved in order display and trade execution can be facilitated by the use of computer technology.

Order Display

Various systems that are used to display orders are surveyed in Chapter 2. As is clear from the discussion in that chapter, the amount of information displayed varies considerably. For existing call markets, investors away from the trading floor receive little or no information at all until after the market has been called. In continuous trading, best market quotes are typically announced in dealer systems. This is true for both over-the-counter dealers and exchange specialists in the United States markets. Board systems typically display the full array of orders at the best and second best market quotes.[18] Order book systems such as that used by the Tokyo Stock Exchange display the complete limit order book to traders on the exchange floor. The Toronto Stock Exchange's and the Tokyo Stock Exchange's automated trading systems (CATS) also display the full array of orders to traders. In addition to the information disseminated by the market centers themselves, systems such as Instinet and AutEx also collect and distribute market information and indications of trading interest to subscribers.

Trading information can be made available by face to face contact, through telephone communication, by board display (the physical posting of prices and order sizes), and/or by electronic equipment. The use of electronic equipment for display purposes has increased dramatically in the last decade and will continue to do so.

Order Execution

Order execution can be handled in a variety of ways. Trades can be arranged by telephone (this is the standard way in dealer markets) or by direct person to person contact (this is a standard way in exchange trading) or can be executed automatically according to predetermined rules in an electronic system.

As noted, electronic technology has been used with much success for information display and order routing. The computer, however, has not for the most part been successfully applied to trade execution itself, although there are exceptions. Trade execution has been automated for (1) small orders (for instance, MAX, the Midwest Stock Exchange's automated execution system and SOES, the NASD's automated small order execution system), (2) issues that generally do not attract large orders (for instance, the CATS on the Toronto and Tokyo exchanges), and (3) a market that feeds off the prices set in another market (for instance, the Cincinnati Stock Exchange, which operates within a context provided by the NYSE). One of the more sophisticated systems to date is Instinet, which along with feeding off prices set in other market centers, allows participants to gain privacy on the screen and to negotiate their trades.

The Matching Process   Trades are executed by a matching process in call market trading. As discussed in the previous section, orders that accumulate

---

[18]Multiple prices are also revealed on the trading floor for cross-listed stocks in the Intermarket Trading System (ITS).

over a period of time are matched against each other and then executed at a price that clears all crossing orders. As noted, the opening procedure of continuous markets such as the NYSE and Amex is a matching process.

The Auction Process   Trades are executed by an auction process when quotes are posted in a continuous trading system. The U.S. exchange markets are auction systems. In the auction process, specialists, limit order traders, and floor traders compete with each other in the setting of quotes.[19] Trades are then made by market orders executing against the best quotes (the highest bids and the lowest asks).

The Negotiation Process   Trade execution is by negotiation when buyers and sellers meet (in person or by phone) and reach agreement about the terms of the trade. Because of the cost involved, the negotiation process is mainly confined to larger trades.

Small orders (one or a few round lots) are typically written with the minimum of instructions. The trader simply sets the type (market or limit), price, and size of the order and submits it to the market to be executed in a matching or auction system. To do more with a small order is prohibitively expensive.[20]

Orders of intermediate size (up to 10,000 shares) are commonly worked on the floor of an exchange. For the most part, this is a negotiation process. Floor traders generally reveal their orders piecemeal to each other and to the exchange specialist. They bargain for price and hold on to all or part of an order if they feel the counterpart bid is too low (or ask too high). At times a specialist stops a price (guarantees the execution) while the floor trader shops around for a better price.

Block trades (10,000 shares and more) are typically negotiated off the floor in the upstairs market. Although the specialist sometimes participates in the process, these deals are commonly arranged without the market maker. After agreement is reached, the orders are executed on an exchange as put throughs. Limit order protection is effectively (but not as yet officially) provided for orders on the book. That is, all limit orders at a price better than the negotiated price are included as part of the block.[21]

---

[19]In these auction systems, a quote must be good for at least 100 shares.

[20]A number of additional instructions can also be specified, however: execute at the opening, at the close, fill or kill, etc. (see Chapter 3).

[21]Assume the market for a stock is $50\frac{1}{4}$ bid, $50\frac{3}{8}$ ask, 200 by 300. If a trade is negotiated at 50, the 200 shares to buy on the book at $50\frac{1}{4}$ execute at 50. Failure to protect limit orders results in *gap pricing* (which is much the same as overreaching). In practice, gap prices occur only infrequently.

Electronic Trading

The power of the computer is well known. For years electronic technology has been used successfully by the airlines industry to provide flight information around the world and for making reservations. To book a flight, one gives an order to an agent, the order is entered in a computer, and a seat is reserved. The process is not as simple in the securities markets.

The factor that differentiates the airlines market from the equity markets is that the price of a plane seat is set in advance. The potential traveler learns the price and either accepts or rejects the offer. In the equity markets, the price of shares is determined as trading itself progresses, and prices continually change. Therefore, strategies are used in equity trading that are not relevant to a passenger reserving an airline seat.

Orders that do not require delicate treatment in the equity markets are called "no brainers." No strategy is used in working the no brainers. These orders can be handled by a rookie trader or even by an electronic trading system. As noted, electronic systems are now being used to execute small orders automatically and by markets (such as the Cincinnati Stock Exchange) that price off other markets (such as the NYSE). In electronic systems such as the Toronto and Tokyo CATS, the issues traded are small, and the order flow comes mainly from small traders. Therefore, CATS is not unduely perturbed by, and need not accommodate, the strategic actions of the big investors and traders.

Large orders are worked because their size in relation to the market creates price pressure (the market impact effect) and because improper order placement can result in unfavorable executions (the information signaling and options effects). To be successful, a computerized system would either have to reduce these undesirable effects sufficiently or else enable traders to cope with them as well electronically as they currently can via direct person to person communication.

Computerized systems by and large have mimicked existing markets. Continuous markets are prevalent in North America and the Far East, and the computerized systems developed in these countries have been based on the principle of continuous trading (for example, the Cincinnati Exchange's NSTS, the Toronto and Tokyo exchanges' CATS, and Intex's computerized system for trading futures contracts). Little thought appears to have been given to an alternative possibility: computerized call market trading.

Speculation About an Electronic Call Market

An electronic call can best be discussed in relation to a specific model. For this purpose, assume that:

1. The market is called once per hour for actively traded issues and less frequently for less actively traded issues.
2. Orders can be accepted and stored in the system at any time.
3. A short period (perhaps five minutes) before each call, the array of stored orders is displayed to all traders who have subscribed to the call's order information system. An indicated clearing price is also displayed by the system.
4. Traders can enter orders piecemeal or all at once as the market forms during the brief precall period.
5. Specialists play an active role in the system.
6. When the market is called, the system sequentially searches for a market clearing price, starting at a value above (or below) the indicated clearing price. As the price moves sequentially lower (or higher), traders and a specialist are given a moment to enter new orders at each potential price. If the arrival of the new orders causes the market to clear at the new price, the process stops and the call is complete. The specialist can stop the call at any price and clear orders at that price or at the previously called price. The specialist then absorbs any market imbalance or gives partial execution on the heavy side of the book according to a secondary trading priority rule.
7. A continuous market exists for trading basket securities (that is, futures or options on stock market indexes and submarket indexes). This market may or may not be electronic.

Block traders need not be precluded from negotiating in the upstairs market prior to a call. Rather than agreeing on a specific trade, however, the block traders extend guarantees to each other as to how they will enter orders at the next electronic call. They may also communicate the terms of their agreement to the specialist, who then implements the agreement as their agent at the next call. Thus institutional traders may gain assurance that the contra side of the market is not thin. More generally, the electronic call, combined with prior communications with other large traders, gives institutional investors an orderly way to approach the market.

The electronic call also conveys an advantage to medium size traders. Because orders are batched, intermediate size orders become small orders. Traders do not have to work these orders because one price is established for all trades.

Specialists should have a key role to play in an electronic call. The decisions to be made by a market maker include (1) the sequence followed by the price scan procedure, (2) the determination of the call price itself when an exact cross is not found, and (3) the determination of whether to influence price by an inventory purchase or sale or to allocate executions on the heavy side of the market according to a secondary priority trading rule. The specialist may also be informed of the prenegotiated block trades and can be given the responsibility for entering the large orders into the electronic call. In carrying out these functions, the specialist sees the orders first, controls the speed with which the scan is moved from one price to the next, determines when the call is complete, and can commit his or her own capital to improving the breadth, depth, and resiliency of the market.

We have previously established that the costs of temporally batching orders are limited accessibility, limited information dissemination, and increased price volatility resulting from traders' using reservation prices. These costs can be appreciably reduced, and perhaps eliminated, in an electronic call market:

- Accessibility to the market can be increased by having frequent calls (one an hour may be viable for thick stocks in an electronic system). The cost of inaccessibility can be reduced by having a well functioning continuous market in basket securities to enable traders to hedge positions between market calls.
- Order flow information, price indications, and the price scan can be widely disseminated off the trading floor by electronic information systems linked to the electronic execution system.
- The inflated price volatility that attends the use of reservation prices can be reduced by encouraging large traders to enter multiple orders (two or more orders at two or more prices).[22] The price scan procedure further counteracts the tendency of traders to submit orders at reservation prices, because traders who enter orders during the scanning period state the exact number of shares they would like to buy or to sell at the price that is being called. In so doing, they pick orders from their normal (rather than reservation) buy or sell curve.[23]

There may be important advantages in a gaming situation to having other players reveal their orders first. Consequently, the trading system must be structured so that all orders are entered in a timely fashion. The computerized call system can handle this problem by the price scan procedure. A call price is struck at any time during the scan that an acceptable cross is found; consequently, a large trader who does not reveal an order at a price that is being called may miss the market. Therefore, uncertainty as to when the call will be complete gives market participants an incentive to step forth and announce their trading desires. This incentive may be rein-

---

[22]Entering multiple orders keeps reservation prices closer to prices on the normal demand curve (see Chapter 8).

[23]This statement is only approximately true for large traders who have market power. These traders tend to undersize their buy orders at prices higher than they think the market may reach and undersize their sell orders at prices lower than they think the market may attain.

forced by use of the time priority rule to ration executions on the heavy side of the market.

No system is perfect, and some participants in the market always find reason to grumble. Our example is meant to suggest, however, that possible solutions do exist. One feature of particular interest about the example we have chosen is that it electronically mimics one of the oldest and most basic approaches to trading: the live interaction of traders on an exchange floor.

THE NEED TO STABILIZE

This section considers the design of a trading system in relation to the stability of a market. The following aspects of a market's architecture are intended to stabilize short-term price movements: specialist/dealer intervention (see Chapter 12); halting of trading during periods of major informational change, imposition of limits on allowable price changes, and the institution of special opening procedures for the continuous market (see Chapter 2); spatial consolidation of the order flow (see the first section of this chapter); and temporal consolidation of the order flow (see the second section of this chapter).

The difficult questions concern not just *how* to stabilize, but also *whether* to stabilize a market. A fine line distinguishes price stabilization from price controls that are antithetical to free-market operations. Furthermore, price limits and other trading restrictions can themselves contribute to volatility if the blockages break down when a market is under stress. However, price instability is costly to traders and to the broader market, and some control is called for. In this section, we consider price volatility in two contexts: (1) the general level of instability that characterizes normal day-to-day operations, and (2) the extraordinary instability that can characterize a market under abnormal stress.

Price Volatility Under Normal Market Conditions

We consider price volatility under normal conditions in relation to a specific transactions record. Table 13.1 presents such a record for CBS stock for the first half hour of trading on March 1, 1985. No press release or unusual news event concerning the company occurred around this period.[24] For our purpose here, CBS was selected essentially at random.

Table 13.1 shows the bid and ask quotations for CBS; the stock's bid-ask spread; the price of each transaction for the period; an indication of whether each transaction was at the bid (B), the ask (A), or within the spread

---

[24]March 1, 1985 was the first day of the sample period for the study of market liquidity and execution costs discussed in Chapter 11.

(M); the size of each transaction (transaction volume); and the time of each transaction recorded to the nearest half minute. Although time distinctions are not available for multiple transactions that occur within a 30-second interval, the transactions themselves are ordered in sequence.

On March 1, 1985, the New York Stock Exchange's trading floor opened at 10:00 A.M.; the market for CBS opened at 10:30:02. At the opening trade, 171,500 shares of CBS common changed hands at a price of 86. The opening trade comprised all crossing orders from (a) the limit order book, (b) the trading crowd on the floor, and (c) orders delivered to the specialist's post by the Opening Automated Report System (OARS).

Table 13.1   TRANSACTION RECORD FOR CBS FIRST HALF HOUR OF TRADING, MARCH 1, 1985

Bid	Ask	Spread	Transaction Price	Bid (B) Ask (A) or Midspread (M) Transaction	Transaction Volume	Time
			86.000		171500	10:30:02
85.750	86.250	0.500				10:30:32
86.000	86.250	0.250				10:33:02
			86.250	A	2000	10:34:32
86.000	86.500	0.500				10:34:32
			86.250	M	1500	10:35:02
			86.250	M	1500	10:35:02
86.000	86.500	0.500				10:35:02
86.000	86.250	0.250				10:35:02
86.000	86.500	0.500				10:35:32
			86.250	M	5000	10:35:32
86.000	86.500	0.500				10:36:32
			86.500	A	2000	10:37:02
			86.500	A	2000	10:37:02
86.250	86.750	0.500				10:37:02
			86.500	M	100	10:37:02
86.500	86.750	0.250				10:37:32
86.250	86.750	0.500				10:38:02
86.500	86.750	0.250				10:38:02
			86.500	B	2000	10:38:02
			86.750	A	2000	10:40:02
86.750	87.000	0.250				10:40:02
86.500	87.000	0.500				10:40:02
			86.750	M	1000	10:40:02
86.750	87.000	0.250				10:41:02
86.750	87.000	0.250				10:41:02
			86.875	M	1000	10:41:02
86.750	87.000	0.250				10:42:02
			87.000	A	2000	10:42:32
			87.000	A	2000	10:42:32
86.750	87.250	0.500				10:42:32
			87.125	M	5000	10:44:02
			87.125	M	5000	10:44:02
87.125	87.375	0.250				10:44:32
			87.125	B	5000	10:44:32

Table 13.1 TRANSACTION RECORD FOR CBS FIRST HALF HOUR OF TRADING, MARCH 1, 1985 (*Continued*)

Bid	Ask	Spread	Transaction Price	Bid (B) Ask (A) or Midspread (M) Transaction	Transaction Volume	Time
87.000	87.375	0.375				10:46:02
			87.000	B	10000	10:46:02
86.750	87.250	0.500				10:46:02
			87.125	M	400	10:47:02
87.000	87.125	0.125				10:47:02
87.000	87.250	0.250				10:47:02
			87.000	B	700	10:48:02
86.750	87.000	0.250				10:48:02
87.000	87.125	0.125				10:48:02
86.750	87.000	0.250				10:48:32
			86.750	B	5000	10:50:03
			87.000	A	1600	10:50:03
			86.750	B	4400	10:50:03
			86.750	B	25000	10:50:33
86.500	87.000	0.500				10:50:33
			86.750	M	2000	10:51:03
			86.750	M	1300	10:51:33
86.500	87.000	0.500				10:52:03
86.500	87.750	1.250				10:54:04
			86.625	M	1500	10:54:04
86.500	87.750	1.250				10:54:04
			86.750	M	5000	10:54:04
86.500	87.750	1.250				10:54:04
			86.500	B	7600	10:54:34
86.250	87.750	1.500				10:55:04
86.250	86.750	0.500				10:55:34
			86.625	M	100	10:57:04
			86.500	M	2600	10:57:04
			86.625	M	600	10:58:34
86.500	86.750	0.250				10:59:04
			86.625	M	600	11:01:34

Source: Data were collected electronically by a firm under contract to the American Stock Exchange and supplied by the Amex.

The opening price of 86 reflected these orders and the specialist's assessment of the market at the time. After the opening trade, the quotes were established at 85.750 bid, 86.250 ask. As trading progressed for the next 30 minutes, prices changed appreciably for CBS. How accurate were the opening prices in light of subsequent events? What might explain the ensuing fluctuations? Let us consider the record.

The first two events after the opening were an increase of the bid to 86.000 and a 2000 share transaction at the ask (86.250), after which the quotes were set at 86.000 bid, 86.500 ask. At 10:35:02, two 1500 share orders transacted at a midspread price of 86.250. Next the ask was adjusted down a quarter, then up a quarter, and another midspread transaction of

5000 shares was recorded at 86.250. This completed the first five minutes and 30 seconds of trading in CBS common.

Transactions continued mainly at midspread prices and at the ask until 10:44:32. Sixteen transactions in total occurred during the first 14 minutes and 30 seconds after the opening transaction. Except for the smallest (100 shares at 10:37:02), trades were in the 1000–5000 share range. The transaction price rose from the morning opening at 86.000 to 87.125. The spread, while also rising, fluctuated between a quarter and a half a point. There were only two transactions at the bid: 2000 shares at 86.500 at 10:38:02, and 5000 shares at 87.125 at 10:44:32.

Sixteen transactions were realized from 10:46:02 to 11:01:34. One was at the ask, six were at the bid, and nine were midspread executions. During this period, the bid decreased from 87.000 to 86.500, the ask decreased from 87.375 to 86.750, and the transaction price dropped from 87.125 to 86.625. The spread, which fluctuated more during this interval than during the first 15 minutes of trading, widened to a point and a half at 10:55:04.

The record for the overall period can be summarized as follows:

1. Total number of trades: 32
2. Transactions at the ask: 7
   Transactions at the bid: 8
   Midspread transactions: 17
3. No transaction was made outside the quotes; that is, no block purchase was negotiated at a price above the ask, and no block sale was negotiated at a price below the bid.
4. Most trades were of intermediate size; however, a 10,000 share block executed at the bid at 10:46:02 and a 25,000 share block executed at the bid at 10:50:33.
5. Trades at the same price as the previous transaction: 14
   Transaction-to-transaction price changes of ⅛ point: 11
   Transaction-to-transaction price changes of ¼ point: 7
   Transaction-to-transaction price changes over ¼ point: 0
6. The transaction price increased 1.3 percent (from 86.000 to 87.125) during the first fifteen minutes of trading. The transaction price decreased 0.6 percent (from 87.125 to 86.625) during the second 15 minutes of trading.

Let us consider the sixth point more closely. Given the brief intervals over which the changes occurred, they are indeed appreciable. To assess them in a specific context, assume an investor with a one-year holding period who expects (and is willing to accept) a 13 percent return on CBS stock. On March 1, 1985, CBS opened at 86; 15 minutes later the stock traded 1.3 percent higher, at 87.125. Consequently, 10 percent of the investor's expected annual return would have been realized after 15 minutes if he or she had participated as a seller in the trade at 10:44:32. On the other hand, if the investor had participated in this trade as a buyer instead of having bought at the opening, 10 percent of his or her annual return would have been lost.

In addition, the realized one-year return would be reduced again if a poor sell execution is obtained at the end of the year. We thus see that because of the level of volatility observed, the annual return realized by an investor is very sensitive to slight variations in the timing of the investor's buy and sell transactions.

The importance of price volatility can also be assessed in relation to changes in shareholder wealth. During the first subperiod (10:30:02–10:44:32), price increased 1.125 points. On the morning of March 1, the number of shares outstanding of CBS common totaled 29,734,091. Multiplying this number by the dollar price change shows that the 1.3 percent price increase represented a $33.4 million wealth increase. It is interesting to see how this change in wealth is distributed between shares that were traded and shares that were not traded.

Consider, for instance, the 100 share trade at 86.500 at 10:37:02. Using the opening price of 86.000 as the base, profits realized on the sale of these shares are $100(86.500 - 86.000) = \$50$. Then, using 86.500 as the base, profits realized on the purchase of these shares are, as of the end of the first subperiod, $100(87.125 - 86.500) = \$62.50$. For all 16 trades during the first subperiod, the profits realized from the sale of shares, π_S, are

$$\pi_S = \sum_{i=1}^{16} N_i(P_i - 86) = \sum_{i=1}^{16} P_i N_i - 86 \sum_{i=1}^{16} N_i \qquad (13.1)$$

Similarly, the profits for the shares bought, π_B, can be computed as

$$\pi_B = \sum_{i=1}^{16} N_i(87.125 - P_i) = 87.125 \sum_{i=1}^{16} N_i - \sum_{i=1}^{16} P_i N_i \qquad (13.2)$$

Table 13.2 shows the number of shares traded and the dollar value of each transaction for the first subperiod of the transaction record; Table 13.3 shows comparable values for the second subperiod. As seen in Table 13.2, 39,100 shares traded in the first subperiod, and the total dollar value of these transactions was $3,392,150. Substituting these values into equations (13.1) and (13.2) shows that during the first subperiod, the dollar profit for shares sold was $29,550 and that the dollar profit for shares bought was $14,437. These values are displayed in Table 13.4, along with comparable figures computed for the second subperiod, using the values given in Table 13.3 and equations equivalent to (13.1) and (13.2).

Table 13.2 DOLLAR VALUE OF CBS TRANSACTIONS MARCH 1, 1985:
            10:30:02–10:44:32

Transaction Price	Transaction Size (No. of Shares)	$ Value of Transaction	Time
86.250	2,000	172,500	10:34:32
86.250	1,500	129,375	10:35:02
86.250	1,500	129,375	10:35:02
86.250	5,000	431,250	10:35:32
86.500	2,000	173,000	10:37:02
86.500	2,000	173,000	10:37:02
86.500	100	8,650	10:37:02
86.500	2,000	173,000	10:38:02
86.750	2,000	173,500	10:40:02
86.750	1,000	86,750	10:40:02
86.875	1,000	86,875	10:41:02
87.000	2,000	174,000	10:42:32
87.000	2,000	174,000	10:42:32
87.125	5,000	435,625	10:44:02
87.125	5,000	435,625	10:44:02
87.125	5,000	435,625	10:44:32
Total for Period	39,100	$3,392,150	

Table 13.4 also shows the change in wealth for shares that were not traded. As noted, 29,734,091 shares of CBS were outstanding on the morning of March 1. Subtracting the number of shares traded from this figure and multiplying the price change over a subperiod gives the change in the total value of the shares that were not traded. For the first subperiod, the total value of shares not traded increased $33.4 million; for the second subperiod, the total value of shares not traded decreased $14.8 million.

The change in wealth for shares not traded far exceeds the funds committed to and withdrawn from the market by traders. Furthermore, the larger the price changes caused by the trades, the larger the disparity becomes. The change in the value of shares not traded is a pure addition to, or subtraction from, the aggregate value of financial assets. The change affects investor wealth and can potentially affect investor confidence.

Having assessed the magnitude of the price fluctuations, let us next consider their cause. In part, the price movements can be attributed to the bid-ask spread. For instance, at 10:38:02, 2000 shares executing at the bid established a transaction price of 86.500. Then, at 10:40:02, 2000 shares executing at the ask established a transaction price of 86.750. The quotes were unchanged for these two transactions—only the quarter point spread, and the juxtaposition of (presumably) a market order to sell and a market order to buy caused the price increase of 0.250.

The movements in the transaction price would have been more pronounced if large orders had executed outside the quotes. This did not occur, however, in our 30-minute sample period. On the other hand, the bouncing

Table 13.3 DOLLAR VALUE OF CBS TRANSACTIONS MARCH 1, 1985: 10:46:02–11:01:32

Transaction Price	Transaction Size (No. of Shares)	Value of Transaction	Time
87.000	10,000	870,000	10:46:02
87.125	400	34,850	10:47:02
87.000	700	60,900	10:48:02
86.750	5,000	433,750	10:50:03
87.000	1,600	139,200	10:50:03
86.750	4,400	381,700	10:50:03
86.750	25,000	2,168,750	10:50:33
86.750	2,000	173,500	10:51:03
86.750	1,300	112,775	10:51:33
86.625	1,500	129,937	10:54:04
86.750	5,000	433,750	10:54:04
86.500	7,600	657,400	10:54:34
86.625	100	8,662	10:57:04
86.500	2,600	224,900	10:57:04
86.625	600	51,975	10:58:34
86.625	600	51,975	11:01:34
Total for Period	68,400	$5,934,024	

of the transaction price between the bid and the ask was mitigated by trades executing at midspread prices. Midspread trades are often accounted for by floor traders who regard the midspread price as fair, given the current market. The specialist may also give a market order trader a midspread execution.[25]

The spread accounts for only a small part of the price movements

Table 13.4 CHANGE IN WEALTH IN CBS STOCK DUE TO CHANGE IN SHARE PRICE MARCH 1, 1985: 10:30:02–11:01:34

	Change in Wealth	
	10:30:02 to 10:44:32	10:46:02 to 11:01:34
For shares sold	$ 29,550	$ − 25,326
For shares bought	14,437	− 8,874
For shares not traded	33,406,865	− 14,832,845
Total	$33,450,852	$ − 14,867,045

[25]For instance, at 10:54:04, with the current ask at 87.750 and the last transaction price at 86.750, a market order to buy would have caused a one-point price change. At that time and given the price, the specialist presumably was not looking to sell (otherwise the ask quotation would have been lower); however, an execution at the ask would have caused an unacceptably large price increase. Therefore, the arrival of a market buy order at this time could have forced the market maker to give a midspread execution because of the specialist's affirmative obligation to make a fair and orderly market.

observed in Table 13.1. Might one infer from the price record that even though there were no explicit news announcements at the time, informational change had in fact occurred during the first half hour of trading? As trading progressed during the first subperiod, the order flow did push the stock's price higher, and at 10:44:32 an observer might have suspected either that news had been released or that the specialist had opened trading in CBS at too low a price. The events of the next subperiod negate this impression, however. At 10:44:02, the stock traded for a third time at a high of 87.125, but the transaction was at the bid, which means it was triggered by a sell order. Then, from that point on, trades were mainly at the bid or at midspread prices, and by 11:01:34, the market had settled back to the 86.500–86.625 level. By the end of the second subperiod, the opening price seemed more in line with market conditions.

Therefore, what caused the price movements? Most likely, the initial increase and subsequent decrease were manifestations of the dynamic process by which price moves in a continuous market about an equilibrium level that is itself continuously subject to change. In this dynamic process, price movements signal information to traders, affect the order flow, and have an impact on subsequent price movements. After the opening trade and the market had been established at 85.750 bid, 86.250 ask, a buy order triggered a transaction at the ask. The quotes rose and three midspread trades were made at the same price. Then two more transactions at the ask were triggered by buy orders, and price continued to rise. The rising price could have been pulling more buy orders in at the time. If so, the price path could have been different if the first trade after the opening had been triggered by an order to sell at the bid rather than by an order to buy at the ask. It is in this sense that the dynamic interaction of the orders can affect the behavior of the transaction price.

Note that the exchange's trading system may itself have contributed to the *orderliness* of the price movements. After 15 minutes, price did move back toward its opening value, which suggests that the opening price was a reasonable assessment of the market at the time. The preponderance of midspread transactions occurred because floor traders did use the current market quotes as pricing guides. The midspread transactions also explain why almost half (14 of 32) of the transactions in the continuous market were at the same price as the previous transaction. Further, specialist operations and the existence of orders on the book explain why 11 of the 32 trades resulted in price changes of only an eighth of a point, and why no transaction-to-transaction price change was greater than a quarter of a point.[26]

One further observation must be underscored. After the price of CBS

---

[26]For this particular sequence, 78.2 percent (25 of 32) of the trades occurred with no price change or with the minimum price change of ⅛ point. In 1986, 90.2 percent of all trades on the NYSE occurred with no price change or with only a ⅛ point change. See the *New York Stock Exchange Fact Book,* 1987.

common had risen sufficiently from its morning opening, the higher values appear to have attracted sell orders to the market. If the price had decreased below its equilibrium level, the fall would presumably have attracted buy orders to the market. The ability to attract stabilizing orders from public traders is characteristic of a resilient market. As we shall see next, this quality of the market may be lost under abnormal conditions of stress.

Price Volatility in a Market Under Stress

We consider volatility under abnormal stress in relation to the changes experienced on and around October 19, 1987. The markets during these weeks experienced price swings and trading volume that far exceeded previous experience and expectations.

Table 13.5 shows the Dow Jones Average of 30 industrial stocks, close-to-close changes in the index, percentage changes of the index, and trading volume for the four-week period from Monday, October 12, through Friday, November 6. Table 13.6 shows how the index changed over hourly intervals during the most turbulent four day part of the period, October 16 and October 19–21.

Table 13.5 DOW JONES INDUSTRIAL AVERAGE AND NYSE TRADING VOLUME
OCTOBER 12, 1987–NOVEMBER 6, 1987

Day	Dow Jones Industrial Index	Point Change from Previous Close	Percentage Change from Previous Close	Number of Shares Traded (Millions)
MON OCT 12	2471.44	− 10.77	− 0.43	141.9
TUES OCT 13	2508.16	+ 36.72	+ 1.49	172.9
WED OCT 14	2412.70	− 95.46	− 3.81	207.4
THUR OCT 15	2355.09	− 57.61	− 2.39	263.2
FRI OCT 16	2246.74	− 108.35	− 4.60	338.5
MON OCT 19	1738.74	− 508.00	− 22.61	604.3
TUES OCT 20	1841.01	+ 102.27	+ 5.88	608.1
WED OCT 21	2027.85	+ 186.84	+ 10.15	449.4
THUR OCT 22	1950.43	− 77.42	− 3.82	392.2
FRI OCT 23	1950.76	+ .33	+ 0.02	245.6
MON OCT 26	1793.93	− 156.83	− 8.04	308.8
TUES OCT 27	1846.49	+ 52.56	+ 2.93	260.2
WED OCT 28	1846.82	+ 0.33	+ 0.02	279.4
THUR OCT 29	1938.33	+ 91.51	+ 4.96	258.1
FRI OCT 30	1993.53	+ 55.20	+ 2.85	303.4
MON NOV 2	2014.09	+ 20.56	+ 1.03	176.0
TUES NOV 3	1963.53	− 50.56	− 2.51	227.8
WED NOV 4	1945.29	− 18.24	− 0.93	202.5
THUR NOV 5	1985.41	+ 40.12	+ 2.06	226.0
FRI NOV 6	1959.05	− 26.36	− 1.33	228.3
Change from Oct 12 Close		− 512.39	− 20.73	

Table 13.6 **DOW JONES INDUSTRIAL INDEX AT HOURLY INTERVALS OCTOBER 16 AND OCTOBER 19–21**

		Dow Jones Industrial Index	Point Change from Previous Value	Percentage Change from Previous Value
FRI., OCTOBER 16	OPEN	2363.90	+8.81	+0.37
	10AM	2355.09	−8.81	−0.37
	11AM	2347.91	−7.18	−0.30
	12 NOON	2340.40	−7.51	−0.32
	1PM	2323.11	−17.29	−0.74
	2PM	2268.44	−54.67	−2.35
	3PM	2297.00	+28.56	+1.26
	CLOSE	2246.74	−50.26	−2.19
MON., OCTOBER 19	OPEN	2046.67	−200.07	−8.90
	10AM	2178.69	+132.02	+6.45
	11AM	2040.63	−138.06	−6.34
	12 NOON	2103.79	+63.16	+3.10
	1PM	2061.85	−41.94	−1.99
	2PM	1974.54	−87.31	−4.23
	3PM	1958.88	−15.66	−0.79
	CLOSE	1738.74	−220.14	−11.24
TUES., OCTOBER 20	OPEN	1949.77	+211.03	+12.14
	10AM	1863.06	−86.71	−4.45
	11AM	1858.75	−4.31	−0.23
	12 NOON	1726.46	−132.29	−7.12
	1PM	1825.27	+98.81	+5.72
	2PM	1760.28	−64.99	−3.56
	3PM	1878.98	+118.70	+6.74
	CLOSE	1841.01	−37.97	−2.02
WED., OCTOBER 21	OPEN	2016.08	+175.07	+9.51
	10AM	1947.28	−68.80	−3.41
	11AM	2036.14	+88.86	+4.56
	12 NOON	2003.15	−32.99	−1.62
	1PM	2008.12	+4.97	+0.25
	2PM	2028.35	+20.23	+1.01
	3PM	1992.21	−36.14	−1.78
	CLOSE	2027.85	+35.64	+1.79

Our discussion focuses on the Dow Jones index because it is broadly followed and widely understood. Note, however, that index returns, as is true of portfolio returns in general, are less volatile than the returns on individual stocks. Furthermore, the variability of an index typically understates the volatility of a market over very short intervals because of nonsynchronous trading.[27] The Dow Jones Industrial Average itself does not cover the broad market, but rather 30 major blue-chip companies. There-

[27]Nonsynchronous trading in individual stocks causes positive index autocorrelation and hence reduces short period variance.

fore, the short period volatility of the Dow may not be as affected by nonsynchronous trading, because price adjustments are generally most rapid for these firms.

For the nation, 1987 marked the fifth year of economic expansion. Inflation was low, and stock market indexes had risen to record levels. The Dow reached its peak of 2722.42 on August 25 of the year. In the fall of 1987, expectations of quarterly earnings reports were bullish. But along with the optimism, were major economic uncertainties. Of particular concern was the federal budget deficit that, although at the time somewhat lower, had reached $221 billion in 1986, and a trade deficit that stood at $169.7 billion in 1986. Interest rates had risen substantially throughout most of 1987, and there was a threat of renewed inflation. Foreign buying at the U.S. Treasury auctions had helped to finance the federal budget deficit, and large sums of foreign capital had been invested in U.S. equities during the market's rise; these funds could be withdrawn rapidly if U.S. interest rates and/or the U.S. dollar fell.

On October 6, the Dow dropped a record 91.55 points to 2548.63 because of mounting fears of higher interest rates and a wave of computerized sell programs. On October 14, a trade deficit of $15.68 billion was announced for the month of August. Although lower than the previous month's figure of $16.47 billion, the deficit was larger than expected and the news rattled an increasingly nervous investment community. The dollar declined in foreign exchange markets, interest rates surged, and the Dow responded with another record point drop of 95.46.

The market experienced yet another substantial decrease on October 15 and then a sharp decline on Friday, October 16. As shown in Table 13.6, the market decline on the 16th occurred mainly between 1:00 P.M. and 2:00 P.M., and in the last hour of trading before the weekend. The Dow lost 235 points for the week, and closed 476 points below the peak it had reached in August. The pressures that would push the market far lower were building.

Three other developments jolted the market at this time. First, a tax bill under consideration by Congress contained provisions that could seriously hinder corporate takeover activity, particularly the leveraged takeovers. Second, comments over the weekend from Washington suggesting the United States would let the dollar fall if West Germany did not reverse a recent rise in interest rates, reinforced concern that *anticipation* of a declining dollar would drive foreign money from U.S. markets. Third, at 8:33 A.M., before the NYSE opened on Monday, October 19, news was reported that warships thought to be American had bombed an Iranian oil platform in the Persian Gulf. For the markets, the tinder was dry and the match had been lit.

On Monday in Tokyo, prices fell from the opening bell. Then the

London market opened sharply down. In New York, a barrage of sell orders rocked the NYSE even before opening trades were made on the Big Board. For instance, the indicated opening price for IBM was $125, compared to a Friday close of $134.50; the indicated opening price for Merck was $170, compared to a Friday close of $184. As shown in Table 13.6, the New York market opened on October 19 at 2046.67, down 200.07 points, or 8.90 percent. Takeover stocks plummeted. Portfolio insurance sell programs triggered in Chicago put enormous pressure on index futures. The price of the futures fell below the price of shares on the NYSE, and arbitrage programs were activated that drove the New York prices lower. Volume exploded; traders were losing track of what was happening. As prices spiraled downward, new rounds of portfolio insurance programs were activated in Chicago; in response, selling pressure was intensified in the New York market by traders anticipating that more arbitrage programs would be run. The market was in full flight.

A trader quoted in *The New Yorker* described the scene as follows:

> Half of the Dow stocks couldn't open for trading this morning. They didn't open for an hour or more. We were frozen in front of our screens. There were just no bids. I.B.M., General Electric, Merck—some of the biggest blue-chip stocks on the Dow—and we couldn't open them! I did some trades on Merck today. You know what a downtick is? When a stock goes down an eighth of a point, a quarter of a point? I was watching Merck on my screen, and it started trading on downticks four points at a time. Then it downticked eight points.[28]

In one 15-minute period the Dow dropped 50 points. In a 45-minute period it fell 100 points. From 10 A.M. to 11 A.M. it fell 138 points. Between 3 P.M. and its close the Dow plunged 220 points. Laszlo Birinyi, Jr., chief equity strategist at Salomon Brothers, was quoted by *Newsweek* as saying, "What does the market know that we don't?" *Newsweek* added, "He got no answers. Just blank stares and shrugs."[29]

Only once before had the market experienced an equivalent fall—in October 1929. But the 1987 drop was faster. The Dow had previously declined 23 percent in a two-day period, October 28 and 29 of 1929; in October 1987, the Dow lost 22.6 percent of its value in a single day. And the fall was worldwide.

In London, the Financial Times average of 30 stocks fell 10 percent. In Tokyo, the Nikkei 225-share index was down 7.3 percent. The market index dropped 7.14 percent in Frankfurt, 11.3 percent in Zurich, 4.65

---

[28]*The New Yorker*, November 2, 1987, pp. 33, 34. Reprinted by permission. Copyright © 1987 The New Yorker Magazine, Inc.

[29]*Newsweek*, November 2, 1987, p. 24.

percent in Paris, 7.81 percent in Amsterdam, 10.5 percent in Brussels, 12.2 percent in Singapore, and 11.3 percent in Toronto. In Hong Kong, the market fell 11.1 percent on October 19, at which point the exchange was closed. When it reopened on October 26, Hong Kong's Hang Seng index lost one-third of its value in one of the most severe session-to-session declines in stock market history.

Trading on the U.S. markets remained extremely heavy and enormous price fluctuations continued for the next several days. On October 20, after several wild swings (see Table 13.6), the Dow closed up 102.27 points. On October 21, the market opened up 175.07 points and held on to close with a 186.84 point gain for the day. Thus in two days, the Dow recouped almost 300 points of the 508 point loss. On Friday the market closed up .33 points; traders were exhausted, the Exchange was closed at 2:00 P.M. to ease back office operations, and the session was quiet by then-current standards—only 245.6 million shares were traded.

The price swings remained large through the last week of October, and then dampened somewhat during the first week in November. On Friday, November 6, the market closed at 1959.05, about where it had been on Friday, October 23, at the end of the most tumultuous week in the Exchange's history.

Having reviewed the record, let us examine the causes of the instability. Three factors need to be considered: (1) informational change, (2) technical factors pertaining to the market, and (3) the dynamic process by which prices change in a financial asset market.

Informational Change   Information concerning the earnings power of individual companies was relatively constant during the period and, as noted, expectations for fourth quarter financial reports were generally bullish through the first two weeks of October. Some might have previously argued, and the experience has thus far confirmed, that by October 12 when the Dow was at 2471.44, five years of a bull market had pushed prices unsustainably high. Nevertheless, according to a report in *Newsweek*,[30] "Few of the nation's thousands of financial gurus had called the crash correctly; by one count, a mere five newsletters came anywhere close."[31]

Yet informational change did change the expectations of those investors who were holding the shares at that time: Prospects for higher interest rates and renewed inflation were strengthening, and uncertainty in the financial markets had increased. The market responded—future earnings were

---

[30]*Newsweek*, November 2, 1987, p. 16.

[31]The NYSE's Chairman, John Phelan, Jr., did foresee the possibility and in fact predicted the chain of events—the advent of bearish news, a broad market decline, the triggering of portfolio insurance programs, and then free fall. See *The Wall Street Journal*, October 27, 1987, p. 34.

discounted at a higher rate, and share prices were adjusted down. By the end of our sample period, on Friday, November 6, the market closed at 1959.05, some 512 points and 21 percent below the value it had closed at on Monday, October 12. If the Dow on October 12 and on November 6 reflected reasonable assessments of the market at these times, then the 512 point decrease was a reasonable assessment of informational change over the four-week sample period.

But how accurately did the specific path that prices followed reflect the pattern of informational change? The wild swings experienced, particularly during the week of October 19, suggest that investor expectations were changing, not only as a reaction to new information concerning the basic determinants of share value, but also in response to the order flow itself, and the market's own price behavior.

Market Factors The price movements observed during the sample period, and in particular on October 19, suggest that certain market factors affected the instability. Although extensive analysis will be required to sort out the elements, one factor appears to be particularly instrumental at the current time. At critical moments of stress, computerized sell programs triggered in the Chicago futures market placed substantial additional downward pressure on the price level. Arbitrage programs interacting with the portfolio insurance programs transmitted the added sell pressure back to the New York market. Consequently, prices that kept falling were fed into electronic systems that in turn kept giving back additional *sell* orders.[32]

In addition, during the wildest moments on October 19, the pace at which market events occurred had so accelerated that traders could not remain sufficiently informed about market conditions. Nor could they adequately digest the import of the events that were taking place so rapidly. Electronic technology had increased the speed with which sell decisions were made, the speed with which the orders were transmitted to the market, and the speed with which the resulting trades were reported. In this context, the widespread use of electronic technology could well have contributed to the instability of the market.

The problem, however, may not reside with technology, but rather with market design. The continuous market appears to have been unnecessarily destabilized by traders overresponding to the stressful market conditions. An acceptable means of halting trading in destabilized conditions would have helped. However, there was no way during the crisis, because to have closed the NYSE could have created panic. The Exchange's chair-

---

[32]In contrast, additional *buy* orders have to be attracted by a price decrease, if prices in a free market are to attain equilibrium values.

man, John Phelan, Jr., showed great courage by keeping the market open at that time.

Certain features of the exchange system stabilized the market and prevented an even more disastrous collapse. The exchanges' computerized order handling and information dissemination systems, though severely tested and perilously close to running out of capacity, handled the order flow with remarkable success. And most importantly, the Exchange specialists committed an enormous amount of their own capital to the market, losing as much as $750 million on October 19 and 20, according to a *New York Times* estimate.[33]

The following passage from *The New York Times* quotes Donald Stone, specialist and senior partner of Lasker, Stone, and Stern, a leading NYSE specialty firm:

> I was in combat during World War II and the feeling you had in your stomach was the same as when you were under fire, except here you didn't risk your life—just all your assets.[34]

The *Times* further reported that Stone traded over a million shares of Johnson & Johnson on Monday and another 1.2 million on Tuesday, in the process "committing some $75 million in just that one stock." The article also quoted James A. Jacobson, an NYSE director and specialist: "The market was going to go down, and no one was going to stop it. The specialists accumulated an enormous amount of inventory, over 10 times the normal load."[35]

The benefits of having specialists commit capital at a time when the market is otherwise in free fall cannot be overstated. In a continuous market trading system, investors must be able to come to the market and sell. If they cannot, confidence in the system can be destroyed and the collapse can be far worse.

Dynamic Price Behavior   The most critical aspects of a market under stress involve the conditions under which the dynamic behavior of prices can result in the free fall experienced on October 19, 1987. The demand curve developed in Chapter 7 and used to present the Grossman-Stiglitz price signalling model in Chapter 9 can be used to gain insight into the matter.

We have previously reasoned that an investor's demand curve to hold shares of a risky asset will be downward sloping under normal circum-

---

[33]*The New York Times,* October 22, 1987, p. D14. Copyright © 1987 by the New York Times Company. Reprinted by permission.

[34]*The New York Times,* ibid.

[35]*The New York Times,* ibid.

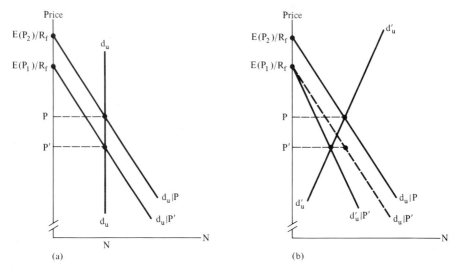

Figure 13.6 Demand of uninformed investor with price signalling. (a) Decrease in price is not associated with increased uncertainty. (b) Decrease in price is associated with increased uncertainty.

stances, but have noted the possibility of a slope reversal under unusual conditions. One such condition is if a decrease (increase) in price conveys a sufficiently strong negative (positive) signal to investors.[36] We now discuss this possibility with reference to Figure 13.6, which presents the demand curve of an uninformed investor with price signalling.

Assume the market generally comprises an adequate number of informed traders, and that an association has been well established between a current price of P and a relatively bullish information set, and between a current price of P' and a relatively bearish information set (where P' is less than P). Figure 13.6(a), with minor notational changes, reproduces Figure 9.2(a). The downward-sloping curve labeled $d_u|P$ shows what the demand of an uninformed investor would be if he or she possessed the relatively bullish information associated with P being the equilibrium price in the current period. The downward-sloping curve labeled $d_u|P'$ shows what the demand of an uninformed investor would be if he or she possessed the relatively bearish information associated with P' being the equilibrium price in the current period.

Note in Figure 13.6(a) that the price intercept of the "bearish" curve is below the intercept of the "bullish" curve, and that the two slopes are the same. The bearish information could lower the price intercept by decreasing the price expected at the end of the investment period [$E(P_1)$ could be less than $E(P_2)$], and/or by increasing R_f-1, the risk-free rate of interest used in the demand model to discount the future expected price.

[36]Also see equations (7.58) and (7.61) and the related discussion in Chapter 7.

As shown in Figure 13.6(a), a current market price of P signals information associated with the demand curve $d_u|P$ and, given this demand curve and the current price of shares (P), the uninformed investor wants to hold N shares. Alternatively, a current market price of P' signals information that results in the demand curve $d_u|P'$ and, given this demand curve and the current price of shares (P'), the uninformed investor also wants to hold N shares. Therefore, with price signalling, the changing price does not affect the number of shares the uninformed investor wishes to hold. Hence this investor's demand curve is the vertical line labeled d_u in Figure 13.6(a).

As discussed in Chapter 9, the infinitely inelastic demand curve is attributable to the special form of the model presented. Most importantly, for both informed and uninformed investors, it assumes that the slope of the demand curve given the information set is the same, regardless of the height of the curve.[37] More generally, one would expect that, all else constant, the variance of the end-of-period price would be greater the *higher* the price, and that the increase in uncertainty would be more for investors who are not directly informed of the bullish information than for those who are. Under these conditions, the demand curve of the uninformed investor would be downward sloping, as it is shown to be in Figure 9.2(b).

Alternatively, assume that a decrease in price from P to P' conveys not only a bearish signal, but also increased uncertainty. In this case the demand curve of the uninformed investor conditioned on the price P' is steeper than the demand curve conditioned on the price P, as shown in Figure 13.6(b) by the curve labeled $d_u'|P'$.[38] If the price-conditioned demand curve becomes steeper as it shifts to the left, the number of shares demanded at a price of P' is less than the number of shares demanded at a price of P. In this case, the demand curve for the uninformed investor is upward sloping, as shown in Figure 13.6(b) by the positively inclined curve labeled d_u'.

The analysis can be applied to the events of October 19, 1987. Consider the demand of investors to hold shares of the market portfolio. Initially, the changing economic environment caused the risk-free rate to rise (due to the increased level of interest rates) and the risk premium to rise (due to the increased level of uncertainty). These changes shifted down the

---

[37]Because the slope is constant for the informed investors, the dollar change in the present value of the end-of-period price must equal the dollar change in the current price (see Figure 9.1 and the related discussion). Note that with $E(P_2)/R_f - E(P_1)/R_f = P - P'$, we must have $d_u(P) = d_u(P') = N$, as shown in Figure 13.6(a).

[38]We showed in Chapter 7 that the slope of this demand curve is given by the present value of the risk premium to hold one share, where the risk premium equals one-half of the investor's coefficient of absolute risk aversion times the dollar risk attributable to holding one share of the risky asset. Thus, increasing the variance associated with the end-of-period price increases the slope of the investor's demand curve to hold shares.

informed investors' demand to hold shares of the market portfolio and caused the curve to be more steeply inclined. Consequently, prices fell in the New York market. Trading accelerated, and prices were pushed down further as computer sell programs were triggered in the Chicago market.

As prices dropped and the general level of uncertainty increased, the risk premium of the uninformed investors increased, and their demand curves became upward sloping. As the pace of events sped up, increasing numbers of professionals became bewildered and joined the ranks of the uninformed. At this point, a lower price was attracting insufficient buy orders from the dwindling number of investors who still believed themselves to be informed. When the positively inclined demand of the uninformed overwhelmed the market, price went into free fall. Virtually the only buyers remaining were the specialists, who were buying because of their affirmative obligation. Professionals like Laszlo Birinyi of Salomon Brothers could only observe and wonder, "What does the market know that we don't?" The answer to his question is "not much."

Reconsidering the Issues

The market drop on October 19, 1987 was the most damaging event in stock market history since the crash on October 29, 1929. Many questions have been raised following it, and analyses of the event, its causes, and its implications will be continuing for a long time to come. At this point, we can attempt some preliminary assessments.

The Market for Financial Assets   The turbulence experienced in October 1987 was unusual, but only because of its magnitude. Financial asset markets are inherently complex and volatile. The reason is twofold: Trading is a manifestation of disequilibrium behavior (investors seek to trade only when they hold unbalanced portfolios) and prices signal information. Consequently, the markets are typically volatile, and institutional arrangements to control price movements are needed, not only at times of particular stress, but also under normal conditions. This point is illustrated by the half-hour trading record in March 1985 for CBS stock.

The Informational Efficiency of Financial Markets   Financial economists have generally believed that the equity markets are efficient in the sense that share prices fully and accurately reflect the information set. As previously discussed (see Chapter 9), one way in which informational efficiency has been tested is by assessing whether or not above-normal returns can be realized using decision rules based on historic price changes. The evidence suggests that such returns cannot be realized because price movements conform too closely to a random walk.

Price movements that are both predictable and exploitable would indeed imply the informational inefficiency of an asset market. The converse proposition does not necessarily hold, however: Unpredictability need not imply efficiency. Recognizing this, the efficiency of the market should be reexamined in light of the enormous price swings experienced in October 1987.

Alternative Market Systems   As previously discussed (see Chapters 5 and 11), the exchange system has competed intensely in recent years with the OTC markets for new listings. Each system has claimed to provide the most efficient market. The exchanges stress their advantages as agency/auction markets, and emphasize the importance of their specialist system. The NASD points to the advantages of their competitive dealer system. Currently, much attention is being given in various market centers around the world to these alternative systems, and decisions being made today will determine the course of future developments.

Comparisons made when the systems are under stress are far more meaningful than comparisons made in periods of relative calm, and the events of October 19, 1987 will provide important evidence. Although the record has not, as yet, been adequately studied, we have been able to note the critical role played by NYSE specialists on the day the Dow dropped 508 points. The financial press has not been as supportive of the over-the-counter dealers. Alison Leigh Cowan wrote in *The New York Times,*

> . . . the Nasdaq market's inability to cope with the crush of customer orders in the Oct. 19 market rout has raised fresh questions about whether it can maintain an orderly market amid a virtual panic. . . . As the market tumbled on Monday of last week, frantic customers could not get through to many of the dealers responsible for making markets in over-the-counter stocks. . . . Some customers asserted that panicky market makers abandoned their posts. "It's clear a number of market makers saw their capital impaired and ran for cover," said Edward J. Mathias, president of the T. Rowe Price New Horizons Fund, a mutual fund specializing in emerging growth stocks."[39]

In another *New York Times* article, Vartanig G. Vartan wrote,

> Did some dealers responsible for making markets in over-the-counter stocks deliberately fail to answer their telephones during the heat of the historic landslide in prices?
>
> As both listed and unlisted stocks continued to tumble yesterday, the teeming over-the-counter market is juggling this additional hot po-

[39]*The New York Times,* October 30, 1987, p. D1. Copyright © 1987 by the New York Times Company. Reprinted by permission.

tato regarding its essential role as an arena for buying and selling equities.

"As long as these dealers don't pick up the phone, they don't have to make a bid to buy over-the-counter stocks from potential sellers," said the head trader for one mutual fund group. "I suspect the move was deliberate in some cases—especially on Monday and Tuesday of last week, when the entire equity market began to cave in. . . . Sometimes you could hear a dealer pick up the phone and then click off without saying anything," the trader added.[40]

The record will be examined carefully in the coming months. Much insight may be gained by contrasting the actual transaction records of leading OTC and exchange-listed issues. The OTC system should not be faulted if its electronic capacity was incapable at the time of handling the enormous, unexpected surge of the order flow. Rather, it is the willingness of the OTC market makers to commit capital to the market that is critical. If a trading system does not ensure that its dealers fulfill this obligation, no amount of electronic technology will solve the problem.

Technology The use of computer technology to trade options and futures has been and will be carefully examined as a cause of the market drop. We have already noted (a) the destabilizing effects of the computerized sell programs that were triggered in the Chicago market and (b) the chaotic price movements that occurred when the rapidity of computer-driven events forced traders to respond to new information before it had been properly digested.

Various possibilities exist for controlling the negative effects of electronic technology. After the crash, the NYSE placed restrictions on program trading that were not totally eliminated until Monday, November 9. The Chicago Mercantile Exchange announced that daily price limits will be imposed on its stock-index futures and options contracts. Other possible controls include limits on the maximum positions individual traders may take in stock-index futures and options contracts, and increasing the Mercantile Exchange's margin requirement from its current level of 7 percent.[41]

The point must be stressed, however, that existing electronic technology, while no doubt contributing to the increased volatility of the market, is neither the only cause nor even necessarily the primary cause. Rather, as this book has emphasized, instability is endemic to a financial asset market. Recognition of this reality is of even greater importance now that a network of markets, both domestic and international, is electronically

---

[40]*The New York Times,* October 27, 1987, p. D16. Copyright © 1987 by the New York Times Company. Reprinted by permission.

[41]Margin requirements are currently 50 percent on the NYSE.

linked. The fundamental problem resides with the architecture of the markets, however, not with the equipment per se that is used.

Adequate structural safeguards are missing. Consequently, primary attention should be directed toward developing a technology that does not yet exist, rather than to finding fault with the equipment that does.

Corporate Share Repurchase   Major support was given to the market as early as October 19, and more widely on October 20 when the Dow recouped 102 points, by listed corporations repurchasing their own securities. The repurchases directly supported prices and were a signal to investors that the 508-point drop on October 19 was an overreaction.

Corporate trading to stabilize the price of their own shares has historically been viewed with great caution because of the opportunity it provides for price manipulation. Yet price variability is undesirable for shareholders, and a corporation might be able to reduce its cost of capital by dampening the returns variance for its equity shares. Corporations do, in fact, indirectly control their price volatility by determining the primary market center where their shares are traded. Should they be allowed to have a more substantial impact?

Cohen, Maier, Schwartz, and Whitcomb (1977 and 1986) have argued that allowing corporations to determine and to pay for the specific amount of stabilization desired would internalize the benefits of stabilization activities on the corporate level and result in a more nearly social optimal amount of stabilization. Share repurchases during a market decline, along with the issuance of additional shares during a market rise, would do just that.[42]

Consideration, therefore, should be given to how corporations might supply capital to market making by establishing a fund that would be augmented by issuing shares in a rising market, and drawn on by buying shares in a falling market. A corporation might be allowed certain controls over the total size of its stabilization fund, but specialists or other exchange officials should be entrusted with managing daily operations to ensure that the result is stabilization, not manipulation.

The Need to Control Price Volatility   Volatility is one of the most serious problems faced by a free-market economy. Volatility characterizes the equity markets, and the cost is tremendous. For the economy, an estimated loss on the order of $500 billion was realized in a single day of trading, on October 19, 1987.[43] In addition, the damage done to the confidence of investors and to the larger population of producers and consumers is unmeasurable.

[42]Share issuance has now been facilitated by the institution of SEC Rule 415, the shelf-registration rule (see Chapter 14).

[43]W. Greider, "Annals of Finance (The FED—Part I)," *The New Yorker*, November 9, 1987, p. 54.

Perhaps the loss in share values reflected an accurate reassessment of the financial worth of the listed firms. On the other hand, the loss might also be attributable in part to the dynamic behavior of prices searching for an equilibrium level and badly missing the mark. Unfortunately, however, a falling price might carry its equilibrium value down with it. With increased uncertainty, decreased financial wealth in the economy, and earnings forecasts that had suddenly turned bearish, the lower share prices may have produced their own justification.

CONCLUSION

This chapter concludes our analysis of the design features of an equity market. We have concentrated on four issues of fundamental importance: spatial consolidation of the order flow; temporal consolidation of the order flow; order display, trade execution, and use of computer technology; and price stabilization.

One cannot comprehend the strengths and weaknesses of a market's architecture without understanding the interaction between the trading system and investors' trading strategies. Account must also be taken of the fact that the more frequently trades are made, the thinner a market becomes on the margin that separates buyers and sellers.[44] If the market is thin enough, even a 100 share order affects the share price of a giant such as IBM. For instance, IBM shares may trade at a one-quarter spread. When this occurs, a 100 share order may increase the bid or decrease the ask. A second 100 share order may then trigger a trade at the new price. Therefore, the value of all IBM shares outstanding, evaluated at the last transaction price, can be altered by the crossing of just two 100 share orders. The result is attributable to the market's being thin because of the dispersion of the order flow.

This chapter has pointed up the considerable advantages of counteracting market thinness by consolidating the order flow, both temporally and spatially. The use of electronic technology to accomplish these ends has been considered as well. Electronic trading, however, despite its enormous potential, has had significant limitations. The major challenge regarding computer technology is the economic problem of structuring a system within which major traders in the premier markets are willing to operate. Traders do not want to expose their orders so as to be exploited by other traders (''shot at'' is a term used on the Street). Large traders must be able to negotiate, and they must be free to exercise reasonable strategy in the placement of their orders.

The solution to electronic trading may be to computerize the call

---

[44]This is because the execution of trades eliminates orders from the market.

market rather than the continuous market. It also appears that the problems of call market trading may in turn be resolved by the proper use of electronic technology. A major benefit of consolidating the order flow, both spatially and temporally, is that order batching reduces the size of each order in relation to the market and thus substantially eliminates the need to work orders on the floor of an exchange. As far as blocks are concerned, the institutional trading desks may be willing to enter their orders into a time batched system if such a system is properly designed with regard to their needs. In the example considered in the third section of the chapter, large traders can reduce their uncertainty by negotiating trades off the market and then bringing the orders to the call for execution, much as they do in the continuous markets of today.

The sketch of a computerized call that is presented in this chapter suggests how such a system might work. The system would accept orders at any time, would display orders to subscribers during a precall period, and would accept additional orders during the call itself. The call would consist of a price scan procedure, wherein traders are asked for their buy and sell orders at specific prices. The call would be regulated by a specialist who controls the price scan, establishes the clearing price, enters negotiated block orders into the system, activates the secondary priority rule, and enters his or her own buy/sell orders as needed to facilitate the formation of the market and to stabilize the clearing price.

Access to the electronic call can be controlled by the frequency with which the market is called for a stock (once per hour might be desirable for the more active stocks). The cost of inaccessibility would be reduced by further development of the continuous markets for options and futures on market indexes. Electronic linkages would allow traders off the floor to interact with the market as it is being called (the dissemination of information to traders away from the exchange would substantially reduce the transaction uncertainty call markets currently entail). The reservation price effect could be reduced by encouraging large traders to submit multiple orders (which would more closely approximate points on their normal buy or sell curves, rather than the single points on their reservation buy or sell curves). Also, traders would enter orders electronically as the call market is being formed and thus would be more likely to specify their orders in relation to the normal rather than the reservation buy/sell curves (thus eliminating the induced inelasticity of the market buy/sell curves).

Some markets are not large enough to justify the expense of continuous trading, and call market trading is currently used primarily on smaller exchanges. The natural effects of thinness and the less developed information systems that characterize some of the smaller markets have caused call markets to be associated with less sophisticated markets. This is unfortunate; call market trading has some very desirable features.

Our speculation concerning an electronic call suggests that the problems currently associated with call market trading can be either mitigated or solved. Any thoughts concerning systems design, however, must be accepted as preliminary. The complexities of trading are too great for anyone to know how traders will respond to a new system until that system is tested and refined in the marketplace.

The chapter has shown that price stabilization under normal conditions is an important function of a trading system. Relatively small price changes (for instance, on the order of 1 percent) have a substantial impact on returns measured over relatively long periods (for instance, one year), and on the dollar value of investor wealth. But price stabilization is of crucial importance when a market is under stress. As shown by the events of October 19, 1987, price movements in an asset market can get out of control. On October 19 and 20, the market came perilously close to meltdown.

The extraordinary volatility persisted. Along with shifting expectations concerning the federal budget deficit, the trade deficit and the value of the U.S. dollar in foreign exchange markets, equity values were buffeted by a number of market factors: margin calls, corporate share repurchases, mutual fund redemptions, and the full resumption of program trading. Throughout the period, uncertainty prevailed concerning what a reasonable level might be for the market, and apprehension remained that the market might drop precipitously again. The experience showed that a normal level of instability, once lost, is not easily or quickly regained.

David S. Ruder, Chairman of the SEC, subsequently called for a system to provide more liquidity to the markets in periods of excessive stress. His position addresses one of the most fundamental structural defects of our current system. How might the objective be accomplished? Creating a special reserve fund may help, but how would such a fund be financed and administered? Unfortunately, access to a common pool could result in an overuse of the fund by individual market maker firms. Ought the capital requirements of the market maker firms be raised? Unfortunately, this would force more of them to merge with the large brokerage houses, thus further increasing the concentration of power in the securities industry.

Another possibility should be considered. A separate stabilization fund could be established by each listed company and managed by the exchange so that the use of share repurchase and issuance may be formalized as a stabilization device. A corporation might be allowed certain controls over the total size of its stabilization fund, but a specialist or other exchange official should be entrusted with managing daily operations. The funds would be augmented by issuing shares in a rising market, and would be drawn on by buying shares in a falling market. Such an arrangement could provide substantial liquidity and badly needed stability to the markets.

SUGGESTED READING

Y. Amihud, T. Ho, and R. Schwartz, eds., *Market Making and the Changing Structure of the Securities Industry,* Lexington, Mass.: Lexington Books, 1985.

Y. Amihud and H. Mendelson, "An Integrated Computerized Trading System," in Amihud, Ho, and Schwartz (1985).

E. Bloch and R. Schwartz, "The Great Debate over NYSE Rule 390," *Journal of Portfolio Management,* Fall 1978.

E. Bloch and R. Schwartz, eds., *Impending Changes for Securities Markets: What Role for the Exchange?* Greenwich, Conn.: JAI Press, 1979.

K. Cohen and R. Conroy, "An Empirical Study of the Impact of Rule 19c-3," Duke University working paper, 1987.

K. Cohen, R. Conroy, and S. Maier, "Order Flow and the Quality of the Market," in Amihud, Ho, and Schwartz (1985).

K. Cohen, S. Maier, R. Schwartz, and D. Whitcomb, "The Impact of Designated Market Makers on Security Prices: II. Policy Proposals," *Journal of Banking and Finance,* December 1977.

K. Cohen, S. Maier, R. Schwartz, and D. Whitcomb, *The Microstructure of Securities Markets,* Englewood Cliffs, N.J.: Prentice-Hall, 1986.

K. Garbade and W. Silber, "Structural Organization of Secondary Markets: Clearing Frequency, Dealer Activity and Liquidity Risk," *Journal of Finance,* June 1979.

K. Garbade and W. Silber, "Dominant and Satellite Markets: A Study of Dually-Traded Securities," *Review of Economics and Statistics,* August 1979.

T. Ho, R. Schwartz, and D. Whitcomb, "The Trading Decision and Market Clearing under Transaction Price Uncertainty," *Journal of Finance,* March 1985.

H. Mendelson, "Market Behavior in a Clearing House," *Econometrica,* November 1982.

H. Mendelson, "Consolidation, Fragmentation, and Market Performance," *Journal of Financial and Quantitative Analysis,* June 1987.

A. Sametz, "A Modest Proposal Toward a National Market System—From CLUB to CLOB," in Bloch and Schwartz (1979).

R. Shiller, "The Use of Volatility Measures in Assessing Market Efficiency," *Journal of Finance,* May 1981.

R. Shiller, "Do Stock Prices Move Too Much to be Justified by Subsequent Changes in Dividends?" *American Economic Review,* June 1981.

chapter *14*

Regulation

The United States regulatory structure is three tiered. Closest to the operating level are the exchanges and the National Association of Securities Dealers (NASD). The market centers are known as self-regulatory organizations (SROs). The SROs monitor trading and have oversight responsibility for their member firms.

Two major governmental agencies comprise the second regulatory level: the Securities and Exchange Commission (SEC) and the Commodities Futures Trading Commission (CFTC). These agencies monitor trading, police listed companies and market centers with regard to securities law, and set policy for a wide spectrum of issues.

The third regulatory level is the United States Congress. Both the SEC and the CFTC are responsible to Congress, the source of the legislation governing the securities markets.

The goals of regulation are threefold:

1. Assure an honest market
2. Enhance market efficiency with regard to the provision and pricing of broker/dealer services
3. Enhance market efficiency with regard to the pricing of shares traded

As discussed by Schreiber and Schwartz (1985), these three goals are not compatible in all respects: (1) Interdealer competition (which, *ceteris paribus*, reduces spreads and commissions) fragments the order flow (which can impede the efficiency of price discovery). (2) The imposition of trading halts (to enhance the stability and fairness of the market) delays access to the market (which for some traders represents an inefficiency). (3) Prohibitions on insider trading (to safeguard honesty and fairness) limit access to the market for some traders and can delay the impact of new information on stock prices. And so forth. Resolving the conflicts between the regulatory goals is a major problem for the regulators. There is also a deeper issue: attaining the proper balance between the restrictions explicitly imposed by a formal regulatory body and those implicitly imposed by the competitive forces of a free market.

This chapter steps away from the current regulatory structure and considers the conceptual issues involved. The first section focuses on causes of market failure for the equity markets. Next governmental regulation of the markets is considered. Finally four specific regulatory issues—(1) elimination of fixed commissions, (2) prohibition of off-board trading in listed securities by member firms, (3) introduction of shelf registration, and (4) restrictions on insider trading—are assessed.

SOURCES OF MARKET FAILURE

The private market gives socially desirable results under some conditions when traders compete freely with one another while adhering only to certain basic legal requirements such as those defined by contract law. However, for various reasons a market may fail to reach the desired equilibrium with respect to the price established and the number of shares traded even though the broader legal context is well defined. Regulators face a difficult challenge when addressing the manifestations of market failure.

Specification of the Rules of a Market

Specification of the rules of a market is not part of the market process, unless two or more market systems are in competition with each other. The flow of traffic on our roads and highways provides an analogy. Drivers are free to select the points of origin and destination of their travels and the routes that they follow. If multiple routes exist between two frequently selected points, drivers compete with one another in their route selection. They also compete in terms of lane selection and other aspects of positioning. Such competition between drivers tends to even out the flow of traffic. If the competition is efficient, we have a result equivalent to that given by the random walk of stock prices: when traffic is heavy, expected transit times are similar for various alternatives, and any one driver can select his or her route by random process. This is because it is not possible in a fully arbitraged equilibrium to predict what the better alternative will be.

The desirability of this result in no way implies that traffic should not be governed by a regulatory authority. Indeed, speed limits should be set, traffic lights should be installed at busy intersections, certain types of vehicles should not be allowed on some roads, and so on. The competitive environment cannot determine these rules; traffic regulations must be set by the body politic. So too must the laws that govern equity trading. For instance, if spatial consolidation of the order flow is desirable, one of the rules should be that all orders for a security must be routed to the same market center.

The regulators cannot avoid making certain decisions. It is tempting in a complex situation to ''let the market decide.'' However, there are some things that the market cannot decide. To avoid setting certain rules by legislative authority could be as disastrous as turning off the traffic lights in the financial district of lower Manhattan.

Market Power

Market Power Vis-à-Vis Competitors *Market power* in microeconomic analysis typically refers to the ability of a selling firm, because of its size in relation to the aggregate of all other sellers in an industry, to realize excess profits by increasing price above the value that would prevail under competitive conditions. Equivalently, a buyer who is large in relation to other buyers in aggregate realizes excess profits by depressing price below the competitive equilibrium. All traders benefit from having this power; all wish to be large in relation to their own side of the market. In the securities industry, the economic units thought to have this market power are the suppliers of marketability services.

In the 1970s, the premier securities markets in the United States were the two national exchanges (NYSE and Amex),[1] and the key participant in these markets was the specialist. Each stock listed on an exchange was then, as it is today, assigned to one specialty firm. Until May 1, 1975, the commission structure was fixed. Members of the NYSE were required to take their orders for listed securities to an exchange for execution. Institutional traders, along with other public traders, were not (and still are not) permitted to enter their orders directly.[2] A decade ago, the NYSE and the Amex were considered clubs that only the privileged few could join.

---

[1]The NASDAQ market has also emerged in recent years as a premier trading arena.
[2]A broker who is an exchange member must serve as intermediary.

Control over price, order flow, and membership in the club gave the exchanges an enviable position of power. For the investment community, this power implied monopoly control of the market for dealer services. Accordingly, the price of marketability services (commissions and spreads) was deemed too high, and market maker profits were thought to be excessive.

Market Power Vis-à-Vis the Other Side of the Market   Market power affects the outcome of trading in the equity markets in another way as well. Some traders are large vis-à-vis the other side of the market (some buyers are large in relation to sellers, and some sellers are large in relation to buyers). Size in this context results in the market impact effects considered in Chapter 10. No trader wants this kind of power; all would rather be price takers than have their orders push price in the wrong direction.

How is it that individual traders can have a price impact in a market that comprises a large number of participants? Taking transaction costs into account, if most investors are sufficiently satisfied with their holdings and do not seek a trade, their buy/sell propensities are not expressed in the marketplace. Therefore, those orders that are taken to the market can have an exaggerated price impact.

Transaction costs reduce transaction rates in all markets. The imposition of a sales tax on milk, for instance, reduces consumer demand for milk and hence the purchase of milk from the market. Nevertheless, an individual who wishes to consume milk at some rate still has to buy the milk at that rate.[3] This is not the case with financial assets. Financial assets yield utility by being held rather than by being consumed, and the rate of purchases and sales for such assets is determined by the frequency with which investor demand curves to hold shares shift.[4] Consequently, trading is thin if the market for an asset is in reasonable balance, even though a large number of market participants have invested in the asset and are affected by its price behavior. This thinness results in the (adverse) market power of those who do seek to trade.

Externalities

Externalities, along with market power, are the cause of market failure most widely recognized by economists. A classic example of a negative exter-

---

[3]The time rate of purchase for services and goods that are consumed must on average equal the time rate of consumption.

[4]Participation in the secondary asset markets is a manifestation of disequilibrium behavior; trading in these markets is an equilibrium repairing process. Participation in most other markets (such as the market for milk), on the other hand, need not be inconsistent with equilibrium behavior.

nality is the soot generated by a production process. For instance, a power company that produces electricity is not responsible for the particles of dirt that exit its smoke stacks, and thus the social cost of this air pollution is not taken into account in the output and pricing of electricity. Because *all costs* associated with the production of electricity are not taken into account by suppliers, electricity is overproduced in the free market.

Externalities exist in trading. Investors who post orders on the market convey a benefit to the market in aggregate. Limit orders stabilize market prices, facilitate price discovery, and act as catalysts that attract other orders to the market. Limit order traders are not, however, separately compensated for providing this service. Because *all benefits* associated with the placement of orders are not taken into account by the decision makers, an undersupply of limit orders can be expected in the free market.

The market failure implied by the externalities of market making provides economic justification for the affirmative obligation of the specialist. This market maker is responsible for supplementing the order flow so as to provide orderliness to the price formation process.

Public Goods

Public goods are similar to externalities in that their production is not governed by the market forces that attend the standard exchange of goods and services. Classic examples of public goods are a lighthouse in a harbor and military defense. As noted in Chapter 13, the characteristics shared by these goods are the following: (1) one person's consumption does not reduce the amount available for others, (2) people who do not pay for the good cannot be excluded from consuming it, and (3) whatever quantity is made available of the public good is available for all consumers. These attributes of public goods lead consumers to misrepresent (understate) their demand for them in the marketplace and prevent the private market from supplying these goods in socially optimal amounts. Consequently, the decision concerning the output of a public good must be made collectively by the body politic.

The public goods–type services of a securities market are identified in Chapter 13. They are the services that provide a fair and orderly market: (1) market surveillance to protect against exploitation, fraud, manipulation, and other violations of the rules; (2) price discovery; and (3) price stabilization.

A broad range of investors benefit from a fair and orderly market. The prices established in the premier asset markets signal information to investors. Assets are evaluated for various legal purposes in relation to prices established in the major market centers. Price basing is used for the redemption of equity mutual fund shares and for the evaluation of estate held shares. Prices set in the futures markets are used to establish prices in associated cash markets. A fairer, more efficient secondary asset market reduces the cost to corporations of raising capital in the new issues market. And so on.

The benefit any individual trader realizes from the public goods aspects of market making does not reduce the amount available for others. A single quantity of each of the public goods–type marketability services is provided to the market, and individual investors benefit from these marketability services even though they may not have paid for them. Accordingly, these services would be undersupplied in the free market. This provides further justification for dealer, specialist, and regulator interference in the operations of the equity markets.

Asymmetric Information

Trading in securities markets is motivated by informational change and by changing liquidity needs. Informational change generates informational asymmetries. Insiders (particularly corporate management) have more information than public traders. Some public traders (''informed traders'') have more information than other public traders (''liquidity traders''). Informed public traders may also be better informed than professional market makers (dealers and specialists).

Informational asymmetries are a particularly vexing and costly problem. Because dealers and specialists widen their bid-ask spreads to protect against the advantage that better informed traders may have (see Chapter 12), informational asymmetries increase the cost of transacting for liquidity traders. Further, if the dissemination of information consistently favors some investors over others, those at an informational disadvantage may reduce their participation in the market. This reduction causes markets to be thinner, resulting in a further deterioration of the quality of the marketplace.

It is not possible to eliminate informational asymmetries totally. There are, however, various approaches to dealing with the problem: (1) impose trading restrictions on those who can be identified as having superior information (the so-called insiders); (2) improve the systems used to disseminate information; and (3) change from continuous trading to time batched (call market–type) trading to allow news to be disseminated and assessed before trades are made. Each of these approaches is not a costless solution, however.

Transaction Price Uncertainty

Transaction price uncertainty, which is endemic to the equity markets (see Chapter 8), affects the flow of orders to the market. The order flow itself establishes the transaction prices that are realized *ex post*. Therefore, the realized transaction prices generally differ from equilibrium values (see Chapters 9 and 13), and a community of traders does not achieve an equilibrium distribution of share holdings after any round of trading. This is most easily understood in relation to call market trading.

Assume, for instance, that when they write their orders, the majority of investors anticipate a clearing price that is higher than the equilibrium price. This upward bias in expectations increases the number of sell orders that are attracted to the market, and discourages buy orders. The batching of orders at the call can thus result in a realized clearing price that is below the equilibrium value.[5] The unexpected realization of this lower price leaves some investors wishing they had bought more shares and allows for the possibility of recontracting. With transaction costs, however, there is an insufficient (and inaccurate) amount of recontracting, and errors made in the first round of trading may not be corrected.

Technological Inertia

Inertia in a dynamic environment inhibits technological change. Inertia need not imply the laziness of economic agents, but rather may be due to the cost of adopting a new technology.

Consider, for instance, the introduction of a typewriter with an improved configuration of the keyboard. The standard typewriter keyboard is known as the *qwerty* keyboard, because of the six keys on its upper-left-hand side. An alternative keyboard known as *Dvorak* has been scientifically designed, is reputedly more efficient, but has not succeeded in the marketplace. The reason may lie in the following observations:[6]

- Countless people currently know the touch system with the current ordering of keys. People acquainted with the qwerty keyboard would profit from learning the Dvorak keyboard only if the new system has a sufficient *differential advantage* over the old, discounted over the remaining years for which they expect to be using a typewriter.
- People just learning to type will realize a return on their investment from the *total benefit* of knowing the new system.[7]

---

[5]It is also possible for the distribution of buy and sell orders to result in a clearing price that is between the expected price and the Walrasian equilibrium value.

[6]The typewriter analogy was suggested by Seymour Smidt. My thanks to Gautam Vora for calling my attention to the Dvorak keyboard.

[7]People just learning to type are also younger (on average) than those already acquainted with the existing system and hence have more years to benefit from their knowledge (which increases their return on the investment).

- There are advantages to all typists' knowing and using similar equipment. The benefit to any individual of knowing the new system may therefore be large if the market in aggregate converts to the new system, but small if the market in aggregate does not.

Consequently, the failure of existing typists to convert to the new system reduces the benefits of the superior technology to new typists, new typists therefore learn the older system, and the new and better typewriters are not produced even though the social benefits may in aggregate outweigh the costs. This technological inertia is attributable to the inability of the new typists to compensate current typists adequately for their cost of learning the new technology.

Technological inertia is most likely to occur when change is comprehensive rather than partial. Comprehensive change affects an entire system (for instance, the full array of typewriter keys); partial change involves the components of a system (for instance, the introduction of one key with a changeable head). It may be possible in certain situations to achieve a comprehensive change by a series of partial changes, but such a switch in technology often is not possible.

There has been substantial technological change in the securities industry in recent years (see Chapter 5). Most prominent has been the introduction of electronic equipment to route orders and to disseminate information. Computer technology has also been applied to trade execution, but only to a limited extent and in the face of much resistance from traders (see Chapters 5 and 13). Thus far, trades in the premier markets are still made by person to person contact, either face to face or by telephone.

Computerized trading represents a comprehensive change from the current system.[8] The change requires that professional traders adapt to an entirely new way of operating. Some whose style is suited to the current system would not fare well in an electronic system. Consequently, even if a viable electronic system were developed, technological inertia could delay its adoption significantly. Those involved with systems design are aware of the enormous resistance they would meet, and of the problems that would be encountered in instituting a comprehensive change. Thus inertia also dulls the incentive to develop a new trading system in the first place.

New technology, of course, may eventually make its way in the market. The compact disc, for example, is replacing 33 rpm records, just as the 33 rpm's eventually replaced the old 78's. But change takes time. Any market may indeed fail to incorporate a new technology at a socially optimal rate.

---

[8]The use of electronic equipment for order routing and information display, on the other hand, is partial, not comprehensive change, and market professionals have had far less difficulty in accepting and adapting to this change.

THE REGULATORY PROCESS

In the presence of market failure, one typically considers turning to governmental regulation to achieve the socially optimal production, distribution, and pricing of resources. Unfortunately, the political process is itself flawed, and governmental interference may not enhance the efficiency of a marketplace.

The political process involves a different incentive structure than the private market: the maximization of votes rather than the maximization of financial wealth. And political power (the ability to win votes) differs from economic power (the command of financial resources over real resources). Consequently, the political process operates very differently than the private market. Our discussion of the regulatory process begins by noting several causes of "government failure."

Government Failure

The Distribution of Political Power   The distribution of power across participants in the political process differs from the distribution of power in the market process. Some who are large in the private market are small in the political arena. The political process typically admits outsiders whose main concerns are not the fortunes of a particular industry or the pros and cons of a particular issue. As a consequence, considerations that are not germane to the operations of a specific industry may enter political decisions, and the solutions attained by political consensus may be distorted.[9]

Inadequate Procedural Safeguards   Procedural safeguards in the governmental process differ from those implicit in the market process. The private market itself is a strict regulator—those who do not operate profitably typically do not survive. Unfortunately, government officials who do not regulate well may nonetheless survive as regulators. Instituting effective procedural safeguards is at best costly; at worst, it may be impossible.

Jurisdictional Disputes   The governmental process may involve competition between rival government authorities for regulatory turf. For instance, the growth of futures and options trading in the early 1980s caused confusion as to which agency, the SEC or the CFTC, would have jurisdiction over these new products.[10] At the current time, change in both the securities and banking industries is generating territorial disputes between the SEC and the bank regulators.

---

[9]See Stigler (1971) for further discussion.
[10]See Scarff (1985).

Regulated firms typically have some freedom to choose their regulators, and regulators typically compete for their constituency.[11] This competition affects the decisions regulators make, may prejudice the outcome of the political process, and further diminishes one's confidence that governmental intervention will enhance the economic efficiency of the regulated industry.

The Cost of Regulating   Regulation is costly, and government funds are limited.[12] The fact that government funds are allocated by a budgetary process embedded in a political environment further suggests that funds may not be distributed efficiently across competing governmental projects.

Imperfect Knowledge   More than some may realize, regulators often do not fully understand the problems encountered by an industry and do not know how best to develop and to institute reasonable solutions. In recent years, both the SEC and the CFTC have solicited opinions, held hearings, and deliberated long and hard about certain critical decisions. However, much remains that is not known about the nature of competition in the equity markets. The problems outlined in the preceding section of this chapter, for example, are not easily perceived and, when perceived, are thorny to resolve. All told, the boundaries of knowledge are among the toughest limitations faced by those who seek to govern the market process.

The Evolving Regulatory Focus

Despite imperfections in the political process, regulation of the securities markets is needed and has grown substantially since the Securities Acts of 1933 and 1934. As noted in the beginning of this chapter, the regulatory goals for the securities markets are threefold: (1) assure an honest market, (2) enhance efficiency with regard to the provision and pricing of broker/dealer services, and (3) enhance efficiency with regard to the pricing of shares traded. We now consider how the regulatory emphasis has changed among these goals since the 1933 and 1934 Acts.

Honesty   To operate efficiently, a market must, first and foremost, be honest. The honesty of a market entails guarding against manipulation of information, prices, and trading volume and preventing abuses of position by insiders and professionals.

---

[11]See Bloch (1985).

[12]The expense of improving market efficiency by governmental intervention can be viewed as a transaction cost that is paid by the government (and financed by tax revenue) rather than paid directly by market participants.

Federal regulation of the securities markets began with the Securities Act of 1933 and the Securities Exchange Act of 1934. The primary motivation for this legislation was to ensure reasonable information disclosure and to prevent dishonesty and market manipulation (see Chapter 5). The acts were designed to protect the ignorant from being exploited by those who might distort reality and entice the gullible into undesirable transactions.

The SEC has been particularly concerned with the fairness of the information flow, and the agency has devoted major resources to preventing the abuse of power by insiders. For those involved with the activities of a corporation (with positions ranging from top management to the proofreader in a print shop), information is a freely generated by-product of some other activity. The primary objective of insider trading regulations is to prevent those for whom information is a free by-product from making excess trading profits at the expense of others who do not have a fortuitous position vis-à-vis the information flow.

The SEC's concern with the honesty and timeliness of the information flow has led the agency to one of its more recent projects, the development of the Commission's *Electronic Data Gathering, Analysis, and Retrieval System* (EDGAR). The Commission receives nearly six million pages of disclosure documents per year under the federal securities law.[13] These documents are commonly prepared in an electronic format, but then delivered to the SEC in hard copy. EDGAR has been developed to enable the electronic transmission and analysis of this information. The system's purposes are threefold: (1) facilitate the corporate filing procedure (by using electronic filing rather than hard copy filing), (2) facilitate the processing and analysis of the information by the Commission staff, and (3) allow direct public access to information in the disclosure documents.

EDGAR has presented the Commission with several interesting regulatory questions. The information contained in EDGAR is clearly of substantial value from both the private and the public points of view. EDGAR, however, is expensive—it is expected to entail an operating cost of between $50 and $70 million a year.[14] Should the cost be financed through general tax revenues or by end user fees? Should the Commission market the information itself or contract with a private vendor for the development and implementation of the operational system? How will the marketing and financing decisions affect the speed with which information is disseminated to the investment community? These questions will be answered as the SEC gains experience with the system. It is clear, however, that although modern technology will greatly facilitate the flow of corporate

[13]Cox and Kohn (1986).
[14]Cox and Kohn (1986).

information to investors, it will also challenge the Commission with some complex regulatory issues.

Efficiency of the Market for Broker/Dealer Services   The second regulatory objective is to enhance market efficiency with regard to the provision and pricing of broker/dealer services. This aspect of efficiency entails keeping commissions and spreads competitive and ensuring the financial responsibility of broker/dealer firms.

Concern about the competitive efficiency of the markets developed with the back office crisis of the 1960s (see Chapter 5). The unexpected increase of the order flow in the 1960s led to a substantial increase in brokerage firm failures, as the houses could not keep up with the paperwork and the number of fails to deliver mounted.

The growing number of failures and the inadequacy of the trust funds established by the SROs, led Congress to pass the Securities Investor Protection Act of 1970. This act established governmental insurance of customer accounts. With the insurance, came enhanced government interest in controlling the industry to prevent the continuing failure of broker/dealer firms. Congressional involvement in operational issues and the competitive structure of the markets was thereby established.

In the 1970s, commissions charged for handling large institutional orders had become exorbitant, and institutional traders were fragmenting the markets in their efforts to avoid these rates. Related issues concerning the competitive efficiency of the markets included the absence of spatial integration among various parts of the industry, the quasi-monopoly position of various market makers (primarily the stock exchange specialists), and the restrictions on entry into certain market centers (primarily the two national exchanges).

Congressional concern about the competitive efficiency of the market for broker/dealer services resulted in the enactment of the Securities Acts Amendments of 1975. The legislation had two provisions of particular import: (1) as the first governmental step in deregulation, it precluded the securities exchanges from imposing fixed commissions, and (2) it mandated the development of a national market system (see Chapter 5).

Efficiency with Regard to the Pricing of Shares Traded   The third regulatory objective is to enhance market efficiency with regard to the pricing of shares. This aspect of efficiency entails improving the market's architecture in order to facilitate the price discovery process.

The Commodities Futures Trading Commission has recognized price discovery as a major function of a securities market, because prices discovered in the futures markets are commonly used for price determination in associated cash markets. Indeed, a major economic rationale for the futures markets is their price basing function. For instance, the price of cocoa is believed to be more accurately determined by the meeting of many buyers and sellers in the market for cocoa futures than by the meeting of a far smaller number of firms that buy and sell the cocoa itself. Therefore, cocoa traders look to the futures markets to set their spot prices.

Price discovery has not as yet been fully recognized as a function of the major equity markets (see Chapter 15). Nevertheless, as has been emphasized throughout this book, price discovery is a major issue. Clearly, a $.25 (or even less) discrepancy in the price of a stock can exceed the brokerage commission on a transaction. In addition, there are further costs of inaccurate price discovery. As noted, prices established in the major market centers signal information to traders, are used for price basing in related markets, and are used in the evaluation of estate held shares, equity mutual fund shares, and so on.

Efficient price discovery is the most difficult of the three regulatory goals to comprehend and to implement. However, it is the objective that pertains most closely to the attributes of the equity markets that make these markets unique. Given the importance of accurate price discovery, the objective should be given more attention by regulators.

THE ELIMINATION OF FIXED COMMISSIONS

The most significant change in the securities industry in the United States since its early development was the elimination of the fixed commission structure on May 1, 1975. At the time there was much concern about the effect the change might have; some people thought it would be disastrous. The industry, however, has prospered under negotiated rates. Today, the success of the deregulation is universally acknowledged.

Commission income accounted for roughly half of the gross income of member firms of the NYSE in the period 1971–1974.[15] As one might expect, broker/dealer firms competed fiercely for this income. Brokerage firms offer a package of services—order handling, record keeping, custodial services, advisory services, dividend collection, and research. In the era of fixed commissions, commission dollars alone typically paid for the entire package. The components other than order handling were in essence a rebate to customers in the form of services, rather than in hard dollars.

Therefore, a brokerage firm was able to lower the price it charged for order handling by bundling services. A major ancillary service included in the brokerage package was research. The array of research reports may not have been nearly as valuable as direct dollar rebates, but as part of the package the reports were a free good, and as a free good they were accepted.

[15]NYSE *Fact Book,* 1974, 1976.

The Securities Exchange Act of 1934 had exempted the NYSE from certain statutes in the U.S. antitrust legislation and, until the 1975 Amendments, the Exchange had been free, subject to permission from the SEC, to set minimum commission rates on stock transactions.[16] In 1968, the NYSE appealed to the Commission for a rate increase. To the Exchange's surprise, the U.S. Department of Justice intervened by presenting to the SEC a brief that not only questioned the need for the requested rate increase but challenged the very existence of fixed minimum rates.[17] This brief set into motion the events that led to the total elimination of fixed commissions on May 1, 1975.

Three undesirable consequences of the fixed commission structure had become increasingly apparent with the growth of institutional trading:

1. The level of the minimum rates was excessively high (purportedly, the excess portion of commissions in relation to the cost of order handling ranged as high as 90 percent for large orders).[18]
2. The market was being fragmented by large traders' turning to regional exchanges and the third market to escape the fixed commission structure.
3. Ancillary services (research, and so forth) were being oversupplied.

After the SEC had opened its investigation of the issue, the burden of proof lay with those who sought to retain the fixed commission structure. The NYSE, as leader of the defense, advanced four main arguments:[19]

1. *Destructive competition in the brokerage industry:* The Exchange argued that because of economies of scale in brokerage, more efficient brokerage houses would drive less efficient houses out of business in a fully competitive environment. The elimination of fixed (high) rates would therefore lead to increased concentration in the brokerage industry. According to the Exchange, the price of brokerage services would then actually be higher for customers because of the enhanced market power of the large firms.
2. *Price discrimination:* The Exchange argued that competitive rate setting would cause the price of brokerage services to be lower for large traders than for small traders because of the greater bargaining power of the institutional traders. Therefore, prices would not be

[16]On April 24, 1972, commissions on trades in excess of $300,000 became subject to negotiation between customers and brokers.

[17]U.S. Department of Justice, *Inquiry into Proposal to Modify the Commission Rate Structure of the NYSE,* SEC Release No. 8239, Washington, 1968.

[18]Summer (1979, p. 41).

[19]The arguments presented by the Exchange, along with an assessment of their validity, have been set forth in West and Tinic (1971) and Tinic and West (1980). This subsection draws heavily on both of these papers.

proportionate to costs for traders of different size, and the price discrimination would unfairly disadvantage small investors.

3. *Ancillary brokerage services:* The Exchange argued that fixed minimum commissions were required to ensure that certain essential services other than order handling be provided by the brokerage houses. The primary concern expressed by the Exchange was that the quantity and quality of research would be impaired if competition were allowed to drive commissions to a level that just covered the cost of order handling.

4. *Market fragmentation:* The Exchange argued that fixed minimum commissions were needed to keep the market from fragmenting. Under the fixed commission structure, member firms were given a rate discount for orders brought to the exchange floor. The NYSE believed that this pricing advantage provided the incentive needed to retain its membership; that without fixed commissions it would lose membership and the order flow would fragment; and that with fragmentation various exchange services such as market surveillance could not be adequately provided.

How valid are these arguments in light of economic theory, the realities of the marketplace, and recent history? With regard to the first argument, might commission rates ultimately be higher if big firms were allowed to drive weaker firms out of business and then impose noncompetitive prices? This could indeed occur if average costs for a securities firm are negatively related to volume because of economies of scale in brokerage. It was not inappropriate, therefore, for the NYSE to attempt to establish empirically that average costs do fall with firm size in the brokerage industry.

However, what would the advisable economic policy be if economies of scale do exist in brokerage? The efficient regulatory solution in such a case would be to allow only a few firms (the biggest and the best) to be the providers of the service and then to regulate those firms. That is, rather than establishing a *minimum* commission at a high price to ensure the existence of inefficient firms, a *maximum* commission should be stipulated at a low value to keep the price of brokerage in line with the cost of providing the service. The economies of scale argument, therefore, does not support the Exchange's case.

Furthermore, the Exchange's empirical findings with regard to economies of scale have been challenged by a number of subsequent studies,[20] and, in fact, an alarming increase of concentration did not occur in the brokerage industry in the years after the deregulation in 1975. Firms of varying size have coexisted, and specialty firms have found their niche in

[20]See West and Tinic (1971) for analysis and further references.

the industry. According to Tinic and West (1980), there is no evidence that the elimination of fixed rates has enabled larger brokerage firms to improve their relative position in the industry. Let us turn, therefore, to the Exchange's second line of defense: the price discrimination argument.

Because the fixed commission structure itself clearly implied price discrimination (against the large traders), price discrimination was a tenuous argument for the Exchange to advance. Furthermore, with negotiated rates the price discrimination argument does not hold on theoretical grounds if sufficient competition exists between the brokerage firms. The reason is that, with competitive pricing, prices are set in relation to costs, irrespective of demand elasticities in different market segments.

Table 14.1 shows commission rates for selected months from April 1975 through December 1978. Rates did fall appreciably over the period for institutional orders of all sizes and for the larger orders of individual traders. Rates for individual orders in the 200 to 999 share range remained essentially stable however, and rates actually increased for individual orders in the 0 to 199 share range. Is this realignment of the rate structure the consequence of differential demand elasticities and price discrimination against small traders? Given the evidence that the brokerage industry is reasonably competitive and that there are economies of scale in order handling,[21] these adjustments are more likely to have been attributable to cost relationships and to the elimination of price discrimination against large traders.

The NYSE's third line of defense focused on the provision of ancillary services. Whether bundled or not, the ancillary services would in theory be provided in optimal amounts in a competitive environment so long as no cause of market failure were operative. A market failure argument is possible, however, because the production and use of one of the services, research, may involve externalities. The reason is that the prices set in the markets depend on the information set; the prices in turn signal information to traders and to the firms whose securities are traded and may be used for price basing in related markets. Therefore, a decline in the quantity and quality of information production may distort security prices and so be unacceptable to the community in aggregate.

Would a sufficient amount of information be produced as a private good in a free market? Was information being overproduced when commission rates were fixed? These are difficult questions to answer because the empirical evidence is fragmentary and conjectural. All told, however, there is little indication that either the quantity or the quality of research has diminished appreciably with the introduction of negotiated rates. Furthermore, individual investors now have the freedom not to obtain, and not

[21]Economies of scale in order handling cause costs per share to be lower for bigger orders, but do not necessarily imply that average costs for a brokerage firm decrease as its trading volume expands, *ceteris paribus*.

Table 14.1   COMMISSION RATES, APRIL 1975 THROUGH DECEMBER 1978[a]

	0–199		200–999		1,000–9,999		10,000 +	
	Cents per share	% of prin- cipal	Cents per share	% of prin- cipal	Cents per share	% of prin- cipal	Cents per share	% of prin- cipal
Rates for institutions by order size								
Apr 1975	59.6	1.50	45.7	1.28	27.6	.83	15.0	.57
June	54.5	1.30	36.8	1.06	21.3	.63	12.1	.46
Sept	51.7	1.30	34.5	1.03	20.4	.59	11.5	.42
Dec	48.9	1.19	31.9	.99	18.9	.57	10.4	.38
Mar 1976	50.3	1.15	33.8	.94	19.0	.54	10.8	.36
June	50.0	1.13	33.4	.93	19.5	.53	10.9	.35
Sept	46.7	1.11	31.1	.87	18.4	.50	10.2	.33
Dec	47.0	1.11	31.2	.91	17.6	.51	10.0	.33
Mar 1977	44.3	1.01	28.8	.83	16.0	.46	9.8	.33
June	43.7	1.07	28.1	.85	15.5	.47	9.7	.33
Sept	40.4	1.05	26.1	.83	14.5	.46	9.1	.32
Dec	40.4	1.07	25.4	.83	14.0	.45	8.9	.33
Mar 1978	40.2	1.09	25.0	.84	13.9	.47	8.1	.33
June	43.1	1.10	27.0	.83	14.4	.44	8.5	.30
Sept	42.5	1.03	26.9	.79	14.4	.43	8.7	.30
Dec	40.7	1.03	24.5	.78	13.7	.44	7.8	.31
Rates for individuals by order size								
Apr 1975	50.1	2.03	32.6	1.86	19.5	1.38	8.8	.76
June	51.0	2.06	32.3	1.85	19.0	1.33	7.7	.60
Sept	51.1	2.07	31.3	1.81	17.9	1.24	8.2	.51
Dec	47.2	2.17	29.1	1.87	16.3	1.26	5.9	.25
Mar 1976	50.7	2.07	32.1	1.85	18.4	1.34	5.9	.57
June	53.2	1.97	33.2	1.74	18.8	1.22	7.3	.45
Sept	51.7	2.01	32.7	1.73	18.3	1.18	7.3	.49
Dec	49.5	2.05	31.6	1.76	17.4	1.19	5.3	.43
Mar 1977	51.4	2.02	32.5	1.76	17.4	1.18	5.6	.23
June	51.6	2.05	32.7	1.78	17.8	1.15	4.6	.35
Sept	51.3	2.07	32.4	1.74	17.1	1.06	6.1	.32
Dec	48.7	2.11	30.8	1.77	16.1	1.09	5.7	.35
Mar 1978	52.5	2.23	33.1	1.86	17.7	1.16	5.4	.35
June	54.8	2.15	35.0	1.78	19.1	1.15	7.8	.49
Sept	56.0	2.01	35.1	1.72	19.0	1.12	6.5	.35
Dec	52.8	2.10	32.7	1.76	17.9	1.10	5.9	.48

[a]April 1975–September 1978 figures were revised; October 1978–December 1978 figures are preliminary. Table from Tinic and West (1980). Original source: *Survey of Commission Charges on Brokerage Transactions*, Office of Securities Industry and Self-Regulatory Economics, Directorate of Economic and Policy Research, Securities and Exchange Commission (July 26, 1979), Tables A-12, -13, and -14.

to pay for, research that is not desired. As Tinic and West (1980, pp. 39–40) indicate, ''Under fixed rates and the bundling of services, many investors 'consumed' research for which they would not have paid hard cash. If they were now unwilling to buy these services outright, who would want to say that this was bad?''

The Exchange's fourth argument, that the elimination of fixed commissions would cause the market to fragment as the Exchange lost members, is totally unsupportable. The market fragmentation that gave impetus to the deregulation was in fact attributable to the fixed commissions. That is, rather than holding the Exchange's membership together, the umbrella of fixed commissions created unjustifiably high rates that drove institutional orders away from the exchange markets.

The Exchange never did, and does not now, need fixed commissions to hold its membership together. As seen in numerous places throughout this book, order flow attracts order flow, and, *ceteris paribus,* bigger market centers operate more effectively because they are bigger. The NYSE had failed to appreciate this. The Exchange lacked confidence that its attractiveness as a market center was due to the orderliness of the markets that it provided. The reality is the NYSE never needed a fixed commission structure to survive, and it lost neither members nor order flow in the years following the introduction of negotiated commissions. In fact, the order flow is more concentrated on the floor of the NYSE today than it had been in the years preceding 1975 (see Chapter 5).

We now have had more than a decade of experience with negotiated commissions. As seen in Table 14.1, the deregulation did, for the most part, cause the rates to fall appreciably. The changing rate structure has primarily benefited the larger investors, but there is no reason to believe that small investors have been treated unfairly. By and large, the brokerage industry appears to be competitive, the Exchange has not lost membership, and the markets have not fragmented. There is no evidence that the quantity or quality of research has declined, and individual investors are now free to select the package of brokerage services they prefer. The change from fixed to negotiated rates must, on all counts, be deemed successful.[22]

In the early months of 1975, the advent of negotiated rates had caused great concern in the industry. But reasons were not then, and have not since, been advanced that would justify this concern on the basis of the market failure arguments considered in the preceding section. Fortunately, with regard to this particular deregulation, Washington was correct.

THE ELIMINATION OF OFF-BOARD TRADING RESTRICTIONS

The fixed commission structure was not the only arrangement that caused the exchange markets to appear noncompetitive—there were also off-board trading restrictions.[23] These restrictions, of which the best known is NYSE

---

[22]An equivalent elimination of fixed commissions was instituted in England in October 1986. The British deregulation is referred to as the "Big Bang."

[23]Fixed commissions and off-board trading restrictions were both established by the *Buttonwood Tree Agreement* signed by 24 securities brokers on May 17, 1792 (the buttonwood tree was located at what is now 68 Wall Street).

Rule 390, require member firms to take their orders for listed securities to the floor of an exchange for execution. This forces consolidation of the order flow and limits competition between dealers and market centers.[24]

The debate over off-board trading has been far more heated, prolonged, and complex than the deliberations over the elimination of fixed commissions. To this date, these trading restrictions have not been entirely removed, although they have been considerably reduced in scope.

As of 1975, NYSE Rule 394 prohibited both agency and principal executions away from the Exchange floor. After the Securities Acts Amendments of 1975, the rule was modified (and its number changed to 390) to allow agency transactions away from the Exchange floor. Member firms, however, were still prohibited from participating as principals in off-board trading. This prevented these brokerage houses from assuming a dealership function and thereby kept them from making their own markets in listed stocks. Then, in 1980, member firms were allowed on an experimental basis to make off-board markets for all issues listed after April 26, 1979 (see Chapter 5).

More recently, regulatory attention has turned to a consideration of alternative order exposure rules for stocks traded off-board. It is not clear which of several proposed rules would most effectively prevent some of the undesirable effects of market fragmentation, or even whether an explicit rule is required to assure order exposure. Thus far, no one rule has been adopted.

The Exchange's off-board trading rule first came under scrutiny in a 1965 SEC confidential staff report. The SEC did not call for repeal of the rule, however, until the Commission was charged, by passage of the 1975 Amendments, "with an explicit and pervasive obligation to eliminate all . . . competitive restraints that could not be justified by the purposes of the Exchange Act."[25] At the time, the NYSE was considered by many an exclusive club that only the privileged could join, and the Exchange's fixed commission structure had recently been found anticompetitive and unjustified. In this context, the off-board trading restrictions appeared to be another anticompetitive barrier that the Exchange had erected to protect its narrow self-interest. Consequently, in June 1977, the SEC announced that it would mandate the removal of Rule 390 by the end of the year.

In response, a cry of alarm was sounded by many market participants, certain academicians, and some members of Congress. The fears concerning removal of the off-board trading restrictions carried far more conviction than the concerns voiced about the end of fixed commissions. It quickly

---

[24]The conceptual issues involved in the consolidation/fragmentation debate are discussed in Chapter 13. We review the matter here from the regulatory viewpoint.

[25]Securities Acts Amendments of 1975, *Conference Report*, House of Representatives Report No. 94-229, May 19, 1975, p. 94.

became apparent that the off-board trading issue was not as straightforward as the elimination of fixed commissions. In early December 1977 the SEC postponed the elimination of the rule.

In July 1980, the SEC instituted Rule 19c.3, which freed Exchange members to make off-board markets for issues listed on the Exchange after April 26, 1979. The day before this rule became effective, *The Wall Street Journal* (July 17, 1980, p. 3) reported that Morgan Stanley and Merrill Lynch had both announced plans to trade in-house what have come to be known as "19c.3 stocks." The article stated that "Most major broker-dealers say they will begin trading listed stocks if competitive pressures make such a move advisable." At the time, it appeared that substantial order flow might be diverted from the exchange markets.

By mid-1983, however, Merrill Lynch, Morgan Stanley, Paine Webber, Goldman Sachs, and virtually all of the other large firms had stopped making markets in 19c.3 stocks. In-house market making is an inherently costly operation because of the considerable amount of financial capital that market making requires. The design of the 19c.3 experiment biased the results because in-house market making in the newly listed, 19c.3 stocks was not as profitable as market making in the established volume leaders such as IBM and Exxon might have been. In part, the stock exchange specialists simply had more fire power and so won the war: brokerage houses that competed with the specialists by making in-house markets for 19c.3 stocks might have received unfavorable treatment by the specialists when they turned to the exchange markets to rebalance their inventory positions. Whatever the reason, the experiment did not succeed. The debate concerning the total removal of off-board trading restrictions, however, has continued.

Although the SEC's 19c.3 experiment failed to increase competition between market makers and did not resolve the consolidation/fragmentation debate, the Commission's involvement with the issue was successful in certain respects. To understand this, the following must be recognized:

1. The Securities Acts Amendments of 1975 mandated the development of a national market system, but did not say precisely what such a system would be. Rather, the Act set forth certain broad goals to be achieved. One of the goals was fair competition among brokers, dealers, and markets; another was the opportunity for investors' orders to meet without the participation of a dealer.[26] These goals are vague and inconsistent in certain respects. Understandably, the SEC had difficulty achieving them.
2. Furthermore, the SEC had not been involved with the design of the market's architecture before the 1975 Amendments. Rather,

---

[26]For further discussion, see Williams (1985).

the Commission has historically been responsible for setting rules and procedures to prevent conduct contrary to the public interest and for overseeing and policing the markets. Accordingly, the new design responsibilities assigned to the SEC were not easily carried out by the Commission.

3. The design and implementation of a national market system was impeded by the myriad conflicts of interest that prevailed among dealers, specialists, traders, exchange officials, issuing corporations, brokerage houses, self-regulatory groups, and the SEC itself. Thus the SEC was responsible for achieving a vaguely formulated goal in the face of extensive opposition.[27]

4. The legal power to mandate the removal of NYSE Rule 390 gave the Commission considerable control over the NYSE and various other groups in the industry. Whether by intention or by luck, the Commission's most successful move was to threaten, but not to put into effect, the total removal of the off-board trading restrictions.

Thus the Commission used its authority to remove Rule 390 to get the industry to move itself forward. The threat, made credible by the recent and successful elimination of fixed commissions, worked. The exchanges have opened their doors to new members, the clublike atmosphere of the NYSE has largely disappeared, and an intermarket linkage system (ITS) is now in place. Today, the belief is widespread that we have achieved a national market system. Nevertheless, NYSE Rule 390, though diminished, still stands.

The experience with off-board trading has been very different from the experience with fixed commissions. Rate fixing was clearly anticompetitive and undesirable, but off-board trading restrictions appear to have some justification. Wherein lies the difference?

As noted, there are externalities in trading, and there are public goods aspects to market making. Traders benefit from a market in which orders are consolidated, trading priority rules are enforced, prices are set with reasonable accuracy, price movements are kept orderly, and trading is closely monitored. The superiority of such a market may not, however, guarantee its existence. The reason is that individually traders may have an incentive to turn to off-board markets.

As discussed in Chapter 13, an off-board market may compete with a national exchange by guaranteeing timely executions at competitive prices.

---

[27]In the Securities Acts Amendments, Congress had established the National Market Advisory Board (NMAB) to carry out the design function for the SEC. The board failed to achieve its objective within the two years it had been given. On December 12, 1977, after much wheel spinning and in the face of increasing impatience in Congress, the NMAB had its last meeting.

Furthermore, because it does not assume the affirmative obligation to make a fair and orderly market, and because it does not provide the stock watch, market surveillance, and other services of an exchange, an off-board market may charge lower commissions than the exchange market. Assume this to be the case and that, consequently, an appreciable part of the order flow is diverted from a major market center. What might then ensue?

Price discovery on the exchange could become less accurate, and the investor protection provided by the exchange's stock watch and surveillance systems could deteriorate. In addition, spreads might increase and prices could become more volatile because of the reduced order flow. These changes would in turn cause the exchange to be a less desirable trading arena; accordingly, the order flow to the exchange could decrease further, and the output of exchange services could be further impaired. In such an event, the quality of the in-house markets would also suffer; consequently, the detrimental effects would be widely felt. Nevertheless, the prospect of this occurring would not be taken into account by investors when they make their individual trading decisions. This is because of the externalities involved, and because of the public goods aspects of market making.

The SEC has been involved with the off-board trading issue since 1975. Over the years, the Commission has invited opinions, held hearings, and monitored its 19c.3 experiment. Throughout, it has acted with caution. Given the importance of the issue and its complexity, the Commission is wise to have done so.

SHELF REGISTRATION (SEC RULE 415)

In 1982 the SEC relaxed its constraint against shelf registration for both equity and debt issues and, with the institution of Rule 415, allowed a corporation to file for a security to be issued, at the corporation's discretion, anytime during a period of up to two years.

Share registration is a statutorily mandated prerequisite to a public primary distribution. An SEC requirement for registration is that investors be provided with current information about an issuer and the securities to be offered. The Commission believed that the public might not have this information if securities could be sold "off the shelf." Thus the Commission's position had been that securities could be registered only if the shares were to be presently offered for sale to the public.

However, a massive effort by the issuer, the underwriters, legal counsel, and the SEC staff is involved in a registration, even for the most repetitive public offerings of major companies with widely traded securities. The process may involve weeks or, occasionally, months. In the meantime, prices fluctuate in the securities markets, and the payoff for an issue is not known until the moment of clearance is reached. Not surprisingly, issuing companies sought to change the regulatory constraint against shelf registration. The deliberations that ensued have taken account of the following:

1. *Transaction costs:* The transaction costs (legal fees, underwriter's spread, and so on) may be lower for a 415 offering because the fixed cost of a registration can be distributed over a series of issuances, and because competitive bidding between investment banks is more aggressive when shares are taken to the market with minimal delay.

2. *Flexibility:* When shares are on the shelf, a corporation is free to decide during a two year period just when they may be issued and can adjust the terms of a debt offering (for example, a bond's maturity) without filing an amendment to the original registration statement.

3. *Market timing:* With shelf registration, an issuer can sell shares quickly after contacting an investment banker (often on the same day). Direct placement may also be facilitated when shares are sold from the shelf. In contrast, an issuer must wait at least 48 hours for SEC approval after filing a registration statement for a traditional sale.

4. *Due diligence:* An underwriter has the due diligence responsibility to ensure the accuracy and completeness of a registration statement. With a 415 offering, however, an official underwriter is not typically named at the original filing, and the speed with which shares can be offered from the shelf may prevent underwriters from providing adequate due diligence after they have been appointed.

5. *Competition between investment banking firms:* Syndicates are smaller for 415 offerings, and it takes considerably less time to form them. This favors the large investment banking firms and can result in regional dealers being excluded from the market.

6. *Market overhang:* Because the market demand to hold shares of an issue is negatively inclined, an increased supply of shares exerts downward pressure on price.[28] The particular problem associated with shelf registration is that the additional shares "hang over" the market without the realization of additional earnings potential, because the funds have not yet been received by the issuer.

7. *Liquidity:* The broader impact of Rule 415 on the liquidity and stability of the market has been questioned because of the speed with which shares can be offered from the shelf. A 415 issuance, like a traditional issuance, may be stabilized by an underwriter. Nevertheless, Rule 415 has more closely integrated primary and

---

[28]A number of studies have found evidence that the issuance of new shares exerts price pressure; for instance, Asquith and Mullins (1986), Dann and Mikkelson (1984), Hess and Frost (1982), Marsh (1979), and Mikkelson and Partch (1985).

secondary market operations, and some concern has been expressed that this may disrupt the liquidity and stability of the secondary markets.

The debate over Rule 415 was intense but relatively brief. In March 1982, the SEC adopted a temporary *shelf registration rule*. In November 1983, Rule 415 was made permanent by the Commission by a vote of four to one. The major difference between the final rule and the temporary rule is that only a limited number of large, widely followed corporations are now allowed to use shelf registration.

The use of 415 offerings since March 16, 1982, is shown in Table 14.2. Shelf registration has been favored for debt issues, but not for equities. This may be because the total dollar value of new debt issues far exceeds the total dollar value of new equity issues (new equity capital is largely generated internally by net income), and avoidance of the fixed costs of an offering is a consideration only when a corporation turns regularly to the financial markets for funds.

Table 14.2   USE OF RULE 415 OVER THE PERIOD MARCH 16, 1982–DECEMBER 31, 1984

	Number of issues		Total dollar amount ($ Millions)	
	Nonshelf	**Shelf**	**Nonshelf**	**Shelf**
Straight debt	830	1,073	70,799	105,153
Convertible debt	228	22	11,797	1,381
Straight preferred stock	151	48	10,344	2,464
Convertible preferred stock	79	26	3,743	947
Exchange listed common stock	370	135	18,426	7,555
OTC common stock	232	2	4,375	27

Source: SEC Memorandum, "Use of Shelf Registration in the Issuance of Debt, Preferred Stock and Common Stock," February 22, 1985.

With regard to issuance costs, the evidence suggests that the savings attributable to a 415 offering are indeed substantial. Kidwell, Marr, and Thompson (1984) have estimated that issuance costs are approximately 30 basis points lower for a shelf registered bond issue than for a traditional bond issue.[29] In dollar terms, the saving for a $90 million,[30] 15 year bond issue with a 12 percent coupon is about $342,000 per year, or $2.3 million in present value terms over the life of the issue. Findings with regard to equity issues suggest that costs for shelf registered offerings are lower by

[29]A basis point is one one-hundredth of 1 percent.
[30]$90 million is approximately the average sized bond issue in Kidwell, Marr, and Thompson's sample of 83 Rule 415 issues, and 73 non-415 issues.

approximately 0.63 cents per dollar as compared to traditional syndicated equity offerings.[31] Furthermore, for equity issues, there is no evidence that the negative price reaction to a 415 offering differs from that associated with a regular offering [see Moore, Peterson, and Peterson (1986)]. Consequently, market overhang does not appear to be a serious problem for a 415 offering.

As with the debate over off-board trading (NYSE Rule 390), the SEC appears to be concerned primarily with the effect of the deregulation on the cost of issuing shares (transaction costs and market overhang). However, the dissenting vote of Commissioner Barbara S. Thomas did reflect her belief that the shelf registration of equity shares could jeopardize the stability and liquidity of the markets. Further, because of concern about information disclosure, the permanent rule has restricted shelf registration to only large corporations for which information release is in any event expected to be considerable.

Compared to the arguments involving off-board trading, those concerning shelf registration are not complex. Transaction costs are always a major concern to market participants. Price uncertainty is harmful to corporations, just as it is to traders. Because the shelf registration rule enables a corporation to reduce the price uncertainty involved in a new offering, it effectively makes the markets more liquid for the corporate issuer. The questions of information release and the concentration of power in investment banking are important considerations; however, in the absence of a clear market failure argument, the SEC should let the market decide whether or not 415 offerings are more efficient than traditional offerings. For the larger corporations, the Commission has.

INSIDER TRADING[32]

The primary objective of regulation is to assure an honest market. To this end, restrictions on insider trading have been instituted to prevent abuses of position. The pertinent legislation is Section 10(b) of the Securities and Exchange Act of 1934 and SEC Rule 10b-5.

Corporate insiders have a fiduciary responsibility vis-à-vis public shareholders. However, the ability to "produce" information presents a corporate insider with an opportunity to profit at shareholders' expense. For instance, the management of a profitable corporation could, if unrestricted, realize personal gain by selling shares short while jeopardizing the profitability of the firm. Insiders, being better informed than public investors,

---

[31]The savings vis-à-vis a nonsyndicated offering were 1.36 cents per dollar. See Bhagat, Marr, and Thompson (1985).

[32]Case material contained in this section draws on Dunfee, Gibson, Blackburn, Whitman, McCarty, and Brennan (1984) and Whitman and Gergacz (1985).

are also in a position to profit from the advantages offered by an asymmetric distribution of information.

Studies have shown that corporate insiders indeed realize abnormal profits when they trade the equity shares of their own firms.[33] Evidence presented by Givoly and Palmon (1985) suggests, however, that excess returns are usually attributable to superior general knowledge, not to insiders keying their transactions to particular announcements or events. Such returns are perfectly legal. What is not allowed is for insiders to trade on information that has not yet been made public.

Gross abuses of positions of power should be disallowed, from the viewpoint of both fairness and efficiency. In extreme cases, the harm done to uninformed traders has no justification. As stated by John Shad, former chairman of the SEC, insider trading "is the few taking advantage of the many. If people get the impression that they're playing against a marked deck, they're simply not going to be willing to invest."[34] If disgruntled traders do cease to participate in a market, prices are depressed and trading becomes thinner, to the detriment of all.

In the United States *insiders* are defined as the officers and directors of a corporation and as any investor who owns more than 10 percent of a corporation's outstanding shares. Such individuals are required by the 1934 Act to report any transaction in the stock of their host corporation within 10 days after the month of the transaction. This information is contained in the *Official Summary of Securities Transactions and Holdings,* which is published monthly by the SEC. Corporate insiders are also prohibited from selling shares short and must return all short run (six months or less) profits realized from trading their host company's stock.

Further, it is illegal for anyone to participate in a transaction that takes advantage of "inside" information that is unavailable to others involved in the trade. This restriction, imposed by SEC Rule 10b-5, has provided the foundation for most federal enforcement concerning fraudulent conduct.

The wording of Section 10(b) of the 1934 Act encompasses a wide spectrum of securities fraud that the Securities and Exchange Commission may proscribe by the rule making authority granted to it. Rule 10b-5, known as the *disclose or abstain rule,* was set forth by the SEC in 1942. A key provision of 10b-5 is that it applies to any transaction by anybody, not just to a corporate insider.

The specific criteria for determining fraud under Rule 10b-5 have subsequently been established by the federal courts. Most importantly, to be in violation of the rule, the information used by a trader must be found to be material. That is, if revealed, the information would have to affect a

---

[33]For instance, Jaffe (1974a, 1974b), Finnerty (1976), and Givoly and Palmon (1985).
[34]*The Wall Street Journal,* November 17, 1986, p. 28.

contra party's trading decision. The trader must also know that the information is unavailable to the public. An individual in possession of such nonpublic information has an obligation to disclose it before participating in a trade based upon it. A failure to disclose such information thus constitutes fraud. And it is fraud that Section 10(b) of the 1934 Act was intended to prevent.

An example is provided by the Texas Gulf Sulphur case.[35] Texas Gulf Sulphur had kept secret a major ore discovery made in November 1963, while it tried to purchase the remainder of a section of land surrounding the find. The corporation issued pessimistic news releases that denied the discovery and depressed the value of the company's stock. Meanwhile, certain corporate insiders and some outsiders who had been given the information purchased shares of the corporation. At the time of the initial discovery, Texas Gulf Sulphur stock was trading at the $17 level. On April 16, after information on the find was publicly released, the stock traded at $36\frac{3}{8}$. By May 15, the share price had risen to $58\frac{1}{4}$. The Second Circuit Court of Appeals found that the information was material, that it was secret, and thus that trades based on it were in violation of the 1934 Act.[36]

Another case involving insider trading under the 1934 Act involved a stockbroker (Gintel) who was not an insider of the corporation to which the information pertained.[37] From November 6 through 23, 1959, Gintel bought approximately 11,000 shares of Curtiss-Wright stock for discretionary accounts under his control. On November 24 and 25, he started selling some of these shares. On the morning of November 25, the directors of Curtiss-Wright—including a member (Cowdin) from Gintel's firm—approved a reduction in the quarterly dividend from $.625 per share to $.375 per share. During a recess in the directors' meeting, Cowdin telephoned a message to Gintel about the dividend cut. Gintel, upon receiving the news, transmitted two orders to the Exchange—one to sell 2000 shares for 10 accounts, and one to sell short 5000 shares for 11 accounts. The orders were executed at 11:15 A.M. and at 11:18 A.M., at prices of $40\frac{1}{4}$ and $40\frac{3}{8}$, respectively. News of the dividend cut appeared on the Dow Jones ticker at 11:48 A.M.. Shortly thereafter, trading was halted on the Exchange because of the large number of sell orders received. The price was $36\frac{1}{2}$ when trading resumed; Curtiss-Wright closed on November 25 at $34\frac{7}{8}$.

Cowdin's relationship with Curtiss-Wright prohibited him from selling the shares without disclosing the news. The SEC held that, by extension,

---

[35]401 F.2d 833 (2d Circuit, 1968).

[36]Interestingly, the standard of business behavior imposed on the securities transactions differed from that imposed on the purchase of land surrounding the site of the ore discovery. Texas Gulf Sulphur was free to purchase the land without any obligation to release information about the discovery.

[37]Cady Roberts & Co., 40 S.E.C. 907 (1961).

it was in contravention of insider trading restrictions for Gintel, a stock-broker in Cowdin's firm, to have acted on the information supplied directly by Cowdin. Gintel had clearly accelerated his selling activity before the news was publicly announced, and the damage was material. The SEC held that Gintel's clients should not have expected him to pass on the benefits of the inside information to them, at the expense of the public. Consequently, the Commission ruled that Gintel's actions were in violation of Section 10(b) and Rule 10b-5.

The extent of liability for noncorporate members acting on nonpublic information has subsequently been the object of much debate. The SEC has taken the position that no one who possesses nonpublic information may trade on the basis of the information until it has been made public. This position has been modified in the courts, however. In *Vincent F. Chiarella* v. *United States,* the United States Supreme Court limited the applicability of Rule 10b-5 by confining the definition of an insider to one who has a "relationship of trust and confidence with shareholders."[38]

Chiarella, as a printer for Pandick Press in 1975 and 1976, handled various documents that contained announcements of corporate takeover bids. Although the names of the companies involved were concealed until final printing, Chiarella was able to deduce corporate identities from other information in the documents. He realized more than $30,000 in profits from trades based on his deductions.

Chiarella was convicted for violating Section 10(b) of the 1934 Act and SEC Rule 10b-5. The court of appeals affirmed his conviction. The Supreme Court, however, reversed the decision in 1980. The reason for the reversal was that Chiarella was not a fiduciary or agent for any of the corporations involved, hence was under no obligation to disclose information before trading on it, and therefore his use of the information was not fraudulent. The decision established that "a duty to disclose under Section 10(b) does not arise from the mere possession of nonpublic market information." In the opinion of the court, financial unfairness per se does not constitute fraud. Although Section 10(b) is a catch-all provision, "what it catches must be fraud."[39]

The Supreme Court further restricted the class of outsiders who could be in violation of the 1934 Act in another landmark case, *Dirks* v. *Securities and Exchange Commission.*[40] Dirks, an officer of a broker/dealer firm specializing in investment analyses of insurance company securities, was informed by a former officer of Equity Funding of America that the fund's

---

[38]*Chiarella* v. *U.S.*, 45 U.S. 222 (1980).
[39]Statements by Justice Powell; see Dunfee, Gibson, Blackburn, Whitman, McCarty, and Brennan (1984).
[40]*Dirks* v. *Securities and Exchange Commission,* U.S. Supreme Court 103 S. Ct. 3255 (1983).

assets were greatly overvalued. Dirks investigated the allegations, found them to be correct, and openly discussed the information with various investors and clients. Over a two week period, while Dirks pursued his investigation, the price of Equity Funding shares decreased from $26 to $15. Shortly thereafter, Equity Funding's records were impounded by the California insurance authorities, and fraud was established.

The SEC held that Dirks was in violation of the 1934 Act because of his repeated allegations of fraud to investors who subsequently sold their stock in Equity Funding. Upon being censured by the SEC, Dirks sought review in the court of appeals, which then also entered judgment against him. In 1983 the decision was reversed by the United States Supreme Court.

The Supreme Court based its decision on the following. No monetary or personal benefit was received by an Equity Funding employee for revealing information to Dirks; rather, their motive was to expose a fraud. Therefore, no employee of Equity Funding had violated his or her duty to the corporation by passing information to Dirks. Hence there could be no derivative breach of duty by Dirks, who himself had no fiduciary obligation to Equity Funding's shareholders.

The Dirks case established that disclosure constitutes a breach of an insider's fiduciary duty only if it is motivated by personal gain.[41] Further, if there is no breach of duty by an insider, there is no derivative breach by an outsider (for example, the security analyst). The Supreme Court's determination in the Dirks case therefore allows an analyst to "dig out" information about a corporation and to trade on that information without its being publicly revealed.

A distinction is now made between "private" information and "inside" information, and trading on the basis of private information is now allowed. This is essential to the informational efficiency of the marketplace. The trading profits a stock analyst can generate are an incentive for information to be brought to light in the first place. Without this incentive, an insufficient amount of information may indeed be supplied in the marketplace.

The SEC has pressed forward in recent years in its efforts to control insider trading. In the spring of 1986, the Commission exposed an enormous insider trading scandal: on May 12, Dennis B. Levine was charged with making $12.6 million from trading illegally on inside information concerning corporate takeovers. Six months later, on November 14, Ivan F. Boesky agreed to pay a penalty of $100 million to settle charges of trading on information illegally obtained. In February and early March of 1987, a

---

[41]A tip given to a relative or friend may also constitute an unjustified exploitation of nonpublic information. The court would view an insider who makes a gift of confidential information to a family member or friend as equivalent to the insider's trading personally on the information and then making a gift of the profits to the family member or friend.

succession of further, major charges were made by the SEC. Then, on March 19, 1987, Boyd L. Jefferies agreed to plead guilty to two charges that involved securities law violations. The SEC's investigations are continuing. The full extent of insider trading operations has yet to be uncovered.

The dollar sums involved in the recent cases are huge, and the people and firms involved are prominent. Levine was a managing director at Drexel Burnham Lambert. Boesky and Jefferies were both founders and chief executive officers of well known firms that carried their names. Others caught were associated with respected brokerage houses, including Kidder Peabody, Merrill Lynch, and Goldman Sachs.

The current wave of insider trading is largely related to the takeover action of the 1980s. Much of the trading activity centers on risk arbitrageurs such as Boesky, and on people in frequent contact with them, such as Levine and Jefferies. Corporate restructuring is typically arranged with extensive participation from investment bankers. The investment banking firms, however, are also involved in arbitrage and other trading activities for their own accounts and for the accounts of institutional investors. Sophisticated communication systems have been developed to bring clients together, and to trade large blocks of stock.

The arrangement of a single takeover is now far more complex than it was just a decade ago. According to Sterngold,[42] "Ten years ago, those involved in the secret planning for a takeover, even a big one, would have barely filled a table for eight at the Four Seasons. But the simple days are gone. The complexities and aggressiveness of Wall Street's takeover activity today require battalions of specialists who, in the normal routine of their jobs, arrange the deals and must resist the temptation to buy and sell the stocks before the takeover is announced.[43] These deal makers are Wall Street's new 'insiders.' "

Extensive efforts are now being made by securities firms to disguise the names of merger candidates, to protect or to shred sensitive documents, and to control the flow of people and of information into and out of offices. But it is not an easy matter in the current environment of communications networks and complex financial operations to control the flow of information and to police those who might use information for their personal gain. Berg wrote in a *New York Times* article, "Wall Street is a warren of in-

[42]J. Sterngold, "Wall Street's Army of Insiders," *The New York Times,* May 18, 1986, section 3, p. 1.

[43]Sterngold continued (p. 8), "At each company involved, the chief executive and his most trusted advisers usually know of the impending deals, and the board of directors, often numbering a dozen or more, must be allowed to debate and vote on the issue. The company's outside law firm is alerted, and at times the board of directors will have its own set of lawyers." And the list grows longer, for it also includes specialists and lawyers at the investment banking houses and at the commercial banks.

formation 'networks'—cliques that exchange information regularly to win out over investors who are not part of any clique.''[44]

The financial community has been shocked by the recent scandals. The feeling of the Street is reflected in a statement by Max Chapman, Jr., president of Kidder, Peabody & Co.: "I'm saddened [by the revelations of insider trading on Wall Street]. But I'm not ready to condemn the industry. This business is still based on a person's word and reputation; we do billions of dollars of business every day, on the telephone. This industry is based on good faith and honesty of the players. I still believe in that.''[45]

The SEC and Congress have responded to the insider trading scandals by considering further legislation. The key legislative rule under which many prosecutions have been made, Rule 10b-5, was set forth by the Commission in 1942, with relatively little discussion and only a limited realization of the extensive array of abuses to which it would subsequently be applied. To date, the government's chief reliance has been on case law that has evolved from court decisions such as those we have considered. The foundation for many of the SEC's cases has been the concept of *misappropriation of information*. The Commission, however, has in the past resisted offering a precise definition of insider trading because of a belief that doing so would restrict its flexibility in prosecuting violators.

Then, in August 1987, the SEC changed its position and, for the first time, advanced a definition of insider trading to be used in proposed legislation, new Section 16A of the Insider Trading Act of 1987. The SEC's proposal would forbid trading by those in possession of nonpublic information that is material and that has been wrongfully obtained by, among other things, bribery, theft, or the breach of confidentiality arising from any contractual, fiduciary, personal, employment, or other relationship with the issuer, current or potential investors, various government officials, and others. The following excerpt from the proposed Insider Trading Act of 1987 was reported in *The New York Times* on August 8, 1987 (p. 34):

> It shall be unlawful for any person, directly or indirectly, to purchase, sell, or cause the purchase or sale of, any security while in possession of material nonpublic information concerning the issuer or its securities, if such person knows or recklessly disregards that such information has been obtained wrongfully or that such purchase or sale would constitute a wrongful use of such information.

The SEC's proposed definition of "wrongful" is intended to cover situations currently encompassed by the concept of misappropriation. The

---

[44]E. Berg, *The New York Times,* May 16, 1986, p. D2.
[45]Columbia Business School *Annual Report,* 1986, p. 18.

proposal would also lighten the burden of proof for prosecutors by replacing a ''use standard'' with a ''possession standard.'' That is, the Commission would have to prove only that an individual *possessed* inside information, not that the person actually *used* the information, when participating in a questionable trade. The legislation would further remove any personal benefits test (the demonstration of ''benefit,'' which may be intangible, has often in the past proved extremely difficult). In addition, the new definition would eliminate the condition that someone who has passed information in question to others must have done so in anticipation of realizing a personal benefit; thus a tipper would be liable for the trades of tippees, even if the latter are not themselves liable.

A fundamental economic question still remains unanswered, however: do the insider trading restrictions increase or impair the efficiency of the marketplace?[46]

Manne (1966) was one of the first to argue against the trading restrictions. According to Manne, the profits realized through insider trading should be allowable as a reward for entrepreneurship. Manne and others have argued further that insider trading, although admittedly causing losses for those who are contra parties to the insider trades, benefits the broader community of investors by keeping prices more closely aligned with the underlying determinants of share value.

The unavoidable vagueness of any legal definition of insider trading, conflicts of interest caused by the law, and the formidable problem of enforcing the restrictions have also been advanced as reasons for changing the law. Consider the problem of vagueness, for instance. Assume an outsider deduces that merger talks are taking place between two companies because some employees have let slip that at each company top management had participated in weekend meetings. It would not be allowable for the outsider to pay for this information. But what constitutes payment? A kind word? Flowers? Football tickets?

What constitutes information? Knowledge, for instance, that an important line of credit is being requested from a commercial bank is not inside information. But what if the bank indicates that the request is likely to be honored? What if the bank indicates that the request will be honored in three business days?

Insider trading restrictions have resulted in conflicts of interest. One department of an investment bank may, for instance, be in possession of information concerning a client firm that is relevant for customers of another department of the bank. The bank's fiduciary responsibility to the client firm dictates that the information be kept secret, but the bank's fiduciary

---

[46]Controls to prevent egregious abuses of position are without question needed. There is scant disagreement, for instance, that short selling by insiders, price/volume manipulation, and the release of false information must be prohibited.

responsibility to customers calls for disclosure. Securities firms have attempted to avoid such conflicts of interest by separating various departments by an information barrier known as a *Chinese Wall*. Nevertheless, investment banks at times find themselves in a no win situation with regard to information that a client is unwilling to make public.

Bloch (1986) reports an example: *Slade* v. *Shearson, Hammill & Co., Inc.* [CCH Fed. Sec. L. Rep. 94,329 (1974)]. The registered representatives of Shearson, Hammill & Co. promoted the stock of Tidal Marine at a time when the investment banking department of the securities firm knew a large part of Tidal's fleet was damaged. Tidal was unwilling to allow Shearson to divulge the information; a Chinese Wall at Shearson prevented the investment bankers from passing the information on to the registered reps; and Shearson was not allowed to solicit customers without revealing all of the information that the firm had. Shearson, of course, could have stopped trading in the client's stock. However, the very act of not trading would itself have signaled the existence of new information to the market. It appeared that whichever way Shearson could have turned, it would not have fully satisfied the dictates of the law.

Trading based on inside information is difficult to control. In a global environment, trades can be made in countries where restrictions do not exist, and funds can be transferred into and out of foreign banking accounts.[47] The six month trading restriction can be circumvented by negating a long position in equity shares with an offsetting position in an option written on the stock. These actions are difficult to detect. In addition, an insider can, without restriction, exploit information relating to his or her own firm by trading the equity shares of a competitor, supplier, or customer firm that is also affected by the information.

The arguments both for and against insider trading restrictions are substantial. At the heart of the issue is a market failure—the failure of the free market to achieve an efficient and equitable distribution of resources when the distribution of information among market participants is asymmetric. The complexity of the question is compounded by the fact that government failure is also involved—the problems attributable to informational asymmetries are not well understood, and controlling insider trading is costly.

Nevertheless, the insider trading scandals of 1986 and 1987 have underscored an important fact. Substantial resources are now being devoted to arranging complex financial packages and to trading. Longer term pro-

---

[47]In September 1982, the SEC established with Switzerland a system for handling SEC requests for information on insider trading. Prior to this understanding, bank secrecy laws in Switzerland would have prevented the disclosure of information concerning trades in U.S. stocks that were made on the basis of nonpublic information. Other countries with bank secrecy laws include the Bahamas, Panama, Bermuda, and the Cayman Islands.

duction and investment goals can, unfortunately, be overlooked when undue attention is paid to realizing the quick profits of a trader. In addition, the positions established by certain traders—in particular, the risk arbitrageurs and market makers such as Jefferies—are giving professionals whose economic function should be to make better markets the power to influence corporate structure. Perhaps the exercise of this power does keep share prices more closely aligned with the fundamental determinants of corporate value. Nevertheless, the social cost is high, both in terms of fairness and because resources are diverted from more fundamental activities relating to production and investment.

Ultimately, the best way to control insider trading would be to create an environment where the act of trading is diminished in importance. This calls for simplifying the process. Continuous trading systems are dynamically inefficient in the very short run. News is neither instantaneously disseminated nor immediately understood. Consequently, traders respond asynchronously to informational change. Because they do, continuous trading accentuates the importance of minutes and even seconds. This is not desirable. Alternatives to the current system should be considered.

CONCLUSION

This chapter has considered how the efficiency of the equity markets might be improved by government regulation of the industry. Regulation may be called for if an unregulated market would fail to achieve an optimal distribution of resources at theoretically desirable prices. The rules of a market system must be set collectively by the body politic. In addition, the causes of market failure that pertain to the equity markets include the market power of some traders, dealers, and market centers; externalities; the public goods aspects of marketability services; informational asymmetries; transaction price uncertainty; and technological inertia.

The regulatory process is itself imperfect, however. We have considered how government failure results from the way in which political power is distributed and the incentive system structured, the inadequacy of procedural safeguards, the existence of jurisdictional disputes, the cost of regulating, and the imperfect knowledge of the regulators.

Despite the shortcomings of the regulatory process, government has played an important role in the evolution of the securities markets. First and foremost, the regulatory authorities and the industry's own self-regulatory organizations (SROs) have sought to insure an honest market. In addition, starting in the 1970s, Congress and the SEC have been concerned with the competitive efficiency of the market for broker/dealer services. Some attention has also been given (primarily by the SROs) to the accuracy of the share prices being set in the market centers. Price discovery is a difficult goal to comprehend and to implement, however, and for the most part it has not received much attention in the debates concerning the design of trading systems.

This chapter has presented a more detailed consideration of four prominent regulatory issues: the elimination of fixed commissions in 1975, the partial removal of off-board trading restrictions in 1975 and 1980, the introduction of shelf registration in 1982, and the continuing debate over insider trading restrictions. The history pertaining to each of these issues gives insight into the workings of the legislative process.

Economists have studied many markets over the years. No single industry has received the depth or breadth of analysis the securities industry has received. This is explained by the tremendous importance of the securities markets to the economy and by the intricacy of their microstructure. There is a further reason: the designers of the trading systems and the regulators of the market do in fact have the power to improve the efficiency of the market's operations.

SUGGESTED READING

Y. Amihud, T. Ho, and R. Schwartz, eds., *Market Making and the Changing Structure of the Securities Industry,* Lexington, Mass.: Lexington Books, 1985.

P. Asquith and D. Mullins, Jr. "Equity Issues and Offering Dilution," *Journal of Financial Economics,* January/February 1986.

S. Bhagat, M. W. Marr, and G. R. Thompson, "The Rule 415 Experiment: Equity Markets," *Journal of Finance,* December 1985.

E. Bloch, "Multiple Regulators: Their Constituencies and Policies," in Amihud, Ho, and Schwartz (1985).

E. Bloch, *Inside Investment Banking,* Homewood, Ill.: Dow Jones-Irwin, 1986.

E. Bloch and R. Schwartz, eds., *Impending Changes for Securities Markets: What Role for the Exchange?* Greenwich, Conn.: JAI Press, 1979.

C. Cox and B. Kohn, "Regulatory Implications of Computerized Communications in Securities Markets," in Saunders and White (1986).

L. Dann and W. Mikkelson, "Convertible Debt Issuance, Capital Structure Change and Financing-Related Information," *Journal of Financial Economics,* June 1984.

T. Dunfee, F. Gibson, J. Blackburn, D. Whitman, F. McCarty, and B. Brennan, *Modern Business Law,* New York: Random House, 1984.

J. Finnerty, "Insiders and Market Efficiency," *Journal of Finance,* September 1976.

F. D. Foster, "An Empirical Investigation of the Agreement Among Underwriters and the Selling Contract: The Effects of SEC Rule 415," working paper, Duke University Fuqua School of Business, 1987.

D. Givoly and D. Palmon, "Insider Trading and the Exploitation of Inside Information: Some Empirical Evidence," *Journal of Business,* January 1985.

A. Hess and P. Frost, "Tests for Price Effects of New Issues of Seasoned Securities," *Journal of Finance,* March 1982.

J. Jaffe, "The Effect of Regulation Changes on Insider Trading," *The Bell Journal of Economics and Management Science,* Spring 1974a.

J. Jaffe, "Special Information and Insider Trading," *Journal of Business,* July 1974b.

D. Kidwell, M. W. Marr, and G. Thompson, "SEC Rule 415: The Ultimate Competitive Bid," *Journal of Financial and Quantitative Analysis,* June 1984.

A. Kyle, "Continuous Auctions and Insider Trading," *Econometrica,* November 1985.

L. Loss, *Securities Regulation,* Boston: Little, Brown, 1961 (Supplemented 1969).

H. Manne, *Insider Trading and the Stock Market,* New York: Free Press, 1966.

P. Marsh, "Equity Rights Issues and the Efficiency of the UK Stock Market," *Journal of Finance,* September 1979.

W. Mikkelson and M. Partch, "Stock Price Effects and Costs of Secondary Distributions," *Journal of Financial Economics,* June 1985.

N. Moore, D. Peterson, and P. Peterson, "Shelf Registrations and Shareholder Wealth: A Comparison of Shelf and Traditional Equity Offerings," *Journal of Finance,* June 1986.

A. Saunders and L. White, eds., *Technology and the Regulation of Financial Markets,* Lexington, Mass.: Lexington Books, 1986.

D. Scarff, "The Securities and Commodities Markets: A Case Study in Product Convergence and Regulatory Disparity," in Amihud, Ho, and Schwartz (1985).

P. Schreiber and R. Schwartz, "Efficient Price Discovery in a Securities Market: The Objectives of a Trading System," in Amihud, Ho, and Schwartz (1985).

W. Silber, "Innovation, Competition, and New Contract Design in Futures Markets," *Journal of Futures Markets,* Summer 1981.

S. Smidt, "Can We Get There from Here?" in Amihud, Ho, and Schwartz (1985).

G. Stigler, "The Theory of Economic Regulation," *Bell Journal of Economics and Management Science,* Spring 1971.

A. Summer, Jr., "Comments on Professors Bloch, Lorie and The Future," in Bloch and Schwartz (1979).

S. Tinic and R. West, "The Securities Industry Under Negotiated Brokerage Commissions: Changes in the Structure and Performance of New York Stock Exchange Member Firms," *Bell Journal of Economics and Management Science,* Spring 1980.

R. West and S. Tinic, "Minimum Commission Rates on New York Stock Exchange Transactions," *Bell Journal of Economics and Management Science,* Autumn 1971.

D. Whitman and J. Gergacz, *The Legal and Social Environment of Business,* New York: Random House, 1985.

S. Williams, "The Evolving National Market System," in Amihud, Ho, and Schwartz (1985).

chapter *15*

Price Discovery

Three objectives motivate much of the analysis presented in this book:

1. To demonstrate that prices established in equity markets and the number of shares traded generally differ from the desired theoretical values that would be attained in a frictionless market environment
2. To demonstrate that differences between actual and desired prices, and between actual and desired trading volume, depend on the design of a trading system
3. To consider how equity markets might be designed and regulated so as to improve the quality of price determination

This statement of the objectives suggests that many of the issues pertaining to the microstructure of the equity markets relate to the efficiency of price discovery.[1]

This chapter reviews the conceptual framework as it relates to price discovery. It considers why accurate price discovery has not attracted more attention from economists or others concerned with market performance.

---

[1]As noted in Chapter 3, the operations of a market center include, along with price discovery: order handling and trade execution; monitoring the integrity of member firms, of listed firms, and of traders; and development of new financial instruments and of improved trading systems.

The chapter also highlights various questions concerning price discovery for which answers do not, as yet, exist.

THE PRICE DISCOVERY PROCESS

Nonoptimal trades at disequilibrium prices may occur in a securities market because of the following:

- Investors have inaccurate and/or incomplete information upon which to base their investment decisions because of the cost of acquiring and processing information (including the opportunity cost of time).
- Investors do not maximize their expected utility of wealth given the information they possess because of decision costs (which include the opportunity cost of time).
- Traders do not communicate their complete buy/sell order functions to the market, because of a broad spectrum of trading costs (transaction costs, execution costs, and the opportunity costs of buying at a high price or of selling at a low price).

This book deals with the effect of trading costs.[2] Narrowing the focus is useful for analyzing their impact on the behavior of investors in the marketplace and the effect of the market's architecture on the price and size of trades. The analysis has been structured as follows:

- Information costs are abstracted from by assuming that individual investors make utility maximizing decisions based on publicly available information that is possessed by all.
- Decision costs are abstracted from by assuming that each market participant knows his or her own continuous, negatively inclined demand curve to hold asset shares.
- The effect of trading costs is represented by allowing each investor to submit only a single point order (one quantity of shares to buy or to sell at a single price) at any trading session. The point order is determined in relation to (1) the transaction price the trader expects to prevail on the market, (2) his or her own demand curve,

---

[2]The effect of information and decision costs has been well established and widely explored by economists. Stigler (1961) first examined the effect of search costs and imperfect information on market equilibrium. Akerlof (1970) established that an asymmetrical distribution of information can lead to market failure. Simon (1959) examined the nonmaximizing behavior of decision makers. For a recent discussion and further references, see Haltiwanger and Waldman (1985).

and (3) the market architecture that determines how orders are handled and translated into trades.[3]

- One particular source of market failure is assumed absent: no one
investor is assumed to have market power.

As discussed in Chapter 9 for a call market, the theoretically desirable
price and quantity of shares traded would be determined at any trading
session by the intersection of market buy/sell curves that are the aggregate
of the buy/sell order *functions* of all traders. The realized market clearing
price and quantity, on the other hand, are determined by the intersection
of market buy/sell curves that aggregate *the single order points* of traders.
The two solutions, in general, are not equal.[4] When they are not equal,
investors participate in nonoptimal trades, and a desire to recontract exists
after any round of trading.

Therefore the market, in aggregate, makes mistakes. It does so because expectations concerning market outcomes, and the trading system
itself, affect the orders that are placed, and the orders that are placed in
turn determine market outcomes. In short, the mistakes are the combined
effect of three factors:

- Because of the rapidity with which information and the desires of
investors to hold asset shares change, transaction prices are volatile
in the dynamic environment of the securities markets.
- Price determination and transacting are concomitant processes; because of this relationship, and given that prices are volatile, traders
may not know the prices at which they can or will transact when
writing their orders.
- Trading costs prevent investors from revealing their complete buy/sell
order functions to the market; thus traders are forced to make strategic decisions when they seek to trade. These decisions affect the
price and size of orders submitted to the market and the market
clearing prices that are established.

The impact of investor trading strategies is further seen in a continuous
market in relation to the bid-ask spread. A market spread exists, even in a
market comprising a very large number of traders, because *for strategic*

[3]More realistically, but with no gain of generality, we might have assumed that a
single point describes each investor's demand to hold shares of a financial asset (for example,
if price is greater than some value P_0, no shares are to be held; if price is P_0 or less, then
Q_0 shares are to be held) and could have allowed that any individual may not seek to trade
at any given trading session.

[4]Two unlikely conditions have to be satisfied for realized transaction prices to equal
theoretically desired equilibrium prices: (1) individual investors must each have rational
(unbiased) expectations concerning the market clearing price, and (2) the set of investors
must be distributed symmetrically according to the individual demand curves to hold shares
of the asset.

reasons, no trader would, even if it were feasible to do so, post a limit order at a price infinitesimally close to that of a counterpart order already established on the market (Chapter 10). This underscores the fact that prices set in the market are not simple statements of what individual traders believe shares of an asset are worth; rather, prices also reflect the response of traders to the market process.

A fair and orderly price would accurately reflect the demand propensities of all traders. Such a price would not be distorted by sudden jolts in the order flow or be biased by an asymmetric distribution of information. Neither would such a price be perturbed by transitory thinness in the market or be affected by the market's architecture. Economists have generally believed, externalities aside, that prices set in markets comprising many sellers and buyers are fair and orderly. Consequently, little attention has been devoted to an analysis of a market's mistakes, and market outcomes (the price and size of trades) have not, by and large, been related to real world trading systems.

However, the dynamic environment of the equity markets accentuates the impact of trading frictions and calls attention to those market design features that have been instituted to mitigate the problem of transaction price uncertainty: the special market opening procedures used by the exchanges, the role of dealers and specialists in setting quotes, the network of trading desks that constitutes the upstairs markets, the imposition of trading halts after major informational change, the extensive electronic systems that provide rapid dissemination of floor information to the investment community, and so forth. In no other market have institutional arrangements been as elaborately developed as in the securities markets. The systems and procedures have not been established simply to help buyers and sellers find each other and trade. The systems have also been instituted in response to inefficiencies and inequities, so that fair and orderly prices may be found as trading progresses.

PRICE DISCOVERY—AN UNDISCOVERED ISSUE[5]

When once asked what primary service is provided by a stock exchange, William Batten, the former chairman and CEO of the New York Stock Exchange, replied, ''We produce the price.''

Only in recent years has awareness of the price discovery function of a securities market emerged, and efficient price discovery still remains an essentially unarticulated objective. There are several reasons why. Some people believe that financial assets have intrinsic values and therefore that prices need not be discovered by the trading system. As we have seen,

---

[5]Material in this section is based on Schreiber and Schwartz (1986).

however (Chapter 9), this is not the case. Individual analysts may indeed determine what they think shares of an asset are worth (or equivalently, the number of shares they might wish to hold at any given price). However, if the community of investors has heterogeneous expectations and trading propensities, the equilibrium price for an asset must be determined in the marketplace. Finding that price is not a simple task.

Some observers of the market believe that orders simply reflect what traders individually believe shares of an asset are worth. If this were correct, it would imply that the equilibrium market price would be between the highest bid and the lowest ask in a continuous market, or where the market buy and sell order functions cross for a call market. However, the order flow is not exogenous to the trading system (Chapter 8). Rather, the orders investors submit to the market are written in relation to investor demand curves, to expectations concerning the clearing price, and to knowledge of how orders are handled in the market. When these factors are taken into account, it is apparent that market clearing prices will deviate from Walrasian equilibrium values (Chapter 9). Thus the equilibrium price may not fall within the spread (for a continuous market) or be at the cross (for a call market).

Price discovery may not appear to be a problem in light of the literature that confirms the efficient market hypothesis. However, this too is a misunderstanding; the efficient market hypothesis refers to *informational efficiency,* not to *design efficiency* (Chapter 9). Consequently, the EMH is not violated by serial dependence in stock returns if the patterns cannot be profitably exploited. The empirical evidence now suggests that substantial serial dependence does exist in security returns. The patterns are diffuse, and it is not clear that profitable trading strategies could be formulated in relation to them. Nevertheless, the serial correlation is evidence that prices deviate from equilibrium values (Chapters 10 and 11).

Modern equity markets appear to provide reasonably fair and orderly prices under normal market conditions. Therefore, price discovery is not an obvious issue much of the time the market is open. The quality of prices that are set is of particular interest, however, when the market is suddenly jolted by informational change. Empirical studies have not as yet adequately analyzed the stress points. It is hoped that this deficiency in the literature will be overcome as intraday returns data become increasingly available in machine-readable form. As discussed in Chapter 14, the extraordinary volatility experienced on and around October 19, 1987 presents a special opportunity to study the markets under stress.

The Commodities Futures Trading Commission (CFTC) has recognized price discovery as an important function of the futures markets, although the Securities and Exchange Commission (SEC) has not taken much account of price discovery in the equity markets. A reason for the difference of regulatory focus is that, for the equity markets, it has not been clear how to assess observed prices because base prices against which to contrast them do not exist.

We can, however, infer the quality of prices (Chapter 11). The returns generation process is such that, if prices were always to attain equilibrium values, the variance of logarithmic returns would increase proportionately with the length of the interval over which returns are measured, and market model beta coefficients would be invariant with respect to measurement interval length. On the other hand, price fluctuations around equilibrium values would (1) cause returns variance to increase less than proportionately with the returns measurement interval and (2) cause beta coefficients obtained from short run returns to be biased downward for stocks that tend to lag the market and to be biased upward for stocks that tend to lead the market. The empirical evidence is that, for the large majority of stocks traded in the major U.S. secondary markets, short period returns variance is greater, in relation to longer period variance, than would be expected if equilibrium values were generally attained. Also, short run betas are biased, with the bias being positively related to issue size[6] (Chapter 11). This evidence emphasizes the importance of taking efficient price discovery into account in relation to market design (Chapters 12 and 13) and as a regulatory objective (Chapter 14).

UNRESOLVED ISSUES

Recognizing that price determination may be imperfect in a market comprising many atomistic traders answers some questions but raises others. This section considers some of the more important unresolved issues.

The Response of Market Participants to Transaction Price Uncertainty

The behavior of individual traders can be analyzed from a positive (descriptive) or from a normative (prescriptive) point of view. This book has focused primarily on the former. Our analysis of the order placement strategy of an expected utility (of wealth) maximizing trader in a simplified environment shows that traders take account of transaction price uncertainty and that their response depends on the design of the market (Chapter 8).

The demonstration leaves a number of questions unanswered. In particular, further positive analysis of the decisions made by traders who, because of the size of their orders, work their orders on the trading floor or negotiate them in the upstairs market (Chapter 4) is needed. Further

---

[6]Lead/lag relationships are not directly observable, but are thought to be related to issue size: price adjustments should be faster for larger companies because these companies are more closely followed by security analysts, and because the markets for their shares are generally more liquid.

normative analysis is also needed with respect to the way investment managers and traders *should* respond to trading friction and to the excessive short period price volatility which is its manifestation.

Thus far, the conventional wisdom is that portfolios should be rebalanced infrequently because trading is costly. However, an optimal response may involve more frequent trading. The more unbalanced a portfolio becomes before adjustments are made, the greater is the intensity with which an investment manager wishes to trade when he or she does approach the market. Being eager to trade, the institutional investor is more willing to accept a large execution cost (buy at a relatively high price or sell at a relatively low price). On the other hand, a manager of a reasonably balanced portfolio can post limit orders on the market and accept the risk that the orders will not execute. Few investment managers currently do this. Nevertheless, because of the lower (and possibly negative) execution costs involved, attention should be given to pursuing a relatively frequent, but more passive, trading strategy.[7]

The cost of trading in a particular market center is of concern to the corporations whose securities are traded there (Chapter 1). Market architecture affects short run price behavior, and market architecture differs considerably between alternative market centers (Chapters 2 and 3). Therefore, the choice of where to be listed (for instance, on one or more exchanges or in the NASDAQ/NMS) is an important corporate decision. Companies currently give much attention to the visibility and prestige of a listing. A more important (and enduring) factor, however, may be the quality of price determination in the various market centers. Further investigation of the matter is needed.

Market Structure

Questions concerning market structure have been raised throughout the book. Major unresolved issues relate to the desirability of strengthening interdealer competition, of geographically consolidating the order flow, of charging a designated market maker (such as a stock exchange specialist) with the affirmative obligation to make a fair and orderly market, and of batching orders over time for simultaneous execution at periodic market calls.

Other questions concerning market design also remain unanswered. Although electronic small order execution systems have been introduced, an electronic trading system that adequately satisfies the special requirements of institutional traders has not as yet been developed. Large traders are afraid to expose their orders in a computerized market (Chapter 13).

---

[7]*Passive trading* involves the placement of limit orders and passive waiting for the arrival of a contra party to the trade; *active trading* involves the placement of market orders or active searching for the contra party. For a further discussion of these alternatives, see Schwartz and Whitcomb (1988).

They are aware of the adverse signals their orders can convey and are fearful of being exploited by the market. The difficulty with computerized trading is that most electronic systems have not as yet accommodated the search and negotiation process with the delicacy required by large traders.[8]

Most trades continue to be arranged by direct person to person contact on an exchange's trading floor or by telephone contact in the over-the-counter and upstairs markets. Consequently, despite the extensive use of electronic equipment for order handling, information dissemination, and post-trade clearance operations, contemporary equity markets remain labor intensive (Chapters 3 and 4).

The problems associated with electronic trading could possibly be overcome by using the computer to mimic a time batched (call market) system rather than a continuous system. The batching itself would bring orders together so as to reduce the market impact of any single order. Furthermore, an electronic negotiation process could precede, or be incorporated into, the market call. Essentially, this is what a Walrasian *tâtonnement* achieves in theory and what call markets such as the Paris Bourse achieve for traders present on the floor of the exchange. Little thought is currently being given, however, to designing a computerized call. Further investigation would be desirable.

Regulation

Questions concerning market regulation have been raised throughout the book. Major unresolved issues relate to geographic consolidation of the order flow, to strengthening of interdealer competition, to effective monitoring of trading in an increasingly automated environment, and to institution of efficient secondary priority trading rules.

Some of the thornier regulatory questions pertain to the distribution and use of information. Superior returns are the incentive that motivates investors to undertake those information gathering activities that keep stock prices in line with the fundamental determinants of share value. However, an asymmetrical distribution of information leads to trading inequities that are unfair from the viewpoint of the investing public.

The problem exists in part because direct trader to trader connections, which have been developed to arrange block transactions in the upstairs market, also provide conduits through which news is disseminated within the community of professional traders. The news could be knowledge of a large order being worked by an institutional trader, and it might be exploited by a strategy called *front running*—buying before a block purchase or sell-

---

[8]The Instinet system does allow two counterpart traders to gain privacy on the screen while conducting a two-way electronic negotiation (Chapter 4).

ing before a block sale, and then unwinding the position quickly after the block transaction has pushed price temporarily higher or lower.

Consolidating orders in an electronic system could reduce the industry's reliance on person to person networks. Furthermore, making the computerized system an electronic call would, because of the batching process, provide time for news to be disseminated and digested before orders could be placed and trades executed.[9] Therefore, an electronic time batched system could give all traders more equal access to the information flow and so reduce the need to regulate the market. Given the turbulence of the market and the complexity of price discovery, continuous trading may not, all said and done, be superior to periodic time batched trading.

Insider trading has received much regulatory attention in recent years; however, monitoring insider trading has become increasingly difficult with the development of derivative assets such as option and future contracts and with the globalization of trading. Continuing consideration needs to be given to determining the extent to which insider trading should be and can be controlled.

The globalization of trading is raising new regulatory questions. What corporate information should a foreign company be required to release when its stock is traded in U.S. markets? How should technological interfaces be constructed between different systems (for instance, the continuous markets in the United States and the call markets in France)? Should the affirmative obligation of exchange specialists be relaxed if an appreciable proportion of trading volume for an exchange listed issue is captured by a foreign market? How should clearing house operations be developed to cope with the growing volume of international settlements? What is the economic impact of 24 hour trading? To what extent is price discovery facilitated when, as with 24 hour trading, the market is never closed?

Stabilization

Share values should reflect the import of an underlying information set. Therefore, if information and/or investor expectations based on that information change, then so too must security prices if an efficient allocation of resources is to be attained in the marketplace. For this reason, price stabilization has been widely frowned upon by economists; it may interfere with the efficient operations of a competitive market.

Financial asset markets, however, are inherently thin,[10] and share prices signal information. Furthermore, in the dynamic environment of the

[9]Allowing time for the dissemination and assimilation of information is the reason that trading is halted in continuous markets after the advent of major news.

[10]Trading is a manifestation of disequilibrium behavior, and investors seek to trade only when their portfolios are sufficiently unbalanced for the benefits of trading to outweigh the costs.

securities markets, price fluctuations also reflect market processes and investor trading strategies that are based on expected market outcomes. In turn, the orders of individual (atomistic) investors affect market prices. Consequently, equilibrium prices are not instantaneously attained.

The path a security's price follows while adjusting to informational change is of critical importance along with a market's static efficiency.[11] If market thinness, price signalling, and investor responses generally cause prices to overadjust to informational change, then interference with the free market to stabilize prices may be justified.

The elimination of uncertainty is clearly desirable for most market participants, and various arrangements have been designed for that particular purpose—for instance, specialist/dealer intervention in trading, the imposition of trading halts following major news announcements, the use of price limits, and the institution of special market opening procedures. Nevertheless, instability continues to characterize the equity markets, even under reasonably normal conditions. Most critically, instability has the potential to cause the markets to fail when under stress, as was demonstrated on October 19, 1987, the day 604.3 million shares traded on the New York Stock Exchange and the Dow Jones Industrial Average dropped 508 points.

The turbulence of October 1987 underscored the complexity of the financial asset markets and highlighted the reality that market outcomes can affect the investment decisions of firms, as well as consumer confidence and spending decisions. The market's plunge also demonstrated that market performance depends in part on market design (see Chapter 13). However, the broad effect of a market's architecture on the behavior of participants and on market outcomes is not easily understood. Financial economists have paid increasing attention to the microstructure of the markets in recent years, but much is not yet known about how best to control price movements in a free market environment. Further insight into the problem is essential. The development of feasible solutions is of paramount importance.

Liquidity

Three points are uncertain about liquidity: (1) its definition, (2) a method to measure it empirically, and (3) the importance of taking it into account in explaining asset pricing.

The Meaning of Liquidity *Liquidity* is generally taken to refer to the ease with which an asset can be exchanged (bought or sold) for money. Assets that can be traded *quickly* at *reasonable prices* are considered liquid. Money itself—cash and demand deposits—is perfectly liquid.

---

[11]Because information and expectations are continuously subject to change, equilibrium prices, if not instantaneously found, may never be attained.

For all but the large blocks, trades for exchange listed or OTC securities can be made within minutes of an order's being communicated to a broker. Does this mean that shares of a highly volatile, thinly traded stock are liquid? Most people would agree that it does not; as just noted, shares also have to be bought or sold at *reasonable* prices for a market to be liquid.

"Reasonableness," however, is an ambiguous concept. If a trader happens to buy shares of a highly volatile security at a relatively high price, is the price unreasonable? If a trader happens to sell shares at a low price because the trade involves 25 percent of the total number of shares outstanding, is the price unreasonable?

Market participants are likely to consider markets illiquid if they are *volatile* and/or if large trades cause adverse price effects. When so used, the term does not describe the operational efficiency of the market, but rather the product being traded. That is, a stock's price may be volatile because the company's earnings are subject to substantial uncertainty, or the equilibrium price of a stock may be changed by a large order because the market demand curve to hold shares is downward sloping.

Liquidity should be defined in relation to the operational efficiency of the market. Illiquidity is the result of trading costs; all assets, no matter how risky or how noncompetitive their markets, would be perfectly liquid if the marketplace itself were a frictionless environment. Traders who are willing to risk their orders' not executing can avoid execution costs (bid-ask spreads and the temporary market impact of large orders) by placing limit orders instead of market orders and/or by breaking up large orders and working them over time. Therefore, when incurring an execution cost, a trader is paying the price of transacting quickly in an illiquid market. If there were no trading friction, this cost would be nonexistent, regardless of the asset's price volatility or the size of individual orders in relation to the total market.

The Measurement of Liquidity   Defining liquidity is one thing; measuring it is another. In a recent article, Lippman and McCall (1986) have defined liquidity with respect to the time it takes to transact. As we have seen, however, this definition would not be helpful with regard to the equity markets, because transactions in these highly organized markets can be obtained almost instantaneously. Rather, we focus on the facet of the previous definition that concerns "the reasonableness of transaction prices."

The accuracy of price discovery in the equity markets is not easily measured. The variance and market model beta analyses presented in Chapter 11 suggest an approach, but questions still remain. In particular, further evidence on the market impact of large orders would be desirable. Does the random arrival of a series of buy orders push price temporarily higher? Does the random arrival of a series of sell orders push price temporarily lower? Do prices quickly return to equilibrium values when they become sufficiently out of line? In short, further analysis of the depth, breadth, and resiliency of a market is needed.

Assessment of a Risk/Return/Liquidity Tradeoff   Defining and measuring liquidity is one thing; assessing its effect on asset prices is another. Currently, much attention is given to asset pricing in a risk/return framework. This, of course, should be sufficient for a frictionless environment. With trading friction, however, the equilibrium configuration of prices across assets might also reflect execution costs.

Are execution costs appreciable enough to have a significant impact on security prices? Spreads are, indeed, consequential, and the bid-ask spread itself has been studied extensively by financial economists. For the months of March and April 1985, percentage spreads for Amex, NYSE, and NASDAQ/NMS stocks averaged approximately 1.34, 1.06, and 1.93 percent, respectively. For an investor with a one year holding period who expects a 10 percent return on an investment, round-trip trading costs of this magnitude are indeed sizable.

The dynamic behavior of the spread and the ability of traders on the Amex and NYSE to obtain executions between the quotes suggest that the spread itself is an imperfect measure of execution costs. Hasbrouck and Schwartz's estimates of execution costs for March and April 1985, averaged approximately 0.12, 0.15, and 0.44 percent for Amex, NYSE, and NAS-DAQ/NMS stocks, respectively (Chapter 11).[12] These estimates probably understate execution costs for larger block orders, for which the market impact effect is believed to be appreciably greater.

Because liquidity is largely affected by the market's architecture and is not fundamentally an attribute of an asset itself, does liquidity differ between assets traded within a market center? Theory suggests, and empirical analysis substantiates, that liquidity does differ from asset to asset. The reason is that the impact of friction on the price behavior of a security depends on the thinness of the market for the particular security. *Ceteris paribus,* thinner stocks are expected, and have been observed to have, wider bid-ask spreads, greater short period price volatility, and market model beta coefficients that are more downward biased because of price adjustment delays (Chapters 10 and 11). We conclude, therefore, that in a nonfrictionless environment, the thinness of a market matters, and thus that liquidity differs from stock to stock within a market center.

Do liquidity differences between assets traded within a market center have an appreciable effect on asset prices? Attention is just beginning to turn to this question, and further research is needed. However, a recent

---

[12]Execution costs are the costs of a purchase or a sale, while the bid-ask spread is related to the cost of a round trip (purchase at the ask and then subsequent sale at the bid). The bivariate correlation between the estimated execution cost and the percentage bid-ask spread is .614 in the Hasbrouck-Schwartz study.

paper by Amihud and Mendelson (1986) presents compelling evidence. These authors measured illiquidity by the cost of immediate execution, which they took to be the bid-ask spread. Their theoretical analysis predicted, and their empirical results confirmed, that assets with wider percentage spreads do yield higher average returns, and that investors with longer holding periods (and consequently for whom execution costs are less important), should, all else constant, select assets with wider percentage spreads. These findings strongly underscore the importance of the provision of liquidity by secondary markets in order to reduce the cost of capital for issuing firms (Chapter 1). They also call attention to the need to expand traditional capital asset pricing theory from a two-dimensional risk/return framework to a three-dimensional risk/return/liquidity framework.

Empirical Analysis

The informational content of stock prices is obscured by the bouncing of transaction prices between the bid and the ask, by the market impact of large orders when counterpart orders on the market are thin, by market maker intervention to reduce the size of transaction-to-transaction price changes, and by short period price changes that occur as the market searches for a new equilibrium after the advent of news (Chapter 10). The effect of the market process on stock price movements is clearly evidenced by the inflation of short period returns variance for most issues, and by the bias in market model beta estimates obtained from short period returns data (Chapters 10 and 11). These and related effects need to be analyzed further.

Various anomalies have been observed in stock returns data. The most intriguing of these is that risk adjusted returns appear to be larger for smaller firms, particularly for the month of January.[13] Returns distributions have also been observed to be approximately lognormally distributed, with the exception that very large positive and very large negative returns occur with greater frequency than would be expected on the basis of the lognormal distribution. The prevalence of large absolute returns has been technically explained as evidence either that returns distributions are nonstationary or that returns are generated by a mixture of distributions.

Little thought has been given to the effect of market microstructure on the observed behavior of returns. Would the small firm and January effects disappear if liquidity as well as risk were properly adjusted for? Would the mixture of distributions hypothesis be supported by an analysis of the differential price impacts (and arrival rates) of large and small orders and of liquidity and informationally motivated orders?

---

[13]For a discussion and further references, see Elton and Gruber (1986) and Thaler (1987).

The increasing availability of intraday data will allow more sophisticated empirical tests to be undertaken in relation to microstructure issues. In addition, financial economists who use short period returns data (a few days or less) for more general purposes will increasingly need to understand and to take account of the impact of a market's microstructure on returns generation.

The Greater Generality of the Problem of Transaction Price Uncertainty

This book deals with trading in one particular marketplace: an equity market. But transaction costs exist in all real world markets; demand/supply conditions in all markets are unstable over long periods of time; all markets require some mechanism for finding the prices at which trades are made. How unique might the equity markets be?

Market conditions change rapidly in the equity markets, and transaction costs are high enough to impede trading and to cause price determination to be a complex, imperfect process. Market conditions may not change as fast in other markets; but if trading frictions are greater, price determination in other markets may be affected, and prices may generally not achieve desired equilibrium values in a competitive environment. Consider, for example, labor markets in which long term contracts are negotiated.

A labor contract is written initially because of the cost of transacting; then, once in effect, the contract is itself a market friction. One may question, therefore, how participants in labor markets respond to friction, and how the response affects wage determination and employment. Assume a large number of firms (in possibly different product industries) and a large (but not necessarily homogeneous) labor force. Let each firm sign a multiyear contract with its employees at a wage rate that is related to the general level of wages. Then consider the following:

- What is the actual process by which the general level of wages is determined?
- Do transaction costs impede the disclosure of demand/supply functions in the labor market as they do in the stock market?
- Does uncertainty exist concerning the level of wages that would clear the market in the current period, and, if so, how do the firms and workers respond to this uncertainty?
- What institutional arrangements for dealing with price discovery exist in labor markets? For instance, does staggered contracting in labor markets facilitate tracking an equilibrium wage, much as con-

tinuous trading facilitates tracking equilibrium prices in the equity markets?[14]

- Is unemployment in labor markets evidence that, because of transaction price uncertainty, the market in aggregate makes mistakes?
- Does change in the magnitude of transaction price uncertainty (caused in part by alterations in aggregate economic policy) cause fluctuations in employment, unemployment, and output?

CONCLUSION

Prices lead individuals to use resources optimally, given aggregate demand/supply conditions. Prices also signal information and are the means by which information is aggregated in the marketplace. What we seek in a trading system is a mechanism for reaching equilibrium prices, and a means of enabling traders to trade optimal amounts at these prices.

Assuming no externalities and that no individual trader is large enough to have market power, the unimpeded forces of demand and supply are sufficient to produce desired equilibrium prices if markets are frictionless. However, when trading costs prevent market participants from revealing their full set of orders to the market, and when frequent shifts in demand/supply relationships introduce transaction price uncertainty, a market comprising atomistic traders generally fails to find the desired equilibrium price, trades are generally made at disequilibrium prices, and a demand to recontract typically exists after any round of trading. In such an environment, the microstructure of a market matters.

This chapter has reviewed many of the issues discussed in the book in relation to price discovery in the equity markets. Coping successfully with transaction price uncertainty is the objective of traders. Avoiding transaction price uncertainty is an objective of investors and listed companies. Minimizing transaction price uncertainty and its impact should be a goal of market architects and regulators. And yet, until recently, relatively little attention has been given to the fact that price discovery is indeed affected by the institutional arrangements that define a trading system.

If prices that approximate equilibrium values are not established, any market will fail to achieve an optimal distribution of resources. Markets, however, may not easily rectify their mistakes. A broader spectrum of economic problems may, therefore, be attributable to friction in the marketplace and to imperfections in existing trading arrangements. The continuing development of microstructure analysis should yield further insight into the processes of trading, price determination, and resource allocation in a nonfrictionless world.

---

[14]Contracts are staggered when they are not negotiated and do not expire at the same moments in time for a set of firms or industries. Staggered contracts are more common in the United States than in Europe, where contracts tend to be negotiated concurrently.

SUGGESTED READING

G. Akerlof, "The Market for 'Lemons': Quality Uncertainty and the Market Mechanism," *Quarterly Journal of Economics,* August 1970.

Y. Amihud, T. Ho, and R. Schwartz, eds., *Market Making and the Changing Structure of the Securities Industry,* Lexington, Mass.: Lexington Books, 1985.

Y. Amihud and H. Mendelson, "Asset Pricing and the Bid-Ask Spread," *The Journal of Financial Economics,* December 1986.

E. Elton and M. Gruber, *Modern Portfolio Theory and Investment Analysis,* third edition, New York: Wiley, 1986.

K. Garbade and W. Silber, "Price Movements and Price Discovery in Futures and Cash Markets," *Review of Economics and Statistics,* May 1983.

J. Haltiwanger and M. Waldman, "Rational Expectations and the Limits of Rationality," *American Economic Review,* June 1985.

J. Hasbrouck and R. Schwartz, "Liquidity and Execution Costs in Equity Markets," *Journal of Portfolio Management,* Spring 1988, forthcoming.

S. Lippman and J. McCall, "An Operational Measure of Liquidity," *American Economic Review,* March 1986.

J. Merrick, "Price Discovery in the Stock Market," working paper, New York University Graduate School of Business Administration, 1987.

S. Phillips, "Regulation and the Futures Markets," in Amihud, Ho, and Schwartz (1985).

P. Schreiber and R. Schwartz, "Efficient Price Discovery in a Securities Market: The Objective of a Trading System," in Amihud, Ho, and Schwartz (1985).

P. Schreiber and R. Schwartz, "Price Discovery in Securities Markets," *Journal of Portfolio Management,* Summer 1986.

R. Schwartz and D. Whitcomb, *Trading Strategies for Institutional Investors,* Monograph Series in Finance and Economics, Salomon Brothers Center for the Study of Financial Institutions, New York University Graduate School of Business Administration, 1988, forthcoming.

H. Simon, "Theories of Decision-Making in Economics and Behavioral Sciences," *American Economic Review,* June 1959.

G. Stigler, "The Economics of Information," *Journal of Political Economy,* June 1961.

R. Thaler, "Anomalies: The January Effect," *Journal of Economic Perspectives,* Summer 1987.

M. Theobald and V. Price, "Seasonality Estimation in Thin Markets," *Journal of Finance,* June 1984.

Index

The letter *n* after a page number indicates that the reference is in a footnote.

530

ACRONYMS AND ABBREVIATIONS

(continued from front)

INTEX	Bermuda-based automated futures exchange
IOC Order	Immediate or cancel order
IPO	Initial public offering
IRA	Individual retirement account
ITS	Intermarket Trading System
LIONs	Lehman Investment Opportunity Notes
LSE	London Stock Exchange
MAX	The Midwest Stock Exchange's automated execution system
MEC	Market Efficiency Coefficient
NASD	National Association of Securities Dealers
NASDAQ	NASD's Automated Quotations System
NASDAQ/NMS	NASD's National Market System
NMAB	National Market Advisory Board
NMS	National market system
NSCC	National Securities Clearing Corporation
NSTS	Cincinnati Stock Exchange's National Securities Trading System
NYFE	New York Futures Exchange
NYSE	New York Stock Exchange
OARS	NYSE's Opening Automated Report System
OTC	Over-the-counter
PACE	Philadelphia Stock Exchange's automated order routing system
PSE	Pacific Stock Exchange
RCMMs	Registered competitive market-makers
REITS	Real estate investment trusts
R4	NYSE's Registered Representative Rapid Response Service
SCOREX	Pacific Stock Exchange's automated order routing system (an improvement over COMEX)
SEC	Securities & Exchange Commission
SIA	Securities Industry Association
SIAC	Securities Industry Automation Corporation
SOES	NASD's automated small order execution system for NASDAQ securities
SOFFEX	Switzerland's planned computerized Options and Financial Futures Exchange (1988)
S&P	Standard and Poor's
SRO	Self-regulatory organization
SuperDot	NYSE's automated small order execution system (an improvement over DOT)
TIGRs	Merrill Lynch's Treasury Investment Growth Receipts
Tokyo CATS	TSE's Computer Assisted Trading System
TSE	Toronto Stock Exchange or Tokyo Stock Exchange